RITUALS IN ABUNDANCE

Liturgia condenda 17

1. Gerard Lukken & Mark Searle, *Semiotics and Church Architecture. Applying the Semiotics of A.J. Greimas and the Paris School to the Analysis of Church Buildings*, Kampen, 1993
2. Gerard Lukken, *Per visibilia ad invisibilia. Anthropological, Theological and Semiotic Studies on the Liturgy and the Sacraments*, edited by Louis van Tongeren & Charles Caspers, Kampen, 1994
3. *Bread of Heaven. Customs and Practices Surrounding Holy Communion. Essays in the History of Liturgy and Culture*, edited by Charles Caspers, Gerard Lukken & Gerard Rouwhorst, Kampen, 1995
4. Willem Marie Speelman, *The Generation of Meaning in Liturgical Songs. A Semiotic Analysis of Five Liturgical Songs as Syncretic Discourses*, Kampen, 1995
5. Susan K. Roll, *Toward the Origins of Christmas*, Kampen, 1995
6. Maurice B. McNamee, *Vested Angels. Eucharistic Allusions in Early Netherlandish Paintings*, Leuven, 1998
7. Karl Gerlach, *The Antenicene Pascha. A Rhetorical History*, Leuven, 1998
8. Paul Post, Jos Pieper & Marinus van Uden, *The Modern Pilgrim. Multidisciplinary Explorations of Christian Pilgrimage*, Leuven, 1998
9. Judith Marie Kubicki, *Liturgical Music as Ritual Symbol. A Case Study of Jacques Berthier's Taizé Music*, Leuven, 1999
10. Justin E.A. Kroesen, *The Sepulchrum Domini Through the Ages. Its Form and Function*, Leuven, 2000
11. Louis van Tongeren, *Exaltation of the Cross. Toward the Origins of the Feast of the Cross and the Meaning of the Cross in Early Medieval Liturgy*, Leuven, 2000
12. P. Post, G. Rouwhorst, L. Van Tongeren & A. Scheer, *Christian Feast and Festival. The Dynamics of Western Liturgy and Culture*, Leuven, 2001
13. Veronica Rosier, O.P., *Liturgical Cathechesis of Sunday Celebrations in the Absence of a Priest*, Leuven, 2002
14. A. Vernooij (ed.), *Liturgy and Muse. The Eucharistic Prayer*, Leuven, 2002
15. P. Post, R.L. Grimes, A. Nugteren, P. Pettersson, H. Zondag, *Disaster Ritual. Explorations of an Emerging Ritual Repertoire*, Leuven, 2003
16. Johann Hausreither, *Semiotik des Liturgischen Gesanges. Ein Beitrag zur Entwicklung einer integralen Untersuchungsmethode der Liturgiewissenschaft*, Leuven, 2004

Liturgia condenda is published by the Liturgical Institute in Tilburg (NL). The series plans to publish innovative research into the science of liturgy and serves as a forum which will bring together publications produced by researchers of various nationalities. The motto *liturgia condenda* expresses the conviction that research into the various aspects of liturgy can make a critico-normative contribution to the deepening and the renewal of liturgical practice.

The editorial board: Paul Post (Tilburg), Louis van Tongeren (Tilburg), Gerard Rouwhorst (Utrecht), Ton Scheer (Nijmegen), Lambert Leijssen (Leuven), Marcel Barnard (Utrecht), Ike de Loos (secretary – Tilburg)
The advisory board: Paul Bradshaw (Notre Dame IN), Paul De Clerck (Paris), Andreas Heinz (Trier), François Kabasele (Kinshasa), Benedikt Kranemann (Erfurt), Martin Klöckener (Fribourg CH), Jan Luth (Groningen), Nathan Mitchell (Notre Dame IN), Susan Roll (Ottawa)
Honorary editor: Gerard Lukken (Tilburg)

Liturgisch Instituut
P.O. Box 9130
5000 HC Tilburg
The Netherlands

RITUALS IN ABUNDANCE

CRITICAL REFLECTIONS ON THE PLACE, FORM AND IDENTITY OF CHRISTIAN RITUAL IN OUR CULTURE

Gerard Lukken

PEETERS
LEUVEN – DUDLEY, MA

Library of Congress Cataloging-in-Publication Data

Lukken, Gerard.

   [Rituelen in overvloed. English]
   Rituals in abundance : critical reflections on the place, form, and identity of Christian ritual in our culture / Gerard Lukken.
      p. cm. -- (Liturgia condenda ; 17)
   Includes bibliographical references (p.) and indexes.
   ISBN 90-429-1517-X (alk. paper)
    1. Ritualism. I. Title. II. Series.

BV180.L8513 2004
264--dc22   2004050563

Published with financial support from the Netherlands Organisation for Scientific Research (NWO)

Revised and expanded edition of 'Rituelen in overvloed. Een kritische bezinning op de plaats en de gestalte van het christelijke ritueel in onze cultuur', Kok, Kampen 1999

D. 2004/0602/120
ISBN 90-429-1517-X

TABLE OF CONTENTS

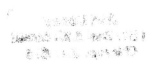

INTRODUCTION

Rituals are closely linked with culture. They are deeply defined by space and time. Rituals differ depending on geographic location. Although they are often characterised by repetition, they change over the course of history. This book is a consideration of Christian ritual in 'our culture'. For me, that will mean contemporary Western culture, and indeed primarily Western European culture. Despite a number of common features, this present-day Western European culture is differentiated. This book was originally written particularly with an eye to the ritual developments in The Netherlands. I therefore realise that the ritual field of vision here is limited. But to my mind, that is a benefit for anthropological observation and reflection. Rituals are simply not free-floating ideological constructions, but concrete, culturally defined practices. Moreover, in a certain sense the developments in The Netherlands are representative. A Dutch psychologist specialising in culture and religion recently remarked, 'nowhere are there so many unchurched, nowhere so many different religious groups, nowhere are the church-goers so active, and nowhere is there so much interest in New Age-related developments. The Netherlands is an experimental station for religious change and development unique for Europe.'[1] With the English translation in mind I have on the one hand included pertinent new literature, and on the other hand widened the focus of my reflections at a number of points to go beyond the Dutch situation.[2]

---

[1] J. JANSSEN: 'Religie: privé-bezit of sociaal kapitaal', in *De Bazuin* 84 (2001) 25, 26.

[2] The perspective chosen necessarily implies that the literature cited will frequently be in Dutch. On the one hand, I realise that this literature will not be as accessible as that in English; on the other, Dutch certainly deserves a place of its own alongside languages such as German, French, Italian and Spanish, and Dutch covers a larger language region than is often realised. In addition to The Netherlands, it is also spoken in a part of Belgium, in the Dutch Antilles, Aruba, Surinam and Indonesia; moreover, it is understood in South Africa: Afrikaans is derived from Dutch, and is also spoken by 60% of the population of Namibia.

In the 1960s there was in Dutch society – as in other European countries – a serious crisis in ritual. The situation was paradoxical. While
under the influence of the Second Vatican Council and the Liturgical
Movement, in the Catholic churches there was great creativity with
regard to ritual, ritual was gradually disappearing from the society,
and participation in Christian ritual was rapidly draining away. A religious void arose. At the same time rituals were being discovered by
psychotherapy. Therapists began prescribing certain rituals for clients
in order to break through impasses at critical transitions from one
phase of life to another. Sometimes what society deprived a person of
had to be made up for through clinical ritual. In this context of the
crisis of ritual, in 1984 I wrote a small book entitled *Geen leven zonder rituelen. Anthropologische beschouwingen met het oog op de christelijke liturgie* (No life without rituals: anthropological reflections
with Christian liturgy in mind). It apparently met a need, and was
reprinted twice.[3]

In 1987 the subject of rituals was the theme for the a series of public
lectures at the Tilburg University. In my introduction I once again
dealt with the crisis in rites, and noted that words such as 'rite' and
'ritual' often had a negative connotation in our society.[4] They were
regarded as a purely formal and stereotypic framework which easily
lead to dishonest and insincere conduct. I once again drew attention to
the then already well established tendency among sociologists to speak
disdainfully of ritualised behaviour.[5] But I also noted that it would
be wrong to discuss the crisis in rites in a one-sided, negative manner,
and pointed to the creation of protest rituals, the revival of rituals
surrounding birth, marriage and death, the great interest in rituals
within the feminist movement and the striking attention of historians
for rituals, who were seen as a gold mine for historical anthropology.[6]

[3] G. LUKKEN: *Geen leven zonder rituelen. Antropologische beschouwingen met het oog
op de christelijke liturgie* (Tweede serie Geestelijke Volksgezondheid 2-24), Baarn 1984,
Hilversum 1986[2], 1988[3].
[4] Published under the title 'Ritueel en menselijke identiteit', in A. DE RUIJTER a.o.:
Totems en trends. Over de zin van identificatiesymbolen, Hilversum 1988, 20-34.
[5] O. VAN DER HART: *Rituelen in psychotherapie. Overgang en bestendiging*, Deventer
1984 (second and augmented edition of IDEM: *Overgang en bestendiging: Over het
ontwerpen en voorschrijven van rituelen in psychotherapie*, Deventer 1978).
[6] LUKKEN: 'Ritueel en menselijke identiteit' 20-21.

Still, it was my opinion at the time that the negative side of the crisis still had the upper hand, because on the one side there was often a lack of rituals, and on the other the new rituals often seemed so transitory that one had to ask if they could even properly be called rituals.

I did not realise then that the positive elements I listed heralded the 'ritual explosion' of the 1990s. The situation has fundamentally changed. There is now a counter-movement which began in the mid-1980s. People have rediscovered ritual, so much so that there are now rituals in abundance. This is the case for both general human ritual and religious ritual. The renewal of ritual in the Christian churches has also progressed still further. It is redundant to argue for rituals now. There is no longer a crisis in ritual in the sense of their crumbling and disappearing. But in my opinion, critical reflection on the present situation is certainly necessary. There remains a crisis in the original sense of the word. Crisis comes from the Greek *krinein*, which means 'to judge' or 'to distinguish'. In the increasing abundance of rituals it is important to clearly distinguish between the false and the authentic. One could say there is a muddle of rituals, in which one at times loses one's way. In this book I intend to delineate the directions ritual is going and set out ritual signposts. It is important to identify the peculiar characteristics of ritual, develop an eye for the shifts that have occurred in ritual and further define the identity of various rituals. What are the place and the shape of Christian ritual within this whole? Does Christian ritual have its own identity within this abundance of rituals?

In dealing with these questions I will again take as my point of departure the same starting point used in *Geen leven zonder rituelen*. This is, specifically, the anthropological approach. It is important to elaborate on this. There is all the more reason to do so because particularly in the second half of the 1980s important developments took place in the field of the scientific study of ritual. People began to speak of 'ritual studies' as a separate discipline, and it acquired its own periodical, the first issue of which appeared in 1985 under the title *Journal of Ritual Studies*. Of course, in the past the study of ritual had not been neglected. This had taken place in all sorts of disciplines. What was new was the attempt to make research into rituals an interdisciplinary undertaking: ritual studies bestrode the wide realm or stage on which disciplines like psychology, sociology, cultural anthropology, European ethnology, dramaturgy, musicology, phenomenology, semiotics, religious studies and liturgical studies come together.[7]

[7] The term 'ritual studies' was first used in 1977; see R.L. GRIMES: *Beginnings in Ritual Studies*, Washington 1982, Preface. The following is a selection from recent literature in the field: B.C. ALEXANDER: 'Ritual and Current Studies of Ritual', in S.D. GLAZIER: *Anthropology of Religion: a Handbook*, Westport Conn./London 1997, 139-160; T. ASAD: *Genealogies of Religion. Discipline and Reasons of Power in Christianity and Islam*, Baltimore 1993, 55-79; M.B. AUNE & V. DEMARINIS: *Religious and Social Ritual: Interdisciplinary Explorations*, New York 1996; L. BAKKER, L. BOER & A. LANSER: *Rituelen delen. Een verzameling ideeën om geloven vorm te geven*, Kampen 1995; M. BARNARD: *Liturgiek als wetenschap van christelijke riten en symbolen*, Amsterdam 2000; M. BARNARD & P. POST (eds.): *Ritueel bestek. Antropologische kernwoorden van de liturgie*, Zoetermeer 2001; C. BELL: 'Ritual, Change, and Changing Rituals', in *Worship* 63 (1989) 31-41; IDEM: *Ritual Theory, Ritual Practice*, New York/Oxford 1992; IDEM: 'The Authority of Ritual Experts', in *Studia Liturgica* 23 (1993) 98-120; IDEM: *Ritual. Perspectives and Dimensions*, Oxford 1997; A. BELLIGER & D.J. KRIEGER (eds.): *Ritualtheorien. Ein einführendes Handbuch*, Wiesbaden 1998; B. BOUDEWIJNSE: 'The Conceptualisation of Ritual. A History of its Problematic Aspects', in *Jaarboek voor liturgie-onderzoek* 11 (1995) 31-56; *Breekbaar als glas. Over de broosheid van symbolen en riten: Tijdschrift voor Geestelijk Leven* 54 (1998) no. 2; D. COHEN: *De cirkel van het leven. Menselijke rituelen uit de hele wereld*, Utrecht/Antwerpen 1991; D. DE COPPET (ed.): *Understanding Ritual*, Londen/New York 1992; R. DEVISCH a.o.: *Le rite, source et ressources*, Brussel 1995; J. DRIESSEN & H. DE JONGHE (eds.): *In de ban van de betekenis. Proeven van symbolische antropologie*, Nijmegen 1994; L. ELSBREE: *Ritual Passages and Narrative Structures*, Bern 1991; F. FRIJNS: *Rituelen. Rituelen in het dagelijks leven van mensen in het bijzonder van mensen met een verstandelijke handicap*, Best 1996; R. FULGHUM: *From Beginning to End. The Rituals of Our Lives*, London 1996; T. GERHOLM: 'On Ritual: a Postmodernist View', in *Ethnos* 3-4 (1988) 190-203; R.L. GRIMES: *Beginnings in Ritual Studies*, Washington 1982; IDEM: *Research in Ritual Studies. A Programmatic Essay and Bibliography*, Metuchen 1985; IDEM: *Ritual Criticism: Case Studies in its Practice, Essays on its Theory*, Columbia 1990; IDEM: 'Liturgical Supinity, Liturgical Erectitude: on the Embodiment of Ritual Authority', in *Studia Liturgica* 23 (1993) 51-69; IDEM: *Reading, Writing, and Ritualizing. Ritual in Fictive, Liturgical, and Public Places*, Washington DC 1993; IDEM: *Marrying and Burying. Rites of Passage in a Mans Life*, San Francisco/Oxford 1995; IDEM: *Deeply into the Bone. Re-inventing rites of passage* (Life Passages 1), Berkeley/Los Angeles/London 2000; IDEM: 'Ritual', in W. BRAUN & R.T. MCCUTCHEON (eds.): *Guide to the Study of Religion*, London/New York 2000, 259-270 (ch. 18); A. GRÜN: *Geborgenheit finden. Rituale feiern: Wege zu mehr Lebensfreude*, Stuttgart 1997 = IDEM: *Een veilige schuilplaats. Meer levensvreugde door rituelen*, Baarn 1997; S. HAAKMAN (ed.): *Rituelen* (Studium Generale), Utrecht 1989; J.Y. HAMELINE: *Une poétique du rituel*, Paris 1997, 35-49; O. VAN DER HART a.o.: *Afscheidsrituelen in psychotherapie*, Baarn 1981 (English edition: *Coping with Loss. The Therapeutic Use of Leave-Taking Rituals*, New York 1987; revised edition: *Afscheidsrituelen in psychotherapie. Achterblijven en verdergaan*, Lisse 2003); VAN DER HART: *Rituelen in psychotherapie*; H.-G. HEIMBROCK: *Gottesdienst: Spielraum des Lebens. Sozial- und kulturwissenschaftliche Analysen zum Ritual in praktisch-theol-

Since the Second Vatican Council liturgical studies, particularly in
The Netherlands, had already opened itself up broadly for other disci-

ogischem Interesse (Theologie en Empirie 15), Kampen/Weinheim 1993; H.-G. HEIM-
BROCK & B. BOUDEWIJNSE (eds.): *Current Studies on Rituals. Perspectives for the Psychology
of Religion*, Amsterdam 1990; E.G. HOEKSTRA & R. KRANENBORG (eds.): *Rituelen in
religieus Nederland. Gebruiken van joden, christenen, moslims, hindoes en boeddhisten in
belangrijke levensfasen*, Baarn 2001; C. HUMPHREY & J. LAIDLAW: *The Archetypal Actions
of Ritual. A Theory of Ritual Illustrated by the Jain Rite of Worship* (Oxford Studies in
Social and Cultural Anthropology), Oxford 1994; E. IMBER-BLACK & J. ROBERTS: *Rituals for Our Times. Celebrating, Healing, and Changing our Lives and Relationships*, New
York 1992; T. JENNINGS: 'Ritual Studies and Liturgical Theology. An invitation to dialogue', in *Journal of Ritual Studies* 1 (1987) 35-56; J. JOOSSE: 'Symboliseren, rituelen, ritueel en cultuur', in *Liturgiewetenschap*, Vol. 2 (Open Theologisch Onderwijs), Kampen
1991, 8-58; D. VAN KAMPENHOUT: *Rituelen. Essentie, uitvoering en begeleiding*, Amsterdam 1993; C. LANE: *The Rites of Rulers. Ritual in Industrial Society – The Soviet Case*,
Cambridge 1981; A. LANSER: "Geef dat het van ons leert te kijken'. De functie van thuisrituelen in de religieuze socialisatie', in *Praktische Theologie* 23 (1996) 426-438; J. LUIJS:
'Taal, teken, ritueel. Humanisten in dubio', in *Werkmap (voor) Liturgie* 25 (1991) 244-
246; G. LUKKEN: *De onvervangbare weg van de liturgie*, Hilversum 1980, 1984²; IDEM:
Geen leven zonder rituelen; C. MENKEN-BEKIUS: *Rituelen in het individuele pastoraat. Een
praktisch theologisch onderzoek*, Kampen 2000; IDEM: *Werken met rituelen in het pastoraat*,
Kampen 2001; N. MITCHELL: 'The Amen-Corner: the Coming Revolution in Ritual
Studies', in *Worship* 67 (1993) 74-81; IDEM: 'Emerging Rituals in Contemporary Culture', in *Concilium* 3 (1995) 3, 121-129; J. MOINGT: *Enjeux du rite dans la modernité*
(Recherches de Science Religieuse 78 (1990) 4), Paris 1991; R. NIEUWKOOP: *De drempel over. Het gebruik van (overgangs)rituelen in het pastoraat*, Den Haag 1986; J.
PLATVOET & K. VAN DER TOORN (eds.): *Pluralism and Identity: Studies in Ritual Behaviour* (Studies in the History of Religions 67), Leiden 1995; P. POST: *Ritueel landschap:
over liturgie-buiten. Processie, pausbezoek, danken voor de oogst, plotselinge dood* (Liturgie
in perspectief 5), Baarn 1995 = P. POST: 'Paysage rituel: liturgie en plein air, la visite du
pape, action de grâce pour la moisson, rites autour d' une mort subite', in *Questions
Liturgiques* 77 (1996) 174-190 and 240-256; IDEM: 'Zeven notities over rituele verandering, traditie en (vergelijkende) liturgiewetenschap', in *Jaarboek voor liturgie-onderzoek* 11 (1995) 1-30; IDEM: 'Overvloed of deritualisering. Lukken en Grimes over het
actuele ritueel-liturgische milieu', in *Jaarboek voor liturgie-onderzoek* 17 (2001) 193-212;
IDEM: 'Personen en patronen. Literatuurbericht liturgiewetenschap', in *Praktische Theologie* 28 (2001) 86-110; IDEM: 'Ritual Studies. Einführung und Ortsbestimmung im Hinblick auf die Liturgiewissenschaft, in *Archiv für Liturgiewissenschaft* 45 (2003) 21-45.
P. POST & W.M. SPEELMAN (eds.): *De Madonna van de Bijenkorf: bewegingen op de rit-
uele markt* (Liturgie in perspectief 9), Baarn 1997; P. POST, G. ROUWHORST, L. VAN
TONGEREN & A. SCHEER (eds.): *Christian Feast and Festival. The Dynamics of Western
Liturgy and Culture* (Liturgia condenda 12), Leuven 2001; M. RAND: *Ritueel* (Magnum
Images 1), Amsterdam 1990; R. RAPPAPORT: *Ritual and Religion in the Making of
Humanity* (Cambridge Studies in Social and Cultural Anthropology 110), Cam-
bridge/New York/Melbourne/Madrid 1999; *Reclaiming our rites: Studia Liturgica* 23

plines that were occupied with ritual.[8] These further developments only served to enhance this openness. If one is interested in the place of Christian ritual in our culture, one can not ignore the input from other disciplines that more or less come together in ritual studies.

The whole of this book is written with the changes that have taken place in recent years in our culture as a background. Thus I cannot always be exhaustive and comprehensive. What I attempt to achieve is a *Gesamtblick*.

I will be chiefly concerned with three themes in this book. The first question to be taken up is, What is ritual? (Part I). Next I will deal with

(1993) no. 1; B. RIDDER & L. WOLTERING: *Rituelen spelen. Rituelen helen*, Oost-Soeburg 1995; E. RIPHAGEN: *Kinderen en rituelen. Het belang van vaste gewoonten voor opgroeiende kinderen*, Kampen 1997; *Rituelen: Skript. Historisch tijdschrift* 6 (1984) no. 4; *Rituelen: Op Schrift. Maandschrift van de RVU educatieve omroep* 3 (1985) no. 8; *Rituelen en religie: Kultuurleven. Tijdschrift voor cultuur en samenleving* 64 (1997) no. 6; *Rituelen in je leven: Humanist. Maandblad over humanisme en wereld* 52 (1997/1998) no. 12/1; *Rituelen schenken levenskracht. Liturgie met ouderen in de praktijk* (DPC-brochure Rotterdam), Rotterdam 1998; G. ROOIJAKKERS: *Rituele repertoires. Volkscultuur in oostelijk Noord-Brabant 1559-1853*, Nijmegen 1994; C. ROSSEELS: *Rituelen vandaag*, Antwerpen 1995; G. ROUWHORST: '"Ritual Studies": drie benaderingen van een complex verschijnsel ...', in *Tijdschrift voor Liturgie* 86 (2002) 266-280; A. DE RUIJTER a.o.: *Totems en trends. Over de zin van identificatiesymbolen*, Hilversum 1988; A. SCHILSON: 'Fest und Feier in anthropologischer und theologischer Sicht', in *Liturgisches Jahrbuch* 44 (1994) 1, 4-32; IDEM: 'Den Gottesdienst fernsehgericht inszenieren? Die Verantwortung der Liturgie angesichts des ‚Medienreligiösen', in *Stimmen der Zeit* 8 (1996) 534-546; IDEM: 'Das neue Religiöse und der Gottesdienst. Liturgie vor einer neuen Herausforderung?', in *Liturgisches Jahrbuch* 46 (1996) 2, 94-109; IDEM: 'Musicals als Kult. Neue Verpackung religiöser Symbolik?', in *Liturgisches Jahrbuch* 48 (1998) 3, 143-167; D. STRINGER: 'Liturgy and Anthropology: the History of a Relationship', in *Worship* 63 (1989) 503-520; M.D. STRINGER: *On the Perception of Worship. The Ethnography of Worship in Four Cristian Congregations in Manchester*, Birmingham 1999; *Symbolen en riten: Tijdschrift voor Geestelijk Leven* 51 (1995) no. 6; T. SWINKELS & P. POST: 'Beginnings in Ritual Studies according to Ronald Grimes', in *Jaarboek voor liturgie-onderzoek* 19 (2003) 215-238; M. VERHELST a.o.: *Met rituelen het leven spelen. Initiatie – welkom – dank – verzoening – feest*, Kapellen/Brussel 1988; J. DE VISSCHER: *Een te voltooien leven. Over rituelen van de moderne mens*, Kampen 1996; see also the bibliography in: M. ZITNIK: *Sacramenta. Bibliographia internationalis,* I-IV, Rome 1992 and GRIMES: *Research in Ritual Studies.*

[8] See among others G. LUKKEN: *Ontwikkelingen in de liturgiewetenschap: balans en perspectief* (Liturgie in perspectief 1), Baarn 1993; P. POST: 'Liturgische bewegingen en feestcultuur. Een landelijk liturgiewetenschappelijk onderzoekprogramma', in *Jaarboek voor liturgie-onderzoek* 12 (1996) 21-55.

the theme of ritual and culture (Part II). Finally I will try to indicate what the new place and shape and identity of Christian ritual is within the abundance of rituals in our contemporary culture (Part III).

Finally I would like to express my appreciation for the Netherlands Organisation for Scientific Research (NWO), which subsided the English translation, and D. Mader, M. Div., who translated the Dutch text.

PART 1

RITUALS

What are rituals? What characterizes them? What role do they play in the lives of individuals and society? These questions are not easy to answer. There are three reasons for this. First, scholars from many disciplines study rituals – biologists, sociologists, anthropologists, ethnologists, historians, philosophers, linguists, dramaturgists, students of comparative religion, theologians. Each discipline has its own approach. This also remains true even after rituals became the central subject in the new discipline of ritual studies. Second, ritual practices differ from culture to culture. Every culture has its own accents in ritual. What ritual practice is can only be determined from the inside out, from within that culture itself. Views on ritual therefore also change through history.[1] They are in part defined by the times and culture in which one stands. Finally, there has been more written about rituals than anyone who studies ritual can hope to read in a lifetime.[2]

In light of this, Bell warns against the danger of short-circuiting between theories about ritual and the factual, empirical data within various cultures, which are particularly colorful. No split can be allowed between theory and practice.[3] Boudewijnse similarly points out that one should not attempt to construct a sort of 'lowest common denominator' from the various approaches in the literature.[4] Thus it is impossible to collect pieces from the literature and put together an answer as though one were putting together an jigsaw puzzle. The views are sometimes too different to permit this. One would not be doing justice to other views, disciplines and methods. What is understood as ritual must be specified in each particular case.

If one desires to adequately heed Bell's warning, one must really begin with a concrete description of the rituals within the various cultures. This means that I would have to begin with the second part of this book, on ritual and culture; after all, it is there that it becomes clear that rituals can differ considerably from culture to culture. Bell herself however acknowledges that it is more instructive to begin with more general considerations,

---

[1] A good survey of developments and theories can be found in BELL: *Ritual. Perspectives*, part I. With regard to this, I would point out that older theories are not per se superseded by more recent theories (see Bell, page 88). Some older theories remain relevant down to this day. Furthermore, they are not mutually exclusive, and the authors often belong to different schools. All provide insight into the phenomenon of ritual in one way or another.

[2] Thus BOUDEWIJNSE: 'The Conceptualisation of Ritual' 31.

[3] BELL: *Ritual Theory*; IDEM: *Ritual. Perspectives*.

[4] BOUDEWIJNSE: 'The Conceptualisation of Ritual' 35-36.

and that the question of whether one must give priority to concrete data or to theory is ultimately the famous question of what came first, the chicken or the egg. On the one hand, generally we identify data only when we have a theory; on the other hand, we often adjust theories as we clarify them on the basis of data.[5] Therefore there is a reciprocal relationship between theory and practice. Thus in the first part of this book ritual in general will be discussed; in the second part ritual will be examined more specifically in its relation to culture.

In this book I have chosen for an approach from my own discipline – that of theology, and in particularly liturgical studies. But in no sense do I consider theology and liturgical studies as isolated disciplines. As was the case in my previous publications, my own approach will be as open as possible for the anthropological approach found in ritual studies, and to an important degree it is also enhanced by these ritual studies.[6] This approach provides my own discipline with a considerably stronger empirical foundation. Furthermore, I will repeatedly need to clarify the terminology used as much as possible. Indeed, only in this way is it possible to understand one another, to shed light on the matters that concern me, and eventually enter into discussion with those who are perhaps disposed to another view.

In the first part, which deals with rituals in general, the first chapter discusses the many forms of human communication, including communication by way of rituals. I will lay the foundation, as it were, by discussing symbolization as the basis for all ritual. On that basis, in the second chapter I will indicate what elements are characteristic for ritual. In the third chapter, issues raised in the first two will be explored in greater depth from the perspective of semiotics. Subsequently, in the fourth chapter, various specific themes will be examined, such as the presentative character of ritual, ritual in relation to space, time and music, the various categories which are distinguishable within ritual, ritual as feast, and the strengths and weaknesses of ritual. The fifth chapter will round off the discussion with a first, tentative consideration of the religious and Christian dimension of ritual.

---

[5] BELL: *Ritual. Perspectives* 1.

[6] In this connection Bell remarks, 'It is not common... for liturgical studies to concern themselves with the idea of ritual in general'; see BELL: *Ritual. Perspectives* 89.

CHAPTER 1

BASIC ELEMENTS OF RITUAL

The point of departure for this chapter is human communication and the special role that ritual plays in it. Then I will move on to symbolization. The essential components in that process are the symbol, the symbolic act and symbolic language, which are also the foundations for ritual. This process will then be explored in greater depth in a discussion of its double meanings and its presentative character.

1. COMMUNICATION

We easily associate the word 'communication' with means of communication. Radio, television, the telephone, internet, automobile and aeroplane spring to mind. These technical instruments enable us to communicate with one another worldwide. The general conviction that our potential for communication has vastly increased thanks to these scientific developments is justified. We can travel around the world and even into space at will; our reach extends progressively further. Through technology we have discovered much more about the world and its people, including ourselves. For instance, what do we not know about the human body? Medical science has taken great strides forward in the last decades. Science has also uncovered a great deal about the human psyche and human conduct. Our interaction with the world around us and with each other has become much more extensive and nuanced, and that has resulted in progress and increased well-being.

Yet at the same time it must be admitted this is not the whole story, because the 'hard' sciences only bring us in contact with a limited piece of reality, the part that they observe and investigate. All these forms of making contact have one thing in common: they isolate phenomena which are linked with one another. They typically fragment the world of our experience.[7] This can be characterized as split or itemized perception.

---

[7] O. VAN DER HART: *Rituelen in psychotherapie* 136, 237-252.

That leaves us with a pressing question: how do we come into contact with the wider and deeper reality? This can happen in two ways. The first possibility of doing so is by reflecting on that deeper reality. This takes place in the humanities, and especially in philosophy and theology. Philosophy and theology contemplate such questions as the true nature of man and of the world, the purpose and meaning of life, the meaning of death, the nature of religion and of God. In our day, as always, many people are in their own way occupied with these philosophical and theological questions. Indeed, more than ever before people are inclined to think through these questions for themselves and take their own standpoint. The importance of this manner of communicating with reality cannot be denied. But there is another possibility for communication which reaches deeper and is more vital, actually the most vital and integral means. That is to be open to people and the world not through discussion or reason with the intellect alone, but by participating in reality through all the means at our disposal, with the whole of our being, with intellect and emotion and all the senses. There one comes upon a whole different way of communication, which occurs through symbolization. It is important to examine this form of communication more deeply, so that subsequently, with this in mind, we can explore what rituals are.

2. SYMBOLIZATION

In The Netherlands, May 4 is the annual day of remembrance for the dead of World War II. The Dutch writer Ed Hoornik wrote of it:[8]

7:57 p.m.
This is Waalsdorp, the Waalsdorpervlakte. Sand, grass, here and there a copse of pines. Dunes, row after row, and behind them, unseen, sometimes barely audible, the sea.
Against the slope of one of the dunes four crosses... four crosses of birch, painted black. No other sound than the voice of the wind.
Slowly the landscape fills with people. They are coming, alone, sometimes two or three together, sometimes in groups... Eyes downcast, feet that more shuffle than walk. Deeper into the hollow in the dunes, closer

---

[8] E. HOORNIK: *Journalistiek proza en brieven*, Amsterdam 1974, 170-171.

to the place where it happened; where it happened again and again. The lorries carrying those condemned to death pulling up and stopping; the condemned being taken out two by two; the walk to the hollow in the dunes; blindfolds for those who wanted them; the desperate pounding of the heart.

And now: eyes downcast, feet that more shuffle than walk.

And then: the firing squad, the command, the shots, the birds rising. Blood that trickles away into the sand, sand that effaces all traces; sand, nothing more than sand, which the years have passed over, through which feet shuffle.

What we see now is the last thing that those who fell saw. A bit of sky …, a bit of earth …, a bit of Holland.

What we hear now is the last that those who fell here heard. Far away the sea …, the wind along the ground and in the trees …, the cry of a bird high in the air.

Then they fell, not far from one another, their head in the sand.

Death put an end to their suffering.

We remember them.

We remember the dead of 1940-1945.

8:02 p.m.

1940-1945. Years that continue to burrow away in our lives, that disturb our sleep and flit through our dreams. Years that we want to lose and that we keep fetching back, because we *can* not lose them. German years, dead years, the years of Buchenwald and Dachau, Auschwitz and Bergen-Belsen, of Sachsenhausen and Ravensbrück, and of this small valley of death here, which the people now enter. The procession of the living for the dead.

1940-1945. Years to which we go back, again and again, in which our feet continue to walk...

Four black crosses of birch, the experience of the silence, the slow approach of the people, alone, in twos or threes or in small groups, the subdued gaze, walking slowly, shuffling, on the way to the execution site, looking to the sky, the earth, a bit of Holland, listening to the sea, the wind and the birds, processing past the crosses, remembering the dead of the Second World War...

There are all kinds of ways we can relate to the dead of the Second World War. We can read about their imprisonment and execution, do research into the concentration camps and the history of suffering that played itself out in them, and try to uncover the causes and explanations for what took place there. But a very specific way of relating to the dead involves symbolization. In it, we use *things* in such a way that the perspective is sprung and something breaks open. This memorial was marked by silence; words were pointedly absent. But often we also use *words* to recall the dead, words that call up something of our belief in a deeper reality and our relation with them. For instance, sometimes their names are read out one by one, to which those assembled answer each time 'present'. And finally: we *act* in a particular, loaded manner, so as to be able to open up space and admit something of a more distant horizon.

Thus, three elements play a role in symbolism: things, words and acts. These elements can also be designated as symbols, symbolic language, and symbolic acts. It is important to look more closely at these various elements.

2.1. Symbol

Much thought has been given to – and a lot written about – the concept of the 'symbol'. Anyone exploring the literature involved will quickly discover that there is no unanimity whatsoever. There are many views, and these can be confusing. I will not tire the reader with a summary of the differing opinions. What I believe it is important to do here is make clear what ritual is all about. To do that, it is essential to take a further look at the symbol, and it will be necessary to come to an agreement about the terms that will be used. Only in this way can we understand one another, here and in possible further discussion.

Still, I do not intend to set about this arbitrarily. I certainly have my own view of the matter, but that is not disconnected from the views of others.[9] I want to further locate my approach, and thus substantiate it, particularly because it has sometimes been remarked that it is no longer up to date.[10] My principle point of departure is the way the term 'symbol'

---

[9] G. LUKKEN: 'Symbool als grondcategorie van de liturgie. Enkele aanvullende verhelderingen vanuit de semiotiek', in *Jaarboek voor liturgie-onderzoek* 14 (1998) 87-97.

[10] See for instance B.D. SPINKS: 'Review', in *The Journal of Theological Studies* 46 (1995) 808 or G. LUKKEN (eds.: C. CASPERS & L. VAN TONGEREN): *Per visibilia ad invisibilia. Anthropological, Theological and Semiotic Studies on the Liturgy and the Sacraments* (Liturgia condenda 2), Kampen 1994; see also A.C. THISELTON: 'Sign, Symbol', in J.G. DAVIES (ed.): *A New Dictionary of Liturgy and Worship*, Londen 1986, 491-492.

is used in theology, and in particular in liturgical studies, where a distinction is often made between *sign* and *symbol*. One also encounters numerous proponents of this distinction outside of theology. I refer – without the intention of being exhaustive – to anthropologists and philosophers such as Cassirer, Durand, Ortigues, Ricoeur and Turner, and to psychologists (in particular those dealing with religion) such as Fortmann, Jung, Lacan, Vergote and Weima.[11] With regard to contemporary theology, one can for instance cite Baumer, Lawler, Lies and Chauvet.[12] The latter makes this distinction a fundamental point of departure for the development of a contemporary theology of Christian ritual. One can even say more generally that symbol in this sense is a central concept in contemporary sacramental theology and in the theology of liturgy,[13] and more broadly, in theology.[14] I have the impression that the critique of the distinction between sign and symbol is primarily related to the rise of a new

---

[11] E. CASSIRER: *Philosophie der symbolischen Formen*, 3 Vol., Berlin 1923 and further; IDEM: *An Essay on Man: An Introduction to a Philosophy of Human Culture*, New Haven 1944; G. DURAND: *L'imagination symbolique*, Paris 1964; E. ORTIGUES: *Le discours et le symbole*, Aubier-Montaigne 1962; P. RICOEUR: *Finitude et culpabilité*, Paris 1963; IDEM: *Le conflit des interprétations. Essais d'herméneutique*, Paris 1969, 16-17; V. TURNER: *The Forest of Symbols. Aspects of Ndembu Ritual*, Ithaca 1967; IDEM: *The Drums of Affliction. A Study of Religious Processes among the Ndembu of Zambia*, Oxford 1968; IDEM: *The Ritual Process. Structure and Anti-structure*, Chicago 1969; H. FORTMANN: *Als ziende de onzienlijke*, 3 Vol., Hilversum 1965-1968, part 1, 186-187 and part 3a, 161-162; C.G. JUNG: *Psychologische Typen*, Zürich 1921, 384-385; IDEM: *Symbole der Wandlung*, Zürich 1952, 642-647; J. LACAN: *Écrits*, Paris 1966; A. VERGOTE: *Het huis is nooit af. Gedachten over mens en religie*, Antwerpen/Utrecht 1974; J. WEIMA: *Reiken naar oneindigheid. Inleiding tot de psychologie van de religieuze ervaring*, Baarn 1981, 229-247.

[12] I. BAUMER: 'Interaktion – Zeichen – Symbol', in *Liturgisches Jahrbuch* 1 (1981) 25-30; M. LAWLER: *Symbol and Sacrament. A contemporary sacramental theology*, Mahwah 1987, 15-17; L. LIES: *Eucharistie in ökumenischer Verantwortung*, Graz/Wien/Köln 1996, 107-108; L.-M. CHAUVET: *Du symbolique au symbole. Essai sur les sacrements*, Paris 1979; IDEM: *Symbole et sacrement. Une relecture sacramentelle de l'existence chrétienne*, Paris 1988; IDEM: *Les sacrements, parole de Dieu au risque du corps*, Paris 1993. See also the approach of D. BOROBIO (ed.): *La celebracion en la Iglesia, I Liturgia y sacramentologia fundamental* (Lux mundi 57), Salamanca 1985, 413-434.

[13] P. LEVESQUE: 'A Symbolical Sacramental Methodology: An Application of the Thought of Louis Dupré', in *Questions Liturgiques* 76 (1995) 161-181, particularly 177-181.

[14] W. ENGEMANN: 'Semiotik und Theologie – Szenen einer Ehe', in W. ENGEMANN & R. VOLP: *Gib mir ein Zeichen. Zur Bedeutung der Semiotik für theologische Praxis- und Denkmodelle*, Berlin/New York 1992, 3-28. See also LEVESQUE: 'A Symbolical Sacramental Methodology'.

discipline, semiotics (the discipline of the sign). This uses a different and sometimes even antithetical terminology, which can cause confusion, that in turn can lead to misunderstandings. I will return to this later. At that point it will become clear that the semiotic approach in no way contradicts my approach, but rather can further clarify, supplement and elaborate on it.[15]

How, precisely, does a *symbol* work? Actually, it is an everyday thing that you encounter in your immediate environment. Birch wood is given the shape of a cross, and is painted black. By placing four birch crosses in the context of an annual memorial observance, they suddenly acquire an extraordinary expressive power. They remind one of the Second World War, which robbed our people of their freedom, and of the courage of those who actively resisted, of their tragic deaths, of those who were left behind as orphans, of the moments before their death, of the last things they saw: a bit of sky, a bit of earth, a bit of Holland. They unveil the last moment in which these countrymen heard what we also hear during the memorial: the sea, the wind along the ground and in the trees, the cries of a bird high in the air. We remember the concentration camps and the unutterable suffering that took place there, and the many who were murdered in violent ways after them, and so much more… It is not easy to express it all in words. In the symbol, the limited receives an infinite amplitude, almost a universality. The symbol has multiple meanings. It functions as a bridge across boundaries. It refers to a deeper reality, a farther horizon, a wider landscape. More immediately: something of that other, of the symbolized reality, is really present in the thing, which symbolizes.

Thus the reference does not come from outside, from somewhere else: not from a book, nor a commentary, nor from a previously conceived explanation. The latter is, for instance, the case in an allegory. The Middle Ages were the high point for allegory. As examples, the twelve months of the year referred to the twelve apostles, the four seasons to the four evangelists, and the whole year to Christ himself. When silence fell three times during the mass, it was a sign of the three days Christ lay in the tomb. The walnut signified Christ: the sweet kernel was his divine nature, the fleshy outer skin his human nature, and the woody shell between them the cross. Huizinga remarks that a poem like

---

[15] See Part 1, Chapter 3.

Olivier de la Marche's *Le parament et triumphe des dames* stands on the lowest step of symbolism in the Middle Ages. In it, each item of a woman's clothing is compared to a virtue. The shoes are care and diligence, the stockings perseverance, the garter determination, the blouse modesty, and the corset chastity.[16] It is clear that this allegory does not operate at the level of direct perception, but as an intellectual explanation. There is indeed a certain randomness involved. Yet if the explanations take hold, allegories can eventually become symbols. One can refer to the five incense grains on the paschal candle as a symbol of the wounds of Christ or to the medieval preacher, who sometimes paused to stand in silence, with his arms extended in the form of a cross, for a quarter of an hour.[17]

Thus, in a symbol the thing speaks for itself: in this situation and this context, the four black crosses of birch inescapably call up something very specific and sweeping. One might say there is a direct, non-rational communication with another reality. Thus symbols cannot be invented, and when using them you need not reflect on them. The perception is intuitive and touches the whole person, at the level of feelings and the senses. Symbols do not rest on agreements. In one way or another, the thing that is a symbol refers to itself, because it participates in the reality to which it refers. Goethe formulated it aptly: the symbol is the thing without being the thing, and yet is the thing.[18]

So the symbol brings together, unites and gives continuity to what is dispersed. It brings past and future together in the present. It helps one not to react incoherently. In and through the symbol we try to communicate with the land from which we came and with the ground under our feet, but also with the land of our future possibilities. In symbols, our origins and the future toward which we orient ourselves become interwoven with each other in the present.[19]

---

[16] J. HUIZINGA: *The Waning of the Middle Ages. A Study of the Forms of Life, Thought, and art in France and the Netherlands in the Fourteenth and Fifteenth Centuries* (Pelican Books A 307), London/Tonbridge 1955, 207, 210-211.

[17] HUIZINGA: *The Waning of the Middle Ages* 192.

[18] Quotation in T. TODOROV: *Théories au symbole*, Paris 1977, 239.

[19] W. JETTER: *Symbol und Ritual. Anthropologische Elemente im Gottesdienst*, Göttingen 1978, 68-69.

Therefore a symbol is clearly to be distinguished from a *sign*. A sign is just as much of a reference to another reality, but this reference takes place through a rational process. It is the result of agreement. It is clear, unambiguous, efficient and utile. A thing which is a sign does not refer to itself, nor does it participate in that to which it refers. One can think of a traffic sign, crosswalk markings, or a contract. Signs have no purpose of their own, and do not call us to stop, muse or meditate, as would be the case with a photo that is dear to one. Signs pass the reference through. They are a sort of springboard to another reality which has nothing to do with the sign as such. If a sign is no longer clear enough, it is altered by agreement. One must learn signs intellectually. Anyone who drives a car must simply know traffic signs by heart. Understanding, knowledge and learning go with signs.

It is true for all things that they are not merely what they superficially appear to be, but in one way or another are more, and so can become symbols. That is true of the hand, the eye, the foot, the body, a flower, the cross, the gallows, bread and wine, a table, a house, a chair, a child, man, woman, color, light, space, etc. The Brazilian theologian Boff tells us how a perfectly everyday object can become a symbol. He had just come to Munich to study. It was August, a beautiful summer, two o'clock in the afternoon. His first letter from home arrived. Everyone has written. Then the news breaks on him: his father has died at the age of 54. One of the mainstays of his life is gone. The next day he discovers a yellowed cigarette butt in the envelope: the last cigarette his father smoked, just before his fatal heart attack. They have sent it to him. From that time on, Boff preserved it in his desk as a keepsake. The color of the cigarette, the aroma of the south-Brazilian tobacco immediately call to mind his father.[20] Thus the simplest thing can become a symbol, and a symbol can involve all the sense organs, even smell.

Indeed, odors can be very compelling symbols. The smell of the cigarette butt is simply part of the symbol and the way it is perceived. An odor can suddenly call up memories of the home where one grew up and one's native land. Bachelard remarks that the smell of a wet raincoat can bring back bygone school years: you smell the month of October and the school corridors where you once walked.[21] Sometimes, when I

---

[20] L. BOFF: *Kleine Sakramentenlehre*, Düsseldorf 1976, 27-29.
[21] G. BACHELARD: *La poétique de la rêverie*, Paris 1971, 119.

smell the penetrating aroma of an orange, I think suddenly of the beginning of the Second World War, when as children in the second year of elementary school we each received an orange from the Red Cross, carefully peeled it and ate it. That one orange became a symbol of the past, of the Second World War, the shortages that prevailed, the security of the class, the help of others. Odors actually express in a particularly emphatic way what a symbol itself contains. Our sense of smell is powerfully linked with the body itself, and as such is preconceptual. Symbols actually work like smells. In this connection, one could say that symbols have the logic of odors.[22]

Our culture has difficulty with perceiving symbols. We are inclined, rather, to look at the sober facts and to take things literally. Our world has become before all else a field for research.[23] For us, the moon is a landscape of rocks and craters. The world around us is no longer self-evidently laden with an 'other' reality. It consists of factual data, which one can investigate in their regularity. In this context, the thesis propounded by a 1983 Dutch dissertation is pregnant: 'The assertion of the heart surgeon De Vries that the heart is only a pump and thus is not the seat of the soul or the symbol of love has the same implacable logic as the assertion that tears consist only of water and salt, and thus can not be a symbol of grief.'[24]

Our way of approaching the world is also strongly influenced by our behavior as consumers. We look to the utility and the profitability of all things. In the advertising which pours out over us daily – always just a little louder and more blatantly than other things – this perspective on things does not vary. Or, if it does vary, it is only in one direction: that of the product to be acquired and possessed. The ideal image of young men and women, propagated by television, is that of two persons whose life is realized primarily through consumer goods.[25] Of course, we can not do without the sensory organ which concentrates on the sign. It is

---

[22] In this connection see GRIMES: *Reading, Writing, and Ritualizing* 20-21 with reference to D. SPERBER: *Rethinking symbolism*, Cambridge 1975. See also N. MITCHELL: 'The Amen Corner. Smells and Bells', in *Worship* 72 (1998) 539-547.

[23] H. FORTMANN: 'De primitief, de dichter en de gelovige', in H. FORTMANN: *Heel de mens. Reflecties over de menselijke mogelijkheden*, Bilthoven 1972, 261 ff.

[24] Thesis of J. ROERDINK, Utrecht: *NRC Handelsblad* September 3, 1993.

[25] D. SÖLLE: 'The Repression of the Existential Element, or Why So Many People Become Conservative', in *Concilium* 17 (1981) 1, 69-75.

also directed toward humanization. But it is disastrous whenever it becomes so overgrown that its more integral functions of recognition are neglected. Then we degrade ourselves beneath our human level. In perceiving a symbol, a sense organ reaches into the depths and touches the whole of the person. It is the function of recognition possessed by the child, the poet, or an adult in real, concrete life, and also the religious person. An open mind is necessary for this organ of recognition to function. We must arrive at a certain naivety and simplicity. Because naivety and simplicity have been ousted from our culture through the critical approaches of science, one must speak of reaching a second naivety and simplicity. Anyone who perceives symbols has decidedly not devalued research, science and technique. They have merely put them in their proper place.

2.2. Symbolic act

Deeds and acts differ.[26] A *deed* is purely transaction, with an eye to a tangible result. A deed is good if it produces the right result. Deeds must be useful. They are aimed at actually changing things, situations and structures. Thus a deed is always unambiguous. It produces a definite product; it sells the product for an established price. Or it pulls the trigger of a gun and the sparrow falls on the roof. Sport in the West is a chain of deeds, aimed at getting results, at ever improving performances. An *act which is a sign,* is thus more like a deed. It is subordinate to something outside itself, to which it refers. For instance, the actions of a traffic policeman are directed toward keeping traffic flowing efficiently. That is the case for clear, unambiguous actions that are in absolutely no way an end in themselves. They refer to and function as a springboard for something else. One could add to this list the signing of a contract, carrying out a rule, and running a meeting efficiently.

A *symbolic act* is in itself laden with meaning. In one way or another it shares in the reality which it calls up. For example, Japanese archery is not so much aimed at results as at providing one with access to a spiritual path. It is a matter of contact with one's deepest self, concentration, directing oneself toward the one true goal. Other actions in sport can also become authentic human expressions laden with meaning: one can

---

[26] C. VERHOEVEN: *Rondom de leegte*, Utrecht 1967, 11 ff.

think of harmonious actions performed in dressage, figure skating or on the balance beam, which *could* become symbolic acts. The accent *can* shift, so that the perspective springs open. This takes place in a most affective way in modern art, when in a performance the artist's own actions become a work of art, in and through which the reality of the artwork is revealed.

Human symbolic acts can have multiple meanings. In his book *Op weg naar het einde* (On the way to the end), the Dutch author G.K. van het Reve writes of the appalling trip from Amsterdam to London: it is the stupidest route that exists on earth. Having elaborated on this for three-quarters of a page, he adds:[27]

> I would hope that after this it is sufficiently clear to you that I travel to get somewhere, and by no means for the pleasure of the trip itself. If God for once is going to be 'all in all', it seems to me that must imply that everyone will be within walking distance, so that, in a manner of speaking, you never have to go anywhere any more. That will be the most amazing thing yet that we, in giving up our separation from Him, will get to see: the Kingdom of God will look surprisingly like a village, not much bigger than Schoorl: calm weather; making small talk; a man smoking his pipe at the back door; watching the clouds go by. Peace, no quarrels: there is already so much trouble in the world. As I said.

This text is full of shifts in perspective. The meaningless trip turns out to be experienced as an eschatological journey, as a way to a new, peaceful world, which radiates warmth.

Compared with symbols, symbolic *acts* appear to have some peculiarities. Where a symbol relates to things outside us, in all symbolic acts people themselves are at issue: their own actions fulfill the symbolic function as bridges. It is we who lay flowers at the grave or a monument.

Symbolic acts without the express presence of symbolic objects are even more clearly a case of personal action. Or perhaps it would be better to say that here the human body itself, the human eye, hand, foot, etc., functions as a symbol. Kneeling is one such symbolic act, at least in the case of our kneeling to pray and not to scrub the floor, for instance; in the latter case one is dealing with a sign act. Other examples are bowing or shaking hands. One can also note that the symbol

---

[27] G.K. VAN HET REVE: *Op weg naar het einde*, Amsterdam 1963, 68-69.

outside the person can never exercise its symbolic function free from human acts; the symbol is always in one way or another taken up in the human act of symbolization.

Finally: it is possible that one and the same human action at the same time is both a symbol and a sign. Thus enacting a law or chairing a meeting may be actions that are signs, but when at the same time the exercise of authority is emphasized – for instance by ceremonial dress or act of obeisance – the same act also becomes at the same time a symbolic act. I will return to this point in section 2.4.

2.3. Symbolic language

In language the distinction between term and word or symbolic language corresponds to that between sign and symbol, and between acts which are signs, and symbolic acts.

A *term* is unambiguous. Terms are really stripped-down words, artificial products that arise through high-handed approaches to and the overmastering of reality. One could also say that a term is a stiff and lifeless word, with only one meaning. It refers to a splinter of reality that is approached in an ordered way. One can speak of a good term, one that does as much as possible with the least possible difficulty, that is, which refers to its piece of reality with maximum clarity. Just as little as with signs, terms are something with which one does not linger. They have purely the function of a springboard: you pass them as quickly as possible in order to hear or perceive that to which they point. One can also change terms if they no longer fulfil their function. Their realm is knowledge and science, and they have no appeal to a person as a whole. One finds examples of terms primarily in the exact sciences. The reality about which these sciences speak can be communicated easily and without misunderstanding. International exchange is very possible. This is made still easier by the fact that technical terms are often simply taken over from the language in which they arose: one can think of terms such as 'abbot', 'deacon', 'hierarchy', 'roentgenogram', 'polder'. The newscaster also moves in the realm of terms. There facts are dealt with in a businesslike manner, in clear language. The number of victims in a disaster or battle is announced without emotion, and more pleasing news is given the same distant treatment. It is a question of exactness.

Symbolic language is different. When words are used as symbolic expression, they call up whole worlds. For instance, the words 'father', 'mother', and 'light' are polysemic. They cannot be clearly defined. One can pause over them. One uses them with commitment and feeling. They uncover and reveal a deeper reality. They do not separate, but connect. Symbolic language is always opening up new horizons.

In this connection, the original meaning of the word 'say' is revealing.[28] Words that express 'say' regularly also have a meaning associated with 'light'. To say something originally means to bring something to light. *Say* is related to the word *see*, and originally meant to let something come to light, to let it be seen. The Greek *phemi* (to say) is related to *phaino* (to bring to light, to appear) and thus also to *phoos* (light). The Latin *dicere* (to say) is related to the Greek *deiknumi* and the German *zeigen* (let see, illuminate). Thus it appears from etymology that at least one of the characteristics – and perhaps the most fundamental characteristic – of the word is that what is put into words really steps into the light. The word hauls things out of their obscurity. It reveals and brings them to light. It is not random, but has to do with reality itself and takes part in it. In words, in symbolic language, it is a matter of shining through, of making reality transparent, opening something up into deep perspective. Gusdorf writes: 'The word reveals the most intimate nature of the thing'.[29] One might also say: 'Speak, and I shall see'.

Our world could not operate without the language of terms. We need that sort of language in order to have dominion in the world. Without the language of terms no trade would be possible, no economic exchange, no scientific research. The language of terms is as important for our welfare as traffic signs are for transit. But it is equally true that this language is insufficient if one 'wants to lift up his heart and say what is within him, hidden and almost unassailable. If it is a matter of love and death, of God and man, this first language, this manner of speaking, is not only inadequate, but indeed dangerous'.[30] Then symbolic language is needed, a language 'more defenseless and modest than

---

[28] H. SCHMIDT: 'Language and its Function in Christian Worship', in *Studia Liturgica* 8 (1970-1971) 9.

[29] G. GUSDORF: *La parole*, Paris 1968[6], 11.

[30] H. OOSTERHUIS: *In het voorbijgaan*, Utrecht 1968, 237.

the first, the language of what can not actually be said'.[31] This language
does not describe historically checkable facts of our existence, but speaks
out its hidden sense, or the feared nonsense. It is not a matter of the
impersonal, objectifying descriptive speech of the exact sciences. What
is expressed here is not simply a speaking about something; it is speech
in which we ourselves are very strongly involved: confession, proclamation, orientation. It is a matter of speech that treats something deeply
and brings it about.[32] The following epitaph written by Ernesto Cardenal for the grave of a Nicaraguan resistance fighter is a striking example
of this:[33]

> They killed you and have not told us where your body is buried,
>   but since then the whole of our nation's territory has become your grave;
> or better, in every foot of land in which
>   your body is not present, you have risen.
>
> They thought they had killed you with the order: fire!
> They thought they buried you
>   but all they did was sow.

Symbolic language does not have to be high and exalted. It can be very
simple and direct. Is this not the case with young children's prattle?
Their speech is like a babbling brook. The world that surrounds them
must be put into words: the cows and the flowers and the car that drives by. Things reveal themselves in this way.[34] This simple speech can
also be found in adults. The psychologist of religion Fortmann describes
how he once took a two hour bus ride from London to Canterbury.
Behind him sat two women:[35]

> Their conversation lasted two hours, or, subtracting the time for catching
> their breath, an hour and three-quarters. I could not understand anything
> more of their dialect than a thousand times 'yes' and five hundred times
> 'Oh dear'! But it was none the less impressive for that. A waterfall is the
> only fitting comparison. There is ground to suspect that the whole neigh-
> borhood and both families to cousins thrice removed formed the subject
> (…).

---

[31] OOSTERHUIS: *In het voorbijgaan* 237-238.

[32] W. LUIJPEN: 'De erwtensoep is klaar', in *Streven* 22 (1969) 510-526.

[33] K. WELLINGA (ed.): '… *Om Nicaragua te bevrijden…' Poëzie van Ernesto Cardenal*,
Amsterdam 1978, 53.

[34] H. FORTMANN: 'Zonder het woord wordt alles zinloos', in IDEM: *Heel de mens* 73.

[35] FORTMANN: 'Zonder het woord wordt alles zinloos' 74.

Fortmann points to the innocence and benevolence of this conversation. He reserves the term 'high-level speech' for those conversations that are really self-revealing.

Symbolic language is important not only in the religious realm: it first puts its roots down at the interpersonal level.

> May I conclude that there is a lot of loneliness? That many people have no one with whom they can get off their chest the things deep in their heart, things that preoccupy them day and night? That the real questions seldom are answered and an endless series of personal feelings remain locked inside…? It is… really a *rare* privilege to be able to speak about the things of the soul – by which I mean not only religious things, though they are included.[36]

Much has been written about narrative theology. Practicing it is more difficult. How can it happen, as long as the anthropological basis is missing, so long as one's own life story and that of the other cannot be told?

2.4. Double meanings

In contrast to the realm of the sign, the act which is a sign, and the term, stands the realm of the symbol, symbolic acts and symbolic language. They are different ways of relating to reality. These two ways of communication are not interchangeable. One must not confuse them.[37]

The difference between the two realms reveals itself clearly when one places myth next to a scientific report. If one gives a scientific explanation about the origins of the world, it is entirely different than when that origin is told in myth. The book of Genesis occupies an entirely different sphere than a science text. In the latter one finds terms and language which functions as signs; in the former, there is symbolic language. Anyone who reads the creation account in Genesis as a scientific explanation has gotten off on the wrong foot.

And yet it is possible for both realms to be present at the same time without losing their individuality and without exchanging roles. Thus the symbolic pole can stand in the realm of terms, signs and acts which are signs. When for instance someone gives a scientific lecture, he moves in the realm of terms, signs and acts which are signs. But at the same

---

[36] FORTMANN: 'Zonder het woord wordt alles zinloos' 73.
[37] CHAUVET: *Du symbolique au symbole* 61 ff.

time one could speak of the symbolic realm, for he appeals to his listeners to take him seriously as a scientist, to recognize him as such and identify with him. An inaugural address certainly aims at the latter too. So, too, it could be that when someone asks a question after a lecture in order to get further information, he really wants to let himself be heard: 'I am here, recognize me, identify with me'.

Often one can speak of double meanings. Almost always meaning really functions at two levels. Sometimes these gradually merge, and another time the emphasis will lie on one or the other. When I say, 'Nice weather', I am reporting a fact. But the emphasis undoubtedly lies on symbolic communication; I am really saying 'I'm here; speak with me'. The worst thing that could happen is that the other deliberately does not answer what I've said: then my presence, my selfhood is ignored. Thus the strong reaction: 'You could have *at least* answered'.

Many variants are possible in the relation between the two realms: thus a maximum of information can go together with a pronounced stress on the symbolic pole. When someone says 'Bring me that document', he gives some precise information, but at the same time he says that the other person is subordinate. On the other hand, in the realm of the symbol, symbolic acts and symbolic language one can also speak of a cognitive pole. One could even say that this pole regularly plays a part. There are almost always what could be called 'catechetical implications'. However, because this notional process occurs above all at the realm of symbols, the emphasis does not lie strictly on intellectual knowledge. Rather there is what the ancient church termed 'mystagogic catechesis'. Thus it is not a matter of knowing science or theology as such. If this is the case, then the symbolic realm changes into that of the sign, the term, and the act as sign. This is also true for liturgy.

2.5. Presentative and discursive symbolism

Sometimes the whole life of another can reveal itself in objects. For instance, in a discussion group a mother laid a bracelet down in front of her, and began to talk. She had given it as a present to her daughter, who had died young. She had worn it her whole life. Her eyes upon it constantly, she told about this life, from birth to death. Objects can, in one glance, evoke widely separated things in this way: in one moment, in and through the thing, infinitely much presents itself. That is true for the ring of the deceased, a photo of a beloved, a piece of jewellery that you received from someone as a keepsake.

Again and again we encounter what Susanne Langer has termed 'presentative symbolism'. By this, she intends primarily the non-verbal forms of symbolic expression.[38] Presentative symbolism is principally a matter of the symbolism of the visual, of space, light, color, gesture, movement, mime, dance, decoration, clothing, objects, images, sounds, intonation, music, aroma, silence, and so forth. It is characteristic of this symbolism that it does not work in successive steps, but simultaneously. Perception takes place in one glance. Similarly, for instance, we do not perceive a photograph by considering or calling to mind the various components from which it is constructed (color, light and shadow) in a certain sequence. There is a sort of total perception. The photograph makes what it depicts present instantaneously. As well as presentative symbolism, there is also discursive symbolism, in which perception is only possible sequentially. Language is in essence discursive: it involves linking units of meaning in larger wholes. The units of meaning follow one another, as items of clothing are worn over one another, or hang next to one another on a laundry line to dry. It is precisely through placing them next to and after one another that the whole is created. In presentative symbolism our manner of dealing with the world is strongly sensory. Our perception begins with the eye and extends through the other senses. Through this things present themselves to us instantaneously, in their concreteness, conveying a realm of experience that is inaccessible to discursive language. This is clearly the case for music: it permits us to experience that which language cannot evoke.

Presentative symbols and symbolic acts play a primary and indispensable role in human life. Lorenzer points out that they are absolutely fundamental for human beings and their dealings with the world around them.[39] According to him the forms of sensory interaction – and that is

---

[38] S. LANGER: *Philosophie auf neuem Wege*, Frankfurt 1965, 86 ff, particularly 102-105 (English original: IDEM: *Philosophy in a New Key. A Study in the Symbolism of Reason, Rite, and Art*, New York 1942).

[39] A. LORENZER: *Das Konzil der Buchhalter. Die Zerstörung der Sinnlichkeit. Eine Religionskritik*, Frankfurt 1981, particularly 85-94 and 151-167. For Lorenzer, see also A. ODENTHAL: *Liturgie als Ritual. Theologische und psychoanalytische Überlegungen zu einer praktisch-theologischen Theorie des Gottesdienstes als Symbolgeschehen*, Stuttgart 2002, 150-155.

the level at which presentative symbolism plays out – precede the forms of interaction which take place through language. They are thus the foundation on which human development is built. Before a child can speak there have already been countless sensory interactions between the mother and child. These have their repercussions in the child, and each time call up reactions from its side. The expansion of the child's radius of action to the world beyond the mother has its basis in the expansion of the scope of sensory interactions. Objects from the world in which the child engages in play have a large role in this, and beyond them, items of clothing, household furnishings, the home itself, the stairs, the garden, the street, the woods, all in the form in which the child encounters them, as they have been shaped in part by other people.

When a child begins to speak, that ushers in a considerable increase in consciousness. The child can now engage in reflection.[40] Through language the child acquires, as it were, a playground that it can enter and make use of independent of reality and concrete situations. It is exactly language which enables us to imagine ourselves in situations that are not present to the senses here and now. Language makes it possible for us to speak of situations in the past and future as though they were in the present. When we talk about Napoleon, no one expects that the Emperor is present in our midst here and now. We can also speak of a person now living in their absence. If they then unexpectedly arrive, we indicate that by a gesture or by a change in facial expression.

However, what is gained with language is in another sense also certainly offset by a loss. While the child previously was fully absorbed in the situation of the moment, and without reflection could respond spontaneously to different situations, this spontaneity is now limited to a considerable extent. Is that absence of inhibition not precisely a child's charm? Thus, on the one hand there is an increase in consciousness through language, but on the other one must accept that the deepest layer of the self is formed by sensory-symbolic interactions and the emotions connected with it.[41] The visible, audible, sapid, palpable impressions of sensory-symbolic forms of interaction involve tangible images

[40] LORENZER: *Das Konzil der Buchhalter* 85-94, particularly 91-92.
[41] LORENZER: *Das Konzil der Buchhalter* 162-163. Regarding presentative symbolism, see also M. BARNARD: 'Beeld en ritueel', in BARNARD & POST (eds.): *Ritueel bestek* 115-116.

and scenes; the world outside us is received experientially. In love and labor the actions that we designate with words are surrounded by an incomparably greater field of gestures and performances than we are able to denominate; without this field our actions would be barren and lifeless.

Thus it cannot be maintained that symbolic forms of interaction in language make the sensory-symbolic forms of interaction redundant. On the contrary: the interplay of the latter remains of eminent importance. Otherwise contact with the primary structures of the self is lost. In the sensory-symbolic forms of interaction we are dealing with the first layer of subjectivity, with its very basis. This layer is, as it were, the link between the consciousness and the subconscious of man, with its urges.

The conclusion is that one cannot disregard presentative symbolism and the forms of sensory-symbolic interaction corresponding to it without paying a heavy price. Where this does happen, it leads to the disorientation of the self. Perhaps the following example will make what I mean by disorientation understandable. If you enter a room where you spend time daily, and suddenly see that everything there has been put in a different place, you feel completely disoriented. At that moment it becomes clear to what extent the self is supported by spatial-symbolic forms of interaction. What is true for space is also true for light, color, clothing, movement, etc.

Presentative symbolism thus plays a central intermediary role in human life. We are often reminded of the past precisely through presentative symbols or symbolic acts. You hear a melody that played an important role in an event that has had radical consequences in your life, and suddenly the whole event springs to mind.

The following text evokes the past in a striking way on the basis of presentative symbolism:[42]

> We know that [for The Netherlands] the war began on May 10, 1940. But knowing this is not remembrance; without thinking we recall a fact, and nothing more. To truly *remember* May 10, 1940, is another matter. We cannot manage that without the day itself, the day as it began, the

---

[42] J.H. VAN DEN BERG: *Metabletica*, Nijkerk 1957³, 39.

summery spring day, its cloudless blue sky with the metally drone of the airplanes; the early hour, the people in their pyjamas coming out to watch: we need all these attributes of then – we can hardly do without even one – If we are to entice that day to show itself – and suddenly the day is as it was, a thousand impressions are present at the same moment, unabbreviated and in meaningful coherence…

You here encounter the permeation of life by what people in the humanities call material culture. All sorts of objects play a role in our lives, and we begin to be attached to them as a sort of basis for our existence: things in your room, things you inherited from your parents or received as gifts from others, that certain spoon, that little painting; often very small and ordinary things. Material things can also suddenly evoke a certain period of history. That is true for a medieval statue of Mary, but equally for simple objects such as an old zinc washtub, a granite drain-board, an old cooker. It is as if these lifeless things have a soul.[43] Things, even the most ordinary, do not stand alone; they are not purely autonomous but are intertwined with and marked by human use that gives them a particular significance. One might say there is an intensive interaction between us and the things around us. The things tell their own story, and bear the traces of the way in which people have shaped them or handled them. From this perspective it is also very understandable that Roman Catholics in the 1960s lost their orientation and footing when too much of the ecclesiastical material culture disappeared (statues, liturgical and devotional objects), and then even the church buildings in which they had worshipped from their youth were demolished. Humans are physical beings, and the whole of the material world is an extension of that peculiar physicality that we can never do without. We cannot live without presentative symbols, and are attached to them.

With regard to the discursive character of language, one important addition is necessary. Language as such belongs to discursive symbolism. But it must be added that Susanne Langer does not exclude all presentative symbolism from language; especially the language of poetry and myth

---

[43] Compare the semiotic study by A. GESPRINT: *L'objet comme procès et comme action. De la nature et de l'usage des objets dans la vie quotidienne*, Paris 1995 and E. LANDOWSKI: 'En deçà ou au-delà des stratégies, la présence contagieuse', in *Nouveaux Actes Sémiotiques* 83 (2002) 5-44.

has presentative characteristics. A poem is read line by line, and thus one can say there is successive perception (syntax), but at the same time it is true that there is a large degree of simultaneity (paradigm). Jakobson therefore remarks that in poetry syntax and paradigm coincide.[44] Perhaps one could even say that precisely as such symbolic language has presentative traits. Being what it is, it contains within itself a number of sensual elements, while on the other hand this sensual quality is reduced as much as possible to the language of terms or signs when language fulfils its task of conveying discursive meaning. Where one can truly call language expressive or visual, it is accurately designated as 'iconic language use'.[45] Such language use is very expressive and convincing. Precisely because it is richer in imagery, it lies closer to the non-verbal, and therefore touches upon the senses, for instance the visual. You see what is being spoken of before your eyes, as it were. When Margaret Thatcher, the former Prime Minister of England, is spoken of as the Iron Lady, you see her before you. An example of iconic language use is the following description of the burial of Empress Zita in Vienna in 1989:[46]

> It was much more impressive than I had thought. In the Dutch news the Empress Zita disappeared from a history that had already been over for centuries, lying in an sculpture-encrusted hearse drawn by six black horses. The last notes of Mozart's *Requiem* drifted out of the open doors of the Stefansdom in search of one another, for the following performance, as they are immortal... Thus we came to the doors of the Kaisergruft, the Hapsburg mausoleum. The gate was closed. Television showed a feeling for the drama. Cameras were placed inside and outside. In the great silence a functionary knocked on the gate, the dead waiting behind him. Where the dead must wait, life is taken very seriously. We viewers were suddenly inside the mausoleum. There stood an old, somewhat threadbare Capuchin friar, from the humblest order in the Church. The wooden cross that would soon mark his own grave must have already been prepared. "Who asks admission?" he asked on the stranger on the other side of the door. The camera outside took over. "Zita, a mortal and sinful human,"

---

[44] R. JAKOBSON & C. LÉVI-STRAUSS: "Les chats' de Beaudelaire', in R. JAKOBSON a.o.: *Questions de poétique*, Paris 1973, 401-419; A.J. GREIMAS: 'Introduction', in A.J. GREIMAS (ed.): *Essais de sémiotique poétique*, Paris 1972, 6-24.

[45] The term 'icon' is borrowed from Peircian semiotics. See Part 1, Chapter 3, 1 for this concept.

[46] A.L. BOON (= Kees Fens): 'Een sterfelijk, zondig mens', in *De Tijd* April 14, 1989, 40.

answered the functionary. It was again dead silent. The Capuchin knew his role well; he paused for a moment of thought. Then he answered, "She can come in." The doors swung open... The whole of the solemnities would have been less impressive if it had been a bishop in full panoply standing behind that door. But there stood a ragged friar with a lopsided beard, a mendicant, a tatterdemalion by birth. To him is all power given. Nowhere else in European culture had something so splendid been devised.

In light of this, one realizes that people do not have to be educated in order to speak in and understand expressive language. Indeed, quite the contrary. Sometimes the use of language by intellectuals is poorer. This also has consequences for ritual, in which in addition to symbols and symbolic acts, precisely symbolic language is also fundamental.

CHAPTER 2

CHARACTERISTICS OF RITUAL

This chapter will begin with several clarifications. Then I will deal with what appears to be most characteristic of ritual: repetition, and the question of the relation between rite and myth. Finally, ritual will be further characterized on the basis of a number of its additional dimensions.

1. SEVERAL PRELIMINARY CLARIFICATIONS

Before I enter into the question of what rituals are, it is necessary to provide some clarifications with regard to the terms 'ritual', 'rite' and 'ritualization', and the tension between functionalism and symbolism.

1.1. The terms ritual, rite and ritualization

The term 'ritual' in its contemporary significance as a designation for a general phenomenon is rather recent.[1] The word 'ritual' is to be found in the *Encyclopedia Britannica* only around the middle of the 18th century (first edition, 1771). There it is designated as the prescribed order of performing religious services, or the book containing such services. And 'rite' was specified as 'the particular manner of celebrating divine service, in this or that country'. In 1910 a long article on 'ritual' appeared in the *Encyclopedia Britannica* which bore witness to an important development. Here ritual was no longer defined as a book that laid down rules for liturgy, but as the designation for a type of symbolic behavior that one encounters in all religions, and even outside of religions. Thus the focus is now on the ritual act itself, and in a general sense at that. Ritual studies are based on this broad meaning of the concept of 'ritual'. Thus it is true that research into ritual began as a study of religious conduct, but in the course of time the concept of ritual was freed up from its religious context and became a designation

---

[1] In this connection see BELL: *Ritual. Perspectives* 259-267; BOUDEWIJNSE: 'The Conceptualisation of Ritual' 43-52.

for all ritual conduct.[2] This does not imply however that there is unanimity in this. One still encounters the opinion that ritual belongs
exclusively to the terrain of religion.[3] I opt for a broad standpoint: ritual is a general human fact. But I would add to that, that ritual comes
into its own in a very particular way within religion.

Next there is the matter of the terms *rite* and *ritual* as distinct designations. According to some, the word 'rite' in the strict sense designates
only repeated symbolic *acts*. But by others the word 'rite' is used in a
broad sense, and has the same meaning as the word 'ritual', in which
symbol, symbolic act and symbolic language come together. This latter
is even generally the case. Thus we have the expression 'Eastern rites',
which refers to the total of all the rituals of the different Eastern liturgies.[4] In this book I will use the terms 'rite' and 'ritual' as equivalents.

Finally there is the distinction made by Grimes between rite, ritual and
ritualizing, ritualization.[5] According to Grimes *rites* refer to the concrete,
more extended and socially recognized sets of ritual procedures, enacted
at specially chosen times and specially set side places, and which are distinguished from daily behavior. As examples of this, one can think of rituals such as baptism, marriage, funerals, the celebration of Easter, New
Year's, and so forth. *Ritual* refers not so much to concrete rites as to the
general scientific idea (the theory) of actions characterised by a certain
'family' of qualities, which are realized in rites. One can speak of *ritualiz-
ing/ritualization* insofar as animals engage in such behaviour or insofar it

---

[2] BELL: *Ritual. Perspectives* 39, 259-267; BOUDEWIJNSE: 'The Conceptualisation of
Ritual' 52. See also S. MAGGIANI: 'Rito/Riti', in D. SARTORE & A.M. TRIACCA: *Nuovo
dizionario di liturgia*, Rome 1984, 1224-1225; RAPPAPORT: *Ritual and Religion in the
Making of Humanity* 24 ff.

[3] See for instance J. DE VISSCHER: 'Geherbergd in een traditie. Symbolen en rituelen dienen tot niets', in *Tijdschrift voor Geestelijk Leven* 54 (1998) 114.

[4] When speaking of 'Eastern rites', the term 'rite' is often used to mean more than
ritual in a strict sense; in that phrase it can designate all the institutions and conduct
associated with Orthodoxy. For the distinction between ritual and rite from the standpoint of ecclesiastical law, see D.R. WHIT: 'Varietetates legitimae and an African-American Liturgical Tradition', in *Worship* 71 (1997) 504-537.

[5] R.L. GRIMES: *Beginnings in Ritual Studies* 35-51; IDEM: *Ritual Criticism: Case
Studies in its Practice, Essays on its Theory*, Columbia 1990, 9-13; IDEM: *Reading, Writ-
ing, and Ritualizing*, 5, 23-32; IDEM: *Marrying and Burying* 11-12, 225-226; IDEM:
Deeply into the Bone 21-29, 91.

concerns human activities not normally viewed as ritual, but regarded and treated as if they were or might be ritual, for instance, giving birth, house cleaning and watching TV. And finally *ritualizing/ritualization* is the act of deliberately cultivating, inventing or constructing a new rite. Such a rite does not typically garner broad social support; it is rather innovative and creative. One could thus say that ritualising/ritualization can be a phase in the process directed toward the creation of the rite. Ritualizing would thus rather be the foundation of the rite as such and of ritual. Others use the term *ritualize* to free the concept of ritual from its narrow traditional connection with organized religious institutions and worship services, and to emphasize that rituals involve *authentic* activities, or to further extend the concept to rituals in the animal world.[6] Bell notes that today people often use the term in studies which are concerned with ritual in technologically developed societies.[7] This latter appears to be the case with Grimes too.

In this book I do not make a distinction neither between rite and ritual, nor between rite/ritual and ritualization or ritualizing. I use 'rite' and 'ritual' for both the actual pattern of ritual actions and for the general scientific theories about rites. With regard to the concepts of ritualization and ritualizing, I also simply use the terms 'rite' and 'ritual' with regard to certain ordinary actions, certain experimental aggregates of acts, and certain conduct in the animal realm. From the context it will be clear whether these involve rituals in the animal world, previously established and socially recognised rites, general human ritual conduct or rites which are in a phase of chance, experiment or creation. With this it of course remains true that gradual changes can enter into ritual. Not all characteristics and dimensions of ritual will necessarily be present, nor will they always be present to the same degree. My characterization of ritual is oriented to giving an outline of what I would designate as the typical ritual domain.

1.2. Functionalism or symbolism?

In general one can say that a tension exists in cultural anthropology between those who place the accent on the functional social dimension

---

[6] BELL: *Ritual Theory* 88-89.
[7] BELL: *Ritual Theory* 89.

of ritual, and those who stress ritual as a symbolic act that has meaning in itself.[8] Are rituals primarily in the service of social life, or do rituals also have a significance in themselves? By discussing symbolization in Chapter 1, before addressing the question of what rituals are, I have already to a large degree defined my position: before all else, ritual is symbolic action. But at the same time it is true that ritual is not limited to that alone. This symbolic action also serves a function in social life and social structures. Thus it also has a functional social aspect. Therefore I endorse Spiro's view that functionalism without symbolism is blind, and that symbolism without functionalism doesn't stand up.[9] In order to avoid the dichotomy between functional and symbolic views of ritual, in the succeeding I will not speak of the functions of ritual, but more generally about its specific dimensions and aspects.

2. FUNDAMENTAL ASPECTS

The aspect of repetition and the question of the relation between rite and myth seem to me to be most fundamental for ritual. I will discuss both below.

2.1. Repetition

The above makes it clear that symbolization is a human activity. It is connected with the fundamental quality of humanity and with the specific human potential for dealing with reality in a very particular way. When we speak of symbolization, the emphasis lies on human activity, on human creativity and expression. But in dealing with reality, no human being starts from scratch all over again. He is no Robinson Crusoe, but lives with others and can fall back on their creativity. Many have already gone before who, through symbolization, have created an entrance into reality. No person enters the world like Adam on the day of his creation. There are already very many previous givens. These begin with one's

[8] A. TERRIN: 'Antropologia culturale', in SARTORE & TRIACCA (eds.): *Nuovo dizionario di liturgia* 84; BELL: *Ritual Theory*, 53 and 65; IDEM: *Ritual. Perspectives*, 59-60, 61-89.

[9] M. SPIRO: 'Symbolism and Functionalism in the Anthropological Study of Religion', in L. HONKA (ed.): *Science of Religion. Studies in Methodology*, New York 1979, 323, 329; See TERRIN: 'Antropologia culturale' 84.

name: one does not choose it oneself, but it is given by one's parents, and they in turn were dependent on certain customs or trends in doing so. What is true of one's name is also true for one's actions and speech. However creatively one engages in symbolization, in fact it is always part of a greater whole in which one is joined. One can never escape the world in which one is included, shaped by previous generations.

Indeed, the characteristic of ritual is the accent on this aspect of being previously given. Symbol, symbolic acts and symbolic language come together in ritual, but in such a way that the emphasis lies on their nature as previously given, on their derivative state, on repetition. Repetition is essential for all ritual. In accordance with the orientation of ritual, one can speak then of a morning or evening ritual, a baptism ritual, a marriage ritual, a protest ritual, and so forth.

The repetitive aspect that is so essential to ritual may be approached in various ways. For example, Staal, who comes from The Netherlands but now works in America, sees ritual as a formal, self-contained action that concentrates entirely upon itself.[10] Staal conducted detailed investigation into a 3000-year-old Indian ritual. His conclusion is that ritual arises because people subconsciously follow the same syntactic rules in their actions as in learning their native language. Because animals also display this ritual conduct, but do not have language, it must be that the origin of linguistic rules is to be found in ritual, and not the other way around. This self-contained and precisely ordered entity of ritual has no intrinsic structural significance. It is meaningless. Therefore one cannot say that there are symbolic actions in ritual which refer to something else. Those who perform ritual have no symbolic meanings in mind. It is possible for people to assign the most diverse meanings to ritual precisely because ritual is meaningless in itself. The approaches by Tambiah, Wheelock and the Belgian

---

[10] F. STAAL: *Rules without Meaning. Ritual, Mantras and the Human Sciences*, Bern 1989, 239; IDEM: 'The Meaninglessness of Ritual', in *Numen* 26 (1975) 1, 2-22 = IDEM: 'De zinloosheid van het ritueel', in IDEM: *Over zin en onzin in filosofie, religie en wetenschap*, Amsterdam 1986, 295-321. See L. APOSTEL: 'Relationaliteit in ritueel en mystiek. Over Frits Staal', in *Ons erfdeel* 37 (1994) 3, 393-404.

[11] S.J. TAMBIAH: 'The Magical Power of Words', in *Man* 3 (1968) 2, 175-208: W. WHEELOCK: 'The Problem of Ritual Language: From Information to Situation', in *Journal of the American Academy of Religion* 50 (1982) 1, 49-71; I. D'HERT & J. VANDIKKELEN: 'Overgave om niet. Antropoloog Rik Pinxten over riten en sacrale drama's', in *Tijdschrift voor Geestelijk Leven* 51 (1995) 6, 597-606.

anthropologist Pinxten are similar to Staal.[11] The views of these authors
are strongly influenced by logic, analytic philosophy and the linguistic
insights of N. Chomsky, D.J. Austin and J. Searle. Staal and his associates emphasize the singularity of the characteristics of ritual as a 'language' that is an action, which 'does things', and as such is not a vehicle for information. According to Staal ritual is not a language, and
therefore cannot be approached with methods from linguistics. Because
rituals are pure *performative* 'language', they have no meaning.[12]

Because this approach to ritual is rather frequently cited as highly
authoritative, it is important to examine it in greater depth. Among the
objections which can be raised to it are the following. First and foremost, performative language (i.e., language which accomplishes things)
is indeed first and foremost an act, but that in no way excludes that
this act also has semantic content. For example, in The Netherlands a
burgomaster is installed by hanging the chain of office around his or
her neck, but this action also certainly has a semantic meaning. This
semantic meaning can be reinforced and further alluded to by a formula pronounced at the same time, which for the rest can in turn be
equally performative (i.e., a formula which accomplishes something).
There is no antithesis between that which is accomplished functionally
and the symbolic, expressive content of the act.[13] Next, semiotics have
provided more insight into the 'language' of ritual as integral symbolic
act. According to C.S. Peirce the sign is comprised of three elements:
a) it is *representamen*: it is visible and represents something, it comprises a connection with something (the word 'Amsterdam' as such, or
the visible red, white and blue flag); b) it refers to a particular *object*
(the word 'Amsterdam' to the city of Amsterdam, or the red, white and
blue flag to The Netherlands); and c) it generates a new sign in the
mind of the interpreting person (the *interpretant*) (Amsterdam as the
capital of The Netherlands, or with regard to the flag, the Dutch
nation and its history).

Following Peirce, Charles W. Morris also makes a three-fold analysis of the sign, into the syntactic, semantic and pragmatic dimen-

---

[12] See also BELL: *Ritual Theory* 112; IDEM: *Ritual. Perspectives* 69, 71.

[13] BELL: *Ritual. Perspectives* 282, note 28, refers in this connection to R. FINNEGAN:
'How to Do Things with Words. Performative Utterances Among the Limba of Sierra
Leone', in *Man* 4 (1969) 537-552, particularly 548-550.

[14] CH.W. MORRIS: *Foundations of the Theory of Signs*, Chicago 1939; IDEM: *Signs,
Language, and Behavior*, New York 1946.

sions.[14] The syntactic dimension is the mutual relation among signs, the semantic dimension is the relation between the sign and what it stands for, and the pragmatic dimension is the relation between the sign and those who use it. Thus Morris arrived at the division of semiotics into syntactic, semantic and pragmatic. But this threefold division also led to misunderstandings. People began to consider the syntactic, semantic and pragmatic too much as independent entities, and to limit significance too much to the semantic dimension. The consequence was that people lost sight of the unity within the sign that Peirce maintained, and no longer saw the function of syntaxis and pragmatics in bestowing meaning.[15] I have the impression that this is precisely the case for Staal and others. They see ritual only as a syntactic chain of signs that has a pragmatic effect, and separate ritual as a entity of sign from its integral connection with semantics.

The Dutch philosopher C. Verhoeven also speaks about the meaninglessness of the framework of repetition in ritual. But at the same time it is true that for him there is no sense of what one might designate as an implication of 'ritual nihilism'.[16] On the contrary, according to Verhoeven ritual creates the framework within which it can actually develop; it is the preparation for a deeper reality, readiness to experience the actual occurrence. The rite is the magic circle that is drawn around what actually happens. It is something attendant, a schedule, a pattern, something formalized within which the transcendent event can be expected, as a gift.[17] The meaningless frame is thus the preamble to a meaningful occurrence. In this sense Verhoeven accentuates the ritual as a symbolic event. But at the same time it is true that on the other hand he introduces a strong dualism into the approach to ritual as symbolic event. He chiefly accentuates the aspect of diversity in the symbol, the fact that it does not, or even in no way at all coincides with that which it evokes. For him the rite is only a condition for the event, and in that way he too radically disconnects ritual and event. Ritual, as

---

[15] R. VOLP: *Liturgik. Die Kunst, Gott zu feiern*, Vol. 2, Gütersloh 1994, 693 ff; J. HAUSREITHER: *Semiotik des liturgischen Gesanges. Ein Beitrag zur Entwicklung einer integralen Untersuchungsmethode der Liturgiewissenschaft* (Liturgia condenda 16), Leuven 2004, 5.

[16] See the characterization by POST: 'Zeven notities over rituele verandering'.

[17] VERHOEVEN: *Rondom de leegte* 14 ff.

a symbolic event, is a more or less formal repetition which *as such* has
a symbolic pregnancy.[18]

This view can also be found in Nijk, who moreover affords a clarifying
perspective on the aspect of repetition.[19] According to his hypothesis,
rites arose in the first instance from no other cause than the consciousness
of a lacunae, a hiatus, an undefined realization of 'having-to-act-without-
knowing-how'. This realization contained within itself the want of 'something' that would make the act worthwhile. One can think, for instance,
of the void that opens up when someone is confronted with death for the
first time. The question is then, what is one to do? A second moment
must have followed this realization, because it is clear that one is brought
to action through the 'having-to-act-without-knowing-how'. The only
thing that one can initially do is just do something, experimentally. One
can only determine how to act meaningfully by doing, and in this way
discovering which act replaces the realization of 'having-to-act-without-
knowing-how' with the realization of 'this is it'. Evidently individuals and
peoples have been able to find such actions, into which they packed their
deepest reality. And evidently the realization that 'this is it', or 'this is the
ultimate' or 'this is ultimately Him' was so radical that they repeated these
actions with great devotion. Thus rites arose.

In Nijk's case, thus, the repeated act itself is a symbolically charged
event. Man as it were 'knows' the ultimate reality through the act, in the
same way as a dancer who portrays a reality, and who knows this reality
only in the act of his or her depiction.[20] In his hypothesis Nijk explicitly limits ritual to symbolic *action*. In this sense, he is close to Staal. But
to my mind his hypothesis is equally true for *symbol* and for *symbolic
language*, the repetition of which involves words which are then
involved in giving meaning, and which therefore are repeated as formulae of a sort.

---

[18] It is striking that Verhoeven regards the sacrament as an exception to this, when
he says that 'the absolute maximum of ritual and religious meaning, the summum of
sacrality in an act, is achieved in a ritual that is what it denotes and effectuates that for
which it prepares. The divinely instituted sacrament of which theologians speak is such
a ritual' (VERHOEVEN: *Rondom de leegte* 38). To my mind, this however is true not only
for the sacrament, but also in one way or another for every ritual.

[19] A. NIJK: *Secularisatie. Over het gebruik van een woord*, Rotterdam 1968, 256-339.

[20] NIJK: *Secularisatie* 272.

Nijk's hypothesis with regard to ritual as symbolic repetition does not exclude that there can also be an animal origin for ritual.[21] Ethologists point to there being patterns of ritual behavior among animals. The most explicit ritual among animals is certainly the courtship dance. Our own ritual behavior decidedly has a strong bio-genetic foundation.[22] We are 'creatures of ritual' whether we like it or not. One must not forget this foundation, and must not spiritualize ritual prematurely.

On the other hand, it remains true that this biological basis is not sufficient to explain the repetitive character of ritual. After all, there is a qualitative difference between animal and human ritual. According to Cassirer this difference consists precisely in the existence of a system of symbols that interferes in the ritual among humans, which gives this ritual a new dimension.[23]

Now, one can understand the deeper reality which is dealt with in Nijk's hypothesis very profoundly. One is then undoubtedly touching upon central rituals, for instance those dealing with death. But ritual also opens out much more broadly.

---

[21] See particularly J. HUXLEY: 'Introduction. A Discussion on Ritualisation of Behavior', in J. HUXLEY (ed.): 'A Discussion on Ritualisation of Behavior of Animals and Man', in *Philosophical Transactions of the Royal Society*, Series B, 251 (1966) 249-271. See also BELL: *Ritual Theory* 89.

[22] See among others HUXLEY: 'Introduction'; K.Z. LORENZ: 'Evolution of Ritualization in the Biological and Cultural Spheres', in *Philosophical Transactions of the Royal Society*, Series B, 251 (1966) 273-284; E.G. D'AQUILI, C.D. LAUGHLIN & J. MCMANUS: *The Spectrum of Ritual. A Biogenetic Structural Analysis*, New York 1979; E.G. D'AQUILI: 'The Myth-Ritual Complex: A Biogenetic Structural Analysis', in *Zygon* 18 (1983) 3, 247-269; C.D. LAUGHLIN: 'Ritual and the Symbolic Function. A Summary of Biogenetic Structural Theory', in *Journal of Ritual Studies* 4 (1990) 1, 15-39; W. BURKERT: *Kulte des Altertums. Biologische Grundlagen der Religion*, München 1998; N. MITCHELL: 'The Amen Corner. Ritual as *Ars Amatoria*', in *Worship* 75 (2001) 250-259 plus the literature listed there. See also BELL: *Ritual Theory* 73 and IDEM: *Ritual. Perspectives* 30-32. This ethological basis for ritual is not universally accepted. See for example DE VISSCHER: 'Geherbergd in een traditie' 122: 'Animals have no rites, and no ritual dances, as people sometimes believe they have found'.

[23] CASSIRER: *An Essay on Man* 25-28. See FRIJNS: *Rituelen* 45-48, 55-58, 116. It is interesting to note here that according to the ancient Chinese *Book of Rites* 41, it is precisely as *homo ritualis* that man is to be distinguished from animals. Animals have no rites, while humans are to be distinguished from animals because they make clear distinctions between the various generations, ages and classes, and the two sexes, through rituals, in order to channel natural desires. See C. DEFOORT: 'Riten als dijken. Het Chinese Boek der Riten', in *Kultuurleven* 64 (1997) 39. For this distinction see also the approach of Rappaport, below Part 1, Chapter 3, 1.1.

Everyday life is full of rituals. From morning to night life runs
according to rituals. That begins when one rises. Getting up always
takes place according to a very strict repetition: washing one's face,
dressing, opening the curtains. Then there is the breakfast table: people
always sit in the same place, wait to begin until everyone is there, pass
the food around, and tell what has happened. Sometimes the rituals are
individual. Someone recently said to me, 'After breakfast I always stop
to think what I am going to do for the day, how I will go about it'.
Someone else told me about a little boy across the street, who, as he left
for school, always turned back at least five times and called out to his
mother 'See y'all later!'. She in turn always continued to stand outside
until he reached the corner. Still another once told me he had a friend
who has a very laborious, step-by-step procedure for filling and lighting
his pipe in moments when he feels really good. In the evening many
know the rituals of reading the newspaper, watching the news, closing
the curtains, getting the children into bed. Particularly the last is often
a detailed ritual. A mother told of her two-and-a-half year old son:
'Every evening after I have kissed him and held his hand I also have to
kiss the doll he sleeps with, and shake both its hands, and then do the
same with the four feet of a stuffed horse that lies at the foot of the bed.
Once I've done that, he sits up once more and asks that I give him one
more kiss and say good night one last time'.[24]
    The clothing we wear, in all its variants, is permeated with ritual:
clothing for children and adults, for man and woman, for leisure and
work; we dress according to the latest fashion[25] or consciously deviate
from it in protest, but even this protest becomes a ritual conduct. The
clothing of clergy, professionals and the military forms a peculiar variant, each having all of their own differences and distinctions: epaulets,
stars, buttons, ribbons, colors.[26] Then there are rituals of greeting. A
speaker is greeted and introduced according to an established pattern.
When people greet each other in company a number of stereotyped
actions are always performed: men close their suit coat, straighten their
clothing, make sure their hair is in place, stand to shake hands or give a
kiss of greeting, sit in the place indicated, drink a cup of coffee or tea,

---

[24] H. WERNER: *Einführung in die Entwicklungspsychologie*, München 1953, 302-303.
[25] R. BARTHES: *Le système de la mode*, Paris 1967.
[26] J.TH. MAERTENS: *Ritologiques*, Paris 1978, Vol. 4: *Dans la peau des autres. Essai
d'anthropologie des inscriptions vestimentaires*.

and so forth. When we walk down a busy street there are also a number of stereotypical actions that everyone performs: people keep as much as possible to the right, do not walk so close behind others that they bump into them, and avoid eye contact from too close by. There are many more: birthday rituals, the rituals of Christmas and New Year's, those for dedicating a building, the start of a school year, in sports, at protest rallies, etc.[27]

It is clear that in the case of these everyday rituals there cannot each time be repeated contact with the very deepest levels of reality. Rather, one could here speak of meaningful communication with others and with the world around us. This meaningful communication is only possible thanks to ritual. If one were to exclude that, there would arise empty spaces. Only repeating what once was created as a meaningful complex of actions, which has been accepted as such, prevents these small gaps.[28] If people repeatedly had to begin again from scratch, life would become unbearable. One can imagine in the everyday situations mentioned, repeatedly encountering the sense of 'having-to-act-without-knowing-how': upon entering a house, when greeting another person, when putting the children to bed, at table, when saying goodbye. Life would be full of lacunae, and proceed only by fits and starts, in a staccato rhythm.[29] We would be left tense, and dead tired. Thus even everyday ritual arises via a process of trial and error. One time people try this, another that, until they find a way of acting that is meaningful. Bossard and Boll provide a fascinating example of this:[30]

---

[27] Anyone desiring an insight into the wealth of human ritual should read the five volumes of MAERTENS: *Ritologiques*: 1. *Le dessin sur la peau. Essai d'anthropologie des inscriptions tégumentaires*; 2. *Le corps sexionné. Essai d'anthropologie des inscriptions génitales*; 3. *Le masque et le miroir. Essai d'anthropologie des revêtements faciaux*; 4. *Dans la peau des autres. Essai d'anthropologie des inscriptions vestimentaires*; 5. *Le jeu du mort. Essai d'anthropologie des inscriptions du cadavre*.

[28] See also A. HAHN: 'Kultische und säkulare Riten und Zeremonien in soziologischer Sicht', in A. HAHN a.o.: *Anthropologie des Kults, Die Bedeutung des Kults für das Ueberleben des Menschen*, Freiburg 1977, 51 ff. and 67 ff. Hahn too sees the lacuna in actions as criterion for ritual.

[29] In connection with the absence of rituals, A.C. Zijderveld characterizes our society as a staccato culture. See A.C. ZIJDERVELD: *Staccato cultuur. Flexibele maatschappij en verzorgende staat*, Utrecht 1991.

[30] J.H.S. BOSSARD & E.S. BOLL: *Why marriages go wrong*, New York 1958, 195; example mentioned in VAN DER HART: *Rituelen in psychotherapie* 267-268.

On rainy evening, about the second year of their marriage, Mr. and Mrs. Brett were playing cribbage. As the game went on in a desultory sort of way, the conversation between them took an intimate turn, followed also by various little intimate acts, such as playfully touching each other. Finally, as the regular bedtime hour approached, Mr. Brett suggested sex relations, to which Mrs. Brett acquiesced with more than customary willingness. In the following weeks, several more cribbage games culminated in this manner. In each of these cases, the sexual act had been very satisfactory to both husband and wife. Then followed the experience of several sex relationships without the cribbage preliminary. Soon, without any deliberate planning or formal agreement, the cribbage game came to be the regular preliminary to sex relationships. Gradually, additions came to be made. Mr. Brett brought home Mrs. Brett's favorite flowers, and placed them in a vase near the cribbage table. Then Mrs. Brett suggested a highball, to be sipped toward the end of the cribbage game. Since she preferred Scotch whiskey, Mr. Brett bought the best Scotch brand, which was reserved for their own use on these cribbage nights. Gradually, each step leading to sex relations between the Bretts had come to be ritualised around the cribbage game, ranging from the first shy references to cribbage to the final consummation. At the time this information was given by the Bretts, fifteen years had passed since the beginning of the cribbage ritual. They say that there are times when sex relations occur without this particular preliminary, bur agree that this does not "seem so right" as when they lead up to it via the ritual route.

So rituals are directed precisely at making progress in life possible when it threatens to seize up. They are necessary to maintain the continuity and coherence of existence. Even where people wish to free themselves of ritual, there quickly arise other latent but established patterns of action. The first thing that people try to do for young persons who have arrived on the brink of society is to again offer them some framework, some ritual to go by. People simply cannot live without a sort of 'Ordinary'.

In the first chapter I noted that symbols, symbolic acts and symbolic language are the foundation of ritual. Moreover, it appeared that the characteristic feature of symbols is that they speak for themselves, while signs are based on agreements and negotiation. In connection with the element of repetition as a fundamental characteristic of ritual, at this point it will be necessary to make an addition to that. In ritual the symbol also begins to share the characteristics of the sign. The recycling of symbol, symbolic act and symbolic language in ritual in fact rests in part on convention and institutionalization. In ritual there is a link to the past, to tradition, through convention. In ritual one finds 'standard' symbols, symbolic acts and symbolic language.

This aspect of repetition that is essential for ritual should not allow us to forget that ritual is always a matter of symbol, symbolic act and symbolic language. Rituals are not merely entities of signs. One may not give in to making ritual into only a formal, stereotypical and institutional act as sign. The tension that is inherent in ritual as ritual must remain. Thus what we have said with regard to symbol, symbolic acts and symbolic language is also true for ritual. The point is that in and through ritual we actually take part in the reality that is called up through the ritual, that we are really taken up in the far-reaching sense of what is performed in and through ritual.[31] In one way or another the ritual itself also shares in that reality. In itself it carries something of the meaning that it calls up. When we stride along in a protest march, the perspective springs open. Our reason for walking is not simply repetition or convention, nor is it merely the intention to get somewhere; it is not a matter of a purely purposeful and efficient action. Our walking is a 'charged' action: it truly takes strides forward. We carry signs and banners and repeatedly chant the same slogans. In doing so we declare that war is a dead end. Thus, the accent shifts in the direction of symbolism. Such rituals function as bridges across boundaries. No further explanation is necessary. They speak for themselves. We are involved as whole persons. We can express ourselves in what we do repeatedly.

If ritual fans out as far as I have just indicated, we are perhaps faced with the question of what the difference is between a custom and a ritual. The difference comes down to this. If the repeated act is purely functional, and the symbolic disappears entirely into the background, then we are dealing with a *custom*, a routine act, without any referential character. This is clear in eating. For animals eating is purely functional. An animal simply devours its prey. For humans, however, eating is not purely functional, but also ritual: the meal is prepared, served, and if possible enjoyed collectively, and in this aromas, the appearance of the

---

[31] I emphatically say 'in and through ritual'; thus ritual is not merely preparation for this participation. See LUKKEN: *De onvervangbare weg van de liturgie* 22-33.

food and the physical attitudes of the diners are also important. Eating is a complex entity of ritual acts.[32] There are gradations in the ritualisation of family meals. According to Bossard and Boll the lowest level are 'hasty meals'. The family members appear to regard them as a necessary evil, pit-stops for refuelling, to be completed as quickly as possible. Food tends to be served as though eating were a mere physiological compulsion, and gulped down as though the time required could hardly be spared. Conversation is scant, monosyllabic and direct, heavily sprinkled with 'yes', 'no', 'uh-uh', 'salt', 'bread', 'more', etc. One is reminded of a pack of snarling dogs cleaning out a dish. 'In both cases "the meal" is over when the last morsel of food is gone.'[33] Here eating is focused purely on result. But at higher levels one very quickly begins to recognise ritually charged moments in family meals. Such meals can even develop into a comprehensive ritual in which each gesture, and the whole succession of acts, can take on a symbolic character. What is true for meals is also true for rising in the morning, dressing, going to sleep, putting children to bed, etc. The broad expansion of ritual thus does decidedly have its limits. One must beware of labelling purely customary acts as ritual. Not everything is ritual. With reason one can say that it is a short step from the proposition that everything is ritual to the practical reality that nothing is ritual.[34]

From the above one might conclude that rituals arise spontaneously from the bottom up, and can not be invented. This is a conviction which has become widespread particularly since the Second Vatican Council. Rituals cannot be created and imposed from above. Yet this is only partly true. It is indeed true that rituals are not purely concepts that can be devised from behind a desk. They are in no sense intellectual fabrications. Before all else, rituals are preconceptual praxis. I will return to this in section 2.2. But just as for instance with regard to the creation of theatre, discussion is possible about the creation of ritual, in which experts and critics can be involved. History indicates that experts can play a role in various ways in the introduction, preservation and

---

[32] F. FRIJNS: *Rituelen* 1 and 120-121.

[33] BOSSARD & BOLL: *Why marriages go wrong* 184-185.

[34] R. MEYER FORTES: 'Religious Premises and Logical Technique in Divinatory Ritual', in HUXLEY (ed.): 'A Discussion on Ritualisation of Behavior of Animals and Man' 410. See also BELL: *Ritual Theory* 73 and 88-93.

alteration of rituals.[35] This was, for example, the case in Taoism in China in the fifth century, when Lu Hsiu-ching decided to collect and publish a series of texts that had been revealed a century before. With respect to this whole he compiled an important series of liturgical manuals which would form the basis for a great deal of Taoist ritual tradition.[36] Thus it would appear that under certain circumstances ritual experts can exercise an important influence on the form and content of ritual life. The rituals of the former Soviet Union are another striking example. They were created by experts in ritual, including several Jesuits, and subsequently imposed from above.[37] One can also point to the extensive codification of Roman Catholic ritual in the 16th century, after the Council of Trent, and the radical renewal of liturgy after the Second Vatican Council, to which liturgical studies made a significant contribution: the new liturgical books were complied by committees of experts in liturgy. On the other hand, one must note that precisely this method has been strongly criticized – and that this critique has been made in the name of liturgy. Perhaps one must admit that here one comes up against an area of tension in which history shows that sometimes one pole or the other dominates: sometimes the pole of authority, and sometimes that of the 'base'. In all this, however, it is clear that the absence of expertise quickly leads to ritual disorder, and that on the other hand the imposition of ritual from above by experts can inflict damage on the vitality of the ritual. It appears to be beneficial for authentic ritual when people continue to seek a balance between the two poles. I will return to this in the second part of this book in connection with the theme of inculturation of ritual.

The fact that repetition is characteristic for ritual in no way means that ritual is always performed in the same formal and fixed way. When Rappaport speaks of the invariance of ritual, he formulates this carefully: people find messages in ritual, which tend to invariance.[38] In connection with this, one can first note that every ritual also has open places: the one element is more closed than another. Thus within the order of service there are moments of improvisation and moments which are a

---

[35] BELL: *Ritual Theory* 130-140; IDEM: 'The Authority of Ritual Experts' 98-120; IDEM: *Ritual. Perspectives* 223. I return to this *in extenso* in Part 3, Chapter3, 3.3.

[36] BELL: 'The Authority of Ritual Experts' 101.

[37] BELL: 'The Authority of Ritual Experts' 102-103.

[38] RAPPAPORT: Ritual and Religion in the Making of Humanity 52-53.

matter of a precise formula or act. In a baptism service there is a difference between the words of greeting and the baptismal formula. Next,
there are also different types of rituals. A celebration in a small group
will generally have more informal elements than an official public
observance. All sorts of variants can occur, or new elements can be
added that cohere with the expressive, self-referential character of the
ritual and its necessary inculturation. I will return to the expressive character of ritual in 3.6 of this chapter. With regard to the necessary inculturation, I will deal with that extensively in the second and third parts.
My concern now is to point out that the element of repetition in no
way excludes free moments, variants and new elements within this
framework. This creativity which is possible in ritual can lead to a transformation in the ritual.[39] This transformation can be very profound.
The question which accompanies this is then always to what degree and
on which level there is continuity and discontinuity in a particular ritual. A clear example is the celebration of eucharist. If one compares its
Medieval form with that of the ancient Church, one will note considerable differences. Is it then essentially the same ritual, or must one speak
of a disjunction? I will return to the question of continuity and discontinuity in ritual in part 2.

In light of this creativity in ritual, Bell is of the opinion that the element
of repetition is not one of the intrinsic characteristic qualities of ritual
and in this connection she mentions precisely the celebration of the
eucharist.[40] It is, rather, merely a phenomenon that is frequently
encountered in ritual. According to her ritual is characterised only by a
manner of acting which specifically establishes a privileged contrast, differentiating itself as more important and powerful. To my mind, this
privileged contrast however is simply related to the fact that in ritual
symbol, symbolic language and symbolic acts come together. Actually,
in symbol, symbolic language and symbolic act one is dealing with a
special reinforced manner of acting. But this does not alter the fact that
repetition is an intrinsic quality of ritual, on the condition that one does

---

[39] In this connection, see GRIMES: *Reading, Writing, and Ritualizing* 30, who
remarks that improvisation is an essential part of many if not most ritual traditions. Just
as literary work is not written from experience alone, but from other works, similarly
one can recognize the way in which new rites arise from other rites.

[40] BELL: *Ritual Theory* 89-93, particularly 91-92.

not understand this to imply necessarily the more superficial and higher levels of the ritual. As an intrinsic quality it belongs to the deep level.[41]

2.2. The relation between rite and myth

In 2.1 I have broadened Nijk's hypothesis, also including symbolic language within it. This expansion, which touches the relation between rite in its limited sense, namely as repeated symbolic action, and myth, is not self-evident, and demands further explanation and clarification.

Nijk argues that all formation of myth is secondary. He explicitly limits rite to symbolic act, and is of the opinion that rite is structurally the foundation of myth. He sees myth as a continuation of an original rite, in language. The happening in which one enters into contact with 'ultimate reality' in an action is retold in myth as a narrative. This involves a happening in the primeval times, which becomes present in the retelling. Other scholars, on the other hand, right down to the present, are of the opinion that myth is more original than rite. Eliade's classic theory is normally counted within this group.[42] The question is however whether Eliade does not stress both myth and rite. According to him, one cannot consider myth purely as a 'script'. Myth is rather an operational knowledge, and therefore an inseparable part of ritual knowledge.[43] Whatever the case, one here runs up against a discussion that goes back to the beginnings of the investigation of ritual as such. This discussion was focused around the question of whether religion and culture had their origin in myth, or in ritual. As well as the choice for either myth *or* ritual, one also finds the assertion that it lies in both myth *and* ritual.[44] In a certain sense this discussion has become less relevant because of the recognition that there is an intense reciprocity

---

[41] See Part 1, Chapter 3, 2.2 and 3, 2.3. Also G. LUKKEN 2004 in Bibliography.

[42] NIJK: *Secularisatie* 272. See M. ELIADE: *Das Heilige und das Profane*, Hamburg 1957, 56-62 (= IDEM: *The Sacred and the Profane: The Nature of Religion*, London 1959); A.E. JENSEN: *Das religiöse Weltbild einer frühen Kultur*, Wiesbaden 1949; IDEM: *Mythos und Kult bei Naturvölker. Religionswissenschaftliche Betrachtungen*, Wiesbaden 1951; D.J. KRIEGER & A. BELLIGER: 'Einführung', in D.J. KRIEGER & A. BELLIGER (eds.): *Ritualtheorien* 26-27.

[43] Ibidem.

[44] A good summary of this discussion will be found in BELL: *Ritual. Perspectives* 3-22, 43. See also R.A. SEGAL: *The myth and ritual theory: an anthology*, Malden Mass. 1998.

between myth and rite. One can certainly say that the emphasis on rite is a legacy of this discussion, which must be positively valued. Contemporary studies also emphasize the primacy of ritual activity, in light of new data.[45] Nijk's hypothesis therefore undoubtedly remains worth considering. To my mind, research into primitive rituals in Zaire by R. Devisch, an anthropologist and psychoanalyst, affords us an interesting perspective.[46] He comes to the conclusion that in these oral cultures ritual practice is almost never mediated by creation myths. Rather, the rituals involved develop purely from physical actions. Words are subordinate to the ritual acts, with all the senses: sight, taste, smell, hearing, and in this series also the verbal (symbolic language). The dynamic power of this ritual action lies in the body itself as an authentic source of the ritual process. The ritual plays itself out 'beneath' the cognitive level and its representation in texts and stories. 'Participants in the ritual have no need to explicitly state the sense of the things; they bear this in their body, discover it again and come into contact with it in the body of their community and the cosmos'.[47] The ritual is a *praxis* of giving meaning. It is preconceptual. Now, this precognitive from contemporary research is likewise emphasized by Bell.[48] According to her, before all else, ritual is an act.[49] Strategies of ritualization are particularly rooted in the body, specifically in the interaction of the social body within a symbolically constituted spatial and temporal social environment. Extremely basic physical opposites play a role in this interaction, such as right and left, inside and outside, front and back, above and below, center and periphery, high and low, past and present, past and future, slow and fast, regular and irregular, etc. Within various cultures a whole system of ritual assignment of meaning is constructed through these very physically defined opposites.[50] Grimes too notes that rituals,

[45] Thus BELL: *Ritual. Perspectives* 22.

[46] R. DEVISCH: 'Des forces aux symboles dans le rite bantou: l'interanimation entre corps, groupe et monde', in R. DEVISCH a.o.: *Le rite, source et ressources*, Brussel 1995, 11-82.

[47] DEVISCH: 'Des forces aux symboles dans le rite bantou' 75-76.

[48] BELL: *Ritual Theory* 93, 140, 221. See T. MICHELS: *Liturgical Innovation in the Practice of a Marriage Rite and the Sacramental Theology of Chauvet* (M.A. Thesis Theologische Faculteit Tilburg), Tilburg 1996, 66-69, 83.

[49] BELL: *Ritual Theory* 80-81, 148, note 56.

[50] For this semiotic system of ritual opposites and their hierarchies, see for instance BELL: *Ritual Theory* 101-107.

like symbols, work in a very sensory manner; they have an 'olfactory logic'.[51] This might also be called an intuitive operation, similar to intuitively preparing a recipe in getting a meal ready, or finding one's way by hunch.[52] Ritual is a kind of knowledge, that is to say a very specific, namely a somatic knowledge.[53] It is so to speak a blind insight and a cultural sixth 'sense'.[54]

Ritualization is focused on doing what it does without bringing that which it does into the sphere of discourse or systematic thinking. In connection with his position Devisch also refers to authors such as Merleau-Ponty,[55] Lévi-Strauss, Kristeva and Bourdieu. Moreover, he is consistent with Lorenzer, according to whom the sensory forms of interaction are primary and fundamental, and also with Greimassian semiotics, which in its recent development emphasizes that the sensory basis precedes all cognitive perception of differences.[56]

Perhaps some readers are asking themselves what, precisely, is the importance of the preceding disquisition. To my mind, it deals with an approach that is also relevant for ritual today. After all, it is the case that in cultures with writing, the relation between rite and myth is rather the opposite. Myth plays a dominant role, and the rite, in the strict sense, is then subordinate to myth. This also occurs in the religions in which the book plays an important role, such as Islam, Judaism and Christianity. But at the same time it is true that in both the literary cultures and religions of the book, different accents can often be found. Popular culture often seems to lie closer to the origin of the ritual than elite culture. The original anthropological source continues to accompany it, and it is well that it does, because an ascendancy of myth easily leads to intellectualism,

---

[51] See above Part 1, Chapter 1, 2.1; GRIMES: *Reading, Writing, and Ritualizing* 20.

[52] GRIMES: *Marrying and Burying* 25-26.

[53] GRIMES: *Marrying and Burying* 247. See also TH.W. JENNINGS: 'On Ritual Knowledge', in *Journal of Religion* 62 (1982) 111-127; C. MENKEN-BEKIUS: 'De koster had maar één tafeltje voor het bruidsboeket', in *Praktische Theologie* 25 (1998) 357-364 and K. STROEKEN: 'Afrikaanse initiatieriten', in *Kultuurleven* 64 (1997) 58-63.

[54] BELL: *Ritual Theory* 115-116.

[55] According to Merleau-Ponty, the word is a special case of the gesture. See H. ETTEMA: *Verbogen taal. Verplaatste tekens. Semiotische beschouwingen van taal in relatie met psychopathologie*, Groningen 1998, 275.

[56] See Part 1, Chapter 3, 2.7.4.

to the detriment of the ritual. With regard to Christendom, in reaction to the 'ritualism' of the Middle Ages the Reformation strongly accentuated the proclamation of the Word, which after the Council of Trent (1545-1563) led to a hardening of the positions: in the Roman Church the rite, in the strict sense, strongly gained the upper hand, and the word was undervalued, while in Protestant churches the opposite was the case. Although since the Second Vatican Council there has been an effort to attain a certain balance between rite and myth, the word from time to time threatens to gain the upper hand.[57] At the very least one can observe that particularly popular culture continues to stand closer to the original anthropological basis. As such, it can function as an important corrective. In Christian ritual too integral physicality is the source of ritual. When the word becomes detached from its physical-ritual context, faith quickly disintegrates into dogmatism, and loses its indispensable contact with the primary layers not only of that which makes us human, but also of the fundamental fact that Christianity is about the Word become flesh.

3. FURTHER DIMENSIONS

Repetition and the tension between myth and rite are to my mind the most obvious characteristics of ritual. But it is possible to sharpen our understanding of ritual by delineating further characteristic dimensions. These will be discussed in the following.

3.1. Mediation of the past and the future

First, one can point to a dimension of ritual that is closely linked with that of repetition: rituals mediate *the past*. This mediation can take place because rituals are consummate repetitions of acts from a bygone time. But the mediation also occurs when there is an adaptation of the ritual in a new context, or a new ritual is created that has links with the past. In one way or another rituals always carry with them the past from which they come.[58] Rituals are already there. Are there not many similarities

---

[57] In this connection see LUKKEN: *De onvervangbare weg van de liturgie* 95-97. T. Michels correctly points out that at certain places in the theology of L.-M. Chauvet the word appears to be much too dominant; see MICHELS: *Liturgical Innovation* 68-69.

[58] JETTER: *Symbol und Ritual* 96-97; BELL: *Ritual. Perspectives* 145-150 designates this characteristic with the term 'traditionalism'.

between peace marches and old prayer processions? I find what J. Ebbers wrote telling: 'When I read and heard accounts of therapeutic rituals, the stories seemed to make sense... Even now, if I develop a ritual with a client, I often see before me images of earlier church services: the many candles and flowers, and praying people out of Purgatory on All Souls' Day. Sometimes I can nearly smell the odor of incense when I think back to the requiem masses where I served as acolyte'.[59] Rituals play an impressive role as a mediator with the past. In their own peculiar way they hand tradition down, actually in a way which reaches deeper than the attempt to do so through the 'pure doctrine'. Rituals keep tradition alive. This does not in any way mean that rituals cannot be in part *future orientated*. On the contrary, they remind us of our *origin* in a way that is entirely their own, and on that basis offer us confidence in the future. Ritual will further assist in and provide for a safe passage. As something familiar from the past, it helps make the transition to a new future possible, and integrates people into further life.[60] Throughout church history liturgies have always been the most enduring and effective mediators of belief.

In this way rituals guarantee our continuity with the past, and at the same time they are open to the future. Without doubt however it is because of the mediating dimension with the past that rituals sometimes obstinately and wrongly offer resistance against renewal. It can also happen that they continue to lead a life of their own when they are no longer functional. This is true of the changing of the guard at Buckingham Palace, for scores of rituals in high society and the diplomatic service, for the Pope's Swiss Guards, and for all sorts of national customs. They become folklore and protocol. As such, they then often receive a new symbolic value.

3.2. Formalization

Likewise closely connected with the aspect of repetition in ritual is the dimension of formalization.[61] Words and actions become abbreviated, as

---

[59] J. EBBERS: 'Een bevrijding van knellende banden', in O. VAN DER HART a.o.: *Afscheidsrituelen in psychotherapie* 44.

[60] I will return to the tensive relation between past, present and future which lies behind ritual in my discussion of ritual and time, in Part 1, Chapter 4, 3.

[61] BELL: *Ritual. Perspectives* 139-144; RAPPAPORT: *Ritual and Religion in the Making of Humanity* 33-36.

it were, and reduced to essential elements. Speech is not long-winded and elaborate, but stylized. There is no rambling or informal movement, but rather restrained going forward. Things are so reduced that the perspective springs open. Rituals do not have an *elaborated* code, but rather a *limited* code: they use only a limited and precisely organized aggregate of things, words, expressions and gestures. Very little can suddenly evoke a whole lot. Precisely through this limited code rituals are in general simple in structure, and are accessible to all members of the community. You definitely do not have to be an intellectual to understand this code. One might even say that too much intellectualism makes it impossible to understand the limited code. Onno van der Hart cites a telling example of this: 'Alice came from an academic milieu, where that [intellectualizing: G.L.] was carried to great extremes. When her husband kissed or hugged her as a sign of his affection, that "said" nothing to her. No, she was only convinced that he loved her if he said that elaborately in words. He could not summon that up, and felt increasingly blocked. The consequence was that he less and less frequently showed his affection for her, and they had fights about whether or not he loved her.'[62] Through its limited formalized code, ritual can also transmit elaborate social/cultural messages with regard to the hierarchy of relations and social position in a very economical manner.[63] One can think of robes of office and uniforms, decorations, the order of seating at a table, manners of greeting, etc.

3.3. Condensation

In ritual the normal and everyday is accentuated and stylized, so that the perspective on it can alter. Ritual condenses reality. It sets it somewhat apart, and in a certain sense lifts the thing, act or word out of the realm of the ordinary. The contours become more sharply accentuated. The pace is restrained in order to stride ahead. One stays still, creates a private space, keeps distance. One can speak of a certain effect of estrangement with regard to what was actually expected. There is no abundance of bread and wine, but on the contrary a small amount, so that the perspective jumps.[64]

---

[62] O. VAN DER HART: *Rituelen in psychotherapie* 51.
[63] BELL: *Ritual. Perspectives* 141.
[64] CHAUVET: *Symbole et sacrement* 354-355; IDEM: 'Ritualité et théologie', in J. MOINGT: *Enjeux du rite dans la modernité* 198-226.

In a sense, ritual focuses attention on itself in a peculiar way in order in and through that to be able to reach the indefinable reality that it will call up. The condensation thus does not take place for its own sake, but on behalf of the symbolic act: only thus can the participation in the farther-reaching, other world be achieved.

3.4. Relief and channelling

From the foregoing, it appears that rituals function to provide a sort of relief.[65] They relieve us of having to discover anew how to proceed in each case, and constantly having to confer with others. Thanks to rituals we need not repeatedly seek the way again in every new situation or difficulty in life. Rituals are thus an aid in new life experiences. In this way too ritual shields the most personal and intimate side of a person's life. This naturally also entails a risk. It can lead to a superficiality and segregation of personal expression. In ritual one can also, in a way of speaking, creep away from oneself. As rituals become older, time can begin to function as an ally in the further erosion of the ritual: it then becomes an inadequate expression of what affects us.

Immediately connected with the dimension of ritual as relief is the dimension of ritual in channeling the strong emotions that come with any crisis situation. In the case of another's death, ritual fills the lacunae and prevents a blind, random explosion of feelings. It helps one to react sensibly in this situation and actively seek an answer before reaching the point of complete personality disorganization.[66] In this, one must realize that the good ritual does not make one immune to anger, grief and doubt. It does not repress existing conflicts and does not function purely as a sort of lightning rod to lead emotions away. What ritual does is to structure the tension that arises out of the conflict, with all the emotions that accompany it. Thus it is not a matter of repression, but of processing and channeling the emotions, of steering and shaping them.[67] This does not only involve feelings of pain, grief and rage, but

---

[65] JETTER: *Symbol und Ritual* 54-55.

[66] HAHN: 'Kultische und säkulare Riten' 67-68. See also A. HAHN: *Religion und der Verlust der Sinngebung. Identitätsprobleme in der modernen Gesellschaft*, Frankfurt 1974, 72 ff.

[67] F.H. TENBRUCK: 'Geschichtserfahrung und Religion in der heutigen Gesellschaft', in *Spricht Gott in der Geschichte*, Freiburg 1972, 85.

equally overwhelming feelings of happiness, joy and awe. It can be that people are unable to express their feelings about positive occurrences, or do not know how to do so. One can think, for instance, of the overwhelming feelings that accompany the birth of a child. An example of this is found in an interview: 'People can make a lot of things, but not life. "There's no factory for that." Mr. E. experienced that in a special way with the birth of his children. He still remembers very vividly how, after the difficult birth of his first child, he was on his way home and had to pull over and stop, because the experience had so affected him. After the birth of his youngest son, he said: "Something so beautiful has got to have something to do with religion"'.[68] Feelings of awe and joy too must be processed and directed. Ritual makes it possible to express them in actions and absorb them. Rituals are thus equally important on joyous occasions; there too they help us across the border and do justice to our emotional life in a humane way.

3.5. Therapeutic dimension

Grimes notes that the European/American world has historically distinguished what something *does* from what it *means*. 'It has commissioned religion, philosophy, language, and the arts to be custodians of meaning, while assigning biology, chemistry, and physics jurisdiction over efficacy. But this division of labor does considerable damage to the healing arts. As placebo research has demonstrated, what a pill *means* determines, at the least in part, what it can *do* ... In short, ritual gestures deeply embraced have concrete physiological results. Conversely, medicines can be made less effective if they are administered in a way that deprives them of meaning'.[69]

For the rest, rituals are not about that controllable reality which is the business of technology and the empirical sciences. When the faithful pray to be freed from illness or saved from disasters, or for fertile fields, some might say they are using the wrong means for dealing with reality. But rituals are not about technical causality or a manageable

---

[68] L. SPRUIT & H. VAN ZOELEN: *Dopen... Ja waarom eigenlijk? Onderzoek naar de motieven die ouders hebben om hun kind al dan niet te laten dopen in de katholieke kerk*, Hilversum 1980, 77-78.

[69] GRIMES: *Deeply into the Bone* 34.

communication with reality. There is an alternative. In and through ritual people let go of reliance on their own capacities. They permit the reality which surpasses them its own existence. They seek access to the divine source, to the transcendent secret of existence, to the renewing power of mystery. They express hope that the future will be better. Rituals are a praxis of faith and hope, not of might and control.[70] They have to do with a basic fact of human experience regarding society, the world and ourselves. Rituals are thus a key to human existence and to the ground that bears it. They shed light in the vicissitudes of this life. They are comprehensive and powerful. This comprehensiveness and power remain hidden from outsiders who ask for proof. Rituals only reveal themselves *in actu*, to those who perform the rituals with devotion.

It is, then, a matter of the deeper roots of existence. Severing contact with these roots leads to a constricted consciousness, to chaos and dispersion, to the bisection of human existence. Ritual is precisely directed toward neutralizing that dispersion and making people whole. Rituals heal and mend people.

Buitendijk describes in a striking way how indispensable symbolic language is for public mental health.[71] How a child is spoken to in the first years of its life, and how it begins to speak, are of decisive importance. In this process it is first of all the mother who plays a major role. In how the child approaches the mother, her presence in expression, countenance, gesture and voice, lie the question and the expectation of an answer, an answer that meets an original desire for community and contact with reality. Through her presence the mother allows the world to be present for the child. Initially in this process the mother is the only speaker and the child follows everything attentively. The child does not do this purely as a spectator, who wants to establish facts empirically and wants to see the world described in unambiguous language. Rather, it is a matter of words and names that pave the way to life itself, to total reality. The child learns to speak in this way; it learns to give a name to the world, in order to be able to enter in to contact with it in a human

---

[70] R. SCHAEFFLER: 'Kultisches Handeln. Die Frage nach Proben seiner Bewahrung und nach Kriterien seiner Legitimation', in HAHN a.o.: *Anthropologie des Kults* 40-42.

[71] F. BUITENDIJK: 'Taal en samenleven', in *Taal en gezondheid* (Serie Geestelijke Volksgezondheid 40), Utrecht 1969, 9 ff.

way. In this process in which the child learns to speak, we are thus dealing with symbolic language: it is about words, not merely terms. It is a matter of dialogue in which initially the mother speaks and 'brings the things to light' for the child. The child gradually enters into this process, becomes active and joins in the revelation. The time comes when it begins to ask all kinds of questions: What is this? What is that? Everything must get a name and be revealed. In this way the child grows into a mentally healthy person.

As long as the process runs in the way just described, the climate will be right for the child's healthy growth. But when the child is only spoken to with terms, frustrations arise. When a child receives no answers to questions about deeper reality, the threat of deep-seated disorders arises. When, for instance, a child asks where someone goes after death, and only gets a superficial-descriptive answer on the order of 'after his death grandpa is buried in the ground', mischief is sown. One could thus say that a child is in all respects under the influence of language. One must take into account what is broken when a child is only spoken to with terms, in impersonal language. This leads to an impoverished consciousness, loneliness, frustration, fear. The child can no longer find contact with life and with reality. One expressive way that this surfaces is in stammering and stuttering.

What is true for symbolic language is also true for symbols and symbolic acts. I have already noted that according to Lorenzer sensory-symbolic forms of interaction form the basis upon which human development takes place, and that this even takes precedence over language.[72] When breakdowns occur here, they can seriously damage the mental health of the child. As a striking example, Lorenzer cites a film of a mother breast feeding her child. The child involved suffers from a serious drinking disorder. A careful analysis of what is seen indicates that the mother offers the child the nipple, but at the moment that the child wants to begin sucking with his lips, withdraws it again. When the sucking reflex ceases, she once again moves her nipple between the child's lips, only to withdraw it again, and so forth.[73] In this way, the communication is constantly disrupted. The primary participation can-

---

[72] See Part 1, Chapter 1, 2.5.
[73] LORENZER: *Das Konzil der Buchhalter* 153.

not be established. Emotional disturbances that are not easy to remedy arise. It is as if in the first groves on a record one is already on the wrong course. Often considerable therapy is necessary to deal with damage which has occurred so early.

Sensory-symbolic forms of interaction continue to be of primary importance even after speech is learned. We saw that the interplay between the symbolic forms of interaction in language and the sensory-symbolic forms of interaction performs the function of maintaining contact with the primary structure of the self. Thus not only symbolic language, but also the presentative symbol and presentative symbolic actions are indispensable for mental health in humans. It is further important to supplement Buitendijk's observations by noting that the presentative symbol and presentative symbolic act are also primary in so far as they function as a sort of irreplaceable basis for symbolic language.

After these considerations, it is not difficult to see that rituals are indispensable for the mental well-being of individuals and society. After all, it is precisely in rituals that symbolic language, symbols and symbolic acts come together. Moreover, I must emphasize that merely the coming together of symbolic language, symbol and symbolic act as such, is not sufficient. It is clear from the foregoing that there must be a balanced confluence of the three.

Thus, when a society lacks rituals it loses contact with the fullness of reality. People then get into a tight corner, and there is a danger to mental health. Without ritual, there is no life. Rituals simply are a part of the equipment of a healthy human being and a healthy society. Martin makes this point more sharply in regard to the rituals of feast. When celebration of feast is lacking, people become *untergesund:* one can speak of a *sub-sanitas,* which leads to apathy, a reduction of experience and emotionality, a narrowing of horizons. The characteristic of all true feast is that it is marked by *Übergesundheit (super-sanitas)*: one can speak of openness, renewal of consciousness, the presence of spirit and self-awareness.[74]

The contribution of neurophysiology with regard to ritual is interesting in this connection. According to Laughlin, McManus and d'Aquili the

---

[74] M. MARTIN: *Fest und Alltag*, Stuttgart 1973, 24-28, 77.

principal neurophysical effect of ritual behavior is to block the activity
of the dominant cerebral hemisphere and to neutralize the functioning
of the analytic conceptual mode.[75] The non-dominant right hemisphere, which is the locus of holistic comprehension, becomes predominant in contrast to the left hemisphere, in which speech and the linear
analytic thought are located.[76] The biological effects are not limited to
brain functions. The tempo of a drumbeat may approximate that of the
heartbeat, and 'as it synchronizes the movements of dancers and unifies
their voices into the unison of hymns, it may seem to entrain their
breaths and heart rhythms, and thus seem to unifie the congregation's
separate members into a single larger, living being'.[77] Ritual participation indeed has neurophysiological consequences. Finally, the integration of the holy arises from a union of the function of both cerebral
hemispheres. The simultaneous functioning of the left and the right
hemisphere accomplishes 'the unification of opposites, of harmony with
the universe, of Oneness with the other members of the congregation,
and even of the Oneness of the self with God'.[78]

It is understandable that in the 1970s when many of the rituals in Western society, and particularly in The Netherlands, were disappearing,
therapists began using rituals in their psychotherapy. They came to the
idea of prescribing rituals for particular clients in order to break through
the impasses at critical transitions in life, such as divorce or the loss of a
loved one. Striking examples can be found in the book by Onno van der
Hart, et al., *Afscheidsrituelen in psychotherapie* (Rituals of parting in psychotherapy).[79] Actually, this was a remarkable phenomenon. While the

---

[75] E. D'AQUILI & C.D. LAUGHLIN: 'The biophysical determinants of religious ritual
behaviour', in *Zygon* 10 (1975) 32-57; IDEM: 'The neurobiology of myth and ritual', in
D'AQUILI, LAUGHLIN & McMANUS: *The Spectrum of Ritual*; C. LAUGHLIN, D.J.
McMANUS & E. D'AQUILI: *Brain, Symbol and Experience*, New York 1990.

[76] RAPPAPORT: *Ritual and Religion in the Making of Humanity* 226-230.

[77] RAPPAPORT: *Ritual and Religion in the Making of Humanity* 227.

[78] RAPPAPORT: *Ritual and Religion in the Making of Humanity* 229-230.

[79] VAN DER HART a.o.: *Afscheidsrituelen in psychotherapie*. Also: IDEM: 'Relaties en
rituelen', in K. VAN DER VELDEN a.o.: *Directieve therapie*, Deventer 1977; IDEM: 'Therapeutische rituelen: twee voorbeelden', in VAN DER VELDEN a.o.: *Directieve therapie*;
IDEM: *Overgang en bestendiging: Over het ontwerpen en voorschrijven van rituelen in psychotherapie*, Deventer 1978; M. DE LANGE-SNELDERS: 'Een pleidooi voor rituelen', in R.
LAFAILLE a.o. (eds.): *Zelfhulptechnieken. Wat het individu zelf kan doen aan zijn
lichamelijk en geestelijk welzijn*, Deventer/Antwerpen 1981, 9-10.

society was in the midst of a crisis of rites, particularly with regard to rites of passage, these were discovered by psychotherapy. The rituals were transposed, and no longer performed in life as a whole, but were used in a clinical situation. They were transplanted from their natural environment, as it were, and turned into a sort of sticking plaster. In this way the rituals, like so much in our society, were subjected to scientific and practical control, for a very specific goal: healing arrested development or disordered lives. P. Vandermeersch warns of the danger of using religious rituals in psychotherapy, because it easily leads to a confusion of the tasks of the psychotherapist and the pastor.[80] On the other hand one can argue that the concept of ritual can be understood more broadly than only applying to religious rituals. It is beyond my competence to decide upon the value of the use of secular rituals in psychotherapy. To my mind, they can have a therapeutic effect. In addition to Van der Hart, Canda and Moore, inspired by Turner, also point to the importance of rituals in psychotherapy.[81] Moreover, the chance of confusion is gradually decreasing because within individual pastoral practice rituals have also been discovered as a possible means of healing.[82] Not long ago A. Mulder argued for developing rituals with a therapeutic purpose, focused on the pastoral client. In this it is important to work

---

[80] P. VANDERMEERSCH: 'Psychotherapeutic and Religious Rituals: The Issue of Secularisation', in HEIMBROCK & BOUDEWIJNSE (eds.): *Current Studies of Ritual* 151-164 = P. VANDERMEERSCH: 'Psychotherapeutische Rituale', in BELLIGER & KRIEGER (eds.): *Ritualtheorien* 435-447 = P. VANDERMEERSCH: 'Psychotherapeutische en religieuze rituelen', in *Werkmap (voor) Liturgie* 25 (1991) 79-91. 1990; see also P. VAN DER VEN: 'Religieus ritueel is geen gereedschap voor de therapeut', in *Trouw* February 1989.

[81] E.R. CANDA: 'Therapeutic Transformation in Ritual, Therapy and Human Development', in *Journal of Religion and Health* 27 (1988) 3, 205-220; R.L. MOORE: 'Contemporary Psychotherapy as Ritual Process: An Initial Reconnaissance', in *Zygon* 18 (1983) 3, 126-143; IDEM: 'Ministry, Sacred Space and Theological Education: the Legacy of Victor Turner', in *Theological Education*, autumn 1984, 87-100; IDEM: 'Space and Transformation in Human Experience', in R.L. MOORE & F. REYNOLDS (eds.): *Anthropology and the Study of Religion*, Chicago 1984, 126-143.

[82] L. VAN DER VEER: 'Een pastorale week. Verslag van een gecomprimeerde vorm van pastorale hulpverlening, waarin gebruik gemaakt wordt van rituelen', in *Praktische Theologie* 8 (1981) 230-239; F.J. VAN TIENEN: 'Een verterend vuur', in *Praktische Theologie* 8 (1981) 240-243 (see VAN DER HART: *Afscheidsrituelen in psychotherapie* 53-59, and W.J. BERGER: 'Opdat wij niet, na anderen gepredikt te hebben, zelf verloren gaan', in *Praktische Theologie* 8 (1981) 244-249). See also (inspired by V. Turner): U.T. HOLMES: 'Liminality and Liturgy', in *Worship* 47 (1973) 286-297; MOORE: 'Ministry, Sacred Space and Theological Education'.

with what are termed self-symbols, basic symbols that express the inner-most feelings of the client.[83] One finds the same argument in the pas-toral theologian Menken-Bekius.[84] Another objection by Vandermeer-sch must however be taken into account, namely that such rituals easily become too individual, and lose the suprapersonal character that is typ-ical of them. But it seems to me this objection is not insurmountable. Here we again encounter the tension between the repetitive character of ritual, which points to larger linkages and a broader context, and the creativity within ritual, which is linked to certain limits. I will return to this in the following point (3.6). Furthermore, it can also be questioned whether precisely in our culture the exclusivity of the concept of collec-tive ritual has not been breached. This will be discussed in Part 3, Chap-ter 3, 3.2.

3.6. Expressive dimension

Rituals are givens passed on to us. Yet at the same time, and necessarily, they are expressive of ourselves. That expressiveness is of essential importance. If we could not discover anything of ourselves in ritual, it would remain external to us and inert. However, ritual helps us precisely in giving a face to what we experience and helping us understand our-selves. Because it does so, we need ritual. If we kept our experiences only in our inner self, they would never become an integrated part of us. They would remain uncertain, unstable, searching, sealed in themselves. Ritual helps us really experience that which has happened to us.[85] Thus ritual is an expression of our selves and what preoccupies us.

---

[83] A. MULDER: *Pastoraat en ritueel. Verslag van een verkennend onderzoek naar het gebruik en effect van therapeutische rituelen, beschreven binnen het concept van communi-catief pastoraat* (M.A. Thesis Theologische Faculteit Tilburg), Tilburg 1991.

[84] C. MENKEN-BEKIUS: 'Een angstige bedevaartganger. Tussen pastoraat en psy-chotherapie', in M. VAN UDEN, J. PIEPER & E. HENAU (eds.): *Bij Geloof. Over bede-vaarten en andere uitingen van volksreligiositeit* (UTP-katern 11), Heerlen 1991, 125-138; IDEM: 'Als het hart een moordkuil wordt... Een ritueel als pastorale hulpverlening', in *Werkmap (voor) Liturgie* 25 (1991) 108-116; IDEM: 'Een kanaal voor onze emoties. Rituelen rond de dood', in *Rondom het woord* 38 (1996) 2, 30-37; IDEM: 'Rituelen houden niet op bij de begrafenis', in *Rondom het woord* 38 (1996) 2, 37-44; IDEM: *Rit-uelen in het individuele pastoraat*; IDEM: *Werken met rituelen in het pastoraat.* See also R. NIEUWKOOP: *De drempel over*; M. VAN UDEN: *Rouw, religie en ritueel*, Baarn 1988.

[85] A. ULEYN: 'Drie idealen waardoor groepen zich laten leiden', in *Speling* 27 (1975) 95; VERGOTE: *Het huis is nooit af* 121.

The expressive function of rituals operates not only for the more central rituals, but also for everyday rituals. In the latter, who we are, how we deal with one another and what our world image is also comes to the fore. Our everyday rituals collectively form a great ritual book. To study it is very fascinating, because it brings our selves to light in relevant ways.[86] This is not true only for the present, but likewise for the past. For instance, Schmitt did an impressive study of gesture as the mirror of the Medieval soul.[87] He begins with a discourse on gesture in classical rhetoric. There it was a matter of the consciously 'beautiful gesture' that must not only fit with the subject being spoken of, but also must express the self-control and inner nobility of the orator. With regard to the Middle Ages, Schmitt points out that for instance, according to the Medieval author Hildemar of Civatek, when pruning the branches of grape vines monastics were supposed to express their humility in their physical posture, and thus, even if they had to stand on tiptoe to reach the highest branches, at least in their thoughts their head had to be bowed. Also, the children in the monastery learned how they had to approach guests poised and without raised voices, while at the same time looking them directly in the eye.

Ritual can be an expression of our self, even when it is rehearsed literally. Then it is a matter of performing the ritual with true devotion and not just formally or by rote, because, according to the rules, that is how it must be. But because ritual is also an expression of those who perform it, that automatically brings with it the fact that variants appear in the ritual. This breathes life into the established framework. That happens, first and foremost, because these persons are involved in the ritual, which automatically leads to their personal accents in its performance. This is even the case where the ritual is performed in a very formal way, as literally as possible, as it were. Sperber correctly points out that the same ritual will have different participants each time, and if only by reason of the new performance, that old concepts in the ritual will be reconstructed in a different way, new links will be woven among the participants, and new information from daily life will be integrated into the symbolic field of the ritual.[88]

---

[86] JETTER: *Symbol und Ritual* 116-117.

[87] J.-C. SCHMITT: *La raison des gestes dans l'occident médiéval*, Paris 1990. See the review by M. DE JONG: 'Het gebaar als spiegel van de middeleeuwse ziel', in *NRC Handelsblad* March 21, 1992, Zaterdags bijvoegsel (Saturday Supplement), 4.

[88] SPERBER: *Rethinking symbolism* 151.

Next, there is the fact that certain parts of the ritual as such can be more open and variable. One could think, for instance, of the sermon in the Christian liturgy; even in the absolutely regulated liturgy between Trent and Vatican II, this variable remains present.[89] A third possibility is that new elements will be brought into the ritual. Thus, for example, at a funeral an object can be placed on the coffin of the deceased that characterises his or her life. To the degree that the singularity of a ritual is emphasized, more new and individual elements will be present. In this it is striking that people in our culture have more interest in the one-off and the informal character of ritual. Finally, there is the possibility of the emergence of an entirely new ritual. What is new within a ritual may not, however, reach the point at which the repetitive aspect, at least at the deep level, entirely disappears. This is true objectively, for the ritual as such. But it is also true for the experience of those taking part: for some, the familiar thread is lost more quickly than for others. Here one encounters a tension which must always be borne in mind. The individualization of ritual has its bounds. If it is overdone and the ritual becomes too informal, it can erode the suprapersonal character of ritual. I can image that the following quote will not be equally accessible as an illustration for everyone, but it certainly contains a kernel of truth which should be taken seriously:[90]

> In an era in which people strive for individualization it appears such pre-formed acts are in conflict with the ideal of self-realization and personal choice. The formal is out. The original is in… The sort of toe-curling gaucherie to which this can lead is to be heard with distressing regularity in civil marriage ceremonies across the land. The city clerk, stripped of the fig-leaf of a fixed text, babbles whatever comes into his or her head. At the worst, there are moments in which he or she – I've seen this now a couple of times – offers excuses for the pair of formal sentences that remain because according to the law they must still be pronounced. Almost literally: "Now, I'm going to ask you a couple of questions. You know what they're going to be, eh? A bit official, but we have to be for a moment." Or: "Yes, and now the official bit of this happening. Don't worry, it's brief. We still have to be formal when it comes to the marriage vows. I hope that won't scare you off!" "Look, take a moment now to give each other a kiss." And: "As you can see, in this marriage record there is room for the names of many children. A bit old-fashioned, eh?"

---

[89] W. JETTER: Symbol und Ritual 257 ff.
[90] R. KOHNSTAMM: 'Beschutting van rituelen', in *NRC Handelsblad* April 11, 1998.

And I myself have heard a Dutch city clerk respond to the couple's 'Yes, I will' two times with 'O.K., that's done.' Even in Christian ritual from time to time too great a degree of informality and individualization will creep in.

I will conclude by remarking that in ritual, creativity is always commanded. In literally rehearsing a ritual, this command is fulfilled by the creativity in the attitude of devotion with which the ritual is performed, and through which personal accents will appear. In the rise of a new ritual, this is primarily expressed in the newly created forms themselves, which must be performed with devotion. Between these two extremes, many variants are possible.

3.7. Invocatory dimension

When we symbolize, the perspective springs open. There is, so to speak, a 'transfinalisation': things, acts and words change meaning; they get a new sense, full of import. A watch that I inherited from my father and that I now have on the mantelpiece is in no visible way distinguishable from other watches, but through the fact that he wore it, it has been transmuted. It has obtained another meaning and has become a symbol of his life, of how he dealt with time. It also calls up his relation to his grandchildren: how he sometimes held the watch by their ear in order to let them listen to its soft ticking.

But symbolism can happen in entirely different ways. It can be a 'definalisation'. It can reverse a chance of nature. This is the case when it is directed toward opening up perspectives in order to dispel evil. This aspect too is indispensable in human ritual. We cannot live life without invoking and exorcising. There is constantly occasion for this. Despite all progress, the natural environment is still always a threat to us. We still experience destructive floods. Hurricanes cause great destruction. Volcanic eruptions cost thousands of lives. We are dependent on the weather; ultimately we have no control over it. Not all diseases are under our control, and certainly not death itself. Then there are power structures that are more powerful than we would want. How many are ruthlessly oppressed? How many suffer hunger? How will we resist the genocide that again and again threatens to take place somewhere in the world?

The meaning of invocation and exorcism today appears to be that through them we 'definalize' the negative powers. We deprive the mystery of evil of its terrifying power by expressing in a ritual way that this does not have the last word. We call evil by its name in order to banish it.[91] We avow our powerlessness, but at the same time express our conviction that this can not and may not be our future. Christians do this in the realization that in God's name, in Jesus' name, evil cannot and may not have the last word. Huub Oosterhuis tells the following story about the birth of his son: 'My son Tjeerd-Pieter was born on Christmas Eve, 1971. I immediately gave him a kiss on his forehead and said, "You are Tjeerd-Pieter David and bogeys don't exist"'.[92] This is exorcism speaking.

Ritual invocation is thus in no way something that only is at home in primitive cultures. After it has been subjected to criticism by our culture, it remains possible and even necessary, in a second innocence. That's just the way we are as humans. At the launch of the first Atlas rocket at Cape Kennedy, all the technicians shouted 'Go, Atlas, go!', constantly repeating it as a litany. Even there, where only technical control can set things in motion, people suddenly realized that there are powers we do not control, but must invoke.[93]

3.8. Ethical dimension

What is symbolized in ritual refers to a deeper reality. In that sense, ritual is a window through which one as it were perceives unsuspected perspectives and something of that other reality enters in our life.

But symbolization does not stop there. What ritual symbolizes also penetrates life itself. Ritual thus also has an import for non-ritual actions. It can help us to better come to terms with the dark, frightening, angry and impenetrable in life.[94] However, it can also be an impulse setting us to work for a humane community. When one encounters a full-grown

---

[91] G. LUKKEN: 'Enkele kanttekeningen over het exorcisme', in *Tijdschrift voor Liturgie* 52 (1968) 259-260.

[92] N. BERGHKAMP: 'Huub Oosterhuis, 'Een lijk verbranden is vreselijk'', in *De Gelderlander*, Saturday October 21, 1972, 4. This Tjeerd-Pieter is now, together with his sister Trijntje Oosterhuis, part of the musical group *Total Touch*.

[93] See HAHN: 'Kultische und säkulare Riten' 62.

[94] JETTER: *Symbol und Ritual* 101.

and authentic ritual, then something of what is experienced in and through the ritual almost of its own accord also permeates life itself. The ritual really need not repeatedly or expressly say anything that declares this connection with life; this connection is simply inherent in a good ritual. Thus ritual influences our ethical acts. It must not be distorted into an ethic, but will have everything to do with ethics even as it remains itself. Where a division occurs between ritual and ethics, ritual should be revised, or it has been performed with too little devotion.

One could say that as ritual is a source and norm for a humane perspective on life – Christians translated this into the maxim *lex orandi lex credendi* (the norm of prayer is the norm of faith) – so ritual is also the source and norm of authentic human action – In Christian terms, *lex orandi lex agendi* (the norm of prayer is the norm of action).[95] Thus, for example, the peace movement was strongly inspired by peace rituals.[96]

3.9. Social dimension

In the study of ritual as such, very quickly the question raised of what role ritual plays in society. Or to put it differently, one poses the question of the 'function' of ritual. This question is about ritual as a social phenomenon. It is not surprising that this interest coincided with the rise of sociology as a new discipline. The term 'sociology' as a name for social science was first used by Comte around 1838.[97] But it was chiefly Durkheim (1858-1917) who first went further into the question of ritual as a social phenomenon. Together with Marx and Weber he is one of the three classic sociologists.[98] After him, a large number of theories about the relation between ritual and society were developed. I will forego dealing with them in detail,[99] and content myself with a global overview of the social dimension in ritual.

---

[95] See T. BERGER: 'Lex orandi – lex credendi – lex agendi', in *Archiv für Liturgiewissenschaft* 27 (1985) 425-432.

[96] M. MORESON: 'Symbolen en riten in de vredesliturgie', in *Tijdschrift voor Liturgie* 70 (1986) 218-226.

[97] See F. VAN PEPERSTRATEN: *Samenleving ter discussie. Een inleiding in de sociale filosofie*, Bussum 1995³, 174.

[98] VAN PEPERSTRATEN: *Samenleving ter discussie* 174.

[99] A good overview will be found in BELL: *Ritual. Perspectives* 23-60; see also BELLIGER & KRIEGER: *Ritualtheorien* 14-17.

Ritual is not purely directed toward the I. To be sure, ritual can be expressive of one's self, but as such it is just as much directed toward the other. In ritual one expresses oneself in a way recognizable to oneself. But this is done within a structure of communicative acts that have been handed down to one, and can be recognized by others. The ritual is, as it were, a call to the other to enter into communication. It awakens collectivity. By definition, rituals have a social function. That is true for the I and for the Thou that will communicate with each other. It is also true for the small group and the larger community. As the self finds identity in and through ritual together with the other, so the members of a group or larger community, precisely as members of that group or community, find their identity in and through ritual. The way people dress and the possessions they carry or own play an important role in this formation of groups. 'An anarchist will have a difficult time of it in his own circle if he wears an expensive three-piece suit and shows up at the 'action' in a sports car.'[100]

The community needs ritual precisely in order to be a community. Without ritual the community would disintegrate. It realizes itself in and through ritual. Without the structure of communicative acts in and through which it expresses and at the same time repeatedly encounters its particular face, a community simply could not exist. You can not imagine a political party without programmatic and more or less festive party gatherings that constitute or affirm and strengthen it. The same is true for family celebrations. If one studies the rituals of a community, one will come to realize how vital the social function of ritual is. A community better instructs one about itself by its celebrations than by an investigation of the buildings or of social structures. One could try to find out about the views on marriage of, say, a Zambian by interviewing him or her, but one could unquestionably immerse oneself more deeply in Zambian culture if one merely studied a Zambian wedding feast itself, or took part in it. A people reveal themselves in the most vital way when they celebrate a religious feast, and perform their ritual dances. One of the foci of ritual is also that it integrates the individual into the community, each time in a different way: as a newborn, as an initiate,

---

[100] P. LOMANS: 'Symbolen in de samenleving. Tussen hakenkruis en hostie', in *Het Nieuwsblad* October 22, 1991, 19. See M. VERKUYTEN: *Symbool en samenleving. Over symbolen en hun rol in het sociale leven*, Zeist 1990.

as a married person. At each of the important transitions of life the individual is assisted in finding his or her place in the community in a new way through a socially acknowledged rite.[101]

The social function of ritual reaches still further. Precisely because the dimension of repetition is essential for ritual, it also brings us – exactly because of the fact that it has been handed down to us – into contact way in a vital way with the generations before us, with the past of our own community. The social function of ritual thus also extends to those who have preceded us. And does it not also touch in another way on the future of our community: is ritual not preserved, renewed and handed on for the sake of those who will come after us?

Ritual cannot be eradicated as a social phenomenon. For instance, a radical renewal of rituals took place in Russia after the October Revolution of 1917.[102] In the former Soviet Union, and later in countries which became subject to it, religious rites were replaced by new rituals which were to express and strengthen the unity of this socialist society. One new celebrated the birth of a citizen into the socialist society, the registration of the child's name, the *Jugendweihe*, a peculiar manner of marriage and burial, May Day, the anniversary of the Revolution on November 7, the feast of harvest, of spring and summer, of the hammer and sickle, of the ear of grain, of agriculture, of animal husbandry.[103] All sorts of rituals surrounding labor and the laborer also arose, with all sorts of distinctions, of which the Order of Lenin was the highest. Everywhere one found portraits and statues of Lenin. His mausoleum near the Kremlin became a central shrine, visited since 1924 by more than a hundred million pilgrims, and above which on May 1 and November 7 the leaders of the country appeared to the people and took the salute of the parading forces.[104] On the basis of the Marxist ideology and frequent materialistic analyses, Western observers

[101] For the role of 'acceptance' in the social dimension of ritual, see Part 1, Chapter 3, 1.2.

[102] B. CHICHLO: 'Le pouvoir des rites en U.R.S.S.', in MOINGT: *Enjeux du rite dans la modernité* 171-192. See also LANE: *The Rites of Rulers*; BELL: Ritual. Perspectives 225-229.

[103] See also LUKKEN: De onvervangbare weg van de liturgie 33-35 and the literature listed there.

[104] CHICHLO: 'Le pouvoir des rites en U.R.S.S.' 183, note 185.

were of the opinion that everything turned on the economy. But more recent analyses by anthropologists have observed the opposite. Religious ritual mentality was transformed by a magical/religious ritual, and stimulating labour was more relevant symbolically than economically. Despite the great natural wealth of the country, the economy actually remained primitive; only to a small extent was it autonomous and secularized. Because of this it descended ever more deeply into crisis. Rituals played an exceptionally large role in keeping together this unusually pluriform and multicultural society, which was comprised of the most varied peoples and languages, even having a number of different alphabets. During *perestrojka*, at the end of the 1980s, this ritual gradually began to collapse, leaving behind a void. In this vacuum people are at this moment busily seeking new rituals, where on the one hand there is a return to Christian rituals, but on the other also a considerable ritual pluriformity, both in the secular and religious perspective. Especially now, it is extremely interesting for anthropologists to follow the ritual developments and their social components.

3.10. Political dimension

The political dimension of ritual is closely linked with the social dimension of ritual. Rituals play an important and obtrusive role in establishing, expressing and promoting the power of political institutions such as monarchy, the state, education, and also the church.[105] Monarchs ascend the throne via rituals, presidents and judges are sworn in, professors installed, and so forth. Thus power is conferred through rituals. This can sometimes be most impressive; striking examples are the coronation of the monarch in England or The Netherlands, or the Japanese emperor. The actual exercise of power is also accompanied by ritual: military parades, the opening of a parliament, royal appearances on balconies, etc. On the other hand, institutional power can also be threatened by means of symbols. This is the case when a national flag is burned in protest, when groups walk out from negotiations, diplomats are recalled, protocols broken, or a mob seizes a parliament building, to name just a few examples. How much of a role rituals can play institutional politics is made clear in the conflict that led

---

[105] BELL: *Ritual. Perspectives* 128-135; see also Krieger & BELLIGER: 'Einführung' 15-17.

to the American president Woodrow Wilson sending troops into Mexico in 1914.[106] As a result of a mistake and smear campaign, the crew of an American whaling ship was arrested, questioned and released by the Mexican military. The affair escalated, and an American admiral demanded a formal apology and the assurance that the Mexican officer responsible would be severely punished. He also demanded that the American flag would be raised at a prominent place on the beach and honoured with a 21 gun salute, after which an American ship would respond to the salute in a fitting manner. When the Mexican president refused this, negotiations followed. The recommendation was that the Mexicans and Americans would fire a salute simultaneously. President Wilson rejected this compromise and demanded that the Mexicans would fire their salute first. But they refused. Several days later American troops invaded Mexico.

Especially in the 1960s we in Western Europe became more conscious of the political dimension of ritual. Existing rituals were criticized as purely a confirmation of the establishment and repressive institutions. As a counterpoint people performed all sorts of protest rituals, which often consisted of a more or less frivolous parody of existing rituals. Thus the political dimension of ritual too demonstrates how powerful and pervasive ritual can be.

---

[106] For this example, see BELL: *Ritual. Perspectives* 133.

CHAPTER 3

SEMIOTIC FOUNDATIONS

Particularly since the 1960s a new science has been developing, namely
semiotics. One can describe this discipline as the science in which signs
and the process of signifying as such are examined. The addition 'as such'
is important. There are of course many sciences in which signs, *among
other things*, are dealt with. Think for instance of human sciences, philosophy and theology itself with its many subdisciplines. Semiotics, however,
concerns the science of signs and signifying *as such*. Thus, although semiotics already has a long previous history, we may say that only in the last
decades has semiotics established itself as an internationally acknowledged
and firmly constituted discipline. At this moment it is practised from and
within almost all disciplines, from biology and physics to philosophy and
theology. Semiotics is in this sense an umbrella discipline and a foundation
for the human sciences. According to P. Maranda semiotics is a science that
coincides with the science of mankind, or with anthropology: 'There is no
semiotic object that is not at the same time already an anthropological
object; and there is no semiotic method that has not already previously
been taken up and used by anthropologists'.[1] It is clear that particularly the
discipline of Ritual Studies can not do without semiotics.

After all, concepts such as symbol, symbolic language, symbolic act
and their effect play a central role there. In this we are however confronted by the difficulty that on the one hand semiotics itself does not
speak unequivocally about these concepts, and on the other that it often
defines these concepts in differing ways. Still, on the basis of semiotics it
is possible to further clarify and deepen what we have said to this point.[2]

---

[1] P. MARANDA: 'Semiotik und Anthropologie', in *Zeitschrift für Semiotik* 3 (1983)
2/2, 227-249. So A.J. Greimas in an interview: H.-G. RUPRECHT: 'Ouvertures métasémiotiques: entretien avec Algirdas Julien Greimas', in *Recherches Sémiotiques/Semiotic Inquiry*
4 (1985) 1, 1-22. See also E. POPPE: 'Omtrent 25 jaar semiotiek van de film', in *Versus.
Tijdschrift voor film en opvoeringskunsten* 7 (1992) 2, 103.

[2] SEMANET (ed. G. LUKKEN): *Semiotiek en christelijke uitingsvormen. De semiotiek van
A.J. Greimas en de Parijse school toegepast op bijbel en liturgie*, Hilversum 1987; G.
LUKKEN & J. MAAS: *Luisteren tussen de regels. Een semiotische bijdrage aan de praktische
theologie*, Baarn 1996; LUKKEN: 'Symbool als grondcategorie van de liturgie'.

In the broad field there are two principle directions: what is termed Peircian semiotics, originating with C.S. Peirce (1839-1914), and Saussurian semiotics, which grew from the work of the Swiss author De Saussure (1857-1913). They lived at approximately the same time, but they never met. They probably did not even know of each other's existence. Both of them stand at the beginning of their respective school of semiotics. One can speak of Peircian and Saussurian semiotics. It is difficult to harmonise the two directions. The difference between these directions is linked to the fact that Peirce was a philosopher and De Saussure was a linguist: he is indeed the founder of the general science of language. Peircian semiotics has spread primarily through the English-speaking world and Germany, while one finds Saussurian semiotics primarily in countries with Romance languages, and in Finland and Lithuania. This follows in part from the fact that Saussurian semiotics – via the Dane L. Hjemslev – was further developed by the Lithuanian Greimas (1917-1992), who soon settled in Paris and gathered around himself what is termed the Paris school. In The Netherlands one finds both the Peircian and the Saussurian direction in semiotics. The distinction between the Saussurian and the Peircian views has also had wider effects. For instance, in the philosophy of language one can distinguish two different lines of development: the French line, which began with De Saussure, and which through structuralism underlies the thought of philosopher such as Derrida, Foucauld and Lyotard, and beside it the Anglo-Saxon line, which runs from Peirce via Wittgenstein, Austin and Searle to Habermas.[3] Within semiotics itself there have been attempts in recent years to bring the two currents closer together.[4]

1. PEIRCIAN SEMIOTICS

I have previously noted that Peirce distinguishes three elements in the sign, namely a) the visible sign as such (*representamen*), b) the sign in relation to the *object*, and c) the sign in relation to the symbol that is generated in the mind of the interpreting person (*interpretant*).[5] In

---

[3] F. VAN PEPERSTRATEN: *Samenleving ter discussie* 340.

[4] E.J. VAN WOLDE: *A Semiotic Analysis of Genesis 2-3. A Semiotic Theory and Method of Analysis Applied to the Story of the Garden of Eden* (Studia Semitica Neerlandica 25), Assen 1989; J. FONTANILLE: *Sémiotique du discours*, Limoges 1998.

[5] See Part 1, Chapter 1, 2.1.

connection with ritual it is particularly the second aspect that is important. In the relation of the sign to the object, Peircian semiotics has a further tripartite classification within the sign, namely that of the sign as *icon, index* or *symbol. Icon* has bearing on a sign in so far as it can be related to an object on the basis of a resemblance. Examples of this would be a photograph as referring to a particular person, a drawing as an illustration of an object, visual advertising for a product, or the 'iconic language use' of which I previously spoke. An *index* is a sign which refers to the object by being really affected by the object, because it is dynamically connected with this object. One can distinguish two sorts of indices:[6] 1) indices which have only an indirect relation to the object, as for instance a finger pointing north; 2) true indices in which there is a perfect correspondence between the sign and the object and either a cause-effect or part-whole relationship. In other words: a true index is a sign that is either an effect of, or an aspect of, or a part of its object. Thus a rash is an index of measles, the weathervane indicates the wind's direction, a Rolls Royce is a sign of the wealth of its owner and the March on Washington of November 15, 1970 indicated the size and social composition of opposition to the war in Viet Nam. Finally, *symbol* is a sign associated by law or convention with that which they signify. Examples include language in general, traffic regulations, legal regulations, etc.

1.1. Two important observations

In the context of our approach, two observations are important:

a. Previously I remarked that the critique of the distinction which I make between sign and symbol is primarily connected with the rise of semiotics, which uses a different and sometimes antithetical terminology. What I have denoted as a sign, is, on the contrary, designated as a symbol by Peirce, and what I have defined as a symbol in Peirce corresponds rather to the categories of icon and index. In schematic form:

| Chapter I: | sign | <--> | Peirce: | symbol |
| Chapter I: | symbol | <--> | Peirce: | icon and index |

---

[6] RAPPAPORT: *Ritual and Religion in the Making of Humanity* 54-68, also for the following.

b. For Peirce there is no ironclad distinction between the sign as icon, index and symbol. It is rather a case of which aspects in the sign are being especially accented. We already saw earlier that through the element of repetition the symbol, as I have characterised it, in ritual also takes on the conventional dimension of the sign.

1.2. Peircian semiotics and ritual: Roy Rappaport

Peircian semiotics still has not been applied very frequently to ritual.[7] At this point the wide-ranging and fundamental study by R. Rappaport (1926-1997), *Ritual and Religion in the Making of Humanity*,[8] is of particular interest. Rappaport interprets ritual principally in terms of the Peircian concept of symbol; in other words, he begins from the conventional character of ritual. He describes ritual as 'the performance of more or less invariant sequences of formal acts and utterances not entirely encoded by the performers'. According to Rappaport, in human ritual one can distinguish two classes of messages: *self-referential* and *canonical* messages. In all rituals, both animal and human, there are self-referential messages: the participants transmit information concerning their own current physical, psychic or social states to themselves or to other participants. One should here think of what I previously designated as the expressive dimension of ritual. There is thus a radical distinction between human and animal rituals, in so far as the message content of all animal rituals is *only* self-referential. But in human rituals one finds additional messages, *not encoded* by the performers of the ritual themselves. These messages, which tend to invariance, cannot *in themselves* be self-referential and cannot *in themselves* represent the performers' contemporary states.[9] The *Shema Israel* of Jewish ritual – 'Hear, O Israel, the Lord our God, the Lord is One' – is an example of such a canonical message. We are here dealing with an invariant message, which may not have changed in 3000 years. It is a core-message of Jewish ritual, what Rappaport characterises as an Ultimate Sacred Postulate. These highest and most sacred

[7] See among others SCHIWY: *Zeichen im Gottesdienst*; R. VOLP a.o.: *Zeichen . Semiotik in Theologie und Gottesdienst*, München/Mainz 1982; H. WEGMAN: 'The rubrics of the Institution Narrative in the Roman Missal 1970', in P. JOUNEL a.o. (eds.): *Liturgia opera divina e umana; Studi sulla riforma liturgica offerti a S.E. Mons. Annibale Bugnini in occasione del suo 70 compleanno*, Rome 1982, 329-338.

[8] RAPPAPORT: *Ritual and Religion in the Making of Humanity*.

[9] RAPPAPORT: *Ritual and Religion in the Making of Humanity* 52-53.

ritual formulations are eternal truths that support the whole ritual order. They are unreachable by human logic. Ultimate Sacred Postulates are peculiar in that they are typically absolutely unfalsifiable and objectively unverifiable. Nonetheless they are taken to be unquestionably true. Moreover, they are immaterial.[10] They exercise the highest authority and are characterised by invariance. The Creeds are examples in Christian ritual. It is these Ultimate Sacred Postulates that, despite all the variations in the order, guarantee unity in it.

It is clear that in canonical messages the accent lies on the conventional, delivered character of ritual, thus on the symbol in its Peircian sense, while self-referential messages are primarily characterised by the sign as icon and index. But here one must also take into account that there are no ironclad distinctions between icon, index and symbol. Self-referential messages can nevertheless rest on agreements, and thus have a 'symbol-character'. And certainly canonical messages can be simultaneously iconic and indexical. Their quality of perdurance and their sacred character can iconically and indexically be signified by the apparent and age-long invariance of their transmission and by the condensation of their utterance. This even appears to be true for Ultimate Sacred Postulates. Rappaport notes the fact that while the *Shema Israel* 'may not have changed in 3000 years (…) is one thing, that a particular person recites it on a particular occasion is another. The *Shema* remains unchanged, but those who utter it, and thus place themselves in relationship to it, continue to change as circumstances change and as generation succeeds generation'.[11] In other words, even with all the invariance of the Ultimate Sacred Postulates, one can still speak of self-referentiality. Or, to put it differently, even with Ultimate Sacred Postulates one is not dealing purely and only with symbols in Peirce's sense, but also with indexicality. Indeed, I must question if this expressive dimension of ritual itself does not penetrate still deeper into Ultimate Sacred Postulates. As literal texts from the past, Ultimate Sacred Postulates are purely and totally symbol, but as such they can take up into themselves expressive forms that are peculiar to various cultures, forms which are indexical and iconic. One can think for instance of the Latin Nicene/Constantinopolitan Creed. This has all kinds of melodies, from Gregorian to baroque, romantic and modern. In these musical

---

[10] RAPPAPORT: *Ritual and Religion in the Making of Humanity* 277-312.
[11] RAPPAPORT: *Ritual and Religion in the Making of Humanity* 53.

forms of expression the conventional text, passed down to us by tradition, is linked to us in iconic and indexical ways. This goes still further. The Latin text is translated into the expressive forms of other languages and then set to music again. In this way referentiality thus penetrates into the old *text* itself. This enables the Christian creed to evoke the core of Christian sacred history in a representative iconic and indexical manner. This can even lead to the question of whether some things may not be changed within the old text as such. I will return to this in Part 2, where I will go into continuity and discontinuity in ritual.[12] It is also important to realise that self-referential messages and canonical messages are not transmitted in separate rituals, but that their strands are interwoven throughout all liturgical orders. One can however say that the canonical stream is carried by the more invariant aspects or components of these orders and that self-referential messages are conveyed by whatever variation the liturgical order allows or demands.[13] In the case of the former the central stress lies on the sign as symbol, in the latter on the sign as icon and index.

In ritual there is a tension between the canonical and self-referential streams. To my mind, this also touches on what one might call the objective and the subjective sides of liturgy. In this connection I would note that there is a difference in accent between Rappaport's approach and mine. Because I have taken symbolisation (in the non-Peircian sense) as my starting point, and only thereafter have come to discuss the characteristic of repetition, in what follows in this book ritual as human expression, the importance of inductive ritual and the necessity of the emergence of new rituals will stand out all the more sharply. The advantage of Rappaport's approach is that he has a good eye for the institutional and objective side of ritual. Moreover, his approach clarifies the anthropological basis of what one in classic sacramental theology designates as the 'validity' of the sacrament. These are aspects that I would in no way want to exclude. It is rather a matter of a difference in emphasis. Rappaport also has a good eye for the variability of ritual. I will return expressly to that in the second part.[14] In any case, our approaches

---

[12] Part 2, Chapter 3, 5.

[13] RAPPAPORT: *Ritual and Religion in the Making of Humanity*, particularly 53-54, 383-385.

[14] See Part 2, Chapter 3, 5.

complement each other. For the rest, Rappaport makes very also clear that performers of the ritual participate in or become part of the ritual orders themselves. As transmitters-receivers they become fused with the messages they are transmitting and receiving. In conforming to these ritual orders they become indistinguishable from those orders; they become parts of them. Since this is the case, for the performers of the ritual it is self-contradictory and impossible to reject the ritual orders being realised by their own participation. Therefore, by performing a ritual order the participants *accept* – and indicate to themselves and to others that they accept – whatever is encoded in the canonical message of that order.[15] In other words, anyone who swears an oath cannot subsequently say that he has not bound himself – and it is not for nothing that perjury is punished. Anyone who takes part in the marriage ritual as a bride or groom can not subsequently say that he or she is not married. The participation as such implies acceptance, although there can be disparity between the act of acceptance and the inward state associated with it. Insincerity does not nullify acceptance. Ritual orders are *public* orders and therefore participation in them constitutes an acceptance of this public order *regardless* of the private state of belief of the performer. The acceptance is not only public, but also clear. One either participates in a ritual or one does not. The choice is free of ambiguity. The inevitable acceptance of a liturgical order by the performer does not guarantee that the performer will abide by whatever message, rules or norms that order encodes. The primary function of the order is to establish conventional understandings, rules and norms with which everyday behaviour is *supposed* to proceed. Participating in a ritual of marriage, in which a prohibition against adultery is enunciated, does not prevent a man from committing adultery. But it does establish for him this prohibition, which he himself has accepted. He has obligated himself to do so. This goes even further. To perform a liturgical order is not only recognise and accept the authority of the conventions it represents, it gives them their very existence. In the absence of performance the liturgical orders are dead letters. The order of marriage establishes the conventions of marriage itself, and the divinity of the God in whose name

---

[15] RAPPAPORT: *Ritual and Religion in the Making of Humanity* 117-138; see also R. RAPPAPORT: 'The obvious Aspects of Ritual', in R. RAPPAPORT: *Ecology, Meaning and Religion*, Richmond 1979 = R. RAPPAPORT: 'Ritual und performative Sprache', in A. BELLIGER & D.J. KIEGER (eds.): *Ritualtheorien* 191-211.

man and woman are joined. The performance of the ritual itself constantly maintains that which is accepted. Here the importance of the
canonical stream of ritual orders becomes apparent. Acceptance would
be meaningless or even logically impossible if the canon were made up
afresh by each participant for each performance. Thus we can conclude
that personal conviction cannot exclusively serve as the foundation of
public social orders. However, is true that a ritual order which is not
supported by the conviction of at least some of the members of a congregation is in danger of gradually falling in desuetude or becoming a
dead letter. Conviction is, in the long run, indispensable to the perpetuation of ritual orders.[16] Here we encounter the demand for the inculturation of ritual, which I will discuss at length later.

Finally, I wish to note one more fundamental point in Rappaport's
semiotic approach. He emphasises that the emergence of language as a
system of conventional symbols was the most radical development in
human evolution.[17] With language an entirely new form of information
appeared in the world. Language belongs to the domain of the symbol
(in its Peircian sense). It permits thought and communication to escape
from the concrete and solid actualities of here and now, to discover
other realms, for instance those of the possible, the plausible and the
desirable. Language makes such thought inevitable. In other words,
humankind is a species that lives and can only live in terms of meanings
it must itself invent. The world in which humans live is not only constituted by natural and organic processes, but also of symbolically conceived and performatively established cosmologies, rules and values. But
the consequences of the emergence of language and its concomitant culture were not unambiguously advantageous. When a sign is only con-
ventionally related to what it signifies, as in Peirce's sense of the symbol,
it can occur in the absence of its referent. This makes lying possible. The
possibility of the lie is a fundamental problem for human society. The
survival of humankind depends upon social interactions, characterised
by some minimum degree of order. Human communication must
achieve some minimum level of reliability. If not, social life becomes
increasingly disordered. Nor is the lie the only vice intrinsic to language.
A second problem of language is the alternative. This problem arises as

---

[16] RAPPAPORT: *Ritual and Religion in the Making of Humanity* 396, 419.
[17] RAPPAPORT: *Ritual and Religion in the Making of Humanity* 7-22.

much or more from the ordering of symbols through grammar. Grammar makes it possible to conceive of alternative worlds and orders. This ability is not, on the face of it, problematic. It makes possible adaptive flexibility to respond to changing conditions. This flexibility however also has a dangerous concomitant: it implies increased grounds for disorder. In the face of this, it may be said that aspects of religion, particularly as generated in ritual, can ameliorate the problems of falsehood and unbridled flexibility intrinsic to language. Religious rituals can establish the true word to stand against the corrosive forces of power and of many words; they can stand against falsehood and Babel. The union of sacred words and the human experience of the numinous, enacted in ritual, induces in man the notion of the divine. The further development of this theme runs like a thread – a sometimes unruly thread – through Rappaport's study. He argues that religion, particularly as enacted in rituals, is central to the continuing evolution of life, although it has been displaced from its original position by the rise of modern science. Religion, as enacted in ritual order, brings us in contact with the world of the divine. In this way, in the ritual order the 'holy' takes shape as an all-embracing religious phenomenon, and subsequently also the holiness of this world and its history.[18]

2. GREIMASSIAN SEMIOTICS

A wholly different manner of supplementing and deepening the preceding chapters is possible from Saussurian semiotics. I have already noted that Saussurian semiotics was chiefly further developed by A.J. Greimas and his Paris school. For that reason people also speak of Greimassian semiotics.

It is my belief that particularly this semiotics, still so little known in the English-speaking world, is especially suitable for further illuminating ritual.

2.1. Signification in all sorts of discourses

Unlike Peirce's, this semiotics does not start from a typology of the separate signs. It focuses on integral discourses as such and seeks to uncover

---

[18] See particularly RAPPAPORT: *Ritual and Religion in the Making of Humanity* 23 ff. and 277-461.

their signification. Greimassian semiotics concentrates on the signification in all sorts of discourses: texts, but also photographs, pictures, comic strips, paintings, statues, theatre, dance, architecture, rituals etc. According to Greimas 'meaning' (Fr. *sens*) is only attainable through discourses, which people create. These discourses mediate 'meaning' through the process of signification, which is behind it. Therefore the question of the meaning of a ritual can be translated into the semiotic examination of the process of signification of the ritual. How do rituals give meaning? Is it possible to describe the characteristics of their system of signification?[19]

---

[19] G. LUKKEN: 'Semiotics of the Ritual. Signification in Rituals as a Specific Mediation of Meaning', in LUKKEN (eds. CASPERS & VAN TONGEREN): *Per visibilia ad invisibilia* 269-283. For the semiotics of the ritual, see also among others.: M. HAMMAD: 'L'architecture du thé', in *Actes Sémiotiques. Documents* 9 (1987) no. 84-85, 1-50; HAUS-REITHER: *Semiotik des liturgischen Gesanges*; J. JOOSSE & P. DE MAAT: 'Semiotische analyse van de opening van het 'Amsterdamse doopritueel'', in *Jaarboek voor liturgie-onderzoek* 1 (1985) 2-67; IDEM: 'Semiotische analyse van de tussenzang van het 'Amsterdamse doopritueel'', in *Jaarboek voor liturgie-onderzoek* 2 (1986) 86-118; G. LUKKEN: 'Het binnengaan in de kerk in de Romeinse huwelijksliturgie. Een semiotische analyse', in *Jaarboek voor liturgie-onderzoek* 1 (1985) 69-89; IDEM: 'Semiotische analyse van de huwelijkssluiting in het post-tridentijnse Rituale Romanum', in *Jaarboek voor liturgie-onderzoek* 3 (1987) 41-85; IDEM: 'Semiotics and the Study of Liturgy', in W. VOS & G. WAINWRIGHT (eds.): *Gratias Agamus. An ecumenical collection of essays on the liturgy and its implications. On the occasion of the twenty fifth anniversary of Studia liturgica (1962-1987)* (Studia liturgica 17), Rotterdam 1987, 108-117; IDEM: 'De nieuwe Romeinse huwelijksliturgie', in SEMANET (ed. LUKKEN): *Semiotiek en christelijke uitingsvormen* 155-226; IDEM: 'De plaats van de vrouw in het huwelijksritueel van het Rituale Romanum en van Vaticanum II. Van ondergeschiktheid van de vrouw naar een zekere evenwaardigheid van man en vrouw', in *Jaarboek voor liturgie-onderzoek* 4 (1988) 67-89 = IDEM: 'Die Stellung der Frau im Trauungsritus des *Rituale Romanum* und nach Vaticanum II. Von der Unterordnung der Frau zu einer gewissen Gleichwertigkeit von Mann und Frau', in LUKKEN (eds. CASPERS & VAN TONGEREN): *Per visibilia ad invisibilia* 311-334; IDEM: 'De constituering van het subject in het ritueel discours', in *Versus. Tijdschrift voor film en opvoeringskunsten* 4 (1989) no. 2, 34-42; IDEM: 'Les transformations du rôle liturgique du peuple. La contribution de la sémiotique à l'histoire de la liturgie', in C. CASPERS & M. SCHNEIDERS (eds.): *Omnes circumadstantes. Contributions towards a history of the role of the people in the liturgy*, Kampen 1990, 15-30 (= *Sémiotique et Bible* 18 (1994) 27-48); IDEM: 'Un chant liturgique néerlandais analysé comme objet syncrétique', in *Jaarboek voor liturgie-onderzoek* 6 (1990) 135-154; N.M. SENGSON: *Research on the Sacramental Process of Penance and Reconciliation. Semiotic Approach to the Orationes of Medieval Rites of Penance* (Thèse de doctorat, Institut Supérieur de Liturgie, Paris), Paris 2001; W.M. SPEELMAN: *The Generation of Meaning in Liturgical Songs. Analysis of Five Liturgical Songs as Syncretic Discourses* (Liturgia condenda 4), Kampen 1995; L. VAN TONGEREN: 'Analyse d'un rituel: Introduction dialoguée de la préface romaine', in *Sémiotique et Bible* 9 (1983) no. 32, 19-26. Also M. SEARLE in Bibliography.

2.2. The deep level of signification

The participant in a ritual perceives a directed totality, which is rather complex. Many 'languages' act upon our senses at one and the same time. This participation is not a single perception of a text in a book, but perception of a complex action with all the senses together: a synaesthesia (*sun-aisthèsis*). We then experience this perception as being meaningful, because we perceive manifold differences, or at least shadows of differences. The colours 'say' something to us, because we recognise them in their mutual differences. Without the perception of these differences there would be one obscure mass. The same is true for sounds, shapes, music, movements, colours, scents, etc. We therefore only perceive meaning by discovering differences gradually. In his recent works Greimas has returned to this starting point and elaborated it further.[20] He says that the problem of the elementary structure of signification was the one over which he had to rack his mind the most.[21] Regarding the discovering of the elementary structures of meaning, he uses the image of a child who begins to perceive shadows of differences and similarities in the pluriform world and thus comes to the conclusion that one thing is not the same as the other: e.g. 'black' is not the same as 'non-black'. This is the beginning of the coming into being of what is called the semiotic square, which shapes the elementary structure of meaning. Greimas explicitly states that the child does not remain stuck at the mere observation that one thing is not the same as the other (as he believes Derrida does, with his ideas about the deconstruction of meaning).[22] On the contrary, what is essential for the elementary structure of meaning is the fact that the negative term is a turning point to a positive contrary term: from 'non-black' one comes to the conclusion that one has to do with the colour 'white'. In a semiotic square:

---

[20] A.J. GREIMAS: *De l'imperfection*, Périgueux 1987; A.J. GREIMAS & J. FONTANILLE: *Des états de choses aux états d'âmes. Essais de sémiotique des passions*, Paris 1991 = A.J. GREIMAS & J. FONTANILLE: *The Semiotics of Passions. From States of Affairs to States of Feelings*, Minneapolis/London 1993.

[21] M. ARRIVÉ & J. COQUET: *Sémiotique en jeu. A partir et autour de l'œuvre d'A.J. Greimas*, Paris/Amsterdam/Philadelphia 1987, 312.

[22] ARRIVÉ & J. COQUET, *Sémiotique en jeu* 312. See also R. SCHLEIFFER: *A.J. Greimas and the nature of meaning. Linguistics, semiotics and discourse theory*, London/Sidney 1987.

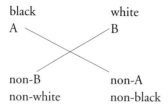

black   white
A   B

non-B   non-A
non-white   non-black

It is essential therefore that one does not remain stuck at the absence ('non-black'), but that an absence calls a presence ('white') into being. Greimas says:[23] 'I am not a philosopher, but it is aporias of this sort which I, as a semiotician [for whom 'signification' is therefore the central issue (G.L.)], had to solve and which I had to face in my way.' In this most elementary system of differences (A – non-A – B – non-B – A, and the movement between these poles) Greimas classifies the fundamental axiologies which lie behind human objects on the deep level.[24]

2.3. Higher levels of signification

On the basis of the elementary system of signification an extensive system of differences is established at higher levels: we find elementary narrative structures at what is called the surface level, and at what is called the level of discursive structure this narrative web is further enhanced with time, places, actors, themes and references to the natural world. Thus from the depth level, rising through the surface level and the discoursive level, meaning is formed at what is termed the level of manifestation, i.e. the level which we perceive immediately. In a diagram:

    level of manifestation: the text, or ritual, as a whole
    discoursive level
    surface level
    deep level

If one wants to have any 'understanding' of meaning as it receives shape in rituals, one should not stop at the first perception. One has to map its systems of signification.

[23] ARRIVÉ & COQUET: Sémiotique en jeu 314.
[24] For further developments with regard to the semiotic square, see J. FONTANILLE & C. ZILBERBERG: Tension et signification, Sprimont 1998, 45-70 and J. FONTANILLE: Sémiotique du discours, 51-73.

2.4. The elementary narrative scheme in rituals

Rituals have a development in which one usually is able to recognise the elementary narrative scheme which Greimas has brought to light for discourses. It is important to sketch this narrative scheme briefly. I will present this scheme by illustrating it at the same time with a ritual: namely the post-Vatican II Roman marriage ritual, as it was published in Dutch.[25] The first phase of the narrative scheme is the manipulation by a destinator of a destinatee with an act, which has to be performed in view. The marriage ritual begins which such a manipulation by the priest as destinator, with respect to the bridal couple as destinatee. In an introductory speech he invites the bride and groom to marry and he prepares a second elementary phase, viz. that of competence. The competence may consist of a wanting to, a knowing how to, a having to and a being able to. In the marriage ceremony we find this phase of competence in the three questions asked the couple regarding their freedom, their faithfulness and their willingness to accept children and raise them in the faith. Thus the couple is made competent for the performance of the ceremony: the exchange of the vows (the 'I want to'). In this act the bridal couple is joined with what is termed the object of value, in this case matrimonial union. Finally in a fourth phase a sanction upon the performance is provided by the priest as destinator: also on behalf of the community present, which is in fact his co-destinator, he evaluates the performance positively: 'From now on the community of the Church will see you as married people...'

In human discourses we do not always find a 'neat' succession of the four phases of the narrative scheme as we do in the ritual examined here; neither are all four phases always expressed. While in the prayer of supplication the phase of manipulation has a dominant role (compare the marriage blessing, which follows upon the contracting of the marriage), in a prayer of praise the phase of sanction is emphasised (we praise and give thanks to God) and in sacraments the act to be performed receives the main accent. However, even if the other phases may not be present explicitly, they are always logically implied. Thus the

---

[25] NATIONALE RAAD VOOR LITURGIE: *Het huwelijk* (Liturgie van de sacramenten en andere kerkelijke vieringen 7), Hilversum 1977. See for analyses LUKKEN: 'Het binnengaan in de kerk in de Romeinse huwelijksliturgie'; IDEM: 'De nieuwe Romeinse huwelijksliturgie'; IDEM: De plaats van de vrouw in het huwelijksritueel' = 'Die Stellung der Frau im Trauungsritus'.

prayer of supplication presupposes that God is competent to perform the act asked for, and the prayer is directed at the execution of what is being asked, and often a thanksgiving for the granting of what is prayed for is pronounced beforehand. The web of ritual acting is thus characterised by different distinguishable phases. In this context we may mention that Christian ritual is rather often described as *actio sacra*. With this people indicate that it is an 'acting'. Through semiotics a more specific characterisation is possible. Semiotics can indicate what kind of acting is involved and which phase of the narrative scheme is predominant in various rituals.

The narrative scheme is, so to speak, a diagram in which the elementary order within the discourse is revealed in its successive stages. This 'skeleton' is always completed further with specific values. Now, in the analysis of the marriage ritual above, it emerges that in the joining in marriage a transition is performed from the values /informal/, /private/, /initial/, /provisional/, /open/, /inclusive/, /fusion without differentiation/ to the values /official/, /public/, /complete/, /permanent/, /enduring/, /closed/, /exclusive/ and /unity of two without separation/.[26] These values may be represented at the deep level in an elementary square as follows:

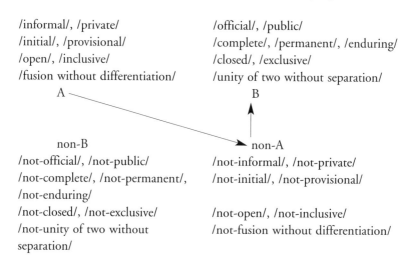

/informal/, /private/   /official/, /public/
/initial/, /provisional/   /complete/, /permanent/, /enduring/
/open/, /inclusive/   /closed/, /exclusive/
/fusion without differentiation/   /unity of two without separation/
    A   B

    non-B   non-A
/not-official/, /not-public/   /not-informal/, /not-private/
/not-complete/, /not-permanent/,   /not-initial/, /not-provisional/
/not-enduring/
/not-closed/, /not-exclusive/   /not-open/, /not-inclusive/
/not-unity of two without   /not-fusion without differentiation/
separation/

In this square it becomes clear what the system of fundamental values looks like and how the fundamental movements in the marriage ritual

---

[26] For the analyses see LUKKEN, 'De nieuwe Romeinse huwelijksliturgie'.

under consideration develop: from A via non-A to B. In the 'story' of the ritual event as it is initiated by the destinator, a certain fundamental pattern of values plays an important role. In his manipulation the destinator tries to bring the destinatee around (to persuade, to tempt, to force, etc.: there are many possibilities) to acceptance of this pattern of values. And in the sanction the main issue is whether the pattern of values has been realised by the subject of doing: 'From now on the community of the Church will see you as married people... What God has united, let no man separate.'

2.5. The destinators of ritual

In rituals, then, one recognises the narrative scheme. But the narrative scheme of the ritual goes further. It is also valid for the – If I may call it that – broader horizontal line of the ritual: for those elements which precede the ritual, with which the ritual is united inseparably, such as the institution narrative, the scenario and the script. It is important to look into these elements and to return then to the system of the ritual *in actu* as a complex discourse with many 'languages'.

2.5.1. Institution narratives

When analysing Christian rituals one often comes upon institution narratives. These can occur at many different places in the ritual: in the readings from Scripture in the liturgy of the Word, in the sermon, in the prayers, in the central act. The last mentioned is the case when in the middle of the Eucharistic prayer the institution narrative is recited: 'On the night he was betrayed, he took bread...', with the related 'do this in memory of me'. But elsewhere as well an institution narrative can play a large part. Thus in the rite of the blessing of the baptismal water, reference is made to the command of Jesus to baptise. In regard to our ritual of marriage, in the nuptial blessing it is called to memory how God created human beings as man and woman and how he united them: on this basis God is asked to bless this marriage. And among the readings we find the Old Testament texts about the institution of marriage 'in the beginning' and the institution narratives regarding marriage from the New Testament. It is here that we again come upon the elementary narrative scheme. In fact we are dealing with the first phase of the narrative scheme: the institution narratives constitute the phase of manipulation of the ritual. The main actors who play a role in these narratives have the role of destinators *vis-à-vis* the actors in the ritual, and also give competence to these actors for its performance. These destinators also determine the pattern of values of the act which the actors of the ritual have to perform. The whole set of values that is involved in the ritual is traced back to its original divine destinator through the institution narrative. We could say that institution narratives constitute the fundamental orientation and the fundamental framework of values of the ritual. References are often made to the institution narratives in the more reflexive introductions to the ritual in the service books. Further, they have a fixed position in the theological treatises of sacramental theology. In all this the issue is to keep the link between origin and ritual. Does the ritual comply with the original pattern of values or does it deviate from it? Secondary deviations from the pattern of values appear to be possible, but fundamental deviations are judged negatively. Semiotic analysis of rituals will probably reveal that fundamental deviations always involve a disturbance in the pattern of relation of the values on the deep level. In this context semiotics may have an important part to play in sacramental theology. The question with regard to the part of the divine destinator (God, Christ), the apostolic Church and the post-apostolic Church in the determination of the 'direction of meaning' of the sacraments[27] doubtless might be clarified in a new way with the use of semiotics.

The semiotic articulation of ritual just described does not appear to be valid for Christian ritual alone. It is rather a specific elucidation of the characteristic role that repetition and myth play in ritual.[28] The symbols, symbolic actions and symbolic language that once, when performed, provided meaning for a void in life are, in semiotic terms, destinators of recapturing that meaning in a new situation, in a characteristic, ritual manner.

2.5.2. Scenario and script

In rituals, as in theatre, we can often distinguish between scenario and script. By *scenario* we may indicate the ritual service book as it is officially published. The *script* is the same textual corpus as it is edited and

---

[27] For the concept 'direction of meaning', see E. SCHILLEBEECKX: *Marriage: Human Reality and Saving Mystery*, London/New York 1976, 142-155.

[28] For the specific role of 'invented tradition' as a destinator, see Part 2, Chapter 4, 4.

amplified with details by the *ceremoniarius* or a responsible group for the purpose of the celebration of the ritual. From a narrative point of view, the scenario functions as destinator for the detailed script, and as the agency which provides competence. Scenario and script together are the destinators and agencies which provide competence to the actual performance of the ritual (the ritual *in actu*). The scenario can be preceded by an introduction, in which a link is made between the ritual which is described and the institution narrative or the origin of this ritual. Earlier ritual shapes of the ritual through the ages are often also mentioned here. These may be very multiform, as was for instance the case with the Christian marriage rituals in the West which preceded the post-Vatican marriage ritual. The comparative study of this in Christian liturgical studies (*liturgie comparée*) is of importance here, to determine the extent to which variants in the pattern of values and in its expression occur. By such research one tries to determine to what extent the rituals of the past are normative narratively speaking as destinators for the service book today, and for adaptations of the ritual to a new culture. In this way it becomes clear that between the institution narrative and the ritual *in actu* there can be many intermediate destinators, which act as so many agencies providing competence with regard to the knowing how, the being able to and also the having to of the ritual performance. In cultures without writing, this role of intermediate destinator is fulfilled by oral tradition. Here one encounters again the repetitive character of the ritual, which does not preclude creativity at all, but does restrict it.

The scenario and the script are text-books in the literal sense of the word. In these text-books one can distinguish two types of texts, semiotically speaking. One finds the language of the rubrics in them: indications as to how the ritual has to be performed. This language is close to scientific language, which is cognitive and intended for making known, and through this making known, for acting. It is much more impersonal, and as clear and unambiguous as possible. Next to this one finds in the scenario the liturgical texts themselves, which have to be pronounced. Some of these are rubrical in nature, as for instance 'Let us pray', 'Let us stand', 'Let us kneel down'. Most of them are, however, more literary or poetical texts. Semiotically, we are dealing here with texts which on the level of content contain a great wealth of meaning. Often at the actual level of discursive structures there is a network of different thematic lines (called thematic isotopes), which means that the perspective can move from one line to another and vice versa. Emotions (joy, sadness, awe, honour, modesty, etc.) play a larger role in these texts as well. To this must be added that the system of the texts as regards content is greatly supported and motivated by the *form of the expression*. Because of this, these texts not only have a cognitive dimension, they are also pathematic in character: intended to generate emotions, and linked to corporality and the senses. Moreover, one often finds texts in the scenario which are combined with music, which usually strengthens their pathematic character.

2.6. Relationships between form of expression and form of content

I have just mentioned the operation of the expression form. At this point it is necessary to go into more detail about the Greimassian view of the sign, as it is not familiar for most of us. Up to this point we have been discussing the content form of the signification, which creates meaning. We have to realise that we were talking all the time about one level of the sign, i.e. the signified. Greimassian semiotics distinguishes two levels in the sign: the signifier (the expression) and the signified (the content).[29] In the same way that in the signified we are concerned with the discovery of the content form, in the signifier we are concerned with the expression form.

To determine the signification in an object it is of great importance to understand the relation between the form of expression and the form of content. According to Greimassian semiotics there are three possible relationships between the form of the expression and the form of the content.

1. In what are called *symbolic systems* the two levels are linked by forms of expression and content that completely match each other, so that each element of the form of the expression has a corresponding element in the form of the content. Examples can be found in formal sign-systems such as algebraic symbols, or street signs with their flashing lights, traffic signals, and pedestrian crossings. In such instances the degree of conformity between content-level and expression-level is

---

[29] J. COURTÉS: *Analyse sémiotique du discours. De l'énoncé à l'énonciation*, Paris 1991, 25-26; G. LUKKEN: 'De semiotiek van de Parijse school', in SEMANET (ed. LUKKEN): *Semiotiek en christelijke uitingsvormen* 21-23.

so complete that it is hardly worthwhile or even possible to differentiate them.

2. A second possible arrangement is represented by *semiotic systems in the strict sense*, such as languages. In a language there is little or no connection between the two dimensions of sound and meaning, and consequently it is essential to study each dimension separately. This is certainly the case where natural languages in general are concerned, for phonology (form of the expression) itself offers little or no clue to meaning (form of the content). The relation is arbitrary. To formulate this simply: the expressions *vrouw*, *Frau*, *femme* and *donna* all indicate the content 'woman', and the word 'table' can indicate both a piece of furniture and the multiplication table.

3. A third possible relationship between the level of the expression and the level of the content is found in *semi-symbolic systems*. What these systems have in common is that in all of them there is some correspondence between the form of the expression and the form of the content, but it is not a correspondence between individual elements of the one and individual elements of the other, but between categories. In other words, there is a correspondence between, on the one hand, the way certain elements in the form of the expression are related and, on the other, patterns of elements in the form of the content. For example, in the language of gesture there is a conventional opposition between verticality and horizontality on the level of expression, which corresponds to an position between affirmation and negation on the level of the content. One can find these semi-symbolic systems not only in the language of gesture, but also in discourses like architecture, sculpture, iconography and film. Even in language, a semi-symbolic system can be in operation, as in poetry. Semi-symbolic systems are also abundantly present in rituals.

2.7. Semi-symbolic relations between form of expression and form of content in rituals

It is clear that Greimas's terminology does not fully correspond with the distinction made in the first chapter between sign and symbol. What in my approach was denoted as 'sign', is on the contrary termed a 'symbolic system' by Greimas, and his 'semiotic systems in the strict sense' are also concerned with the context of the sign. What I denote as 'symbol' Greimas terms a 'semi-symbolic system'. But at the same time it is true that Greimassian semiotics does not contradict the distinction made. On the contrary, it can considerably clarify and deepen our understanding of this distinction. If one must consider the symbol, symbolic act and symbolic language as belonging to semi-symbolic systems, this means that there the expression has influence on the content in an entirely characteristic manner. It is important to go into this more deeply.

2.7.1. Semi-symbolic relations in ritual texts

So long as Greimassian semiotics was strongly focused on texts, it devoted little attention to the form of the expression, its structures and its influence on the form of the content. Texts were considered as semiotic systems in the strict sense, which means that the relation between expression and content was seen as a random relation. This view of the expression of the text as standing in an arbitrary relation with the form of the content is more fitting for the context of the language of signs than that of symbolic language (in our sense). It does too little justice to texts that include symbolic language. Indeed, one can read a text without devoting special attention to the forms of expression. Then the ultimate concern is exclusively for the form of the content. In such a reading of a text one as it were looks right through the expression. That is really how we are accustomed to read. Sometimes you do not know yourself whether you have read a text in your own language or in a foreign language. Our eye only registers the text itself if we encounter an error in spelling or printing. A difficulty in correcting proofs is that you always spontaneously stray away from the text itself.

But to the degree that semiotics of the Paris school devoted more attention to 'language' in the broadest sense, and also involved non-linguistic objects (painting, photography, film, music, dance, ritual, etc.) in its sphere, interest in the form of expression grew. With regard to linguistic expression itself, people became interested in the peculiar relations between expression and content. In this the focus was initially primarily on poetic texts. In poetry, by its nature, the design of the expression is very relevant. Expression is one of the determinants for the form of the content. Sounds, rhythm, rhyme, metaphors, structural forms and such in the form of expression play a major role there.[30] Greimas remarks that

---

[30] GREIMAS: 'Introduction'.

in poetry language tries to escape the randomness of linguistic signs, and tries to find an original motivation again, such as that involved in imitative signs like onomatopoeia (words such as 'hiss', 'buzz' or 'bang') or, in the most extreme case, the human scream. These are attempts by the subject to rediscover the materiality of language, and have as their sensory effect the generation of a stronger consciousness of reality.[31]

But it is not only in poetry that the semi-symbolic relation between the form of the expression and the form of the content plays a role. The question of this relation arises in all literary texts. There can also be semi-symbolic relations in prose, though perhaps in a less obvious and more refined way. For instance, R. Jakobson notes: 'Why do you always say only Jeanne and Marguerite, and not Marguerite and Jeanne? Is it that you prefer Jeanne over her twin sister? Absolutely not; but it sounds better that way'.[32] There is still considerable research called for in this connection. Willem Marie Speelman and Johann Hausreither made an important contribution to this in their dissertation, in which they expressly include the literary expression forms of liturgical songs in their relation to the literary form of the content in their analysis.[33]

The less a text is comprised of unambiguously defined terms, the greater is the importance of the expression, and the more the expression supports the content in one *irreplaceable* manner or another. The relationship can become so close that the expression as it were motivates the content. One might also say that the expression as it were takes the content into itself, and that it participates in the content in its own manner. Therefore this form of expression cannot be replaced by another at random, as can indeed happen when a text is written in the closely defined terms of language of signs.

With regard to texts, in view of the relations between the form of the expression and the form of the content one could introduce a gradual gradation reflecting the extent to which the text moves from a semiotic system in the strict sense to a semi-symbolic system. Academic texts will

---

[31] A.J. GREIMAS: 'Réflexions sur les objets ethno-sémiotiques', in A.J. GREIMAS, *Sémiotique et sciences sociales*, Paris 1976, 182. See also IDEM: 'Introduction'.

[32] R. JAKOBSON: *Essais de linguistique générale*, Paris 1963, 218.

[33] SPEELMAN: *The Generation of Meaning in Liturgical Songs*; HAUSREITHER: *Semiotik des liturgischen Gesanges*

tend to belong to a semiotic system in the strict sense. The form of expression will play only a slight role in them. The relation between the form of the expression and the form of the content is arbitrary. For instance, in a theological paper the same content may be articulated in different ways of expression without affecting the meaning. It does not make much difference whether I say that according to Scripture, for instance the *Magnificat*, God is more sensitive to the cry of the poor than of the rich, or that God discriminates against the rich in favour of the poor. The language of academic texts is therefore rather that of terms, or of the language of signs. With non-academic texts – and everyday conversational language is included in this – the form of the expression in its relation to the form of the content however quickly becomes relevant. Whatever the case, with literary texts the relation between expression and content is undoubtedly intense, and in this the relation in poetry, compared to prose, is the most intense. These verses of the *Magnificat* say the same thing as our academic paper above, but in a way which makes the form of the expression far less arbitrary, and therefore much more difficult to replace:[34]

6   [God] hath showed strength with his arm;
      he hath scattered the proud in the imagination of their hearts.
7   He hath put down the mighty from their seat,
      and hath exalted the humble and meek.
8   He hath filled the hungry with good things,
      and the rich he hath sent empty away.

Here the expression form touches upon the content form. We may for instance note that in verses 6-8 we are dealing with three sets of two lines. We might ask, does the order of the three sets have bearing on the signification in the content level, as the relation between God's preference for the poor and his scorn for the arrogant rich? We find that we cannot in any way change the order and put verse 7 in front and let it be followed by verses 6 and 8. Nor can you arbitrarily transpose verses 7 and 8, or the halves of these verses. It seems that in one way or another there is a relation between patterns of relation on the level of expression and patterns of relation on the level of content. Such a relation is technically called a semi-symbolic system.

---

[34] *Magnificat*, verses 6-8 in the King James Version, set to a Gregorian form in the service music section of *The Hymnbook*, Richmond, etc. 1955.

But there is more to be said with regard to symbolic language. I became aware of this when I was working together with exegetes on a semiotic analysis of the *Magnificat*. As a liturgist I wanted to also involve the layout in the analysis, while they wanted to forego that. For them it was much more important to begin from an academically responsible text with notes, than deal with the question of how the lines are arranged on a page. But to the degree that a text contains more symbolic language, it is also more important to involve *visual expression* in the perception of the content. The way in which the exegetes wanted to analyse the *Magnificat* ultimately reduced this text to a scientific specimen. A positivistic/scientific approach of this sort simply lies in the sphere of terms – or the language of signs. But the specimen decidedly contains more. In addition to the literary form of expression already mentioned, visual layout also plays a role in determining the content of a text. One becomes conscious of that when you arrange the same text in different ways. I would take as an example the following farewell text for a deceased individual:[35]

> Brothers and sisters, we are gathered together here around this dead body, all that is left to us of this man, to pay our last respects to him and to do justice to his life and death. Keeping our eyes fixed on the cross of Jesus Christ we say in groping faith that this is not the end, that our God is a God of the living. Rather than his body we are left with the name of this man, … which we speak now with reverence and affection and pray Lord God, remember this name which he was given by other people and by which he is known even though he is dead, the name that you have written on the palm of your hand. As a sign of our hope that God will give a new and immortal body to this man and to all of us and to bear witness to our faith in the resurrection, I bless this dead body in the name of the Father and of the Son and of the Holy Spirit. Let us now go in peace and take him, whom we have had among us during this past hour for the last time, to his grave. We let him go out of our keeping and place him in the earth, in the care of the living God, in the name of the Father and of the Son and of the Holy Spirit. May our prayers accompany him.

This text only really affects you as symbolic language when you maintain the layout given it by the author, and this layout does its work together (syncretism) with the literary form of the expression:

---

[35] H. OOSTERHUIS: *Your Word is near. Contemporary Christian Prayers*, New York 1968, 91-92.

Brothers and sisters,
we are gathered together here
around this dead body,
all that is left to us of this man,
to pay our last respects to him
and to do justice to his life and death.
Keeping our eyes fixed
on the cross of Jesus Christ
we say in groping faith
that this is not the end,
that our God is a God of the living.

Rather than his body
we are left with the name of this man, ...
which we speak now with reverence and affection
and pray
Lord God, remember this name
which he was given by other people
and by which he is known
even though he is dead,
the name that you have written
on the palm of your hand.
As a sign of our hope
that God will give a new and immortal body
to this man and to all of us
and to bear witness
to our faith in the resurrection,
I bless this dead body
in the name of the Father and of the Son
and of the Holy Spirit.

Let us now go in peace
and take him, whom we have had among us
during this past hour
for the last time, to his grave.
We let him go
out of our keeping
and place him
in the earth, in the care of the living God,
in the name of the Father and of the Son
and of the Holy Spirit.

May our prayers accompany him.

At this point one can once again introduce a gradation. In an academic text the layout is indeed important, but at the same time it is true that it is the communication of the content that comes before all else. It is already something different in didactic texts: these are presented much more with blocks, italic texts and texts in the margins: the form of expression makes it easier to distinguish between main points and details in the text, between definitions and further explanations, etc. The expression takes you by the hand, as it were, and makes more intensive following and understanding of the text possible. The visual form of the layout in liturgical texts is even more important. It is precisely through the visual expression as semi-symbolic system that the text, which actually belongs to discursive symbolism, also begins to share in presentative symbolism. Thus, alongside the linguistic form of expression the visual form of expression may play a role in signification in a scenario and script of a ritual. Texts are printed bold or thin, in italic or roman, in small or large type, in red or black, with consecutive lines or arranged line by line, with line spacing, centred, etc. This visual form of expression can strengthen and support the textual forms of meaning, and thus makes them more persuasive, but it can also change the content or disturb it. Thus in the post-Vatican II service books the red-black relation points to the relation of contents: rubrics (i.e. instructions for acting) – text. And it is possible to emphasise the import of a biblical text *vis-à-vis* the other texts by printing it in italics, while the other texts are in roman type. For signification on the content level it is therefore not irrelevant whether a prayer is printed on a narrowly folded sheet of normal office paper with all the lines set consecutively, or that a layout is provided which correlates with the content form of the prayer. An incorrect arrangement of the lines may change or obscure the contents.

To the extent that visual expression expands further, it also becomes richer as a semi-symbolic system. For example, one can include a text in a large book with an icon on the cover, which is displayed to those present beforehand, and one can begin sections of the text with illuminated letters. It is really remarkable that liturgical studies can consider the texts of old manuscripts without including facts about the iconography in their study. One exception is Palazzo's introduction to the old sources of the liturgy, which also discusses the illustrations in the sources concerned.[36] But in liturgy the semi-symbolic character encompasses even

---

[36] E. PALAZZO: *Le Moyen Age. Des origines au XIIIe siècle*, Paris 1993.

more. One can surround the text with symbolic acts such as censing it, surround it with candle light, etc. The semi-symbolic expression then becomes a multiform synthesis (syncretism) of many expressions that together enrich the content of the text. That makes this expression all the stronger and more authentic.[37]

2.7.2. Semi-symbolic relations in spoken ritual texts

To this point I have dealt with written texts in connection with symbolic language, and not with the spoken word. However, in the liturgy *in actu* the text becomes a spoken word – and the spoken word almost always and inescapably operates at the level of the semi-symbolic system. After all, it is coupled with intonation, the timbre of the voice, the volume of the sound, facial expressions, gestures and a particular place from which it is spoken. All these not strictly linguistic expressions are related to the content of what is said. In this sense, spoken symbolic language is almost always syncretic; that is to say, the convergence of many expression forms. Regarding intonation, it has been correctly observed as the difference between a Protestant and a Catholic service. The connection between the reading of a text at a reciting tone and at a vivid tone could point to a distinction between a more sacred and a more secular use of the text. In the Roman liturgy of the period before Vatican II, there was a refined distinction between speaking aloud, speaking half-aloud, speaking under breath and the inaudible whispering of the priest when reciting the words of the consecration. Thus, with regard to the sound, there was a form of expression which plausibly corresponded to a content form of, on the one hand, laical speaking addressed to the community and, on the other hand, exclusively priestly, sacred speaking addressed to God. Only a precise analysis within the context of the ritual itself could reveal whether or not my interpretation is correct. At any rate, various elements in this practice in a celebration deserve closer analysis, and they are semiotically of relevance.

2.7.3. Text and music

A special place in the scenario is occupied by those texts which are set to music. It is the strength of Greimassian metalanguage that with one and the same set of instruments it can analyse both text and music with

---

[37] GREIMAS: 'Réflexions sur les objets ethno-sémiotiques' 182.

regard to expression form and content form. In this way it is possible to study in a refined way the signification of text and music as one web in their mutual interaction in the various genres of liturgical songs. This is something new, because until now the analysis of text and music were done according to different methods, and it was therefore very difficult to attune these analyses to each other.[38]

2.7.4. Analysis of non-verbal ritual expression

To this point I have also always proceeded from symbolic language, and I have discussed semi-symbolic relations involving non-verbal liturgical expressions as such only in this context. It is also possible to discuss the latter separately, and in that way to examine symbols and symbolic acts as such. With semiotics one can observe and analyse these non-verbal liturgical expressions very precisely.

One can for instance think of the symbolism of *space*. Semiotics makes it clear that the interrelation between ritual and space or architecture is so fundamental that we may speak of the spatial or architectonic dimensions of a ritual.[39] Thus the meaning of a church building is strongly determined by the way in which the inside-outside relation has been given shape, and is it possible to consider various elements of the design, such as the nave, the altar and the ambo, as destinators and competence providing agencies for the ritual. The narrative course of the ritual is strongly determined by the architecture. It is important to call to mind in this context that the acquisition of certain powers (the competence of being able to) is linked to certain demarcated places. The altar is the place of the one who is competent to preside, the ambo is intended for the one who has the competence to read (perhaps just this one time), etc. In this context the entrance procession of the bridal couple, which was introduced as an option in the post-Vatican marriage ritual, is interesting. The couple are greeted at the door (on the threshold) of the church by the priest, who is dressed in his official vestments and is

---

[38] SPEELMAN: *The Generation of Meaning in Liturgical Songs*; HAUSREITHER: *Semiotik des liturgischen Gesanges*.

[39] G. LUKKEN: 'Die architektonische Dimensionen des Rituals', in *Liturgisches Jahrbuch* 39 (1989) 19-36 = IDEM (eds. CASPERS & VAN TONGEREN): *Per visibilia ad invisibilia* 360-374 and IDEM: 'Les dimensions architectoniques du rituel', in *Sémiotique et Bible* 16 (1991) 5-21.

accompanied by his assistants. Semiotic analysis shows that here a transition is performed from informal and private to official and public acting.[40] Then a spatial trajectory is followed from the door of the church through the nave to the altar. This is done in a solemn, organised procession, in which the assistants, the priest, the bridal couple itself, and sometimes also the witnesses, the parents and even others participate. The bridal couple is led to the altar: the central place for official acts. Thus the couple is established as the proper subject of doing in the marriage service and is made competent to act publicly and officially. Then, during the contracting of the marriage the priest, as official destinator, has his place opposite the bridal couple, which as the proper subject of doing is surrounded by the witnesses, family, friends and the community as official co-destinator of the performance. Thus fundamental values, which play a decisive role in the marriage ritual, are expressed clearly in a non-verbal way by the design of the architectonic space, by movements and positions in space, and by the connection of actors with specific places in the space.

We may also note that in practice there are rather large differences between what I simply call modern and older churches. In older churches the threshold between inside and outside is usually considerably higher than in modern churches. One goes through several doors before one is inside. At the same time it is true in most cases that the altar in older churches is considerably higher than the nave. This difference in architecture interferes in the signification of the aforementioned entrance ritual of the bridal couple. In the old architecture the expression of official competence of the bridal couple comes across as much more of a sacred act than in a modern church.

I would also like to mention the 'language' of *gestures*. Just before the exchanging of the marriage vows, the bride and groom join mutually their right hands and hold them together during the pronunciation of the marriage vows. In this performance the transition from /open/, /inclusive/ and /fusion without differentiation/ to /closed/, /exclusive/ and /unity of two without separation/ is expressed. After the exchange of the vows follows the performance with the rings. The bride and groom put a ring on each other's finger as an enduring material sign expressing the values of faithfulness and permanence. This expresses the transition from a relation between a man and a woman, which was

---

[40] LUKKEN: 'Het binnengaan in de kerk in de Romeinse huwelijksliturgie'.

/open/, /inclusive/, /initial/, and /temporary/ to one, which is /closed/, /exclusive/ (i.e. excluding all others), /final/ and /enduring/.

Just how multifaceted and wide-ranging ritual is can be illustrated from a semiotic analysis of the Catholic *funeral procession*.[41] The classic order of succession in this funeral procession is as follows. As a rule, at the very front comes the undertaker. Then the procession is opened by an acolyte or cleric who carries the cross, and is accompanied by two acolytes with candles. There are also acolytes bearing incense and holy water. After them possibly follows a choir, and in any case the presiding priest with possible assistants. It is increasingly the custom that flowers are carried just before the coffin, or at the beginning of the procession. Behind this whole group of persons the coffin with the deceased person is carried. After it the family and friends, and other parties involved, join in the procession.

When one examines the form of expression of the procession more closely, the first thing that strikes one is that the procession is divided into two parts, *the group before the coffin* and *those who follow the coffin*. The second thing is that while the procession moves forward by itself, and is characterised by an upright posture, the motionless deceased is carried in a horizontal position, and that the coffin with the deceased forms the central point of the procession. One can correlate these forms of expression with pairs of antitheses involving content. The opposition in form of expression /before/ and /after/ the coffin corresponds to the content oppositions of /functional/ and /serious/ (the undertaker, clergy, their assistants, etc.) versus /relational/ and /grieving/. The forms of expression /vertical/ and /in motion/ versus /horizontal/ and /motionless/ can be paralleled with the opposition in content /living/ versus /dead/. Those carrying the flowers in front of the coffin can be seen as partly /relational/ and partly as /functional/. In that sense they form a sort of transition to those who follow the coffin.

It is further conspicuous that those who precede the coffin are uniformed, that is, they wear liturgical clothing. Further, the colour of their clothing is official: black, dark, grey or (since the Second Vatican council) white. Those who walk behind the coffin are more or less formally

---

[41] See more extensively G. LUKKEN: 'Het ritueel van de christelijke begrafenis. Een semiotisch-theologisch onderzoek', in *Jaarboek voor liturgie-onderzoek* 12 (1996) 118-135.

dressed. In this, the general rule applies that those who are closest to the deceased also wear the most explicitly formal clothing, either mourning dress or more or less dignified clothing. Farther back in the procession one finds more and more everyday clothing, particularly when it is a long procession. The colour of the clothing behind the coffin runs from black and dark to everyday, colourful clothing. With regard to the pall-bearers, one finds either the uniform clothing of the undertaker's staff, or – if family and/or friends are bearing the coffin – formal clothing. In comparison with the group who follow, the group preceding the coffin are also distinguished by the 'attributes' they carry with them: the liturgical objects of the cross, light, incense and holy water, and flowers. These appear to be a adumbration of the coming programme at the grave. The objects involved lend a specifically Christian significance to the beginning of the procession, a significance that will only reveal itself fully at the actual burial. Within the movement of the funeral procession one could point to this whole as an expression of an intended Christian programme of burial. It involves an autonomous programme which however is subordinate to the main programme of the committal itself, and that as such in Greimassian semiotics would be termed an auxiliary programme. With regard to the group in front of the coffin, this programme is functional, and with regard to those who follow the coffin, it is indicative of a programme of wanting to participate in it. As such, the attributes involved give a characteristically Christian identity to the whole funeral procession. One realises the importance of the attributes mentioned for giving meaning to the funeral procession. If they were absent, and the burial procession was only preceded by the undertaker, the procession would be deprived of an important part of its Christian signification.

The funeral procession is accompanied by the sound of bells: a typical auditory form of expression that contrasts with the din of everyday life. The expression of this sound is strikingly characterised by the Dutch poet Achterberg:[42]

> They are buried here with a haste
> as if death were snapping at their heels.
> And what most surprises the onlooker
> is that the procession has almost no tail;

---

[42] G. ACHTERBERG: *Ode aan Den Haag*, 's-Gravenhage 1953; See IDEM: *Verzamelde gedichten*, Amsterdam 1985, 827.

of course, a distant relative
with whom one races to the grave
to get back quickly from the ride,
for each remains themselves the closest relative.

Where I come from, they toll the bell for hours.
Every child knows what is going to happen.
People fall in behind the bier in deepest silence.

And long thereafter a chill hangs over the village,
which pierces one to the bone,
like the recovery from a severe shock.

The classic funeral procession was a part of a pregnant ritual in which all the senses were involved, including the insistent sound of the church bell that penetrated the ears. It is the expression of death as something that touches the whole community, and reaches further than the participants in the funeral procession alone. It situates the funeral procession spatially too, as an event within the larger space of life, which pauses for a moment, and it continues to dominate the village or city until the deceased is buried. Only after the ecclesiastical committal, when through ritual acts of all sorts the transition is completed for both the deceased and those remaining behind, does life again return to normal.

In diagram

Signifiant / Expression	after	coffin with deceased	before
	formal clothing		uniformed or liturgical clothing
	colour: from black and dark to colourful		colour: black, dark, grey, white
	vertical	horizontal	vertical
	moving of itself	motionless	moving of itself
	funeral bell	funeral bell	funeral bell
			liturgical attributes
Signifié / Content	relational		functional
	grieving		serious
	living	dead	living
	participating in proposed programme of Christian burial		functional with regard to proposed programme of Christian burial
	death	death	death

It is also interesting to further consider the procession *after the coffin*.[43]
First, in the form of expression one can point to the distinction between
those who walk close behind the coffin and those who follow at a
greater distance. This opposition of /close by/ versus /distant from/ can
in the level of content be correlated with the social relation these persons had with the deceased. Behind the coffin come first the members
of the immediate family and then more distant family, friends, acquaintances, and finally representatives of the wider circles of business relations, the place or town. This reflects the opposition in content between
a close and a more distant social link with the deceased. This is also
expressed in the manner of walking: those who come close behind the
coffin are clustered closer together than those who are further removed
from it. This is true both when one examines the procession in terms of
its length and when one considers it in transverse section. There is a spatial division of /closely following/ and /close together/ versus /with space
between/. I will return yet to discuss the interaction in the cross section.

Next, there is a minimum of gesture on the part of those who walk
close behind the coffin: they restrict themselves almost entirely to walking straight ahead, without head movements; to the degree that people
are farther from the coffin, one sees more gesture and more movement.
Moreover, there is a contrast between the silence that prevails close
behind the coffin, and the buzz of conversation near the end of the procession. There is also a difference in mood: while close behind the coffin there are often tears, at the end of the procession there are sometimes
even smiles. Everyone who has walked in a funeral procession knows
that there is often conversation at the end of the cortege – certainly if it
is long. Finally, the clothing close behind the coffin is often more
adapted to the funeral (mourning clothing or at least formal clothing)
than that in the ranks at the end. This all touches upon relational patterns involving the form of the expression (the *signifiant*).

The question is then, what corresponds to this at the level of the
form of the content (the *signifié*). It appears that we here encounter the
opposition in content of /death/ versus /life/. The walking close
together, the minimum of gesture, the silence, the tears, the mourning
or formal clothing are all forms of expression that are connected with
the thought of death. Taken in itself, any one of these elements of
expression would suffice: think, for instance, of the ritual of one

---

[43] COURTÉS: *Analyse sémiotique du discours* 30-33.

minute's silence for the dead. But the profusion of various forms of expression undoubtedly reinforce experience and perception, and is characteristic of ritual. Moreover, one can not speak of /death/ without referring to /life/. That makes the conduct at the end of the procession more understandable: there simply is a close relation between the level of the expression and that of content. As opposed to the nearness of family and friends with respect to the deceased who is being borne away, the end of the procession is further removed from the deceased, which is also reflected in the forms of expression that refer to /life/.

Courtés makes another interesting observation in this connection.[44] With regard to funeral processions, he points to the distinction between personal interactions over its length and those in its transverse section. Its length connects all with the deceased, whether they are walking close behind the coffin or at a greater distance. Although the procession does tend to stretch out more toward its end, its basic characteristic remains that people join into a procession that forms up behind the deceased.

The interaction that one finds in the transverse section of the procession is different. Such transverse interaction is not often found toward the head of the procession, but more toward the end. Among those toward the end of the procession there are conversations, but in each case it is striking that these take place with persons to the right or left, and not with those walking before or behind. In this way the involvement with the deceased is maintained. Whatever the case, that there is also an involvement with the living in the procession can perhaps for some be a source of annoyance, but it is simply a fact that in all circumstances /death/ and /life/ continue to be linked with one another. Although the deceased is found at the centre of the procession, it is an undeniable fact that the procession consists of the living.

These forms of the expression can be correlated not only with /death/ and /life/, but also with an opposition that involves the emotional dimension. The oppositions in the form of expression are connected with the categories /sorrow/ versus /cheerfulness/ and /joy/.

Furthermore, all sorts of nuances are possible between the /sorrow/ close behind the coffin and the /cheerfulness/ at the end of the procession: a gradual transition can be identified. This does not so much

---

[44] COURTÉS: *Analyse sémiotique du discours* 33.

involve the discontinuity that is expressed in the oppositions we have noted, as the continuous line that one can also observe. This continuous line concerns the tensities of a discourse, namely gradual transitions. In the discourse 'funeral procession' one can, with regard to the *signifiant*, point to the gradual transition from the front to the back of the procession from tears, through serious and peaceful faces, to the smile, and this would appear to correlate with the transition from /sorrow/ through /seriousness/ and /serenity/ to /joy/ as *signifié*.

In diagram

Signifiant / Expression	behind	in front
	with spaces	close together
	gestures	minimum of gestures
	sound	silence
	smiles. laughter	tears
	coloured or informal clothing	black or formal clothing
	priority for the transverse axis	priority for the longitudinal axis
Signifié / Content	diffuse social link	close social link
	life	death
	joy	sorrow

From the foregoing it becomes clear that in ritual, both in spoken symbolic language and in the symbol and symbolic act, one can very quickly speak of a widely inclusive object in which various layers can be distinguished and analysed. One or more of the senses – the ears, eyes, taste and smell – are involved in the perception of this object. This broadly sensory expression is inseparably and intrinsically linked with the content. We saw that according to Lorenzer the sensory forms of interaction are primary and fundamental. This is confirmed by Greimassian semiotics, which in its recent developments likewise places emphasis on this sensory basis that precedes all cognitive perception.[45] However this may be, anyone who does not take sensory expression seriously devalues that to which the symbolic world ultimately refers.

It is important to have an eye for the many 'languages' which come together in various ways – each time differently – in ritual. This is the

[45] J. FONTANILLE: *Sémiotique du visible. Des mondes de lumière*, Paris 1995; FONTANILLE: *Sémiotique du discours*; J. FONTANILLE & C. ZILBERBERG: *Tension et signification*, Sprimont 1998; P. PERRON & J. FABBRI: 'Foreword', in GREIMAS & FONTANILLE: *The semiotics of passions* I-XVI.

reason rituals appeal to the integral human being and can be salutary in a holistic way. Greimassian semiotics offers the possibility for a comprehensive and careful analysis of ritual, and affords a precise insight into its complexity. In particular, it makes one sensitive to the fact that what is involved here is more than texts and words.[46] The non-verbal contributes as much or more to the signification of ritual. Because of this awareness, semiotic analysis of ritual can also perform a critical-normative function. To give a concrete example: the cross that precedes the funeral procession that accompanies the deceased to the grave appears to be an extremely important element when it comes to a Christian burial. Precisely because words at the cemetery are so easily blown away, this non-verbal element has an irreplaceable significance. And anyone with an insight into the funeral procession as such will realise that the composition and the succession cannot be altered without cost.

[46] It is remarked in a recent article that the limitation of the Greimassian semiotic approach is that the 'acting' of the actor remains outside of the field of vision (see A. SCHEER, 'Ut duo sint... A theory of acts approach to marriage liturgy', in POST, ROUWHORST, VAN TONGEREN & SCHEER (eds.): *Christian Feast and Festival* 601). From the above it will be clear that, on the contrary, this 'acting' is brought out in many, and very nuanced manners.

CHAPTER 4

SPECIAL THEMES

It is also possible to further clarify the characteristics of rituals on the basis of a number of special themes. We will successively deal with the place of presentative symbolism, ritual and space, ritual and time, ritual and music, the classification of ritual, the theme of feast and the strengths and weaknesses of ritual.

1. THE PLACE OF PRESENTATIVE SYMBOLISM

It is actually remarkable that in the past those who have studied Christian ritual have been preoccupied especially with the books in which the texts and instructions for the rituals are written down. In liturgical studies, as in dramaturgy, study centred on the examination of *written* texts. In their training liturgists learned to handle the very complicated sources for liturgy, past and present, as dramaturgists did with the published plays of Shakespeare, Pirandello, Pinter and so forth. As noted in the preceding chapter, with regard to the printed or written text there was a distinction made between scenario and script. By scenario we indicate the liturgical book as it is published. The script is the same textual corpus, but amplified with details regarding the celebration of the liturgy. Both forms of text were characterised by discursive symbolism. What was important was the written word. Within this, it is clear that the script was a richer whole than the scenario. But even when the script is the focus of attention, there is actually a severe limitation, because ritual in no way concerns the books involved as such. Books of ritual have no purpose in themselves. They are only the destinators of the actual performance of the ritual. They are intended as 'pace setters' for the performance of ritual. Ritual is, before all else, a praxis.[1] The result of our 'classic' way of looking at things is that people easily see the ritual *in*

---

[1] This is constantly emphasised by C. Bell in both her books, from 1992 and 1997; see also KRIEGER & BELLIGER: 'Einführung' 9-17.

actu as a mere 'decoration' of the written scenario and script. For a long time this has also been the point of view in theatrical studies. The performance (the *mise en scène*) was seen as the translation of the published text. In a way, the actual performance was of secondary importance to the play. The interpretation of the printed text was put first, and the performance was considered merely as the support of a linguistic discourse by a non-linguistic discourse.[2] But today's semiotics of the theatre have a different view. The performance is a completely separate and new discourse, in which many 'languages' come together.[3] The same is true for rituals. In these it is not a matter of written language, but of spoken language, which moreover is determined by various other languages: by the language of a space, architecture, the spatial relations between the different objects and actors, the movements in the space, the gestures, the music, the scents, the climatological circumstances, the materials which are used, which are oriented to the tactile sense, etc. I myself did not realise how unaccustomed we were to this different way of seeing things until one of my students, Jean Pierre Niati, from the Democratic Republic of Congo (Zaire), wanted to do a thesis on the revised Congolese (Zairean) liturgy.[4] When I suggested that he start from the new service book of the Zairean rite, he objected. He explained to me that the service book is no more than a tool and a starting point, and that the real subject was the celebration itself of the Zairean rite. Therefore we decided to take a videotape of an actual performed liturgy as the primary source for the research project. This is after all a celebration in a culture that is first and foremost an oral culture. To this very day in Congolese culture the emphasis still lies on oral transmission and oral communication. When something of the ritual is put into writing, the manuscript will be seen as a deposit of the oral performance in the culture, much more so than the other way around. In oral cultures it is rather the liturgy *in actu*, handed down by tradition, which is the destinator and the agency providing competence, more so than the written scenario. In contemporary theatre we may note attempts to return to this tradition. An example of this in my country is the *werktheater*, which is given shape in the actual performances. And

---

[2] P. PAVIS: *Problèmes de sémiologie théâtrale*, Montréal 1976.

[3] Precisely as performance, ritual therefore has a number of characteristics that remind one of theatre. In this connection see BELL: *Ritual. Perspectives* 74-75.

[4] J.P. NIATI: *La messe zaïroise: efforts d'une église africaine en vue d'une liturgie inculturée* (M.A. Thesis Theologische Faculteit Tilburg), Tilburg 1994.

we may also think of the farmers' theatre as it took shape when Ernesto Cardenal was minister for culture in Nicaragua.[5] In a certain sense the same occurs in the wider performing arts, for instance when in television programmes people prefer live broadcasts.

In our culture, which is so dominated by typography, printers and copying machines, seeing things this way is anything but obvious. On the contrary. We are inclined to read old manuscripts with the eye. But they are much more sensory. Behind the manuscripts lies a living, an aural, possibly a dictated word.[6] There is thus also something auditory about them. In Arab culture that is obvious. They read the written word out loud, so that the movement, the rhythm and the breathing of the written word can be reconstructed. Only then can one understand a text. Whatever the case, the *living* word is written in a different way, and has its own sense of time. You look up in surprise when you read that it took three years to dictate the *Summa Theologiae* of Thomas Aquinas. There was a day when books were very rare, and the written book extremely valuable. The greatest owners of books in the Middle Ages were the monastic libraries.[7] But that fact must not call up mental images of large halls with full bookcases along the walls. One of the richest libraries of the early middle ages was to be found in the abbey of Reichenau. In 822 it owned the then respectable number of 415 codices. In the next twenty years another 48 titles were added to this. A century later, it is reported that between 960 and 1016 (in other words, a bit over a half century) thirty new books had been written. In the 13th century, the largest university library, that of the Sorbonne in Paris, still had not reached 1000 volumes, and in the 14th century this had risen to 1722 volumes.[8] The cause of this rarity of the book is that they had to

[5] J. VAN LIESHOUT & M. MERCX: *Spelenderwijs revolutie maken. Volkstheater in Nicaragua*, Nijmegen 1986.

[6] M. ZUMTHOR: 'Le texte médiéval entre oralité et écriture', in H. PARRET & H.-G. RUPRECHT (eds.): *Exigences et perspectives de la sémiotique. Recueil d'hommages pour Algirdas Julien Greimas*, Amsterdam 1985, 826-843.

[7] J. VAN LAARHOVEN: 'Het boek van de Middeleeuwen', in *Kohelet. Faculteitsblad Theologische Faculteit Tilburg* 5 (1988) 1, 6-7.

[8] F. VAN OOSTROM: *De waarde van het boek*, Leiden 1994; IDEM: *Handgeschreven wereld: Nederlandse literatuur en cultuur in de Middeleeuwen*, Amsterdam 1995; see also IDEM: 'Niets nieuws sinds Jacob van Maerlant. De waarde van het boek', in *NRC Handelsblad* February 12, 1994, Boeken, 3 and his lecture on the occasion of the 419th dies natalis of the Rijksuniversiteit Leiden, on February 7, 1994: *NRC Handelsblad*, February 9, 1994, 9.

be written by hand, and that this complicated and protracted production process could take years of drudgery. When one compares with that the fact that, with a total population of 15 million, the total number of books in Dutch households in 1994 came to more than 1.5 billion, that there are another 90,000,000 books in Dutch libraries, and another 86,000 titles are delivered to bookstores every year,[9] one can imagine how the view of oral culture, which is so essential for ritual, has been considerably altered. The turning point came after the discovery of printing with moveable type by Johannes Gutenberg in 1450. While in the 15th century there were still only 50,000 manuscripts produced, by the end of this same century there were an estimated 10,000,000 books in existence.[10]

I have previously noted that Judaism, Christianity and Islam are the religions of the book. That means that the written word plays a larger role for them than it does in religions without a written Scripture. In these books one finds the 'Ur-myths' that share in defining their ritual in a fundamental way. These books are therefore regularly used in the rituals of these religions. But in ritual they do not function as books that one must read and study in a library; it is a matter of sacred texts being made to speak by actually reading them aloud in the midst of those who are participating in the ritual.[11] This ritual context for the book has been honoured and preserved especially in the Eastern liturgies. At the same time, the book is there still always seen as a icon of the divine world, and surrounded by a rich ritual of its own.[12] But in our 'book culture' these roots have slowly atrophied. The Bible no longer finds its true 'home' in the liturgy, and has gradually become a manual for theology and preaching. Another consequence of the increasingly strong book culture was that rituals themselves were reduced to books, and that the interest focused primarily on the texts of the rituals. With printed liturgical books one could also carry out liturgical renewal, in which moreover the stress was laid on (the mastery) of textual innovations. Liturgical studies also became first and

[9] VAN OOSTROM in his lecture on February 7, 1994 (see previous note).

[10] A. KAVANAGH: 'Textuality and Deritualisation: the Case of Western Liturgical Use', in *Studia Liturgica* 23 (1993) 72.

[11] G. LUKKEN: "Zo spreekt de Heer'. De Schrift als levend boek', in *Schrift* 30 (1998) 178, 119-122.

[12] KAVANAGH: 'Textuality and Deritualisation' 73.

foremost a 'textual' discipline, which further limited itself to the officially published printed texts. But ritual is not about the reading, but the reading of the holy book aloud in he community, as a living proclamation. And it is even less a matter of reading printed liturgical texts, but the living word, in its full liturgical context. The expression 'to read mass' was actually in conflict with the essence of the eucharistic ritual.

I have previously noted that the word itself, despite its discursive character, precisely as symbolic language already has a certain relationship with presentative symbolism.[13] This is all the more the case when one is dealing with the spoken word. The spoken word is connected with the person who speaks. It takes shape in his or her unique physicality, his or her personal history. You hear a voice, and recognise the person immediately, without having seen them. Everyone speaks with an intonation and timbre peculiar to themselves. Sometimes, on the basis of the 'tone' that is struck, you can recognise a particular acquired subculture, for instance that of the official spokesperson. Thus, as we have already remarked, it is not without reason that people speak of the characteristic difference in tone between the Reformed and Roman Catholic worship service. Further, speaking is most closely linked with the breath of life. It is permeated by the process of breathing, and thus with the feeling of that breathing: it can be quiet, harried, short-winded, clipped, inspired, intent, engaged. Speaking is also linked with the physical movements of the mouth. It is 'visible'. That is the foundation for lip-reading among the deaf. We articulate in different ways. The sounds are formed physically. They are also coupled with facial expressions. One can speak of an open or closed expression. Then there are still the other physical movements. What is the posture of the speaker? Upright or bowed down, relaxed and free or not? Is the speaker seated, and if so, how? What gestures and bodily movements are made? Articulation, facial expression, gestures can all very clearly be involved with what is being said. The logic of the remark 'Let me put on my glasses because I want to hear you' may not be obvious, but it is very true.

Finally, there is the clothing. That also resonates with the spoken word. It can make the word official, or sacred. It can give the word the quality of being spoken from afar, from on high, from a strange world,

---

[13] See Part 1, Chapter 1, 2.5.

or from nearby. Time also plays a role: is it language from the past, a
language we no longer speak, the language of a previous generation, of
older or younger people, contemporary language, current slang? And
where is it spoken? From a high chancel, or in the middle of the community? In what space? In a church? What sort of church? A high
Gothic church, or an intimate contemporary meditation centre? What
sort of lighting is there?[14] Is there the scent of incense or unguent? What
is the temperature in the space? That can also contribute to how the
word functions. Steenma recounts how in the past Protestant churches
in The Netherlands were warmed by coals and small fires in foot warm-
ers, so that the warmth rose pleasantly under skirts and up pantlegs.[15]
That was certainly beneficial to the preaching.

The observations of the anthropologist M. Jousse in connection with
the spoken word are striking:

> When you read me in the future, you will no longer see me live before
> you. The book will not be able to give you the whole of my poor, patient
> existence, that strove so for the search for truth… for all that is a part of
> living human expression. You will no longer have at your disposal my
> whole vital and trembling being – for man thinks with his whole body. In
> the written word a different mechanism is at work. From that moment on
> there is no longer direct contact, from person to person. The idea is
> launched, the creation is finished, but each interprets the thought for
> themselves. Thus one could say that every disciple is more or less a traitor.
> But it is perhaps at that moment that we begin to live on, when our idea
> is passed on to each of these individuals, who recreate it in their own
> image and likeness… Each makes it his own truth… Interpretation is the
> way the creator lives on.[16]

Thus it would appear that the spoken word in ritual is most closely linked
with, and rooted in other non-verbal 'languages' which by definition are

[14] On the importance of light in ritual, see G. LUKKEN: "Ik heb geen wortels dan in
het licht' (Hans Andreus). Een semiotische beschouwing over het licht in de liturgie', in
A. MULDER & T. SCHEER (eds.): *Natuurlijke liturgie* (Liturgie in perspectief 6),
Baarn/Heeswijk-Dinther 1996, 68-90.

[15] R. STEENSMA: *Opdat de ruimten meevieren*, Baarn 1982, 39.

[16] M. JOUSSE: *L'anthropologie du geste*, Vol. 1, Paris 1974, 30. For the very specific
approach of this anthropologist, see also IDEM: *L'anthropologie du geste*, Vol. 2, *La manducation de la parole*, Paris 1975 and *L'anthropologie du geste*, Vol. 3, *Le parlant, la parole
et le souffle*, Paris 1978.

presentative. This presentative character gives ritual a strongly sensory and physical basis. That foundation is essential. Where it is absent, ritual misses its mark, and becomes a purely rational and intellectual happening. In ritual all the senses are important, bar none.

Through its limited code, presentative symbolism has a broad sphere of action.[17] Augustine therefore correctly observes that the sacraments are an easy yoke and light burden, easy to support, and yet of consummate significance.[18] This does not mean that what is shared is also simple. Precisely in its simplicity, presentative symbolism can have many senses and be rich in meaning. Moreover, it penetrates man deeply: it touches man in life and limb. D. Van Brederode's remark is apposite: 'I can sometimes still feel the cross of ashes on my forehead. My body still understands all too well the ominous whisper "Remember, o man, that thou art dust, and to dust thou shalt return"'.[19]

2. RITUAL AND SPACE

We normally speak of ritual without taking space into account. In liturgical manuals one can for instance sometimes find something about the funeral procession and its order, but nothing about its spatial effects. These manuals also do discuss church buildings, but in a separate chapter, without relation to the ritual itself. It is therefore not surprising that one of my students, who wished to write his doctoral dissertation on cremation rituals, asked himself whether, and if so where information about the architecture of crematoria should be included. I answered that he should begin with it, because the space is such an essential and fundamental part of the ritual itself.[20]

---

[17] See for the concept *limited code* Part 1, Chapter 2, 3.2.

[18] AUGUSTINE: *Epistola* 54, 1, 1.

[19] D. VAN BREDERODE: *Ave verum corpus*, Amsterdam 1994, 79.

[20] For a more extensive discussion of this matter and further literature, see LUKKEN: 'Die architektonische Dimensionen des Rituals'; IDEM: 'Ritueel en ruimte', in *Werkmap (voor) Liturgie* 25 (1991) 132-140; G. LUKKEN & M. SEARLE: *Semiotics and Church Architecture. Applying the Semiotics of A.J. Greimas and the Paris School to the Analysis of Church Buildings* (Liturgia condenda 1), Kampen 1993; IDEM: 'Liturgische ruimte en haar vormgeving: ter inleiding', in *Werkmap (voor) Liturgie* 29 (1995) 2-5; IDEM: 'Het ritueel van de christelijke begrafenis; IDEM: 'Hoe krijgt de ruimte betekenis in het

We are so much defined by space that we can not think or speak without constantly using spatial references.[21] For instance, we always think in terms of a framework of verticality, and order our experiences according to a scheme of above to below. We stand tall, speak about the highest good, say that prices are rising, and so forth. We seldom realise how much our communication with one another is defined by the space in which we move. When I go to the city, my route is determined by the roads that others have built. Along those roads stand countless signs. The space is carefully ordered according to different movement patterns. Automobiles, bicycles and pedestrians are kept apart and directed by traffic lights, bicycle lanes and auto roads, zebra crossings, speed bumps, traffic islands – and numerous traffic signs. Space plays a special role in architecture. The door determines where I enter, and if the doorway is very wide many can come in at the same time. Then you are undoubtedly dealing with a public building. Further, there are corridors which determine where I can go, and rooms and halls that are situated in a particular manner. Thus the building defines my actions in an intrusive manner. You cannot escape from communication patterns defined by space.

Space also plays a large role in ritual. The space in which a ritual takes place is bounded. This is certainly more obvious for rituals which take place indoors, for instance in a church building. But it is also true for rituals which are performed outdoors. On a pilgrimage people travel by a certain route, and memorial and funerary rituals take place at a certain spot. The space is also always subdivided in a particular way, and the divisions determine in part the roles that are played. This articulation of the space can be indicated by clear boundaries, but it can also be mental or more or less fluid. For example, the space can be articulated by the way in which the participants arrange themselves at the beginning of a ritual. In my view, *ritual* human actions are even more pervasively and fundamentally defined by space itself than are general human actions. One can think of the spatial articulation of a church building, which

ritueel?', in J. MAAS & A. SMEETS (eds.): *Werktekeningen. Semiotische constructies in blauwdruk*, Tilburg 1999, 39-52; IDEM: 'Mystagogie van de ruimte', in H. LOMBAERTS, J. MAAS & J. WISSINK (ed.): *Beeld en Gelijkenis. Inwijding, kunst en religie*, Meinema, Zoetermeer 2001, 28-41.

[21] H. HERMANS (ed.): *De echo van het ego. Over het meerstemmige zelf* (Annalen van het Thijmgenootschap 83, 2), Baarn 1995, 11 ff.

rigorously determines the course of the ritual: the place where people enter, the positioning of the actors, the movements from one place to another, the competencies that are exercised, etc. Thus, if spatial – and in particular architectural – dimensions are an integrating and fundamental component of human communication strategies, this would be true to an even greater degree for the communication pattern of ritual. The space itself, with its articulation, and its furnishings are a part of the ritual programme. They influence the actors in the ritual, and in part define their competencies with regard to one another. The spatial dimension is thus the ultimate integrating component of the ritual. One might say that the ritual is not only defined by the textual script, but likewise by the space itself, which just as much functions in its part as a sort of script for the ritual.

One particular element still deserves attention in connection with space: *movement* in space. In ritual the movements are generally more stylised than in everyday life. They are performed with special attention and a higher degree of concentration. In ritual one does not walk as if wandering around, but one marches. There are also patterns of movement that are performed in a particular way, according to the ritual: one can think of the way in which the gesture of blessing is made, the exchange of rings by a bridal couple, the procession to a cemetery, or the movements in St. Vitus's Procession at Echternach. Ritual acts are linked with movement in all cultures.[22] In the Old Testament one has the waving movements of the hands of the priests during the sacrifices, stylised movements that one still finds preserved in Eastern liturgies. Another familiar movement is the circumambulation of, or dancing around a point that is regarded as holy. One finds this today in striking form in the Congolese (Zairean) Eucharist rite. In the later case, as also in marching and in the St. Vitus's Procession, one is dealing with something that can be characterised as *dance*. From ancient times dance has been connected with ritual. One danced at the birth of a child, at marriage, at all of the important transitions in life. Through the media we know just how much South American and African ritual conduct has

---

[22] M. VAN AMSTERDAM: *Hoe welkom zijn op de bergen de voeten van de vreugdebode (Jesaja 52, 7)... Dans binnen de liturgie...?* (Liturgie in perspectief 4), Baarn 1995, 61 (with reference to K. GOLDAMMER: *Die Formenwelt des Religiösen. Grundriss der systematischen Religionswissenschaft*, Stuttgart 1960, 354).

dance as an integrating component. Who does not remember the demonstrations against apartheid in South Africa, which were full of dance movements, and at a particular moment followed by images of Bishop Tutu, dancing in his room at the news of Mandela's release? 'Dance may be called the oldest ritual language of man'.[23] Very aptly Grimes remarks, 'What divides us into white and black, native and non-native, perhaps even man and woman, is not only economy, country and politics, but also dance. There is a deep chasm between those who dance for the sake of relaxation or health, and those who do this as a manner of embracing the world.'[24]

3. RITUAL AND TIME

In addition to space, time is also a fundamental category in ritual.[25] In connection with the repetitive character of ritual I have previously noted the mediating dimension of ritual with respect to the past. Here, however, we are dealing with the category of time as an integrating component of ritual. Ritual in fact takes place not only in a particular, limited space, but also in a special time.

Time is one of the most fundamental elements in human life. Everyone experiences the passing of hours, days, months and years. Days have their own course, a beginning and an end, even as life does. We experience time in the beat of our pulse, in our breathing in and out, in the rhythm of rising and going to bed. Time gives us a realisation of brokenness and discontinuity, of finiteness and mortality. What was, yesterday, is now no more. Time allows things to slip away from us, and

[23] VAN AMSTERDAM: *Hoe welkom zijn op de bergen* 62. About dance and ritual, see also M. VAN AMSTERDAM: 'Over lichamelijkheid en dans', in BARNARD & POST (eds.): *Ritueel bestek* 104-109; R. BEURMANJER: 'Ritueel en dans: de eerste stap', in BARNARD & POST (eds.): *Ritueel bestek* 110-114.
[24] GRIMES: *Marrying and Burying* 247.
[25] For further literature see, among others, H.-J. AUF DER MAUR: *Feiern im Rythmus der Zeit, I: Herrenfeste in Woche und Jahr* (Gottesdienst der Kirche. Handbuch der Liturgiewissenschaft 5), Regensburg 1983, 16-25; K.-H. BIERITZ: 'Das Kirchenjahr', in H.-C. SCHMIDT-LAUBER & K.-H. BIERITZ (eds.): *Handbuch der Liturgik. Liturgiewissenschaft in Theologie und Praxis der Kirche*, Leipzig/Göttingen 1995, 453-489; HEIMBROCK: *Gottesdienst: Spielraum des Lebens* 73-80; RAPPAPORT: *Ritual and Religion in the Making of Humanity* 169-235; L. VAN TONGEREN: 'Beleving en rituele vormgeving van tijd', in BARNARD & POST (eds.): *Ritueel bestek* 63-68.

makes us lose our grip on our life and the world. It is precisely in ritual that man seeks coherence and continuity. We try to link past, present and future. Ritual is about a form of action in time in which past, present and future come together and are involved with one another in one or another way. The past is evoked, to become actual in and for the present, and this in tension with the future. In this way people try to hold fast to the sense of what was once experienced as meaningful. Ritual is an attempt to bring back the past, as it were, to experience it again and give it meaning. We want to link both joyful and sorrowful events with the present and the future. What was salubrious is recaptured as a source of vitalisation for the present and the times to come. Vital events are commemorated and made present in life today. People mark their birthday once a year; they celebrate the beginning of their marriage, the founding of their city or country, the new year, the beginning of a new millennium, and so forth. But rituals also seek to give meaning to tragic events from the past. Ritual is directed at processing these, to fill in what is missing, as it were. Rituals try to complete what alas still remains unfulfilled. We continue to bring to mind that in life which has been baleful. On Aids Memorial Day we commemorate the millions who have died of this fatal illness. We commemorate the countless victims of the concentration camps. The war cemeteries lie full of young men who were never able to complete their life. You read it on the crosses: age 18, 19, 20... The annual commemorations focus on still giving their senseless deaths meaning. They died for our freedom, they live on in our memory. During the memorial ritual a child stands before every grave and lays flowers upon it, out of thankfulness for what they did for us. With regard to the commemoration of the disastrous battle for Arnhem in 1944, in which many British and Polish soldiers died, J. van der Heyden writes,

> From the very first children... were involved in the performance... of the memorial. During the memorial service in Oosterbeek they lay flowers on every grave. In Arnhem they take part in the silent procession and in Driel the children sang Polish songs during the memorial. There is a double innocence involved here. On the one hand the schoolchildren symbolise innocence, the new, the unsullied: hope for the future. On the other hand, many of the soldiers died at an age not much different from theirs. The children therefore honour the victims who risked their own future and innocence for the future in freedom for them, the children. They must be made aware of the nature of the sacrifice that was made here, for what

purpose the battle was fought... that it was 'not for nothing'... a continuing point for reflection. It is about giving meaning to the suffering, and in that to give meaning to the past for the present.[26]

At other memorials for the Second World War we read off the names of the dead one by one, and each time answer with 'present'. In the same way the Chileans, under the oppressive military regime of General Pinochet, in their stadiums would spontaneously call out 'Presente!' on hearing the name of their murdered president. The dead are not dead. They live on at least in and with their people. And on the graves of unidentified soldiers we place the text 'Known to God'. We continue to bring to mind that in life which has been baleful. In rituals we seek to call the past into the present, and in doing so to give it meaning, so that the way to the future remains passable.[27]

Thus, in ritual we deal with delineated time. That time can have different parts that extend over longer periods. But it is always true that this involves a time which is different than ordinary time. In and through ritual we step outside of everyday time. We then no longer experience time in an instrumental way: the purpose of ritual is not to produce as much effect as possible with as few means as possible. Authentic ritual is not oriented to the rational 'time is money' principle. On the contrary, in and through ritual we create our own fictive space, in which we as it were have all the time in the world, and in which time is experienced first and foremost as a gift.[28] In ritual we 'celebrate' time, as it were. We elevate time above itself. Ritual has a special, alternative time, within which other rules apply than those in everyday life, and the course of things is interrupted. Thus all peoples have their calendar of rituals, of special observances and feasts.

The experience of ritual time has both a cyclic and linear dimension. The succession of day and night, of the weeks, months and seasons repeats itself again and again. By the same token there is a linear dimension, the movement from past through the present to the future. The experience of ritual time is not the same in all cultures. Archaic cultures have an experience of time that is predominately cyclic. Although we also experience a

[26] J.O. VAN DER HEIJDEN: 'Symboliek en ritueel van een herdenking', in *Werkmap (voor) Liturgie* (Vieringen (Rituelen) buiten 1) 30 (1996) 21.

[27] See also N. SCHUMAN: 'Gedenken', in BARNARD & POST (eds.): *Ritueel bestek* 181-193.

[28] HEIMBROCK: *Gottesdienst: Spielraum des Lebens* 73-80.

cyclic pattern, a linear experience of time dominates our culture. This last began with the Chaldeans in the 8th century before Christ, very quickly spread further, and is characteristic for the Jewish, Islamic and Christian religions. I will return to these cultural differences in Part 3.[29]

4. RITUAL AND MUSIC

Intonation usually plays a very specific role in ritual speaking. Ritual speech has many variants, but it is clear that the 'tone' of this speech has its peculiar formalities. The tone of everyday conversation is simply different from that in the performance of a ritual. There are children's rhymes in which one can really find the basic elements of what we could call ritual music. For instance as a counting out rhyme children chant 'Enie menie miney moe, / catch a pigeon by the toe /, if he hollers let him go – / enie menie miney moe'. The world of children is full of this sort of ritual music. But this ritual music is likewise found in the adult world. The cries of the street vendors, shouting 'rags!' and 'hares and rabbits' skins!' have disappeared, but anyone who visits a farmers' market will note how stall-holders still often hawk their wares in chant. And then there are the cheers and singing in football stadiums during matches. Contemporary rapping is likewise a very elementary ritual music. In days gone by manual labour was also often accompanied by ritual music. Van der Leeuw points out that driving piles, pumping, rowing, sowing, all work which demands a regular rhythm, each had their songs. *Wenn beim Brauen nicht gesungen wird, geratet das Bier nicht* (If one doesn't sing while brewing, the beer doesn't turn out well), according to an old German proverb.[30] A modern variant might be the Muzak piped into offices, programmed to be up-tempo at times when the workers' energy would be flagging. Ritual music has its own results. A lullaby increases the effect of rocking a child to sleep. The trumpets of the Children of Israel made the walls of Jerico tumble down. Thus music plays a fundamental role in ritual. It is an integrating component of ritual, an indispensable element of ritual itself, precisely as it is also the Ur-language of religion. Rappaport says:

> a sense of union is encouraged by the coordination of utterance and movement demanded of congregations in many rituals. To sing with others, to move as they move in the performance of a ritual, is not merely to

---

[29] AUF DER MAUR: *Feiern im Rythmus der Zeit, I*, 20. See Part 3, Chapter 9, 2.
[30] G. VAN DER LEEUW: *Wegen en grenzen*, Amsterdam 1948², 155.

symbolize union. It is *in and of* itself to reunite in the reproduction of a larger order. Unison does not merely symbolize that order but indicates it and its acceptance. The participants do not simply communicate to each other *about* that order but *commune with* each other *within* it.[31]

Like ritual movement – and particularly dance – ritual music has the power to invoke a different, deeper world for a group and permit them to become part of it. As such, ritual music is therefore the basis for music in Christian ritual.[32]

5. CLASSIFICATION OF RITUAL

There is little unanimity with regard to the classification of ritual. One finds all sorts of arrangements.[33] In my view, one is best served by a global, and not too detailed classification. I will limit myself to a division of rituals into three groups: crisis rituals, cyclic rituals and rites of passage.[34] Although particular rituals are sometimes assigned to different groups, to my mind this division is quite enlightening and entirely adequate. Moreover, there is considerable agreement with regard to this global classification. I will now examine the various groups.

5.1. Crisis rituals

Most anthropologists characterise crisis rituals on the basis of their effect in helping people come to terms with crises.[35] Situations which are

---

[31] RAPPAPORT: *Ritual and Religion in the Making of Humanity* 220.

[32] A. VERNOOIJ: *Muziek als liturgisch teken* (Liturgie in perspectief 10), Baarn/Heeswijk 1998; IDEM: 'Musiceren en luisteren', in BARNARD & POST (eds.): *Ritueel bestek* 145-154.
Because music is such an integral component of ritual itself, Wilderbeek prefers to speak of ritual music rather than of liturgical music. See H. JONGERIUS: 'Op de vierkante meter die je gegeven is doen wat je meent te moeten doen... Een gesprek met Jos Wilderbeek', in *Inzet* 21 (1992) 1, 12.

[33] See for instance BELL: Ritual. Perspectives 93-137.

[34] TERRIN: 'Antropologia culturale' 85-92. This does leave the question of what category one should place rituals such as the blessing of things and persons into. One could create an entirely separate category for them, but generally they are assigned to one of the three listed here. One can consider the blessing of the bride and groom as part of a rite of passage, the blessing of a house or child as a cyclic rityal, and the blessing of the sick as a crisis ritual.

[35] TERRIN: 'Antropologia culturale' 85-86, 89-90.

uncontrollable often occur in society. One can think of the drama of incurable disease, natural disasters such as floods and draughts, or the threat of war, but also of uncertainty about success in an examination, the outcome of a contest, or the result of a harvest. By means of ritual people then try to process and relieve the individual and social crises to which these events lead.

Malinowski notes that it is not easy to distinguish the magical, religious and technical-instrumental elements in these rituals.[36] His example is fishing among the Trobriand islanders. For them, fishing in the open ocean, as opposed to fishing in the lagoons, is full of dangers and uncertainties. Significantly, they only take refuge in ritual with regard to fishing at sea, and the technical-instrumental, religious and magical are closely interwoven with each other in this ritual. In this connection one can also think of the classical rite of unction, which in the ancient church was directed to both physical and spiritual healing. Moreover, in this context one should reread what I have written in a previous chapter on the prophylactic (exorcizing) dimension of ritual.[37] This experience is still topical in our time, particularly among those who opt for a relationship with nature that is not purely and simply technological, but also experience nature in a ecological-religious manner.[38] Rituals such as lighting a candle before a saint's image or crucifix, and pilgrimages to holy sites can also be placed in this category.

According to Malinowski these rituals also have a secondary instrumental effect, to the extent that they decrease anxiety. Opinions however differ on this. For instance, according to Geertz rituals of this sort do not per se dispel anxiety and suffering, but are rather a reaction to the anxiety about the vacuum that accompanies a crisis.[39] Thus one cannot speak of an instrumental effect with regard to dispelling anxiety, but rather of the search for meaning by way of symbols. From what has come before it will be clear that it is also my view that the symbolic effect is the most fundamental level in crisis ritual. Even where the anxiety is not exorcised, these rituals give real meaning to life.

---

[36] B. MALINOWSKI: *A Scientific Theory of Culture and Other Essays*, Chapel Hill 1944; IDEM: *Magic, science, and other essays*, Glencoe 1948.

[37] Part 1, Chapter 2, 3.7.

[38] TERRIN: 'Antropologia culturale' 85-86.

[39] C. GEERTZ: 'Religion as a Cultural System', in M. BANTON (ed.): *The Relevance of Models in Social Anthropology*, London 1965, 1-46. See TERRIN: 'Antropologia culturale' 85.

With regard to the blending of the symbolic effect of the ritual with its instrumental effect, I find Rappaport's interpretation of the ritual slaughter of pigs in New Guinea particularly instructive.[40] Various peoples in New Guinea keep pigs as domestic animals. They kill them only under special circumstances, and within a ritual context. Such a ritual slaughter is organised when the number of pigs has grown so large that the amount of work involved in keeping them and the amount of food they need is too great. The pigs are then a problem rather than a benefit to the community. Further, in time of war pigs may only be killed and eaten by the warriors; the protein and salt the warriors acquire this way is thus of benefit to the whole community, which they after all must defend. Thus through ritual the killing of pigs is formalised and limited to special circumstances. In this way the ecological balance is maintained, the conflict is kept limited, and overpopulation prevented. It is an open question whether advisors trained in economics or ecologists could have arranged matters better than precisely this ritual context. Our rationalised society with its bio-industry perhaps must come to the realisation that rituals even nowadays can often be more efficient in managing crises than purely objective regulation imposed from above.

5.2. Cyclic rituals

In the group of cyclic rituals we are dealing with rituals that further articulate important points in time. Within these rituals one can distinguish those rituals which are connected with the seasons, and rituals which are focused on commemoration.[41]

Seasonal rituals mark the beginning and end of seasons, the year, the century; they regulate time in a society and in part define the calendar of feasts.[42] They are primarily directed to introducing order into time and the cosmos, and giving these meaning in a particular way. They impose, as it were, cultural programmes over the order of nature.[43]

---

[40] RAPPAPORT: 'The obvious Aspects of Ritual' 41. See BELL: *Ritual. Perspectives* 29-30.
[41] BELL: *Ritual. Perspectives* 103-108 speaks of Calendrical Rites.
[42] TERRIN: 'Antropologia culturale' 91-92.
[43] GRIMES: *Marrying and Burying* 196-197; IDEM: *Deeply into the Bone.*

Memorial rituals involve the evocation of important events and persons from the past. One can here think of both national holidays and ecclesiastical holy days such as those honouring heroes and saints. One also finds quite a few feasts in which seasonal and commemorative rituals come together, such as for instance Christmas, Easter and Pentecost. Seasonal and memorial rituals define both the civil and the religious and ecclesiastical calendar, and because they recur regularly one can class them as cyclic rituals. They give meaning to the always recurring cycle of days, months and years. They order time in a general manner, in contrast to rites of passage, which apply to the individual life cycle.

5.3. Rites of passage

Rites of passage involve rites which are related to the transition from one phase of life to another: the birth of a child, the beginning of a course of study (be it primary school, high school or college), first love, engagement, marriage, the noviciate, entering a religious order, ordination, beginning a major journey (for instance a pilgrimage), farewells, old age, or burial. These are rituals that on the one hand recur for people, and in that sense may appear to be cyclical, but which on the other hand occur only once in each individual's biography.[44]

The term 'rite of passage' goes back to Van Gennep (1873-1957).[45] One might be inclined to think that there are two elements in these rites of passage: the phase left, and the phase entered. However, according to Van Gennep there are always three phases in a rite of passage: a. detachment, in which the individual is in a ritual way separated from the earlier social position (*rites de séparation* or *rites préliminaires*) ; b. an intermediate stage (*rites de marge* or *rites liminaires*), in which the ambiguity of the individual's position is ritually expressed and made bearable; and c. integration into the new group, in which the entry into the new position is ritually celebrated (*rites d'agrégation* or *rites postliminaires*). Furthermore Van Gennep indicates that a particular accent can be placed upon any one of these three elements. For instance, in rituals

---

[44] A. VAN GENNEP: *Les rites de passage*, Paris/Den Haag 1969 (first edition 1909); see J.-Y. HAMELINE: 'Relire van Gennep... Les rites de passage', in *La Maison-Dieu* (1972) 112, 133-143; IDEM: 'Les *rites de passage* d'Arnold van Gennep', in *La Maison-Dieu* (2001) 228, 7-39.

[45] VAN GENNEP: *Les rites de passage* 13-15.

concerning death, it is on detachment; in marriage, on integration; in engagements, the noviciate and the catechumenate, the intermediate stage. Grimes warns that one must be careful in using Van Gennep's scheme. Particularly when dealing with initiation one must take into account that the transition may occur in a more complex manner.[46]

It is true that rites of passage involve phases in the life of an individual, but they also have an important social component. After all, they also involve people taking on a new social role, with all the rights and obligations that brings with it. Some scholars even place all the emphasis on this social-symbolic function of the rite of passage. This is particularly the case for Victor Turner (1920-1983), who took over Van Gennep's framework with his own content.[47] His views are still highly influential. Turner provides a further specification of the three phases: a. the phase of destructuring, in which the individual leaves the existing structure; b. the phase of 'liminality', in which the individual passes over the threshold (L.: *limen*) and enters a 'border situation', leaving the zone of the strong structures of the social order and entering a phase of anti-structures in which there is a symbolic purity, and in which the individual participates in a community (*communitas*) that is characterised by the relations of I, Thou and we; and, c. the phase of restructuring, in which the individual again enters the social structural models.

Although Turner has many followers, in my view there are quite a few critical questions which can be posed to his approach. Turner narrows the approach of Van Gennep somewhat.[48] All emphasis lies on the phase of liminality. The anti-structure of this phase represents the authentic reality. But why should one limit authentic symbolic power to a non-structural, liminal phase? The effectiveness of symbols never stands apart from structural elements. Furthermore, Van Gennep's *période de marge*, termed the liminal phase by Turner – examples would be the noviciate, engagement, a retreat, entering a seminary or military academy, being suspended or taking a sabbatical – has its structural side.[49] Also, in the

---

[46] GRIMES: *Deeply into the Bone* 103-107.

[47] TURNER: *The Forest of Symbols* and IDEM: *The Ritual Process*. For Turner see among others B. BOUDEWIJNSE: 'The Ritual Studies of Victor Turner. An Anthropological Approach and its Psychological Impact', in HEIMBROCK & BOUDEWIJNSE (eds.): *Current Studies on Rituals* 1-32.

[48] TERRIN: 'Antropologia culturale' 86-87.

[49] D.J. AUSTIN: 'Born again... and again: Communitas and Social Change among Jamaican Pentecostalists', in *Journal of Anthropological Research* 37 (1981) 3, 226-246;

first and third phase there can be just as much authentic symbolic effectiveness, particularly with regard to the relation between life and death.[50] Thus in some cases there will be a symbolic death performed in the first phase, after which follows a period of symbolic transition between death and life in the second phase, and being reborn in the third phase. To my mind, Turner's perspective can easily lead to a certain dualistic view with regard to the relation between liturgy and social reality. Turner considers the detailed and complex ritual of the liturgy between Trent and the Second Vatican Council, including the strangeness of the Latin, a pure example of 'liminality', while he sees the innovations after the Second Vatican Council, including the introduction of the vernacular, as a too thorough accommodation to secular culture.[51] It has a want of anti-structure. This view of Turner's not only coincides with a overly dualistic concept of ritual, but also with the question of to what extent rituals as such can be subject to radical changes. In this regard Turner has a rather static view of ritual. In his opinion, true rites of passage belong to pre-industrial cultures.[52] I will return to this in Part 2.[53]

The anthropologist and psychoanalyst R. Devisch has also provided a fundamental critique of Turner.[54] Like Turner, Devisch has carefully studied the rituals of Central African tribes. According to Devisch, Turner looked at ritual too much from the outside and too intellectually. He is fascinated by the rite as a micro-social drama that is intended to resolve social and emotional conflicts in a ritual manner and strengthen the community. He makes the peculiar creativity of ritual dependent on its functionality for the regular social order, while ritual is inherently creative and transforming, from its corporeal and sensory

---

B. MORRIS: *Anthropological Studies of Religion: an Introductory Text*, Cambridge 1987, 258-260; M.J. SALLNOW: 'Communitas Reconsidered: The Sociology of Andrean Pilgrimage', in *Man (N.S.)* 16 (1981) 163-182. See BOUDEWIJNSE: 'The Ritual Studies of Victor Turner 16-17.

[50] TERRIN: 'Antropologia culturale' 87.

[51] V. TURNER: 'Ritual, Tribal and Catholic', in *Worship* 50 (1976) 504-526.

[52] GRIMES: 'Liturgical Supinity' 64-65. This involves the fixed nature of pre-industrial rituals as such. In another respect, one can concur with GRIMES (*Deeply into the Bone* 121) in his observation that Turner 'was largely responsible for a radical reconception of ritual... For him ritual was not the guardian of the status quo or a means of garnering social consensus, as it had been previously under the influence of the French sociologist Emile Durkheim. Rather ritual became deeply subversive and creative'.

[53] Part 2, Chapter 2, 2.

[54] DEVISCH: 'Des forces aux symboles' 59-77.

interior. He considers ritual too much as a meta-commentary on the social order, as a statement of the eternal social drama in which conflicts must be resolved.[55] Devisch notes that Turner's mother was an actress, and that Turner himself loved theatre. This has influenced him in his view of ritual. From his literary culture he developed a theory about the manner in which social drama and drama on the stage are connected with each other. Ritual thus takes on the same qualities as theatre. But ritual has its own sensory and immediate vitality. Those who participate in it in principle have no need to further interpret the meaning of the symbols. That is only a secondary question. It is a matter of a world in which they live, of the happening itself, and not of the knowledge or a 'reality' that rests on representation. Ritual is a praxis of conferring meaning. With this we return to what was said above in connection with the primary presentative symbolism of ritual.[56] This appears fundamental for all three phases of a rite of passage.[57]

I have pointed out that rites of passage are involved with the individual life cycle, but also that people encounter them regularly, and that they have an important social component with regard to new social roles. Thus, precisely as collective events, rites of passage are only possible when the transition between social positions, which it accomplishes from the point of view of the society, ends in a rather predictable way. Rituals that are valid for the whole of the community presuppose a certain consistency in situation among different individuals: despite the fact that for one particular individual it will be a one-time occurrence, the situation is still considered a repetition within the larger community. In a certain sense, the ritual must be possible irrespective of the individuals.[58]

This presents certain difficulties in our culture, for it is highly diverse, shattering the possibility for collective ritual. At the same time, we are challenged by new voids, which must be filled by actions which

---

[55] V. TURNER: 'Social Dramas and Stories About Them', in *Critical Analysis* 7 (1980) 141-168.

[56] Part 1, Chapter 1, 2.5. and Chapter 4, 1.

[57] Turner also applies his approach to the ritual of pilgrimage. But here too critical questions arise, and there is a certain departure from, and at least a broadening of his views. In connection with this see J. PIEPER, P. POST & M. VAN UDEN: *Bedevaart en pelgrimage. Tussen traditie en moderniteit* (UTP-katern 16), Baarn 1994, 229-231, 259-260, 263-264, 272-273.

[58] HAHN: 'Kultische und säkulare Riten' 70-72.

must ease the transition from one situation to another. The consequences of this for rites of passage will be discussed in Part 3.

6. FEAST

The subject of 'feast' is presently the centre of attention. Studies on the
topic appear from all sorts of disciplines. Recently the results were published of the Dutch national research program (1995-2000) 'Liturgical
Movements and Feast Culture'.[59]
   The French dictionary *Petit Robert* is famed for the clarity of its definitions. Let me begin with the definition of 'feast' one finds there.[60] On the
basis of usage, feast is to be understood as: 1. a ceremony or joyous event
with a commemorative character; the day devoted to this ceremony; 2. a
day in the church calendar commemorating a saint; 3. public and periodical joy commemorating an event or person; 4. a joyful event that is organised for an occasion; 5. 'fêtes galantes', as a term for a genre in French
painting; 6. a joyful event within the family, among friends. What strikes
one in all these definitions from usage is that according to this dictionary
joy is a characteristic of the feast. When a ritual involves a sad occasion, it
is indeed difficult for us to call it a feast. We do not, for instance, speak of
a 'funeral feast'. We are just as little inclined to term a prayer service
against the threat of war a feast. This means that the concept of feast is
closely connected with the perspective of the positive and joyful.
   We do also peak of 'celebrating a feast'. The concept of 'celebration'
appears to have a broader meaning. We can speak of celebrating a funeral
liturgy, and we can term the prayer service against war a celebration. S.
Maggiani however remarks, following J. Potel, that the concept of feast
can also be applied where the feast has a sad character, as in the case of a
memorial for the dead or a funeral ritual. Rituals of this sort do indeed
have aspects of the feast, because they take place in a special time, and
contribute to introducing a rhythm in time, as reference points in the calendar. Moreover, these rituals allow people the opportunity to enter into
a new relation with time and history by means of a return to the past, to

---

[59] POST, ROUWHORST, VAN TONGEREN & SCHEER (eds.): *Christian Feast and Festival.*
For literature, see particularly p. 27-42, 66-71. See also POST: 'Liturgische bewegingen
en feestcultuur' and IDEM: 'Feest', in BARNARD & POST (eds.): *Ritueel bestek* 171-180.
[60] *Le nouveau Petit Robert. Dictionnaire alphabétique et analogique de la langue
française*, Paris 1994, 911-912.

the origin, and give them a prospect on the future and the ultimate meaning of life. They also are an opportunity to create wider community among relatives and friends, and for important economic exchanges (flowers, gifts).[61] He closes with the following description of feast from Isambert: the symbolic celebration of an object (event, person, God, cosmic phenomenon, etc.) in a consecrated time with predominately collective activities that have an expressive function.[62] This description is close to the working definition of the Dutch national research program, which is as follows: 'By 'feast' we refer to the moment in which, or the occasion on which people, in the structuring of time and the course of an individual's life cycle, as groups or as society, give special (that is to say, in an way which breaks through the everyday) ritual form to occurrences that mark personal and social existence, doing so from faith, a religious, philosophical or ideological orientation which makes sense of life'.[63] Post summarises this description in a clear and operational way, where he, by way of a normative-critical perspective, mentions the following four qualities or dimensions of feast:[64] 1. Contrast with regard to the everyday: feast is other, it stops the rat race, it is a refuge. 2. It lives by the grace of memory: something or someone is remembered and therefore there is something or someone to celebrate. This is the myth of feast, the content. 3. It is a ritual. The memory is kept going through a ritual setting. The anamnestic and sacramental dimensions are linked in the ritual performance: feasting is something you *do*, performed in word and action. 4. It is inseparably linked with group culture. Feast stands or falls with group solidarity; feasting is done *together*.

7. STRENGTHS AND WEAKNESSES OF RITUAL

Rituals play a very particular role in our communication with reality. They give us an access to reality that comes only in this way, and in no

---

[61] J. POTEL: *Les funérailles une fête*, Paris 1973, 120. See also S. MAGGIANI: 'Festa/Feste', in SARTORE & TRIACCA: *Nuovo dizionario di liturgia* 568.

[62] F. ISAMBERT: 'Fête', in *Encyclopedia Universalis* VI, Paris 1970, 1047.

[63] POST: 'Liturgische bewegingen en feestcultuur' 35; IDEM: 'Liturgical Movements and Feast Culture. A Dutch Research Program', in POST, ROUWHORST, VAN TONGEREN & SCHEER (eds.): *Christian Feast and Festival* 37 and 42.

[64] P. POST: 'Introduction and Application: Feast as a key concept in a liturgical studies research design', in POST, ROUWHORST, VAN TONGEREN & SCHEER (eds.): *Christian Feast and Festival* 71.

other. This has important consequences. In particular, it means that without rituals a part of reality remains veiled for us. It is impossible to gain access to that part of reality in any other way, because it is only uncovered through ritual. In one way or another ritual is itself a part of that reality, because it participates in it. Thus rituals are irreplaceable. You cannot do without them, under penalty of losing contact with reality and impoverishing human experience.

Perhaps the comparison with a work of art can make this clearer. You can try to convert a work of art into concepts, but the reality represented in the artwork reaches further. You can only reach that through the mediation of the artwork itself. You cannot translate a work of art. When you try to tell someone about it and evoke it in words, it is necessarily impoverished. The unique character of the mediation is thus far from accidental. An artwork is, after all, itself the carrier, participant and representation of what it calls up. There is thus no other immediate communication possible with the reality that the artwork represents.[65] In the same way in and through ritual we also gain an access to reality that is entirely in a class of its own and irreplaceable. It has a very specific *power*.

When rituals are not performed, experience of reality is lost, and this loss is all the more radical because it involves the impoverishment of an experience of reality that touches human existence as such. Rituals, after all, involve precisely the mystery of human reality: our person, our relations with others and with the world. They touch that reality which is not to be grasped and which cannot be authenticated, the transcendent reality where the religious also finds its point of contact.

Nevertheless the words 'rite' and 'ritual' for some people in our society retain a negative connotation. People put up resistance against rituals or are offended by them, because by definition rituals have to do with the purely formulaic and stereotypical. They cover up and conceal. They lead to dishonest and hypocritical behaviour. Rituals deal with an unreal world, or they are directed at maintaining power. Here one runs up against the ambiguity of ritual. Precisely that which is the power of ritual can also become its *weakness*. It is important to expand upon this point. Rituals in a certain sense are like Pandora's box.[66] If you open

---

[65] L. KOLAKOWSKI: *Geist und Ungeist christlicher Traditionen*, Stuttgart 1971, 90 ff.

[66] GRIMES: *Reading, Writing, and Ritualizing* 158. In this connection, see also ODENTHAL: *Liturgie als Ritual* 127-167.

them up, you discover not only virtues and health, but also mischiefs and sickness. Even the purist ritual intentions are not able to produce an act that is free of the danger of infection. Certainly now that the attraction of ritual is growing again, critique of ritual is also important. I would closely connect this critique with each of the fundamental characteristics and dimensions of ritual that I have sketched above.

There are possible deviations in ritual that are connected with its *repetitive character*. Through this characteristic rituals can easily deteriorate into pure routine and the ordinary. Then they are performed without any devotion or creativity. This can be the case in the secular rituals of burial or marriage at the city clerk's office, but it is equally well a possibility in every religious ritual. The ritual can be rushed through. Then it loses much of its meaningfulness. It flies on automatic pilot. Rituals can also become compulsive actions at the moment of repetition. When I have forgotten to lock the door of my car several times, the inclination can arise to perform this action again even if it is certain that I have locked the car. Religious rituals also lend themselves to compulsive actions: for instance, those with excessive scruples may repeatedly confess their sins and receive absolution.

Ritual has a *dimension of relieving and channelling*, but the other side of this coin is that this can lead to superficiality and escapism. It may be that ritual, rather than channelling feelings, only formalises and covers them up.

The *healing dimension* can lead to magical use of ritual. One then employs it as an almost infallible and instrumental means of accomplishing healing and manipulating higher powers. And the healing function can also be reversed. Then one encounters rituals that come out of black magic or from satanic sects. These are undoubtedly a threat for the spiritual health of the individual.

One can lose oneself in ritual: it has an *expressive dimension*. But this too has its shadow side: that of narcissism or that of the attempt to make it into the most individual expression of the most individual emotion. In the latter case one erodes the social dimension of ritual, and its repetitive nature. In the case of narcissism, the ritual becomes locked up in itself. It becomes a theatrical confirmation of the I.

As far as *the dimension of condensation* is concerned, rituals can become so isolated that they lose touch with everyday life and ethical acts. They then communicate with a purely vertical reality, without taking into account the horizontal dynamic of that which the depth of reality hands on.

Finally, rituals have a *mediating dimension with regard to the past*. But they can be fatally stubborn and resist adaptation, precisely when this is necessary. They can be means of propping up the existing order.

We said that ritual can also have a *prophylactic, an exorcizing dimension*. This protective element serves to express that people hope to banish what they cannot control. But it can also take on a more or less magical character, or an expression of a certain superstition. That can be rather innocent. Everyone knows of rituals with regard to the number 13 and the custom of not walking under a ladder. People also seem to expose a wonderful creativity. For instance, when at Ajax the Dutch soccer player Johan Cruyff always tapped goalkeeper Gerd Bals on the waistband of his shorts when they went onto the field, and Wim van Hanegem at Feijenoord always let a red and white ball bounce three times in the stadium tunnel: if the ball bounced to the ceiling, they were sure to win.[67] The Dutch goalkeeper Hans van Breukelen says,

> All dates that are divisible by seven are lucky dates. Germany, Hamburg, that 1-2 on the 21st. The number seven is important. Russia and Benfica both on the 25th. Two and five is seven. Real Madrid, last season, on the 18th, eight minus one is also seven. I also often take a 25 guilder note in my pants pocket, because two and five is seven.[68]

Italian men wear a small horn around their neck or on their watch to protect their fertility. And everyone knows that in religion ejaculatory prayers, medals and relics sometimes become magic formulas and objects. I again cite Hans van Breukelen:

> I inherited a medal of Pope John XXIII from my granddad. A big, bronze medal. I always wore it. Until I lost that medal in an away fixture at Zeist. I really did comb both penalty areas for an hour after the match was over, but I never recovered my precious medal. I felt less of a goalkeeper after that, and furthermore never won another championship again. Until, about four years ago, on my father's birthday, my uncle Frans heard this story. Uncle Frans is also a deep believer, had just been to Rome, and, I swear to God, had that medal of Pope John XXIII hanging on a golden chain. He gave it to me. Everyone knows the results since. Although I don't keep goal any more with that medal, I always keep it with me, in my football bag, in a pocket on the right side.[69]

---

[67] R. KAGIE: 'Topsport en geluksrituelen', in *NRC Handelsblad* April 5, 1991, 18.
[68] H. VAN BREUKELEN: *Het Engeltje van Hans van Breukelen*, Hoornaar 1989, 67.
[69] VAN BREUKELEN: *Het Engeltje van Hans van Breukelen* 66-67.

Thus one can not say that magic is an element that one finds exclusively in primitive cultures and religions, and that that it has been conquered by higher religions such as Christianity or by science.[70] Magic rituals are of all times. Moreover, one must approach them in a nuanced way. For example, Douglas points to a remarkable parallel: the positive evaluation of the ethical religion of the ancient Hebrews in its contrast to the magical religions of the surrounding peoples gets equated with the Protestant's positive judgement of the ethical view of religion in the Protestant churches, in contrast to the magical style of the Roman Catholics. In essence, however, this is a matter of two differing styles of ritual conduct that coincide with two different types of social organisation.[71] There appears to be a certain critical view by Protestants of Catholic ritual based on strongly ethical grounds, while in fact there are two different manners of authentic religious conduct. In linguistics some make a distinction between metaphoric and metonymic ritual conduct. There is a metaphoric relationship when A is treated as if it were B (pouring out water as a representation of rain), and a metonymic relationship when A is treated as if it was a part of B (a relic of the Cross as sharing in one way or another in the holiness of Christ himself). One is clearly dealing with metonymic relationships in the case of relics, not only those of the Cross, but also those of saints, and with objects that are connected with Sacred Blood miracles.[72]

An illustrative example of the peculiarly metonymic 'logic' of ritual comes from ancient and medieval China. There in times of great heat waves the people hauled the images of the gods out of their cool temples and set them in the burning sun, when their prayers for relief were not answered. In this way they let the gods experience at first hand, as it were, the suffering of the people, and asked them urgently to do something about it.[73] Then there is the story of the woman who lighted

---

[70] For a survey of the various views and approaches, see BELL: *Ritual. Perspectives* 46-52.

[71] M. DOUGLAS: *Purity and Danger. An Analysis of Concepts of Pollution and Taboo*, New York 1966, 18-19. See BELL: *Ritual. Perspectives* 49.

[72] See in connection with this for instance G. SNOEK: *Medieval Piety from Relics to the Eucharist: A Process of Mutual Interaction* (Studies in the History of Christian Thought), Leiden 1995 = IDEM: *Eucharistie- en reliekverering in de Middeleeuwen*, Amsterdam 1989.

[73] For this example, see BELL: *Ritual. Perspectives* 115, who refers to A.P. COHEM: 'Coercing the Rain Deities in Ancient China', in *History of Religions* 17 (1978) 3-4, 249-250.

candles in front of a picture of a saint in her room, but turned it face to the wall when her prayers were not answered. Is this a superstitious, magical act? This seems, rather, to be striking and expressive ritual conduct. This sort of 'magical' ritual conduct perhaps occurs more often in popular piety than in that of the elite, and it cannot be denied that it can deteriorate into magic. But even educated theologians will acknowledge that this sort of ritual expression is not foreign to them.[74]

Ritual can also be placed too much in the service of *myth* or *ideology*. I earlier discussed the rites of socialist societies. It is familiar to all that in the former Soviet Union rituals were expressly designed also from Marxist ideology. In this connection it is interesting that, for example, in 1963 certain ritual innovations were designed by a sub-department of the Central Committee of the Communist Party: the Committee for Ideological Affairs.[75] National Socialism also placed rituals expressly in the service of its ideology. On November 9, 1923, Adolf Hitler staged a *putsch* in Munich, in which sixteen of his henchmen died, and he himself was arrested and imprisoned. After he came to power in 1933 he made turned this event into a 'celebration of victory and national resurrection', a celebration that in 1943 was elevated into a national memorial day for the dead. In this ritual people sang about 'the banners for which the first standard-bearers fell, glorious and holy as a sacrament'. At the end of this ritual the *Führerehrung* took place, in which they pledged, 'Führer, the mystery of your leadership rests in our own deeds. You are us, and we are you. All thee words that you find are taken from our mouths, because you say what we believe. And you are the one who impresses the form of life so supply that it... envelopes us like God's wide mantle'.[76] The whole of this ritual is full of idolatry of the Führer as a messianic and almost divine figure. It is a ritual in the service of the ideology of nationalism and racism. One can also think of Napoleon. Under his regime a new saint was discovered, namely St. Napoleon. He

---

[74] See in connection with this Part 3, Chapter 7, 3.

[75] A. WENGER: 'La nouvelle campagne antireligieuse en URSS', in *La Croix* 85 (1964) February 17-19.

[76] H.J. BECKER: 'Liturgie in Dienst der Macht. Nationalsozialistischer Totenkult als säkularisierte christliche Paschfeier', in *'Totalitarismus' und 'Politische Religionen'. Konzepte des Diktaturvergleichs* 2 A, Paderborn 1997, 37-73; W. FREITAG & C. POLL (eds.): *Das dritte Reich im Fest. Führermythos, Feierlaune und Verweigerung in Westfalen 1933-1945*, Bielefeld 1997.

was supposed to have been a Roman officer, who in the third century died a martyr's death for his faith. It so happened that the birthday of Napoleon, August 15, was the Assumption of St. Mary, the most important Marian feast. This day now became the feast of the newly discovered St. Napoleon, and at the same time was proclaimed a national holiday. Napoleon had already produced an imperial catechism 'to bind the conscience of the people to the august person of the Emperor through religious sanctions'.[77] With the new holy day he reinforced this political ideology in an insistent manner.[78] Thus it would appear that religious rituals can be taken into the service of an ideology: nationalism, racism; one can think too of apartheid in South Africa, and of dictators front and centre, in a special place during church services commemorating a coup. I myself remember a photograph of a Portuguese bishop who during the decolonisation of the Portuguese territories in the 1960s was standing on a tank, blessing weapons and soldiers. And what are we to make of the ghastly rituals accompanying so-called 'holy war'?

Ritual can also be in service of ecclesiastical institutions. This is sharply and strikingly described by the psychologist of religion H. Fortmann.[79] He writes:

> What great fashion houses do for women, Rome had done for centuries for its power elite: canons in purple-with-white habiliments, canons in purple-with-mouse grey habiliments, bishops with white mitres high as towers. And see around them… the chic of Rome in black and white, knights of this and of that in green and grey, halberdiers with bunches of red plumes on their helmets, in orange and blue. O what a Church Visible we have!… We are waiting now for the pope. He enters precisely on time. White mitre, white robe, red mantle… See him stand during the passion song with folded hands, motionless… Pope Paul corresponds – just as did Pius XII, who had himself photographed at his prie-dieu as if it were a preliminary study for his grave monument – to the Roman *Idee-an-sich* of 'pope': immovable, infallible, and wiser than all the experts of the world. He may be as modest as possible, but an office that isolates someone so is always bad for the person. It gives the impression of super-humanity… Nowhere does one experience more strongly how great is the power of institutions than in Rome.

[77] B. CASCOIGNE: *De christenen. Geschiedenis van een wereldreligie*, Amsterdam/Brussel 1977.

[78] See also A. COBBAN: *A History of Modern France*, Vol. 2: *From the first Empire to the second Empire 1799-1871*, Hammondsworth 1965, 32.

[79] H. FORTMANN: *Hoogtijd. Gedachten over feesten en vasten*, Utrecht 1966, 64-69.

He then argues not for the abolition of the office of pope, but for this office as a modest brotherly service for the local churches, and nothing more, but also nothing less than the evangelical yeast in the dough.

How even existing, authentic ritual can be drafted into the service of a particular religious ideology can be seen in the ordination of the conservative bishop J. Gijssen on February 13, 1972. He had been named by Rome to 'put the house in order' in The Netherlands. Against the wishes of the Dutch archdiocese his ordination took place in Rome; Cardinal Alfrink was 'summoned' by Paul VI to be co-consecrator, but representatives of the diocese of Limburg, to which he was being ordained, were absent. In this way the new ritual from after the Second Vatican Council, which expressly assigns a function to the local church, was undermined.[80]

In Rome there are – quite correctly – different congregations for rites and for the orthodoxy of doctrine. They are co-equal. But when the latter congregation begins to exercise control over Christian liturgy, it is generally at the cost of ritual. In point of fact, ritual involves a primary orthodoxy, in the sense of authentic worship, and not the secondary orthodoxy of correct doctrine. True ritual is never speculative or purely dogmatic, but is characterised by the elusiveness of the symbol, symbolic language and symbolic act. Perhaps this can best be made clear by the following example. Some time ago, among other objections against a Dutch project involving baptismal rituals, it was noted that the concept of original sin was lacking.[81] But the objectors sought too much for the speculative concept, ignored the metaphors and also neglected to songs which accompanied the ritual. As in the old liturgy, in which the concept of original sin as such is also absent, these spoke of the lame, blind and sick humanity: symbolic language which was apparently not understood.

One here also encounters the ambiguity of *social and political dimension* of ritual. Ritual binds people together, gives identity to groups, communities and nations. But feast can also degenerate into orgy. Ritual can also become too subservient to the rulers. One has only to think of the initiation rituals of Nazism, fascism and socialism, of the rituals

[80] L. ENGELS: 'Een bisschopswijding en de afwezigheid van de plaatselijke kerk', in *Tijdschrift voor Liturgie* 56 (1972) 218-240.
[81] This concerns TH. KERSTEN: *Gedoopt voor mensen. Werkboek voor katechese en liturgie*, Nijmegen 1983.

of mass demonstrations and military parades and of the bread and circuses of the Roman Empire. A study by C. Lane, *The Rites of Rulers*,
appeared in 1981.[82] The cover has a striking photograph of the May
Day military parade in Moscow, but the book does not deal only with
the exercise of power via ritual in the former Soviet Union, but also with
rituals of power in England, the United States and post-colonial communities. The same ambiguity discussed here can also be a concern in
Christian mass liturgies, such as previously took place at the end of Pax
Christi marches, and to this day take place with papal visits to all sorts
of countries. For example, the mass celebration of Eucharist on a papal
visit can 'assume the character of an *adventus*, where power is propagated, legitimised and confirmed'.[83] In this context, H. Häring notes
that, in part under the influence of papal trips, in various countries
there is a revival going on in participation in large ecclesiastical and religious events: organised mass demonstrative gatherings employing modern means of communication and organisational aids. Although there is
no need to reject these in principle, they still contain within themselves
the potential to work purely for the stabilisation of the established order.
This is all the more true for papal visits, because in his trips the pope
regularly makes use of the privileges and possibilities that a head of state
enjoys. Through this, the ritual sometimes openly contributes to legitimising unjust and oppressive systems, although this is generally unin-
tentional. Whatever the case, with Christian ritual one must guard its
characteristic features carefully. For instance, the Eucharist is the celebration of a meal, and it is questionable if the scale of this can be
expanded at will without degenerating into magic. The massality of a
gathering with the dimensions of a stadium or an airport becomes a sort
of spectacle, at which one must ask oneself if it indeed does sufficient
justice to that which is actually involved in the celebration of the Lord's
Supper.[84]

One also finds this ambiguity in simple civil rituals. An example is
the opening of the academic year at Dutch universities. This is still
always accompanied with an official ritual in which professors in gown
and regalia take part. This ritual is in a certain sense rather innocent,

[82] LANE: *The Rites of Rulers*.
[83] POST: *Ritueel landschap* 30.
[84] H. HÄRING: 'Tussen 'civiele religie' en godsdienstkritiek', in *Tijdschrift voor Theologie* 24 (1984) 348-354.

but it still radiates authority and power. Particularly in the 1960s the power aspects of rituals of this sort were strongly criticised. For instance, at the opening of the academic year in 1968 at the Tilburg University, two students came up the side aisles of the auditorium, with white pocket handkerchiefs around their neck as academic bands. They sat down among the professors and during the opening address repeatedly tried to involve them in dialogue. In the meantime a banner was unfurled in the auditorium with the text 'Authorities requiescant in pace'. In this connection it is important to note that every ritual is exposed to the danger of becoming manipulative. This danger is related to the question of how power is distributed. The more power is divided and shared out together, the smaller this risk is. To more power resides in the hands of a few, the greater the danger of ideology and domination. For example, the ritual of the opening of the academic year is at this moment more in balance than it was in the 1960s, because it has as its counterpart a number of rituals of dialogue that were introduced with the democratisation of the universities.

With regard to the social dimension, when it involves the relation between men and women, one encounters the ambiguity of ritual in a very specific way. It cannot be denied that in the past rituals were to an important degree created and controlled by males. This has led to rituals having contributed to emphasising the peculiar identity of males in an insistent way, and expressing male domination over women.[85] This was the case with civil rituals, but no less so with religious rituals. One may think of the fact that among the Jews, only boys undergo the initiation rite of circumcision,[86] that the marriage blessing was only pronounced over the woman, and that women were excluded from the office of priest. It is thus not surprising that an altered view of the role of men and women in our culture has also had radical consequences for rituals. I will return to this in Part 3.

In the preceding it has become clear to what degree ritual can be intertwined with ideologies, and, as such, how much harm it can do to freedom and the rights of those who take part in it willingly or unwillingly. To what extent can ideologies be enforced by means of rituals, and is

---

[85] In connection with this see GRIMES: 'Liturgical Supinity'.

[86] See in connection with this L.A. HOFFMAN: 'How Ritual Means: Ritual Circumcision in Rabbinic Culture and Today', in *Studia Liturgica* 23 (1993) 78-97.

social control possible by way of rituals? One here encounters the problem of *power and ritual.* It is discussed in a particularly nuanced manner
by Bell.[87] According to her insights, this question is generally approached
far too simplistically. It is therefore important to go into this more
deeply.

Generally people see power as something that the one in fact possesses, and another does not. Power is considered as something that
gives someone a certain form of control over others. It is then characterised as the denial of power to others. But one finds a new approach
with Foucault.[88] According to him, power is relational, and depends on
the moment in time. It is no fixed thing, but is constantly being organised and realised in mutual interrelationships. It is a question of directing the activities of the other. As such, power relationships are deeply
embedded in the network of social relations, and fundamental for every
society. To this he adds that power relationships do not operate purely
and simply from the top down, but equally in the other direction. There
can be no movement from the top down without a counter-movement
from the bottom up. For instance, the power of a monarchy likewise has
its roots in pre-existing forms of conduct. Power is always exercised over
free subjects, and to the extent they are free; which is to say, subjects can
always act differently. Even in cases of physical restraint, the subject is
capable of resistance, perhaps not physically, but inwardly. Now, rituals
play a major role in the realisation of power relationships. They create
special relational patterns. Power relationships are enacted within the
social body: between man and woman, teacher and pupil, government
and subject. Ritual is an effective social strategy in these. Consciously or
unconsciously, by means of rituals special relations of domination, consent and resistance are realised.

One must realise two things about this. First, certain forms of domination by ritual are not realised only from above, but likewise from
below, simply because people take part enthusiastically. Second, most
ritual practices of domination and control inevitably have their boundaries. Processes of ritual domination are necessarily coupled with

[87] BELL: *Ritual Theory* 169-218, particularly 197-218. See also *Ritual and Power*:
Journal of Ritual Studies 4 (1990) 2.
[88] Among others M. FOUCAULT (ed. C. GORDON): *Power/Knowledge: Selected Inter-
views and Other Writings 1972-1977*, New York 1980; IDEM: 'The subject of Power', in
H.L. DREYFUS & P. RABINOW (eds.): *Michel Foucault: Beyond Structuralism and
Hermeneutics*, Chicago 1983[2], 208-226.

processes of assent, resistance and negotiatory appropriation.[89] When people participate in a ritual in a totalitarian state, there is perhaps assent in terms of physical presence, but this in no way means that there is inward assent. People appropriate a ritual in their *own* individual way, and do so in a manner that serves their personal wellbeing. This also applies for Roman Catholic rituals with regard to the pope in Rome as the centre of unity. One can think of the enthusiastic crowds at many papal visits. This conduct is rather frequently regarded as hypocritical, because the same Catholics do not wish to accept papal pronouncements about sexuality. But in this people forget that such rituals do not per se imply absolute obedience. There is on the one hand assent, but at the same time there can be resistance and personal manners of appropriation. That is characteristic of the power relationships with rituals. You simply can not negotiate during the performance of the ritual itself. The only solution then is the negotiation by means of appropriation.

Thus one could say there is a flexible strategy: assent in public, but nothing more than that. This is simply the characteristic quality of these rituals, and it is also precisely what makes them possible and effective. It can not be denied that this approach to ritual and power by Bell is in all respects worth considering. One can not simply propagate and impose ideologies through public rituals. They are limited by the fact of individual appropriation. Rituals are simply a different way than physical violence. But at the same time it remains true that real totalitarian rituals are dangerous. One must not gloss over their negative side, and resistance against then is necessary – even public resistance, either in the form of not participating in them, or by counter-rituals.

---

[89] The concept of appropriation is a technical term in the humanities, which goes back to M. de Certeau, see W. FRIJHOFF: 'Toeëigening: van bezitsdrang naar betekenisgeving', in *Trajecta* 6 (1997) 2, 99-118; P. POST: 'De creatie van traditie volgens Eric Hobsbawm', in *Jaarboek voor liturgie-onderzoek* 11 (1995) 90, and the literature listed there (in note 46); also IDEM: 'Religious Popular Culture and Liturgy. An illustrated Argument for an Approach', in *Questions liturgiques* 79 (1998) 14-59 and in J. LAMBERTS (ed.): *Religion populaire, liturgie et évangélisation – Popular Religion. Liturgy and Evangelization* (Textes et Études Liturgiques/Studies in Liturgy 15), Leuven 1998 = IDEM: 'Religieuze volkscultuur en liturgie. Geïllustreerd pleidooi voor een benadering', in J. LAMBERTS (ed.): *Volksreligie, liturgie en evangelisatie* (Nikè-reeks 42), Leuven/Amersfoort 1998, 19-77, here 35-36. See also P. POST, 'Interference and Intuition: on the Characteristic Nature of Research Design in Liturgical Studies', in *Questions Liturgiques* 81 (2000) 1, 59, note 22 (literature).

It is clear that a tensive relation exists here between this approach by Bell, and that of Rappaport.[90] It involves the tensions between the objective public and the subjective private aspects of the ritual. When Rappaport speaks of the acceptance that participation in the ritual assumes as self-evident, this involves particularly the objective character of the ritual. After participating in the ritual of marriage, the bride and bridegroom can not say that they are not married, and that this ritual did not have the consequences that the ritual implies. But at the same time, it is true that the bride and bridegroom can appropriate the ritual in their own way. Normally it is assumed that the subjective and objective sides of the ritual correspond with one another. Ideally they are in balance with each other, and that the one aspect does not function at the expense of the other. But this can happen. Rappaport therefore is correct when he observes that a ritual order which is not supported by the conviction of at least some of the members of a congregation is in danger of gradually falling in desuetude or becoming a dead letter, and that conviction is, in the long run, indispensable to the perpetuation of ritual orders.[91]

The preceding has consistently dealt with ritual as such, which is characterised by the coming together of symbol, symbolic acts and symbolic language. It dealt with that which reaches to the depth of reality, even if it appears that it can concern that depth in a negative sense. Ritual can however deviate in another way. That is the case when it becomes *sign*. It then degenerates into superficiality. It is *used* in the service of other things. Then it becomes something merely instrumental, a sign that, so to speak, must be passed as quickly as possible.

This is the case when a ritual is only performed in the name of *ethics*: because it has to be. For instance, before the Second Vatican Council some Christians went to church only because that was required. Sunday church attendance then becomes a sign of good conduct. But ordinary rituals of getting on with others can also be performed purely because they are required. One thinks of certain rules of etiquette that have been strongly formalised. They are performed in what one might say was an

---

[90] See Part 1, Chapter 3, 1.2.

[91] RAPPAPORT: *Ritual and Religion in the Making of Humanity* 396, 419. See Part 1, Chapter 3, 1.2.

entirely 'empty' way. I must, however, note that sometimes such a strongly formalised and 'empty' repetition receives again a symbolic character. This can be seen in the case of protocol: by sticking to it in a very precise and formal way, one can take part in that private world that is protected and delimited by protocol. Military exercises like marching, standing at attention and presenting arms, precisely because of their formal and mandatory character, suggest discipline, strength and power. Now that religious rituals are no longer so strongly prescribed, another possibility through which rituals can decline into bodies of signs reveals itself. The ritual can be put into the service of a certain ethical or political strategy. Such a subordination misunderstands the basic character of ritual.

Ritual can also assume a purely sign value because it is placed in the service of *commerce*. This happens with a number of contemporary rituals: sport, vacation, fashion, song festivals, Father's Day, Mother's Day, feasts such as St. Nicholas, Christmas and Carnival, and even with rituals involving the dead. In the case of the latter, one is correct in speaking of the funeral industry. You also encounter an ambiguity typical of this situation. Even where these rituals have become almost totally subordinate to economic ends, it can be that participants reinterpret them on another wave length where the economic aspect is absent, or at least does not predominate.[92] It is precisely in this connection that Baudrillard makes a distinction between sign and symbol.[93] Also, rituals that are strongly defined by economics can be appropriated in an authentic way, and thus be experienced in a symbolic manner. Examples of this are the rituals of Christmas and of Mother's and Father's Day. I will return to this later.[94]

In connection with the subject of the strength and weakness of ritual, I want to make three final remarks.

The first concerns the importance of 'ritual criticism'. With reason Grimes notes that such criticism is possible only if we consider rites to be human artefacts subject to the usual human flaws and manipulations. Ritual criticism is based on the premise that rites, however noble in intention or sacred in origin, are imperfect.[95] It is important that rituals are constantly re-evaluated in this regard.

[92] L. VOYÉ: 'Le rite en question', in DEVISCH: 'Des forces aux symboles' 118.
[93] J. BAUDRILLARD: *Pour une critique de l'économie politique du signe*, Paris 1972.
[94] See Part 3, Chapter 2, 2.
[95] GRIMES: *Deeply into the Bone* 293. See also IDEM: *Ritual Criticism.*

Second, I wan to call attention to a remark that the authority on comparative religions Sierksma made during a discussion. He noted that in the animal world, both hypertrophy and atrophy of rituals can be found. This would suggest that this phenomenon can also appear among people. One could think of individuals, but also of various cultural eras. One might for instance ask if during the centuries before the Second Vatican Council one might not speak of ritual hypertrophy in the Roman Catholic church. In that period, a considerable amount of training was necessary in order to learn to command the complicated ritual of the liturgy. Thus, for example, from the moment he entered the sacristy until he returned there, the priest was captive in a network of very precise rules, right down to the different hand towels with which he had to dry his hands *ante* and *post* (before and after the Mass). If an error was made during the execution of the rubrics, another ritual went into effect. In the *Tractatus de defectibus missae* (Tractate on defects in the Mass) he could find what he had to do then. One could speak here of top-heavy ritual, in the same way that one can use that term for the manners of the Victorian era and in the etiquette books of the previous century. The weakness of ritual can also thus express itself in hypertrophy. But we must be cautious about all too quickly judging this hypertrophy from the perspective of our own culture, which with regard to ritual rather aims at some moderation, and is more informal.[96] Cultures and cultural periods can differ from one another rather considerably with regard to the density of ritual.[97]

Third, I will once again underscore how intrusive the power of ritual is. It is very arrestingly and expressively characterised by Ronald Grimes as follows:

> Effective ritual knowledge lodges in the bone, in its very marrow. This metaphor first struck me with force while in a discussion with an archaeologist. He was explaining how certain values and social practices can be inferred from ancient bone matter. An archaeologist can deduce from bone composition that the men of a particular society consumed more protein than the women. On the basis of bone size and shape, it may be evident that in some cultures women habitually carried heavier loads than men. Certain social practices are literally inscribed in the bones. Even

---

[96] In Part 1, Chapter 4, 5.3 I noted that Turner on the other hand admired the complicated ritual from before the Second Vatican Council as authentic ritual.

[97] See for this also Part 3, Chapter 2.

though we imagine bone as private, and deeply interior to the individual body, it is also socially formed.

Of course ritual is not really a something that dwells in a literal some-where. Rites are choreographed actions; they exist in the moments of their enactment and then disappear. When effective, their traces remain – in the heart, in the memory, in the mind, in texts, in photographs, in descrip-tions, in social values, and in the marrow, the source of our lifeblood.[98]

[98] GRIMES: *Deeply into the Bone* 7.

CHAPTER 5

THE RELIGIOUS AND CHRISTIAN DIMENSION:
AN OVERTURE

In this final chapter of the first section, I will briefly reflect on the religious and Christian dimension of ritual. In doing so I will anticipate
what will be addressed comprehensively in the third section. However,
it appears to me to be important to provide a first introduction here; it
can put the reader on the track of the perspective through which this
book will ultimately move.

The deeper reality toward which ritual is oriented can remain purely
within this world. For instance, funeral rituals can be oriented toward
parting from the dead, channelling feelings, getting through the period
between the separation and integration into and the processing of the
new social status as widow or widower. Ritual can concern purely
human values, which remain within this world: the experience of peace,
reconciliation, security, trust, and justice. That is no small matter. On
the contrary. This is a matter of a 'to be or not to be' of fundamental
human values. To focus this in on our culture: 'If we do not birth and
die ritually, we will do so technologically, inscribing technocratic values
in our very bones. Technology without ritual (…) easily degenerates
into knowledge without respect. And knowledge without respect is a
formula for planetary annihilation. It matters greatly not only *that* we
birth and die but *how* we birth and die'.[1]

But ritual can reach beyond that. In November 1970 one of the
largest peace marches ever took place: the protest march on Washington, against the Vietnam War. Forty thousand people, each with a sign
with the name of a dead soldier on their chest, marched past the White
House. Every time someone passed by there, through the microphone
he shouted the name of a dead soldier. After that they sang in a massive
gathering the songs *All we are saying is give peace a chance* and *Where
have all the young men gone?* In a sort of intercession, they prayed for the
end of the terrible war, and for money no longer to be spent on

---

[1] GRIMES: *Deeply into the Bone* 13.

weapons, but on the struggle against poverty. They laid the names of the fallen soldiers in a coffin and marched to the national cemetery to bury them, led by seven drummers with black-shrouded drums and the widow of one of the dead soldiers. During the event, reporters asked participants about their experience. One woman said this was the most religious experience she had participated in over the past years. Characteristically, the Dutch subtitles on the program left out the word 'religious'. Whatever the case, what for one person is only a radical human experience, can have a great religious import for another.

The same is true for other rituals. Very ordinary rituals can call up religious experiences. One could even say that it is precisely rituals that contribute to religious experience. 'Rituals are the mother tongue of religion'.[2]

If you go back to the source, possibly the distinction between religious and non-religious ritual behaviour is purely artificial. The etymological root is 'rta'.[3] In our culture we have been taught to make the distinction. But the fact remains that there is a hidden meaning present in human rituals, through which they have a religious import when seen from a particular point of view. It is also true that it is precisely rituals that are able to awaken religious experience. This is connected with the revelatory character of ritual. Symbolic communication has characteristics that one could call 'meta-communicative', to use Habermas's term.[4] Precisely because of these qualities, ritual is the language that pre-eminently fits religion, and conversely, ritual is first and foremost a religious phenomenon. This at the same time implies that religion touches us most deeply, and comes closest to us, precisely through ritual. After all, ritual gives a very physical form to the experience of the holy.[5] Therefore

---

[2] JETTER: *Symbol und Ritual* 93.

[3] JETTER: *Symbol und Ritual* 93-94. A different view is presented by H. Stoks in his Review of J. PLATVOET a.o. (eds.): *Pluralism and Identity*, in *Tijdschrift voor Theologie* 36 (1996) 3, 325-326. Regarding the words 'rite' and 'ritual' he remarks that etymologically these are not so much to be connected – as it has been argued in this book, in note 15, page 28 – with the Indo-Germanic root 'r(e)i', which means something on the order of 'to flow', but rather with the long stem '(a)rei' (to count), derived from the root 'ar' (to add); 'this in contrast to what E./ V.W. Turner believed, sadly enough taken over in this book again'.

[4] J. HABERMAS: 'Habermass', in H.E. BAHR (ed.): *Religionsgespräche. Zur gesellschaftlichen Rolle der Religion*, Darmstadt 1975, 29.

[5] J.W. DIXON: *The Physiology of Faith. A Theory of Theological Relativity*, San Francisco 1979, 188, speaks of ritual as 'the somatic embodiment of the experience of the holy' (quotation in GRIMES: *Beginnings in Ritual Studies* 269).

religion is rather a choreography of physical acts such as walking, bowing, kneeling, laying on of hands, etc.[6]

It would be going too far afield here to treat the question of what precisely is being indicated by the word 'religious'. It is sufficient to establish that in the experience of the religious we are dealing with values that in some unknown way are distributed above humans themselves. People experience a greater, a majestic but unapproachable dimension of existence. It involves the experience of the absolute. Thus the experience does not have to be oriented toward an approachable person in order to be denoted as religious. It is true, however, that religious experience comes to its fullest development when the transcendent, absolute reality also is given a name.

In several religions the transcendent, absolute reality is identified as a personal Thou: as Someone over and against us, who addresses us and toward whom we can direct ourselves. Here we touch upon the Christian dimension of ritual.

Christian ritual is oriented toward the revelation of a God who has shown Himself in history, first in Israel, but particularly in one of that nation: Jesus of Nazareth, who chose the side of the poor and the weak, who was ignominiously executed, and has become the first-born from the dead. According to the Christian faith, in Him we are saved. Christians believe that He gives the world, history and life its ultimate meaning. All Christian ritual is directed toward Jesus of Nazareth, in whom God, full of compassion, regards humankind, and in whom He is constantly at work for us. In and through this person, it is possible to approach God.

Thus in Christian ritual the cross stands central, either in the presentative symbolic language as especially in the Reformation, or as a central 'presentative' material symbol of what has happened in Jesus of Nazareth, as particularly in Roman Catholic liturgy. In the East, one finds the icon, with its infinitely varied representations in which the Christ-figure is none the less always central: a presentative symbol of what Christian ritual is aiming at. I use the word 'presentative' here with deliberation.[7] It means that Christian ritual does not purely look back to the past as past, but to that past as being contemporary and present in our tangible world and history. This all then occurs in the field of

---

[6] GRIMES: *Beginnings in Ritual Studies* 88.
[7] See Part 1, Chapter 1, 2.5 and Chapter 4, 1.

tension present in symbolism. In other words, one can speak of a comprehensive presence in and through tangible ritual, but this presence is not such that it coincides with the ritualised: one can also speak of a non-presence that compels further acts and a look toward the future. Presentative ritual thus gives real ground under foot, but at the same time is a marching-order toward the future.

In Christian ritual we encounter a symbolism in which one can speak of an inversion of values (*Umwertung aller Werte*). One does not realise this when one sees the cross only at the apex of church spires, as a decoration on the vestments of a person of authority or as a frequently hung wall ornament. The subversive character of the cross only forces itself upon one when realises it is an instrument of torture. The cross is like the gallows, the guillotine, the garrotte, the firing squad, the electric chair, the gas chamber.

In Christian ritual, the central figure is the man of sorrows, his eyes glazed in death. The oppressed in today's world rightly depict him with deep wounds and infinite sorrow in his eyes, as one cast aside. It was *because of* his suffering and death that God has exalted him and given him a name that is greater than any other name (Phil. 2:9). This executed man lives by God. Christian ritual expresses, in all sorts of nuances, variations and keys, that there is no salvation through anyone other than Jesus of Nazareth, who was crucified, but whom God has raised from the dead; no other name is given to us in which we – according to God's plan of redemption – are saved (Acts 4:10-12).

As noted, in Part 3 I will return at length to Christian ritual, and to its place and shape in our culture. But first, in Part 2, I will examine the subject of ritual and culture.

PART 2

RITUAL AND CULTURE

In Part 1 we sought to answer the question of what rituals are, what their place is, and what their characteristics are. Our concern there was a general outline of ritual. Rituals are a universal human given. They belong to the nature of our being human, as it were. But this does not mean that rituals are always the same in all times and all places. Already in the first part we every now and then unavoidably encountered developments that had to do with culturally determined elements in ritual. Rituals vary with cultures. Every culture gives shape to ritual in its own way.

In the second part I will now go further into the subject of 'ritual and culture'. First I will make clear in an inductive manner, on the basis of concrete examples, that rituals are always culturally determined (Chapter 1). In the following chapter I will attempt to provide a further description of what one can understand by the term 'culture', and indicate how ritual is closely related to culture, which has radical consequences for the dynamic of change in ritual (Chapter 2). In a separate chapter I will go into the theological problematic of inculturation (Chapter 3). Finally, in the last chapter of Part 2, I will discuss several specific research problems with regard to ritual and culture (Chapter 4).

CHAPTER 1

CULTURAL DETERMINATION OF RITUAL

In studying the lives of various peoples in the past and present one encounters an unimaginable variety of rituals. It is not possible to even come close to sketching out this wealth. What I do propose to do is to give some sense of the role of culture in determining the form of this ritual. This cultural determination begins very close to home.

1. THE PAST

First, one must note the enormous differences between past and present with regard to *the most ordinary of rituals*. Today there is little difference between the ritual by which a king or queen gets up in the morning, and that of his or her countrymen. But in the time of Louis XIV that was different.[1] If one wishes to situate this ritual, one must first realise the presentative symbolism of space. One needs to imagine the huge palace of Versailles, which is still visited by hundreds of thousands annually. In his power the French king stood above the nobility, the high clergy and the upper echelon of civil servants. This was symbolically expressed in the fact that no one was able to – and no one was permitted to – build a house like that of the king. The size, the magnificence and the decoration of the royal residence exceeded all else. One does not enter this structure directly; one must first cross a wide, vast courtyard. In doing so, one passes between two long wings, one to the right and one to the left. These were intended for ministers of state. At the end of the courtyard lies the actual palace. In this palace the spaces are so arranged that they enclose one another as squares within squares. The king and his court lived in the innermost space, on the first storey. It was there that the daily ritual of *le lever du roi* (the rising of the king) took place.

[1] A. LORENZER: *Das Konzil der Buchhalter*, with reference to N. ELIAS: *Die höfische Gesellschaft*, Darmstadt 1977, 126 ff.

Normally the king was awakened at eight in the morning. This was done by the First Valet, who slept at the foot of the royal bed. The king always slept with a small wig on his head; the protocol was that he might never be seen without a wig. The doors were opened by his valets. In the meantime one of them gave a sign to the royal Chaplain, the Grand Chamberlain and the First Chamberlain. A second valet warned the kitchen to prepare the royal breakfast, and a third stood by the door in order to admit those who had the privilege of being present at the rising of the king: these included (among others) the king's cousins, princes and princesses, the king's physician, the king's surgeon, the First Chamberlain, the Grand Officers of the Chamber and the Wardrobe, certain noble gentlemen, the Royal Herald and the Royal Steward, the Great Almoner, ministers and secretaries of state, officers of the royal bodyguard, and the marshals of France. This ritual of entering the royal bedroom was very precisely regulated. There were no less than six different *entrées*. The sixth entry had a special rank. These people did not come in through the main door, but through a side entrance. This *entrée* was intended for the sons of the king, including the royal bastards, with their families, and the powerful palace steward. These were the persons who could always come into the king's chamber, so long as he was not in a meeting, and could also remain in the chamber when he was ill. During the various entries the valets laid out the royal clothing. Two valets helped him out of his night-shirt, and helped him put on his day shirt, the one valet taking responsibility for the right sleeve and the other for the left. He was similarly assisted in putting on the remainder of his clothing and shoes. The king then stood up, and a dagger was belted on at his side. When the king was dressed, the First Almoner pronounced a prayer, while the rest of the courtiers waited in the great gallery behind the bedroom. It was a ritual that suited an absolute monarch. Anyone who before the Second Vatican Council experienced the ritual of a papal and episcopal pontifical Mass can somewhat imagine this ritual; the pope and bishops were also dressed in a pontifical manner, and in public, before the Mass, even changing their shoes.[2] But at the same time it is true these rituals seem to belong to another culture, so that they are alien to us. For instance, it is also known that people in France in that time found it a most normal matter that the king

---

[2] The changing of shoes had its origin in the time when the pope or bishops arrived by horse, with riding boots.

conducted important state business in the presence of the court while sitting on the toilet.[3]

There are also great differences between the past and the present with regard to *more central rituals*. I will give two examples. An important part of the baptismal ritual in the early Church was the renouncing of Satan and sealing a covenant with Christ. Just before baptism the person receiving baptism turned to the west. In the Greco-Roman culture the west, where the sun set, represented decline, destruction and death. Hades, the realm of the dead, also lay to the west. Facing the west, the baptisand renounced Satan. The renunciation of Satan was coupled with a more plastic rite: the person spit toward the west. It is a well-established custom for people to spit at persons or things they despise. In the time of Tertullian people were so familiar with the symbolism of spitting that *despuere*, the Latin verb for spitting, was used as a synonym for contempt or loathing.[4] After the renunciation of Satan the baptisand turned to the east, the place where the sun rises. The east is the direction of hope, life and light. He now bound himself with Christ, who is the Rising Sun. Neither the experience of turning to the west or to the east, nor the gesture of spitting in contempt, which were so familiar to the Romans, can be found in our culture.

Another example comes from marriage, which receives a extraordinary range of shapes in various cultures, so vast that it is difficult to survey its various developments briefly.[5] The Romans married in the presence of family, by the man and woman exchanging their mutual consent. Until into the fourth century Christians married in the same way. They performed the marriage rituals in the ordinary way, within

---

[3] A. HAHN: 'Kultische und säkulare Riten' 53.

[4] TERTULLIANUS: *Ad Nationes* 1, 10: CC 1, 25. See F. DÖLGER: *Der Exorzismus im altchristlichen Taufritual. Eine religionsgeschichtliche Studie*, Paderborn 1909, 118.

[5] See more extensively G. LUKKEN: 'De geschiedenis in vogelvlucht', in A. BLIJLEVENS & G. LUKKEN (eds.): *In goede en kwade dagen*, Baarn 1991, 41-43 (= *Werkmap (voor) Liturgie* 12 (1978) 369-373). Further: K. RITZER: *Formen, Riten und religiöses Brauchtum der Eheschliessung in den christlichen Kirchen des ersten Jahrtausends* (Liturgiewissenschaftliche Quellen und Forschungen 38), Münster 1982[2]; J.B. MOLIN & P. MUTEMBE: *Le rituel du mariage en France du XII au XVI siècle* (Théologie historique 26), Paris 1974; G. DUBY: *Le chevalier, la femme et le prêtre. Le mariage dans la France féodale*, Paris 1981; P. ARIÈS: 'La naissance du mariage occidental', in *La Maison-Dieu* (1982) 149, 107-112; K. STEVENSON: *Nuptial Blessing. A Study of Christian Marriage Rites*, Londen 1982.

the family circle. An ecclesiastical ritual did develop of veiling the bridal couple, or only the bride, before the actual exchange of vows, but it was not regarded as obligatory. Until the end of the 11th century the marriage rites within the family circle remained the real marriage ceremony. Under the influence of German culture the primary act was the conveyance of the bride by her father to the bridegroom, after which the couple entered the bridal chamber. Sometimes one saw the priest participate in the ritual of the handing over of the bride. Slowly ecclesiastical interest in the closure of marriages increased, and the rites of marriage began to be performed either in front of the church building (where other public contracts were also closed) or in the church itself, before the altar. These rites were not obligatory, Thus one has the famous painting by Jan van Eyck from 1434 of a bridal couple in a bedroom. The man and woman have joined hands, while at the same time the man has raised his right hand, a gesture that people in the Middle Ages also made in courts of law. This painting depicts the ritual of sealing the marriage of the Arnolfinis, an Italian couple who lived in Brugge for many years. They are apparently concluding the marriage at home, in the bridal chamber, without the presence of an official from the municipality or of a representative of the Church. You can indeed see in the mirror that two persons are just entering the room. They are apparently the witnesses. The man is dressed in impressive clothing, and has a wide-brimmed hat on his head. It is notable that he has no shoes on. This is a sign that the bridal chamber is a sacred place. From this – and from still other details – one can conclude that the painting depicts the sacramental sealing of a marriage between two Christians.[6] Only in 1563 was the ecclesiastical marriage liturgy prescribed. Marriage before a municipal official developed parallel with that. In our own time both the church and civil marriage ceremonies are still undergoing rapid development. The ritual of marriage remains extremely sensitive to cultural determination.

2. THE PRESENT

In the present there is a great diversity in rituals at the same time. One *everyday ritual* is social calling. In Japan a traditional ritual that is alien

---

[6] W. SWAAN: *Glorie der gotiek*, Amerongen 1977, 113 and 116.

to us is still very much practised.[7] When someone wants to receive a good friend, he leads him to a room that is called the *zashiki*. In the course of this he has his friend pass through a number of rooms that usually lie one behind another. The richer the host is, the more successive rooms that will be passed through. The host does not lead his visitor through all these rooms to show off his wealth, because the rooms involved are as good as empty. He does it because he can reflect the rank of his visitor in this way. The more distinguished the guest, the more rooms he must pass through. Finally the guest arrives in the actual room where he is offered the place of honour, and the host goes to sit in the lowest place. In this way, in a very sensory and spatial manner, the host makes clear that he is placing his home at the disposal of his guest.

Cultural factors shape all sorts of everyday rituals. In France it is customary to shake one another's hands before every meal. The frequency of this ritual differs among French, Germans, Americans and Dutch.[8] In our Western culture we nod our heads up and down for 'yes' and shake our heads from one side to the other for 'no'. But Abyssinians do it differently; they say 'no' by moving the head only to the right, and 'yes' by moving the head up and to the back, and lifting the eyebrows. In Western Europe it is not customary that you clap along when others are applauding you. To do so would indicate immodesty. A Russian does join in when others applaud him; for him not to do so would be improper. Among us sitting cross-legged, 'Indian style', or squatting down is not really a relaxed position. In other cultures, for instance in the Middle East, it is. Maori women in New Zealand learn from the time they are children to walk with emphatic hip movements. You see that also, for that matter, in Latin America. But what is a normal manner of walking there is regarded as provocative in Western Europe and North America. And while on the topic of walking: some Russians from the steppes walk in what is for us a very unusual manner, alternatively moving their left arm and left leg forward at the same time, and then the right leg and right arm.[9]

---

[7] M. HAMMAD: 'Définition syntaxique du topos', in *Le Bulletin* 3 (1979) 10, 25-27.

[8] D. DE LOOF: 'A Comparison of Selected German and American Emblems', in *Kodikas Code* 3 (1981) 101-102.

[9] Examples from FORTMANN: *Heel de mens* 158 ff.

With regard to *more central rituals*, among us the ritual of marriage is limited to the actual day of exchanging the marriage vows; we have the performance of the marriage before a civil clerk or judge, and the church ceremony, possibly preceded by a 'bachelor party' and almost always followed by a wedding reception and a honeymoon trip. But in Africa the ritual of marriage is a long process, which moves on step by step. It includes the choice of the partner, the submission and approval of an official marriage proposal, a trial period for those who are going to marry, the actions through which the man and woman acquire the social status of husband and wife in the eyes of the groups present, the bringing of the bride to the home of the groom, festivities, living together as man and wife, and the birth of the first child. In the view of Africans the marriage ritual is thus much more than just the exchange of vows between the partners.[10] Thus the marriage ritual can differ widely from culture to culture. In Vientiane in Laos the exchange of rings is unknown as a marriage ceremony; rather, the groom ties a cord around the bride's wrists. Several years ago a missionary from Flores, in Indonesia, told how he had assisted in the performance of a marriage as the official representative of the church, using the official Roman Catholic marriage ritual. But subsequently it appeared that the couple did not experience this liturgy as a real wedding ceremony, because the bride had appeared without the customary festive clothing, had not had the proper hairdo, and the dowry was not handed over at home. How would people be able to know that she was married? The groom shared this opinion.

Another example is cremation. In the West the body is simply left behind in the auditorium of the crematorium after the memorial or prayer service, and burned in an oven in the absence of next of kin. But among Hindus cremation takes place outdoors and is surrounded by an extensive ritual. However, in contrast to India, in the West outdoor cremation is generally forbidden. Yet Hindus in The Netherlands attempt to remain as close as possible to their own ritual. They gather at the funeral home, where the *pandit*, or house priest, preaches and the family prays.

---

[10] 'Naar een verinheemsing van het christelijk huwelijksritueel. Document van het symposion van de bisschoppenconferenties van Afrika en Madagascar, Acara September 15, 1976', in *Archief van de Kerken* 32 (1977) 725-729 (Source: *Documentation Catholique* April 17, 1977); P. ROUILLARD: 'Liturgies en Afrique', in *La Maison-Dieu* (1977) 130, 129-146; TH. REY-MERMET: *Ce que Dieu a uni... Le mariage chrétien hier et aujourd'hui*, Paris 1974, 265-284.

There they light a *dia*, a small dish with a wick of absorbent cotton drenched in pure butter, and pour out a copper bowl of water, an offering to the deceased. The cremation itself is led by the oldest son, who has shaved the hair from his head. After the deceased is laid out and washed, while mantras are being said the *pandit* places five egg-shaped balls formed of rice flour, honey, milk, butter and sesame seed around the deceased, as offerings to him. The components of these balls symbolise the original elements of the creation, earth, water, air, fire and ether. People enter the crematorium in procession, led by the oldest son in a loincloth. After further preaching and singing, the oldest son lights a *dia*, with which he walks around the coffin five times, and touches the mouth of the deceased. Traditionally this is the beginning of the outdoor cremation; here that takes place in a symbolic manner. Subsequently people say their farewells, and lay grains of rice and flower petals on the coffin. Then the coffin is accompanied to the oven. The cremation as such has deep symbolic significance. It is intended to allow the body to merge back into the original elements.

With regard to the present, one can also point to the differences among *subcultures* within one and the same culture. For instance, we are familiar with the peculiar rituals of high society: precisely because there are these differences, night-club comics can amuse their audience with them. Youth have their own rituals. What applies for the young can also be seen with all sorts of groups and categories in our society. How small the geographic distance between different rituals can be, is strikingly sketched by Van Kilsdonk in an article on greetings. 'When as a village child I visited the city – in my case Nijmegen – for the first time, more or less hand in hand with my mother, so far as I can remember it was not the high and also more stately houses that impressed me, nor the trams in the traffic, but the strange observation that here people did not greet one another. For me our greeting one another in the village streets was so much second nature that with every passer-by hastening along the pavement I almost had the feeling that I had to bite back a greeting or we would be given a cold stare. Thus the city is a world where people don't greet one another. A village stops being a village, in a social sense, when people no longer say good-day to one another.'[11]

[11] J. VAN KILSDONK: 'Groeten in Amsterdam', in *De Bazuin* 65 (1982) 15 (April 9), 2; see also IDEM: *Met het licht van jouw ogen … zegen mij*, Amstelveen 1982, 32.

It is remarkable that people are often not conscious of how rituals are culturally determined, right down to ordinary body movements. Rituals are generally seen as self-evident and natural patterns of action.[12] It is for that reason that we experience the rituals of other cultures as all the more strange and incomprehensible. We often have the inclination to regard rituals from other cultures as suspect, primitive, barbaric and exotic. Europeans are not the only ones who react that way. The response of the native Americans to our use of pocket handkerchiefs was to think that Europeans collected their mucus and carried it around in their pockets.[13] A Chinese who visited the United States described the people there as wild and bad: they pay no attention to the moral precepts of Confucius and the Elders; they do not pay honour to their ancestors, but claim to be wiser than their fathers and grandfathers. Worse yet, men and women are so shameless as to walk arm in arm along the streets in broad daylight! And dinner parties are unbecoming because a man there must be prepared to shake the hand of a strange woman, offer her his arm, and even converse with her.[14] Since film and television regularly confront us with the rituals of other peoples, knowledge of these is no longer the preserve of explorers, missionaries and scholars, and the realisation of how culture determines ritual is growing.

Cultural prescriptions effect even the most *elementary nature symbols* such as earth, water, air and fire.[15] One might think that water is the same symbol everywhere and throughout the ages. But that would be mistaken, and is the result of an incorrect and all too mechanical view of our own perception. Our perception is in no way like a general who oversees everything surrounding him. Even the objective world of the natural sciences appears to be an illusion. For a long time people had no understanding of the law of gravity, until Newton formulated it. That meant that people were suddenly able to perceive natural phenomena in a different way. Laws of nature have to do with the interface between reality and perceptive consciousness. We can not perceive naked reality.

---

[12] BELL: *Ritual Theory* 94-104 and 109; IDEM: *Ritual. Perspectives* 167-169.

[13] BELL: *Ritual. Perspectives* 260-261, with reference to S. GREENBLATT: 'Filthy Rites', in *Daedalus* 111 (1982) 3, 1-16.

[14] BELL: *Ritual. Perspectives* 260-261, with reference to R.D. ARKUSH & L.O. LEE (eds.): *Land without Ghosts. Chinese Impressions of America from the Mid-Nineteenth Century to the Present*, Berkeley 1989, 16 and 55-56.

[15] JETTER: *Symbol und Ritual* 58 ff.; CHAUVET: *Du symbolique au symbole* 56 ff.

Our perception is always coloured and limited by our culture. Nor are our 'news reports' and 'documentaries' ever completely objective. They are always coloured by the individual's perspective, assumptions and selection. In fact we know that full well. An accident is perceived in different ways by different people, so that we recognise that differing testimony about it is not per se evidence of intent to deceive. In the same way, our perception is always strongly defined by the paradigms of our own culture. It is strongly culturally determined. That is also true for nature symbols such as water. The way in which we regard, experience and interpret water varies in from culture to culture. It is like our perception of a landscape, which varies constantly, according to the hour of the day and the weather, or the way the same decor varies according to the lighting. In the same way, people perceive water out of differing socio-cultural backgrounds. Pure, undetermined perception simply does not exist. Our perception is always thoroughly pre-structured by the socio-cultural milieu in which we live. The Eskimos are a striking example of this: they perceive snow differently than we do. This is demonstrated by the fact that they use dozens of words for snow. The cultural network from which they perceive enables them to perceive the realm of snow more precisely, differently, and with more nuance than we do.[16] In the same way Dutch has different words to express the distinctions between pouring rain, driving rain, periodic rain, rain squalls, drizzle, rising and thick mists, and people of the Sahara have various words for the means of desert transport par excellence, the camel. It is thus never the case that we can perceive reality without the intervention of culture. Reality is only present for us as a construct arising from the network of the culture in which we live.[17] Thus a natural symbol such as water is taken up in human history through the various ways in which people interpret it: the natural element becomes an historic given that enters again and again in to varying cultures. In this manner the symbol itself also changes constantly. Thus symbols are transitory, in the sense that they participate in our history, within which cultural modifications continually take place. In this respect, certain symbols also can disappear, and new symbols can arise. What is said here of the symbol applies a fortiori for symbolic

---

[16] E. CLAES: *Het netwerk en de nevelvlek. Semiotische studies* (Argo-studies 1), Leuven 1979, 4-15.
[17] CHAUVET: *Du symbolique au symbole* 19.

acts and symbolic language, the historic involvement and determination of which appeals to most of us much more directly.

For a solid perspective on ritual it is important to delve more deeply into this. I will do this from *semiotics*. In Part 1 reference was already made to the distinction between *sign* and *symbol*. I indicated that one of the characteristic differences between the two was that symbols speak for themselves, while signs are based on understandings or negotiation. The sign has something arbitrary about it, and rests much more on agreement. When this are no longer clear, people must then replace it with another sign. One can think of traffic signs that do not produce the desired results because they are not clear. With the symbol as such it is a different matter. The Ur-symbol of water can not be replaced by another symbol just like that. The symbol is not 'makeable', and was there long before I was. I can not become its master. Thus it is not random. There is a connection between what I see, hear and so forth (the expression) and that which it evokes (the content). But none of this implies that the symbol is purely 'natural' and unchanging. It is always part of a broader whole that interprets the symbol through actualising one or another of its symbolic potentials.[18] One might say that a symbol is not 'natural', but is always 'cultural'. It is to some extent determined by culture. Symbols are thus decidedly also founded on human creativity and convention. One settles in to them in a certain culture, they 'fit' and are 'fitting'. Particularly the use of the concept of symbol in the Peircian sense makes us conscious of that, as appeared in Part 1. Symbols also have something institutional about them, so much so that in Christian culture people can speak of the institution of the sacraments.[19] Also, although one can thus speak of a giveness in the symbol that one must definitely take into account, it in part receives its form and content from the concrete interchange among the subjects in a particular culture. The symbol is always part of a greater whole in which it assumes a particular place, which can vary according to this whole. For this reason therefore no really universal symbolic system exists. One must even acknowledge that the fundamental symbols such as earth, water, air and fire do not function as such in all cultures, or in any case that they receive a different significance. For instance in China air is not

[18] VERGOTE: *Het huis is nooit af* 147-148.
[19] VERGOTE: *Het huis is nooit af* 150-153.

among the basic symbols, but wood and metal are.[20] So it appears that the meaning of symbols is to an important extent in part determined by the way in which they function in a culture in their concrete expressions (denoted in semiotics as 'enunciations'). In that sense one can say that people can only understand them from the 'enunciative praxis' of a culture. In this connection I would also want to refer back to what I noted previously with regard to material culture.[21] The symbolic referential power of material objects is always strongly determined by the peculiar place that they take within the culture in which they function. Objects have their place, and receive their meaning through the enunciative praxis itself within the culture in which they are used. Therefore, as separate objects they have the capacity to suddenly evoke the whole of such a culture. The extent to which symbols, symbolic acts and symbolic languages are interwoven with the total culture is undoubtedly one of the reasons that having an understanding and feeling for rituals from other cultures demands so much empathy and investigation.

[20] J. COURTÉS: *Du lisible au visible. Initiation à la sémiotique du texte et de l'image*, Brussel 1995, 21.
[21] Part 1, Chapter 1, 2.5.

CHAPTER 2

THE CLOSE RELATION BETWEEN RITUAL AND CULTURE

In this chapter I will first attempt to give a characterisation of the term
'culture', and work out what the relationship between ritual and culture
is. This will reveal that ritual is closely connected with culture, and even
occupies a central place in it. With this we encounter a tension that presents itself in this context: precisely because ritual is so strongly characterised by repetition, the question arises: when cultures change, must
one hold fast to the old rituals, or is innovation possible? In fact, this
question touches on the issue of ritual change, or, to put it otherwise,
the theme of the unavoidable and necessary inculturation of ritual.

1. CULTURE: AN ATTEMPT TO FURTHER CHARACTERISE THE TERM

The rather recent discipline of cultural anthropology has punctured the
old myth about culture, and worked out the concept in a manner which
rather differs from the traditional view.[1] In the traditional view culture
was synonymous with extensive knowledge and understanding. A man
with culture was someone who knew many things well. Moreover, that
knowing was primarily logical/rational, abstract, intellectual. The intellectuals in particular were considered to be the bearers of any culture.
This reductive view arose from a Eurocentrism that had a preference for
the Greek *logos*, and undervalued other forms of life, acting and thinking. Through ethnological studies, beginning from the early years of the
last century, this concept of culture was thrown into a state of crisis.

---

[1] C. DI SANTE: 'Cultura e liturgia', in SARTORE & TRIACCA: *Nuovo dizionario di
liturgia* 71-92. For this section see G. LUKKEN: 'Inculturatie van de liturgie. Theorie en
praktijk', in J. LAMBERTS (ed.): *Liturgie en inculturatie. Verslagboek van het twaalfde
liturgiecolloquium van het Liturgisch Instituut van de K.U. Leuven – oktober 1995* (Nikè-
reeks 37), Leuven/Amersfoort 1996, 15-30 – IDEM: 'Inculturation de la liturgie. Théorie
et pratique', in *Questions Liturgiques* 77 (1996) 1-2, 10-39 and in J. LAMBERTS (ed.):
Liturgie et inculturation. Liturgy and Inculturation (Textes et Études Liturgiques/ Studies
in Liturgy 14), Leuven 1996, 10-39.

That is the negative delineation of culture – but what then is culture, seen positively? It is not so simple to precisely define this new concept of culture that rises above the Eurocentric myth. One finds quite a lot of definitions in cultural anthropology, even many times the more than 150 definitions that the American anthropologists Kroeber and Kluckhohn collected in 1952[2] The concept is too complex to be defined in a few words. It therefore seems preferable to indicate a number of elements over which scholars are in agreement:[3]

a. A first important element is that the cultural does not involve only the rational, the intellectual, but every human practise; from the practise of the language through the preparation of food, construction of houses, agricultural practices, establishment of temples, prayer to a divinity or divinities, etc. Culture deals with the way in which language, the body, space and time are used. The language forms a specific, coherent entity of its own in every culture. The rules for conduct and the social mobility of the body, particularly the face and hands, always form another discrete whole. The design and use of space also form another peculiar, coherent entity. Finally, the way time is apportioned reveals the hierarchy of human activities: the relations among work, free time and time spent together with others, in meals, meetings, feasts, etc.[4]

The new attitude in ethnology that one should not make a distinction within a culture between the cultures of the elite and of the mass of people is closely connected with this vision of culture. When one speaks of popular culture, one must not think in terms of this division, but realise that what is being referred to is the commonplace and everyday culture that people share with one another, often unconsciously. It is however the case that often a certain tension continues to exist between the prescribed order and practices as they are performed.[5]

---

[2] A.F. KROEBER & C. KLUCKHOHN: *Culture. A Critical Review of Concepts and Definitions* (Papers of the Peabody Museum, 1952, 47), New York 1995. See P. KLOOS: *Culturele antropologie. Een inleiding*, Assen 1995 (sixth revised edition), 16-19.

[3] I here follow the line of DI SANTE: 'Cultura e liturgia', supplementing this article on a number of points.

[4] M.-C. KOK-ESCALLE: *Instaurer une culture par l'enseignement de l'histoire de France 1876-1912. Contribution à une sémiotique de la culture*, Berne/Frankfurt am Main/New York/Paris 1989, 10-11.

[5] POST: 'Religieuze volkscultuur en liturgie' 31-39. See also Part 3, Chapter 7, 3.

b. Culture extends beyond what are generally termed the arts. The concept is still often limited to them. The French have a minister, and the Dutch a secretary of state for culture. It is clear that their responsibilities are more limited to the arts, than inclusive of all the areas mentioned above.

c. The cultural is not the opposite of the natural. One does not have the natural man first, and then the cultural man. In reality we are always dealing with a cultural man. His nature and culture are so deeply interwoven with one another in this state that one often thinks of something as natural, when in fact it is cultural. For example, our manner of walking and sitting, of rising and going to bed are not natural, but culturally determined. The same is true, for instance, for those behaviours which we term typically male or female.

d. Human beings create culture, but the opposite is also true: human beings are created as humans by culture. Thus: without mankind, no culture, but equally, without culture, no mankind.[6]

e. The cultural is not univocal. Therefore one should never speak of only one culture, but there are always many cultures, both in succession to one another (diachronic) and simultaneously (synchronic). No one culture thus has absolute value, and every culture is only relative.

f. Symbols play a decisive role in culture. Culture is thus not purely a matter of mediation by instrumental signs, but of mediation through symbols in the true sense of the word. With Chauvet and others, one can correctly designate culture as a symbolic order.[7]

---

[6] C. GEERTZ: 'Impact of the Concept of Culture on the Concept of Man', in J.R. PLATT (ed): New Views of the Nature of Man, Chicago 1965, 116.

[7] CHAUVET: Du symbolique au symbole; IDEM: 'L'avenir du sacramentel', in J. MOINGT: Les sacrements de Dieu, Paris 1987, 81-106; IDEM: Symbole et sacrement; IDEM: 'Ritualité et théologie'. See also D.S. AMALORPAVADASS: 'Theological reflections on inculturation (Part 1)', in Studia Liturgica 20 (1990) 41. One finds the concept of 'symbolic order' earlier in J. Lacan. For this see for instance A. MOOIJ: Taal en verlangen, Meppel 1975 and P. MOYAERT: 'Het ik en zijn identificaties', in DE RUIJTER a.o.: Totems en trends 52-77.

g. Their culture is the only starting point for really learning to know people. In this process ritual practices, more than any other cultural practices, are able to reveal who people actually are. This coheres with the fact that rituals are among the most deep-seated human activities. Ritual is in one way or another the matrix out of which other cultural activities such as art, medicine and education gradually emerged, differentiating themselves from one another[8]

h. One point which is very important in connection with out topic: On the one hand one must distinguish culture from sectors such as economics, politics, social life and religion. Economics, for instance, is simply a separate sector, with its own laws and competence. But on the other hand the economic sector is also a component of culture, and certainly to the extent that it also functions in a symbolic manner. Culture as such is not economics, but the way in which we deal with money and goods is certainly part of our culture. The same is true for the other sectors. Every culture is thus ultimately all-inclusive.[9] After all, there is also a deep interrelationship among the various levels of economics, politics, social structures and religion. Thus radical cultural changes can be caused by changes in social-economic structures. By the same token, the manipulation, control and exploitation of people by social-economic-political systems, for instance, will likewise be accompanied by cultural domination.

i. Closely related to the foregoing is the fact that on the one hand people can distinguish religion as a separate sector alongside that of culture, as is also the case for economics, politics and social life. But on the other hand religion, as a symbolic order, is likewise a part of the total culture. As such, it is even a very central component of the culture. In turn, ritual takes a central place in religion. Thus, religious ritual – the cultus – is the heart of culture, its deepest and most dynamic element. Anthropologists, and also representatives of all sorts of other disciplines, have repeatedly pointed to the fact that religious rites play a central role in every culture. This coheres with

[8] GRIMES: *Deeply into the Bone* 13.
[9] See also AMALORPAVADASS: 'Theological reflections on inculturation (Part 1)' 41 and 44. The Second Vatican Council also employed a broad concept of culture: see *Pastoral Constitution on the Church in the Modern World Gaudium et Spes*, Città del Vaticano 1965, no. 53.

the irreplaceable and deep-seated place rituals – and in particular religious rituals – occupy in every culture. As a religious expression, the cultus is a central, integrating element in culture, but it is also true that culture in turn conditions the practise of the cultus in a very profound way. I will here limit myself to a reference to the abundant literature on this.[10]

j. The various elements of a culture do not come together randomly, but form a coherent structure. Every culture has its own fabric of relations, and has a characteristic internal coherence. Every culture has its own specific symbolic order. Therefore cultures always possess peculiar qualities by which they can be distinguished one from another. An important consequence of this inner structural coherence is that any change at one point in the culture will have its repercussions for the whole system, which must then restructure itself globally. For theology, this means that changes in social, political or economic life have their repercussions for religion, and thus

[10] Some literature: M. BARNARD: 'Dynamiek van cultus en cultuur', in BARNARD & POST (eds.): *Ritueel bestek* 47-62; A. BERGAMINI: 'Culto', in SARTORE & TRIACCA: *Nuovo dizionario di liturgia* 333-340; *Catechism of the Catholic Church*, Città del Vaticano 1994, 1204 ff.; COHEN: *De cirkel van het leven*; *Culte et culture: La Maison-Dieu* (1984) no. 159; VAN DER HART: *Rituelen in psychotherapie*; VAN DER HART a.o.: *Afscheidsrituelen in psychotherapie*; HEIMBROCK: *Gottesdienst: Spielraum des Lebens*; HEIMBROCK & BOUDEWIJNSE (eds.): *Current Studies on Rituals*; G.J. HOENDERDAAL: *Riskant spel. Liturgie in een geseculariseerde wereld*, Den Haag 1977, Chapter VII (Cult and Culture); LANE: *The Rites of Rulers*; LUIJS: 'Taal, teken, ritueel'; LUKKEN: D*e onvervangbare weg van de liturgie*; IDEM: *Geen leven zonder rituelen*; G. MARTINEZ: 'Cult and culture. The Structure of the Evolution of Worship', in *Worship* 64 (1990) 406-433; MITCHELL: 'The Amen-Corner: the Coming Revolution in Ritual Studies'; MOINGT: *Enjeux du rite dans la modernité*; NIEUWKOOP: *De drempel over*; P. POST: 'Het verleden in het spel? Volksreligieuze rituelen tussen cultus en cultuur', in *Jaarboek voor liturgie-onderzoek* 7 (1991) 79-124; D. POWER: 'Cult to Culture. The Liturgical Fundation of Theology', in *Worship* 54 (1980) 482-495; RAND: *Ritueel*; *Reclaiming our rites*; *Rituelen: Skript*; DE RUIJTER a.o.: *Totems en trends*; DI SANTE: 'Cultura e liturgia'; A. SCHEER: 'Het dilemma: cultuur-cultus', in *Jaarboek voor liturgie-onderzoek* 7 (1991) 159-168; IDEM: 'Liturgiewetenschap: cultus en cultuur in dialectiek', in *Praktische Theologie* 22 (1995) 80-99; TERRIN: 'Antropologia culturale'. See also ZITNIK: *Sacramenta*.
      The central role of ritual also prevails in 'popular culture'. See in this connection D. EBERHARD: *Kult und Kultur. Volksreligiosität und kulturelle Identität am Beispiel der Maria-Lionza-Kultes in Venezuela* (Beiträge zur Soziologie und Sozialkunde Lateinamerikas 23), München 1983; W. HARTZINGER: *Religion und Brauch*, Darmstadt 1992; POST: 'Religieuze volkscultuur en liturgie' 40-49.

also on liturgy. If that does not happen, it means that the coherence of the symbolic order has been broken, and condemns religion to marginalisation. Was that not precisely the drama of Western theology in the past centuries, a drama which is still not over? Another consequence of the structural coherence within cultures is that one can only understand a culture well when one makes a point of perceiving the culture in its totality. Achieving a basic understanding of one of its sectors only makes sense if that happens for the other sectors as well. This makes investigation of cultures far from simple.

k. Every culture is exposed to the danger of becoming manipulative. This danger is related to the question of how power is distributed. The more power is divided up and shared out together, the smaller that risk is. The more power is in the hands of a few, the more the culture is in danger of becoming an ideology, and instrument of domination. As a cultural phenomenon, religious ritual, including liturgy, contains this risk too; liturgy can become an ideology and instrument of power that oppresses people. If this occurs, they can no longer express their deepest religious feelings and convictions, and become religiously frustrated or search for other ways, for their own religious subculture.

l. Finally, it is extremely important to recognise that every culture is a *dynamic* fabric of relations. There is a constant process of creation and transformation. New practices are integrated, and existing practices ossify and are dropped.[11] It is precisely this dynamic process of rejection and creation of particular practices that makes a culture specific: the coherence of culture arises in part through this process of integration, exclusion and ongoing rearrangement of the hierarchy of values.

2. RITUALS CHANGE WITH CULTURE

Rituals are closely tied up with the community, the place and time from which they arose and in which they function. They are interconnected with certain social-cultural areas. They reflect their era, and are even

---

[11] KOK-ESCALLE: *Instaurer une culture* 10 and 15.

subject to wear as time goes by.[12] Even though they may deal with the same universal events such as birth, marriage, death, greetings and saying farewells, rituals are seldom universal. One can not simply transplant African rituals to Europe, or vice versa. When that does happen, they remain alien for the participants, and easily lose their vital significance. The more universal a ritual becomes, the greater is the danger of this loss of intensity and import. In recent church history Western rituals of Christendom were exported to mission fields outside Europe. The consequence was, for instance, processions in which Africans walked with as much self-constraint as the most staid Europeans. In doing so they deny their own nature: in their movements Africans simply are not Europeans; in a procession they dance.

Because rituals are strongly socio-culturally determined, they are also extremely characteristic of a certain community in a particular time. If, for instance, you can understand the initiation rites of a particular primitive community from the inside out, you have penetrated deeply into the soul of such a community. Their peculiar identity is expressed in these rites. This has the consequence that rituals also enforce divisions. In and through its ritual this community distinguishes itself from the others. Rituals therefore also often mark geographic boundaries. The remark of Andrieu, the famous publisher of the *Ordines Romani* and the *Pontificalia*, which are invaluable for the study of Western liturgy from the past, is interesting here: 'That the border between Poland and Russia was never successfully erased… is largely due to the great difference between the Latin and Byzantine rites. It is largely due to their liturgy that the Poles have preserved their national identity, despite all attempts at amalgamation and absorption that had the benefit of the ethnic relationship. For this same reason, after World War I there were constant difficulties which arose between the government in Warsaw and the Ruthenian Catholics of the Byzantine rite, who were incorporated into Poland at that time.'[13]

The great world religions give form to the ritual element, each in their own way, and to a great extent this defines their identity. Quite correctly

---

[12] JETTER: *Symbol und Ritual* 58 ff., 98 ff., 149.
[13] M. ANDRIEU: *Les Ordines Romani du haut moyen-âge* (Spicilegium Sacrum Lovaniense 23), Leuven 1948, XV, note 1.

therefore, people normally visualise the characteristics of such religions in terms of their ritual. Thus we find it typical of Muslims that they go to a mosque and pray to Allah. You have long rows of men before you, who kneel down on their heels and repeatedly bow forward. And at the entrance of the mosque you have the shoes that they took off before going in. Likewise, it is characteristic that only males are present in the mosque; the women remain outside, and are veiled. Then there is Ramadan, the Islamic month of fasting. Christians are characterised by the cross, the Bible from which they read and are read to, their churches, and the rites there around the altar and baptismal font. Grimes aptly remarks that the differences between religious traditions are just as much choreographic and kinaesthetic as they are conceptual and doctrinal. It is even the case that the choreographic and kinaesthetic elements are more fundamental and lasting, and define religious competence more than verbal elements.[14]

It is also obvious that the rituals of the great world religions are socio-culturally determined. Yet that is not self-evident to everyone. One here runs up against the tension between one's own identity, one's own *Anliegen*, and the socially-culturally determined ritual forms in which and through which this peculiar *Anliegen* is expressed and performed. This tension is peculiar to all ritual, but it comes to the fore in religion in a particularly intense way. There the original rituals are sometimes declared sacrosanct in their concrete design. Fundamentalism easily concentrates on rituals, because these mediate their origins in such an intense way, and because it is precisely in ritual that the element of repetition plays such a vital role. First and foremost this involves the holy books themselves, as ritualised word. For fundamentalist Muslims, Christians and Jews the message is identified with the letter of the Koran or Bible in this way. For them their scripture has an ultimate sacred status in its entirety, as absolutely and literally true. This results in an overspecification of the sacred, which threatens to disgrace sanctity itself.[15] For such a position, any confrontation with other cultures unavoidably leads to insistent questions. For instance, Islam in the West is in this way confronted with the question of whether it is essential for Islam that women wear a headscarf. Fundamentalist Jews encounter the question of whether circumcision, which is only performed

---

[14] GRIMES: *Marrying and Burying* 249.
[15] RAPPAPORT: *Ritual and Religion in the Making of Humanity* 489-490.

on males, does not in the final analysis relegate women to a second-class status in Judaism. Modern Jews therefore argue for having both boys and girls initiated into the covenant of the people of Israel on the eighth day, and if the child is a boy he is then at the same time circumcised.[16]

The tension between ritual fundamentalism and openness for change in rites is to be found very early in the history of Christianity. One of the first serious conflicts played itself out around rites. The question was to what extent pagans who became Christians must conform to Jewish rites. Must they be circumcised? May they eat meat that is forbidden to Jews? This conflict was settled at the first Church council, held at Jerusalem (Acts 15). Pagans who became Christians did not have to be circumcised; for them baptism was sufficient. And the ritual prescriptions with regard to eating meat were altered. One may, James said, not impose any unnecessary burdens.

This was an inconceivably important decision, which also had a deep emotional impact. The conflict between Peter and Paul was actualised at a later point in time, when Peter still appeared to go along with those who held a fundamentalist standpoint, and kept aloof from table fellowship with Christians of pagan background (Gal. 2:11-14). Paul then 'withstood him to his face' (Gal. 2:11).

Christians thus do not have to profess their faith in cultural forms which are alien to them. From its beginning Christianity has been open to all cultures, and is oriented universally. This affects the rituals in a very radical way, because it is precisely in and through these that Christianity is experienced in such an irreplaceable and intense way. Christian rituals are not absolutely linked with a particular culture. On the contrary: in Christianity there is a fundamental openness for ritual renewal.

Yet one can also point to ritual fundamentalism and an ossification of rites in Christianity. The Roman Catholic church has just left behind a long period in which existing and historically determined ritual forms were fixed. Between the Council of Trent (1545-1563) and the Second Vatican Council (1963: Constitution on liturgy) the Roman liturgy was an inflexible whole. For four long centuries the official liturgy remained almost unaltered.[17] The actual culture, however,

---

[16] HOFFMAN: 'How Ritual Means' 96-97, with reference to D. POLISH (ed.): *Rabbi's Manual*, New York 1988.

[17] For nuances to this, see J. HERMANS: *Benedictus XIV en de liturgie*, Brugge/Boxtel 1979.

was undergoing far-reaching changes during this period. That which cannot happen fair, however, happens foul. The new culture forced its way in, to closely envelope the sacrosanct block of the official liturgy: the style of church buildings was culturally determined, there was contemporary music (from Bach and Mozart to Perosi and Tippett, and that was true also for the songs of the people), and the more distant accoutrements of the liturgy took the forms of the baroque, Enlightenment, Romanticism and the neo-styles: one can think of the clothing, the decoration, the images, the interior design of the church buildings. But the official liturgy – aside from the sermon – remained inviolable. It became isolated. The link between liturgy and life was broken, and the liturgy as such lost its social relevance. Only by treating it as a sort of mnemonic could the believers make a connection with actual life: in participating the liturgy they expressed their intention to live as true Christians, and by renewing this intention from time to time, it remained virtually valid in ordinary life. Sunday was connected with Monday in an artificial manner.

There was another reason which made this way an unsafe and dangerous path. In the period between Trent and Vatican II the ritual, determined though it was by time, all too easily came to be identified with the divine itself. One might speak of supernaturalism. The forms were spiritualised, and the human in the efficacy of the ritual was reduced to a minimum. The physical acts were practically reduced to acts which were technically necessary to receive the sacrament. A rigidly regulated formalism arose, which made natural human expression impossible.[18] The legal approach came to dominate: every last detail was prescribed in the rubrics. The liturgy came to under heavy ethical pressure. Infringements of the rules for the ritual were very quickly seen as serious offences. For instance, in the manuals of ethics one could find expositions on mortal sins and venial sins in connection with the liturgy. One could read, for example, 'One who celebrates without paraments, or without alb, or without chasuble, has committed a mortal sin.'[19] According to most such manuals, the same is true for celebrating without stole or maniple. And: 'One who speaks the words of consecration aloud, commits a venial sin.

---

[18] A. VERGOTE: 'Christian Misreadings of the Human', in *Concilium* 18 (1982) 5, 16-22.

[19] *Notae morales et canonicae ad tractatum de sacramentis in genere*, Sint-Michielsgestel 1947, 109.

But one who speaks them so softly that the himself cannot hear them, commits a mortal sin because of the danger of invalidity.'[20] Alphonsus Liguori (1696-1785) lists more than 100 mortal sins that can be committed in the performance of the liturgy.[21] The faithful were also constantly urged in moralising tones to approach the ritual worthily. Vergote remarks, 'The effect of supernaturalism on the sacrament has been disastrous, and we are still subject to its ruinous consequences. The decrease in participation in the worship service in Western Christianity is undoubtedly for a part due to the degeneration of its forms in the old liturgy.'[22]

Thus one can say that the ritual forms became strongly divinised. This was so much the case that a considerable proportion of Roman Catholic believers before the Second Vatican Council were of the misapprehension that the celebration of Eucharist as it in fact existed went directly back to Christ. In fact it was however a ritual design that was prescribed in the missal of Pius V (1570), after Trent, the product of centuries of development. It is this historically determined liturgy of Pius V that is now being declared the only true and orthodox liturgy by the followers of Lefèbvre. In their opinion the renewed Roman liturgy deviates from the provisions and doctrine of the Council of Trent. This is unquestionably an instance of liturgical fundamentalism. There is basically no difference between this and the ritual fundamentalism that one encounters in other religions.

In Part 1 it appeared that Turner, from the ritual standpoint, sketched a very positive image of post-Tridentine Christian ritual, and pronounced a rather negative judgement on the renewal of the liturgy after the Second Vatican Council.[23] One gets the impression that this famous anthropologist still had a rather static conception of ritual. Or is it the case that in his view ritual can indeed undergo changes, but not that which belongs to our culture? I will return to this in Part 3.[24] Whatever the case, in contempo-

---

[20] *Notae morales* 111.
[21] K.-H. PESCHKE: 'Die Sünde in den Traktaten über die Sakramente', in LEKTOREN IN ST. AUGUSTIN (ed.): *In verbo tuo. Festschrift zum 50jährigen Bestehen des Missionspriesterseminar St. Augustin bei Siegburg, Rheinl. 1913-1963*, St. Augustin 1963, 235-246; A. ANGENENDT: *Liturgik und Historik. Gab es eine organische Liturgie-Entwicklung?* (Quaestiones disputatae 189), Freiburg/Basel/Wien 2001, 147.
[22] VERGOTE: 'Christian Misreadings of the Human' 16-22.
[23] See Part 1, Chapter 4, 5.3.
[24] See Part 3, Chapter 3, 3.1.

rary anthropology people are generally convinced that rituals are subject to change and that new rituals can arise. Most rituals, including those which we now view as classic or traditional, grew up from below.[25] The view that ritual resists change from the inside out, or that the survival of ritual depends on the pure repetition of the ritual tradition, must be revised.[26] Liturgy is always embedded in a cultural process. That entails risks. In any case, men can sometimes correctly consider liturgy as a model *for* a particular culture, but it can likewise be the model *of* a culture, thus sharing in all the weaknesses, flaws and contradictions of that culture. It can embody oppressive structures, nationalism, racism and sexism.[27] Here one encounters the problem of what is termed inculturation of liturgy.

2. THE CONCEPT OF INCULTURATION

For sixteen centuries, from late Roman times to our own, the Christian churches had a purely mono-cultural view of the world. In their view there was only one universal culture: that of Europe. Mission proceeded from that culture. In our century however the Christian churches have gradually become aware of culture as a pluriform phenomenon, and in the mid-1970s the concept of inculturation began to play a central role in this rising consciousness. Initially all sorts of terms were used interchangeably with one another, such as adaptation and accommodation, revision, incarnation, indigenation, contextualisation, acculturation and enculturation;[28] ultimately all of these were displaced by the term inculturation.[29]

[25] MITCHELL: 'The Amen-Corner: the Coming Revolution in Ritual Studies'.

[26] BELL: 'Ritual, Change, and Changing Rituals'; IDEM: *Ritual Theory*.

[27] GRIMES: 'Liturgical Supinity' 58-59, 63.

[28] For these various terms and their exact meaning, see among others L. AMAFILI: 'Inculturation: its Etymology and Problems', in *Questions Liturgiques* 73 (1992) 170-188; A. CHUPUNGCO: *Liturgical Inculturation. Sacramentals, Religiosity, and Catechesis*, Collegeville 1992, Chapter 1; A. SHORTER: *Towards a Theology of Inculturation*, London/New York 1988; N. STANDAERT: 'L'histoire d'un néologisme. Le terme 'inculturation' dans les documents romains', in *Nouvelle Revue Théologique* 110 (1988) 555-570.

[29] J. MASSON: 'L'église ouverte sur le monde', in *Nouvelle revue théologique* 84 (1962) 1038-1039. Compare also the title of the journal founded in 1994, the *Journal of Inculturation Theology*, published by the Catholic Institute of West Africa in Port Harcourt, Nigeria.

With regard to the concept of inculturation, see further among others: H. BAUERN-FEIND: *Inkulturation der Liturgie in unsere Gesellschaft: eine Kriteriensuche, aufgezeigt an*

It is important to define the meaning of the term carefully. It was used in theological literature for the first time in 1959 by Segura and Sohier.[30] The term began to make headway in the mid-1970s, largely

den Zeitzeichen Kirche heute, Esoterik/New Age und modernes Menschsein (Studien zur Theologie und Praxis der Seelsorge 34), Würzburg 1998; A. CHUPUNGCO: 'Liturgy and Inculturation', in A. CHUPUNGCO (ed.): *Handbook for Liturgical Studies*, Vol 2: *Fundamental Liturgy*, Collegeville 1998, 337-375; G. EVERS a.o.: 'Annoted Bibliography on Inculturation', in *Theologie in Context. Supplements*, Aachen 1984 (Annoted Bibliography on Inculturation); FÉDÉRATION LUTHÉRIENNE MONDIALE: *Culte et culture en dialogue. Consultations internationales de Cartigny (Suisse, 1993) et de Hong Kong (1994)*, Département des études, Genève 1995; LUKKEN: 'Inculturatie van de liturgie'; LUTHERAN WORLD FEDERATION; 'Nairobi Statement on Worship and Culture. Contemporary Challenges and Opportunities', in *Studia Liturgica* 27 (1998) 88-93; IDEM: 'Chicago Statement on Worship and Culture: Baptism and Rites of Life Passage', in *Studia Liturgica* 28 (1998) 244-252; IDEM: (ed. S.A. STAUFFER): *Baptism, Rites of Passage, and Culture*, Genève 1999; G. ROUWHORST: 'Inculturatie en verandering in de westerse cultuur', in *Inzet* 25 (1996) 5, 108-115; IDEM: 'Inculturatie en verandering in de westerse cultuur', in *Inzet* 25 (1996) 5, 108-115; A. SCHEER: 'Liturgische taalvernieuwing als culturatievraagstuk', in *Tijdschrift voor Liturgie* 82 (1998) 289-302; S.A. STAUFFER (ed.): *Worship and Culture in Dialogue*, Genève 1994; IDEM: (ed.): *Christian Worship. Unity in cultural diversity*, Genève 1996; IDEM: 'Worship and Culture. A Select Bibliography', in *Studia Liturgica* 27 (1997) 102-128 (this bibliography contains almost exclusively English language literature); L. VAN TONGEREN: 'De inculturatie van de liturgie tot (stil)stand gebracht? Kanttekeningen bij een Romeins document over liturgie en inculturatie', in *Jaarboek voor liturgie-onderzoek* 12 (1996) 164-186; IDEM: 'Liturgie in context. De vernieuwing van de liturgie en de voortgang ervan als een continu proces', in *Tijdschrift voor Liturgie* 81 (1997) 178-198; IDEM: 'Een onafscheidelijk driespan. Liturgie en kerkbouw in de context van de cultuur', in P. POST (ed.): *Een ander huis. Kerkarchitectuur na 2000* (Liturgie in perspectief 7), Baarn/Berne 1997, 30-38; IDEM: 'Liturgical Renewal Never Ends', in M. LAMBERIGTS & L. KENIS: *Vatican II and its legacy*, Leuven 2002, 365-384; M. TRIACCA: "Inculturazione e liturgia': eventi dello Spirito Santo. A proposito di alcuni principi per il progresso dell'approfondimento degli studi su 'liturgia e culture", in *Ecclesia Orans* 15 (1998) 1, 59-89; A.M. TRIACCA & A. PISTOIA (eds.): *Liturgie et cultures* (Bibliotheca Ephemerides Liturgicae 90), Rome 1997.

[30] Normally people cite the Jesuit Masson as being the first to use the term. Masson writes: 'Today there is a more urgent need for a Catholicism that is 'inculturated' in a variety of forms' (MASSON: 'L'église ouverte sur le monde' 1038). See AMAFILI: 'Inculturation' 174. Chupungco incorrectly dates the first use to ten years later, in 1973, by the Protestant missionary G.L. Barney (A. CHUPUNGCO: 'Liturgical Inculturation', in *East Asian Pastoral Review* 30 (1993) 2, 110, note 4). According to V. NECKEBROUCK: 'Progressistische theologie en inculturatie', in LAMBERTS (ed.): *Liturgie en inculturatie* 76, note 4 the term had however already been used three years before Masson, by R.P. SEGURA: 'L'initiation, valeur permanente en vue de l'inculturation', in J. MASSON (ed.): *Mission et cultures non-chrétiennes*, Brugge 1959 and A. SOHIER: 'Inculturation dans le monde chinois', in MASSON, *Mission et cultures non-chrétiennes*.

under the influence of the Jesuits, and as being relevant not only for the Third World, but also for all local churches.[31] In 1975 the term was used for the first time by Paul VI,[32] and in 1977 it received wide official recognition through the fifth synod of bishops, after which, beginning in 1979, it was used with increasing frequency by Pope John Paul II.[33] The term also came to be generally adopted in theology of liturgy and missiology. It must be said that the Congregation for Worship long held fast to the term adaptation; only in 1990, in a discussion of a draft text of the document on inculturation in liturgy, was it suggested that the term inculturation should be used![34]

The term was unknown in anthropological literature. It is a neologism. The term enculturation was however familiar in anthropology. This term denotes the learning process through which, beginning in childhood, an individual gradually becomes an integral part of his or her culture.[35] The new word however received a totally different meaning from the word that preceded it. It denotes the interaction or dialogue between the gospel and culture. By inculturation one is to understand the dynamic relation between the Christian message and the culture – or better, cultures. It concerns a continuing process of mutual and critical interaction and assimilation involving both sides.[36] It is also important here to be conscious of the difference between *inculturation* and *acculturation*. Chupungco makes the difference between the two clear in this way.[37] In acculturation you are dealing, as it were, with the

---

[31] For instance, P. Arupe, Superior General of the Jesuits, writes that the need for inculturation is universal: see J. AIXALA (ed.): *Other Apostolates Today: Selected Letters and Adr.*, St. Louis 1981, 173.

[32] PAULUS VI: *Evangelii nuntiandi*, Città del Vaticano 1975, 20, 62-65.

[33] 'Commentarium alla quarta istruzione per una corretta applicazione della costituzione conciliare sulla sacra liturgia', in *Notitiae* 30 (1994) 155-156.

[34] 'Commentarium alla quarta istruzione ' 155-156; F. TRAN-VAN-KHA: 'L'adaptation liturgique telle qu'elle a été réalisée par les commissions nationales liturgiques jusqu'à maintenant', in *Notitiae* 25 (1989) 864-883; CRONACA: 'Cronaca dei lavori della 'plenaria' 1991', in *Notitiae* 27 (1991) 82-83.

[35] SHORTER: *Towards a Theology of Inculturation* 5-6; AMAFILI: 'Inculturation' 181-182, 184-186.

[36] G.A. ARBUCKLE: *Earthing the Gospel: An Inculturation Handbook for the Pastoral Worker*, New York 1990, 17 and 34; M.C. DE AZEVEDO: *Inculturation and the Challenges of Modernity*, Rome 1982, 11; SHORTER: *Towards a Theology of Inculturation* 11.

[37] A. CHUPUNGCO: *Cultural Adaptation of the Liturgy*, New York 1982, 81 and 84; IDEM: *Liturgical Inculturation* 27-29, 111-114; see also SHORTER: *Towards a Theology of Inculturation* 12-13.

formula A+B=AB. In other words, the two cultures exist side by side without mutual assimilation and enrichment; A and B come together, but continue as separate entities. They undergo no substantial or qualitative change. A clear example of this in the history of liturgy is the baroque period. The Tridentine Mass was protected by the rubrics from incursions from outside, and as a result the baroque culture remained stuck at the periphery of the liturgy. Inculturation is different. There the formula is A+B=C. This is not a matter of two things that remain together purely externally, but of mutual penetration. Concretely, on the one hand there is an inward transformation of authentic cultural values through integration into Christianity, and on the other hand Christianity puts down roots in the culture.[38] There is thus mutual enrichment, through which A is no longer A, and B is no longer B. A new totality, C, is formed. A good example would be the classic Roman liturgy between the fifth and eighth century, which took shape through a close interchange involving Greco-Roman culture and the Christian liturgy.

One must realise that inculturation is a profound process. It is not purely and merely an interchange involving the religious rites of a culture and Christian liturgy. Culture is, as we have seen, an extremely inclusive entity, which encompasses the whole of human life, in all its layers.

To take a concrete example: think of the year 1000, the period of Romanesque culture.[39] What did the *social-political* layer look like then, in general terms? Power was in the hands of feudal lords. All others were subject to them. You could serve such lord as a vassal or liege. You then took an oath to life-long fealty, and must perform your services for that lord. You were thus a tributary of his. In return for that you enjoyed the protection of the feudal lord. He provided your sustenance. Most vassals were soldiers. It was a world of warriors, where things could be very rough. Lots of blood was shed. On the other hand, there were positive virtues: courage, loyalty and munificence. Few men then were literate, and people appreciated grand gestures. These were experienced as being highly 'charged'. The rite in which the vassal entered into his life-long contract with the feudal lord was also 'charged'. He knelt down before him, and swore an oath of loyalty. That was a decisive gesture, which

---

[38] Compare the description by the Synod of Bishops in 1985, closing statement, D 4.
[39] G. DUBY: *Le temps des cathédrales. L'art et la société de 980 à 1420*, Paris 1976.

had profound implications for his life. Alongside the social-political layer, in that culture there was an *economic* layer. The vassals had to perform labour for the feudal lord, and pay taxes to him. In this way the feudal lords enriched themselves on the backs of the people, via the vassals, and had great wealth at their disposal. Finally, there was a *religious* layer in the culture. This was closely linked with both of the previous layers. Men imagined God as a sort of feudal lord. Man was in service to God, as a sort of feudal lord. Like liege men, they knelt before God and took their oath of fealty to God himself. With that, from his side God gave help and protection to his liege men, just as a feudal lord would do. In a culture such as this the image of God as a feudal lord was unavoidable, although at the same time people experienced that God was essentially greater and different.

Christian ritual formed the knot, as it were, which brought together the various layers of the culture in a very intense way. For instance, in the ritual of the oath that the vassal took to the feudal lord, he knelt down before him, laid his hand on the cross, on a Bible or on a bag of relics; then he laid both his hands in those of the lord, and swore his oath of loyalty. Three contracts come together in this Christian ritual: the social-political, the economic and the religious. Thus Christian ritual reflected all layers of the culture, even those of economic, social and political life.

From the perspective of ritual, the following is also important. We still admire the many monasteries and churches that Romanesque culture produced. These monasteries and churches were financed by the feudal lords. This was done not only from munificence, which was a virtue in that time. They also offered their wealth as a means of acquiring the favour of the almighty feudal Lord. Building churches and monasteries was a gesture of fundamental Christian piety. The feudal lords financed these buildings in order to achieve eternal salvation through the intercession of the saints in heaven and the saints on earth (the monks). Thus again the ritual gesture of the financial offering reflected all the layers of culture as a sort of nerve centre.

The Nigerian theologian Upkong therefore is correct in pointing out that the economic, social and political aspects of the culture are also

---

[40] J.S. UKPONG: 'Towards a Renewed Approach to Inculturation Theology', in *Journal of Inculturation Theology* 1 (1994) 8-24.

included with inculturation.[40] It involves the integration and transformation of the economic, political, social and religious life of a people. He gives the Eucharist as an example. It is not sufficient to Africanise the celebration of Eucharist, but it is also a matter of the impact of the Eucharist on the economic, political and social life of the community.[41] For instance, the Eucharist as a meal evokes the whole reality of the material, the bodily, the economic, and the social customs and usages that inescapably accompany eating and drinking in all cultures. With this, one immediately confronts the issue of the inculturation of the substance of the Eucharist: in Africa, bread is simply equated with Western food, and grape wine is a luxury product from capitalist culture. Is it not then more obvious to think in terms of what is everyday food in Africa for the substance of the Eucharist? In Africa, would rice, corn or manioc cakes and local palm or banana wines not be more credible as the material for the Eucharist?[42] The remark of B. Botte that according to the gospels Jesus did not take a plate of rice and a cup of tea at the Last Supper does not appear to be relevant.[43] Even when using local foodstuffs one can say that Jesus took up bread and wine; this is every bit as possible as speaking of Zion and Jerusalem as our destination, and thinking of Paul's letter to the Corinthians as directed to us.[44]

---

[41] UKPONG: 'Towards a Renewed Approach' 22.

[42] A. HASTINGS: 'Western Christianity Confronts other Cultures', in *Studia Liturgica* 20 (1990) 26-27; F. KABASELE: 'Eucharistiefeier in Schwarzafrika', in L. BERTSCH (ed.): *Der neue Messritus im Zaire. Ein Beispiel kontextueller Liturgie* (Theologie der dritten Welt 18), Freiburg im Breisgau 1993, 170-178; G. LUKKEN: 'New Rites around Communion in Present-day Western Culture', in C. CASPERS a.o. (eds.): *Bread of Heaven. Customs and Practices Surrounding Holy Communion. Essays in the History of Liturgy and Culture* (Liturgia condenda 3), Kampen 1995, 206; W. DE MAHIEU: 'Anthropologie et théologie africaine', in *Revue du Clergé Africain* 25 (1970) 383; A. THALER: 'Inkulturation der Liturgie. Am Beispiel der Mahlelemente', in *Diakonia* 20 (1989) 172-179; R. JAQUEN: *L'Eucharistie du mil. Languages d'un people, expressions de la foi*, Paris 1995; R. GASE N'GANZI: 'Débat autour des matières eucharistiques en contexte africain: état de la question', in B. HALLENSLEBEN & G. VERGAUWEN (eds.): *Praedicando et docendo. Mélanges offerts à Liam Walsh o.p.* (Cahiers œcuméniques 35), Freiburg 1998, 49-73; IDEM: *Les signes sacramentels de l'Eucharistie dans l'Eglise latine. Etudes théologiques et historiques*, Freiburg 2001; P. GIBSON: 'Eucharistic Food. May We Substitute?', in *Worship* 76 (2002) 445-455. For further literature see H.B. MEYER: *Eucharistie. Geschichte, Theologie, Pastoral* (Gottesdienst der Kirche. Handbuch der Liturgiewissenschaft 4), Regensburg 1989, 383, note 104.

[43] B. BOTTE: 'Le problème de l'adaptation en liturgie', in *Revue du Clergé Africain* 18 (1963) 320.

[44] Thus KABASELE: 'Eucharistiefeier in Schwarzafrika' 178.

CHAPTER 3

THE THEOLOGICAL PROBLEM OF INCULTURATION

As inculturation operates at such profound levels, the question immediately arises of whether one should not be extremely cautious and wary about inculturation. Could inculturation not easily proceed at the cost of the gospel itself? You here run up against the central problem which presents itself in every inculturation. The infamous example is that of the *deutsche Christen* during the Nazi era in Germany.[1] They inculturated into the resurgent Germanic culture to such an extent that they also accepted the ideology and practice of National Socialism. A milder example is that of the Danish national church, which is so Danish that the Lutheran theologian Aagaard has questioned if more realisation of catholicity might not be good medicine for that church.[2] And are there not, for instance, numerous elements in our Western culture that cannot be considered as candidates for inculturation. One might think of our economic structures, which lead to exploitation of the Third World and bring about exaggerated consumptive behaviour, and also of the lopsidedly rationalised approach to matters of all sorts in our culture, up to and including even the use of rituals of birth and death in advertising and commerce.

So it is entirely possible that inculturation can erode the identity of the gospel. Thus inculturation of the gospel must always involve a *critical* symbiosis between the gospel and culture. The following issues seem to me to be important in relation to this.

1. TWO ATTITUDES

In the history of Christian conversion there have been two antithetical attitudes, for which historically Pope Gregory I and the missionary

---

[1] R. SCHREITER: 'Inculturation of Faith or Identification with Culture?', in *Concilium* 30 (1994) 2, 26; A. WESSELS: *Kerstening en ontkerstening van Europa. Wisselwerking tussen evangelie en cultuur*, Baarn 1994, 214.

[2] H. WITTE: 'Kerken kunnen té geïncultureerd zijn', in *Een-twee-een* 22 (1994) 23-24.

Boniface may stand as models.[3] The missionary Boniface wished to dispense with the religions he encountered. He had little sympathy for culture. In 20th century terms, he was in the camp of Karl Barth, who argues that God's message is squarely opposed to human experience. His was a very characteristic spirituality, which is possible and undoubtedly has its *raison d'être*. Pope Gregory worked differently. In sending missionaries to England he tried to arrive at an inculturation of Christendom, and to preserve what was not directly in conflict with the gospel. Christian missionaries to Great Britain at the end of the sixth and beginning of the seventh centuries, in apparent compliance with the spirit of Gregory the Great, adapted their liturgical calendar to the previously existing cycle by emphasising saint's days coinciding with pagan festivals and times of sacrifice. And pagan temples were reconsecrated for Christian worship.[4] You can compare this with what Pope Boniface IV (not to be confused with the missionary Boniface!) did in 609. He received the Pantheon, the old Roman temple of all the gods, from the Byzantine emperor Phocas, and consecrated it to the Virgin Mary and all martyrs. This is the current which appears most accepted within the Catholic tradition, and you find it from the ancient Church. Christianisation had as it were a personal and social system peculiar to it that apparently appealed to many.[5] Those who know the history of the ancient Church know that the legacy of Greece and Rome was so thoroughly taken up into the Church that some of what we know of Greece and Rome we know through the Church. In the past the Christian message was accepted and spread through Europe chiefly because the Church was able to connect with that which was peculiar to the culture. Roman, Gallic-Celtic and Germanic treasures were brought into the new Jerusalem[6]

---

[3] WESSELS: *Kerstening en ontkerstening van Europa* 20 ff.

[4] See in this connection RAPPAPORT: *Ritual and Religion in the Making of Humanity* 192-193, 339, 490-492.

[5] T. VAN DEN BERK: *Mystagogie. Inwijding in het symbolisch bewustzijn*, Zoetermeer 1999, 64-82. R. STARK: *De eerste eeuwen. Een sociologische visie op het ontstaan van het christendom*, Baarn 1998 estimates the growth of Christianity in the first four centuries at 40% per decade. This means that around the year 350 of an estimated population of 60 million about 34 million were Christians. That is over 56%.

[6] WESSELS: *Kerstening en ontkerstening van Europa* 219-220. For the history of the inculturation of the liturgy see further among others J. ALDAZÁBAL: 'Lecciones de la historia sobre la inculturación', in *Phase* (1995) 96-100; ARBUCKLE: *Earthing the Gospel*; CHUPUNGCO: *Cultural Adaptation of the Liturgy* 3-41; IDEM: *Liturgical Inculturation*;

It is indeed true however that the Christian revelation does not merge seamlessly with the varying perspective of human rites. In one manner or another there remains a specific *gap*, an unbridgeable opening or jump, namely to the Christian mystery, which must also always be expressed in inculturation.[7]

2. THERE IS NO PURE MESSAGE

Because of this 'jump', some place their emphasis on the sovereign power of the gospel which, free and autonomous, can go its own way in the transformation of a culture during the inculturation process. They accept the transcendence of revelation, from which faith can critique every culture.[8] But if you work in that way, you approach the view that revelation is antithetical to culture. Then you all to easily forget that the revelation as we know it in faith itself has always been inculturated. That already inculturated faith will stress certain characteristics of the message, and will necessarily accentuate others less. A pure message simply does not exist. The gospel cannot do without people and their expressions, linguistic and otherwise, and these are, whether one likes it or not, always tied to time and place, and thus culturally determined. A cultureless Christianity does not exist. Every expression of Christianity is culturally charged, including that of the very first Christian communities.[9] It is not as if you can separate the core from the rest of the apple. No, everything is intertwined.

3. MAGISTERIUM

Nor is the magisterium of the Church a meta-institution that, as it were, floats in a storm-free region above culture. Inculturation is therefore a

---

P.M. GY: 'The Inculturation of the Christian Liturgy in the West', in *Studia Liturgica* 20 (1990) 8-18; E. MUNACHI EZEOGU: 'The Jewish Response to Hellenism: a Lesson in Inculturation', in *Journal of inculturation theology* 1 (1994) 2, 144-155; P. SCHINELLER: *A Handbook on Inculturation*, New York 1990, 12 ff.; SHORTER: *Towards a Theology of Inculturation* 104-176.

[7] I will return to this point *in extenso* in Part 3.
[8] SCHREITER: 'Inculturation of Faith' 24-25.
[9] T. GROOME: 'Inculturation. How to Proceed in a Pastoral Context?', in *Concilium* 30 (1994) 2, 125.

difficult search in the midst of our history, performed in dialogue with one another. Guarding Christian identity is a very laborious process, as actually can be seen in the way that the first council in Jerusalem wrestled with the issue, and the conflict between Peter and Paul, of which I already spoke. It is a matter of a collective, active and creative transmission (*tradere*) of the message in an ever-living tradition. The question of how we should preserve identity in the course of that process of searching is thus not purely a question just for doctrinal authority or leadership, but one of collective responsibility in which everyone has their own role and expertise. What is necessary is that the search is carried on in constant dialogue, recognising both ideology and superficiality as dangers.

4. THE DANGER OF NOSTALGIA

A critique of culture on the basis of the gospel and Christian tradition is therefore justified. But that cultural critique may never have its origin purely and simply in a resistance to culture itself because of nostalgia or an exaltation of a previous culture. The critique must flow out of the inculturation of the gospel into that culture itself. One thus always must take the particular culture extremely seriously, and not reject its manifestations a priori.

5. CONTINUITY AND DISCONTINUITY WITH TRADITION

I have noted the insistent question of how, in the course of the process of searching that is involved in inculturation, we are to preserve the identity of the message that has been handed down to us. At this point the problem arises of the continuity and discontinuity of Christian ritual within the tradition.[10] It is a complicated problem, which one may not simplify. The fact is that one must realise that no culture whatsoever can consider itself as an the absolute site for the expression of truth. In one culture elements and perspectives may come to the fore that in another culture may be less accessible, or not accessible at all. Every culture is necessarily always also a selection, and that has consequences for

---

[10] G. LUKKEN: 'Liturgiewetenschappelijk onderzoek in culturele context. Methodische verhelderingen en vragen', in *Jaarboek voor liturgie-onderzoek* 13 (1997) 138-144.

the expression of Christian faith. For instance, in the past the subordinate role patterns of women were also expressed in Christian ritual, and
one had the blessing of weapons. Ritual was also intertwined with the
'natural' institution of slavery; a painful reminder of this being the following article: 'To cover the expenses of the church, the king is required
to provide two slaves each year to be sold for the purchase of wax, wine,
oil and hosts.'[11] Through the development of our culture aspects which
previously were not open to question have been illuminated, while at
the same time we must be aware of the fact that our culture also has
only a limited vision, and needs correction from the tradition.

Fitzpatrick rightly points out that the church sometimes has the inclination to suggest more continuity with the past than is in fact the case.
The past is then adapted to the present, or one might say there is selective memory. One example is furnished by the condemnation of Berengar of Tours in the 11th century, who struggled against crassly realistic
conceptions of the Eucharist, and in opposition advanced a more or less
symbolic-sacramental view. He withdrew his view, and twice made a
confession of faith in which he met the objections – and these confessions were accepted. The first confession however was considerably
closer to his standpoint than the second. This milder confession was
never included in the much-consulted reference work on confessions by
Denzinger, until it finally appeared there as late as 1963.[12] The encyclical *Mysterium fidei* by Paul VI,[13] in which newer views of the Eucharist
were rejected, speaks of the unanimous condemnation of Berengar, but
only mentions his second confession; the first is passed over in silence.
In my view, elsewhere in this encyclical too one might say there is a
selective appeal to tradition. In its critique of the new approach to the
Eucharist as symbolic reality, the encyclical cites Theodore of Mopsues-
tia (no. 44) and Johannes, Bishop of Constantinople (no. 50), who both
reject the 'symbolic' approach. But these two texts are an exception in
Greek patristics, which on the contrary always maintained symbolic terminology when discussing Christ's presence in the Eucharist! It is therefore difficult to endorse what the encyclical says at the end (no. 74),

---

[11] Article 7 of an agreement between the apostolic prefect of the Capuchin missionaries and the Congolese king Pedro IV, July, 1700.
[12] H. DENZINGER & H. SCHÖNMETZER: *Enchiridion Symbolorum*, Barcelona 1963,
690 and 700; P.J. FITZPATRICK: *In Breaking the Bread. The Eucharist and Ritual*, Cambridge 1993, 221-222, 226-227.
[13] PAULUS VI: *Mysterium fidei*: *Acta Apostolicae Sedis* 57 (1965) 753-774.

when it speaks of 'the venerable churches of the East, from which so many illustrious Fathers of the Church have come, whose testimony to the Eucharist we have recorded with pleasure in this encyclical.'

In dealing with the problem of continuity and discontinuity, it is important that one does not prematurely neutralise the discontinuity. This is particularly the case when a culture is actively developing. What is true in this respect for society as such is likewise applicable for Christian faith. Life and doctrine are often not so straightforward as people think, and quite erroneously people sometimes try to reduce the tension between the past and present by justifications or adjustments, certainly when the tension between one era and another is great, as in the Roman Catholic Church, which has a long and varied history.[14] Many Christians are asking themselves today how it was possible that people thought in such a way. Or they say they feel deceived by the past. It was not all that long ago that older brothers or sisters of the same families were forced to break off their courtship because their perspective marriage partner belonged to a different Christian church, and will now attend the celebration of a full church wedding of a younger sibling in exactly the same situation, where the difference is no longer a obstacle. Times change, and that is also true, in a very radical manner, for rites. If we had films from the past, we would definitely have problems discovering the line in the history of the celebration of the Eucharist: there would be images of the Last Supper, of the simple gathering around the table in one house or another that followed it, of the Mass with the elevation of the Host in a medieval cathedral – celebrated by the priest far from the people, at a High Altar hidden from their eyes by a rood screen, or in private at a side altar –, of the Reformed Lord's Supper, of a baroque Mass during the performance of a mass by Mozart, through to the simple service of Word and Table in a modern church.

In connection with the question of continuity and discontinuity in tradition, it seems to me that liturgical studies can go one of two directions. The first is that of the hierarchical dimensions of the ritual or liturgical order, as is elaborated by Rappaport. The second is the way of comparative ritual and theological verification, which I have worked out little by little in the past. The two ways in no way contradict each other; on the contrary, they can supplement each other.

---

[14] FITZPATRICK: *In Breaking the Bread* 225-246.

Rappaport notes that for religions with universal aspirations, segregation of the fundamental from the contingent in liturgical orders is very important, because their Ultimate Sacred Postulates must gain acceptance from individuals of different societies. Supra-cultural acceptance is facilitated by the separation of universal postulates from social particularities. The separation of the fundamental from the contingent enhances flexibility and at the same time assures the continuity of the ritual. This separation of the fundamental from the contingent does not necessarily imply a separation in time and space. Often, if not always, these elements can be distinguished within the same ritual.[15] In connection with the distinction between the fundamental and the contingent Rappaport speaks of an hierarchical organisation in liturgical orders. There are four levels in this hierarchy:[16]

a. The level of the Ultimate Sacred Postulates, such as the Jewish declaration of faith called the *Shema Israel* and the Christian Creeds. These involve eternal truths which sustain the whole liturgical order. Rappaport limits these Ultimate Sacred Postulates to truths formulated in language. One can however ask if certain fundamental non-linguistic elements do not likewise belong to these sustaining elements of the liturgical order. One might think, for instance, of the central acts of the Lord's Supper. Whatever the case, these involve elements that are asserted to be ageless and are of long duration. As we have already noted above, the *Shema Israel* has endured for 3000 years. Likewise, the Nicene Creed has remained unchanged since 325. The first level thus involves long duration.[17] It includes the most invariable dimension within the ritual order, which guarantees unity.

b. The second level concerns assumed notions about the world called 'cosmological axioms'. These involve assumptions about the fundamental structure of the world (cosmology). This level is closely associated with the Ultimate Sacred Postulates. These cosmological axioms deal with certain relationships such as those between warmth and cold, light and dark, land and sea, God and man, man and woman. The manner of their expression is more general and varied. Whereas Ultimate Sacred Postulates are in themselves either devoid of explicit social

---

[15] RAPPAPORT: *Ritual and Religion in the Making of Humanity* 271-272.
[16] RAPPAPORT: *Ritual and Religion in the Making of Humanity* 263-276.
[17] See also RAPPAPORT: *Ritual and Religion in the Making of Humanity* 328-343.

content or very vague in this regard, cosmological axioms are more specific; often they have explicit and substantial political, social and ecological import. They also serve as the logical basis from which specific rules of conduct and proprieties of social life can be derived. Those accepting these cosmological axioms may regard them as being as enduring as Ultimate Sacred Postulates, but they are probably less so. They can change or even be radically altered by environmental or historical conditions without Ultimate Sacred Postulates being affected.

c. The third level concerns rules that translate cosmological axioms into conduct for the relations (for instance) between cold and warm foods, man and wife, etc. These rules are expressed in the rituals and are more concrete and specific than the cosmological oppositions as such. For example, the opposition man – woman can lead to the rule of exclusion of women from serving Mass. It is clear that these rules of the third level are likely to be shorter-lived. They can be changed, while the cosmological axioms remain unchanged.

d. Whereas the first three levels refer to the order itself and are then imposed upon the world external to them, the fourth level concerns the import of understandings of the external world. On this level the order is continuously adapted to indices of prevailing conditions. It is the most changeable level. Here one can for instance refer to the liturgical prayers and the sermon, but also to the differences in the communities enacting the order.

It is clear that the possibilities for inculturation and, with that, of change increase to the degree that a 'more superficial' level is involved.[18] The deepest level, that of Ultimate Sacred Postulates, is characterised by Rappaport simply as that of 'invariance'. It forms an unchanging ground upon which all else can change without loss of order. One can paradoxically say that the invariable, which constitutes the sacred, nurtures flexibility.[19] In Part 1, however, with regard to the exclusive invariance of the Ultimate Sacred Postulates as emphasised by Rappaport, I posed the question of whether change does not sometimes penetrate to the first level itself.[20] I pointed to the Nicene-Constantinopolitan Creed, which has

[18] In this connection, see also RAPPAPORT: *Ritual and Religion in the Making of Humanity* 419-437.

[19] RAPPAPORT: *Ritual and Religion in the Making of Humanity* 427.

[20] See Part 1, Chapter 3, 1.2.

been given all sorts of musical forms of expression, from Gregorian to baroque, romantic to modern, and the Latin text of which has been translated into numerous languages, so that one can question whether changes have not indeed been possible within the old text as such. Within the Christian order Barnard lists two indices in our culture that penetrate to the first level, and thus affect it at its most fundamental and enduring dimension.[21] The first is that of feminism. This is clearly at work in the third and fourth levels. But it also touches the second level. Feminism objects to the cosmological axiom of the man-woman opposition. It rejects the fundamental thinking in dichotomies. And feminism even seeps through to the first level. People are demanding that formulations of faith not be written in exclusively masculine language, and are seeking to have the image of God the Father replaced with that of God the Mother and Father. People also argue for the rewording of the baptismal formula in inclusive language. The second index is the relation between the Church and the Jewish people. Barnard points out that the growing realisation of the consequences of the Holocaust and its permanent topicality have penetrated to the first level. Thus the discussion is ongoing whether the *Shema Israel* should be included in the Christian service of worship. Here and there sounds the call to reformulate the creeds, because the Old Testament, and with that the relation between the Church and the Jewish people, is too briefly stated: 'I believe in God the Father, and in Jesus Christ…' It is being asked whether after God the Father there are not further references to the Old Testament that should be added.

The second way that one can travel in connection with the question of continuity and discontinuity of the tradition is that of comparative ritual and theological verification, as I have gradually elaborated it in the past,[22] and further underpinned it in recent years.[23]

---

[21] BARNARD: 'Dynamiek van cultus en cultuur' 53.

[22] For this see particularly G. LUKKEN: 'De liturgie als onvervangbare vindplaats van de theologie. Methoden van theologische analyse en verificatie', in H. BERGER a.o.: *Tussentijds. Theologische Faculteit Tilburg. Opstellen bij gelegenheid van haar erkenning*, Tilburg 1974, 317-332 = G. LUKKEN: 'La liturgie comme lieu théologique irremplaçable. Méthodes d'analyse et vérification théologiques', in *Questions liturgiques* 56 (1975) 317-322 and (with additions) LUKKEN (eds. CASPERS & VAN TONGEREN): *Per visibilia ad invisibilia* 239-255.

[23] POST: 'Interference and Intuition'; IDEM: 'Introduction and Application'; IDEM: 'Programm und Profil der Liturgiewissenschaft. Ein niederländischer Beitrag', in W. RATZMANN (ed.): *Profile und Perspektiven der Liturgiewissenschaft*, Leipzig 2002, 81-100.

I very deliberately use the adjective 'comparative', knowing that it calls up associations with the classic work of Anton Baumstark, *Liturgie comparée*.[24] For a proper understanding it is necessary to situate Baumstark's method in the context of his time.[25] In the course of the 19th century the consciousness arose in Western Europe that change is an essential aspect of all forms of life: not only social and political, but equally biological and linguistic. This coincided with the rise of historiography, which also exerted a great influence on liturgical studies. Between 1817 and 1840 Catholic theologians at Tübingen attempted to integrate the rising historical consciousness into theology, but after 1840 came a reactionary countercurrent which isolated history from theology. Neo-Scholastic theology got the upper hand. It made a strict distinction between nature and grace, and separated the theological terrain from human reason. According to this theology, human inquiry could only investigate the natural world. It distinguished two orders of knowledge: that of theology, which is certain, and characterised by constancy, unity and consistency, and that of the humanities and natural sciences, which is uncertain and characterised by change, plurality and contradiction. In short: theology stands above history. Or in the words of Louis Billot (1846-1931): 'Dogmas have no history'.[26] It will be clear that neo-Scholastic theology considerably complicated the work of historians of liturgy. It was in this context that Baumstark emphasised that the study of liturgy belonged to the field of the human sciences. For him it was a matter of studying liturgy as history, and not as theology. To the extent that liturgy does deal with God, it does belong in the field of theology, and only theology can study it. But it is also possible to investigate liturgy as a purely historical phenomenon. Just as studies in comparative grammar only analyse the language and not that to which the language

[24] A. BAUMSTARK: *Liturgie comparée. Conférences faites au Prieuré d'Amay*, Chevetogne 1939; IDEM: *Liturgie comparée. Principes et méthodes pour l'étude historique des liturgies chrétiennes*, Chevetogne 1953[3] (edition revised by B. BOTTE); IDEM: *Comparative Liturgy*, London 1958 (English edition of the previous publication). See also A. BAUMSTARK: *Vom geschichtlichen Werden der Liturgie* (Ecclesia Orans 10), Freiburg/B 1923. Baumstark (1872-1948) taught in Bonn, Münster, Nijmegen and Utrecht.
[25] F. WEST: *Anton Baumstark's Comparative Liturgy in its Intellectual Context I* (Dissertation Notre Dame University, promotor Marc Searle), Ann Arbor 1988; IDEM: *The Comparative Liturgy of Anton Baumstark* (Joint Liturgical Studies 31), Nottingham 1995.
[26] For this quotation, see R. AUBERT: *The Christian Centuries. A New History of the Catholic Church*, Vol. 5: *The Church in a Secularized Society*, London 1978, 179.

refers, similarly comparative liturgy can analyse liturgy, and not that to which it refers, namely God. It studies a liturgy, the referent of which is God. In this way Baumstark laid the foundation for the method of comparative liturgical studies, a method which according to him did not differ from the comparative method of the definite sciences. Its object belongs simply and solely to theology. Baumstark was correct in fearing that theological a prioris could play havoc with the empirical data of historical liturgical study.[27] In this way he ran the risk of coming into conflict with theology. Baumstark himself mentions, as one instance of a potential conflict, the absence of the words of institution in the eucharistic prayer of Addaï and Mari. With regard to this he remarks, 'We are not justified in conjuring the fact away. It is the theologian, not the liturgist, whose business it is to relate the historical datum to the unchangeable character of dogma.'[28] Baumstark proceeded from the assumption that no fact discovered can ever contradict the *depositum fidei* of the Church. He believed this in connection with the model of harmony. After Baumstark the method of *liturgie comparée* was further adapted, particularly by the school of the liturgist Juan Mateos (1917-2003), and after him by Robert Taft (1932).[29] Recently the method has

[27] BAUMSTARK: *Liturgie comparée. Principes* 3: 'Par ce rapprochement, on entend délimiter nettement la place occupée par l'histoire de la liturgie dans l'ensemble des sciences. Seul son objet appartient à la théologie. Mais le travail à faire sur lui ne diffère pas du travail comparatif des sciences'.

[28] BAUMSTARK: *Comparative Liturgy* 8. It would be another sixty years before history and theology would really encounter one another in the question of the absence of the words of institution in the eucharistic prayer of Addaï and Mari. A ruling of July 20, 2001 (promulgated October 26, 2001) allows members of the Chaldean Catholic Church and members of the Assyrian Church of the East (its orthodox counterpart) to receive Communion at each of their liturgies. Theologically this ruling means that the Vatican recognizes the legitimacy of the Eucharist as practiced by the Assyrians, including their eucharistic prayer of Addaï and Mari. In regard to this Taft remarks that this is 'perhaps the most significant decision out of the Holy See in a half-century... This moves us beyond a medieval theology of magic words. The document recognizes the enormous advances made in studies concerning the evolution of the Eucharistic prayer' (J.L. ALLEN JR.: 'Rome', in *National Catholic Reporter*, November 16, 2001). See also M. SMYTH: 'Une avancée oecuménique et liturgique. La note romaine concernant l'Anaphore d'Addaï et Mari', in *La Maison-Dieu* (2003) 233, 137-154 and R. TAFT: 'Mass Without the Consecration? The Historic Agreement on the Eucharist between the Catholic Church and the Assyrian Church of the East Promulgated 26 October 2001, in *Worship* 77 (2003) 482-509.

[29] R. TAFT: 'The Structural Analysis of Liturgical Units: An Essay in Methodology', in *Worship* 52 (1978) 314-329 = IDEM: *Beyond East and West. Problems in Liturgical Understanding*, Washington 1984, 151-164.

been rightly defended and expounded anew by Taft.[30] All this however does not exclude that it can be supplemented in a fundamental way, particularly with regard to theology.

In the meantime the historical dimension had also penetrated theology deeply, and liturgy had been rediscovered as a characteristic locus for theology. Now that liturgical studies can enter into theology in an adult manner, an important addition to Baumstark is not only possible, but also necessary. This addition is not intended to in any way erode the peculiar value of *liturgie comparée* in Baumstark's sense. This retains its own unique value. It is rather a matter of complementing his method with that of comparative *theological* verification. The method of comparative ritual and theological verification consists of a careful analysis of the *integral* rituals (in other words, not just only their texts!) of past and present, both in their formal components and their content (thereby involving different methods) as primary theological sources, and the confrontation of these *primary* liturgical sources with the *secondary sources* of theological and liturgical reflection. In doing this, one must take into account that both the primary and secondary sources are deeply intertwined with the culture in which they arose. Furthermore, in referring to these sources Post makes the distinction between the levels of *designation* and *appropriation*: this means that rather than the unilateral emphasis on their designation by, for instance, academic or ecclesiastical elites, the accent shifts to the broad process of production, distribution and consumption of culture: from the prescribed order to the lived, celebrated practice. So the research accent shifts fundamentally, from top down to bottom up: the community is seen as the central locus in which culture is shaped.

The levels of designation and appropriation can be interrelated with the categories of liturgical meaning suggested by Hoffman.[31] According to Hoffman there are various levels of meaning in ritual: a. private: the meaning individuals give to rites; b. official: the interpretations of ritual experts; c. public: the shared views about the meaning of certain rites in spite of their 'official' interpretations; and d. normative: how people see

---

[30] R. TAFT: 'Comparative Liturgy Fifty Years after Anton Baumstark (d.1948): A Reply to Recent Critics', in *Worship* 73 (1999) 521-540. I would also note the extensive collection R. TAFT & G. WINKLER: *Acts of the International Congress Comparative Liturgy fifty years after Anton Baumstark (1972-1948)* (Orientalia Christiana Analecta 265), Roma 2001.

[31] HOFFMAN: 'How Ritual Means'.

the world and themselves as a result of celebrating a rite.[32] Bradshaw also observes that the concern of liturgical theologians has too much been only with 'official' meanings, and he refers to Hoffman's categories.[33]

The model just outlined is an important expansion of the classic research design of Baumstark's *liturgie comparée*.[34] According to this model of comparative ritual and theological verification the 'theological sources' ('loci theologici') involved can illuminate and critique one another, in which the interest is not seeking their identity in the literal sense of the word – after all, it is never purely a matter of repeating what was previously said and done – but of congruity. In the process one can see that expressions, relationships and emphases shift, and all sorts of surprises can occur, but one must be especially alert for contradictions.

Wegman has advanced a series of critical questions in regard to this approach. He argues for the relativisation of tradition as such, including Scripture.[35] What he hopes to achieve by this is a more dynamic conception of tradition, in which the confessions of faith from the past are seen as source documents, while in the liturgy we will be able to give our own confessions of faith a chance as sequels to the biblical story, without being called to order with regard to their orthodox character. I have the impression that Wegman sought to emphasise primarily the right of that which is new in liturgical inculturation.[36] It is my view, however, that the concept of congruity does not in any sense have to exclude such an accent.

---

[32] See also M.E. JOHNSON: 'Can We Avoid Relativism in Worship? Liturgical Norms in the Light of Contemporary Liturgical Worship', in *Worship* 74 (2000) 135-155. Johnson points out that Hoffman was not the first to argue that liturgists need to pay attention to multiple meanings in ritual performance or to suggest various meanings to which attention should be given. He refers to M.M. KELLEHER: 'Liturgy: An Ecclesial Act of Meaning', in *Worship* 59 (1987) 482-497; IDEM: 'Liturgy and the Christian Imagination', in *Worship* 66 (1992) 125-147; IDEM: 'Hermeneutics in the Study of Liturgical Performance', in *Worship* 67 (1993) 292-318.

[33] BRADSHAW: 'Difficulties in Doing Liturgical Theology'.

[34] BAUMSTARK: *Liturgie comparée. Principes.*

[35] H. WEGMAN: 'Liturgie en lange duur', in L. VAN TONGEREN (ed.): *Toekomst, toen en nu. Beschouwingen over de ontwikkeling en de voortgang van de liturgievernieuwing* (Liturgie in perspectief 2), Heeswijk-Dinther 1994, 11-38. Regarding Wegman's approach see G. ROUWHORST: 'Herman Wegman. Een terugblik op zijn leven en werk', in *Jaarboek voor liturgie-onderzoek* 12 (1996) 17-20.

[36] In this connection see also J.F. WHITE: 'How Do We Know It Is Us?', in E. ANDERSON & B. MORRILL (eds.): *Liturgy and the Moral Self: Humanity at Full Stretch Before God*, Collegeville 1998, 55-65.

In this connection I would want to examine three points further.

First, in comparative ritual and theological verification the critical-normative dimension does not have to function purely and simply from the past toward the present; the present can also contribute to a critical-normative examination of the past. The process can be a two-way street, rather than just a one-way street.[37] In this context, Post introduces a new concept, namely that of 'interference'.[38] Interference is a term which has its roots in the natural and physical sciences, and is being used with increasing frequency in the humanities. It denotes mutual influence. It emphasises the dynamic and back-and-forth nature of a movement. At the same time, the term has a normative and critical implication. Thus, there must be a mutual confrontation and verification of the primary and secondary sources of the past and the present.

Next, there is the adage *Lex orandi lex credendi*.[39] This accentuates the entirely unique, privileged and irreplaceable place of liturgy among the other *loci theologici*. Liturgy can bring to light what remains more or less hidden in other *loci*, and can act as a supplement and corrective with regard to other *loci*. Wegman is correct in arguing for the primacy of ritual as a *locus theologicus*, especially in its peculiar, continuing and contemporary creativity. This is generally – and unjustly – subjected to the norms of, and constrained by secondary loci. But it is not only secondary loci that are involved. I have the impression that Wegman is likewise referring to with the officially sanctioned – and heavily inculturated – primary loci from the past, *and* the officially sanctioned loci from the present, the *editiones typicae*. He is correct to the extent that he identifies undeserved restraint and defends the irreplaceable value of the primary liturgical current. This cannot function without its own, peculiar *élan vital*. In that sense this current of the long duration sets its own norms and legitimises itself. But this does not mean that one can elevate the primary liturgy of past and present – particularly in its appropriated form – to the ultimate normative structure, without confronting it with, and letting it enter into a process of interference with, the many other *loci theologici* in a critical manner. To not do so would be one-sided.[40] It would treat liturgy as too

---

[37] BRADSHAW: 'Difficulties in Doing Liturgical Theology' 188.

[38] POST: 'Interference and Intuition'

[39] For a bibliographic survey of the literature on this adage K. IRWIN: *Liturgical Theology: A Primer*, Collegeville Minnesota 1990, 11-14; IDEM: *Context and Text: Method in Liturgical Theology*, Collegeville Minnesota 1994, 3-43.

[40] See also JOHNSON: 'Can We Avoid Relativism in Worship?' 144.

independent of the total of the other loci, which all have their *raison d'être*. Even as one may very correctly have serious objections to the separation of the magisterium from the total of the loci, and against elevating it to a unique, sanctifying norm, so one may not isolate the primary liturgical stream in its appropriation from the whole. But taking this into account, one can still say that liturgy has a peculiar, irreplaceable norm-giving role, which moreover functions in both directions, in theological comparative verification of the past with the present, and the present with the past.

Indeed, in this process the normative character of the liturgy from the past with regard to the present is a more complicated matter than is sometimes suggested. Wegman correctly points to the contingency in the growth of Western liturgy. What is now characterised as belonging to the *lex orandi* in essence rests on chance.[41] The question thus arises at every turn, of what the criteria are by which a concrete liturgy from the past, or parts thereof, can be regarded as *lex credendi*. How is it we are to understand *the* liturgy in this adage? That of the universal church, east and west? That of the Western or Eastern church? That of the majority of local churches? That of some influential local churches? Wainwright has occupied himself with questions of this sort, and has come up with no conclusive answers.[42] What is more, when discussing the normative character of the *lex orandi* of the past, he points to the authority of the critical exceptions to the near-universality of some liturgical practices. For instance, the rejection of particular, separate sacraments by the Quakers has pointed the way for an authentic sacramental view of the whole of human life. Certainly the ecumenical and transcultural liturgical *ordo*, suggested by Lathrop, is interesting. It is based on the post-resurrection appearances of Jesus, the description of baptismal and Sunday worship by Justin, the traditional confessional documents and current ecumenical convergence in liturgical practice and interpretation.[43] Whatever the case,

[41] WEGMAN: 'Liturgie en lange duur'; see also VAN TONGEREN: 'Liturgie in context' 190-191.

[42] G. WAINWRIGHT: *Doxology. The Praise of God in Worship, Doctrine and Life. A Systematic Theology*, Westminster 1982², 251-283; see also B. VAN DIJK: *Zoek het Levend Water waar het zich vinden laat: in bronnen. Een studie naar het gebruik van de liturgie als zoek- en vindplaats in de bilaterale dialoog tussen de Lutherse Wereld Federatie en de Rooms-Katholieke Kerk* (M.A. Thesis Theologische Faculteit Tilburg), Tilburg 1991, 80-88.

[43] G. LATHROP: *Holy Things. A Liturgical Theology*, Minneapolis 1993; IDEM: *What are the Essentials of Christian Worship?*, Minneapolis 1994. See JOHNSON: 'Can We Avoid Relativism in Worship?' 137-139.

the adage *lex orandi, lex credendi* definitely has considerable value, but with regard to its application one runs into a complex problem, and constant critical reflection, with an accent on the two-way traffic between the past and present, and on the importance of collective dialogue – in an ecumenical framework as well – remains necessary.

Third, there is the question of what is to be understood by congruence and identity in the literal sense of the word. An initial answer might be that identity, in the literal sense of the word, is to be understood as 'being the same in about the same way' – that is to say, dressed in the same cultural clothing – while congruency refers to 'being the same in a new way', in another culture. The next question then arises: how do you determine that something is in essence the same in the new cultural expression (both linguistic and non-linguistic)? It cannot be denied that over the last decades hermeneutics have made an important contribution on this issue. I will limit myself, so far as liturgy is concerned, with a reference to the investigation by Schillebeeckx with regard to the new approaches to the *realis praesentia* in comparison with the classic approach by way of transubstantiation.[44] In this connection I would also refer to my approach to the question of what was and is intended during and after the Second Vatican Council by the substantial unity of the Roman rite, and whether or not this substance goes beyond that which is culturally determined about this ritual.[45] In both cases hermeneutics, which is heavily defined by cognitive intuition, plays a decisive role in the approach. The question is whether here too further clarification and augmentation is possible through a more controllable semiotic approach. I wish to address this question further.

In my opinion, from the perspective of semiotics congruity is a matter of the deep structures of the discourses being compared with one another. This can make it clear that the same or analogous deep structures, with their contrasts and contradictions at the more concrete superficial level of narrative structures and the even more concrete discursive level of figurativity can be given shape in rather distinctive and varied manners.[46] Within groups of discourses one often encounters

---

[44] E. SCHILLEBEECKX: *The Eucharist*, New York 1968.

[45] LUKKEN: 'Inculturatie van de liturgie' 34-42.

[46] For the technical terms see LUKKEN: 'De semiotiek van de Parijse school'; IDEM: 'Semiotische analyse van de Schrift in homiletisch perspectief. Semiotische vragen aan de (bijbel)tekst', in LUKKEN & MAAS: *Luisteren tussen de regels* 32-70.

specific models of discursive enunciative praxis that are characteristic of a particular culture or subculture. In this, it can happen that the contemporary enunciative praxis is surprisingly new, and can even serve as a touchstone with regard to the enunciative discursive praxis of the past: it can clarify, nuance, critique or supplement this. It is here important to underline that in this case it is not the past which serves as the touchstone for the present, but precisely the other way around: the present as a touchstone for the past.

Each time it is attempted, penetrating deep structures from the concrete, manifested enunciative praxis demands careful and laborious semiotic analysis. But this is necessary to gain insight into the continuity of the similar elements. In essence, this is the semiotic translation of the question of *longue durée*. When radical shifts appear at the level of deep structures, theology generally becomes cautious. But that is not enough. It can be that there are shifts in the deep structures of the discursive enunciative praxis – for instance, in contrariety or contradiction – which at first sight appear radical, but ultimately, after further analysis, are only marginal, or only shifts in emphasis.[47] Here, it seems to me, one encounters the question of the hierarchy of values, which one can homologise with that of the *hierarchia veritatum* (hierarchy of truths).[48] In this light, one can make distinctions between central and more peripheral deep structures.

When Wegman emphasises the contingency of the liturgy of the past and the discontinuity between the liturgy of the past and present, one realises that in liturgical literature and in ecclesiastical pronouncements discursive structures or superficial structures as such are rather often declared necessary constants, and in that, deep structures. Is that not the case, for instance, when people declare a certain family of rites sacrosanct? Viewed from the perspective of semiotics, it is always a matter of deep structures, and even there one must introduce a hierarchy. Bradshaw's observation should be taken to heart. According to him, 'the "deep structures" running through liturgy are very few indeed, if we apply the test of universal observance to them. There are very few things that Christians have consistently done in worship at all times and in all

---

[47] An example of this is to be found in J. COURTÉS: 'Sémiotique et théologie du péché', in J. COURTÉS: *Sémantique de l'énoncé: applications pratiques*, Paris 1989, 178-224.

[48] See for instance E. SCHILLEBEECKX: 'Ruptures dans les dogmes chrétiens', in *Bulletin ET. Zeitschrift für Theologie in Europa* 8 (1997) 1, 28-29.

places.'[49] I believe that the deep structures can in every case be opened up for discussion and tested, in part from contemporary liturgical enunciative praxis. This is a creative process that takes contemporary liturgical praxis with the utmost seriousness, subjects it to further in-depth analysis, and employs it in a critical-normative manner with regard to the past, but on the other hand is also prepared to take the past seriously as a touchstone. What is involved here is thus a dynamic theological verification, the point of departure for which is not exclusively located in the past, nor exclusively in the present, but which in continual dialogue does justice to the tensive relation in time, with its unavoidable trio of past, present and future. Furthermore, in liturgical research the realisation can be active in the background that it is a question of doing justice to the right praise (*orthodoxia*) of the anamnesis:[50] the process of giving shape to the memory of the central acts of salvation of Jesus' death and resurrection, every anew, in every culture, in the present, not purely as events that remain in the past and slide toward oblivion, but as vital today, and into the future. This is the ultimate and in a certain sense simple deep structure that encompasses all the others. It is simple however only in a certain sense, because discovering this deep structure in the actual enunciative praxis demands a repeated, careful and labour intensive semiotic analysis, which to an important degree can supplement hermeneutics and always should precede this hermeneutics.

When this semiotic analysis is performed in community it is generally more reliable than an individual analysis. One can also formulate this more broadly. The questions about continuity, discontinuity and congruence are ultimately questions which can never be answered by any single individual; there is always a struggle in which all sources for theology come into play, including the whole contemporary Christian church community – or rather, church communities – in all their parts, in mutual dialogue.

Perhaps the following diagram will clarify the integral and open research design that has been sketched above:

---

[49] BRADSHAW: 'Difficulties in Doing Liturgical Theology' 184-185.

[50] In the early Church and especially in the East, the liturgy was known as *theologia prima* and dogmatic speculation as *theologia secunda*. The first meaning of 'orthodoxy' was also right praise (*ortho-doxia*) in the liturgy and it is only in the secondary, derived sense that it came to mean teaching. See G. LUKKEN: 'The Unique Expression of Faith in the Liturgy', in *Concilium* 2 (1973) 9, 19.

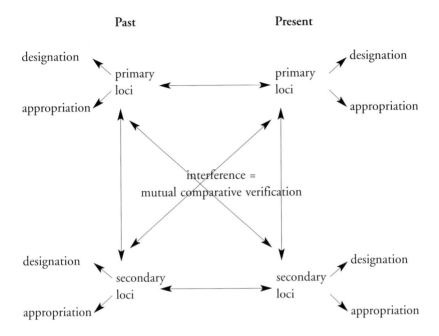

CHAPTER 4

SEVERAL SPECIFIC PROBLEM AREAS IN RESEARCH

To close this section, I wish to go into several specific problem areas with regard to ritual and culture. These involve the question of research in ritual in the context of culture, the role of the researcher, the difference between oral and written culture, and the role of history.

1. RESEARCH AND CONTEXT

From the foregoing it is clear that research into Christian ritual is wide-ranging and complex, for one can only do justice to it in its integrity if one studies the ritual as an inculturated object. This means that one must involve the whole cultural context of the ritual in the research, including all the layers and sectors that are linked with the culture, and including too the reception, appropriation and actual experience of the ritual. At this point it seems important to me to remind readers that the concept of *inculturation* has gradually replaced the concept of *contextualisation*.[1] Thus, to speak of ritual as an *inculturated* object is synonymous with speaking of it in its *integral* context.

Such research is however so sweeping and complex that a careful delineation of the object will be necessary every time work is undertaken. I would here call upon semiotics for clarification on this point. Careful delineation of the object is ordinarily necessary for any responsible scientific research. In a certain sense one could endlessly expand the context of the ritual to be investigated, as will appear from my remarks on the concept of culture and on comparative verification. If the investigation is not to be purely intuitive, it will be important to always determine which context – that is to say, which layer of the culture and of the comparative verification – will be involved in the research. Once the object is *delineated*, then the question becomes whether one can still speak of context within

---

[1] For the various terms and their exact meaning see the literature cited in Part 2, Chapter 2.2, note 28.

the delineated object, because the true further context is that which lies outside the delineated object, and the object itself can be considered as one structural whole, one integral symbolic order, within which the status quo and developments can be studied. This study can be:

a) diachronic: through the syntax with its destinators (senders, causes, reasons, critics, etc.), actors (subjects of doing), value objects, aspectualizations (lines of approach), points of view, passions and emotions, etc.;
b) synchronic: through investigation of mutual relations, differences and tensions in the semantics;
c) performative: through the traces that the act of utterance (enunciation) have left behind in the delimited object, which can be a reflection of and a reference to the context presumed by the object.[2]

If however for the interpretation of the delimited object one calls upon the help of a context that is not reflected enunciatively in the delineated object itself, one is in fact further expanding the object of investigation. In doing so, one enters into an endless process which will only end when the integral inculturated object is studied. If one still wishes to involve a wider context in the object, it is better to expand the object and once again define it carefully and precisely, than to fall into the danger to which Greimas has correctly drawn attention: namely that the indeed insufficient but in any case certain information that the analysis of the delineated expression produces affords us 'more clarity with regard to the enunciation than the sociological parameters that one produces somewhat randomly and in unlimited numbers, like a magician pulling rabbits from his hat.'[3]

2. THE ROLE OF THE INVESTIGATOR

Completely objective research is impossible. There is always a personal angle in an investigation.[4] This can be a particular method or approach

---

[2] For an elucidation of the semiotic terms used here, see A.J. GREIMAS, A.J. & J. COURTÉS: *Sémiotique. Dictionnaire raisonné de la théorie du langage*, Tome 1, Paris 1979 = A.J. GREIMAS & J. COURTÉS: *Semiotics and Language. An Analytical Dictionnary*, Bloomington 1982 = A.J. GREIMAS & J. COURTÉS: *Analytisch woordenboek van de semiotiek*, Vol. 1, Tilburg 1987. See also LUKKEN & MAAS: *Luisteren tussen de regels*.
[3] GREIMAS & COURTÉS: *Sémiotique. Dictionnaire*, 391, sub verbo 'sociosémiotique'.
[4] COURTÉS: *Du lisible au visible* 260-262, also for the following.

within the whole of simultaneously acknowledged possibilities, for instance the literary/historical method, a feminist approach, a semiotic approach, etc. It can also be the limitation in the researcher's approach that is unavoidable as a result of his or her own culture. All these lines of approach are paradigms, as it were – that is to say, frames of reference that are specific; they involve the exclusion of certain parameters in favour of others which one believes to be more productive for the research. For instance, there is the paradigm of official medical science, which explains physical problems first and foremost as a result of physiological causes that must be treated in an organic manner, while certain alternative therapies on the contrary give preference to psychological causes and treatments based on that approach. Within liturgical studies there is at this moment a growing conviction that intra- and interdisciplinary research in the framework of ritual studies is the most adequate (or in any case, is a very adequate) method. Whatever the case, it is clear that even the most objective academic research is preceded by a 'belief' rather than real knowing. Therefore science rests on the order of subjective beliefs, possibly of a very extensive community, rather than on objective knowing. Every researcher is unavoidably shaped by the social-cultural, geographic and historical limitations of his or her own time. Every era, every culture therefore has its own 'myths' as presuppositions. Courtés points out that in the Middle Ages levitation was the object of scientific discussion, according to the insights of the time, but that levitations slowly disappeared once the law of gravity was formulated. The most recent miracles appear to be those of Lourdes: these involve miracles that withdraw from the bio-physiological terrain that is still not yet completely dominated by science. Thus, we can only perceive what our culture *permits* us to perceive. It is simply the case that our communication with reality always takes place through our corporality, which is necessarily defined by time and place, and therefore is also very limited. What is involved is always *my*, and *our* perception, here and now, within the framework of the paradigm, selected by the researcher and necessarily limited by the cultural situation.

One could thus say that the researcher himself or herself always is at least some part of that which is observed, and that already before any analysis there is interpretation. It is however the case that there is a gradation recognised in anthropological research into ritual. The researcher can investigate ritual as an outsider; he can also engage in participatory research, which is to say research in which he both participates in the ritual and thereafter, and in its context, reflects upon it. In this connection, Grimes distinguishes the following 'layers':[5]

1. prereflective participation in a ritual,
2. reflective participation, as that of a priest, rabbi or educated layman,
3. sympathetic participatory observation, such as that of a field researcher,
4. distanced observation and description,
5. taxonomy, classification and categorisation,
6. theoretical interpretation,
7. reflection on theories and/or theoreticians.

To my mind, ritual studies concentrates upon the third layer, and subsequently moves in the direction of 1-2 and 4-7.

After the foregoing it should be clear that the participatory research of which Grimes speaks can also be qualified as scientific, although on the condition that one explicitly and precisely declare the relevant expansion of the object, and distinguish the layers carefully.

In what I have presented here I have tried to clarify some fundamental research problems with regard to liturgy in the framework of ritual studies through Greimassian semiotics. The ideal always remains a rigorously academic approach, according to which one must precisely justify the delimited object, and the framework (paradigm) within which the research is to take place must be indicated. This is what is always sought for in the formulation of criteria for the assessment of research. But at the same time it is true that this is an ideal. Even in the most rigorous application of scientific methods it is easy to overstep boundaries, and from time to time to make intuitive judgements. That is definitely permitted. But one must realise that it is in fact not right to formulate these as certainties or conclusions, because they are only hypotheses which must be tested by further research.

In these considerations my concern was a problem with which all researchers are confronted with – perhaps all the more when they enter into a field of intra- and interdisciplinary research, and wish to study ritual in the context of culture. These considerations will also have their own paradigm, and it therefore cannot be concluded that what I have said is the last word on the subject. What I have said here must also be regarded as a challenge to further discussion.

---

[5] GRIMES: *Beginnings in Ritual Studies* 162.

3. THE DIFFERENCE BETWEEN ORAL AND WRITTEN CULTURE[6]

Bell has pointed out that most studies on ritual have their roots in ethnographic observations of oral cultures.[7] Consequently people sometimes forget that the ritual life in oral societies is considerably different from societies that are familiar with writing and printing. Cultural change has a different dynamic in each of the two. In stable oral cultures the transmission of myth is accompanied by constant adaptations, the purpose of which is to assure that the myth remains relevant to the aims of the society involved, in a balanced manner. The way in which the transmission of the royal genealogies took place in traditional Tahiti is interesting. When a change of dynasties happened, the traditional myth had to be adapted to conform with the new political situation. To accomplish this the priests would make small, insignificant 'errors' each time the genealogies were recited, until the adaptations were completed. Thus nothing changed in the ritual officially, but in fact there was almost constant change.[8]

According to Bell, in an oral society change is a constant and relatively unproblematic matter, because that which is the closest to the Ur-myth, an Ur-genealogy or Ur-ritual is there stored in the memory of the people, with all the variants thereof which are shaped in a particular situation. People can routinely introduce changes into the ritual, because they do not have documents with the 'original' and 'true' version. For example, among the Dayaks of Borneo there was a custom of killing a slave as a foundation offering during the construction of certain buildings. The slave was placed in the hole that was dug for the main supporting pillar of the structure, and slain when the pillar was erected.[9] During the Dutch colonial period this was forbidden. This led to a change in the ritual: people sacrificed a water buffalo instead of a slave, and the myth was adapted in this spirit: in the time of the forefathers

---

[6] In relation to this, see also Part 1, Chapter 4.1.

[7] See, also for the following, BELL: 'The Authority of Ritual Experts' 104-109; IDEM: *Ritual Theory* 130-140; IDEM: *Ritual. Perspectives* 202-205.

[8] In this connection see BELL: 'The Authority of Ritual Experts' 105 refers to (among others) the Dutch authority on comparative religion P. VAN BAAREN: 'The Flexibility of Myth', in A. DUNDES: *Sacred Narrative: Readings in the Theory of Myth*, Berkeley 1984, 218.

[9] BELL: 'The Authority of Ritual Experts' 106 also refers here to VAN BAAREN: 'The Flexibility of Myth' 219.

the slave who would have been thrown into the hole was changed into a water buffalo. Considerable discussion arose among the Dayaks about this change, but ultimately people reached a consensus. Apparently for an oral society the agreement between ritual and what precisely happened at a certain moment in the past was not the most important issue. There tradition is something that only exists in the flexible embodiment of memory and contemporary cultural life. In oral culture ritual confirms tradition, even where it transforms that tradition in the specific circumstances of each ritual performance.

The rise of writing however has important consequences for the perception of tradition and the place of authority with regard to rituals. Written documents lead to what one can call an historical consciousness: the realisation that life today differs considerably from what it was in the past. Moreover, writing is accompanied by ritual being turned into text, which subsequently begins to function as prescription and norm. Through this, tradition comes to be understood differently: it is no longer immediately embodied in customs and actual practice, but is something which must be reproduced and protected against change. As the distance between the past and present becomes greater, complex institutions of experts arise who mediate between the past and present through their explanations and interpretations. They connect the unchanging historical sources with the changing community of today. Authority now resides in the written rules and with those who know and interpret them. It no longer resides in what is done in actual practice, but in the written word. In the same way that writing defines social-religious authority and tradition differently and in a new manner, so ritual is viewed and used in a different way. It is no longer a matter of performing that which the people are always assumed to have done, but of performing in a 'correct' way that is laid down in texts. Prayers are repeated and recited, and liturgy is followed or read in this context. With regard to changes: in an oral culture, as the embodiment of tradition ritual can change in a flexible manner in order to remain in harmony with the community; ritual changes without necessarily calling up the image of change as such and problematising the change. But in literate societies with written models change very quickly becomes a problem that threatens tradition and authority. On the one hand, the written ritual traditions can more easily prevent and check on changes there, because the texts have authority as such, and function as a standard in case of any deviation. On the other hand, a textual, written tradition facilitates more open access to liturgical knowledge and explicit questions about the meaning, legitimacy and originality of the tradition. This encourages the rise of experts who can enter into discussion with one another. Compared with an oral society, literate societies are the scene of much more consultation and discussion, and within them there are controversial standpoints, including fundamentalist views.

Turning ritual into text and the rise of authoritative directives which accompanies that, can be connected with a number of other developments. Among these Bell lists the establishment of what are asserted to be universal values above the more local and particular, the organisation of bureaucratic and centralised institutions, and the rise of concepts such as orthodoxy versus heterodoxy, codified doctrines and formal dogmas.[10] In this way textual ritual inevitably leads to a tension between a centralised liturgical tradition and local ritual life.

Following Goody, Bell remarks that it is a misunderstanding to simply divide societies into oral and literate societies, because literacy never completely replaces oral transmission.[11] This unquestionably has consequences for ritual. Even in literate societies some parts of communal life always remain overwhelmingly oral. This means that there are layers which compete with one another, and various kinds of ritual experts. One can, for example, distinguish literary experts with official positions, and experts who are closer to the base community.[12] I have the impression that in liturgical studies at this moment interest in the oral layer of liturgy is increasing rather than decreasing, and that a growing number of experts are emphasising its importance. In any case, this is what I have stressed in Part 1; it is, so to speak, a parameter that in part determines my reflections on ritual in general, and that on the basis of the preceding I wished to make more explicit. Moreover, I believe that illuminating the difference between oral and written culture with regard to ritual can give a clearer insight into the way in which the renewal of liturgy after the Second Vatican Council was launched precisely by experts, and into the many tensions that have arisen, and continue to arise during this process of renewal. I will return to that in Part 3.

---

[10] BELL: 'The Authority of Ritual Experts' 108.
[11] BELL: 'The Authority of Ritual Experts' 107, note 19. See J. GOODY: *The Interface Between the Written and the Oral*, Cambridge 1987, XII.
[12] BELL: 'The Authority of Ritual Experts' 108.

4. The role of history

In the first Part it appeared that the experience of ritual time is not the same in all cultures. I pointed to the distinction between the cyclic experience of time in archaic cultures and the linear experience of time which began with the Chaldeans in the eighth century before Christ, which very quickly spread, and is characteristic of the Jewish, Muslim and Christian religions.

In the cyclic experience of time people seek contact with sacred occurrences of the Ur-time in and through ritual by separating themselves from changeable time, and thus participating in the sacred Ur-events, divine occurrences that took place in the Ur-time. The community departs from chronologically ordered time into another time which lies at the beginning of all things, but by the same token can be endlessly repeated.

In the linear experience of time however there is a different form of ritual remembrance of the past. In and through ritual people seek contact with sacred acts that took place in the past. These events are not outside of chronological time, but took place within our history. There is no question of stepping out from the present into a sort of timeless state. The 'then' and the salvific acts which then took place are celebrated as contemporary today, in a tension reaching into the future. For example, the Jews celebrate the mighty salvific acts that JHWH performed for the Jewish people within our history, and Christians celebrate especially the salvific acts in and through Jesus of Nazareth, born of the Jewish people and died under Pontius Pilate. They remember this Jesus, who was crucified, but whom God raised from the dead and appointed as Lord and messiah (Acts 2:36). With him has come the fullness of time, while history is still in full swing. It will only reach its fulfilment when the Lord returns, at the end of time. This future is also 'remembered': Lies aptly characterises this as *Blick des Voraus im Zurück* (Glance ahead into the past).[13] In and through the liturgy the Christian community enters into the sacred events which were performed in that time (*in illo tempore*), which once again become contemporary, and will someday be a full reality. There is no sense of cyclically recurring events, but rather a linear movement which embraces the past, present and future. This manner of commemoration among Jews and Christians is denoted with the technical word *anamnesis*: remembrance.

---

[13] Lies: *Eucharistie in ökumenischer Verantwortung* 52.

Thus time is a fundamental category in all ritual, and in our Western culture that involves linear time. People seek coherence and continuity in and through rituals. They seek to link and involve past, present and future with one another. In this way people attempt to hold on to the meaning of what was once experienced as meaningful. Ritual is, as it were, an attempt to recover the past, experience it and give it significance again. That which was salutary is taken up again as a source of vitalisation for the present and the time which is to come. Rituals attempt to perfect that which alas remains incomplete.[14]

The original events of 'then' always play a decisive role in the commemoration of the past. Rituals are therefore always connected in one way or another with the foundation narratives through which they were set in motion, as it were. That which happened then is a stimulus to remembrance in the present, in a tension reaching into the future. It is in this context that the concepts of *invention of tradition* and *invented tradition* play a role.[15] As it happens, from time to time the appeal to tradition, to foundation narratives, rests on non-authentic, invented or manipulated stories, promoting alleged, supposed or created traditions. Thus it is for instance sometimes suggested that people have celebrated Carnival for long generations in a particular place, while this ritual is actually of a rather recent date there.[16] When De Coubertin began the international Olympic Games in 1896 as a ceremony and ritual of international competition and community peculiar to itself, he appealed to the tradition of the Greek Olympic games in ancient Athens.[17] The ritual of crowning the British monarch, which in fact dates from the end of the 19th century, is regarded as having been handed down from time immemorial: a tradition that must be at least a thousand years old. Even the skittish horses that disrupted the funeral of Queen Victoria were immediately incorporated into the old ritual.[18] If something is a ritual, it must always have existed; it is thus even possible to create 'age-old' rituals while people watch.[19] In connection with this invented tradition, one could also note that already in the early church there were from

---

[14] See Part 1, Chapter 4, 3.
[15] BELL: *Ritual Theory* 118-124; IDEM: *Ritual. Perspectives* 223-242.
[16] C. WIJERS: *Prinsen en clowns in het Limburgse Narrenrijk. Het carnaval in Simpelveld en Roermond 1945-1992*, Amsterdam 1995.
[17] Extensively on this, BELL: *Ritual. Perspectives* 231-235.
[18] BELL: *Ritual. Perspectives* 148.
[19] BELL: *Ritual. Perspectives* 149.

time to time appeals to apostolic tradition with regard to rituals, even if the ritual involved in fact did not go back to the time of the apostles. In this way authority was bestowed on the ritual involved. And in contemporary Islam one for instance finds all sorts of movements that pretend to be returns to the purer Islam of the past, but which in fact give an entirely new shape to the Islamic tradition.[20]

The concepts of invention of tradition and invented tradition are derived from Hobsbawm, who together with Ranger edited a collection in 1983 entitled *The Invention of Tradition*.[21] Post however points out that through a critical rereading of Hobsbawm important nuances are possible.[22] Viewed in this perspective, the concept essentially expresses the ever-changing ways men have of dealing with the past and the constant construction of traditions. Ultimately it becomes a matter of recognising that every way of dealing with the past is a construct.[23] That has always been the case. It is also important in this context to note that in much of the academic literature on early Christianity one can observe a thoroughgoing mythologisation of the period in which the Church arose. In many cases, according to Rouwhorst, the reconstruction of the early Church found there is deeply influenced and coloured by certain idealised images that have their roots in the researcher's ecclesiastical or confessional context.[24] Among Protestant authors the motif of *sola scriptura* often plays a major rule, consciously or unconsciously, and among Roman Catholic authors there is frequently the inclination to assume a greater continuity between the early phase of Christianity and later periods. The early phase then serves to more or less expressly legitimise later

---

[20] J. TENNEKES: *De Bierkaai en de Bron. Antropologische kanttekeningen bij hedendaags christendom*, Kampen 2000, 139.

[21] E. HOBSBWAM & T. RANGER (eds.): *The Invention of Tradition*, Cambridge 1983; see therein E. HOBSBWAM: 'Introduction. The Invention of Tradition' 1-14. See also GRIMES: *Reading, Writing, and Ritualizing* 5-22 ('Reinventing ritual').

[22] P. POST: 'Traditie gebruiken. Sint Hubertus in Muiderberg', in VAN UDEN, PIEPER & HENAU (eds.): *Bij geloof,* 191-211; IDEM: 'Het verleden in het spel?'; IDEM: 'De creatie van traditie volgens Eric Hobsbawm'; IDEM: 'Zeven notities over rituele verandering'; IDEM: 'Rituals and the Function of the Past: Rereading Eric Hobsbawm', in *Journal of Ritual Studies* 10 (1998) 85-107; IDEM: 'The Creation of Tradition: Rereading and Reading beyond Hobsbawm', in J.W. VAN HENTEN & A. HOUTEPEN (eds.): *Religious Identity and the Invention of Tradition. Papers Read at a Noster Conference in Soesterberg, January 4-6, 1999* (Studies in Theology and Religion 3), Assen 2001.

[23] See also TENNEKES: *De Bierkaai en de Bron* 136-150.

[24] G. ROUWHORST: 'A la recherche du christianisme primitif', in *Bulletin ET. Zeitschrift für Theologie in Europa* 8 (1997) 2, 181-195.

ecclesiastical practices. In both cases, however, people run the risk of projecting idealised images onto early Christianity which do little or no justice to the actual history. As examples Rouwhorst discusses the role of ecclesiastical offices in the period during which the Church came into being, research into the early Christian celebration of Eucharist, and the image in many liturgical studies of the liturgical traditions of the city of Rome. He therefore argues that the study of early Christianity not be considered as closed, but that it be a continuing task, in which the researchers at all times make their own positions and assumptions clear.

Following from the foregoing, one might say that our view of the past is always coloured by the paradigm of our own culture. History is written with the conscious or unconscious concern for creating meaning, with an eye to continuity or discontinuity with the events the past. Historiography too is a constructed narrative. It involves a knowing of the past that is consciously or unconsciously represented and recycled according to the value patterns of one's own culture. Thanks to dealing with the past in this way, people can orient themselves in time.[25] According to Veyne, history exists only 'through the questions that we pose. Materially it is written with facts, bur formally with a problematic and with concepts.'[26] From this view of history, one can also perhaps better understand the differing ways that oral and written cultures deal with history, as discussed above. The way we have of dealing with the past is in part, in one manner or another, determined by our search for identity, both individually and collectively, and either way a creative handling of tradition plays an important role in it. Such creative handling can take many forms. This pluriformity is the result of the distinctions between the various cultures – for instance, oral and literate cultures – but equally the different points of view within one and the same culture. It is important to take as thorough a census of these points of view as possible, certainly when radical shifts in a culture are occurring, as is the case in the West at this moment. Between the extremes of a fundamentalist handling of the past and the pure invention of the past lie many degrees. Furthermore, it is always important to keep sight of the various literary genres involved. The ritual of news reports is more strongly connected with facts from the past than the ritual of carnival is. But even with the ritual of news reports one must

[25] KOK-ESCALLE: *Instaurer une culture* 22-23.
[26] P. VEYNE: *L'inventaire des différences*, Paris 1976, 9.

realise that construction and selection are involved. With regard to this, in the genre of the documentary even more is possible than in news reports. For example, there was a documentary about an attack in Ireland that began with images of a jeep riding past houses in Germany, while it was suggested that one was in Ireland all the time. Analysis after the fact has revealed that the filmed report of the execution of the presidential couple in Romania, the Ceausescus, which was broadcast worldwide on television in 1990, was not live, but constructed.[27] According to expert criminological research the couple must have already been executed several hours before the images were made in the same place. With an awareness of the creativity within ritual, it is therefore important to have insight into the various 'literary' genres: ritual is a matter of stories and play rather than the bare facts and literalness. On the other hand, it remains true that rituals are also bound by certain limits, either precisely as ritual, or, as I have indicated above, as ritual within a particular, for instance Christian tradition.

The interrelations of ritual and culture have far-reaching consequences when a radical cultural transition takes place, as is now happening in our Western European culture. That calls up many questions, which will be dealt with further in Part 3. This is especially true for Christian ritual. The primary question is whether the experience of the Lord as the firstborn from the dead is possible here today in a worthy manner.

---

[27] J. POST: *Optische effecten in de film. Aanzetten tot een semiotische analyse*, Leuven 1998, 152-160, 212.

PART 3

CHRISTIAN RITUAL IN OUR CULTURE

Particularly since the end of the 1960s, The Netherlands and many other Western European countries have been subject to a radical cultural shift which has had important consequences for both ritual in general, and for Christian ritual. What can be said about ritual in this culture, and in particular about the place, shape and identity of Christian ritual? That is the topic which I will take up in this section. Following the line of the preceding anthropological considerations, in the course of this I will be discussing Christian liturgy as Christian ritual, or, as the case may be, as the ritual of Christian churches. I realise that in doing so I will be accentuating one specific approach, namely that of anthropology.[1] I will return to the question of the legitimacy *and* the limitations of this approach at the end of this section.

First I will attempt to sketch the outlines of contemporary culture (Chapter 1). Then follows a chapter regarding the development of ritual since the 1960s: from a crisis in ritual to an abundance of rituals in recent years (Chapter 2). This is succeeded by a chapter discussing ritual in our culture (Chapter 3). The chapter which follows discusses the new place of Christian ritual in the midst of many rituals (Chapter 4). A very specific development is that of Christian ritual at a distance (Chapter 5). In the sixth chapter I emphasise the importance of an inductive and adequate liturgy. After that I discuss the renewed attention for the presentative character of Christian ritual (Chapter 7). An extensive examination of the new rites of passage from birth to death follows in Chapter 8, after which several important dimensions and themes in contemporary Christian ritual are taken up (Chapter 9). This third section will be rounded off with a reflection on the peculiar identity of Christian ritual (Chapter 10).

---

[1] BELL: *Ritual. Perspectives* 218, remarks: 'The term "liturgy" comes from the Greek *leitourgia*, meaning an act of public service or ministry. It has been the preferred term for Christian scholars talking about their own rites and ritual tradition, although these scholars are increasingly comfortable with the neutral and more embracing term 'ritual'. That Christian scholars can situate their liturgies within the broad context of human ritual in general represents an important development in their liturgical tradition'.

CHAPTER 1

CONTEMPORARY CULTURE

It is not easy to provide a brief characterisation of contemporary culture.[2] Yet I wish to make the attempt. In doing so I will limit myself to
the most obvious characteristics. These will involve developments which
are unavoidable and ubiquitous, although not always present in the
same degree, either in The Netherlands or in Western Europe. In general one can characterise our culture on the basis of two concepts:
modernity and post-modernism. But there are also new developments
which are appearing and ushering in a new phase of interdependence
which might be characterised as the emergence of a 'network culture'
and of globalisation, and there are signs of a revival of religion.

1. MODERNITY

We may join many sociologists in first pointing to the modernisation of
our society.[3] A number of changes have taken place which we have all
experienced personally, and although they have not penetrated all parts
of society to an equal degree, in global terms one can say that they can
still always be seen as characteristics of Western culture.

Modernity is characterised by a far-reaching process of change resulting in
differentiation.[4] This involves the development of relatively autonomous
sectors or subsystems within the society as a whole, which will include the

---

[2] G. LUKKEN: *Inculturatie en de toekomst van de liturgie* (Liturgie in perspectief 3),
Heeswijk-Dinther 1994 = G. LUKKEN: 'Inculturation et avenir de la liturgie', in *Questions Liturgiques* 75 (1994) 113-134.
[3] L. HALMAN: *Waarden in de Westerse Wereld. Een internationale exploratie van de
waarden in de westerse samenleving*, Tilburg 1991; see also J. VAN DER VEN: *Ecclesiologie
in context*, Kampen 1993, 18-31, 136-140.
[4] In characterising modernity, I have used as my guide L. LAEYENDECKER: 'De keerzijde wordt zichtbaar – Problematische kanten van de moderniteit', in S.W. COUWEN-
BERG (ed.): *Westerse cultuur: model voor de hele wereld*, Kampen 1994, 40-47.

economic system, science, politics, social life and religion. Specific actions are performed within each of these sectors, and these take place on the basis of specific criteria and patterns of values which are operative only within their own sector. For instance, the criteria for science are determined within the sector of science itself. What actions are medically responsible is ultimately decided only within the medical sciences themselves. The adage is that religion must not interfere with economics and politics – and that applies for every sector with regard to every other. The autonomy of the various sectors has isolated the sectors involved from outside influences, and one of the consequences of this is that they have been able to develop as strong individual entities. Their autonomy has led to better performance, both in terms of quality and quantity.

But at the same time something remarkable occurred. In one sense every sector has its own norms and values. One would expect that between themselves the sectors would respect the peculiar norms and values of each sector, or at least be in constant dialogue about them. But in fact this was not the case. In comparison with the previous situation, a radical change took place. The role which religion had previously played as the umbrella spanning the whole of culture and all its layers was now taken over by three sectors which were deeply intertwined with one another, namely economics, science and technology. They have a specific, instrumental manner of dealing with reality, an approach which is purportedly as rational as possible. Means must be attuned to the ends as efficiently as possible.

If one desires to get a better insight into modernity, one must realise what changes have occurred in our economic system. Traditional societies based on agriculture and ownership of land have become industrialised societies. Rather than land, now money, capital, has become the defining factor. This is a radical change. Land was very visible and tangible. Money, capital, is much less so – and even what visibility and tangibility is associated with money is decreasing steadily with the advent of telebanking, payment with plastic cards and investing with electronically traded shares. What we do have is a very *rationally ordered economy*, which moreover has achieved more extensive sway through the globalisation of finances. This economy is oriented to constant growth, in the most efficient manner possible. The goal is to produce ever more, as cheaply as possible, in order to then sell the products at as high a price as possible. The fundamentals of the free market are the organising principle in this, the liberal economic system which is based on competition and the law of the jungle. Since what is produced must be sold, marketing and advertising are therefore an important component of this economic system. The consumer is constantly hammered to buy products. In that process it is sometimes necessary to create a need among consumers for particular products, so that they will buy them. Whatever the case, increasing the field for sales will in turn lead to more production, and thus to more profit. The cycle endlessly repeats itself.

This economic system is by no means a holy cow. It is sharply criticised within our culture. People question if allowing the strongest to carry all before them is just, and about the fate of the weak, be they individuals or groups (whether they are the economically disadvantaged, those who are less talented, the handicapped, ill or elderly), or whole peoples. Is it not the case that in addition to, or as opposed to the survival of the fittest the humane counterpoint of the salvation of the weakest has as much, if not more justification? Whatever the case, it is precisely this salvation of the weakest that touches the core of the biblical message, which is essentially about a very humane culture of compassion for the weak and about charity.[5] At the time this is being written eighty percent of the resources on earth (energy, raw materials) are consumed by the rich nations; that is to say, by twenty percent of the world's population. Furthermore, there is a question of whether limits must be set on 'growth' and competition in order to avoid exhausting energy, natural resources and the environment. Problems are already on the horizon, the basis of which has been illustrated by the ecologist W. Rees in the following compelling image: if everyone on earth at this moment were to enjoy the same standard of living that the West has, we would need two more worlds to sustain the situation. If one calculates the present consumption of resources by the population of The Netherlands in relation to the area they occupy, they would need a territory fifteen times the size of their country – a territory the size of France.[6] In 1994 the Group of Lisbon, under the leadership of R. Petrella, produced the report *Limits of Competition*, in which they argue for the replacement of the principle of ruthless free competition in the market

    [5] B. VAN IERSEL: 'Bible and Evolution. Two Codes – Two Messages', in *Concilium* 36 (2000) 1, 102-111; see also H. HÄRING: 'The Theory of Evolution as a Megatheory of Western Thought', in *Concilium* 36 (2000) 1, 23-34, particularly 30.
    [6] W. REES & M. WACKERNAGEL: *Our Ecological Footprint. Reducing Human Impact on the Earth*, Gabriola Island BC 1998; J. VAN WORKUM: 'Acht aardes, en nóg niet genoeg', in *Roodkoper* 2 (1997) 5, 8-9.

economy with that of cooperation: we must adopt the social contract of a consultation economy internationally.[7] Then it would no longer be a matter of blind faith in the natural and beneficial operation of a market which is governed by an invisible hand, but of open, visible negotiation leading to a regulated economy that meets the needs of all, in which all factors and interests are carefully weighed.[8] Such a model would hold the middle ground between the neo-liberal market model and the centralised economies of communism. Whatever the case, the market mechanism can only do its work well if the economic subjects are conscious of their moral responsibility; its operation within a framework of democratic nations operating under the rule of law and a political system with social-ethical objectives would contribute to that.[9] It would not be just to say that the neo-liberal market model is totally without norms. As the Dutch Liberal European Commissioner Frits Bolkestein has explained, Adam Smith, the father of economic liberalism, argues that man by nature feels sympathy with the lot of his fellow man; the basis of the liberal economy is not conflict and the display of power, but cooperation and competition on the basis of equal rights.[10] But quite correctly the Conference of Bishops of England and Wales recently noted that the Catholic doctrine of the general interest cannot be reconciled with the unlimited free market. The central dogma, as formulated by Smith, is the conviction that in a completely free economy each citizen, by striving to realise his own self-interest, is led by an invisible hand to contribute to a goal which he had never imagined, namely the flourishing of society. That is sometimes the case, but to say that it is always so is a form of economic superstition. Smith himself apparently believed that this rule did not always apply, because he also remarks that by striving for his own self-interest, he *often* serves the interests of society. The Christian doctrine that it is more valuable to serve others than

---

[7] GROUP OF LISBON: *Limits of Competition*, Cambridge, Mass. 1995 (= R. PETRELLA a.o.: *Grenzen aan de concurrentie*, Amsterdam 1994). See also B. GOUDZWAARD & H.M. DE LANGE: *Genoeg van te veel, genoeg van te weinig. Wissels omzetten in de economie*, Baarn 1991 (third revised and augmented edition); H. NOORDEGRAAF & S. GRIFFIOEN (eds.): *Bewogen realisme. Economie, cultuur, oecumene*, Kampen 1999.

[8] See also R. WELTERS: 'De prijs van de markt (Interview with Henk Tieleman)', in *De Bazuin* 78 (1995) (January 20), 8.

[9] V. ZSIFKOVITS: *Wirtschaft ohne Moral?*, Innsbruck/Vienna 1994.

[10] F. BOLKESTEIN: 'Normloosheid is liberalisme vreemd', in *NRC Handelsblad* March 29, 1997, 7.

yourself appears definitely not to be in accordance with the ethos of a capitalist economy.[11] To my mind, the middle position of the Group of Lisbon seems more adequate in this connection.

It is in no way my intention to give a complete sketch of our economic system here. It is just as little my place to propose fully-developed alternatives. What I do wish to do is draw attention to the fact that in our society we are dealing with a very specific economic system that is open to debate, and in which there is a certain fundamental tendency that exercises great influence. This economic system – certainly in its amalgamation with science and technology – comprises an unusually powerful network of organisations, business firms and institutions which define our existence, whether we like it or not. It forms a compulsory context, as it were, for all life.[12] Despite all critique, it is difficult to break through its fundamental tendency. This has important consequences, because this tendency necessarily penetrates the other layers of our culture. It strongly defines our social/political life, and likewise our ethics and conduct. As a rule, the chief interest of the media is the economy: twenty-four hours a day media broadcasts discuss economic growth, rising or falling wages, exchange rates for the dollar and euro, prevention of inflation, the closing prices on the Dow Jones and FTSE indices. One could argue that the economy dominates all sectors of society more than it did previously. This was acutely formulated by the Dutch ethicist Schroten on the Dutch television programme 'Buitenhof': 'Once theology was the queen of the sciences, and now that is economics.' The woman interviewing him restated and aptly reformulated his point: 'Thus economics is the new theology of the sciences.'[13] This formulation is not far from that of Rappaport, when he notes that economic rationality is not only given free rein but is elevated to the status of a general organising principle, and may even claim sanctity.[14] Monetized epistemology becomes a theology, and as such is

[11] CATHOLIC BISHOP'S CONFERENCE OF ENGLAND AND WALES: *The Common Good and the Catholic Church's Social Teaching*, Manchester 1996 = BISSCHOPPENCONFERENTIE VAN ENGELAND EN WALES: 'Verklaring: Het algemeen welzijn en de sociale leer van de katholieke kerk', in *Een-twee-een. Kerkelijke documentatie* 25 (1997) 2/3, 23-24.
[12] L. LAEYENDECKER: 'Kerk en tegencultuur', in *Praktische theologie* 23 (1996) 258.
[13] Television programme *Buitenhof*, June 1, 1997.
[14] RAPPAPORT: *Ritual and Religion in the Making of Humanity* 450.

highly sanctified. It is raised to the status of an 'Ultimate Concern'.[15] Or put in another way, fundamentalism is not only a problem in relation to religious groups; the most important, and most perverse fundamentalism of our time is economic.[16]

We are not always conscious of this, but in fact our norms and values are strongly defined by our economic system. This is true for the political sector, but equally for social sectors such as health care and care for the elderly, sports, education and training, the arts and sciences, and even for religion. All sectors work with quantification and cost-effectiveness calculations. As an entrepreneur must produce as much as possible or go under, so an academic must 'publish or perish'. Similarly there are ongoing discussions of how, based on criteria such as the frequency with which they are cited and weighing the academic publications in Europe, one can arrive at a list of the best economists – a top ten or top fifty –, to then determine where the best economic research centre is. The social relevance of the research in question is hardly a point of discussion in this; it deals rather, and before all else, with whether, amid all the competition, one brings in as many grants for university research as possible, publishes as much as possible, or where students achieve the highest grades. Then there is also the calculation of man-hours for students, of units of credit and the number of class-hours and other tasks a lecturer has, in order to optimise the productivity of education. In such a situation one can understand the following lament: 'Is there really no way back to the way scientific investigation was conducted in the past, with generous time for personal research in the literature and thorough preparation for education, away from 'subsidiological' life on the present university expressway?'[17] And with regard to care for the ill and elderly, there too one finds ever more influence from the market mechanism. For instance, in The Netherlands 'home care' has recently been consigned to the market, and since then has been more and more bound to the principle of doing as much as possible as quickly as possible for the least money. A team must process a certain number of clients in a specified

[15] RAPPAPORT: *Ritual and Religion in the Making of Humanity* 455, 497-498.

[16] JUNG MO SUNG: 'Evil in the Free Market Mentality', in *Concilium* 33 (1997) 5, 24-32.

[17] D. MOSSEL & C.B. STRUIJK: 'De macht van het kleine. Verrukking en vrees in balans', in J. DE VISSCHER (ed.): *Mosterdzaadjes van het bestaan. De waarde van de kleine dingen*, Baarn 1996, 43.

time.[18] In the health care sector the quality of medical treatment is rightly strictly regulated and monitored; at the same time it is also true that an administrative culture devoted to the bottom line is developing there too, which is at the expense of care for the persons themselves.[19] Cost calculation and production are also central in sports: it is no longer a matter of the elegance of the play, the beauty of the moves, but of constant breaking of records, notching up as many points as possible. The trainer of a team with a losing record is fired. The profit motive also leads to such pronouncements as 'Football is war'. It is therefore not surprising that the aggression of the teams on the pitch also provokes aggression among the fans. There is even an effort in our culture to employ our free time as economically as possible, and we have seen a market created for combating the stress that the market itself creates. Of course, one must not paint a totally black picture. It cannot be denied that our rational economy and our cost-calculating approach have led to prosperity. But at the same time it seems that that which is a powerhouse in our culture is also its weakness, certainly when it becomes separated from the larger context.

---

[18] THUISZORG: 'Thuiszorg neigt steeds meer naar 'stopwatch-zorg'', in *NRC Handelsblad* March 20, 1997, 8. In the NCRV television broadcast *Het is onze zorg*, April 14, 1997, the following work schedule for home care by Utrecht's visiting nurses was presented: shower, $\frac{1}{2}$ hour; administering eye drops, ten minutes; feeding, $\frac{3}{4}$ hour; washing and dressing, 40 minutes; removing support hose, ten minutes. One of the nurses remarked: 'Before you had a quarter of an hour for removing support hose, now it's ten minutes, and they would rather you only took five. Sometimes we don't even take off our coats, which is very unsociable.'

[19] H. DE DIJN: *De herontdekking van de ziel. Voor een volwaardige kwaliteitszorg* (Annalen van het Thijmgenootschap 87, 3), Nijmegen 1999. What I am referring to here is striking revealed in the following citation: 'About four years later a woman visited the student pastorate, a very well-educated woman, also – and precisely – in a theological sense, mother of five children, wounded and at her wits end with anxiety and disappointment about her two sons, who were not unknown to me. The younger of the two, once thriving and creative, looked grey from addiction. Without premeditation our visitor reported, "I have already had a couple of conversations with the psychiatrist Vlaar. He is not all that much older than my sons." Dr. Vlaar, said the theologian, "listened as if my story was the first that he ever heard. At a certain point, as a mother I could no longer hold back my tears. After a few minutes I looked up and saw in a flash that his eyes too were glistening with tears." For all her book-learning, according to the erudite woman: "That moment was a revelation for me. His listening struck me as a way of giving...!"' (J. VAN KILSDONK: *Met het licht van jouw ogen ... zegen mij. Toespraken*, Heeswijk 2000, 119-120; see also 33-34, 196-203).

I have already noted the great influence of the *empirical and exact sciences*. This has brought with it the fact that in our culture the world has primarily become a field for research. The exact sciences have played a large role in this. The world is viewed in terms of verifiable results. Technology has increased our capacities immensely. The rise of science and technology has meant enormous progress. They have brought us well-being. But there is also a down side. The dominance of empirical observation has produced a narrowing of our field of vision. A one-dimensional perception has begun to predominate. We have become desensitised observers of nature, who view and manipulate a lifeless cosmos from outside, and without respect.[20] We see, as it were, with only one eye. We have lost our perspective. The world has become grey. We no longer perceive its hues. We have lost a sense of the world's wholeness. Goal-oriented and utilitarian actions prevail. Labour is no longer a meaningful expression for man, but an alienating, impersonal compulsion to be busy that reflects our one-dimensional existence in the world. Our free time too is in service of unequivocal achievement. It has itself become work, or at least is in the service of work: we rest only so that we can work better.[21] Being without work makes us totally desperate.

Modernity has also led to thoroughgoing urbanisation. Steadily increasing concentration of the population makes space more valuable. In an *urban society* work is precisely divided according to function. This has certain major advantages. But at the same time it is true that work is in this way separated from family life. These have become separate sectors, and the family reduced to the small core of parents and children, or other small relation patterns. As a result, relations are no longer direct and all-inclusive as in agrarian cultures, but rather functional and impersonal, and social control decreases; on the other hand, through pushing affective relations back into the private sphere, the smaller relation patterns become more intimate.

It cannot be denied that modernity has had *positive results*.[22] One must acknowledge that progress has occurred. Dozens of illnesses have disappeared. Life expectancy has increased. Technology has made our world

[20] C. Dessaur, C.: *De droom der rede. Het mensbeeld in de sociale wetenschappen. Een poging tot criminosofie*, Den Haag 1982.
[21] Jetter: *Symbol und Ritual* 140 ff.
[22] Laeyendecker: 'De keerzijde wordt zichtbaar' 41.

both larger and smaller. We can travel to distant places with greater ease. The potential for communication has expanded. Larger concentrations of people have resulted in a more efficient infrastructure for transportation, traffic, energy production, education and services. Labour is less heavy and tiring. Individuals can develop their talents and interests better and more freely. The distinctions between social classes have narrowed. One can argue that greater human equality has been achieved. We have a democratic society, with an efficient and rationally organised administration. Authority should be functional, a service to society. It is precisely in that way that it must prove itself. Dialogue is indispensable for accomplishing this. One can observe however that there is a tendency for government to become increasingly bureaucratic and centralised. The historian Von der Dunk characterises The Netherlands as a velvet-covered ball of iron regulations.[23] It is difficult to keep democratic principles and this tendency toward the centralisation of government in balance with one another, but, whatever the case, that is indeed the aim. People strive for greater justice. Human rights have been recognised by international treaty. We are becoming more attentive to the peculiar rights of children. International tribunals are being established. Increasingly the law enforcement apparatus is not oriented only to punishment, but to re-educating perpetrators and protecting the rights of victims. Humane values have clearly enjoyed a victory. On the other hand, it is also true that it is precisely modernity that has brought new crises with it, in well-being, health, water and air pollution, the felling of tropical forests, overcrowding, hectic lifestyles, the lack of time and place for reflection. In this connection, there are also counter-movements, particularly with regard to care for the environment.

In view of our theme, it is important to look more deeply at the consequences of modernity for *religion*. In an agrarian society religion occupied a dominant and overarching place. In Western Europe one could say that Christianity had hegemony over all sectors: politics, social life, economy, education. At the village level the priests and Protestant clergy had an influence on every corner of life, and the villages were dominated visually by their church towers and audibly by the sound of the church bells. In rationalised modern society however religion has lost its

---

[23] H. VON DER DUNK: 'Nederland wordt een fluwelen regelstaat', in *NRC Handelsblad* September 7, 1993, 8.

place as penetrating and influencing all spheres of life, and has become at best one sector of life among many. Rather than church towers, it is the towers of the banks and insurance companies that define the skyline of our cities. They function as the new sacred buildings which offer security for life now, and life to come. Churches have had to surrender their power and social control. Modernisation has forced religion into a marginal position. It lost the scope in society that was once regarded as self-evidently its due. Religion was, as it were, toppled from its throne.

In addition to this, it came under severe criticism, and new and radical questions were posed to it. Modernity also brought with it the *process of secularisation*. It is quite correctly noted that the word 'secularisation' is used in many, and often contradictory, ways.[24] One must use the term carefully. Yet this is a key word representing what many in our culture experience. The word refers to a process which affects our society across the board. On all sides a process is underway, moving from a closed, static society to an open, dynamic society. Taken on its own, this is a neutral phenomenon, but it does have radical consequences for religion. Because of secularisation, people in our culture place more emphasis on the world as *saeculum* than on the world as *kosmos*. If one conceives of the world in terms of the Greek concept of *kosmos*, the world is a static, spatial order. But in the concept embodied in the Latin word *saeculum*, the accent is more on the dynamic of history. In the cosmic world view, God is experienced as the first orderer, the eternal law. Man, in all his doings, is dependent on nature as an objective order given by God. Religious thinking orients itself toward an absolute, unchanging, preordained and supra-historical set of norms and values.[25] In this view of the world the secular aspect has a more or less unfavourable significance: it is the transient, changeable, finite, corporeal, as opposed to the genuinely religious, which is unchanging, immortal, non-corporeal and spiritual. Now, in this view Christian ritual, the liturgy, belongs in the realm of the divine. It is an inviolable and divinely ordained entity, constituted by God's own intervention, and through those who stand closest to the divine world, the 'spiritual fathers'. There is a clear separation between the sacred and profane, between the church service and the

[24] NIJK: *Secularisatie*.
[25] M. PLATTEL & C. RIJK: 'Het geseculariseerd mens- en wereldbeeld in verband met het godsdienstig verschijnsel', in *Werkmap Katholieke Studentendagen 1969 Tilburg*, Tilburg 1968.

world. But our culture looks at the world differently. It considers the world as *saeculum*. In this world view the concept of 'history', and with it the transient, changeable and dynamic, takes on a particular accent. In this vision people find it unacceptable that the sacred be lifted out of history in an almost dualistic manner. Life in the dynamic of history – or to put it differently, the world of labour, family, marriage and social engagement – no longer has to be coupled with the non-sacred. The sacred now functions differently: it functions together with the dynamic of the tension between past, present and future and together with human responsibility. The sacred is thus not something fixed. Man must continually seek it, as a ground under his feet, as a hand that holds him fast, as a perspective that beckons. The sacred is no longer linked with holy places, sacred objects or clothing, or prescribed sacred acts.

For some, in the 1960s the secularisation process led to the conviction that the end had come for Christianity. Others preferred to speak of the end of 'conventional' Christianity, of a Christianity which moved in an all too elevated sphere, a space and time alongside our world. Whatever the case, the process of secularisation led to the loss of the 'obviousness' of Christian religion. Christianity – or, more broadly, religion in general – lost its structure of plausibility. The churches emptied. There arose a tremendous sense of emptiness, an emptiness that would be pointedly expressed in God-is-dead theology.[26] All of this led to a sharp polarisation within the church. Some chose for the way back. They pursued the apparently safe path of restoration. Those who took the culture seriously however opted for a dialogue between Christianity and culture. They took up the challenge of inculturating Christianity: over against 'God-is-dead' theology there arose political theology, followed by critical theologies such as black theology, the theology of revolution, liberation theology and feminist theology. These in turn contributed to the theology of hope, a theology of the Spirit, theology which emphasised the warm and mystic current of Christianity, charismatic theology, theology of creation (ecological theology) and theologies of inculturation. At the same time the pluriformity of the system by which meaning was assigned grew. With regard to the religious sector, people began to speak

[26] See for example T.J.J. ALTIZER: *The Gospel of Christian Atheism*, Philadelphia 1966; T.T.J. ALTIZER & W. HAMILTON: *Radical Theology and the Death of God*, Indianapolis/New York/Kansas City 1966.

of a market situation (indeed in economic terms!) in which Christianity had to compete with other systems of values and meaning.

2. POSTMODERNISM

A belief in the possibility of controlling and reshaping nature, society and the individual was characteristic of modernity. It was generally accepted that continual progress was possible, in the sciences, technology and the world economy, and also for people in the struggle for freedom and equality.[27] This belief in progress was accommodated in various coherent systems of meaning such as socialism, Marxism and enlightenment philosophy. Although modernity continues as a force in our society, since the 1980s the modern idea of progress has been afflicted by crisis, a crisis which has undoubtedly been amplified by the collapse of Marxism in the 1990s. Our culture began to be characterised as postmodern, a term which had begun its career already in the 1960s, then applying primarily to architecture and literature.[28] The term was now applied to the whole of Western culture; among the most influential philosophers involved in this analysis were Derrida, Baudrillard and Lyotard. In both art and philosophy, postmodernism has many guises.[29] A general characteristic of postmodernism in each case is that it casts doubt on the belief in progress, the strength of human rationality, the authority of modern science, and on the great ideologies, including those of religions. It resists the manner of thinking in which all phenomenon are ultimately traced back to one fundamental source, and stresses differences. It is not possible to postulate one original principle which covers them all. The time of the 'great stories' is past, according to Lyotard. Among these 'great stories' he counts not only philosophies of history from Hegel to Marx, but also the idea that the aim of history is to realise the development of the free market economy or representative democracy.[30] These philosophies are very much

---

[27] MODERNITY: *The Debate on Modernity: Concilium* 28 (1992) no. 6.

[28] See among others I.N. BULHOF & J. DE VALK (eds.): *Postmodernisme als uitdaging*, Baarn 1990; W.A. DE PATER: 'Het postmodernisme nog eens uitgelegd', in *Nederlands Theologisch Tijdschrift* 50 (1996) 3, 177-202; J. BLOECHL & S. VAN DEN BOSSCHE: 'Postmoderniteit, theologie en sacramententheologie. Een onderzoeksproject toegelicht', in *Jaarboek voor liturgie-onderzoek* 13 (1997) 21-48.

[29] VAN PEPERSTRATEN: *Samenleving ter discussie* 329.

[30] VAN PEPERSTRATEN: *Samenleving ter discussie* 331.

under the influence of the concept of progress, and proceed too much from a fixed idea. Only fragmentary knowledge is possible, and our power over the world is relative. We must learn to live with more tentative insights, and a more modest attitude would befit us.[31] We must learn to recognise our limitations, and accept them. No coherent system of meaning is possible any more. Therefore there is a recognition of a plurality in meaning. Coupled with the phenomenon of individualism, this means that people no longer allow themselves to be led so easily by institutions. The tractable individual now speaks for himself and determines his own course. Among the most striking examples of this phenomenon are the temporary agency and the 'living apart together' relationship: people seek jobs of a different nature rather than following a single career, and they no longer easily enter into long term personal commitments; with the latter, the number of singles in The Netherlands has increased sharply, to the point where today one in three households consists of a person living alone. In all sorts of contexts people seek a second chance: in work, in relations, in politics, in religion (hence the popularity of reincarnation rather than belief in a Last Judgement[32]).

However one may evaluate postmodernist theories, it is clear that our world does exhibit a large number of postmodern characteristics. We live in a fragmented and post-ideological society. There is a quest in the midst of many questions, modest, hesitant, here and now, in the midst of history – a history in which there is the acknowledgement of vast suffering and massive and senseless deaths of victims who often remain anonymous. One here recalls the two great wars of the twentieth century, the Holocaust, the brutal war in Vietnam, the killing fields of Cambodia, the victims on the Square of Heavenly Peace in Beijing, the corridor of death during the first Gulf War, the ethnic cleansing in the former Yugoslavia and the deep wounds of Srebrenica, the famines and conflicts in Somalia, the genocide in Rwanda, the war in Chechenia, victims of earthquakes and hurricanes, of AIDS. There is absurd death on a massive scale. Tomorrow and the day after that there will apparently be still other unexpected and gruesome scenes that pass before our eyes.[33] Where then are the great stories of progress? History is generally other than our preconceived ideas. One must accept the challenge and

[31] BULHOF & DE VALK (eds.): *Postmodernisme als uitdaging.*
[32] JANSSEN: 'Religie: privé-bezit of sociaal kapitaal' 27.
[33] SPECTRE: *The Spectre of Mass Death: Concilium* 29 (1993) no. 3.

repeatedly open up the closed stories in new contexts, with the realisation that in doing so the perspective will shift each time, and that to which the stories refer ultimately will always remain elusive.

3. A NEW PHASE?

Have there in recent years been developments which point to a new phase in Western culture? While the structural elements of modernism and postmodernism still permeate – and will certainly continue to permeate – our culture, one can at the same time note some developments that seem to indicate that there are important processes of change under way there.

3.1. The World Wide Web and globalisation

It appears to soon to be able to select any one term to denote the culture which is dawning. It might however be provisionally characterised by using one of its main components, the *World Wide Web*, as a metaphor. We may well be able to speak of a network culture. Alvin and Heidi Toffler speak of the 'third wave'.[34] The first wave, they argue, was the agricultural revolution, which was inseparable from developments in farming. Following that there was the second wave, the industrial revolution, which was the basis for modernity. The culture of the third wave is symbolised by the computer, and will spread across the whole world in the next three decades. This culture is particularly characterised by the creation and exploitation of knowledge. One must realise that a single chip can hold an unimaginable quantity of data, and this memory chip capacity is constantly expanding. In only a few years we will have at our disposal pocket-sized devices that will combine the capacity of traditional super-computers with cellular visual telephony and a wireless

---

[34] A. & H. TOFFLER: *Creating a New Civilization. The Politics of the Third Wave*, Atlanta 1994. See also G.S. WORGUL, Jr.: 'Inculturation and Root Metaphors', in *Questions Liturgiques* 77 (1996) 40-51 and in J. LAMBERTS (ed.): *Liturgie et inculturation. Liturgy and Inculturation* (Textes et Études Liturgiques/ Studies in Liturgy 14), Leuven 1996 = G.S. WORGUL, Jr.: 'Inculturatie en basismetaforen', in J. LAMBERTS (ed.): *Liturgie en inculturatie. Verslagboek van het twaalfde liturgiecolloquium van het Liturgisch Instituut van de K.U. Leuven – oktober 1995* (Nikè-reeks 37), Leuven/Amersfoort 1996, 57-74, especially 68-70.

fax/modem. Information, management, advanced technology, software, new forms of education and medical care, financial and all sorts of other services will play an important role in this third wave. A new infrastructure is coming into being which can lead to a more efficient use of space, and which also brings with it new forms and possibilities for creating community. This new culture can also be denoted as the ICT culture: the culture of information and communications technology. With regard to information, at a 1978 symposium at the University of Tilburg it was already noted that three-quarters of all information that has ever been assembled by mankind dated from after the Second World War. In the meantime that information has expanded tremendously, and continues to grow constantly. It is expected that by 2020 mankind will have developed a single memory chip that can hold 6667 times the sixteen volume Encyclopaedia Britannica – or 213,344 books: a complete library on a couple of square centimetres. The question now is not so much where one can obtain information, but what sort of search engine is capable of selecting the information desired. Whatever the case, in our culture the stress lies on the communicative aspects of society. Such a culture is no longer manageable in an hierarchic manner. Its management will have more the characteristics of an archipelago than a pyramid. It is a culture for which a new ethos will be needed, in which virtues such as *Prudentia* (wisdom, prudence) and *Temperantia* (moderation) will have to play key roles.[35]

The culture of the World Wide Web goes hand in hand with what people generally denote as the phenomenon of *globalisation*. Globalisation is the term for economic processes that have the whole world as their realm and that are backed up by the technological developments in the fields of mobility and communication. Faith in the fundamental structures of the free market and free trade play a large role in these processes. The anti-globalist protest movements have been organised against it. They ask if in fact the West is not in this way creating its own free zones, at the expense of the developing and poor countries. This has led to increased discussion about the necessity for a regulatory matrix for the operation of the market and free trade. It involves a complex question in which all kinds of issues are interconnected with one another. For instance, there is the question of how one should respond

---

[35] H. PEETERS: *Over deugden en ondeugden. Vroeger en nu*, Nijmegen 1996.

to the globalisation of the network of capital markets, operating with the aid of modern information and communications technologies, which have enabled ever larger amounts of capital to be moved ever more quickly. National economies appear to have become particularly vulnerable to the caprices of the currency markets. Globalisation also touches the vulnerability of employment, the manner in which firms are organised, business shrinkage and mergers, the mobility of labour, migration, the question of economic refugees, currency speculation purely and simply to accumulate greater wealth, the problem of extravagant salaries for top managers, the urgency of development aid and development assistance and the issue of environmental protection.

Some would rather avoid the term globalisation, because it easily creates the impression that the whole world is being submerged under one common ideological denominator – specifically, that of the West, which is ruled by the law of the jungle. For example, Haars suggests replacing the word 'globalisation' with 'mondialisation'.[36] By this he seeks to emphasise the communicative aspect of globalisation. It is not the play of forces that is central, the domination of a mono-economy, a mono-culture or a mono-political system, but humane, mondial communication. It is about communication among the different components, in which borders are not first and foremost demarcations or dividing lines but on the contrary places of discussion and encounter, points of contact. Rather than being flash points for conflict, boundaries should become meeting places, which then lead to solidarity. At the mondial level this means, for instance, that efforts must be made toward greater justice in the relations between rich and poor countries. The governing principle must be that the underprivileged become 'opportunity-makers', in a double sense. First, they must be taken seriously and accepted as partners in discussions about opportunity; then through that they will be in a position to point out new and unexpected directions to us as well.

The problem of globalisation is high on the agenda of Christian churches everywhere in the world. I will confine myself to referring to the international consultation on globalisation by churches from the North and South in Soesterberg, in The Netherlands, in 2002. There

---

[36] J. HAARS: *Kansanderen. Liefhebben vanuit de marge*, Averbode 2000, especially 82-101. One also finds the concept of 'mondialisation' in place of 'globalisation' in the title of the recent special issue *Globalization and its Victims: Concilium* 37 (2001) no. 5.

the conviction was expressed that the present manner of globalisation, in which the rich and powerful call the tune, is definitely not the only way in which globalisation can take place. There are possible alternatives.[37] The big problem is that particularly over the last twenty years, international trade in goods and services has lagged far behind that in currency and capital, so that money is being created without there being production of goods to balance it. People can become rich without doing anything for their money. At this moment the international trade in money and financial services is 100 times as extensive as that in goods. That is why a revision of the world monetary system in particular is urgently necessary. A possible course of action is the direction indicated as early as 1964 by the Nobel Prize winner Jan Tinbergen. He notes that every well-administered country has three key financial institutions: 1) a central bank that assures that the currency is as stable as possible; 2) the banks which, on the basis of the savings of the citizens, enable businesses to invest, and thus are important for employment; and 3) a ministry of finance that collects taxes and duties and spends them according to priorities. At the world level, we have the beginnings of a central bank in the International Monetary Fund and the beginning of an investment bank in the World Bank. The greatest problem is however that both of these serve primarily the interests of wealthier lands, which have the most votes on their boards, and that the application of democratic principles would demand that both their decision-making process and their attention must be refocused to reflect the needs of the majority of the world's population. In addition to the two institutions mentioned, there would have to be a sort of international ministry of finances, a sort of 'world treasury'. This would have to be coupled with the introduction of a new international currency, based on the value of around thirty commodities, rather than only on gold, or the dollar. This could be supplemented by the proposal of the Nobel Prize winner James Tobin to introduce a world tax of 0.2% on all international financial transactions. Now that money has become a product to the degree it has, it should be taxed just as all other products are. Whatever the case, the poor Lazarus at last deserves a full place at the table of the rich, and a globalisation of solidarity is needed.

[37] L. ANDRINGA & B. GOUDZWAARD: 'Economie in dienst van het leven', in *Een-twee-een* 30 (2002) no. 9, Section 3-21.

3.2. In search of quality and sustainability

At this point the 'globalisation' of our communications structure does not appear to have occurred at the expense of interest in more direct community structures on a smaller scale. On the contrary: from the Dutch Social and Cultural Report 1998 it appears that support among the Dutch population for maintaining or raising social benefits to an acceptable level is relatively high. Assistance to one's neighbours, the elderly and the handicapped is rising. Only seven percent of the Dutch population claim to have never given anything to a charitable appeal. There is also attention for mondial community. Support for Amnesty International, Greenpeace and the Foster Parents Plan appears to be growing, as are the membership figures for environmental and nature organisations. There is an increasing interest in issues such as abortion and euthanasia, and for quality of life. Within the larger communications structure new connections are also being made in the more immediate vicinity.

The Rio Conference was held in 1992, building upon the intuition of the 1960s and the environmental conference at Stockholm in 1972. During the Rio Conference negotiations between the rich North and the poor South of the world on 'sustainable development' took place for the first time in history. One-hundred-twenty countries committed themselves to an agenda for the 21st century.[38]

It appears that one can speak of a growing desire for security, development, harmony with nature, and solidarity. Are we entering a transitional phase from a society which strives for purely economic growth, to a society which strives for quality and sustainability? Although there are also strong counterforces – one may think of the United States absenting itself from the latest international environmental conferences – one must not underestimate the rising undercurrent. It is gaining in power and strength. A growing aggregation of social groups, organisations and movements around the world are beginning to voice what the market has forgotten, and international businesses are beginning to recognise every now and then: slowly the importance of the basic demands of ethical action is coming through. More even than in the 1960s many are

---

[38] R. BECKERS-DE BRUIN: 'Van verlangen naar beweging. Van beweging naar groene politiek', in H. GEERTS (ed.): *Maakbaarheid, macht en matigheid. Korte beschouwingen over het natuurdebat* (Annalen van het Thijmgenootschap 86 (1998) 3), Nijmegen 1998, 72.

realising that the limits of growth really have been reached. Among politicians and the directors of multinationals there is a rising consciousness that the free market must begin to take on a humane shape. The contours of that were already sketched in 1991 by Pope John Paul II in his encyclical *Centesimus annus*, in which he indicates that the market mechanism cannot satisfy a number of essential, collective human needs, and argues for a humane ecology. In all of this, one must realise that fundamental changes in the orientation of a society take a long time to happen. When no one expects it any more, suddenly it is there: democracy across all of Europe, the abolition of apartheid in South Africa, the end of the Cold War…[39] Could the tragic events of September 11, 2001, be a marker for such a change of direction? I will return to this in the following point.

3.3. Resurgence of religion

Before beginning, I would note that with regard to religious developments in our culture there are definitely major differences. For instance, in the United States religion continues to play an important role, despite all secularisation. When I speak of a religious resurgence as a third movement in 'our' culture, I am particularly referring to developments in Western Europe, for which The Netherlands can be seen as a crystallisation point.[40] In the early 1990s there were some who saw signs that as a cultural current postmodernism was already past its peak in Western Europe, and that people were once again searching for greater coherence, for stories which offered a meaningful context for life.[41] Whatever the case, in mid-1996 a remarkable development appeared, particularly in The Netherlands. Since the late 1960s the media had treated religion as though it were a taboo subject. If it did come up for discussion, it was generally in a negative sense. A sort of evolutionary

[39] BECKERS-DE BRUIN: 'Van verlangen naar beweging' 72-74.

[40] In this connection, compare what I said in the Introduction of this book. See also the recent data from the European values research: L. HALMAN: *The European Values Study: A Third Wave. Source Book of the 1999/2000 European Values Study Surveys*, Tilburg 2001; W. ARTS, J. HAGENAARS & L. HALMAN: *The Cultural Diversity of European Unity*, Leiden/Boston 2003.

[41] 'Het postmodernisme voorbij', Supplement of *Werkschrift voor Leerhuis en Liturgie* 13 (1993) 1, 1-52; J. ISAAC: *Arendt, Camus and Modern Rebellion*, Yale 1992; J. DE VISSCHER a.o.: *Hannah Arendt en de moderniteit*, Kampen 1992.

242 CHRISTIAN RITUAL IN OUR CULTURE

scheme appeared to have been tacitly accepted, according to which developments in culture had made religion obsolete. One also finds this view frequently in theories of secularisation. However, this evolutionary scheme is not regarded as tenable by either contemporary scholars in the field of comparative religion, or by contemporary anthropologists. According to them, religion is a component of all cultures. Gradually one also is seeing studies in the social sciences that are tackling such secularisation theories on the basis of empirical evidence.[42] Whatever the case, almost overnight this taboo on religion in the media was broken. In May, 1996, a special issue of the weekly *HP/De Tijd* appeared under

---

[42] J. VERWEIJ: *Secularisering tussen Feit en Fictie. Een internationaal vergelijkend onderzoek naar determinanten van religieuze betrokkenheid*, Tilburg 1998. See also M. GIJSWIJT-HOFSTRA: *Vragen bij een onttoverde wereld* (Amsterdamse Historische Reeks, kleine serie 37), Amsterdam 1997; HELLEMANS, S.: 'Secularization in a religiogeneous modernity', in R. LAERMANS, B. WILSON & J. BILLIET: *Secularization and Social Integration. Papers in honor of Karel Dobbelaere*, Leuven 1998, 67-81; A. VAN HARSKAMP a.o.: *De religieuze ruis in Nederland. Thesen over versterving en de wedergeboorte van de godsdienst*, Zoetermeer 1998; S. HELLEMANS: 'Veranderende religie, veranderende kerken', in *Praktische Theologie* 26 (1999) 315-326; I.N. BULHOF, I.N. & L. TEN KATE (eds.): *Flight of the Gods: Philosophical Perspectives on Negative Theology*, New York 2000; L. BOEVE, A. VAN HARSKAMP & L. TEN KATE: 'Van een God die niet bestaat en de ondoorgrondelijke dingen die Hij doet', in *Tijdschrift voor Theologie* 41 (2001) 337-355; A. SCHILSON: 'Liturgie(-Reform) angesichts einer sich wandelnden Kultur. Perspektiven am Ende des 20. Jahrhunderts', in M. KLÖCKENER & B. KRANEMANN (eds.): *Liturgiereformen. Historische Studien zu einem bleibenden Grundzug des christlichen Gottesdienstes* (Liturgiewissenschaftliche Quellen und Forschungen 88), Münster 2002, 965-1002, especially 968-970. Nevertheless, one still finds in The Netherlands, and undoubtedly in other countries, the view that religion is on its last legs in the Western world. See H. VISSER: *Leven zonder God. Elf interviews over ongeloof*, Amsterdam 2003; A.H. VAN DEN BOEF: *Nederland seculier! Tegen religieuze privileges in wetten, regels, praktijken, gewoonten en attitudes*, Amsterdam 2003. In The Netherlands this view is defended in a strongly polemic manner by the philosophers P. Cliteur and H. Philipse. According to P. Cliteur religion is an activity which should merely be tolerated, in the same way we tolerate the use of alcohol and drugs. See, among others P. CLITEUR: 'Alleen oecumenisch humanisme brengt licht', in *NRC Handelsblad* December 22, 2001, 7. H. Philipse essentially reprises the similar discussion in England, in which it appears that the scientific criteria that were employed against the existence of God were not tenable. According to L. Van den Brom Philipse (see H. PHILIPSE: *Atheïstisch manifest*, Amsterdam 1995) 'attempts to reanimate this dead horse one more time'. See L. VAN DEN BROM: 'Geloof gaat langs de afgrond', in *Rondom het woord* 38 (1996) 4, 26, note 2. The documentation on the English discussion is to be found in A. FLEW & A. MACINTYRE: *New Essays in Philosophical Theology*, London 1955. See also A. AYER: *The Central Questions of Philosophy*, London 1973.

the title 'God returns to The Netherlands', with articles that included 'Beyond De-Christianisation', 'Converts in the 1990s', 'The God of the Christians, Jews and Muslims', 'Can God do everything?' and 'Eighteen questions you didn't dare to ask'. This 'return of God' was taken over by the rest of the media. Even in the broadsheet *NRC/Handelsblad*, which had practically neglected the subject of religion since the 1960s, religion suddenly became a recurrent theme after mid-1996. This trend continued into 1997, so much so that in March of that year 'My God' was the theme for the Dutch National Book Week, which is organised annually by the nation's booksellers' and publishers' association.[43] This theme was chosen because of the increasing interest among authors for religion and the rise in sales of books that took questions about life and its purpose as their subject. One out of every four or five books that Dutch men and women buy appears to be a religious publication.[44]

Considerable attention was also given to the new converts to Catholicism, what were called 'new Catholics'. For some years there had been about 1000 conversions to Catholicism per year.[45] But now this phenomenon was suddenly magnified by the media, to the extent that one got the impression that the number of active adherents to the Catholic Church was on the rise again. This was by no means the case. On the contrary, the institutional church continued to shrink. The first church membership figures which we have for The Netherlands are from 1879. In that year about 0.3% of the population were unchurched. In 1960 that had risen to 18.3% of the population. The great jump came in the years thereafter: according to the Social and Cultural Planning Bureau, by 1991 57% of the population were not affiliated with any church, and in 1999 that had reached 63%, the highest figure in Europe. According to expectations, by 2010 this will reach 67%, and in 2020, 72%. With regard to young people (aged 17 to 30), a 1991 survey indicated that as many as 72% regarded themselves as unchurched.[46] Other

---

[43] The book on that theme, distributed free to anyone who bought another book during that week, was R. DORRESTEIN: *Want dit is mijn lichaam*, Amsterdam 1997.

[44] J. PIJFFERS: 'De godsdealers. Het eigenlijke thema van de boekenweek is koopmanschap', in *De Bazuin* 80 (1997) 5, 16-19.

[45] A. BROERS a.o.: *De nieuwe katholieken*, Gorinchem 2000.

[46] J.W. BECKER & J.W.R. VINK: *Secularisatie in Nederland 1966-1991* (Sociale en culturele studies 19), Den Haag 1994; J.W. BECKER, J. DE HART & J. MENS: *Secularisatie en alternatieve zingeving in Nederland*, Den Haag 1997; J.W. BECKER & J. DE WIT: *Secularisatie in de jaren negentig*, Sociaal en Cultureel Planbureau, Den Haag 2000.

surveys with regard to youth show lower figures.[47] However, it is incontestable that a sizeable majority of the Dutch population is unchurched.[48] Between 1900 and 1960 it was primarily the Reformed Churches which suffered from the outflow of members; but after 1960 the Roman Catholic church was affected too.

With regard to the percentages, they can be the result of one-step and two-step survey questions. The Dutch Central Bureau for Statistics employs a one-step question. Used by most surveys, a one-step question is formulated as 'Of what church, religion or philosophical group do you mainly count yourself a member?' On the basis of this sort of question, the Central Bureau for Statistics comes up with a figure of 40% unchurched. Thus with this manner of formulating the question one arrives at a smaller percentage of unchurched persons than with the two-step formulation, which is '1) Do you consider yourself a member of a church congregation?', followed by '2) If so, which?' Both ways of asking the question are relevant, because from the difference between the two one can arrive at a percentage of 'borderline' church adherents, or the size of the grey area between the churched and unchurched. If one compares the figures from the Social and Cultural Planning Bureau and the Central Bureau for Statistics, one arrives at a percentage of 23% borderline believers. With regard to Catholics, on the basis of a two-step formulation, since 1960 the percentage of the population which is

[47] See for instance J. PETERS: 'Religie in meervoud', in O. SCHREUDER & L. VAN SNIPPENBURG (eds.): *Religie in de Nederlandse samenleving. De vergeten factor*, Baarn 1990, 46-47, and the research reported there. See also the research by the Department of Social Science at Rotterdam's Erasmus University: *Geloof in levensstijl: een empirisch onderzoek onder de Nederlandse jeugd*, Rotterdam 1998. According to this latter research, 56% of the young people between 15 and 24 believe either in a personal God (28%) or in a 'vital spirit or higher power', and 43% count themselves as members of a church community. Note however that this research employs a more spacious definition of religion: namely the availability of answers to questions about the meaning of life. See also: 'Nederlandse jeugd gelovige dan gedacht', in *Een-twee-een* 26 (1998) 9, 332.

[48] Not only in The Netherlands, but also elsewhere in Europe there is a high percentage of unchurched. According to the European Values Survey conducted in 1981, and repeated in 1990, this is particularly the case in The Netherlands, Great Britain, France and Belgium. See L. HALMAN, F. HEUNKS, R. DE MOOR & H. ZANDERS: *Traditie, secularisering en individualisering. Een onderzoek naar de waarden van de Nederlanders in een Europese context*, Tilburg 1987; HALMAN: *Waarden in de Westerse Wereld*; P. ESTER, L. HALMAN & R. DE MOOR (eds.): *The Individualizing Society: Value Change in Europe and North America*, Tilburg 1993.

Catholic fell from 37% to about 24%. The results of a one-step question shows that as 34%, so that the number of borderline Roman Catholics averages around 10%.[49]

In the survey by the Social and Cultural Planning Bureau it is said that it is primarily the unchurched who do not believe in God, and primarily the churched who do. This is a view that one often encounters, but it is based on a rigid conception of religion. The pastoral theologian Van der Ven points out that the researchers involved proceed from the idea that belief in God can be seen exclusively as belief in a *personal God*. But that is far too simple an idea. Often this involves an outdated formulation of the question.[50] There are many more conceptions of God than those which are generally acknowledged in empirical investigations. Among other points he makes is that in our culture the mystery-character of God is often strongly experienced, a situation in which the person of God is nuanced. Images such as Sea, Ocean, Gulf, Desert, Fire, Light and Sun, which are also found in great mystics, are used for God. One further also finds abstract concepts such as Source, Purpose, Ground of Being, Depth of Being, Strength, Plan or Foundation. All of these images transcend the simple division between God as a person and a

[49] KASKI: 'Kerncijfers 1994/1995. Uit de kerkelijke statistiek van het R.-K. Kerkgenootschap in Nederland', in *Een-twee-een. Kerkelijke documentatie* 23 (1995) no. 9 = KASKI: *Kerncijfers uit de kerkelijke statistiek 1994/1995 van het R.-K. Kerkgenootschap in Nederland* (Memorandum no. 291), Den Haag 1995 (KASKI = Katholiek Sociaal Kerkelijk Instituut, Den Haag); PETERS: 'Religie in meervoud' 46-47. Regarding the figures and their interpretation, see also H. HILHORST: 'De godsdienstsociologie op zoek naar nieuwe vormen van religie', in P. STOUTHARD & G. VAN TILLO (eds.): *Katholiek Nederland na 1945*, Baarn 1985, 114-130; H. DE LOOR & J. PETERS: 'Een vergelijkende sociologische analyse van de katholieke en de hervormde kerk sedert 1945', in STOUTHARD & VAN TILLO (eds.): *Katholiek Nederland na 1945*, 144-168; O. SCHREUDER, O.: 'De religieuze traditie in de jaren tachtig', in O. SCHREUDER & L. VAN SNIPPENBURG (eds.): *Religie in de Nederlandse samenleving. De vergeten factor*, Baarn 1990, 17-41; *Waarom lopen de kerken leeg? Over de oorzaken van afgenomen kerkbezoek en kerkverlating in Nederland tussen 1937 en 1995: Sociale Wetenschappen* (1998) no. 2; J.W. BECKER: *De vaststelling van de kerkelijke gezindte in enquêtes*, Sociaal en Cultureel Planbureau, Den Haag 2003.
[50] J. VAN DER VEN: 'Het Planbureau versimpelt het godsgeloof', in *NRC Handelsblad* June 22, 1997, 7; IDEM: 'Faith in God in a Secularised Culture', in *Bulletin ET. Zeitschrift für Theologie in Europa* 9 (1998) 1, 21-45. See also J. DE HART: 'Een bespreking van recente godsdienstsociologische boeken', in *Praktische Theologie* 24 (1997) 334-335.

non-personal force. Rather, what we have is a *dispersal of the church* on one hand and a *religiosity or acknowledgement of the being of God* on the other.

Indeed, the *religious climate* of Western European culture appears to be undergoing a radical change.[51] For a long time the churches, as coherent and delineated institutional entities with symbols and the ritualisation linked to them, had a monopoly on religion. That monopoly has now been broken. Acceptance of ecclesiastical dogma is no longer automatic; for many the morality of the Church is open to debate; ritual practices are being abandoned. The old model of the religious person appears to apply only to a small minority. At the same time one can observe that the boundaries of religion have been shifted. When one makes judgements based exclusively on the old model, one might conclude that religion is disappearing. But those who expand their gaze see that there is definitely a religiosity, expressing itself in new ways. According to the 'God in Nederland' survey in 1997, two-thirds of the Dutch still consider themselves religious, but many are of the opinion that they have no need of a church for this.[52] From the survey on European values it appears that a secular Europe is not the same as an atheistic Europe. Across all of Europe, only 5% of the population call themselves atheists. I have noted above that many in our culture have the experience of the mysterious dimension of existence, of 'something holy', which can be more specifically characterised in many ways: as the inner, the intimate, the hidden, the dynamic force in all that lives.[53] People have the experience of a 'more'. This involves the experience of an absolute, without this being experienced as a person who can be addressed. One can also call this experience religious. 'An experience may be termed religious when a person is existentially involved with his whole being in the experienced reality of the world and history, and thus his sense of depth, future and totality is so sharpened that he interprets and validates his

[51] See, for the following as well, GABRIEL: 'Sehnsucht nach Religion im säkularen Europa'. In this connection J. MAAS & H.-G. ZIEBERTZ: 'Over breukvlakken en bruggenhoofden', in *Tijdschrift voor Theologie* 37 (1997) 384-404 is also of interest.

[52] J. PETERS, G. DEKKER & J. DE HART: *God in Nederland 1966-1996*, Amsterdam 1997.

[53] LUKKEN: *De onvervangbare weg van de liturgie* 37. In The Netherlands some have recently been referring to this general religious tendency disparagingly as 'something-ism'.

connections with this reality as positive possibilities for personal development.'[54]

At the same time it is true that this involves experience of *the holy* or the search for 'the holy', and not *the Holy One*. There is a depersonalisation of the holy, of 'passing God by'.[55] It is in relation to this that the French philosopher Ferry notes that a radical change has taken place in our society with regard to the question of meaning.[56] In our secularised society we can no longer simply solve acute questions about meaning in life experiences, which chiefly arise on the occasion of a radical loss (of a loved one, a job, etc.), by placing the 'I' within, and subordinate to, the larger context of religion. A question about meaning now implies the expression of subjectivity itself at its deepest, and in relation to others. The sacred – that which is ultimately involved – is in one way or another contained in man himself; it is incarnated there. The meaning of life lies in the divine in man himself. In this sense one can speak of a transcendental humanism, which does not offer up the 'I' to God, but knows '*the* holy' as concealed in man himself. What we are dealing with is the sacred with a human face. Only in relation to this sacred can the question of meaning be answered. One could say that under the influence of secularisation we have a repeated, passionate search for the ultimate as found in the here and now, in current contingency, in the uncertainty of human existence with all its randomness and unpredictability, and not proceeding from an all-embracing divine entity. With this, religion has become vaguer and more diffuse. Along with that has come the rise of what Bourdieu has characterised as 'the new clergy'.[57]

---

[54] H. MERTENS: 'Religie als ervaring van de werkelijkheid', in *Tijdschrift voor Theologie* 14 (1974) 128.

[55] See in this connection P. POST: 'Goede tijden, slechte tijden: devotionele rituelen tussen traditie en moderniteit', in P.J. MARGRY (ed.): *Goede en slechte tijden: het Amsterdamse Mirakel van Sacrament in historisch perspectief*, Aardenhout 1995, 15-17, and B. HUIJBERS: *Aan Gij voorbij. Het mysterie bezongen*, Hilversum 1989.

[56] L. FERRY: *L'homme-Dieu, ou le sens de la vie*, Paris 1996; F. GUWY: 'Religie zonder geloof in God. France Guwy in gesprek met de filosoof Luc Ferry', in *Roodkoper* 2 (1997) 2, 6-10.

[57] P. BOURDIEU: *Rede und Antwort*, Frankfurt am Main 1992, 232. See GABRIEL: 'Sehnsucht nach Religion im säkularen Europa' 188.

One cannot say that this provides a clear alternative for the old model, a substitute for institutional Christianity.[58] Until now it was always the case that one complex of concepts made way for another: a clear example of this was, for instance, the Reformation and Counter-Reformation. But now a structure in which the individual goes in search of, and as it were assembles his or her own religion has replaced the old model.[59] Among the churched this can be seen in the fact that some of them have no difficulty integrating the idea of reincarnation, for instance, into their belief system, or follow a different sexual ethic than that officially prescribed. In general, speaking of modern believers as 'reli-zappers' is not without justification: they pick the elements of their philosophy of life from the shelves of the religious supermarket, and the components of their do-it-yourself packet may change from time to time, according to the circumstances.[60] In any case, outside the church there is great pluriformity to be found. The great transcendences have been replaced, as it were, by smaller transcendences which are sought and found through the agency of smaller groups.[61] In this process there are many gurus who function as the 'new clergy'. There are all sorts of new religious movements in the form of New Age, therapeutic or inte-gral healing programmes aimed at passing on knowledge or training persons.

Because the traditional model of religion has been broken open, and with the tendency toward individualisation, a market situation has been created with regard to the range of possibilities. However, it remains true that the traditional churches have a position within this market which is very strong, and one they will apparently retain, on the condition that they sufficiently inculturate themselves in the new culture.

[58] Thus BECKER & VINK: *Secularisatie in Nederland 1966-1991*.

[59] GABRIEL: 'Sehnsucht nach Religion im säkularen Europa' 189 ff.

[60] H. STEKETEE: 'God in Nederland is verhuisd', in *NRC Handelsblad* November 14, 1997, 3; J. DE HART: 'Kerkelijke en niet kerkelijke religie', in *Praktische Theologie* 26 (1999) 277-296.

[61] Perhaps the renewed interest in angels (and saints) can also be counted as part of these 'intermediate transcendences'. See in this connection A.M. WEIGL: *Schutzengeschichten heute*, Altötting 1973[9]; K. KÖSTLIN: 'Die Wiederkehr der Engel', in N.-A. BRINGÉUS (ed.): *Religion in Everyday Life. Papers Given at a Symposium in Stock-holm 1993*, Stockholm 1994, 79-96; H. SCHWALL: 'Engelen: het overschot van ons tekort', in *Tijdschrift voor geestelijk leven* 52 (1996) 1, 37-52; 'Les anges dans nos cam-pagnes', in *L'actualité religieuse* 139 (1995) 17-37; P. POST: 'Engel, bode, advocaat et cetera', in BARNARD & POST (eds.): *Ritueel bestek* 259-274.

They represent a strong religious tradition and religious competency; from the past it can be seen that they were often able to give that tradition a new form in interaction with new cultures. The question which challenges the Christian churches is whether they will now be able to bridge the growing gap between the church and the actual religious beliefs of people. Are they prepared to, and can they succeed in reshaping existing and changing forms of religiosity, or in channelling them?[62] By no means do the churches have to see the new religious movements as competitors. Indeed, in our pluriform culture these have their own indispensable role. They give shape to the search of the religious, in the form of a quest for meaning in the midst of all contingency, and are a challenge to effect a new inculturation of the churches in our culture. In this, the churches will need to be more actively involved in the finding of meaning in the contingent life histories of people than they ever have been before, in a new articulation and representation of the core of Christendom, from the conviction that the divine and holy received its ultimate form in Jesus of Nazareth. This will have to take place in small, self-selected and self-activating groups, in a creative interaction with the pluriformity in its own ranks, in community with other Christian churches and the world religions. A part of this inculturation will also be the acceptance that the church can never again claim a monopoly position. There are all sorts of alternate life philosophies. This will particularly be an adjustment for Western Europe, which is attracting increased migration. Since the Second World War over thirteen million immigrants have come to Western Europe, as a consequence of which other of the world religions are now firmly established here. One might even say that this is the greatest change in the religious map of Europe since the Reformation in the 16th century. It is expected that by 2020 7% of the Dutch population will be Muslim, while all Christians together will comprise 21%, and 72% will be outside the churches or mosques.[63]

An entirely new factor in the process of religious resurgence we have just sketched were the stigmatising events of the attack on the World

---

[62] This question comes to the fore urgently in the research by PETERS, DEKKER & DE HART: *God in Nederland 1966-1996.*

[63] BECKER, DE HART & MENS: *Secularisatie en alternatieve zingeving in Nederland.* In 2002 5.5% of the Dutch population were Muslim and 0.6% Hindu.

Trade Center in New York on September 11, 2001, by Muslim terrorists. Since then the Western world has been confronted with new questions. Does the resurgence of religion not also contain dangers? Is not war being waged in the name of religion too? Indeed, and alas, religion does play a not unimportant role in many violent conflicts. In this connection the 'Declaration toward a Global Ethic' adopted by the Parliament of the World Religions (Chicago, 1993) is an important step. It focuses on the observance of the common ethical principles of all religions. Religions must make the proposition credible that, despite all their mistakes, they are ultimately about human well-being and peace.[64] On the other hand it is also true that the absence of religion has not always promoted world peace. One can think of the genocide committed by Lenin and Stalin, and of Cambodia. A-religious political ideologies can be as dangerous as religions. The dangers of extremism and fundamentalism are present in both religions and a-religious ideologies. With regard to September 11 itself, it is clear that this was a crime against humanity which must be sharply condemned and opposed. But at the same time one can rightly ask whether this deed was perhaps the symbol of something more than just religious fanaticism. Our world is involved in a process of mondialisation and globalisation. Might not one of the seedbeds for religious fanaticism be growing inequality, 'as high as the rising commercial skyscrapers, and a misery as deep as the bottom of the ocean?' Has not 'the rage of the victims reached the point of explosion?'[65] The new questions touch upon religion as such, but equally upon the core of Western culture. The war against Muslim extremism appears to only make sense if it is coupled with a 'war' against the economic fundamentalism of the Western world that leads to the exploitation of the enormous numbers of deprived people in the world. The new world order is not well served when we bomb our enemies back into the Stone Age, especially if they were already there in the first place.[66]

An important impetus for this process might be the Millennium Declaration of September, 2000, drawn up by the world community,

[64] See C. HASSELMAN: 'Chicago Global Ethic Declaration (1993)', in *Concilium* 36 (2000) 4, 26-37.

[65] J. SOBRINO & G.F. WILFRED: 'Globalization and its Victims. Introduction; The Reasons for Returning to this Theme', in *Concilium* 37 (2001) 5, 8.

[66] N. MITCHELL: 'The Amen Corner. Brave New World', in *Worship* 76 (2002) 76.

gathered in the General Assembly of the United Nations. In it the goal was formulated that in 2015 the number of people who have to survive on less than a dollar a day must be cut by half. By that date there must be primary education for all children, with equal opportunities for girls. Figures for infant mortality should be cut to one third of their 1990 level, and women's deaths in childbirth reduced by seventy-five percent. By that date there will be an end to the further spread of HIV/AIDS, malaria and other illnesses. The number of people without access to drinking water will be cut by half. All of this should take place as a result of a lasting working partnership of rich and poor countries, within an open and fair trade and financial system, with a prospect of a solution for the question of international indebtedness, guarantees for the environment and world-wide equality for men and women. Will we succeed in realising this ambitious plan? In March, 2002, in Monterrey, Mexico, as a follow-up to this Declaration the United Nations, joined by the International Monetary Fund and the World Bank, organised the largest conference on development assistance which had even taken place to date. This Financing for Development (FfD) conference was to facilitate the realisation of the Millennium Declaration. As far back as the 1970s the United Nations established the norm that each developed country should devote 0.7% of its gross domestic product to development assistance. Only then could one achieve the objectives by 2015. At present this norm is met only by the Scandinavian countries, Luxembourg and The Netherlands; they indeed exceed it. But at the FfD conference the total aid promised by the countries of the European Union did not exceed 0.39% of their gross domestic product. With regard to the United States – which demands the leadership in the battle against international extremism – aside from having unilaterally pulled out of international environmental agreements, at the moment of all industrialised countries it gives the smallest proportion of its gross domestic product to development assistance, namely 0.15%. There is a very long way to go. According to President Wolfensohn of the World Bank, people will have to begin to realise that the West is no longer a luxury residential area that can be protected from its poor neighbours. Closing the chasm between the rich and poor is a matter of simple humanity, but equally of international security. Will we really succeed in attaining a new world order in the 21st century?

Whatever the case, the appearance of various sorts of fundamentalism – be they economic, political ideological or religious (and not only

Muslim, but also Jewish and Christian) – is coupled with the urgent question of how an authentic religious resurgence can take form in a society that is increasingly multi-cultural and multi-religious. The basis for such a resurgence can only be that it is precisely the religious that is able to challenge the ever-present tendency toward fragmentation in our world, and see the cosmos as an integrated and ordered whole. Essentially, the *homo religiosus* can contribute in a more fundamental manner to the well-being of the cosmos and the improvement of society than can the purely *homo economicus*.[67] There are several interesting observations which accompany this. First, it appears here that the various sectors which have arisen with modernity are being impelled to enter into encounters with one another more again. This in no way involves a new hegemony of religion over these sectors, but a *dialogue* in which the peculiar criteria of the other sectors are respected. This dialogue will undoubtedly touch on a number of new ethical questions such as those with regard to gene technology, genetic manipulation, abortion and euthanasia. Next there is the question of the ecumenical dialogue, which reaches much further than only the Christian community, involving also dialogue among the world religions and all other religious currents.[68]

The disappearance of the taboo on religion has also led to triumphalist noises. Some see secularisation as a phenomenon which reflected no human needs, and a thing of the past. The movements of the 1960s, '70s and '80s are dismissed as 'mistaken' or as really just a tempest in a teacup.[69] Or the remark is heard that at last the situation in Dutch Catholicism has finally gotten back to normal. At the same time the reactionary pole of the polarisation is praised. People forget then that

---

[67] See in this connection RAPPAPORT: *Ritual and Religion in the Making of Humanity* 456-461 with the title: Postmodern science and natural religion.

[68] C. ANBEEK, C. BAKKER, L. MINNEMA & C. MENKEN-BEKIUS (eds.): *Geloven in de interreligieuze dialoog: Praktische Theologie* 29 (2002) no. 1. With regard to the figures for the world religions: there are 1.9 billion Christians (= 31% of the world's population), 1.2 billion Moslems, 811 million Hindus, 360 million Buddhists, 23 million Sikhs and 14 million Jews. The number professing no religion grew from 3 million in 1900 to 768 million in 2000. Figures derived from the *World Christian Encyclopedia*, Oxford 2001.

[69] Sometimes such noises come through as the undertone of remarks like 'now deservedly and happily the post-Vatican II generation of theologians are being replaced by a new, untainted and sincere generation.'

'only that culture can have a future which knows its past, accepts it at its own pace, and is able to evaluate it again'.[70] Only as people take modernity – including the secularisation which accompanies it – and postmodernism seriously and integrate it, can the real inculturation of religion in our culture take place. If these forces are ignored, people will all too easily be stuck in static views with regard to dogma, ritual, morality and ecclesiastical organisation. They will then, for instance, continue to appeal to what is termed Natural Law, not realising that a pure Natural Law is an abstraction because nature is always an inculturated and therefore historically constructed nature. An ecclesiastical answer to modernity and postmodernity has yet to be forthcoming from official church sources. There is still no real inculturation, though this inculturation is vitally important for the credibility of Christianity in our culture; it is essential for what sociologists term the church's plausibility structure. It would be beneficial to express the peculiar identity of Christianity once again in the midst of the many religious currents. In this 'the holy' receives the name of 'the Holy One', of a personal Thou, Someone opposite us Who speaks to us and to Whom we can turn: an Other with a countenance. This is not just the Deity of the philosophers. In this regard we should recall the famous text of Pascal. After his death at the age of 39, a paper was found sewn into the lining of his coat. In several sentences on it he recalls an extraordinary experience he had on the night of November 23, 1654. 'From about half past eleven in the evening to half an hour after midnight' he had the experience of 'Fire. God of Abraham, God of Isaac, God of Jacob, not of the philosophers and scholars. Certainty, feeling, joy, peace...'[71] Christian faith reaches further than the academic or philosophic concepts of God. It focuses on a very concrete God, who has revealed himself in history in his relation to Israel, in Jesus of Nazareth, and also continues to work in the midst of history today. Christianity must give a new shape to his identity, in and through complex interchanges with our contemporary culture. That old structures have collapsed, and that Christianity no longer holds a monopoly position in our culture, is perhaps more of a benefit than a loss in this, because Christianity must therefore abandon all false appeals to power, and must return to its core of compassion, humility,

[70] D.A.A. LOOSE: *Vergeten Ithaka. De odyssee van de moderne tijd*, Vught 1995, 38.
[71] B. PASCAL: *Les pensées de Pascal* (ed. F. KAPLAN), Paris 1982 = B. PASCAL: *Gedachten. I. Tekst*, Amsterdam 1997.

unpretentiousness and service. It is a question of giving shape and expression to the Christian story of suffering, death and resurrection, and to the larger and smaller stories of Biblical justice. As such, Christian inculturation means the difficult realisation of a counter-culture that attacks the peremptory and unilateral influence of the complex of the exact sciences, technology and capitalism.[72] With regard to the place and role of religion in the coming 'network culture', one encounters two challenging questions. Will the various sectors indeed succeed in entering into a productive dialogue with one another? And what place will religion take in the network of the world wide web? It appears that the Vatican, individual bishops, priests, monasteries and parishes are beginning to take their place in this web. Will this increase the possibilities of dialogue?

[72] LAEYENDECKER: 'Kerk en tegencultuur' 259.

CHAPTER 2

FROM A CRISIS IN RITUAL TO RITUALS IN ABUNDANCE

In Western, industrialised society insistent questions are arising with
regard to ritual. Ritual is in a state of flux. Radical changes have
occurred. This will obviously also have consequences for Christian ritual. It is experiencing the repercussions of these wider changes. Christian ritual cannot ignore its anthropological basis. If it is to be credible,
it must be really rooted in our culture. Thus there must be a creative
interchange between liturgy and contemporary culture. This also
implies the question of whether an authentically contemporary Christian liturgy might not be productive of more humane ritual in our society.

The changes with regard to ritual have emerged in The Netherlands
in a radical and almost shocking manner. In the 1960s there was suddenly a radical crisis in ritual, while more recently – really quite
abruptly – there has been an explosion of ritual. It seems to me to be
productive to review these changes more concretely.

1. CRISIS IN RITUAL

In the 1960s the words 'rite' and 'ritual' suddenly acquired negative
connotations in our society. Many began to consider ritual by definition
as something purely formal and inauthentic. Rituals were seen as a cloak
for the real problems of society. People began to consider even protest
rituals as only romantic gestures, as senseless, inefficient and unproduc-
tive. An increasing number of people no longer succeeded in arriving at
meaningful action in traditional rituals. On all sides people encountered
a crisis in ritual which made them uncertain. This was most radically
true for the great rites of passage. They lost their 'natural' significance.
The transition from the one phase of life to another was often no longer
underscored by ritual. The phases themselves lost their significance.

---

[1] H. Cox: *The Seduction of the Spirit*, New York 1973 = IDEM: *De verleiding van de
geest. Persoonlijke overdenkingen over gebruik en misbruik van de religie*, Bilthoven 1973, 33.

Harvey Cox observed that 'our lives run without phases, like an auto-mobile with an automatic transmission which passes from one gear to another imperceptibly. The result is that we no longer know in what gear we are driving.'[1] In The Netherlands there was still some ritual for the birth of a child – birth announcements, serving rusks with blue or pink aniseed comfits, visits by family or friends – but a real rite of pas-sage with any depth was lacking. The ritual of marriage fell more and more into discredit. People just moved in together. A real ritual to mark the transition to life together was lacking. And in 1970 Kok began his book *De geschiedenis van de laatste eer in Nederland* (The history of the last respects in The Netherlands) with the words, 'In this modern world, now that death has taken on another face, or better, has been given another face…, the last remnants of what were once meaningful cus-toms are falling away.'[2] Indeed, the words 'falling away' were not too strong; there came nothing to replace them. Rituals of death as rites of piety and solidarity appeared to be increasingly on the way out.[3] When someone died, it seemed the general rule that the body had to be carted away as quickly as possible, to an often very clean space, the morgue, the funeral parlour, the *chapelle ardente*. The number of private com-mittals and cremations – that is to say, funerals that took place without public announcement, without visitors or presence of even friends – increased. This tendency was strongest among the unchurched in the most urbanised areas, but was almost entirely absent among Roman Catholics.[4] The crisis in ritual thus extended to almost all the important moments in life, from birth to death. But it also had its effects on every-day rituals. Opening ceremonies became shadows of themselves, or dis-appeared altogether. When the school year opened, the courses just began, and the meeting schedule got heavier. There was increasingly less ritual at the transition from the work week to the weekend. 'Sunday best' disappeared. Actually, for many the weekend simply became filled with overtime from the work week, or with other tasks. Some had diffi-culty with commemorations of all sorts. There were discussions about whether we should continue to celebrate national observances. The

---

[2] H. KOK: *De geschiedenis van de laatste eer in Nederland*, Lochem 1970.

[3] G. LUKKEN: 'Kernvragen rond de christelijke dodenliturgie', in *Tijdschrift voor Liturgie* 64 (1980) 146-164.

[4] J. FORTUIN: 'Op verzoek van de overledene… Een onderzoek naar de uitvaartge-woonten aan de hand van overlijdensadvertenties', in G. BANCK (ed.): *Gestalten van de dood. Studies over abortus, euthanasie, rouw, zelfmoord en doodstraf*, Baarn 1980, 45 ff.

transition from one season to another increasingly took place without any event to mark it.

With regard to Christian churches, the situation was paradoxical. Midway through the 1960s a radical renewal of ritual took place. That was true for all the Christian churches, but particularly for the Roman Catholic Church, which in 1963 issued the constitution on liturgy as the first document from the Second Vatican Council. This was an effort to fundamentally renew liturgy. The changes were intended to bring the liturgy into step with the times (*aggiornamento*), and increase the opportunities for active participation. All rituals, from birth to death, were renewed. Furthermore, great ritual creativity was sparked among the congregants.[5] At the same time however it appeared that participation in Christian rituality fell back considerably.[6] This was a trend which had already appeared before the Second Vatican Council, but under the influence of the culture now continued at increased speed. In 1966 64.4% of Catholics still took part in the weekend liturgy. In 1982 this percentage had fallen to 22.7%, in 1988 to 16.9%, and in 2002 to

---

[5] For the countless new rituals in The Netherlands, in addition to the official books of worship of the various Christian churches see, among others, the many books by Huub Oosterhuis, the *Werkmap (voor) Liturgie* (from 1966) and the documentary publications in which material from this portfolio was reissued, the *Servicemap (voor) jongerenliturgie* (from 1971), the *Werkcahiers (voor) vieringen met kinderen* (from 1972), the series *Liturgie in beweging, Een jaar de tijd, Goed voor een jaar*, the publications of the Werkgroep Liturgie Heeswijk, of Midden onder u, of the ecumenical Kompas congregation and H. VRIJDAG: *Zonder beelden sprak hij niet tot hen*, 3 vol., Baarn 1988-1991. See also the *Directorium voor de Nederlandse kerkprovincie* which appears every year, L. DANEN: *Uit goede bron. Literatuurlijst van liturgisch materiaal en achtergrondinformatie* (Liturgische Handreikingen 13), Breda 1987 and L. DANEN & J. JOOSSE: *Literatuuroverzicht liturgie* (Liturgische Handreikingen 24), Breda 1999.

With regard to Protestant liturgy, one can refer to, among others, the material in P. OSKAMP & N. SCHUMAN (eds.): *De weg van de liturgie. Tradities, achtergronden, praktijk*, Zoetermeer 1998, 3ᵉ revised edition 2001, M. BARNARD, M. VAN LEEUWEN, N.A. SCHUMAN & J.H. UYTENBOGAARDT (eds.): *Nieuwe wegen in de liturgie. De weg van de liturgie – een vervolg*, Zoetermeer 2002 and G. WARNINK: *Lezen over vieren: Literatuurwijzer ten dienste van werkgroepen liturgie*, een uitgave van de deputaten voor de eredienst van de Gereformeerde Kerken in Nederland (Postbox 202, 3830 AE Leusden), 1981. See also M. BARNARD & N. SCHUMAN, *Nieuwe wegen in de liturgie. De weg van de liturgie*, Zoetermeer 2001.

[6] Researchers make the distinction between being churched (i.e., being a member of a church) and churchgoing (regular participation in church services). Here we are dealing with the figures for the latter.

8.6%. Of all members of Christian churches, in 1970 67% still attended church once a fortnight, while in 1991 this percentage had fallen to 43%. With regard to weekly attendance, there was a decline from 40% in 1980 to 31% in 1991 to 23% in 1999. Looking at the total Dutch population, the percentage of regular churchgoers fell from 77% in 1966 to 44% in 1996.[7] Participation in the rituals of baptism, confirmation, marriage, unction and funerals showed the same falling line. It did remain true that the liturgy, as compared with other ecclesiastical gatherings, continued to attract the largest number of church members, and that the publicly visible liturgy remained the most central element of Christian worship. In this connection one should recall what I noted in Part 2 with regard to the fact that religions are primarily perceived on the basis of their ritual visibility.[8]

The crisis in ritual also affected everyday Christian rituals. One can think of grace before meals, morning and evening prayer, the blessing of homes and objects, the use of holy water, and devotions to images. Finally, many Christian rituals which were related to folk religion also disappeared: veneration of the Sacrament, pilgrimages and processions, holy medals, veneration of relics; so many statues and images were removed from the churches that people spoke of a new breaking of the images.

Yet at the same time there was evidence of a counter-movement. New rituals also arose. These were often rituals of protest such as the sit-in, the protest demonstration and the protest march in its many forms, the Russell and Vietnam tribunals, occupation of businesses and school offices, squatting in vacant houses, handcuffing oneself to the fences of nuclear power plants or military bases, human blockades, the singing of protest songs, presentation of petitions, marching around the Pentagon or an embassy seven times, as the Israelites had done around the walls of Jericho, self-immolation, setting up fields of crosses as an anti-war protest, disrupting academic gatherings with slogans, banners and songs as anti-ritual, the clenched fist salute, giving the V-sign. There were still others: the forum discussion, the teach-in, placing flowers at graves or memorials, burning candles at the place where someone had been killed, friends and associates themselves carrying the coffin to the grave, the rites of flower-

---

[7] PETERS, DEKKER & DE HART: *God in Nederland 1966-1996*; BECKER & DE WIT: *Secularisatie in de jaren negentig.*

[8] Part 2, Chapter 2, 2. See also SCHMIDT-LAUBER & BIERITZ (eds.): *Handbuch der Liturgik* 13-14 and 572.

power, the hippy culture and punk, pop concerts, dancing together or sitting in circles talking, in The Netherlands hanging out the flag with a schoolbag on the stock as a sign that one had passed graduation exams, the introductory week or the team-building weekend for new students. One can also recall the massive peace demonstrations against nuclear weapons in 1981 and 1983 in Amsterdam and The Hague, at which it appeared just how impressive and effective the new rituals could be.

William Golding's novel *Rites of Passage* appeared in 1980; he received the Nobel Prize for literature in 1983. Nooteboom's *Rituelen* and Silko's *Ceremonie* also appeared in 1980, the latter much read in feminist circles. It was precisely in such circles that a new interest in symbols and rituals grew. There was also a growing interest in rituals in historical disciplines; one may recall the Annales group. For instance, in 1975 Ariés had remarked that rituals were a goldmine for the history of ideas.[9] Among Christians the renewal of rituals that had begun in the 1960s continued unabated, despite the decline in the number of participants; liturgies underwent revision in churches all across the board, and among the congregants there has been a constant flow of renewal in rituals right to the present day, so much so that one can speak of an amazing creativity. Moreover, particularly in the second half of the 1980s there was the rise of ritual studies. As early as 1975 Grimes had founded a ritual 'laboratory' at the Wilfrid Laurier University in Waterloo, Ontario, Canada, that was a first step toward what later became ritual studies.[10] This laboratory did not have liturgy as such as its focus, but was organised in a broader, anthropological manner, and ran for twenty years. For the rest, one must not forget that in The Netherlands too, at an even earlier date, developments in that direction had gotten under way. In 1966 there was planning toward founding a centre for liturgical renewal which was to be organised on a cross-cultural basis, and which would collect and stimulate the activities of liturgical laboratories.[11] Furthermore, in the second

[9] P. ARIÈS: 'Les rituels de mariage', in *La Maison-Dieu* (1975) 121, 143; see also T. VAN ENG & B. SENTIUS: 'Skript-interview met Willem Frijhoff', in *Skript. Historisch tijdschrift* 6 (1984) 237-252.

[10] GRIMES: *Marrying and Burying* 47-53; 135-144.

[11] TH. GOVAART: 'Het liturgisch experiment in Nederland. Informaties en inzichten', in *Tijdschrift voor Liturgie* 50 (1966) 334-335. See also J. JOOSSE: *Eucharistische gebeden in Nederland. Een documentaire studie over de ontwikkeling van de vertaalde en 'eigen' Nederlandse eucharistische gebeden (1963-1979)* Tilburg 1991, 52-53, 519-520.

half of the 1960s various departments of theology offered ritual labs for
theological students, where instructors brought together verbal and
physical expression, comparative religion and liturgy. These involved
not only the discussion of liturgical material at a practical level, but
equally exercises, developing and 'playing' with ritual praxis in an interdisciplinary and anthropological context. These labs were gradually
expanded into more stringent liturgical laboratories with an eye to
training for pastoral duties, in which a broad anthropological basis
continued to play a role. These are still to be found in departments of
theology. In reflection in liturgical studies the anthropological foundations also received particular emphasis.[12] The international breakthrough of ritual studies in the second half of the 1980s, with even its
own journal, therefore connected very well with the preceding developments in The Netherlands.

2. RITUALS IN ABUNDANCE

What is remarkable is that in the 1990s this undercurrent which always
remained present rather abruptly exploded into a spate flowing through
our society. Compared with the polar opposite of the 1960s, one can
hardly imagine a greater contrast. In 1997 Paul Post presented a lecture
with the title 'Every day a festival, or beyond the crisis in ritual'.[13]
Among other matters, in it he offered his impressions from a 'ritual
diary' he had put together in 1996 from his personal observations and
from the media. One could indeed speak of an abundance of ritual.
    This can perhaps be seen most strikingly in regard to rituals sur-
rounding death. Rather suddenly there has been an explosion of great
creativity. People are searching in all directions for meaningful death rituals. The appearance of books such as *Zand erover: afscheid en uitvaart
naar eigen inzicht* (Dust to dust: leave-taking and funerals to one's own
discretion)[14] and *Onder de groene zoden: de persoonlijke uitvaart* (Six feet

---

[12] See among others LUKKEN: D*e onvervangbare weg van de liturgie*; IDEM: *Geen
leven zonder rituelen*; IDEM: 'De 'doorbraak' van de antropologie in de liturgie', in H.J.F.
DEGEN a.o. (eds.): *Herinneringen aan de toekomst. Pastoraat in de geest van Vaticanum II*,
Baarn 1991, 167-176.
[13] P. POST: 'Alle dagen feest, of: de ritencrisis voorbij. Een verkenning van de markt',
in POST & SPEELMAN (eds.): *De Madonna van de Bijenkorf* 11-32.
[14] M. SAX a.o.: *Zand erover. Afscheid en uitvaart naar eigen inzicht*, Amsterdam 1989.

under: the personalised funeral)[15] are apposite expressions of this. There are also new developments with regard to death notices and obituaries.[16] People are expressing a need for more personal graves, and find new, artistic designs for burial clothing, coffins, gravestones and urns or other repositories for ashes, including containers in the form of a medallion that can be worn around the neck. Visiting the cemetery is again in fashion. In the funeral home, more time can be allotted for the leave-taking, and at the crematoria too more possibilities are gradually being offered.[17]

There are also striking public death rituals. For example, viewers were able to follow on television how the last wishes of the pop singer Klijn, who had appeared on the programme hosted by the Dutch celebrity Paul de Leeuw as an AIDS patient, were carried out. The ashes were strewn from a boat in New York harbour by De Leeuw and a friend of Klijn, with the skyline of New York in the background. A newspaper reviewer wrote,

> The way De Leeuw did it, there were no awkward moments; he didn't conceal his nerves. Fumbling and sloppily formulated as usual, but sincerely and looking right in the camera, he explained to the viewer what the intention was. Then there was a feeble attempt at a joke, a downright blunt question ('Have you got over it?' or something to that effect), attention for the urn, surprise at the little number tab that appeared to be in the ashes and the emptying of the plastic sack by Klijn's friend, hanging over the railing. A champagne toast and a comforting gesture rounded off the short film.[18]

Following that De Leeuw joined with List in singing a song from the 1960s familiar to many: 'The land will always be greener on the other side of the hills' (a line which was repeated again and again in the song), which ends with the words 'Perhaps then a new time begins.'

---

[15] J. ENKLAAR: *Onder de groene zoden. De persoonlijke uitvaart. Nieuwe rituelen in rouwen, begraven en cremeren*, Zutphen 1995.

[16] See for instance L. DERKSEN: *Als het donker wordt, wat zal ik dan nog zeggen... Een verzameling rouwpoëzie*, Naarden 1992.

[17] H. VAN WEERDENBURG: 'Een rode kist in een witte lijkauto', in *De Bazuin* 76 (1993) 36, 8-10. See also the interview with the funeral director J. Fiddelaers by N. KOOLSBERGEN: 'Macht over de dood', in *Het Nieuwsblad* September 17, 1993, 25 and E. SCHOOTS: 'Het goede afscheid nemen', in *NRC Handelsblad* November 26, 1993, Weekagenda, 1.

[18] P. KOTTMAN: 'Paul de Leeuw maakte gedenkwaardige televisie', in *NRC Handelsblad* November 29, 1993, 15.

There were also a number of striking death rituals with public participation, chiefly after national disasters such as the crash of an El Al cargo
plane into an apartment block in a suburb of Amsterdam, and a short time
later the crash of a Dutch air force Hercules transport at the Welschap air-
base near Eindhoven, in which practically all members of a military band
were killed. Then there were the numerous commemorative observances:
AIDS memorial day, the fifty-year commemoration of the end of World
War II, the massive White March in Belgium after the discovery of the
children murdered by Dutroux, the silent marches held in various Dutch
cities for young victims of senseless violence, the annual memorial (since
1996) for victims of traffic accidents, the setting up of memorials alongside
highways and streets at the scenes of fatal accidents or murders.

Many of the rituals we have just mentioned can be termed 'disaster rituals'. They form a very specific category within the 'emerging rituals'.[19]
A truly new ritual form in The Netherlands is the silent procession. Paul
Post describes one as follows: 'On the evening of Friday, January 12,
2001, those walking along the dyke at Volendam, a small port city
north of Amsterdam, were not American or Japanese tourists as usual,
but thousands of Dutch people; they had joined in a procession along
the dyke. As a result of a terrible fire in a cafe in the city on New Year's
Eve, a massive procession expressed the sympathy of the population for
the victims and their families. It was not a subject with which the television could fascinate the viewers in the normal way, and yet the procession was shown in its entirety by national and regional broadcasters.
Fourteen young people had lost their lives in the fire, and a number of

[19] P. POST: *Het wonder van Dokkum. Verkenningen van populair religieus ritueel*,
Nijmegen 2000, 107-111; IDEM: 'La marche silencieuse: perspectives rituelles et
liturgiques sur de nouveaux rites populaires aux Pays Bas', in *La Maison-Dieu* (2001)
228, 143-157; P. POST, R.L. GRIMES, A. NUGTEREN, P. PETERSON & H. ZONDAG: *Disaster Ritual. Explorations of an Emerging Ritual Repertoire* (Liturgia condenda 15), Leu-
ven/Paris/Dudley MA 2003 (based on: P. POST, A. VAN NUGTEREN & H. ZONDAG: *Rituelen na rampen. Verkenning van een opkomend ritueel repertoire* (Meander 3), Kampen
2002); C. MENKEN-BEKIUS, L. BAL & M. VAN DIJK-GROENEBOER: 'De kerk en stille
tochten tegen geweld. Praktisch-theologische overwegingen bij een nieuw ritueel', in
Praktische Theologie 28 (2001) 272-277; L. BAL, M. VAN DIJK-GROENEBOER & C.
MENKEN-BEKIUS: 'De stille tocht van Gorinchem. Een sociologische analyse', in *Praktische Theologie* 28 (2001) 278-291; C. MENKEN-BEKIUS, L. BAL & M. VAN DIJK-
GROENEBOER: 'De beleving van de stille tocht van Gorinchem', in *Praktische Theologie*
28 (2001) 292-301; MITCHELL: 'The Amen Corner. Brave New World'.

injured were still being cared for in special burn units in The Netherlands and adjoining countries.[20] He then notes that in the relatively
short time since 1996 the silent procession had become one of our most
conspicuous public and collective rituals. The White March in Brussels
for the murdered children was similarly a disaster ritual. Other forms are
the placement of flowers, stuffed toy animals, drawings and letters at the
scene of an accident or disaster: in Paris where Princess Diana was killed
and outside her home in London, or at the gates of a football stadium
where fans died. Disaster rituals likewise took an American form after the
attack on the Twin Towers and their collapse. Mitchell observes that September 11 reminded us that our powers of 'ritual invention' are intact.
'Many strongly felt the need to *do* something – in public, with others…
In cities and towns across the country people pried themselves away from
TV screens long enough to light candles as dusk fell, to festoon their
homes and cars with flags and tricolor ribbons, to sing "Amazing Grace"
or "God Bless America", to march in patriotic processions.'[21]

A whole different category of rituals have formed around birth. They are
also once again claiming attention. One can point to birth announcements in newspapers, the sending of congratulatory cards, ceremonies
surrounding the registering of the birth at the city clerk's office, visits to
the mother and new-born, giving jewellery to the child and mother (for
example a silver cup or teddy bear, a birth spoon or napkin ring engraved
with the child's name, or a charm for the mother's bracelet), the grand-
parents opening a savings account for the baby, having a ceramic tile
made with the child's name and birth date, planting a tree for the occasion (a pear tree for a girl, an apple or nut tree for a boy), distribution of
rusks with aniseed comfits, and the image of a stork placed in the parents' front garden. There have also been suggestions for a birth-party,
where the child is formally presented to all those attending.

Finally, there is great creativity surrounding marriage ritual.[22] Civil marriage ceremonies are gradually becoming less formalities. The official

[20] POST: 'La marche silencieuse' 143-144.
[21] MITCHELL: 'The Amen Corner. Brave New World' 67.
[22] J. PIEPER: *Rituele veranderingen met betrekking tot de huwelijkssluiting. Een onderzoeksvoorstel Wetenschapswinkel Katholieke universiteit Brabant*, Tilburg 1996; J. PIEPER
& P. POST: 'Rituele veranderingen met betrekking tot de huwelijkssluiting', in *Jaarboek
voor liturgie-onderzoek* 12 (1996) 136-163.

from the city clerk's office appears in a special robe, music is played, poems are read, a suitable site is chosen (romantic, atmospheric castles, manor houses, old churches, or private homes), rings are exchanged, a marriage book presented.[23] Marriages are also occasionally performed during dinner parties.[24] Furthermore, symbols from the old nature religions play a role. Particularly nature and the four basic elements of earth, water, air and fire surface repeatedly in these rituals, and marriages are sometimes performed in a woods, at the holy site of a nature religion, or at a New Age centre.[25] One often encounters a mixture of Germanic, Celtic and Christian elements.[26] One can also point to the rituals of the bachelor party preceding the wedding, the new rituals of gay marriage, and the creation of divorce rituals.

In the impressions in his ritual diary Post further makes reference to the struggle between the Dutch St. Nicholas (who brings Dutch children gifts on his saint's day, December 5) and the Anglo-American import of Santa Claus (who does the same on Christmas), the continuing manger cult, St. Martin's Day processions, Epiphany celebrations involving the three kings, preparations for and the celebration of Carnival itself, the typically Dutch event of the Eleven Cities ice skating marathon, meditation rooms (in a number of diverse places: prisons, schools, university campuses, nursing homes, shopping malls, airports, monasteries, hospitals), the dedication of the Dachau monument in the Amsterdamse Bos, New Age rites, therapeutic rituals, pilgrimage to Santiago de Compostela. To that list one could add rituals surrounding moving into a new home, Gay Liberation parades, Father's Day, Mother's Day, celebrations for the 100th birthday of late parents, Secretary's Day, International Volunteers Day, Valentine's Day, AIDS quilts, pilgrimages to the graves of the pop stars like Jim Morrison (in Père Lachaise Cemetery in Paris) and Elvis Presley (at Graceland, in Memphis), and pop concerts.

---

[23] PIEPER: *Rituele veranderingen met betrekking tot de huwelijkssluiting* 17-19, with among others reference to POST: 'Goede tijden, slechte tijden; PIEPER & POST: 'Rituele veranderingen met betrekking tot de huwelijkssluiting' 149-150.

[24] PIEPER: *Rituele veranderingen met betrekking tot de huwelijkssluiting* 19; PIEPER & POST: 'Rituele veranderingen met betrekking tot de huwelijkssluiting' 150.

[25] PIEPER: *Rituele veranderingen met betrekking tot de huwelijkssluiting* 14-15; J. VAN HOOYDONK: 'Trouwen in het bos?', in *De Bazuin* 80 (1997) 22, 32.

[26] PIEPER & POST: 'Rituele veranderingen met betrekking tot de huwelijkssluiting' 150-151.

Ever more – and often exotic – rituals enter society through training programmes among alternative groups and therapies. For example, in the
guide to alternative health care for the southern Netherlands for 1997
one found shamanistic workshops, Reiki courses, Ki-aidiko training, bio-
release courses, Gnostic get-acquainted evenings, exercises in sacred
dance, meditative dancing, water dancing, reincarnation therapy, chakra
therapy, chakra readings, aroma therapy, colour healing, Bach (flower)
remedies, rebirthing, yoga, tarot, Transcendental Meditation, Zen meditation, tonal meditation, meditation training involving inner light and
sound, and drawing mandalas.[27] The Dutch monthly periodical *Koördanser* offers a complete listing of courses, lectures, workshops and celebrations focusing on personal growth. Among the events listed there are
healing celebrations, Zen archery, 'living heaven on earth', sweat lodge
ceremonies, 'magnified healing' and dancing under the full moon.[28]

From the first section of this chapter it is clear that creativity within the
church with regard to ritual was already fully present since the Second
Vatican Council. What is new however is the onset of interest in pilgrimages,[29] devotional processions, visitation to cemeteries on All Souls'
Day, Thanksgiving and harvest celebrations, blessings of homes, the sea,
fields, animals and vehicles. One can classify these rituals as 'rituals of
popular religion', of 'popular culture', or as 'outdoor rituals'.[30] For the
rest, the trend toward rituals outside of the church building had already
begun earlier. I recall that in the second half of the 1960s we had organised 'reflection celebrations' on Sunday in the small auditorium of the
Municipal Theatre in 's-Hertogenbosch. The director of the Theatre was
himself involved in them, and we tried to relate the celebrations with

---

[27] F. FRANZEN: *Adres-Wijzer voor de Alternatieve Gezondheidszorg voor Zuid Nederland, Periode 1997*, Eindhoven 1997.
[28] *Koördanser. Informatieblad voor persoonlijke groei* (2002) (May), no. 198. Also
Christian spiritual centers are mentioned.
[29] Between 1983 and 1993 the number of pilgrimages to Santiago de Compostela
increased by 3500%, from 2000 to 70,000. See P.L. MALLOY: 'The Re-Emergence of
Popular Religion Among Non-Hispanic American Catholics', in *Worship* 72 (1998) 7.
[30] POST: *Ritueel landschap*; IDEM: 'Zeven notities over rituele verandering' 14;
Vieringen (Rituelen) buiten 1 and 2: *Werkmap (voor) Liturgie* 30 (1996) no. 3-4; PIEPER,
POST & VAN UDEN: *Bedevaart en pelgrimage*; M. VAN UDEN, J. PIEPER & P. POST (eds.):
Oude sporen, nieuwe wegen. Ontwikkelingen in bedevaartonderzoek (UTP-katern 17),
Baarn 1995; P. POST, J. PIEPER & M. VAN UDEN: *The Modern Pilgrim. Multidisciplinary
Explorations of Christian Pilgrimage* (Liturgia condenda 8), Leuven 1998.

performances which had recently taken place in the same theatre. These were not the only events of their kind.[31] One might recall the agape celebrations of Sjaloom, which took place 'in one home or another',[32] home worship, motel services, outreach services in all places of all sorts, the performance of a wedding during the wedding dinner,[33] and 'really' outside, the hikes of students to Chartres, the Franciscans' hiking tours and the walking tours of the international Catholic peace movement, Pax Christi.

The new rituals also have their extravagances. One finds this for instance with death rituals. In 1996 a section of the grass from the pitch of the old Ajax stadium in Amsterdam was removed to Amsterdam's Westgaarde crematorium to serve as a field for strewing ashes. The field is twelve by fifteen metres, with the dugout from the old football field, chalk lines and centre spot, surrounded with grey gravel; in the same way advertising signs surround a football pitch, there are fences with memorial plaques along the sides of this field, all in the Ajax team colours. Some of the deceased want to be dressed in an Ajax shirt at their funeral, and more than one Ajax scarf has gone to the grave with its owner. For that matter, in England the strewing of ashes at football stadiums has been common for years, often on a special plot of grass behind the pitch. Elsewhere people have been buried in classic 1950s Chevrolets or Cadillacs. More than once those present at a crematorium have been treated to a laser show in the darkened auditorium that afforded them a near-death experience. In 1998 The Netherlands witnessed its first 'environmentally friendly' funeral procession by bicycle. The coffin was conveyed in a bicycle trailer drawn by a black bicycle, and followed by a bicycle cortege.[34] In 1996 the Amsterdam artists' association Arti et Amicitiae held a five course 'funeral dinner', each course with its own symbolism, for which popular culture and fairy tales were the ultimate sources. The basic idea was that the survivors should

---

[31] See for instance R. ADOLFS (ed.): *Buiten-dienst. Informele samenkomsten buiten de kerkmuren*, Baarn 1969.
[32] See for literature G. LUKKEN: 'Op weg naar eenheid in verscheidenheid. Modellen van gemeenschapsvorming rondom brood en beker', in E. HENAU & F. JESPERS (eds.): *Liturgie en kerkopbouw. Opstellen aangeboden aan Ad Blijlevens*, Baarn 1993, 92-104.
[33] F. FRIJNS: 'Een bruiloftsfeest. Proeve van een huwelijksviering', in *Tijdschrift voor Liturgie* 55 (1971) 370-377.
[34] P. VAN ANDEL: 'Uitvaart op de fiets', in *NRC Handelsblad* October 2, 1998, 20.

commemorate the deceased by eating heartily, out of honour for the gods, and so that those left behind could go on to a productive future and the deceased would thrive, joining the banquet in the shadow realm.[35] Sometimes the ritual creativity seems boundless. In 1998 the ash capsule was patented, a minuscule container with ash from the deceased that is introduced into the body of one of the next of kin by hypodermic needle: the skin as grave monument.[36] Some have had the ashes of the deceased processed into a diamond. Similarly there have been marriages performed at the bottom of swimming pools, in nightclubs, amidst dolphins or alligators, on top of mountains, hanging from aeroplanes, in free fall before the parachutes open, and at nudist camps.[37]

A new phenomenon are what are being termed ritual agencies, which frequently are managed by theologically trained individuals.[38] Their orientation is broad: they are intended to meet the general human and religious demand, as well as possible Christian demand for rituals. For instance, in its promotional materials Motiev, a Dutch agency for 'ritually designing important moments in life', reports that in addition to celebrations of births it will also provide voyages of growth and discovery, youth ceremonies, partnership ceremonies, celebrations for those reaching their fiftieth birthdays, life reviews, promotion celebrations, anniversary celebrations, wisdom observances and mourning ceremonies.[39] This is part of a wider phenomenon. Belgium recently has been able to boast an agency called 'Rent a priest'. Wagner-Rau notes that in Germany the number of 'ritual designers' is growing, a trend that, particularly in light of the number of unemployed theologians, is only likely to increase. There is ever more competition between ecclesiastical and other sources

[35] D. BLOCH: 'Uit-eten voor een vruchtbare toekomst', in *NRC Handelsblad. Agenda* April 11, 1996, 3.

[36] M. KALSE & P. TIMMERS: 'Veranderende rituelen rond dood en begraven', in *Studio* 72 (1998) 42 (October 10-16), 6-7.

[37] PIEPER: *Rituele veranderingen met betrekking tot de huwelijkssluiting* 19, with reference to J.N.E. PLASCHAERT: 'Het gemeentehuis', in *Burgerzaken en recht* (1995) 2, 29-31.

[38] See among others J. VOSSEBELD: 'Van confectie naar maatwerk. Keuze uit een keur aan kwaliteit op de markt van uitvaart, huwelijk en aanverwante artikelen', in *Mara* 9 (1996) 4, 12-21.

[39] Folder from *Motiev* (A. van Luijk, Melleveld 15, 4724 EK Wouw). One finds a similar assortment at a ritual agency in Vught: see M. SERNÉ.: *Ritueelbegeleiding, hulp bij het maken van een persoonlijke viering*, Vught (Capellebosdreef 13) without year.

of ritual guidance.[40] Ronald Grimes mentions a collective of artists who comprise Welfare State International in Ulverton, England, directed by John Fox and Sue Gill, which has produced large-scale civic celebrations, managed weddings, taught workshops on funeral making and assisted people in planning child-naming ceremonies.[41] He also notes that Joyce Gioia sells ceremonial services in the New York City area and is authorised to perform weddings in the states of New York and Massachusetts. 'She calls herself a multi-faith minister'.[42] In Australia Jim and Meg Boswell run a business called Celebration Ceremonies. Meg bills herself as a marriage and naming celebrant and John as a master of ceremonies and management consultant as well as a naming and funeral celebrant. Meg specialises in family events such as weddings and vow renewals, and John in business and community celebrations such as retirements, achievement and service recognitions, and the induction of new officers.[43] Grimes also points to the danger of a 'purely market-driven ritual economy' among these 'alternative ritual entrepreneurs', who work in the interstices between religions.[44] It is however important to equally emphasise here that there are meaningful ways to fill a ritual gap created as churches lost their monopoly position, leaving many in a ritual no-man's-land. I will return to this.[45]

The transition from the crisis in ritual to rituals in abundance raises the issue of what is termed the density of ritual. This can differ according to the culture, but also within one and the same culture or cultural period, by individuals or by the phase of life for the same individual. All sorts of theories exist with regard to these changes in density.[46] The most familiar in our time is the theory that with the growth of secularisation ritual will decrease. This proceeds from a sort of evolutionary model.

---

[40] U. WAGNER-RAU: *Segensraum. Kasualpraxis in der modernen Gesellschaft* (Praktische Theologie heute 50), Stuttgart/Berlin/Köln 2000, 219.

[41] GRIMES: *Deeply into the Bone* 77-85. Grimes recommends two of their how-to-do books: T. COULT & B. KERSHAW: *Engineers of the Imagination: the Welfare State Handbook*, London 1983 and S. GILL & J. FOX: *The Dead Good Funerals Book*, Ulverston 1996.

[42] GRIMES: *Deeply into the Bone* 307.

[43] GRIMES: *Deeply into the Bone* 308-309.

[44] GRIMES: *Deeply into the Bone* 309.

[45] See among others Part 3, Chapter 4.

[46] BELL: *Ritual. Perspectives* 173-209.

The sketch just given shows how open to question this theory is.[47] Other theories, such as the emphasis on orthopraxis and oral culture as a stimulant for ritual, as opposed to orthodoxy and written culture as a brake, also lend themselves to oversimplifications. In any case, there is no unanimity in the answer to this question. To my mind, the most useful is the careful typology developed by Douglas. According to her, ritual is strongly connected with social organisation in which the stress lies on mutual solidarity within a whole, primarily through group identity, but also through internal hierarchical order. From this basis she arrives at a typology of four kinds of societies with all sorts of variants in ritual density.[48]

[47] See for instance also PLATVOET & VAN DER TOORN (eds.): *Pluralism and Identity.*
[48] Especially M. DOUGLAS: *Natural Symbols. Explorations in Cosmology*, New York 1973. See BELL: *Ritual. Perspectives* 43-45, 183-190.

CHAPTER 3

RITUAL IN OUR CULTURE

This chapter begins with an exploration of the new questions with regard to ritual. Then I will examine the ambiguous situation in which we find ourselves. Finally I will go into several specific characteristics and problem areas of ritual in our culture.

1. A FIRST EXPLORATION: NEW QUESTIONS

In our culture the ritual market is undergoing transformations of all sorts. I deliberately use the term 'ritual market' here. It clearly reflects the economic hegemony in our culture: one finds an almost boundless stock of rituals, from which the consumer can choose according to his or her own taste. Does that not detract from what authentic ritual aims at? Or should this be assessed positively, for instance as the wealth of a pluriform ritual culture? In a certain sense the abundance also strikes one as chaotic. The ritual market offers 'everything including the kitchen sink', as it were. Can one find a line in this? Must one not ultimately speak of a devaluation of ritual? Some find little to be optimistic about in this connection.[1] Are not new rituals often oriented to instrumentality, or theatrics, and as such a surrogate for the search for sense and meaning? Are they not sometimes rather artificial? Is the word 'bungling' sometimes appropriate? Are they not often directed toward the individual, at the expense of the collective? Are not many of the new rituals a cover for narcissistic self-centredness? One can think of what one encounters in rituals purportedly conferring human wholeness and spiritual and physical healing. But this is a question which can be posed not only with regard to therapeutic rituals. Are not public festivals too (the Queen's Birthday, Carnival, sports contests) often captive to our

---

[1] R. NAUTA: 'Rituelen als decor. Over het geheim van de leegte', in POST & SPEEL-MAN (eds.): *De Madonna van de Bijenkorf* 73-95 and, in a number of respects too, GRIMES: *Deeply into the Bone*.

economic system, and as such more oriented to utility and profit than to the 'outsideness' which characterises the feast? And in new ritual, is not the search for the uniqueness of the moment often at the cost of the element of repetition, which is essential for ritual?

To my mind, the new situation is more or less reminiscent of the situation at the time Christianity came into being. There was also a superabundance of rituals in the Greco-Roman world, with regard to gods, the emperor, the institutions of city and state, public festivals, the stadiums and amphitheatres, birth, marriage and death. Sometimes the Christians were fiercely opposed to these rituals. But on other occasions it was just as much the case that Christian ritual sought – and found – its way precisely in interaction with this Greco-Roman culture. It was in this manner that what we now term the classic Roman liturgy arose. For Christians the specific culture has always, repeatedly been a challenge for seeking out new forms for their rituals and the place and function of their rituals within that culture. Why should our culture be less suitable for this than cultures in the past? In the midst of the abundance of rituals, is it possible to catch sight of the place and form of Christian ritual, in interplay with our culture? In the following I will attempt to do precisely this.

2. AN AMBIGUOUS SITUATION

In general, one can say that the situation in our culture is ambiguous. On the one side it affords a strong and positive foundation for authentic ritual; the symbolic order is a centre of attention. On the other side the situation is negative, because the symbolic order is under threat of being overrun, through its domination by the economic order.

2.1. Renewed interest in the symbolic order

I have already noted that one-dimensional perception considerably complicates our symbolic perception.[2] The symbolic order is, after all, by definition multi-dimensional. It is therefore not surprising that in our culture there should be a passionate search for a more extensive meaning.

---

[2] See Part 3, Chapter 1, 1.

Now, it is interesting that in our culture this search is at the same time defined by strongly-held assumptions. In particular, there is a widely accepted conviction that we will never succeed in our search for meaning without the mediation of symbols. It is precisely at this point that radical shifts have taken place in our culture. Especially in psychoanalytic circles, linguistics, semiotics and contemporary philosophy, the insight is now widely accepted that we have no direct access whatsoever to truth or reality, and are always imprisoned in a network of mediators. One such mediator, first, is the network of language. There is no way in which the language that we use can be conceived as a tool by which we give a name to a previously perceived reality. On the contrary, we can only penetrate to reality by designating it, and that designation is always partial, an attempt which is culturally defined and limited. Language can never disclose reality as such to us. It always stands between us and reality, as an imperfect attempt to penetrate to it. Language discloses something of reality to us, but at the same time it must be recognised that this disclosure is only partial: language at the same time obscures. Thus we can never claim to be masters of the world outside ourselves. It is present through language, but only in part. That world will always remain other, the Other, which one cannot command in a pure understanding. We conduct our search in and through the mediation of language, and repeatedly experience tentativeness. What is true for language is also true for non-linguistic manners of dealing with reality, through body language, facial expression, gestures, acts and behaviours. These too are only mediators, which as such are always inadequate, constructed and culturally defined: we can not master reality with them. Reality always remains at a distance as the other, and thus elusive. Our speaking and the way in which we dress, eat, live, travel and work is enmeshed in a network constructed by our culture; thus, for example, we do not simply eat calories, but the dishes which are selected, named and determined by our culture.[3]

We always communicate with reality through our own spectacles, with all the limitations that implies. There is a culturally determined *symbolic order* to which we are captive, and in and through which we must repeatedly and constantly discover and find our identity as human beings. In Part 2 I noted that symbolic order condenses intensively in ritual,[4] so that it plays an essential role in giving meaning to live – both everyday life and

---

[3] CHAUVET: *Du symbolique au symbole* 28.
[4] See Part 2, Chapter 2.

its crucial moments. Rituals are the embodiment, as it were, of the symbolic order. In addition, one is correct to speak of a symbolic order, because in the final analysis the mediation is not purely through instrumental signs, but through symbols in the true sense of the word: symbols that simultaneously reveal and conceal. Our search for meaning thus on one had offers perspective, but because of the mediation is also always patchwork. That is all the more true because the symbols in the symbolic order are always in a specific and limited manner brought into relation with one another in a structured whole, which unavoidably means our search is culturally determined. This insight into the mediation of the symbolic order *and* its limitations is an extremely favourable condition for ritual in our culture now, and for its authentic experience.

2.2. Domination of ritual by the economic system

At the same time, it is true that the situation is not completely favourable. Both secular and religious rituals in our culture are easily dominated by the economic system. They are colonised, so to speak, by the economic system.[5] It is important to look at this further.

Rituals involving free time are strongly dominated by the pursuit of production and growth. The entertainment industry is always inventing new possibilities; amusement parks must expand to continue to draw visitors, and constantly offer more sensational attractions; travel bureaus organise vacations as efficiently as possible in 'off-the-shelf' offers; professional sports is a business run according to hard economic imperatives.

Perhaps sport is the most clear-cut example. What is important there is the book value, the replacement value and the market value of the players.[6] They can also be hired out to other clubs, in which case we speak of lease activity. In fact, football clubs provide a product, and the

---

[5] A very specific area of research in ritual is that into 'consumption rituals'. See C. OTNES & M.A. McGRATH: 'New Research on Consumption Rituals', in *Journal of Ritual Studies* 11 (1997) 2, 35-44 (with bibliography); S. FRIESE: 'A Consumer Good in the Ritual Process: The Case of the Wedding Dress', in *Journal of Ritual Studies* 11 (1997) 2, 47-58; N.A. RUDD: 'Cosmetics Consumption and Use among Women: Ritualized Activities that Construct and Transform the Self', in *Journal of Ritual Studies* 11 (1997) 2, 59-78.

[6] D. WITTENBERG: 'Big business. Het uitgekiende ondernemingsbeleid van PSV', in *HP/De Tijd* May 20, 1988, 16-19.

players are the means of production. Advertising in the stadium is a safe source of revenue, because in television broadcasts it remains in the picture longer than the several short seconds of the advertising commercials as such. Businessmen – particularly from firms which sponsor the club – are given luxury boxes or sideline seating at matches. In the matches themselves, it is more a question of results than of the play. Winning is all that counts. The competence of the trainer is measured by the win/loss record. In all these ways, sport is more dominated by results than by displays of skill or beauty. The beauty and relaxation of sport becomes subordinate to top performances: rather a face contorted in anger or pain than a beautiful move. This despite the fact that in every sport, as I previously remarked,[7] harmoniously performed actions are possible, such as are still found in dressage, ice dancing and gymnastics.

The economy has also taken rites of passage into its service. This is most clearly the case in rituals surrounding death. It is entirely appropriate to speak of a funeral industry. The rites of death are streamlined and professionalised. Funeral parlours are designed with efficiency in mind; visiting hours are precisely set. The coffin must not be carried, but wheeled, on a wagon. At the cemetery one does not go to the graveside; the last rites are performed on a stone patio near the cemetery entrance, and there people take leave of their loved one. There are increasingly few real burials. Happily, one can see signs of a counter-movement: the Christian rituals remain rites of piety and closeness, before all else, and in recent years there are also moves toward authentic creativity with regard to secular death rites.[8] Still, economic influences remain considerable. For some time the American funeral giant Service Corporation International was also active in the Dutch market. This firm professes to maintain an open approach to death as an object of commercial activity,[9] but has acquired

---

[7] See Part 1, Chapter 1, 2.2.

[8] SAX a.o.: *Zand erover*; ENKLAAR: *Onder de groene zoden*; G. LUKKEN: *Op zoek naar een geloofwaardige gestalte van de dodenliturgie* (Liturgische Handreikingen 19), Breda 1994; IDEM: 'Liturgische aspecten: nieuwe tendensen in de uitvaartliturgie', in J. MAASSEN (ed.): *Uitvaarten – een last en een lust voor pastores* (DPC-bundel 4), Rotterdam 1997, 43-64; IDEM: 'Nieuwe ontwikkelingen in het uitvaartritueel', in J. VAN DEN BOUT a.o. (eds): *Handboek Sterven, Uitvaart en Rouw*, Maarssen 2001, III 4.4, 1-16; IDEM: 'Het christelijke dodenritueel in onze geseculariseerde en multiculturele samenleving', in *Speling* 53 (2001) 1, 83-90.

[9] J. ENKLAAR: 'In het rijk van SCI is de dood koning', in *NRC Handelsblad* August 9, 1991.

the nickname of McDeath, as a sort of McDonalds of the funeral world. Their inroads into the Dutch market remained limited, but their market concept still exercised considerable influence.[10]

But there are also other rituals that are influenced by commerce. One encounters this influence for instance in the otherwise positive developments in rising secular birth rituals. The visiting nurse service in Twente, in the northeast of The Netherlands, provides brochures for perspective parents with information about what are being termed 'maternity parties'. In place of weeks of visits to the mother and new-born, the 'Maternity Party Bureau' organises one big party at which all the parents' acquaintances are invited to admire the new-born and congratulate the parents. In addition to the culturally required rusks with aniseed comfits, there are decorations with pink or blue balloons, pink or blue candies, old-fashioned Dutch bridal sweets, pink champagne and a pink and blue, five layer cake. A special play area is created for the children. The cost for this standard packet for fifty adults and twenty children is €270.00.[11]

Analogous phenomena are appearing in marriage ritual. Celebrations such as St. Nicholas's Day, Christmas,[12] New Year's and Carnival have their commercial sides, and even rituals such as Sunday as a weekly day of rest are losing ground under the 'polder model' of negotiated consensus in Dutch politics. Sunday too must be subject to the laws of the market. It is no longer the day on which labour rests.

The influence of our economic system manifests itself in a characteristic manner in advertising. Day in, day out, twenty-four hours a day, we are approached as consumers, as buyers of products. Advertising urges us on constantly to acquire new objects in order to become happier. Sometimes the exchange value of the object is so strongly emphasised that merely its purchase alone would appear to bring satisfaction. In advertising the product is connected to aesthetic symbolic images which

---

[10] J. ENKLAAR: 'Nederlandse uitvaartbranche volgt voorbeeld van 'McDeath'-multinationals', in *NRC Handelsblad* September 5, 2002, 16.

[11] A. VELTHAUSZ: 'Bij de baby op de borrel', in *De Twentsche courant Tubantia* January 4, 1997, 'Leven', 1.

[12] D. MILLER (ed.): *Unwrapping Christmas*, Oxford 1993; *Sinterklaas en de kerstman: concurrenten of collega's? Rituelen – commercie – identiteiten: Volkskundig Bulletin* 22 (1996) no. 3; G. ROOIJAKKERS: 'De kerststal tussen kerk en VVV', in *De Bazuin* 83 (2000) (December 22), 10-13.

promise human autonomy and full manliness or femininity, for instance. The link is completely illusory, but it works on us at a deep level because of the intrusive presentative symbolism, which produces apparent satisfaction and disassociation.

Actually, in this case one can no longer speak of true presentative symbolism, because under the guise of presentative symbolism there are here in fact univocal signs which manipulate people in one direction, and thoroughly and deeply interfere with the capacity for full symbolisation.[13] Thus the things remain prisoners within themselves, as it were. They reproduce themselves, but do not point beyond themselves. The perspective does not break open – or if so, it opens only in the direction of the product to be acquired and possessed. The references remain constantly captive within the growth of the consumer process, and this must have a desymbolising effect.[14]

This ritual of advertising also takes other rituals under its wing. For instance, in advertising even burial and cremation are presented as desirable consumer objects, with 'presentative symbols' such as tranquil landscapes, high mountains, a pyramid or a wind-surfer, that evoke eternity but in fact are hidden, univocal, desymbolising signs of a product that the advertiser wants to sell us. Sometimes this advertising even takes on painful forms; after all, it is intended to grab attention and provoke response. Then you get 'I want a shiny metal coffin', with under it, in parentheses, 'Pilot, age 40', or 'I definitely don't want to be cremated. (Fireman, age 52)'. Or religious symbols are used. Bible verses are quoted: a major Dutch brewer promotes beer with a phrase from Ecclesiastes 3: 'There is a time for…' Adam and Eve are depicted, with the forbidden fruit replaced by the temptation of a perfume or a particular brand of jeans. In the Paris Metro there were posters of Moses on Mount Sinai, with two large tickets for the Metro in his hand. This cultivating of a religious aura in advertising is on the one side fed by a critique of religious systems of meaning; on the other side it bestows a suggestion of authenticity.[15]

---

[13] LORENZER: *Das Konzil der Buchhalter* 167-174; W. HAUGG: *Kritik der Warenästhetik*, Frankfurt 1971; J. BERGER: *Ways of seeing*, Londen 1972.

[14] CHAUVET: *Du symbolique au symbole* 253 ff.; J. BAUDRILLARD: *L'échange symbolique et la mort*, Paris 1976.

[15] M. WALRAVE: 'Religieuze symbolen in de reclame. Rage of postmoderne trend?', in *Tijdschrift voor Geestelijk Leven* 54 (1998) 2, 197-205.

Yet it would be unjust to limit ourselves to only these negative remarks. There are also nuances which can be introduced with regard to the domination of ritual by our economic system. One can note that a relationship between economics and ritual appears unavoidable. There has always been 'sponsoring': many rituals were funded by emperors and kings. Calling a patron a Maecenas, after all, reminds us that the practice goes back to the ancient world. The music for church celebrations such as Christmas and Easter was often written by composers in the service of monarchs. Thus there can be an economic foundation without that detracting from ritual. On the other hand, however, this can also lead to the ritual of 'bread and circuses'.

From the perspective of ritual too, problems can arise when the economy takes ritual in service and begins to dominate it. Among the examples are Mother's Day, Father's Day, Secretaries' Day and Valentine's Day. There ritual is subordinated to considerations of efficiency such as sales and profit. Yet those who engage in these rituals can also experience them in ways that have nothing to do with the economic perspective. The rituals can be appropriated in such a way that their meaning is turned in an authentic direction.[16] In cases like this, the subject puts the commercial aspects between parentheses, as it were, permitting the perception of another expression than the commercial bias. It can happen that those who participate in the ritual are not completely controlled by outside commercial pressures. They also have their own 'power'.[17] With regard to the authenticity of both the ritual itself and those who participate in the ritual, one can employ the following criterion: are the predominate value patterns consumption, possession, results and power: in short, 'having'? Or are they patterns of integrity and integral experience of identity, of an experience of meaning that leaves things open, of value patterns such as mutual relationships, commitment to a better society, in short value patterns that have more to do with 'being'?

Finally, it is also possible to positively value consumptive tendencies, namely as a very particular experience of the symbolic order.[18] Specifically, the question is whether in our culture it is always purely and simply a passive and instrumental consumption that is involved. There is

---

[16] VOYÉ: 'Le rite en question' 114-120.

[17] See what was said previously about 'ritual and power' in Part I, Chapter 4, 7.

[18] SCHILSON: 'Liturgie(-Reform) angesichts einer sich wandelnden Kultur' 972-980 and 994-999; see there for further literature.

evidence that it is not purely and simply a matter of possessing an object, but is at least as much if not more the experience and expression of a certain 'lifestyle'. People acquire things that they find to be 'beautiful', of a certain design: this furniture, this cutlery, that automobile. What is involved is an aesthetic experience of this being. Lying behind this is a very particular symbolic experience of reality which is oriented toward the subject, with an accent on feeling and experience. The objects desired and the possession of them are not the ultimate aim of acts of acquisition. It is much more a matter of the performance of the subject in aesthetic acts focussed on subjective experience and emotion. This contemporary ritual mentality plays a role in all sorts of areas, not only that of the free market, but also those of politics, science and religion. With regard to religion, it forms a major challenge. The question is whether religions can shape their rituals in such a way that on the one hand they will do justice to this need for subjective emotional experience, and on the other side do justice to the peculiar and irreplaceable identity of the religious symbolic order. Religious rituals must be able to break open this experience, to its very deepest. What is found there is nothing less than the elementary vision of a reality of ultimate goodness and clarity, the fulfilment of what the 'marketing cultus' promises.

3. SEVERAL SPECIFIC CHARACTERISTICS AND PROBLEM AREAS

In Part 1 we spoke about the characteristics of ritual in more general terms. There we were dealing with the lowest common denominator, as it were, of ritual in different cultures. In this section we are dealing with ritual – and in particular Christian ritual – in *our* culture. Within this culture ritual takes on its own accent, and there are new problem areas which deserve our attention.

3.1. The dynamic of the new: ritual in constant change

An extensive study on liturgical reform as a phenomenon that is inherent in the history of liturgy recently appeared.[19] It involved a field of investigation that is practically virgin territory. It observes that liturgical

---

[19] KLÖCKENER & KRANEMANN (eds.): *Liturgiereformen*.

reform is an extremely complex phenomenon that runs through the whole history of the church and liturgy. It is a characteristic feature of church life and a wide-ranging phenomenon that not only involves the revision of texts, but also of symbols, symbolic actions, space, music and song. The study demonstrates that liturgical reform has had peculiar characteristics in each period, and in each era has been closely connected with the socio-cultural context. This is also true for our era today. It is therefore important to keep in mind the peculiar characteristics of ritual in our culture. Since the 1960s ritual has been in a thorough state of flux. One can no longer characterise ritual as something which is static over a long period or as a rigidly fixed entity, but instead as something which is constantly undergoing change, like the culture itself. On the one hand, this is related to the fact that the culture itself has undergone a revolution. But on the other hand it is related to the specific characteristics of the new culture. It no longer has the stability of preceding cultures. Greimas has noted that after the Middle Ages one could initially speak of longer cultural periods such as Classicism, the Baroque or Romanticism, but that because of a stress on originality the periods began to succeed one another at ever increasing speed.[20] Rituals are incarnate in a culture which is in constant change, and that fact will have repercussions on these rituals. Much more than before there is now a necessity for ritual innovation and experimentation. In Part 1 I indicated that because of its peculiar characteristics, ritual requires that at the same time there be a limit to this: when *all* repetition disappears from ritual, the existence of ritual as such is in danger. But before that boundary is reached, there is room for more dynamism than was previously thought possible. It is in this that there is a major difference from traditional ritual. While ritual was previously seen as representative of the status quo and the authority of dominant social institutions, now for many it is on the contrary anti-structural, revolutionary and an aid in the deconstruction of institutions and the generation of alternative structures.[21]

It is valuable here to return to the views of Turner. In Parts 1 and 2 I noted that Turner considered the developments in ritual in the post-industrial era, including the liturgical renewal from after the Second

---

[20] GREIMAS: *De l'imperfection* 82-84.
[21] BELL: *Ritual. Perspectives* 257-258.

Vatican Council, as deviations.[22] This flows from the fact that his point
of view was shaped by the ritual of old, tribal cultures, and in particular
his research into the rituals of the Ndembu in Zambia. He had even
undergone the initiation rituals of this tribe, and in 1983 received both
a Ndembu and a Roman Catholic burial.[23] Added to this is the fact that
his research into the rituals of the Ndembu was less detached than one
would expect. Bell observes that Turner at no point notes the dramatic
political context of his research project. He was performing his research
while colonialism was collapsing under the pressure of powerful and
chaotic movements for self-determination. The colonial institutions had
an interest in maintaining a certain influence through less political
means, such as the 'authentic' rituals of the Ndembu.[24] Whatever the
case, Turner took the experimental status that is peculiar to ritual in our
culture too little into account. It is precisely in relation to this that there
is a widespread tension developing in relation to Christian ritual at the
moment.

In Chapter 1 of Part 3 I noted that the Constitution on Liturgy (1963)
meant a radical renewal for Christian ritual. It was intended to bring
the liturgy in step with the times (*aggiornamento*). Under the influence
of this Constitution work began with an amazing energy on the
renewal of all of the liturgical books of the Roman rite. They arrived at
a simple and transparent liturgy, in which there was on the one hand a
return to the sources, particularly focusing on the first millennium of
the Church, but in which on the other hand some room was left within
clearly delineated boundaries for adaptations to the culture in which
the liturgy would function. In 1973 yet, among the tasks for the coming ten years that were sketched out for the worship service by the then
secretary of the Congregation for Worship was the study of the adaptation of the liturgy to the nature and traditions of various peoples, so
that it could arise spontaneously from their heart, and not remain
something which was foreign to their culture and mentality. Liturgy
'... can not but follow the laws of life. Without progress it would begin
to become anaemic. If it does not renew itself, that would mean its

[22] Part 1, Chapter 4, 5.3 and Part 2, Chapter 2, 2.
[23] GRIMES: *Ritual Criticism* 129; IDEM: *Beginnings in Ritual Studies*, 134, 155-156.
[24] C. BELL: 'Ritual Tensions: Tribal and Catholic', in *Studia Liturgica* 32 (2002) 15-
28 (French: 'Tensions à l'intérieur du rite: tribal et catholique', in *La Maison-Dieu*
(2001) 228, 41-61).

death.'[25] The programme outlined in 1973 was never carried through. In fact, stagnation set in rapidly, and since the mid-1970s the official renewal of the liturgy has come almost to a halt. In this way, the official liturgy threatens to remain stuck at the very first steps of the way that it should have gone, if it was really to be integrated into our culture – and this while it gradually became obvious that *aggiornamento* with contemporary culture in fact had radical consequences. In The Netherlands we were very quickly and very sharply confronted by this. Through the sudden cultural revolution from being a static, closed society to becoming an open, dynamic society, characterised by secularism, modernity and post-modernism, very quickly a farther-reaching inculturation got under way than the one which could be found in the official, renewed liturgical books. At the congregational level great creativity appeared. Thus when the publication of the new official liturgical books began in the 1960s, experts argued that this situation had to be taken into account. This could be done both by taking good ritual elements which arose from among the congregations and integrating them in the official books, and by publishing these books in a less definitive fashion: it was suggested they should perhaps be in the form of ring-binders, to which supplements could regularly be added. In fact, however, the new, official books were too little inculturated, and they were published in a fixed form; they were more or less definitive books, provided with the classic red rubrics and place-marker ribbons. More or less: because quite a few of the official liturgical books have since been published in revised editions. Whatever the case, in The Netherlands (but also elsewhere) this state of affairs led to a certain 'two track' liturgy: the official liturgy, which was inadequately inculturated into Western culture, and next to it a much more fluid liturgy at the grass-roots level.

A new development seemed to present itself when in 1994 a document[26] appeared dealing with the fundamental problems of inculturation, which

---

[25] A. BUGNINI: 'Progresso nell'ordine', in *L'Osservatore Romano* December 12, 1973.

[26] CONGREGATIO DE CULTU DIVINO ET DISCIPLINA SACRAMENTORUM: *De liturgia romana et inculturatione. Instructio quarta 'ad executionem Constitutionis Concilii Vaticani secundi de Sacra Liturgia recte ordinandam' (ad Const. Art. 37-40)*, Città del Vaticano 1994 = *Acta Apostolicae Sedis* 87 (1995) 288-314 and *Notitiae* 30 (1994) 80-115 = *De Romeinse liturgie en de inculturatie. Vierde instructie voor de juiste toepassing van de constitutie over de liturgie van het Tweede Vaticaans concilie (bij de nummers 37-40)*, in *Een-twee-een. Kerkelijke documentatie* 23 (1995) 1, 30-46.

had been inherent in the 'spirit' of the Vatican Constitution on Liturgy, but not foreseen by it. It is an extremely generous and open document. The theoretical section of it is a plea for a thorough-going inculturation of the liturgy. Halfway through, however, the tone of the document changes: in the practical section the norms with regard to liturgical reform are sharpened, particularly as they relate to sweeping inculturation.[27] Moreover, it is striking that with regard to the necessity of inculturation a distinction is made between, for instance, India or Africa and Western Europe. The document speaks very negatively of Western European culture. It is portrayed as a culture characterised by indifference and disinterest in religion. Therefore it is not so much inculturation of the liturgy which is necessary, as education with regard to liturgy. But why should inculturation have to stop at the threshold of contemporary Western European culture? First, while it is indeed true that pure humane values are also important for inculturation, one can not say that these are less present in our culture than in preceding cultures. In this connection I refer the reader back to the more extensive description of the concepts of culture and inculturation in Part 2. The document itself also provides a description that reaches further than just the inculturation of pre-existing religious rites. Next, our contemporary Western European culture does indeed have sound, pre-existing religious values. We are becoming more aware of this as we are able to identify the religious with something wider than purely and simply the institutional churches. One can also ask why our culture should be less suitable for inculturation than, for instance, pagan Roman culture, with which the liturgy entered into so deep a process of inculturation that we to this day speak of the Roman liturgy. Bertsch has rightly remarked that both pre- and post-Christians are to be considered as candidates for inculturation.[28] The document on inculturation thus in no way neutralises the tension with the ritual movements at the congregational level. Unfortunately, this document was followed by a supplement that interprets the concept of inculturation more as unilateral 'implantation' of the old Roman liturgy in our culture.[29] This is the

[27] LUKKEN: 'Inculturatie van de liturgie'.
[28] L. BERTSCH: 'Entstehung und Entwicklung liturgischer Riten und kirchliches Leitungsamt', in L. BERTSCH (ed.): *Der neue Messritus im Zaire* 235.
[29] G. LUKKEN: 'Implantatie versus inculturatie? Een nieuwe Instructie over het vertalen van de Romeinse liturgie', in *Eredienstvaardig* 17 (2001) 4, 127-131. See also R. KACZYNSKI: 'Angriff auf die Liturgiekonstitution? Anmerkungen zu einer neuen Übersetzer-Instruktion', in *Stimmen der Zeit* 126 (2001) 651-668; reaction to this: J.

Instruction *Liturgiam authenticam*, of March 28, 2001, regarding the translation of the new Roman liturgy.[30] On the basis of the preceding Instruction on inculturation, one might have expected that this next Instruction would argue for further inculturated translations of the official Roman liturgical books. The opposite was however the case. The recent Instruction takes a very restrictive standpoint with regard to the translation of these books. All translations must be revised, and this must be done on the basis of the criterion that the Roman liturgy must also be maintained substantially in our contemporary culture. For this view, it appeals to article 38 of the Constitution on Liturgy, which speaks of the possibility for adapting the revised books 'while retaining the substantial unity of the Roman rite'. The meaning of this phrase from the Constitution is by no means clear. It has been interpreted in all sorts of ways by liturgists and in liturgical studies.[31] The Instruction opts unambiguously for the most stringent view, namely that in the translation of new liturgical books the substance of the Roman liturgy should be retained in both form and content. It then limits this view still further by bringing it as close as possible to the pre-Vatican substantial unity of the Roman liturgy, which was celebrated in the uniform Latin. In the new Latin liturgical books one finds the authentic liturgy as such, and it is precisely this Latin liturgy which must be reproduced as precisely as possible, even in our culture. It is normative in the literality of its form and content. Further,

RATZINGER: 'Um die Erneuerung der Liturgie. Antwort auf Reiner Kaczynski', in *Stimmen der Zeit* 126 (2001) 837-843. See also R. FALSINI: 'Lo spirito della liturgia da R. Guardini a J. Ratzinger', in *Rivista liturgica* 88 (2001) 3-7.

[30] CONGREGATIO DE CULTU DIVINO ET DISCIPLINA SACRAMENTORUM: *De usu linguarum popularum in libris liturgiae romanae edendae. Instructio quinta 'ad exsecutionem constitutionis Concilii Vaticani Secundi de sacra liturgia recte ordinandum' (Ad Const. art. 36)*, in *Notitiae* 37 (2001) no. 3-4 (= no. 416-417), 120-174. The Instruction begins with the words 'Liturgiam authenticam'.

[31] For the details, see LUKKEN: 'Inculturatie van de liturgie' 34-42. See also among others: N. MITCHELL: 'The Amen Corner. Back to the Future', in *Worship* 73 (1999) 60-69; D. POWER: 'Foundation for Pluralism in Sacramental Expression: Keeping Memory', in *Worship* 75 (2001) 194-209, especially 195; R. KACZYNSKI: 'Anmerkungen zu den nachkonziliaren liturgischen Büchern', in KLÖCKENER & KRANEMANN (eds.): *Liturgiereformen* 1003-1016, especially 1015-1016. Kaczynski notes: 'Die Tatsache, dass noch nie versucht wurde, offiziell zu umschreiben, was unter der "substantialis unitas ritus romani" zu verstehen sei, ist zwar einerseits erfreulich, gibt aber andererseits den römischen Behörden die Möglichkeit, immer dann, wenn ihnen in der Entwicklung der Gottesdienstfeier etwas nicht behagt, festzustellen, dies widerspräche der "Einheit des römischen Ritus im wesenlichen".'

according to the Instruction, this has important consequences for the translation of old liturgical texts. I will return to this in Chapter 7.[32] The Instruction conceives inculturation as bringing this authentic Roman liturgy into contemporary culture. It seems to be forgotten that the old Roman liturgy too, however valuable as a monument to Christian inculturation it is, was nevertheless itself also a dynamic and inculturated liturgy, defined by time and place. As in any inculturated liturgy, in the Roman liturgy too certain things therefore receive more, and others less, emphasis, so that they sometimes are overplayed, and others receive too little attention. Its sacred design definitely also has its limitations.

These restrictions unfortunately do no justice to the generous views of the first part of the Instruction on inculturation, nor to the dynamism of ritual in our culture and the liturgical movement at the congregational level that accompanies it. That is sad, and all the more so when one realises that at the same time there is a reactionary movement which seeks to return to the liturgy from before the Council – a movement which recently seems to be gaining strength.[33] That can be seen, for instance, in the 1996 *Oxford Declaration on Liturgy*, which hopes to be the stimulus to a new Liturgical Movement.[34] The signers of this document are of the opinion that actual official renewal following the Second Vatican Council was on the one hand respectable, but on the other hand that it has betrayed the original principles of the Liturgical Movement. It has broken the continuity with the past; it can not be said to be an organic development from the tradition. Without identifying themselves with traditionalist groups who wish to return to the old Roman missal, the signers do wish to meet such groups half way by putting the brakes on thorough-going inculturation of the liturgy and seeking a liturgy that does more justice to the sacred, stately, beautiful and spiritual character of liturgy. For them the important goal is to have the 'mainstream' of renewal, such as one finds in the Congregation for Worship and academic liturgical studies, shift in a

---

[32] See Chapter 7, 1. For a critique of the document see also P. JEFFERY in Bibliography.

[33] N. MITCHELL: 'The Amen Corner. Reform the Reform?', in *Worship* 71 (1997) 555-563; IDEM: 'Emerging Rituals in Contemporary Culture'. See for instance the book of K. GAMBER: *The Reform of the Roman Liturgy. Its Problems and Background*, San Juan Capistrano 1993.

[34] S. CALDECOTT (ed.): *Beyond the Prosaic. Renewing the Liturgical Movement*, Edinburgh 1998. For a critique, see a.o. G. ROUWHORST and P. POST 2004 in Bibliography.

more conservative direction and re-Catholicise. In that, the authors rather frequently call on Cardinal Ratzinger, who is characterised as the 'leading voice' in the contemporary Liturgical Movement.[35] However, this Cardinal, prefect of the Congregation for Doctrine, is unjustified in complaining, with regard to the post-Vatican liturgical renewal, of the unprecedented step of 'the large-scale replacement of the one liturgy by another'.[36] In his view, the crisis in the Church in which we find ourselves today has a great deal to do with the collapse of the old liturgy. In particular, he is dismayed by the abandonment of the old Tridentine missal of 1570, because change of the sort which has happened after the Second Vatican Council has never before occurred in the Church. His complaint recurs at length in a booklet, the title of which in undeservedly refers to Guardini, pioneer of the Liturgical Movement.[37] His accusations go to the core of the Constitution on Liturgy of the Second Vatican Council and the renewal that was sparked off by this Constitution, and link up closely with the wishes of those who wish to return to the liturgy as it was before the Council. Mitchell rightly notes that Ratzinger's reproaches are not justified, because the Tridentine reformation of the liturgy was perhaps even more radical than that of the Second Vatican Council; after all, it put an end to a tradition that until that time had harboured

[35] CALDECOTT (ed.): *Beyond the Prosaic* 154.

[36] PAULUS VI: 'Damaged Church', in *The Catholic Messenger*, Davenport, IA Vol. 115: 17 (April 24, 1997) 1, 10.

[37] J. RATZINGER: *Der Geist der Liturgie: eine Einführung*, Freiburg 2000. See R. GUARDINI: *Vom Geist der Liturgie* (Reihe Romano Guardini Werke), Mainz/Paderborn 1997 (original edition 1917). For (very critical) reviews of Ratzinger's book, see amomg others A. GERHARDS: 'Review', in: *Herder-Korrespondenz* 54 (2000) 263-268; K. RICHTER: 'Review', in *Theologische Revue* 96 (2000) 4, 324-326; FALSINI: 'Lo spirito della liturgia da R. Guardini a J. Ratzinger', 3-7; P.M. GY: 'L'esprit de la liturgie du cardinal Ratzinger est-il fidèle au concile ou en réaction contre?', in *La Maison-Dieu* (2002) 229, 171-178 (Response by J. RAZTINGER: 'L'Esprit de la liturgie ou la fidélité au Concile. Réponse au père Gy', in *La Maison-Dieu* (2002) 230, 114-120); A. SCHILSON: 'Der Geist der Liturgie – von Guardini bis Ratzinger', in M. KLÖCKENER a.o. (eds.): *Gottes Volk feiert... Anspruch und Wirklichkeit gegenwärtiger Liturgie*, Trier 2002, 92-117; A. HÄUSSLING: 'Der Geist der Liturgie. Zu Joseph Ratzingers gleichnamiger Publikation', in *Archiv für Liturgiewissenschaft* 43/44 (2001-2002) 362-395. See also R. WEAKLAND: 'The Liturgy as Battlefield', in *Commonweal* (New York) January 11, 2002 = IDEM: 'Liturgie zwischen Erneuerung und Restauration', in *Heiliger Dienst* 56 (2002) 83-93 and *Stimmen der Zeit* 220 (2002) 475-487; IDEM: 'The Right Road for the Liturgy', in *The Tablet* (London) February 2, 2002, 10-13.

numerous local variations.[38] Moreover, one can note that the deepest roots of the liturgical renewal of the Second Vatican Council reach back to the tradition of the early Church.[39] It is clear that in a pluriform culture one must be tolerant of groups that adhere to the traditional liturgy. And of course there must also be a place for a liturgy that does justice to the sacred, stately, beautiful and spiritual.[40] But it would not be right to put the brakes on the post-Vatican renewal and thorough-going inculturation.[41] On the contrary. Christian liturgy must take up the challenge of the encounter between the Roman liturgy and modern Western culture.[42] At the congregational level in the church this is already well under way. One must acknowledge that a ritual that is constantly in development brings with it complicated questions. It is highly understandable that some long for quieter times, which afford more ritual certainty. This desire is definitely legitimate, and in contemporary culture is even respected, too. The predilection for the old has its own rituals. I will return to this when I discuss musealisation and folkloreisation.[43] Our culture accepts exactly a great pluriformity. But the question here is that of the illegitimacy of the reactionary tendencies that reject all that is other, including the liturgical renewal of the Second Vatican Council, and particularly the further inculturation of the liturgy in our extremely

[38] N. MITCHELL: 'The Amen Corner. Rereading Reform', in *Worship* 71 (1997) 462-470.

[39] In this regard see F. MCMANUS: 'Back to the Future: The Early Christian Roots of Liturgical Renewal', in *Worship* 72 (1998) 386-403. He remarks (pages 400-401): 'Much too noticeable in the church today is the uninformed dissenting minority alienated by Vatican II. It unhappily includes some educated presbyters and bishops, sometimes in lofty offices and in the Roman clergy, that is, the cardinals of the Holy Roman Church. (...) The language of the opposition to the reform is, to say the least, rash as well as mistaken: 'a break in the history of the liturgy', 'the collapse of the liturgy', the absence of 'a sense of continuity'. For a clear rebuttal to Ratzinger see also H. HÄRING: 'De Schriften, 'ziel van de theologie': Pleidooi voor een herontdekking van de Bijbel', in *Tijdschrift voor Theologie* 38 (1998) 280-283.

[40] See also MALLOY: 'The Re-Emergence of Popular Religion'.

[41] On the reactionary tendencies, see also, among others: MITCHELL: 'The Amen Corner. Back to the Future'; R.G. WEAKLAND: 'Liturgy in the United States these Past 25 Years', in *Worship* 75 (2001) 5-12; R. TAFT: 'A Generation of Liturgy in the Academy', in *Worship* 75 (2001) 46-58, especially 56-57.

[42] See for instance: H. KERNER (ed.): *Gottesdienst und Kultur. Zukunftsperspektiven*, Leipzig 2004.

[43] See Part 3, Chapter 5, 2.

dynamic culture.[44] In real inculturation one will have to respect the contemporary dynamics of ritual.

3.2. Experiments and breaking through the exclusivity of the concept of collective ritual

In Part 1 I discussed Nijk's theories.[45] Ritual comes into being by trial and error, experimentally. The term 'experiment' is thus linked with ritual, certainly in regard to its origins. From this perspective it is obvious that experiment plays a large role in a cultural transition such as ours, in which rites must become incarnate in a new culture. But there is more. One here encounters a phenomenon which is characteristic for our culture as such. I have the impression that ritual experimentation plays a larger role in our culture than it did in preceding cultures. Grimes even calls ritual experimentation the most characteristic post-modern form of ritual actions.[46] As far back as the 1960s experimental circles with regard to ritual came into existence, both in the society in general and within the church. What I am referring to is primarily the search for rituals within an alternative circuit in the society in weekend conferences, workshops, laboratories and therapeutic gatherings. In these the frame of reference might be anthropological, psychological, feminist, theatrical or religious, or a mixture of several of these fields. Next, within the church as well, since that time there have been centres of ritual experimentation which can be qualified as liturgical spawning grounds. All these experiments broke through the established view among anthropologists and liturgists that ritual is per definition collective, and created by the society as such. Ritual experiment on the contrary goes back to individual authors or small groups who create new rituals. The classical view is that rituals are anonymous because they have only a collective author. Thus when in the foreword to the Dutch altar missal in 1970 the authors of the translations of the official and of the newly created eucharistic prayers were listed, this was criticised as 'unliturgical'. This is understandable from the point of view that says rituals are collective.

---

[44] Thus I am not referring here to those who after the Second Vatican Council wish to continue to celebrate the Roman liturgy in Latin. It is precisely in our pluriform culture that this practice also has a right to exist. For this see Part 3, Chapter 6, 3.

[45] Part 1, Chapter 2, 2.1.

[46] GRIMES: *Ritual Criticism* 109-144, 125. See also IDEM: *Reading, Writing, and Ritualizing* 11-19, and BELL: *Ritual. Perspectives* 259-266.

On the other hand, among these 'collective' rituals there was an ancient eucharistic prayer that was denoted as the 'canon of Hippolytus'! Whatever the case, this collectivity applied all the less for the new, created eucharistic prayers that were included in the *Appendix ad experimentum* of the Dutch missal in 1970. After all, a ritual experiment as such is not nameless or anonymous. It is entirely proper that in The Netherlands we speak of the eucharistic prayer by J. Duin or De Boskapel and the liturgy by H. Oosterhuis.

Because of the familiar view that ritual is per definition collective, many reject ritual experimentation by individuals or small groups. Rituals arising in these circles are very quickly characterised as narcissistic or neurotic.[47] Now, it cannot be denied that the alternative circuit has had its wash-outs, and that the danger of ritual narcissism or neurotic applications is present. One does find groups in the alternative circuit who perform therapeutic rituals which purely focus on the I, as if ritual was an entity closed in on itself, without any jump in perspective. It is also true that this ritual lends itself to manipulation and injuring people. But it would be unjust to reduce all ritual experiments to this level.

In our culture there is simply a scale that runs from collective rituals through creativity and inductivity within these rituals to stringent ritual experiment. This experiment is not necessarily focused only on the I. Even purely therapeutic rituals can be orientated to the discovery of oneself and one's own identity through the other, or – and I am here referring to religious rituals – the Other, or the One Who is Other.

People are right to speak of ritual spawning grounds, because although much of what is tried out will not withstand the test of criticism over the long run, it is also true that some of what is today alternative will tomorrow belong to ritual convention.[48] In connection with this individualisation of ritual, one can speak of a new paradigm.[49] The accent is placed on ritual as an expression of inner spiritual-emotional sources and one's own true identity. Thus these rituals are first directed more inwardly than outward, arrive more at the communal from the

---

[47] NAUTA: 'Rituelen als décor' and the remarks of P. Moyaert in: L. LEIJSSEN, P. MOYAERT & L. BOEVE: 'Samenspraak. Rituelen, sacramenten en liturgieën', in *Kultuurleven. Tijdschrift voor cultuur en samenleving* 64 (1997) 5-15.

[48] Thus GRIMES: *Ritual Criticism* 110.

[49] BELL: *Ritual. Perspectives* 241-242.

individual, from the 'I' and 'we', and in the first instance place the stress on achieving wholeness and healing. In this other way they are directed toward the renewal of community, the reshaping of human identity and the recreation of our most existential meaning in this world.[50] But at the same time it is true that precisely along this way the transcendent and redemptive 'other side' of ritual that comes over us receives shape in a probing, trustworthy and innovative manner. I will return to this in my final chapter.

In ritual experimentation in our culture use is often made of sources from many cultures. One can frequently speak of an intercultural, eclectic or interreligious happening. In post-modern society many influences are accepted and undergone simultaneously. As examples one can think of certain feminist rituals, but also of Christian ritual that itself has passed through many cultures and taken in many borrowings from these cultures. In this way the Roman liturgy, about which the documents speak, underwent profound Germanic and Frankish influences in the past.

The views on experimentation which have been outlined here and which immediately also touch on the inculturation of liturgy reach further than the view of experimentation that one finds in the official Roman documents. The document on inculturation in this manner contains the regulations that already were laid down in the third Instruction of 1970. Experiments must be carefully formulated and first presented to Rome. After they have been examined, permission may be granted for the experiment during a fixed period of time. Further, they must be supervised so that the established boundaries of time and place are not exceeded, and the experiment not be publicised in a manner that it might already begin to influence the liturgical life of the country in question. Chupungco is right when he remarks that these rules are not only impractical, but unrealistic.[51] Whatever the case, one must realise that a real experiment cannot be centrally controlled and regulated, but that it rather develops on site, and also must evaluated in that location. This last is also important. Ritual experiment can definitely be coupled

---

[50] BELL: *Ritual. Perspectives* 264.
[51] A. CHUPUNGCO: 'Remarks on the Roman liturgy and inculturation', in *Ecclesia Orans* 11 (1994) 3, 269-277. I will return to this in Chapter 9, 7.

with a critical attitude. Precisely as experiment, ritual is never definitive, and always open to improvement. It is possible to create rituals, and as the same time to provide for a critical, self-assured culture.[52] Here one encounters the specific role of experts in our culture.

3.3. The special role of experts

The view is widespread that rites arise spontaneously as a result of the influence of invisible collective forces. In Part 1 I indicated that rituals indeed do have something to do with the intuitive and preconceptual. In that context it was noted that rites are not devised behind a desk, but arise.[53] But it would be wrong to conclude from this that rites cannot be planned, and that laboratory situations are an absolute corruption of the process. It can equally little be maintained that rites are exclusively collective and anonymous in nature (see 3.2). Here one encounters the question of what role experts can play with regard to the creation and evaluation of rituals.[54]

In answering this question one must make the distinction between oral and written cultures. In oral cultures there is definitely change and innovation in ritual, but this occurs almost without notice. Experts – for instance, priests – can play a role in this, but they are at the same time closely integrated into the ritual process itself, of passing on tradition. Therefore this process of renewal happens almost invisibly, and the role of the expert is less obvious. The role is flexible and intrinsically bound up with the vital, oral transmission of tradition.[55] In written cultures it has traditionally been different. In these experts often play a much more marked and visible role. Back in Part 1 I referred to the striking examples of Taoism in China, of the new liturgical books which were published after the Council of Trent and – likewise under the influence of experts – remained almost unchanged for four centuries, the creation of the new liturgical books after the Second Vatican Council, and of the rituals of the

---

[52] GRIMES: *Ritual Criticism* 127. IDEM: *Deeply into the Bone* 83-85 mentions the following steps in reinventing ritual: attending, imagining, studying, inventing, improvising, evaluating, reinventing. For the elaboration of these fundamental phases of the experiment, see there.

[53] Part 1, Chapter 2, 2.1.

[54] See in this connection BELL: 'The Authority of Ritual Experts'.

[55] See in this connection Part 2, Chapter 4, 3.

former Soviet Union.[56] The more conspicuous role of experts in written cultures is related to the fact that the transmission of tradition in these cultures is more complicated than in oral cultures. I have already mentioned this in Part 2, but will now return to it here in this context.[57] In written cultures rituals are fixed in written texts, and as such they become normative. In these cultures tradition is no longer experienced as being immediately embodied in current practice, but rather as that which is written down in texts. The textual tradition must be reproduced and protected. The written, and not the oral or spoken word, has authority. Ritual *in actu* becomes the concrete performance of the textual book. In this context changes in the ritual are quickly experienced as a threat to the tradition. Therefore interpretative experts are necessary. On the one hand they must preserve the tradition, and on the other they are expected to bridge the gap between the past and present in a responsible manner. In written cultures there is more control possible, and more possibility to curb changes than in oral culture. At the same time however people have a greater knowledge of the ritual tradition, and it precisely because of this that discussion about possible or necessary changes becomes possible. In part because of this, change therefore becomes a complicated process of weighing up the pros and cons. In this bureaucratic and centralised institutions play a special role, and one cannot separate the questions from discussions of orthodoxy and heterodoxy. Moreover, tensions can arise between the centralised ritual tradition and local ritual practice. This is true particularly because at the rank and file level something of the spontaneous, oral culture always remains present.

With regard to our present culture, although we are once again aware of the primary oral character of ritual, one must still acknowledge that our rites have the characteristics of ritual in a written culture. There are various layers of experts who are involved in the design, revision and evaluation of rituals. This include both those who have a peculiar creative talent, and those who are occupied in more academic roles, such as sociologists, psychologists, anthropologists, representatives of ritual studies, theologians and liturgists. Moreover, one must always realise that while the leadership of institutions also has authority, this authority is only functional if it remains in constant dialogue with the experts, and does not isolate itself from them.

---

[56] Part 1, Chapter 2, 2.1.
[57] Part 2, Chapter 4, 3. See also BELL: 'The Authority of Ritual Experts' 107-120.

The most insistent questions concerning changes in ritual are always if and how the new ritual fits and ties in with the primary human processes,[58] and to what degree there is continuity and discontinuity with the tradition. With regard to the former, intuition will play an important role in answering this question, but help from representatives of the disciplines mentioned above is definitely also necessary. With respect to continuity and discontinuity with tradition, with regard to Western Catholic liturgy the question of the substantial unity of the Roman rite will play an important role in answering this. In article 38 of the Constitution on Liturgy it is indicated that the possibilities for adapting new liturgical books are limited by the fact that the substantial unity of the Roman rite must be preserved. At the same time, article 40 of the same Constitution opens the way for more radical inculturation, and leaves open the possibility for the rise of new rites alongside the Roman rite. As has already been noted above, various answers are being given to the question of what is to be understood by the 'substantial unity' of the Roman rite. In the most restrictive view, this means pre-serving both the form and content of the classic Roman liturgy; others understand it more liberally, and in the main limit it to the content of the Roman liturgy.[59] The essential question is to what extent Western Catholic liturgy will preserve continuity with the past. It is obvious that the question of substantial unity with the Roman rite applies much less for the non-Western world: for Africa, Asia, Latin America. Article 40 of the Constitution appears intended chiefly for these regions. Yet the document on inculturation introduces a limitation even for the non-Western world. This does not appear in the theoretical section; from this section one might also conclude that liturgies other than the Roman one might come into being there. But this possibility is pre-cluded in the practical section. Thus the definitive title *Roman Missal for the Dioceses of Zaire* for the inculturated Congolese missal can be com-pared with titles such as the old *Pontificale Romano-Germanicum*. Per-haps one could also say that the document on inculturation will slow the rise of new rites, but that it will not preclude their creation. Ulti-mately article 40 of the Constitution has not been voided.[60] However

---

[58] GRIMES: Reading, Writing, and Ritualizing 280-281.

[59] For more details, see LUKKEN: 'Inculturatie van de liturgie' 34-38.

[60] For this more optimistic interpretation see WHIT: '*Varietetates legitimae* and an African-American Liturgical Tradition'.

that may be, in any case the limitation seems unrealistic for non-Western countries. The future will reveal to what extent Catholic liturgy here and elsewhere will be able to include the 'substance of the Roman liturgy' within itself.

3.4. The role of the media

Modern mass media such as television, video and the internet have a major influence on ritual.[61]

First of all, there is the fact that people are also confronted with rituals through the mass media. The consequences of this are considerable. People first became aware of this in 1952 when the coronation of a monarch – Elizabeth I of England – was broadcast by television for the first time. Ritual now became a world-wide experience. The ritual event had undergone an enlargement, as it were. At the same time the specific ritual gained other dimensions because people could participate via the eye of television in their living room, in the family circle. This permitted people to see all sorts of details that even most of those who were present live could not see. The television viewers could see much more. One might say that they had the best seats. In that sense they came closer to the event. Although the coronation was in fact an event that affected the entire nation and world, it was nonetheless because of participation via television that people had the sense of a real, authentic, collective and intimate involvement. Furthermore, the combination of images and sound in film and television make the audio-visual media the most ingressive media that exist. On the other hand, viewers of such media remain more at a distance, because they are not present live at the event, which as such affects all the other senses too. After all, ritual consists of more than just seeing and hearing. Although the involvement of television viewers can be enhanced by all sorts of visual strategies, they remain first and foremost spectators from outside. Participation in ritual via television is thus completely different from actual, physical participation.

Now, it is also possible to compose rituals in a new manner. For instance, one can make the funeral of President Kennedy into a new narrative, in which the camera constantly zooms in on the blood on

---

[61] See, for the following also, BELL: *Ritual. Perspectives* 242-251.

Jacqueline Kennedy's clothing during the improvised swearing-in ceremony for the new president, and on the salute given before the coffin by
his little son John-John after it was borne out of the church at the
funeral.[62] Another striking example was the wedding of the Dutch
Crown Prince Willem Alexander with the Argentine Maxima Zor-
regueita on February 2, 2002. The event was broadcast in its entirety on
television. Because Maxima's father had been a minister in the Argentine
cabinet during the regime of General Videla, the presence of her parents
at the wedding appeared to be politically unfeasible for the Dutch government. At the end of the church ceremony the Argentine tango 'Adios
Ñoniño' (Farewell, Old Man) was played on a bandore. It resounded as
a leave-taking from her father and her fatherland. Precisely at that
moment the camera zoomed in on the bride, and all the television viewers could see how Maxima could no longer hold back her tears. In the
selection of images from the wedding after the live broadcast it was precisely that moment that was repeated time after time. Within the new
entity, it was this scene, together with the couple's kiss on the balcony of
the palace, which became central moments of the event. Thus the ritual
that had been performed became a new ritual full of emotions, which
could be repeated endlessly. In this way, rituals can be further mythologised through TV. People can participate in this mythologised whole,
although it took place in the past. The distance in time is bridged, as it
were, by a newly composed and insinuative ritual entity.

This new form of participation in ritual does not only involve rituals
on the occasion of national or international events. Television now
makes all ritual accessible: the rituals of other cultures, right back to the
most primitive, the rituals of other religions and the rituals of our own
culture; furthermore, it covers the whole spectrum of rituals, from birth
to death. One must add to that the further-reaching possibilities of
video and the internet. Both the participation itself and the range of
action of the participation are thus considerably broadened, but at the
same time it is true that this is always a peculiar form of participation,
which one can designate as participation at a distance.

Media involvement also brings with it a second form of change,
namely their participation in some functions that were previously

---

[62] This narrative received still another dramatic layer in July 1999, when this John
F. Kennedy, Jr., now age 38, was killed together with his wife in a tragic aeroplane accident.

provided for by rituals.[63] By transforming reality into theatre the media fulfils a role that traditionally was performed by myth and ritual. News takes on mythical-ritual features through our collective and at the same time personal participation in events, through uniform patterns, times of presentation and symbols. This provides a collective feeling of order. Soap operas also seem to fulfil an important ritual-mythological function: they establish and maintain cultural patterns of action and thought, and in that way provide a sense of meaning in life.[64]

[63] BELL: *Ritual. Perspectives* 245-247.
[64] See also G.T. GOETHALS: ,Ritual and the Representation of Power in High and Popular Art', in *Journal of Ritual Studies* 4 (1990) 2, 149-177, particularly 163-177 = G.T. GOETHALS: 'Ritual und die Repräsentation von Macht in Kunst und Massenkultur', in BELLIGER & KRIEGER (eds.): *Ritualtheorien* 303-322, especially 312-322; E. HURTH: *Zwischen Religion und Unterhaltung. Zur Bedeutung der religiösen Dimensionen in den Medien*, Mainz 2001; SCHILSON: 'Liturgie(-Reform) angesichts einer sich wandelnden Kultur' 983-988.

CHAPTER 4

CHRISTIAN RITUAL AMIDST MANY RITUALS: THE
MONOPOLY POSITION BROKEN UP

Christian ritual has lost its hegemony in our culture. With its pluralism in
approaches to life, the significance of the Christian tradition is no longer
accepted as obvious in our Western society. Christian ritual must increasingly compete in the marketplace of meaning with rituals from other great
religious traditions which are now present in our society. Moreover, it must
compete with other rituals which afford meaning, which have arisen outside the church, and indeed outside religion. One could argue that a non-
conventional system of providing meaning has arisen in our society, one
which has been derived eclectically from a difficult to separate blend of elements from non-Christian and pre-Christian cultures. The monopoly
position of Christian ritual has been broken up. For the rest, in this context one must also realise of how recent a date Christian ritual really is. The
moment when the human race appeared has been estimated as having
taken place two-and-a-half million years ago. Little is known about our
ancestors. One can only guess at their ritual conduct. But one must realise
that *Homo erectus*, at least if suitably dressed, would not stand out on any
modern street. At any rate, one can certainly speak of human ritual conduct two hundred thousand years ago among those of our forefathers we
have named *Homo sapiens sapiens*, who are generally accepted as the true
predecessor of modern man. Recent research indicates that ritual conduct
perhaps is still older and even goes back to as much as four hundred thousand years ago. The ancestors of the Neanderthal, who has for a long time
been seen as the primitive predecessor of *Homo sapiens sapiens*, were then
already making fine throwing-spears with which they hunted horses. These
Neanderthal still survived to live alongside *Homo sapiens sapiens*, and certainly had burial rituals a hundred and thirty thousand years ago.[1] With its

[1] T. HOLLEMAN: *De Neanderthaler. Een verguisde pionier*, Amsterdam 1998; see also
F. D'ERRICO a.o.: 'Neanderthal Acculturation in Western Europe? A Critical Review of
the Evidence and its Interpretation', in *Current Anthropology* 39 (1998) Supplement 1-
44; C. MAREAN & S. YEUN KIM: 'Mousterian Large – Mammal Remains from Kobeh
Cave: Behavioral Implications for Neanderthals and Early Modern Humans', in *Current
Anthropology* 39 (1998) Supplement 79-113; see also KLOOS: *Culturele antropologie* 2-6.

two thousand year history, Christian ritual is still very young. If one wishes to go back to the oldest traces of human ritual conduct, one must multiply this period of two thousand years by 100 or 200. This realisation compels us to modesty.

Since the crisis in rites in the 1960s, there has been a certain no-man's-land in ritual in our culture, lying between the artificial psychotherapeutic rituals and Christian rituals. People often opted for Christian rituals because there were no alternatives. But in recent years radical changes have taken place in this no-man's-land: it has slowly filled up with many rituals. Now Christian rituals seek their place in the midst of an abundance of ritual. I will here successively discuss rituals from within the secular world, general religious and finally interreligious rituals that afford meaning for life.

1. WORLDLY OR SECULAR RITUALS

After a period in which ritual was subject to the equivalent of clear-felling, over the last decade there has been growing interest in ritual. One would even be justified in speaking of an 'explosion' of ritual. Numerous new rituals involved with secular sources of meaning are to be found amidst the abundance of rituals in our day. Even the Dutch Humanist Society, which for a long time was very critical of all ritual, recently devoted a special issue of their magazine to the theme of rituals.[2] Moreover, they have their own training in ritual for volunteers who lead rites for entering into relationships and funerals. Such secular rituals actually fill a 'hole in the market'.

One here also encounters those rituals which have to do with civil religion, which can be of immense importance for providing meaning in society. The concepts of civil religion and public religion refer to a more or less coherent aggregate of basic values, focused on the nation, with a religious character.[3] They symbolise, as it were, the identity of the

---

[2] *Rituelen en religie.*

[3] M. TER BORG: 'Publieke religie in Nederland', in SCHREUDER & VAN SNIPPENBURG (eds.): *Religie in de Nederlandse samenleving* 166. Jean Jacques Rousseau had already used the term *religion civile* as far back as the time of the French Revolution. For literature in addition to the footnotes in Ter Borg see also G. DE HAAS: *Publieke religie. Voorchristelijke patronen in ons religieus gedrag,* Baarn 1995.

nation. It cannot be denied that the rituals of civil religion can be dangerous. That is for instance the case when they operate in the service of an extreme nationalism; one can think, for example, of certain rituals during the war in Serbia, or of the rituals of Nazism that I drew attention to in Part 1.[4] These rituals thus share in the ambiguity of all ritual. But in The Netherlands they also function in a very positive manner. In this case these rituals engage with values such as freedom, equality, toleration and solidarity. These values are considered in Dutch society as a sort of Ultimate Sacred Postulate. One might compare this with what Rappaport remarks about the American Declaration of Independence as an Ultimate Sacred Postulate.[5] These Dutch values are expressed in the annual Remembrance Day rituals on May 4, as the most important ritual giving meaning to public life, and books such as the *Diary of Anne Frank*, the writings of Hillesum, Minco's *Het bittere kruid* (The bitter herb) and Mulisch's *De aanslag* (The attack) fulfil the role of a sort of holy scripture.[6] The lines of poetry by the resistance fighter Van Randwijk, inscribed on a wall on the Weteringsplantsoen in Amsterdam, are dear to us:

A people who yield to tyrants
have lost more than life and goods;
then light itself dies.[7]

One can also think of the rituals at fixtures involving the national football team: the supporters wear red, white and blue scarves and hats, and even paint the Dutch tricolour across their faces. Another outstanding national ritual is the Eleven Cities ice skating marathon, as masses of people begin before sun-up on an all day, brutal long distance race along frozen rivers and canals through eleven cities and towns in the north of the country. It is a true national event. 'That's how the Dutch like to see themselves: struggling with the elements, at one with nature in a flat and empty seventeenth century landscape, cheered on by the villagers.'[8] Then there are also symbols such as the Waalsdorpervlakte,[9] the World War II monument on the Dam in Amsterdam, the

---

[4] Part 1, Chapter 4, 7.
[5] RAPPAPORT: *Ritual and Religion in the Making of Humanity* 425.
[6] TER BORG: 'Publieke religie in Nederland' 170-171.
[7] TER BORG: 'Publieke religie in Nederland' 167.
[8] 'Elfstedentocht', in *NRC Handelsblad* January 6, 1997, 7.
[9] About the Waalsdorpervlakte, see Part 1, Chapter 1, 2.

Auschwitz monument, the statue of the Dock Worker in Amsterdam, a monument to the longshoremen and their 1941 strike against Nazi deportations, and Zadkine's sculpture 'The Destroyed City',[10] commemorating the German bombardment of Rotterdam.

The Dutch royal house (the house of Orange) fulfils its own very special role with regard to civil religion. Every year there is the celebration of the Queen's Birthday on April 30, and the opening of the Staten Generaal – the parliament – in The Hague by the Queen on the third Tuesday of September. The Queen addresses the parliamentarians, being driven from her working palace to the parliament building and back in a golden coach. Her annual Christmas address to the nation is also a binding ritual factor.

As collective secular ritual, the rites surrounding the royal house took a very creative and innovative new shape with the marriage of Crown Prince Willem Alexander and Maxima Zorreguieta on February 2, 2001.[11] The event began with a national celebration on the evening before the wedding in Amsterdam's ArenA football stadium. This ritual was a happy invention. A football stadium is precisely *the* place where feelings of joy and sorrow are collectively experienced. The space of the stadium effected a very specific solidarity. Dutch communities sent delegations of their citizens to participate in the event surrounding Willem Alexander and Maxima. The theme of the event was 'Meer Samen, Samen Meer' (More Together, Together More). The multicultural Dutch society was emphatically represented: both traditionally Dutch and immigrant Netherlanders from every province appeared on a giant screen and there unanimously identified themselves as Dutch men and women. Further, as a national wedding present an Orange Fund was presented to the bridal pair, to benefit actions for a multicultural society. In this way the function of the House of Orange as a binding element in a pluriform, multicultural Dutch society was ritually expressed. The presence of Nelson Mandela as a guest was also characteristic: the man who gave his all to resist the tyranny of apartheid and violence, who in his struggle was often supported by The Netherlands, and who for instance could become a model for Maxima's homeland, which (in

[10] There were several other English translations for the title given; Destroyed City seems to be the overwhelming choice on both Rotterdam art sites and Zadkine biographical sites.
[11] J. DE BRUIJN: 'Huwelijk bevestigt het mystieke verbond van God, Nederland en Oranje', in *NRC Handelsblad* February 3, 2002, 9.

particular because of the role of Maxima's father) was so deeply involved in the discussions which preceded the marriage. It was a collective ritual full of hidden meanings. One can add to that the fact that the ArenA is a modern temple of football, where the 'Orange feeling' and national pride are expressed around the high points of sports, and that Willem Alexander, as a member of the International Olympic Committee, is devoted to sport. There were also hints of religious elements: the motto 'More Together, Together More' with allusions to the miracle of the multiplication of the loaves, and especially the national marriage song by the singer Marco Borsato, with its title 'Walking on the Water', also a gospel reference.

The following day there was then the ritual of civil marriage by a municipal official. Although this involved a rite of passage for individuals, as a royal wedding it was at the same time a collective, national ritual. Quite in keeping with the new attention for secular marriage rituals, this ritual was much richer than the old civil marriage ceremony in Dutch tradition, which was merely a thin and formal legal framework. The civil marriage of Willem Alexander and Maxima took place in the former stock exchange in Amsterdam, designed by H.P. Berlage, a prestigious monument to Dutch architecture. It lies close to the Dam, the square containing the national World War II monument and a royal palace, which can be considered the 'heart' of The Netherlands. This place was strictly cordoned off, for the sake of security, but also creating a sort of ultimate holy place. On another side of the square was the Nieuwe Kerk, where the ecclesiastical wedding ceremony would take place.

The burgomaster of Amsterdam made the civil ceremony a particularly meaningful ritual. In his address he referred to Maxima's visit to the Hollandsche Schouwburg, a theatre where Amsterdam's Jews were assembled before being taken way to the concentration camps during World War II. Again there was the allusion to the discussion which had preceded the marriage, and also to Maxima's position with regard to the basic Dutch national attitude of resistance against all tyranny. In his speech Burgomaster Cohen cited what Maxima had written in the guest book after her visit to the Hollandsche Schouwburg: 'Let the 21st century be one of forgiveness, but we will never forget.' The reference to the persecution of the Jews was all the stronger because the burgomaster, who functioned as the municipal official conducting the wedding, is himself Jewish. He closed the ritual with the observation that in a typical Dutch way the bridal couple were now going from exchange to church, from merchant to clergy. Speaking of new collective national ritual…

It would appear that people are becoming attached to the rituals of civil religion to the extent that the influence of organised religion recedes, and the globalisation of Western society increases. However that may be, what is involved here is the creation of new, humane, secular systems of meaning in our culture, with their own symbolic order, as structured and coherent wholes. They are important, and fill a vacuum in the human process of assigning meaning.

2. GENERAL RELIGIOUS RITUALS

As well as secular rituals, there are general religious rituals. These too are indispensable in our culture as a new means of creating meaning. It seems to me that the Christian churches can perform an important service for our society at this point. Precisely at the crucial moments of life and in the face of profound crises and disasters, in our society there is a widespread incapacity, a clumsiness at, and even a fear of expressing deeper religious feelings and thoughts. Well, then, the churches should not withdraw into their shell.[12] They too have their role in making the world whole. Drawing on their tradition and their current activity and experience, churches often have the ability to give shape to new religious rituals. One can think of the inability to find words at the death of a loved one or in the face of the large numbers of fatalities in a disaster. Clergy can help here to find the right words, gestures and acts in order to then express the deeper general religious dimensions. Sometimes images from the biblical tradition, such as hope in the future city of peace, in a time and place where the lion will lie down with the lamb and a child can put his hand in the viper's nest, and the conviction that the seed that falls in the earth and dies will bring forth fruit, are also definitely helpful in this.[13]

---

[12] See for instance G. HEITINK & H. STOFFELS: *Niet zo'n kerkganger. Zicht op buitenkerkelijk geloven*, Baarn 2003.

[13] G. LUKKEN: 'Stoten wij op een muur of is er daarachter meer?', in *Hervormd Nederland* 48 (1992) 34, Section *Voorlopig: Dood en begraven* 7-8.

I am referring here to rituals that in the past I have often designated as 'threshold liturgy'. This term is accurate to the degree that these general religious rituals can function as a step toward, and a preparation for Christian ritual. But they do not have to be that; they can likewise be autonomous elements. To that extent one can better in this case speak of the necessity of developing general religious rituals. In a certain sense one can still say that this is a no-man's-land. Despite the revival of religion and the presence of many religious movements, and the often undifferentiated mixture of all sorts of religious cultural heritages, in our culture there is still no real collective alternative for Christian ritual.[14] Yet this no-man's-land is filling up. Grimes correctly observes that meaningful religious ritual in our post-modern world is no longer the exclusive realm of religious institutions.[15] I have above noted how the resurgence of the religious in contemporary culture is taking place outside the institutional church.[16]

Outside the institutional church, synagogue, temple or mosque there is a revival of religiosity and holism, in all sorts of directions.[17] Naturally, this resurgence will have its rituals. For instance, in research involving parents P. Voll demonstrated that religion as a system of symbols and rites is present in all kinds of ways as a non-thematic (that is to say, not ecclesiastically institutionalised) horizon, in the form of prayers and bedtime stories. Things which are the essential concerns of religion are ultimately being expressed in these.[18] The emerging ritual agencies also serve to fill this need for general religious rituals, particularly for birth, marriage, entering into long-term relationships, and death. Further, it is striking that in marriages performed by municipal officials the religious dimension is also being given form from time to time.

One also encounters here the search for new religious rituals among *young people*. Many people have the experience that young people no

---

[14] HALMAN: *Waarden in de Westerse Wereld* 54-55; T. NUGTEREN: 'De nieuwe kleren van de keizer? Enkele notities over context, inhoud en verwerking van alternatieve zingevingssystemen in Nederland', in B. VEDDER a.o. (eds.): *Zin tussen vraag en aanbod. Theologische en wijsgerige beschouwingen over zin,* Tilburg 1992, 241, 245, 247, 254-255.
[15] GRIMES: *Ritual Criticism* 115.
[16] Part 3, Chapter 1, 3.3.
[17] E. SCHILLEBEECKX: 'Cultuur, godsdienst en geweld. Theologie als onderdeel van een cultuur', in *Tijdschrift voor Theologie* 36 (1996) 396.
[18] P. VOLL: 'Religion im Alltag', in A. DUBACH a.o.: *Religiöse Lebenswelt junger Eltern,* Zürich 1989, 262-300. See MAAS & ZIEBERTZ: 'Over breukvlakken en bruggenhoofden' 398-399.

longer automatically join into the Christian symbolic order in which they are included by baptism, confirmation and first communion. Rather often they become estranged from the symbolic order once they leave primary school. In keeping with the tendencies of contemporary culture, they then take responsibility for their own belief patterns. They have many possibilities to choose from. They are confronted with the great world religions, but also an immense selection of books, trainings and fellowships in the area of alternative philosophies of life.[19] For them the question of meaning also comes to the fore at important moments in life. Opting for Christian rituals at those moments is by no means obvious. What system of meaning, what ritual will they select? Purely secular, humanistic rituals? Empirical research indicates that despite the high percentage of young people who are not involved with any church, the tendency among them is not toward purely secular sources of meaning but rather toward a religious or semi-religious realignment. There are quite a few indications that they have created a third force between the two extremes of institutionalised Christianity and atheism or agnosticism, one in which there appears to be a great receptivity for generally religious or philosophical ideas and conduct.[20] For instance, it is striking that although only 39% of Dutch young people report themselves to be church members, 82% say that they pray on occasion. 'For most young people prayer functions as a coping mechanism, a form of non-directive therapy which they use to keep their life in balance.'[21] In this context the question also arises, for instance, of what general religious experience among the young is connected with the pop concerts which they attend in such numbers.[22] For them religion is much less linked to

[19] NUGTEREN: 'De nieuwe kleren van de keizer?' 245.

[20] J. DE HART: 'Bijgeloof – bij geloof? Christelijke religiositeit en 'New Age'-stromingen onder Nederlandse jong-volwassenen', in *Tijdschrift voor Theologie* 33 (1993) 166-176; J. JANSSEN, J. DE HART & C. DEN DRAAK: 'Praying as an individualized ritual', in HEIMBROCK & BOUDEWIJNSE: *Current Studies on Rituals* 71-85.

[21] JANSSEN, DE HART & DEN DRAAK: 'Praying as an individualized ritual' 71-85; J. JANSSEN J. & M. PRINS: "Let's reinvent Gods'. De religie van Nederlandse jongeren in een Europese context', in J. JANSSEN, R. VAN UDEN & H. VAN DER VEN (eds.): *Schering en inslag. Opstellen over religie in de hedendaagse cultuur. Aangeboden aan Jan van der Lans bij zijn afscheid als hoogleraar godsdienstpsychologie aan de Katholieke Universiteit Nijmegen*, Nijmegen 1998, 132.

[22] K.H. REICH: 'Rituals and social structure: the moral dimension', in HEIMBROCK & BOUDEWIJNSE (eds.): *Current Studies on Rituals* 121-134; J. ZWAGERMAN: *Collega's van God. Portretten en polemieken*, Amsterdam 1993.

themes. For them it is no longer identical with institutional Christian religion. But the religious – and indeed the Christian religious – is in fact present as a horizon, and from this horizon comes to the fore in a special way at key transitions in life.[23]

3. INTERRELIGIOUS RITUALS

Already at the end of the 1960s the centre Interreligio raised the question of whether people in our society would not have to arrive at interreligious celebrations.[24] In recent years there has been a breakthrough in this area.[25] I am referring for instance to the collective mourning service on October 11, 1992, in Amsterdam for the victims of the disaster with the El Al air freighter, to the memorial for the victims of the aeroplane crash in Surinam, to the collective prayer services for peace in January 1992, before the first Golf War, to the World Day of Prayer for peace on October 27, 1986, in Assisi, and the interreligious prayer day on January 24, 2002, against all violence in the name of religion, also in Assisi; these last initiatives of Pope John Paul II brought together representatives of almost all the world religions. These are only a few examples. Particularly at critical moments in our history the need for interreligious observances arises. But they also appear at other, more everyday moments. A form of Christmas observance for diverse religions has been developed at various Dutch schools.[26] Since the early 1990s, for instance, in Zwolle there has been a tradition of holding a joint religious celebration with Jews, Christians and Muslims at the beginning of the New Year. Various mosques and Islamic organisations in The Netherlands have over the course of the years developed the custom of organising special *iftar* meals during Ramadan, to which representatives of other religions are also invited. In The Hague the Council for Life Philosophies and Religion prepares an annual observance on the occasion of the Dutch Remembrance Day, May 4, in which the theme of reconciliation among various groups and peoples is central. And in

---

[23] MAAS & ZIEBERTZ: 'Over breukvlakken en bruggenhoofden' 397.

[24] R. BOEKE: *Dit zal u een teken zijn*, 's-Gravenhage 1987, 157-178.

[25] J. SLOMP: 'Met moslims bidden? Een interreligieuze liturgische vraag', in *Werkmap (voor) Liturgie* 27 (1993) 117-125.

[26] G. SPEELMAN: 'Kerstfeest in een interreligieuze school', in *Begrip Moslims-Christenen*, November 1991, 106.

Genk, Belgium, on World Peace Day, October 4, Christians and Muslims hold a joint, interreligious service. What is striking in this last initiative is that a neutral date has been chosen, rather than one which was already connected with a particular religion.[27] And in the personal sphere, on the occasion of interfaith marriages, there are examples of marriage liturgies in which both a Koran and a Bible are presented to the couple, and there are readings from both during the service.[28]

One the one hand, these interreligious celebrations are linked with modernisation and postmodernism, which make us tolerant of other attitudes toward life and other religions; on the other hand, they are connected with the fact of increased migration. We will increasingly be confronted with minarets and mosques and the ritual spaces of Hindus and Buddhists. Our culture now accepts the conviction that Christianity must not silence the ritual narratives of those who believe differently. Further reflection on interreligious celebrations is under way. It has been said that they are not intended as a step toward conquering deep-rooted divisions and differences, On the contrary, they respectfully make room for the differences in each other's convictions.[29] They have their own autonomous value.

---

[27] K. STEENBRINK: 'Moslims en de kerken. Contacten en dialoog als onderdeel van kerkelijk handelen', in *Tijdschrift voor Theologie* 3 (1997) 56-72. For interreligious celebrations see also *Interreligieus vieren: Werkmap (voor) Liturgie* 28 (1994) 273-327.

[28] G. SPEELMAN a.o. (eds.): *Ik ben christen, mijn partner is moslim*, Kampen 1995, 108-110. See also D. BENTURQUI: *Couples islamo-chrétiens: promesse ou impasse?*, Lausanne 1990, 69-90.

[29] SLOMP: 'Met moslims bidden?'.

CHAPTER 5

CHRISTIAN RITUAL AT A DISTANCE

It is not only because its monopoly position has broken up, and it must now compete with many other rituals that provide meaning, that Christian ritual has assumed a different place in our culture. Its place has also changed to the extent that one can now participate in ritual at a distance. This involves first the possibility of literally participating in Christian ritual via mass media. But it also involves a very special tendency, namely that of participation in Christian ritual as a precious or beloved museum object or folklore from the past, or as a work of art. These are new forms of ritual participation that are tied to developments in our culture. With them comes a different setting for ritual. Finally, one finds a certain distanced participation in ritual when it becomes theatre. Therefore I will be discussing the similarities and differences between theatre and liturgy.

When I speak of participation 'at a distance' this is in no sense meant in a derogatory manner. One can appraise these new forms of participation in a distinctly positive manner. They can have deeply Christian roots.[1]

1. TELEVISION AND THE WORLD WIDE WEB

In Chapter 3.4 above I noted the influence of visual media on participation in ritual and the experience of ritual. In this connection entirely new questions arise regarding Christian ritual in our culture. For several decades now we have become accustomed to Christian ritual having claimed a real weekly place on television, and rituals being broadcast on special occasions such as the marriage or funerals of important persons. There are also broadcasts of rituals such as the *Urbi et orbi* blessing and the massively attended liturgies on the occasion of papal visits to various countries.[2] There are Christians who experience Christian liturgy primarily in this way, and this experience can be very intense. Reflection on the

---

[1] See in this connection POST: 'Religious Popular Culture and Liturgy'.
[2] See in this connection POST: *Ritueel landschap* 28-32.

peculiar nature of television liturgy is slowly getting under way.[3] Through various media strategies it is possible to further intensify this experience.

In addition to television there is the Internet. The World Wide Web will undoubtedly greatly increase the possibilities for participating in ritual through the mass media. Both rituals from distant regions and those from one's own place and region come, as it were, within reach and sight. All sorts of ritual are making their appearance on the World Wide Web. This is also the case with the major rites of passage, especially the death rites.[4] For instance, the World Wide Cemetery, established in 1995, contains 'monuments', listed alphabetically as well as by region and year of death.[5] Grimes notes that the cyber-world is a better substitute for a cemetery than for a funeral, for while the cemetery is a place to 'visit', the funeral enables you to 'do'.[6] The danger of the internet however is the further disembodying of death. This is especially the case with the funeral. In a critical way he discusses the 'virtual' funeral of Princess Diana, and concludes that we need graphic myths rooted in tactile rites and passionate engagement without the requirement of literal belief.[7] It

[3] J. HEMELS: 'Liturgie en massamedia. Na de discussie over televisietoneel is nu ook die over de televisieliturgie ons deel geworden', in *De Bazuin* 65 (1982) 46, 1-2 and 6-7; H. RAKOWSKI: 'Literaturbericht zum Thema "Gottesdienstübertragungen im Fernsehen"', in *Communicatio socialis* 20 (1987) 250-265; J.G. HAHN: *Liturgie op televisie of 'televisie-liturgie'*, Amsterdam 1992; M.K.J. GERTLER: *Fernsehgemeinde: Erfahrung von Kirche durch Gottesdienstübertragungen*, Köln 1999; A. BAZAN: 'Realtà liturgica e comunicazione ciberspaziale. Verso una nuova liturgia?', in *Rivista liturgica* 87 (2000) 137-144; W.M. SPEELMAN: 'Het ware licht. Theologie van de liturgie in de media', in *Jaarboek voor liturgie-onderzoek* 16 (2000) 167-186; M.K.J. GERTLER: 'Wenig Feierlichkeit auf dem Bildschirm. Gottesdienstübertragungen im deutschen Fernsehen', in POST, ROUWHORST, VAN TONGEREN & SCHEER (eds.): *Christian Feast and Festival* 747-774; B. GILLES: *Durch das Auge der Kamera. Eine liturgie-theologische Untersuchung von Gottesdiensten im Fernsehen*, Münster 2001; W.M. SPEELMAN: 'Televisie en liturgie', in BARNARD & POST (eds.): *Ritueel bestek* 123-130;: IDEM: *Liturgie in beeld. Over de identiteit van de Rooms-katholieke liturgie in de elektronische media* (Netherlands Studies in Ritual and Liturgy 3), Groningen/Tilburg 2004.

[4] GRIMES: *Deeply into the Bone* 273-282.

[5] GRIMES: *Deeply into the Bone* 274-275; see also G. SCHWIBBE & I. SPIEKER: 'Virtuelle Friedhöfe', in *Zeitschrift für Volkskunde* 95 (1999) 220-245.

[6] GRIMES: *Deeply into the Bone* 274-275.

[7] GRIMES: *Deeply into the Bone* 275-282. Regarding the funeral of Diana, see also W.M. SPEELMAN: 'The Feast of Diana's Death', in POST, ROUWHORST, VAN TONGEREN & SCHEER (eds.): *Christian Feast and Festival* 775-801.

is indeed true that participation in rituals through television and internet carries with it the risk of manipulation and distortion. It raises new questions which must be examined critically. Participation in ritual through media simply is a considerable dilution of physical participation. On the other hand, it is also true that it opens up new possibilities.

Churches too are seeking a place on the internet. One can surf sites from the Vatican, dioceses and parishes. Some bishops have an internet site of their own that is accessible for mutual contacts and pastoral help. Priests and Protestant preachers put their sermons on the net. In this way one can participate in congregational worship. In June, 1998, the Anglican Church opened a 'virtual chapel' complete with pews, stained glass windows and an altar, where visitors could come and pray. Internet congregants can choose for morning or evening prayer. One can even contact contemplative orders through the internet. Hundreds of convents and monasteries have their own websites. This will all have radical consequences for the place of Christian liturgy in our culture. It is still difficult to foresee what these will be. It is not impossible that small-scale religious communities will blossom in reaction to this 'digitisation of God', resulting in community building as a dissent from the strong commercialisation of society.[8]

Finally, there is also the broader ritual role of the media as such. D. Mol points out that television affords the possibility of religious experience.[9] Television gives the viewer the possibility of creating a worldview according to personal choice. Secular programmes can fulfil the religious function of providing meaning in life. He makes this clear on the basis of a description and analysis of the programme 'All you need is love'.[10] The Christian, biblical dimension can also come up in this process.

2. MUSEALISATION, FOLKLORISATION AND AESTHETICISATION

Other forms of participation in liturgy 'at a distance' have also appeared in our culture. These too involve a reduced mode of participation, and

---

[8] See also S. O'LEARY: 'Cyberspace as Sacred Space: Communicating Religion on Computer Networks', in *The Journal of the American Academy of Religion* 64 (1996) 781-808; B. ROEBBEN: 'Spiritual and Moral Education in/and Cyberspace: Preliminary Reflections', in *Journal of Education and Christian Belief* 3 (1999) 85-95.

[9] D. MOL: *Onze digitale god. Religieuze en pastorale kanten van televisie* (Zin-Speling), Kampen 1997; IDEM: 'De tv als 'pastor'', in *Praktische Theologie* 24 (1997) 41-58.

[10] See previous note.

principally take one of three forms: musealisation, folklorisation or aes-theticisation. Because these forms of participation are becoming increas-ingly frequent, it is important to consider them further.

These new possibilities are undoubtedly related to a development which already started in previous cultural periods, but which has intensified in our culture. It involves the 'splitting off' of the arts. Ethno-semiotics and socio-semiotics distinguish three phases in this process.[11]
    The first is the mythic phase, which is characterised by the active par-ticipation of the whole community in what takes place. The symbolic system which is used here is extraordinarily 'full'. One finds a narrative and poetic texts, music, gesture, dance, etc., all going hand in hand. There are no spectators. The mythic acts are not theatre that is directed to an audience, which attempts to communicate meaning to those who are watching, but is rather a collective happening, in which the individ-ual is integrated into the group. It is clear that liturgy belongs to this mythic phase.
    The second phase is that of folklore. In this phase one no longer finds mythic narrative, sacred dance or sacred music. These are replaced by the folk story, folk dance and folk music. There are still mythic ele-ments to be found in this phase: there is an effort to replicate certain mythic acts in which the community participates; but on the other hand there are also spectators, to whom the actors seek to communicate something. You watch folk dance and listen to folk stories and music.
    The third phase is that of the spectacle, of theatre: there you have architecture and iconography or painting as such, apart from its func-tion in the larger whole, and also the literary narrative or poem, drama, the concert, ballet, opera, cabaret and film. The arts have been split off, and the primary intention is to convey meaning to listeners, viewers and visitors.[12]
    One can situate the processes of the musealisation, aestheticisation and folklorisation of liturgy in our culture within this pattern.

---

[11] GREIMAS: 'Conditions d'une sémiotique du monde naturel' 79; IDEM: 'Réflexions sur les objets ethno-sémiotiques'.
    The same three phases are also denoted with the terms sacred, ludic and aesthetic, respectively.
    [12] GREIMAS & COURTÉS: Sémiotique. Dictionnaire, sub verbo Théâtrale (sémio-tique); E. DE KUYPER: Pour une sémiotique spectaculaire (Doctoral Thesis EHSS), Paris 1979.

2.1. Musealisation

The phenomenon of musealisation involves the third phase, that of the splitting off of the arts. Musealisation adds to this process the characteristic that it deals with the various independent arts as something from the past which individuals will now appropriate with admiration as hearers, viewers or visitors. Recently someone reported to me that he wanted to visit Westminster Abbey in London. A long queue waited at the church doors, and one had to pay an admission fee. But he saw a side door with the sign 'For silent prayer only', and went in through it. A guard asked him what he had come to do. His answer was 'I want to pray', and he was admitted to a side room from which he could admire Westminster Abbey in silence. There is quite a difference if one visits this building to participate in prayer, or as a sort of exhibition space. It is striking that as participation in liturgy declines, at the same time monumental churches are overrun with tourists. That is true not only for Westminster Abbey, but equally for Notre Dame in Paris and the Dom, Santa Maria del Fiore in Florence: tourists shuffle en mass through these churches, and they are as packed as art museums with block-buster exhibitions. In 1995 25% of the Dutch population visited a church one or more times for a cultural reason. Thus churches came third, after historic city centres (31%) and historic villages (30%), but before castles (20%) and significantly ahead of windmills (11%). One can speak of musealisation in our culture.[13] That also applies to religious

---

[13] See in this connection W. DERKSE: 'Het nieuwe heilige? Over de opbloei van geestelijke muziek in een geseculariseerde tijd', in D. VAN SPEYBROECK (ed.): *Kunst en religie*, Baarn 1991, 43-57; J. DE VISSCHER: 'Kunst en religie. Van manifeste verbondenheid naar verborgen verwantschap', in VAN SPEYBROECK (ed.): *Kunst en religie* 100-112; IDEM: *Een te voltooien leven* 7-10; H. LÜBBE: 'Der Fortschritt und das Museum', in *Dilthey Jahrbuch* 1 (1983) 39-56; P.J. MARGRY: 'Accomodatie en innovatie met betrekking tot traditionele rituelen. Bedevaarten en processies in de moderne tijd', in VAN UDEN, PIEPER & POST (eds.): *Oude sporen, nieuwe wegen* 189-191; J. PIEPER, P. POST & M. VAN UDEN: *Pelgrimage in beweging. Een christelijk ritueel in nieuwe contexten*, Baarn 1999; POST: 'Het verleden in het spel?'; IDEM: 'Pelgrims tussen traditie en moderniteit. Een verkenning van hedendaagse pelgrimsverslagen', in PIEPER, POST & VAN UDEN (eds.): *Bedevaart en pelgrimage* 23-30; IDEM: 'The Modern Pilgrim. A Christian Ritual between Tradition and Post-Modernity', in *Concilium* 32 (1996) 4, 1-9; IDEM: 'Post-modern Pilgrimage. Christian ritual between Liturgy and 'Topolatry'', in A. HOUTMAN, M. POORTHUIS & J. SCHWARTZ (eds.): *Sanctity of Time and Space in Tradition and Modernity*, Leiden 1998, 299-315; A. STOCK: 'Tempel en tolerantie. Over de musealisering van de religie', in *Werkschrift voor Leerhuis en Liturgie* 15 (1996) 98-101;

monuments and objects. Images of Christ or Buddha, old sacred manuscripts of Bibles and liturgical books, altar furnishings, relics and images of saints are displayed in museums, and people admiringly attend festivals of religious music; concerts in churches often attract more people than the liturgical celebrations in the same spaces do, in which religious music is obviously also an integral part. In 1994 the Rijksmuseum in Amsterdam even organised an exhibition of objects involved in devotional practices, under the title 'Devotion in Beauty'. One can also think of the Dutch ritual of the annual Open Monument Day, on which churches on the monument list are heavily visited.

One undoubtedly finds here ritual forms that have a religious slant, but at the same time it is clear that these are other ritual forms than that of full participation in liturgy.[14] Compared with the latter, they are a heavily diluted and most distant form of participation. This was brought home strikingly by one of the Dutch bishops when he spoke in 1991 on a VPRO television broadcast about several magnificent gospels in an exhibition at the Meermanno-Westreenianum Museum (The Museum of the Book) in The Hague. He remarked, 'Really a 9th century gospel like this does not belong behind glass. It should be used in the liturgy. The deacon must carry it into the church high above him in the entrance procession, and he should sing from it.' To the surprise of the programmers, he proceeded to do precisely that.[15] Thus one must realise that an image of Christ or of a saint in a museum is really an alien in a strange land. Sacred objects in a museum – and that is equally true for holy objects from primitive peoples as for those of the great religions – are watered down, as it were, when they are taken out of their own context and made into art objects, objects of curiosity, art enjoyment and fascination. They then no longer fulfil their original religious function.[16] Benjamin makes

---

J. VAESSEN: *Musea in een museale cultuur. De problematische legitimering van het kunstmuseum*, Zeist 1986; W. ZACHARIAS (ed.): *Zeitphenomen Musealisierung: das Verschwinden der Gegenwart und die Konstruktion der Erinnerung*, Essen 1990; see also the literature listed in POST: 'Zeven notities over rituele verandering' 18, note 49.

[14] G. LUKKEN: 'Het kerkgebouw als 'totaal kunstwerk': verbondenheid van kunst en cultus', in J. MAAS (ed.): *Beeld en gelijkenis. Bundel voordrachten gehouden bij het afscheid aan de Katholieke Theologische Universiteit te Utrecht van dr. Tjeu van den Berk*, Utrecht 2001, 27-38.

[15] W. DERKSE: 'Het nieuwe heilige?', in *Brabantia nostra. Tijdschrift voor kunst en cultuur* 40 (1991) 5.

[16] GRIMES: *Reading, Writing, and Ritualizing* 91; H. LOMBAERTS & L. BOEVE (eds.): *Traditie en initiatie. Perspectieven voor de toekomst*, Leuven 1996, 102-103.

an emphatic distinction between the cultic value and the exhibition value of an artwork, and he notes that this distinction can already in fact be found in Hegel.[17] Originally the artwork was in service of ritual, but in modern times it has become detached from it. As early as the Renaissance there arose a tendency to collect art. Wealthy gentlemen had their curiosity cabinets, small museums of a sort. Gradually in the 18th and 19th century collections became more extensive, and the end of the 19th and beginning of the 20th century saw the creation of the great public museums as repositories for all sorts of cultural/historic and aesthetic objects. The last few decades have witnessed both the expansion of the great museums and a real explosion in all sorts of small, regional museums. The musealisation of culture has thus led to a radical transformation of the significance of objects, from an absolute stress on their cultic value to an absolute stress on their exhibition value for as large an audience as possible.[18] In this situation it becomes an interesting question, whether in museums one can do more justice to these sacred objects by situating them more in their 'biographical' context, and thus, as it were, personalising them. They then are given a symbolic value that comes closer to that of their origins.[19] With regard to concerts of religious music, this is the case when they are held in the space in which the music originally belonged – the church building itself. This also follows from what I said in Part 1 with regard to the rich presentative significance of objects.[20]

It is not always possible to make a sharp distinction between mythic and museal forms of participation. There are two particular movements possible.

First, it is possible that within the liturgical ritual itself the perspective can jump from the mythic to the museal form of participation. For instance, it can happen that there is an authentic liturgical ritual, but that the participant in this ritual only appropriates it in a museal manner. Post presents a striking example, citing Waldenfels. It involves the

---

[17] J. DE VISSCHER: 'Alsof Genesis 3 niet had plaatsgehad. Het postmodernisme in de hedendaagse schilderkunst en sculptuur', in BULHOF & DE VALK (eds.): *Postmodernisme als uitdaging* 98-113; IDEM: 'Kunst en religie' 100-102. See G.W.F. HEGEL: *Phänomenologie des Geistes*, Hamburg 1952, 523-524.

[18] DE VISSCHER: 'Kunst en religie' 101.

[19] GRIMES: *Reading, Writing, and Ritualizing* 93-96.

[20] Part 1, Chapter 1, 2.5.

story of a prelate from Cologne who on his deathbed, during the performance of the ritual for the dying, took up the crucifix with the remark: '18th century, poor workmanship'.[21] I saw a similar episode not long ago in the celebration of a Byzantine liturgy. I sat toward the back, and behind me sat a pew full of listeners who had the musical score with them. In these cases the ritual itself affords no reason for this reduced participation.

A second possibility is a movement in the opposite direction, from museal to mythic participation. For example, it can be that one experiences the museum as a 'cathedral of art'.[22] For instance, the Boniface Museum in Maastricht, designed by the Italian architect Rossi, draws deep inspiration from the Dom (Santa Maria del Fiore) in Florence,[23] and, according to Henk van Os (at the time he made the comment its director), the Rijksmuseum in Amsterdam can be considered our national cathedral of art, as it were, with Rembrandt's *Night Watch* as the central altarpiece. Of further interest here is the remark by the Canadian museum director MacDonald that he and his colleagues have the 'image' of being high priests of deserted cultural cathedrals, and this fact obsesses them.[24] It cannot be denied that many experience visits to museums, particularly in the case of special exhibitions, as religious events. According to Grimes museums are also quasi-religious institutions, which in part trade upon ultimate values, and one can see a museum visit as a ritual with contemplative elements.[25] Van Os has remarked that, if it were up to him, at the same time they buy their tickets people would be able to rent cushions, on which to sit and meditate before the artworks on the walls.[26] Thus although the emphasis lies on its exhibition value, in one way or another the artwork as such continues to retain something of its original religious/ritual function. But at the same time it is true that the exhibition value dominates in these cases; one is simply in a museum, and there is no way one can speak of

---

[21] POST: 'Pelgrims tussen traditie en moderniteit' 23, with reference to B. WALDENFELS: *Stachel des Fremde*, Frankfurt 1990.

[22] H. VAN OS: *Een kathedraal voor de kunst*, Amsterdam 1997.

[23] POST: 'Post-modern Pilgrimage' See also IDEM: *Het wonder van Dokkum* 119-121.

[24] Thus a quotation in GRIMES: *Ritual Criticism* 81. See also IDEM: *Reading, Writing, and Ritualizing* 96.

[25] GRIMES: *Ritual Criticism* 64; IDEM: *Reading, Writing, and Ritualizing* 96-100.

[26] B. DE KLERCK: 'Het museum een kathedraal', in *NRC Handelsblad* September 26, 1997, 43.

participation in a fully-formed liturgical ritual. Vernooij gives another example with regard to the concert as a sort of religious event. 'Globally speaking, if in the Baroque era the objective link with liturgy was to a large extent lost and the church became a concert hall, it may equally globally be said of the Romantic age that the concert hall in its turn was elevated to being a sacred space where the ritual of the concert was performed... In that time the concert takes on remarkable cultic features: the devotional silence at the beginning, the ritual applause, the doors that shut implacably once the concert begins, the lights that are lowered, the director as celebrant...'[27] In addition to the sports contests themselves, he further offers the opening of the ArenA football temple in Amsterdam on August 14, 1996, as a textbook example of the 'liturgisation' of mass gatherings. It was complete with a specially composed 'hymn', the sacred play of unveiling first the whole space and thereafter the pitch (compare Good Friday), and Trijntje Oosterhuis as a genuine priestess, clad in the liturgical colours of Ajax, white and red.[28]

It is clear that either direction the movement goes, one encounters reduced ritual religious forms. One finds an even much more sharply reduced form where religious objects are included in a profane environment as decoration. For example, I know of a cafe called 'The Eleventh Commandment', where all sorts of saints' images and even a stations of the cross are included in the decor. And one can find religious objects as background sets for soap operas, and Gregorian music is heard as Muzak. These ritual forms seem to mix rather in the profane sphere of street festivals and markets involving old crafts. They belong to the category of what can be called 'reli-culture', 'reli-tourism' and 'reli-shopping'.

2.2. Folklorisation

The threefold distinction from ethno-semiotics and socio-semiotics also makes it possible to situate more or less 'ritual' manifestations more precisely as expressions that belong to the transitional zone that lies between liturgy and the autonomous arts. One should here think

---

[27] A. VERNOOIJ: 'De taal van de ziel', in *Jaarboek voor liturgie-onderzoek* 14 (1998) 233-234.
[28] VERNOOIJ: 'De taal van de ziel' 234.

of all forms of folkloristic religious rituals such as the Sacred Blood procession in Bruges, the St. Hubertus procession in Maastricht, lantern-lit St. Martin processions, *palmpaas* processions on Palm Sunday in the Low Countries, Marian processions, the mounted pilgrimage for the feast of St. Gerardus, manger processions at Christmas, seawater consecrations in Flanders, Three Kings processions, etc.[29] On the one side, for the active participants these remain an authentic mythic event. But at the same time it is true that they attract crowds of spectators who have come to witness a folk custom. It is not without reason that regional and local tourist boards and local radio and television broadcasters include these rituals in their lists of attractions. As such these rituals thus have a certain duality, seen from the perspective of liturgy: there are those who play an active role, and in that sense participate at a mythic level, and there are spectators, who see the whole as the performance of a piece of theatre. Even for those who actively participate, however, it is possible to appropriate the event in various ways. For instance, one can go on a pilgrimage and experience this ritual mythically, but it is likewise possible that one undertakes the whole as a religious tourist. As Mulder indicates in an article on pilgrimage and tourism, various gradations appear possible.[30]

2.3. Aestheticisation

The subject of aestheticisation is unquestionably related to that of musealisation and folklorisation. Yet it is important to separate it out and deal with it specifically. In this manner a number of characteristic elements that play a role in liturgy in contemporary culture can be discussed.

[29] See among others POST: 'Traditie gebruiken'; IDEM: *Ritueel landschap* 20-21 (sub 3.6 'gefolkloriseerde liturgie'); IDEM: 'Alle dagen feest'; IDEM: 'Goede tijden, slechte tijden' (regarding the Silent Procession in Amsterdam); P. POST & J. PIEPER: *De palmzondagviering. Een landelijke verkenning*, Kampen 1992, 59-63; G. ROOIJAKKERS: 'Percepties van bovennatuur. Continuïteit en verandering in de Zuidnederlandse rite-praktijk', in *Jaarboek voor liturgie-onderzoek* 11 (1995) 103-125; *Vieringen (Rituelen) buiten 1 and 2*. See also the literature, listed in POST: 'Zeven notities over rituele verandering' 18, note 49.

[30] A. MULDER: 'Op zoek naar de ware pelgrim. Over pelgrimage en toerisme', in VAN UDEN, PIEPER & POST (eds.): *Oude sporen, nieuwe wegen* 20.

It is an indisputable fact that ritual and liturgy have a special relationship with art.[31] Ritual sites are generally true art works, and ritual itself is characterised by aesthetic qualities. The old adage *bonum et pulchrum convertuntur* (the good and the beautiful are mutually convertible) is undoubtedly true for ritual. As such, aesthetic qualities are an integral part of ritual. But when these qualities are absolutised or when certain aesthetic forms are declared sacrosanct, one encounters the phenomenon of the 'aestheticising' of ritual.

In the years 1948-1950 Van Doornik published two substantial volumes in which converts to the Roman Catholic Church described their experience. One is struck by the fact that in these testimonies, for some the beauty of Romanesque and Gothic churches and the splendour of the Catholic liturgy were a reason for changing their faith. When in 1996 it was noted in the press that every year about 1000 adults were going over to the Catholic Church, it was rather frequently noted that among these new converts too the attraction of the Roman liturgy played an important role. Moreover, in this the stress lay on the beauty of the traditional liturgy. The sociologist Zijderveld observed in this connection that the Catholicism of yore was an audio-visual religion, which preserved the aesthetics of music and image in an exemplary manner. Gregorian music and incense curb the chill intellect. He sketched a picture based on the traditional liturgy, and then opined, 'The best chances for the Catholic Church in the coming religious ferment will be if it is not modernised too much and does not become veiled Protestantism, as promoted by the reform-minded, who, for the rest, are constantly nattering away about this so annoyingly.'[32]

Several months later Kees Fens, a professor of literature, wrote about the way in which the Catholic liturgy had once defined his image of the world:

> Light, music, incense – together, that was God. Later language joined them, Latin, which fixed itself in me as a religious mother tongue... Very much later I would discover that God was not only Catholic, but also Italian. He seemed to still live on there in the churches: the eternal light and odour. I heard the music without it being sung or played. But – and that

---

[31] See among others KRIEGER & BELLIGER: 'Einführung' 11-14; RAPPAPORT: *Ritual and Religion in the Making of Humanity* 384-388.

[32] A.C. ZIJDERVELD: 'Katholiek reveil', in *NRC Handelsblad* June 8, 1996, 9.

was perhaps the most impressive – the light continued outside in a more vivid form. I believe that I always have believed in a southern God, and this did not fit with the grey Dutch light and the jagged Dutch language. When God became Dutch too, I ended up outside the Church.[33]

It was not only Fens who was disillusioned by the renewal of the Catholic liturgy; a large number of the converts from before the Second Vatican Council also fell away or expressed sharp criticism of the post-Vatican II Catholic liturgy. Accusations of a lack of beauty in the new liturgy also came from outside those circles. What strikes me time and again is that people here seem to have a very specific beauty in mind. Fens writes of an Italian beauty and of the beauty of Latin; Turner speaks about the incomparable beauty of the Tridentine Mass as a composition; it is a matter of 'the beauty of Gregorian chant' and other church music from the past.[34] Catholic liturgy is then identified with that beauty. This happens not only among Catholics, but even among those outside the Catholic Church who approach the Roman liturgy in a museal manner. There are two dangers in this view.

The first is that the liturgy becomes identified with aesthetics, with beauty, in a radical manner. Its aesthetic value becomes absolute, as it were. Liturgy becomes 'an art in itself', which in fact is a reduction, at the expense of its mythic character.

An interview with Schillebeeckx, in which he responds to remarks by the professor of musicology Hélène Nolthenius, is interesting in this regard.

> *Interviewer*: In the conversation… with Hélène Nolthenius an image of Catholicism emerges in which, as Nolthenius herself says, 'side issues' play a role: 'A Christmas tree, beautiful liturgy, Gregorian chant, beautiful paintings, Italy'. And, she says, that 'in essence has nothing at all to do with religion'.
>
> *Schillebeeckx*: I recognise that picture. It is a typical intellectual sort of Catholicism, which you – *mutatis mutandis* – also encounter with people like Frits van der Meer, Kees Fens and Cornelis Verhoeven. Not among 'average' believers. You could call it 'aestheticism'. Hans Urs von Balthasar – the well-known German theologian – is also that sort of aestheticist. They are so stuck on forms. And although form and content of course

---

[33] K. Fens: 'God is geur, muziek en licht', in *NCR Handelsblad* December 24, 1996, 24.

[34] See in this connection the articles by the priest/art historian Antoine Bodar which appear in the Dutch daily *Trouw* and other sources.

cannot be separated from one another, I still have the impression that for them the form is more definitive than the content. Nolthenius sees Catholicism as a cultural legacy heavily freighted with the aesthetic... and it cannot be reconciled with it in one way or another.[35]

The danger in this view of liturgy is thus that the tension between form and content, which is peculiar to liturgy, becomes lost. The identity aspect of the symbol becomes over-accented, as it were, at the expense of the equally essential diversity aspect. That brings with it the risk that the peculiar nature of liturgy becomes distanced, so that one must speak of a reduced ritual.

But there is a second danger. Not only is the tension we have mentioned broken, but at the same time people appear to be choosing a very limited form of beauty, one which excludes others. These include not only that of 'the average man' but also forms of beauty which are linked with other cultures. I will go into this further.

What is a beautiful ritual? This should not only be asked of classical art historians, but also of ethnologists. In the paraliturgy of the past people sang simple devotional songs, and they carefully preserved endearing pictures and devotional prints in their missals. In Christian ritual there was also a layer of popular piety that was characterised by sentimentality. One must not overlook these devotional and sentimental sides of the liturgy. They are essential for the liturgy of the community.[36] Most recognise this layer in themselves. It is the layer of the fondly recalled song from days gone by, from the 'rich Roman life' or sung on your mother's lap, of the picture that hung on the wall at home, of the poem from the past. The underside of all this is that of kitsch: the tear-jerker, the song or poem about the harsh realities of life, children who break their mothers' hearts, the dear old mother who sacrificed herself, about loneliness, disappointments in love, injustice – in short, really about the downtrodden.[37] These texts and songs can express a fundamental experience for people; they can be a precious expression of faith. It is certainly the case that you here run up against a boundary, and indeed a boundary which in essence, from the

---

[35] K. Kok: 'Esthetisch katholicisme. Kees Kok in gesprek met Edward Schillebeeckx', in *Werkschrift voor Leerhuis en Liturgie* 10 (1990) 4, 16.

[36] A. Vernooij: "Dan danst de kreupele als een hert..." (Jesaja 35, 6). Over de toekomst van de gemeenschapsliturgie', in VAN TONGEREN (ed.): *Toekomst, toen en nu* 66.

[37] Excellent examples are to be found in H.H. Heijermans: *Snikken en Smartlapjes*, Baarn 1981.

perspective of liturgy, differs little from that of aestheticism. Here too the tension between form and content can be lost. That happens when the sentiment begins to so dominate that one becomes caught up in it. Then the perspective can no longer jump, opening up in the direction of the transcendent. Then one must also speak of a reduced liturgical form.

There are still other views and experiences of the aesthetic, which are related to the changes in culture, and which are of great importance for the experience of liturgy in our culture. A certain ideal of beauty did play a role in the liturgy of the past. Beautiful forms, harmony, balance, the positive aspects of man and the world were important elements in it. Over against that stands an approach to the aesthetic in the light of late-modern art and philosophy after Auschwitz (Adorno, Levinas and Lyotard). This is not so much an aesthetic of the beautiful as one of suffering, death, the monstrous, the accusation. Freyer points out that this aesthetic, inspired in part by the Jewish tradition with its ban on images and its critical attitude toward concepts that turn God into an idol, is a challenge for contemporary sacramental theology.[38] One can of course ask if such theology, from its inclination toward representational thinking, does not too easily accentuate the epiphany of the holy, and do this in line with our own needs and experience of time, at the expense of divine transcendence. Freyer then develops a liturgical aesthetic, drawing especially on Levinas. The sacraments are much more startling signs of the 'passing through of the Lord'. In this the materiality of the sacrament would rather have to be an expression of the metaphors used by Levinas, such as motherhood, vulnerability, responsibility for the other, nearness, being touched. The accent on these dimensions also makes it possible to express the force of the social dynamic of the sacraments in a new way; in the aesthetic view of liturgy this is generally difficult to place.

2.4. The distinction between theatre and liturgy

Reference is often made to the numerous similarities between theatre and liturgy.[39] Indeed, theatre and liturgy have much in common. Both

---

[38] T. FREYER: *Sakrament – Transitus – Zeit – Transzendenz. Überlegungen im Vorfeld einer liturgisch-ästhetischen Erschliessung und Grundlegung der Sakramente* (Bonner Dogmatische Studien 20), Würzburg 1995.

[39] For this see G. LUKKEN: 'Wat heeft de liturgie met theater te maken? Een verheldering vanuit de semiotiek van de verschillen, overeenkomsten en raakvlakken', in LUKKEN & MAAS; *Luisteren tussen de regels* 134-166; IDEM: 'Semiotik des Raums in

can be conceived of as a syncretic object in which many 'languages' come together. Both work with a textual book in which texts and directions are present, and in both this script is secondarily adapted into a detailed scenario for the actual performance. Yet there are also differences. It is important to go more deeply into the similarities, differences, and points of interface. In doing this I will proceed from the present situation in which theatre has become autonomous, as a separate art. Included in this consideration of theatre are other art forms such as the concert, opera, ballet, cabaret, etc.

In theatre one find actors and spectators, opposite one another. They have different roles. The actors exercise influence on the spectators through the 'character' they play, letting that character be seen and heard by the spectators. The spectators from their side are not wholly passive. They watch and listen to what is performed in front of them and exercise influence on the actors by interventions before, during and after the performance. Moreover, the communication between the performers and the audience in a theatre differs from normal human communication. Everyday communication confirms reality as reality, however tragic it may be from time to time. The communication in theatre

Theater und Rituell: Unterschiede, Übereinkünfte und Berühungsebenen', in TH. NISSLMÜLLER & R. VOLP: *Raum als Zeichen. Wahrnehmung und Erkenntnis von Räumlichkeit*, Münster 1999, 55-70. See also E. POPPE: 'De toeschouwer en het spektakel', in *Versus. Tijdschrift voor film en opvoeringskunsten* 4 (1989) 2, 7-33; *Liturgie en theater*: *Werkmap (voor) liturgie* 25 (1991) 129-192; W. FRÜHWALD: 'Zwischen Märtyrerdrama und politischem Theater. Vom spannungsvollen Verhältnis der Kirche zur Theaterkultur', in *Theologie und Glaube* 85 (1995) 35-46; J. JEROENSE: *De speelse kerk. Een pleidooi voor theater in de kerk*, Zoetermeer 1995; K. KOCH: 'Liturgie und Theater. Theologische Fragmente zu einem vernachlässigten Thema', in *Stimmen der Zeit* 120 (1995) Heft 1 (Bnd.213), 3-16; BELL: *Ritual. Perspectives* (particularly 72-76 and 159-164); BELLIGER & KRIEGER (eds.): *Ritualtheorien* 12-14; *La liturgie, un théâtre?: La Maison-Dieu* (1999) no. 219; J. CHILDERS: *Performing the Word. Preaching as Theatre*, Nashville, NT 1998; M.A. FRIEDRICH: *Liturgische Körper. Der Beitrag der Schauspieltheorien und -techniken für die Pastoralästhetik*, Stuttgart 2001; B. REYMOND: *Théâtre et christianisme*, Genève 2002; G. LUKKEN: 'Gottesdienst als kulturelles Phänomen. Zukunftsperspektiven: Gottesdienst und Theater', in KERNER: *Gottesdienst und Kultur* 83-105. C. Bell emphasises especially the similarities, doing so from the fact that in both cases it is a matter of 'performance', that is to say, a realisation *in actu*. To my mind she gives too little consideration to what the differences are. That is also true for the otherwise relevant contributions by J. BESEMER: 'Ieder speelt zijn rol – ieder geeft zijn deel', in J. DE WIT a.o.: *Leve(n) de liturgie*, Baarn 1995, 56-67; IDEM: 'Theater en liturgie', in POST: *Een ander huis* 49-54.

is however entirely different. The actors and spectators are involved in a fictive reality that is evoked there. In the theatre people leave the natural world and enter a fictive space. This world rests on the suspension of disbelief by the spectator, which could be characterised as a form of denial: I know full well that this reality does not exist, that it is imaginary, but I still choose to believe in it. Here in the theatre I will act as if it is really true. Theatre thus assumes a radical separation from the natural world, a separation that involves both the cancelling of real time and actual space: a new order is created, based on reality and the natural world, which is however negated in one and the same breath, in denial. In this very characteristic way, one can say there is a disclosure that transcends everyday reality.

In this communication there is a tension between the actors and spectators, and this tension is essential for theatre. To put this another way: performers and spectators are closely linked with each other, but they must at the same time remain separated from one another. The stage and the auditorium are therefore spatial components which are on the one hand coordinated with and linked to one another, but on the other hand remain separated from one another. In the classic theatre this differentiation has its physical expression in the footlights, but it is also, in an conceptual way, found in street theatre. And even where this boundary is transgressed in avant-garde performances, and the performers intermingle with the audience, this is only a provocation: the transgression of the boundary only establishes its existence, even emphasises it.

Ritual has a different communicative structure. In contrast to theatre, in ritual there is a collective acting agent, which only secondarily can be further subdivided in various ways. It is not a matter, as in theatre, of beginning with a distinction between actors and audience, but all who are present are acting subjects. Although distinctions can also arise in which /letting be seen/ and /seeing done/ play a role, this element is in no way essential for the performance of ritual. Thus ritual can be characterised as an action in which all actively participate. In this sense, there is also no presence of a division between a stage and auditorium, as there is in a theatre building. There are no footlights. There can be distinctions within the space – that of the space where the central ritual action takes place, and that of the community – but this distinction is not intended to focus attention exclusively on the 'actors', while reducing those who are in the space for the community purely to spectators. This boundary is only relative, and furthermore can be overstepped.

The second characteristic is still more important. In ritual there is no denial of the natural world and transformation of it into a fictive reality. On the contrary: one accepts reality, but directs it, and thus penetrates into it, and breaks through it into the transcendent depths as a (to a large extent yet to be revealed) mystery in which one participates in and through the ritual. Thus there is no negation of the natural world, nor any denial of it, but a breaking open of the natural world and history to discover their ultimate, transcendent dimensions. With Speelman, one can characterise the communication structure of liturgy primarily as mystery.[40]

The acting subjects also perform in a different manner than theatre actors do. They step back, as it were, from that which they wish to evoke, and which is experienced as a pre-existent fact. This is expressed most strongly in the *recto tono* recitation of religious texts, which as it were in a implicit manner signals the underlying existence of another 'actual' voice and a 'true' discourse that is spoken by this voice. An interesting illustration of this is found in the list of abuses in the liturgy that was drawn up for the Council of Trent. Among these abuses was the all too theatrical performance in word and gesture during the pronouncement of the words of institution in celebrating the Eucharist.[41] In ritual a certain reticence is apparently desirable. Of course there are certainly gradations. For instance, in Christian liturgy the sermon is preached in

---

[40] W.M. SPEELMAN: 'The plays of our culture. A formal differentiation between theatre and liturgy', in *Jaarboek voor liturgie-onderzoek* 9 (1993) 65-91, especially 76-78.

[41] 'And there are those who, when they come to the words of consecration, with protruding lips slowly speak out the separate sounds, and bow their head forward over the Host and the chalice and move it back and forth and right and left in the form of a cross, puffing repeatedly, as if their play of gestures lent consecrating power to the words of our Lord, or as if the power of the consecration lay in such gesticulation; it is however the case that the words of consecration involved should be spoken over the Host and chalice in a simple way.'(Sunt qui, cum ad consecrationis verba perventum est, prominenti ore ad singulas voces admodum cunctanter expressas ita caput supra hostiam calicemque inclinent atque in crucis modum circumducant, subinde afflantes, ac si suis illi gestibus aliquam consecrandi virtutem illis Domini verbis attribuant aut tota consecrationis vis in similibus istiusmodi gesticulationibus esset collocata, cum tamen verba ipsa consecratoria simpliciter super hostiam en calicem respective proferre deberent) *Concilium Tridentinum* VIII, 916-921. See H. SCHMIDT: *Introductio in liturgiam occidentalem*, Rome 1959, 374.

another tone of voice than that used for the eucharistic prayer. And there is a difference between speaking *recto tono*, cantillation, the lyric tone of the Easter hymn *Exsultet*, the dramatic character of the *improperia* on Good Friday and the plaintive tone of the lamentations of Jeremiah in the Holy Week office. But still, in its essence authentic liturgical music is never theatrical music. And even the rhetoric of the sermon is subject to the rules of the ritual, and is different from a monologue in the theatre.

On the one hand, one thus finds quite a few points where liturgy and theatre touch upon one another, but on the other hand there are clear differences. They are two autonomous entities. Proceeding from this, it is possible to get a better perspective on two movements: that from the original unity of theatre and ritual toward their separation from one another, in which ritual too gradually moves toward being 'distanced', and the counter movement back toward their interweaving one with another. More insight into this can indirectly clarify what we have said about musealisation and aestheticisation.

First, I want to discuss the *movement from unity* between theatre and ritual *toward separation from one another*. In the original Greek drama, the mythical unity was still present. Its links with the cult were of the closest nature. The same was true for traditional Chinese theatre.[42] One also finds theatrical elements in ancient Christian liturgy, but these are subordinate to the ritual itself. For instance, in the Holy Week liturgy there is very emphatically the presence of /letting be seen/. One can think of the ritual of displaying the cross on Good Friday, of the portrayal of the passion narrative on Palm Sunday and Good Friday, in which the one is the narrator, a second the Christ figure, and the third represents the people, and of the Easter Vigil. In these there is a definitely /letting be seen/ and /seeing done/, but the characteristic element of ritual still remains dominant. The distinction between the performers and the viewers is transcended because all participate in the ritual in word and act. There remains a collective acting subject, which is compounded of the roles of priest, deacon, acolyte, choir and all other participants. All present answer; all take part in the veneration of the Cross, all light their candles at the Pascal candle. During the singing of the passion story all kneel for some time in silence after the singing of the text

[42] BELL: *Ritual. Perspectives* 164-166.

'He bowed his head, and died.' The collective active subject which is so characteristic for ritual is thus maintained. Also, the /letting be seen/ in the Holy Week liturgy – however expressive it may be – is not a theatrical enactment of the events, but a controlled and regulated act. The language, the acts, the movements, the singing are all stylised and restrained, in the manner of ritual. Finally, the participants do not focus on a fictive reality, as in theatre, but on the collective acceptance of a 'mystery'. The theatrical elements remain subordinate to the structural elements of ritual.

But also in Christian liturgy at a certain point the theatrical begins to become more autonomous, causing the ritual to withdraw from the mythic fabric, and become more distant. The celebration of the Eucharist in the Middle Ages is one example. One of the greatest changes in the history of the Eucharist was the introduction of the elevation, the raising and display of the Host in the middle of the eucharistic prayer, after the words of institution were pronounced. This radical innovation was already practised before 1068 by the monks of Cluny, and spread quickly throughout the Western church.[43] The central element in the celebration of the Eucharist now became the showing and contemplation of the Host. Moreover, during the Middle Ages the distinction between the priest and the people, between the altar and the nave, had gradually taken place. This division came to be strongly marked architecturally, certainly most emphatically by the construction of a rood screen and rood loft, a richly carved partition between the nave and chancel, across the whole width of the nave. The climax of the ritual of Eucharist was now the display of the Host and its contemplation by the faithful, which further was coupled with the strict separation between the priest as the celebrant and those present as spectators, to such a degree that Klauser speaks of the 'dissolution of the liturgical community'.[44] Viewing the Host was experienced as actual participation in the Eucharist, while people also began to perceive the whole of the celebration of Eucharist as a dramatic representation of the life of Jesus. One can question whether theatrical structures did not begin to dominate the liturgy here, and liturgy did not take on too many features that

---

[43] C. CASPERS: *De eucharistische vroomheid en het feest van Sacramentsdag in de Nederlanden tijdens de late Middeleeuwen*, Leuven 1992, especially 20-21; M. ANDRADE: *The History of the Elevation of the Host in the Mass of the Roman Rite* (Doctoral Thesis San Anselmo), Rome 1995.
[44] TH. KLAUSER: *Kleine abendländische Liturgiegeschichte*, Bonn 1965, 95 and 100.

are characteristic of the theatre. Greimas's remark is relevant in this context, that the liturgical reforms of the Second Vatican Council attempted to transform the Mass, which had become purely theatre, by once again constituting it as collective mythic event.[45]

The development of liturgical drama is also interesting in this connection. A good example of liturgical drama is the *Visitatio sepulchri*, which developed around the middle of the 10th century.[46] At the end of matins, right before it was concluded with the singing of the *Te Deum*, the liturgy switched over into a liturgical drama. A further breakthrough for liturgical drama took place in the 12th century with the *Officium peregrinorum*, which portrayed the encounter between Jesus and the two disciples on the Emmaus road (see Luke 24:13-35). It was characteristic of this liturgical drama that it was enacted in close connection with the liturgy itself. Those which fulfilled liturgical functions as it were changed their role and began to depict that which was being celebrated. Liturgy shifted over into theatre almost imperceptibly. Yet it remains important to keep this transition firmly in mind. In this liturgical drama /letting be seen/ and /seeing done/ is important. The celebrants are now acting a role. While in the celebration itself they still acted in such a way that they *represented in a ritual manner* the deeper Christian reality that is being celebrated, they now cross over into *impersonation and imitation*, the acting of an interpretative and depictive role. One must keep this distinction well in mind. The example which Kurvers gives illuminates this. When the worship leader in the Maundy Thursday liturgy washes the feet of twelve disciples, this is a dramatic form of liturgy, which one can compare with the forms that we have noted above. The ritual is preserved. But when in the *Officium peregrinorum* a priest appears who, in addition to his liturgical attire also wears a pilgrim's hat in order to realistically render the character of Christ in a play, we have the structural elements of theatre.[47]

In this same line of the 'distancing' of ritual, one can also think of what have been termed 'concert masses', that arose in the 19th century, and which have been characterised as 'ecclesiastical concerts with liturgical

[45] GREIMAS: 'Conditions d'une sémiotique du monde naturel' 80.
[46] G. KURVERS: 'Liturgisch drama in de Middeleeuwen: lessen voor nu', in *Tijdschrift voor Liturgie* 79 (1995) 178-196. See also among others J. BÄRSCH: 'Das Dramatische im Gottesdienst. Liturgiewissenschaftliche Aspekte der Osterfeiern und Osterspiele im Mittealter', in *Liturgisches Jahrbuch* 46 (1996) 1, 41-66.
[47] KURVERS: 'Liturgisch drama in de Middeleeuwen' 193.

accompaniment'.[48] For example, one sees posters with announcements like 'Next Sunday: performance of the mass by Mozart by so-and-so, with pontifical attendance by Bishop X'. It has also happened that after the intonation of the Gloria, the bishop, on his cathedra, has been offered a copy of the score.[49] Similar situations can also occur if the choir (adult of youth) gives in to the seductive allure of concert performances, or the family service becomes a performance by the children for their parents. To my mind, the mythic interconnectedness of ritual is also shattered when the leader performs in a narcissistic manner; in which case the accent comes to lie on the leader's own letting himself be seen,[50] or where people reward the choir with applause after the service.[51] A clear-cut example of turning ritual into a purely theatrical spectacle was the staging by performers of a solemn 'mass with three men' in the Paradiso in Amsterdam in 1984, as 'an immortal musical drama', 'a high point of our Western culture'.[52]

[48] O. URSPRUNG: *Die katholische Kirchenmusik*, Potsdam 1931, 219. See J.A. JUNG-MANN: *The Mass of the Roman Rite*, New York 1961, 111-117; IDEM: *Pastoral Liturgy*, London 1962, 80-89.

[49] K. BORNEWASSER: 'Is het waar dat de kerkmuziek van deze eeuw weinig of niets heeft meegenomen van de muzikale ontwikkelingen buiten de kerk?', in *Werkmap (voor) Liturgie* 26 (1992) 241.

[50] The semiotic description of a 'dandy' in DE KUYPER: *Pour une sémiotique spectac-ulaire* 126, is worth noting in this regard: the dandy is characterised by a narcissistic relation in which he is both destinator and his own destinee. He displays himself in order to be seen by both others – and himself. On more than one occasion I have encountered worship leaders who were in love with the sound of their own voice. In this connection see also E.C. KENNEDY: 'The Contribution of Religious Ritual to Psychological Balance', in *Concilium* 7 (1971) 2, 55: 'It is no secret that certain aspects of religious services attract the maladjusted. The Church is no stranger to the minister who worships himself rather than God. When neurotics use these ceremonies to satisfy their own psychological yearnings they can hardly be the developers of ritual which can contribute to the psychological balance of anyone else. They drain off quite narcissistically the energies of the ritual, letting it revolve around themselves more than anything else. It is not unusual to find persons of uncertain psychological maturity deeply interested in the liturgy precisely because it offers them such an opportunity to make themselves the centre of all eyes, the arbiter of a ritual which has a private meaning and frequently unconscious for them. This neurotic orientation separates them from the community which they are supposed to be leading in worship.'

[51] This applause almost automatically calls up the image of a concert hall. Thus, to my mind, we are not dealing here with applause as one found it in the ancient church, for instance with Augustine during his sermons, nor with that found to this very day in the liturgies of congregations in Africa and other countries of the South.

[52] T. OOSTVEEN: 'De schoonheid van de liturgie zonder alle rechtse praatjes', in *De Tijd* March 9, 1984, 53-58.

But in addition to the movement from the original unity of theatre and ritual toward the gradual separation of the two, one can also observe a *movement in the opposite direction*: the theatre or concert becomes intensified into ritual. The separation between liturgy and theatre can to a greater or lesser extent be eliminated, as ritual qualities begin to dominate, and the original unity is approached once again. Turner pointed regularly to the ritual aspects of theatre,[53] and Schechner developed a theory of performance precisely in connection with the theme of ritual and theatre.[54] Grimes has also been occupied with experimental theatre as an example of ritualisation. Ritual theatre was practised in the most explicit manner by the Pole Grotowski (1933-1999).[55] He searched for a form of theatre which strove for extreme austerity. In this connection Grotowski spoke of 'poor theatre'.[56] He has exercised great influence on contemporary theatre directors. In the case of ritual theatre, what is really as such an autonomous art jumps in the direction of mythic participation. To my mind this also happened during Holy Week in 1998, at the Moses and Aaron Church in Amsterdam, when all of those present could join in singing Bach's St. Matthew Passion (with the exception of the parts of the evangelist). That awakened the realisation that the St. Matthew Passion, like Bach's cantatas, was originally composed for liturgy. The Good Friday liturgy in the Lutheran Tomas Kirche in Leipzig consisted of singing and listening to the Passion. When this Passion was rediscovered in the 19th century, it began to be performed as a concert.[57] In my view, one can also consider the oratoria by Oosterhuis

[53] V. TURNER: *Dramas, Field and Metaphors. Symbolic Action in Human Society*, Ithaca 1974; IDEM: *The Anthropology of Performance*, New York 1987; IDEM: *Das Ritual. Struktur und Anti-Struktur*, Frankfurt am Main 1989; IDEM: *Vom Ritual zum Theater. Der Ernst des menschlichen Spiels*, Franfurt/Main 1989.

[54] R. SCHECHNER: *Essays on Performance Theory 1970-1976*, New York 1977; IDEM: *Between Theater and Anthropology*, Philadelphia 1985; IDEM: *Performance Theory*, New York/London 1988; IDEM: *The Future of Ritual*, London/New York 1993; R. SCHECHNER & W. APPEL (eds.): *By means of Performance: Intercultural Studies of Theatre and Ritual*, Cambridge 1995. See also R. SCHECHNER: *Theater – Anthropologie. Spiel und Ritual im Kulturvergleich*, Reinbeck 1990, particularly there: Ritual und Theater: Rekonstruktion von Verhalten (included in: BELLIGER & KRIEGER (eds.): *Ritualtheorien* 415-433).

[55] GRIMES: *Beginnings in Ritual Studies* 164 ff.; IDEM: *Ritual Criticism* 115-118; IDEM: *Deeply into the Bone* 123-125; L. WOLFORD & R. SCHECHNER (eds): *The Grotowski Sourcebook*, London 1997.

[56] J. GROTOWSKI: *Towards a Poor Theatre*, New York 1968.

[57] B. HEFFELS: 'De Matthäuspassion: opgetrokken rond de kruiskreet van Christus', in *Univers* 27 (1996) 10-11.

and Oomen, such as the *Klein Kerstoratorium* (Little Christmas oratorio), the *Nieuwe Kerstoratorium* (New Christimas oratorio), *Het verhaal of een levende* (The story of one who lives) and *Het lied van Lazarus en de rijke vrek* (The song of Lazarus and the rich miser)[58] as being along the same lines as this ritual performance of the St. Matthew Passion. They are closely linked with the core of ritual.

It can also happen that the museal jumps in the direction of mythic participation. On Easter Monday, 1998, in an exhibition space in Rotterdam's Boijmans Van Beuningen Museum, an ecumenical Easter service was held in which the theme of art and belief was given shape.[59] Large tapestries on the theme of justice, designed by contemporary artists and intended for the newly constructed law court in Den Bosch, were being shown. A prayer service was held in the midst of these tapestries. According to the worship leader Marcel Barnard, the intention of this was not to raise the museum to the status of a temple; it was, rather, to place a liturgical exclamation mark at certain aspects of culture. That Christ, as one who was condemned and crucified, effected the acquittal of mankind in his own way, was central. This was a fully formed Christian ritual in a museum. Something similar had already been done in Australia.[60] R. Crumlin organised exhibitions on religious themes in contemporary art in various museums.[61] The exhibitions took place as collaborations among her, the artists and the visitors. Impressions, interpretations and memories were exchanged in open communication. This input was then framed by a ritual observance which integrated what had been evoked. The opposite form is also possible. Modern religious art can be shown in a church building, and liturgical celebrations held in relation to such exhibitions. An example of this was the liturgical celebration with the exhibition of contemporary art 'Met de dood voor de ogen' (Looking death in the eyes), which was held in the Grote Kerk in

[58] Editions of the Stichting Leerhuis en Liturgie in Amsterdam.

[59] M. BARNARD: 'Een kerkdienst in een museum', in BARNARD & POST (eds.): *Ritueel bestek* 56-62; A. GROND: 'Het museum is geen tempel', in *De Bazuin* 81 (1998) (April 3), 32; A. AUGUSTUS-KERSTEN: 'Liturgie in het hol van de leeuw?', in *Eredienstvaardig* 16 (2000) 84-88; E. BEENDER: 'Een vonk kan overspringen. Kerkelijke vieringen in het museum', in *Vieren. Tijdschrift voor wie werkt aan liturgie* 1 (2003) 4, 8-12.

[60] H. LOMBAERTS: 'Weerbaar of weerloos? Godsdienstige tradities in de hedendaagse maatschappij', in LOMBAERTS & BOEVE (eds.): *Traditie en initiatie* 105-107.

[61] R. CRUMLIN: *Images of religion in Australian art*, Kensington 1988; R. CRUMLIN & A. KNIGHT: *Aboriginal art and spirituality*, North Blackburn 1991.

Leeuwarden in 1991.[62] In Cologne Mennekes organised his exhibitions of the work of contemporary artists creating religious art in the late-Gothic Sankt Peter Kirche, and tried to integrate these in the liturgical celebrations.[63]

The movement toward the original unity can also be found in the 'happening' and the pop concert. On the one hand, there one encounters the theatrical elements of /letting be seen/ and /seeing done/, /letting be heard/ and /hearing done/, and the evocation of a fictive reality. On the other hand, they are characterised by mythic elements and a role played by the audience, of a nature which permits one to ask if this audience do not become in part performers themselves, as acting subjects, so that the characteristic qualities of ritual begin to dominate. This new development appeared especially from the 1950s on.[64] It came to be seen particularly clearly in the Woodstock Music and Arts Fair, from August 15 through 17, 1969, where 400,000 fans listened to 32 bands and soloists. People shared hopes and expectations, and enacted the myth of a world ruled by peace and love. The participants did not sit on chairs, but grouped themselves around the stage. In this way people created a strong, mutual community. In later pop concerts this mutual community and active participation was reinforced by the ritual of clapping to the music, raising arms and hands in the air, joining hands, swaying to the rhythm, holding up lighted cigarette lighters, and singing refrains repeatedly. For instance, as the key song at the Live Aid rock festival in 1995 people sang the mythic text about a different, better world, 'We are the world, we are the children...' Something of this sort can also occur at concerts of the classics, such at the last Night of the Proms. Important connections for youth liturgy in our culture are to be found here.

[62] T. SCHOENMAKER: 'Vieren 'Met de dood in de ogen'', in *Jaarboek voor liturgie-onderzoek* 8 (1992) 153-168; R. STEENSMA: 'De receptie van de tentoonstelling 'Met de dood in de ogen' in de Grote Kerk te Leeuwarden', in *Jaarboek voor liturgie-onderzoek* 8 (1992) 169-204; see also G.D.J. DINGEMANS, J. KRONENBURG & R. STEENSMA: *Kaïn of Abel. Kunst in de kerkdienst: twee vijandige broeders?*, Zoetermeer 1999.

[63] F. MENNEKES: *Kein schlechtes Opium. Das Religiöse im Werk von Alfred Hrdlicka*, Stuttgart 1987; IDEM: *Faith. Das Religiöse im Werk von James Brown*, Stuttgart 1989; IDEM: *Altarbild, Geist und Körper. Eine Wettbewerbsausstellung des 90. Deutschen Katholikentags*, Berlin 1990; F. MENNEKES & J. RÖHRING: *Peter Drake*, Köln 1990; IDEM: *Crucifixus. Das Kreuz in der Kunst unserer Zeit*, Freiburg/Basel/Wien 1994. See also LOMBAERTS: 'Weerbaar of weerloos?' 107 and IDEM: 'Kunst zonder religie? Religie zonder kunst?', in LOMBAERTS, MAAS & WISSINK (eds.): *Beeld en gelijkenis* 17-27.

[64] K.H. REICH: 'Rituals and social structure'.

Finally, I wish to point to the possibility of *a double perspective*. It can be that the ritual which is being performed is appropriated in a distanced way. I found an example of this in a review of the 1994 Musica Sacra festival in Maastricht. There one can read,

> Every year the Musica Sacra festival, which took place last weekend, draws two kinds of audiences. The one half come for the Musica, the other half for the Sacra. The first group comes, sometimes from afar, to the basilica of Our Lady, St. Servaas church and a couple of others, to listen to magnificent music with, more or less coincidentally, a religious dimension. Some are surprised by the liturgical entourage, and walk away upset before the first sign of the cross is made. The rest snicker at the kneeling, let the sermon go in one ear and out the other, look on fascinated at the spectacle with the candles, bells, wine and bread that is going on up on the chancel, and become annoyed with the coughing churchgoers who are disrupting 'their' music. The second group, generally folks from Maastricht, go as always to their Sunday church service and there coincidentally hear church music which they otherwise would not go out of their way to hear. They sing along with the Gregorian songs and accept their strange guests, so long as they conform a bit to what is going on. This mixture of music lovers and church-goers gives Musica Sacra a character all of its own, which certainly does not harm the music. On the contrary, the naturalness with which at least a part of the 'concerts' are embedded in the liturgy lends the music a degree of authenticity. The tranquil medieval melodies for one voice and the polyphony from the Renaissance receive an extra dimension if they rise together with incense.[65]

Apparently this liturgy lends itself to two attitudes: the completely a-liturgical attitude of the concert, and the liturgical.

---

[65] P. LUTTIKHUIS: 'Musica sacra zorgt voor verdeeldheid in Maastrichtse kerken', in *NRC Handelsblad* September 19, 1994, 8.

CHAPTER 6

INDUCTIVE AND ADEQUATE LITURGY

If Christian liturgy is to have credibility in our culture, it will have to take seriously certain achievements of modernity and postmodernism. This is true first and foremost for the fact that in our culture the stress lies on the here and now, on the search for meaning in the midst of our history and in the midst of all contingency. Christian liturgy will have to take into account the fact that the great ideological stories have been disposed of. Moreover, it will have to accommodate itself to the pluriformity of convictions and styles: the relation people have with Christian religion can differ considerably, as can spirituality. This will all have radical consequences for Christian ritual in our culture. Successively, I will go into the importance of small things and small stories, the need for an inductive and adequate liturgy, and the importance of the ritual expression of the *praeambula fidei*.

1. THE IMPORTANCE OF SMALL THINGS AND SMALL STORIES

For many there is a growing conviction that the search for meaning, here and now, in the midst of all contingency, is only possible if a certain 'decompression' takes place. It is not possible to conduct such a search with a constantly overloaded agenda and frantic consumption of free time. Nor will the search for meaning be satisfied by seeking out the extravagant and shocking. The extraordinary seems rather to be concealed in the ordinary, in commonplace things and scenes, in the conduct of the child and the adult, in nature and its primal elements of earth, wind, fire and water, in the unfolding of things, in the objects around us. Life is full of scenes in which the perspective can jump. For those who look candidly, there is much that is meaningful and unexpected to be seen.[1] It is even as Herzberg wrote of the common fly:

---

[1] GREIMAS: *De l'imperfection* 89-98 (L'attente de l'inattendu).

This is your life, fly:
what cannot be caught
is circled. Only
stopovers,
no set route,
tasting and sampling,
little discoveries,
never putting down roots.[2]

And of man,

Rising from the chaos of sheets
and premonitions, curtains
open, the radio on.
Suddenly there was Scarlatti
clearly to be heard.
Now all is as it has become,
everything is as it is.
Although it will perhaps
finally somehow be straightened out.[3]

Another author has written,

I was alone, and had spent some time sitting quietly in the shade reading,
but now, having become one with the tranquil environment, I was just
dozing off. When I opened my eyes again, there sat a tiny black fly on my
open paperback. It was smaller than the letters... Shortly before... it must
have been flying around in the vicinity, and suddenly noted the nice white
pages with his wonderful compound eyes, and immediately executed a
perfect turn and a faultless landing. Without taking notice of me, he now
marched self-assured on his six mini-feet, zigzagging at a steady pace over
my book, stopping for a moment here or there to smell or taste it. I suddenly realised that this at first sight insignificant little being possessed a
differentiated gastric system, from mouth to anus, with all the elements
necessary for digestion, that there was a minuscule heart that beat to
pump the blood around, that it had kidneys, that its branched tracheal
system took care of respiration, that hundreds of muscles made the movement of its feet, wings, head, antennae, mouth parts and such possible,
and further that the intensity of its metabolism and the supply of energy
in the tiny organism changed constantly in relation to its activities, such as
walking, flying, sitting still and looking around... that this tiny animal

[2] J. HERZBERG: *Doen en laten. Een keuze uit de gedichten*, Amsterdam 1994, 96.
[3] HERZBERG: *Doen en laten* 15.

also had a nervous system that linked together all the parts of its body with thin nerve fibres and, constantly activating or restraining them, controlled and guided its movements. The nerve centre of this whole body consisted of minuscule brains, where all the signals from the sensory organs came together and were weighed up against one another with lightning speed... After I had reflected on all this, I carefully stretched out my hand and slowly moved my forefinger in the direction of my visitor. He saw me coming, and when I had gotten close enough, he spread his wings and flew away. I never saw him again.[4]

And then there is the story of the hospital patient:

Before an operation, I had to have some x-rays made. I was wheeled to the x-ray department in my hospital bed. Once there I climbed out of the bed rather stiffly. The x-ray nurse asked that I take a seat on a chair, and went immediately to get a pillow to support my back. The same photos had to be made two times in succession. Thin needles were inserted into my body, and I had to sit stock still in the x-ray machine for a quarter of an hour in a highly uncomfortable position. At a certain point it all became too much for me, and I couldn't help but emit a light sigh. Suddenly I felt how the nurse softly stroked my dangling hand in comfort. This evidence of empathy did so much good for me that I will not quickly forget it.[5]

This story reminds me of what the Dutch author Gerard Reve wrote of Sister Immaculata, who for all of thirty-four years washed, changed and fed crippled old people.[6] There can also be an opening out of perspective in stories of suffering, as they become stories of comfort, courage, submission, compassion, of perseverance. People derive life from narratives. The eclipse of the great, legitimising ideological stories in no way means that narratives disappear. Quite on the contrary: when the great stories, in their arrogance, dominated everything, countless little stories could not be heard. But the millions of small

---

[4] J. LEVER: 'Klein, onzienlijk, onvoorstelbaar', in DE VISSCHER (ed.): *Mosterd zaadjes van het bestaan* 23-24.
[5] 'Ligt u lekker?' in *NRC Handelsblad* July 8, 1995, Zaterdags bijvoegsel (Saturday Supplement), 2.
[6] GERARD REVE: *Verzamelde gedichten*, Amsterdam 1987, 80, in his poem 'Roeping' (Calling): 'Sister Immaculata, who for all of thirty-four years now / has washed and changed crippled old people / and fed them their meals, / will never see her name in the papers. / But every unwashed gorilla disrupting traffic / with a placard saying that he is for this or against that / gets to see his mug on the six o'clock news. / Good thing there's a God, isn't it?'

stories that form the fabric of everyday life now have their chance.[7] We tell them to one another, privately, and also publicly, via radio and television. They are small stories, generally open-ended, a constant search for meaning, repeated over and over again. The search for meaning always begins with the here and now, in ordinary life, with love and pain. Some stories are more appealing, reveal more, become scenic overlooks, so to speak, to which people return time and again. The Bible is not one story, but thousands of stories, both in the Old and the New Testament – ordinary stories, often at the same time revealing that which is hidden in the ordinary. The Bible is not a finished book of doctrine, a *Summa theologica*. It constantly approaches things from different angles, and what it is about is always being revealed in different and surprising ways, but at the same time is also concealed. The stories are never entirely transparent. They provoke the reader. Scripture is not one great story, but a book in fragments, which at every turn perhaps momentarily reveal a bit of their depth. Scripture also always begins with the here and now, in history, in what happens to people in their larger and smaller stories. That is the way in which the history of God with his people is told, up through the story – or better, the stories – of Jesus of Nazareth. The stories are always an 'open story'.[8] This in essence is also the 'narrative style' and the 'way of doing' in liturgy. There too it is not a question of doctrine that dots every i and crosses every t, of ideology, of truth delivered ready for use, of the great legitimising story of orthodoxy, but of fragments, experienced again and again, of orthodoxy in the sense of true worship.

---

[7] F. LYOTARD: *Le différend*, Paris 1983. In connexion with the importance of 'little things', see also S. SEXSON: *Gewoon heilig. De sacraliteit van het alledaagse*, Zoetermeer 1997.

[8] For the concept of the 'open story' in connection with speaking of the Christian God in the context of postmodernism, see L. BOEVE: *Spreken over God in 'open verhalen'. De theologie uitgedaagd door het postmoderne denken* (Doctoral Thesis), Leuven 1995. See also IDEM: 'Theologie na het christelijke grote verhaal. In het spoor van Jean-François Lyotard', in *Bijdragen. Tijdschrift voor filosofie en theologie* 55 (1994) 269-295; IDEM: 'Een postmoderne theologie van het 'open verhaal'', in *Onze Alma Mater* 50 (1996) 210-238; IDEM: 'Initiatie en traditie in een postmoderne samenleving. Een theologische verheldering', in *Verbum* 64 (1997) 7-8, 128-135; IDEM: 'Method in Postmodern Theology. A Case Study', in L. BOEVE & J.C. RIES: *The Presence of Transcendence. Thinking Sacrament in a Postmodern Age*, Leuven 2001, 3-17. See also BLOECHL & VAN DEN BOSSCHE: 'Postmoderniteit, theologie en sacramententheologie', especially 40-48. At the end of this section I will discuss the void that goes with this open story.

Liturgy is the story of our repeatedly remembering, confessing, acknowledging, entreating, lamenting, praising, searching and singing in the past and present, looking to the future, as a people who are travelling with their God – a sometimes understandable, but just as often absent or difficult God, an elusive friend. 'What faithful people picture concerning the meaning of their existence, what meaning they will give to their life, what they believe regarding their future, that is all represented in the liturgy in stories, songs and prayers.'[9] Essentially, a culture that cultivates an interest in the here and now and for the small stories, is a favourable time for liturgy.[10] The stories told in it are stories which, despite the division of social life into many sectors, appear to be able to penetrate all these sectors. Even the 'great story' of the market ultimately does not seem to be able to withstand them.

Inculturation of liturgy in our culture thus has consequences for the shape of the liturgy which has been passed down to us. In what follows I will go into the main characteristics of this shape, which is in a process of intensive development. The general characteristics of ritual in our culture have already been discussed.[11] Here I will deal more specifically with the form of Christian liturgy. It is not possible to sketch a complete picture here. As is always the case in the history of liturgy, that will only be possible in retrospect. Here it is our purpose to indicate several main lines trends which appear to be playing major roles.

2. INDUCTIVE LITURGY

The old Requiem Mass was an impressive liturgy.[12] It was a liturgy which was able to give form to the feelings of that stark moment in a dignified manner. The Latin funeral service had a design that was acceptable across the generations. One need think only of the penetrating opening song, 'Lord, give them eternal rest, and may eternal light

[9] H. WEGMAN: *Liturgie in de geschiedenis van het christendom*, Kampen 1991, 9.
[10] In this connexion see D.A. STOSUR: 'Liturgy and (Post)Modernity: A Narrative Response to Guardini's Challenge, in *Worship* 77 (2003) 22-41. Narrative is an important key to both individual and collective participation in liturgy. In Christian liturgy our stories have their ultimate foundation in the *narratio* of the Easter mystery.
[11] Part 3, Chapter 3, 3.
[12] H. FORTMANN: 'Latijnse uitvaart', in FORTMANN: *Hoogtijd* 103-124.

shine upon them', and the closing song, 'May the angels accompany you to paradise'. For centuries the Roman rite marked the departure of the dead with this ritual, superbly comforting those left behind, although one must add that there was also a strong strand of threat and judgement running through the Requiem Mass. It cannot be excluded that some may have experienced more threat than comfort. Whatever the case, the strength of this ritual was that it could be performed without regard to persons. The ritual might be celebrated more solemnly for one than for another, but as such it was the same for everyone. The Latin funeral service was a monumental, prescribed and preformed liturgy. Everyone could make use of it. It could be performed despite the ever-changing circumstances in the world and the different life histories and the varying destinies of individuals. The uniformity and ahistoricity of the ritual was not experienced as a problem. Men simply experienced a certain distinction between the profane and the sacred. It was a liturgy which fit in a cosmic world-view.

One can characterise this liturgy as a *deductive* liturgy: that is to say, as a liturgy from above. The general was applied to the particular. The element of transcendence was expressed as a transcendence from above to below, a sort of trans-*de*-scendence. The descending motion was emphasised. This deductive nature was reinforced still more to the extent that the liturgy became more fixed, which was particularly the case in the last four centuries.

Over against this deductive liturgy stands what I would qualify as *inductive* liturgy. This liturgy works in the opposite direction: it begins with the specific and moves from there to the general. In the case we have been discussing, what is of prime importance would no longer be *the* Requiem Mass, but *this* specific funeral liturgy. Inductive liturgy begins where people are, and not from the other side. It begins with *these* people, who are confronted with *this* death. The next of kin and the deceased have their own history. Pastoral help takes this into account. In pastoral counselling the pastor is not someone who stands over against, but someone who stands next to those who are confronted with the death. He must so to speak constantly keep ahead, searching for the right word or gesture at the right moment. Liturgy stands within the broader context of this pastoral activity. There too the pastor must work in an inductive manner. He will have to deal with questions about meaning. Sometimes he will say what those present would want to say, but dare not.[13] He will have to help those present to move on, to open themselves up, so that in their need they can come to terms with things. In this what is important is deliverance in the light of Christian faith, in the name of the gospel. However, the gospel requires authenticity, and it would detract from it if the pastor would in these circumstances move directly to proclamation of only the pure Gospel.[14] So he tries to give form to a liturgy that fits with *this* situation. From the particular he moves to the general, from here to the other side. The transcendent is gradually discovered and revealed, as it were, from the here and now. There is a rising line, a trans-*a*-scendence. From the particularity of this situation, what was already done before is reappropriated. After all, in inductive liturgy too the ritual element of repetition remains of essential importance. Only, the repetition is less literal, it happens in a freer and more creative manner. This inductive liturgy fits better with our social-cultural situation than deductive liturgy would, seeing as in our society the emphasis lies on the *saeculum*, on individual and collective history with all its weal and woe. Liturgy cannot be separated from that. It is included in the dynamic of history. It can not be static. History implies ever again different, one-off, unique events which demand illumination, and perspective. One can only transfigure and transfinalise them if one begins with the here and now. We are dealing with open stories that offer the here and now the possibility of discovering the other, and the Other. That is the widely shared feeling of our culture.

Let me make this more concrete. In my homiletics course, I empha-sised to the students that they should start from concrete situations. Shortly thereafter one of the students delivered a sermon on the story of the man born blind. He began the sermon with a description of blind-ness. It was a general description. I tried to improve it, and said how I would have done it myself. I would have spoken of how the blind always walk by feel, seeking for the light. To this the students responded that this was equally general. Then came what was to my mind a good sug-gestion. Someone said, 'I know a blind man who lives near me. He is a

---

[13] W. BERGER: 'Uitvaart na zelfdoding. Een vraaggesprek met de voorganger', in *Praktische Theologie* 7 (1980) 351.

[14] J. BOMMER: 'Die Verkündigungsaufgabe der Kasualien Taufe, Hochzeit und Beerdigung', in F. FURGER a.o.: *Liturgie als Verkündigung* (Theologische Berichte 6), Zürich/Einsiedeln/Köln 1977, 195.

medical doctor. I often see him passing by, his cane out in front of him. He always wears dark glasses. He carries his head slightly tipped back, as though searching for the light. That affects me deeply: being a doctor, taking upon oneself a full practice, and being blind.' Beginning like this, there is more chance of touching your listeners. You launch off from the unique, from singularity. The general has been said a thousand times, while the unusual is new and inexhaustible. Thus the Easter mystery is all the more fascinating to the degree that it is given shape not in its generality, but in its specificity. With regard to liturgy, this can happen first of all in the sermon. Let me give an example from a funeral liturgy that I found very striking. A pastor had a conversation with an incurably ill man, not long before his death. The conversation went as follows:

> Pastor: Do you have contact with the other patients?
> Patient: Yes, but those contacts are very superficial. There is one doctor who is hospitalised here who I can talk with, though. But, yeah, there is one disadvantage to that: it's God, God and still more God.
> Pastor: That annoys you?
> Patient: You've got to be careful about that.
> *There follows the story, bit by bit, about how at his work he sometimes had quarrels that started over questions about religion.*
> Pastor: You think it a bit strange that we have not yet spoken about God here, while it's a bit in my job description? What are your expectations from me?
> Patient: That's something different. You're not here to sell me something.
> Pastor: I don't know what I would have to sell to you; you don't seem to have any need…
> Patient: No.
> Pastor: Any need of discussions or such. Because that is always the way it began?
> Patient: Yes, that's so.
> Pastor: You are totally alone before a wall, and you can not look over it, but have to go through it.
> Patient: No, you can't see what is behind it. There is no answer to that.
> Pastor: Would it be all right if I sort of wandered up to that wall with you – as far as that can be?
> Patient: Yes… yes, that would be o.k.
> Pastor: Then we could agree there what to raise in our conversations.
> Patient: O.K.
> *Silence*
> Pastor: You are tired? Is that it?
> Patient: Yes.

Pastor: Shall I come back the day after tomorrow?
Patient: Yes… please. Until then… and thank you.[15]

Several days later the patient died. The pastor had sat by his side in silence one more time, while he was in a coma. In the funeral sermon in a personal manner the pastor involved sketched how this man had lived and suffered. But with the hint of reconciliation in this moment of farewell, he immediately went on to formulations such as 'God is the God of the living, and not of the dead', and so forth, reporting nothing of the last conversation. Why was it not said that this man had difficulty with God, that he did not see God as a hackneyed word or subject for discussions, that he saw death as a wall before him,[16] and was pleased to have a pastor beside him, to accompany him as far as possible? Thereafter the pastor could have expressed his own lived faith: would this man not be surprised, now that he has seen behind the wall, that he had fought the good fight? And he could have asked the relatives and friends if they could now follow him in this faith.

These are just fragmentary suggestions, by which I want to make clear how the Easter mystery can be evoked in the here and now, at this probing moment of the funeral liturgy.

What is true for the sermon is *mutatis mutandis* true for the rest of the liturgy. One thinks first of all of the opening words. A striking example can be found in the funeral of a young woman who had committed suicide.[17] The service was held in the student parish in Nijmegen. A whole spectrum of society was present: the distressed and shocked, believers, doubters and unbelievers, with all degrees of love and involvement with the deceased. In his words of welcome the worship leader touched upon the feelings of those present thus:

> We have come together here because we feel ties to one another. We are here this morning to do the last thing that we can. We have come together in this church. For some among us a space like this is familiar, safe, natural.

---

[15] This is a verbatim transcription from the clinical-pastoral work of Servaas Bellemakers.

[16] In crisis situations people often use symbols to express themselves. They speak then of feeling empty, being in the desert, standing in front of a wall, feeling caged, bound or trapped. This is also distinctly the case with the dying. See P. ZUIDGEEST: 'Mensen leven van beelden', in *Praktische Theologie* 8 (1981) 302.

[17] BERGER: 'Uitvaart na zelfdoding'.

That is good, a feeling like that. Others here will remember it from the past, from a time that lies behind you, from your childhood. Then it was warm, full of character, but now it just doesn't fit any longer, it has lost its interest. That feeling is o.k. too. And perhaps there are also those among us who are embittered, rancorous, full of pain at what the church and faith has done to them. That is not a problem. At this moment everything flows together, because we are first of all here for her, because of what she did for us, that which she meant for each of us personally. Since we learned of it, we have each been intensely confronted with life and death, antitheses which go hand in hand. Her choice has shocked us, touched us, saddened us, angered us. That irrevocable event leaves us powerless.
Why? What was she seeking? What were we unable to give her? How can we convince each other that you did what could be done? So many questions, so many emotions tangled up together.
Coming together here, we have no answer. I don't think that anyone among us expects such an answer.
First and foremost, we are here because of her. But also for ourselves. We comfort and encourage one another by singing, by listening, by – perhaps with great resistance – doing something that seems like praying.

This hour, concentrating around memories of her, will nourish our hope that life is ineradicable, irrepressible, as a child that is born. These flowers, these candles, the incense we burn bears witness to this expectation. She loved these things; through them she was open to the ineffable. May we also be open in the same way during this hour.

Then there are also prayers in which one can take *this* death and *these* survivors into account. But in closing I would want to note the non-verbal elements which because of their presentivity can have a very penetrating inductive effect: flowers, candles, incense, the elements which, it is said in these introductory words, the deceased loved, and in which she found an opening to transcendence. There are also the furnishings of the space, the way light falls, the quiet, the placement of the coffin (the central symbol in the funeral liturgy), kneeling before the coffin as a gesture expressing the uniqueness of this person and respect for him or her as a continuing mystery, friends or family acting as pallbearers, prayer cards, the roles in which and through which those present express their involvement, etc. Even when one sticks with the official order of service, there is still plenty of room for inductive elements.

There is the counselling model for assisting individuals. It seeks to do as much justice as possible to the peculiar feelings and views of the other, as they learn to help themselves. The counsellor attempts to activate an internal dialogue within the counselee, who must begin to listen to themselves. In that way the person will learn to find a way out of their own problems. That model can also – obviously with the necessary alterations – be applied to sermons.[18] In such a sermon one tries to bring into being a relation between the listener's feelings and the Christian message. The listeners enter into internal dialogue with themselves, at the level of faith, to move forward on their own. This model is an important aid for inductive liturgy. In an outstanding way it does justice to the particular feelings and opinions of others. Therefore precisely this model is also suitable for bringing together persons from various views and with varying expectation patterns. Moreover, it is a gradual model. In and through what is evoked in those present, the perspective gradually shifts and disclosure arises. Here too there is the rising line of trans-ascendence, which breaks through one-dimensionality, and everyone can descry the further horizon in their own manner. In the examples which I have just given of the opening words and the sermon from funeral services, it is really the counselling model which is being applied. To my mind, a classical example of a liturgically styled counselling model is to be found in the following opening lines of a 1968 Christmas celebration by Oosterhuis, *Heden en hier en in die dagen* (*Presently and here and in these days*).[19] One realises that with inductive liturgy the opening of the service must be very precisely formulated. With an eye to disclosure, Oosterhuis employs somewhat alienating effects:

Recently a Dutch submission
was declared the most artistic news photo
of 1967:
'One-and-a-half years old, one-and-a-half years hungry'.

Recently hunger strikes took place
in The Hague, Venlo, Maastricht,
Dordrecht, Doetinchem, Zutphen.
Today and tomorrow a number of students in Utrecht
are holding a hunger strike, protesting against
insufficient aid for the hungry of the world.

---

[18] E. LINN: *Preaching as counseling. The unique Method of Hary Emerson Fosdick*, Valley Forge 1966; T. ODEN: *Kerygma and counseling*, Philadelphia 1966; W. BERGER: 'Preken en counselen', in *Tijdschrift voor Pastorale Psychologie* 4 (1972) 35-38.

[19] H. OOSTERHUIS: *Bid om* vrede, Utrecht 1966, 64-65.

Per year our world spends
about two-hundred-fifty million dollars
on weapons.
That is half a million dollars per minute.

On the Oude Zijds Voorburgwal in Amsterdam
an anti-Christmas crèche has been set up.
It's made of torched Christmas trees,
and instead of carols there are audio fragments
from the Vietnam Tribunal.

Napalm is a simple compound
of benzene and a slow burning
syrupy sort of petroleum.
Today napalm is classified
as a conventional weapon.

The tune of our opening song
is not difficult.
Everyone can sing along
as loud as they want.
The text reads,
'Today you shall behold his glory'.

Tomorrow one-hundred-eighty thousand children
will be born, about forty-five in Amsterdam.
Our help is in the Name of the Lord
Who made the heavens and the earth.

In Amsterdam there are
twenty-two thousand guest workers.
In Amsterdam there are
about a hundred and ten thousand senior citizens,
twelve percent of the population.
The Salvation Army runs its Christmas aid programme
all year round.

Presently, today and tomorrow:
conflicts in Israel.
In Bethlehem:
demonstrations by Palestinians
who want to return to their homes.

Grace be with you, and peace,
anyway,

from God the Father, who created us,
but not to mangle each other;
and from Jesus, his Son;
and from the Holy Spirit, dwelling in us.

Hear the glad tidings:
Here is your God.

Let us now sing the opening song,
'Today you shall behold his glory,
here is your God.'
Our Saviour is born today,
Christ the Lord.

The difference between deductive and inductive liturgy can be seen
clearly when one compares the opening of the Good Friday liturgy from
before the Second Vatican Council with that written by Oosterhuis in
1986. After the priest and his assistants have thrown themselves face
down on the ground for several moments (the attitude of prostration),
this prayer follows immediately in the old Good Friday liturgy:

God
through the suffering of the Lord
You have freed us from death,
which oppressed man
since the first sin.
Sanctify us,
who still bear
the image of Adam in us;
pour out your grace
which offers the prospect of heaven,
so that we begin to be like unto your Son
and become an image of Jesus Christ,
our Lord.

Oosterhuis's Good Friday liturgy begins however with the here and now,
in the counselling model:

We have come together
to remember
the death of Jesus of Nazareth.
In the 'thirties...
he was turned over to the foreign occupying forces...

condemned to death
by the Roman governor Pontius Pilate,
was executed as a rebellious slave...
With the gospel of the resurrection
was spread the delusion
that the Jewish people
were guilty of the death of Jesus
and rejected of God.
And through the centuries
this delusion has prompted men
to anti-Semitism and persecution.
In our century we saw and heard
how, with the cooperation of many Christians,
millions of Jews were taken away,
ill-treated and starved in camps,
driven together in gas chambers.
This hour we remember all the slaughtered Jews,
sisters and brothers of Jesus of Nazareth,
killed as he was –
how they were carried to the block
and stood dumb before their shearers.
May this remembrance
be able to prevent
other Jews from being
jeered at and persecuted
because they are Jews,
and that nowhere among us
nor among other men
will that delusion ever find a hearing.
May all who claim
to follow Jesus
begin to see and acknowledge
that they have received
the Name of God from Israel:
'God of liberation,
God of the living,
He alone!'[20]

[20] H. OOSTERHUIS: *Israël, Volhard in hem. Een nieuwe liturgie voor Goede Vrijdag,* Hilversum 1986 = *Werkschrift voor Leerhuis en Liturgie* 4 (1983) 1.

3. ADEQUATE LITURGY

Adequate liturgy is closely connected with inductive liturgy. The term 'adequate' is open to misinterpretation, but I know of no better word to denote what I want to say. One can understand the word in two ways: first in the sense that it refers to a liturgy that exhaustively takes into account the culture, the subculture, the group or individual involved. I am not using the term in this sense. I am concerned with the second meaning of the word: to be adapted to, filling a need or requirement. Thus, for me, this in no way involves a complete equivalence.

Thus adequate liturgy, like inductive liturgy, takes the here and now as the point of departure for giving ritual form. But the concept indicates more specifically the necessity of arriving at gradations in the liturgical selection. Subsequently, it implies that Christian ritual in our society must seek connection with the pluriformity of convictions and spiritualities, and that we in our culture arrive at various models and types of liturgy.

Adequate liturgy *first* and foremost implies that one must take into account the necessity of arriving at *gradations* in the liturgical selection available. In our culture we are quite simply faced with various levels of belonging to the church. I have already pointed to the fact that in Western European society, and particularly in The Netherlands, there is a growing percentage of unchurched persons.[21] With regard to church members, several categories are now distinguished. These are generally the following:

- marginal members (that is to say, those who do not regularly attend church)
- average members (that is to say, those who regularly attend church, but are otherwise not active)
- core members (that is to say, those who both regularly attend church and are members of, and/or perform tasks in church groups).[22]

There are also other terms used to identify the various groups, such as active, passive and selective (i.e., seasonal or feast,[23] 'Christmas and

[21] See Part 3, Chapter 1, 3.3.
[22] See HALMAN: *Waarden in de Westerse Wereld* 81.
[23] For the denomination 'feast-christians, see P. POST, J. PIEPER & R. NAUTA: 'Om de parochie: het inculturerend perspectief van rituele marginaliteit. Verkenning van een onderzoeksperspectief', in *Jaarboek voor liturgie-onderzoek* 14 (1998) 113-140.

Easter' or 'Ashes and Palms') Christians; or core congregants, liturgical congregants and occasional congregants. With regard to the latter group, the English term 'non-practising' (and in Dutch 'marginal congregants') is also used to indicate those who do not participate in church life, without this implying that they consider themselves non-believers.[24]

In most European countries today the largest percentage of *church members* are marginal. The Netherlands has a peculiar position in this: not the largest proportion of church members, but only 22%, are marginal. Among Roman Catholics marginal members make up only 10% of the total. In this respect, The Netherlands in fact assumes a middle position in the religious/ecclesiastical picture, which contrasts with the image that people in general have: according to this image, The Netherlands leads Europe in abandoning religious observance.[25] With regard to average members, among Catholics the figures show that those who attend a weekend liturgy on a weekly basis are declining steadily (1988: 16.4%; 1989: 15.9%; 1990: 14.9%; 1991: 14%; 1992: 13.1%; 1998: 10.2%; 2000: 9.2%; 2002: 8.6%). Because increasing numbers of young people are dropping away, it can be expected that the figures will continue to decline. Ever more church buildings are becoming redundant. The number of marginal church members and unchurched will undoubtedly rise in the future.

How are we to deal with marginal church members, who generally only participate in ecclesiastical rituals at important transitions in life and possibly major feasts? In their participation in church ritual, do they not too much assume the role of consumers? Are these church rituals indeed adequate for them? Is the church not going too far in catering to them? Does the church not dilute its identity by being of service to them only occasionally? Such questions approach the problem in a purely ecclesio-centric manner; one is thinking from the centre of the church. That can be seen in the very categories being used: those who do not go to church regularly are pejoratively designated as 'marginal' members: they

---

[24] See also E. HENAU: 'Verscheidenheid in kerkbetrokkenheid. Een pastorale uitdaging', in E. HENAU & L. HENSGENS (eds.): *Een pastorale uitdaging. Verscheidenheid in kerkbetrokkenheid*, Tielt/Bussum 1982, 18-24.

[25] R. DE MOOR: 'Globalisering van de cultuur en nationale identiteit', in J.J.M. DE VALK (ed.): *Nationale identiteit in Europees perspectief*, Baarn 1993, 32.

really do not belong here, they are on the fringes; not to mention the problems with those who are outside the church and yet sometimes ask for the performance of a rite of passage.

Seen from our culture, as I have sketched it above, another understanding is possible. One can place the rising number of unchurched and marginal church members against the background of an irreversible process of socio-cultural change in which we find ourselves. When we take this as our point of departure, we must take into account the fact that we are confronted with an open society with various systems of meaning, among which people can choose. This means first of all that those who, for instance, choose Christian rituals for important life transitions must be approached positively. In our society such a choice is increasingly less obvious. Much more than in the agricultural society in the past, making such a request indicates a real choice and actual involvement with the church. It is no small thing when people in our culture turn to the church at important moments. Much more than before we must realise that there are different gradations of real involvement with the church, and that these must be taken seriously. Even as in the past it was accepted that not everyone would be come a monk of nun, so today different gradations in religious commitment must be taken seriously. The designation 'marginal church member' is thus in fact less serviceable.

Moreover, it would appear that the designation 'unchurched' is much too wide. Being 'unchurched' has negative connotations. It designates those who do not belong to one of the Christian churches as such. But, as I indicated above, that does not say at all that they have a worldview in which religious dimensions no longer play a role.

In such a situation, a gradation in the selection of liturgy available becomes extremely important. It could be that merely a general religious ritual is adequate. Why should churches not be able to supply that so long as there are, and at the points where there are lacunae in our culture? But also with regard to the Christian dimension, an adequate expression is needed for those who participate in liturgy only at decisive moments in their life. It is not a matter of all sorts of fringes of Christian faith. In the same way that in catechesis the four principle truths were sufficient, rather than a complete and top-heavy catechism, so too in liturgy one can also limit oneself to the core of Christian faith. One must also then seek to express this core in a not too overwhelming manner. In essence, this core is ever again the Easter mystery, which can be put into words and represented in all sorts of ways, including those with a low threshold. Furthermore, one can expand the stock of Christian liturgy available for rites of passage, and could make a distinction between a Christian celebration of birth and baptism, between a Christian celebration on the occasion of a marriage or choosing to live together and the Christian sacrament of marriage, between a farewell for the deceased with an observance of word and prayer, or with the celebration of Eucharist, between a Christian agapè and an Eucharist celebration. I will return to this when I speak of the importance on new rituals for transitions in life.[26]

In a certain sense, people do not have it easy in our culture. Living in various sectors and fulfilling the role patterns connected with them, they have to seek an integrating sense of meaning, and in this it is unavoidable that their choices will differ. Even when they choose the Christian system of meaning, there will be differences among them. If liturgy is to become embedded in our culture, it must take this into account to an increasing degree. Without losing its Christian identity, it will have to connect up with the general and individual pattern of choices that it encounters.

It is thus of importance in our culture that both the general religious dimension and the Christian dimension – and this latter in different degrees – be expressed. In our culture there are many ways with regard to the one way, and all of these ways deserve to be made passable liturgically.

Adequate liturgy not only implies that there must be gradations in the selection of liturgy available. There is also a *second* element. In an adequate liturgy one will also have to take into account various *spiritualities and styles, groups and categories*, which will lead to various *types of liturgy*. After all, in our culture there is on the one side increasing globalisation (we are on our way to being one Europe with one currency, to one world economy, one world culture), but on the other side it is true that there is great concern for separate groups, regional cultures, and retaining or restoring local customs.

First, I would go into the affiliation of the various spiritualities and styles that form subcultures as it were within the broader culture of Christian liturgy. As an example, one can think of a monastic spirituality

---

[26] Part 3, Chapter 8.

like that of Taizé. This appeals particularly to younger people, but not to them alone. But the sphere is broader. There is also the peculiar style of the monastic liturgy in a wider sense. One must also take in that already in earlier periods in history there were some Western Christians who felt particularly at home in Byzantine liturgy. The abbey of Chevetogne in Belgium, where the Benedictines celebrate the Byzantine liturgy daily, is a striking example of this. This interest in Byzantine liturgy has expanded in the West in recent decades. One finds communities for which the ritual expression of the Byzantine liturgy – sometimes in the Dutch language – seems particularly adequate. There are also those who feel more at home in the design of the post-Vatican liturgy in Latin and using Gregorian song. While the monks in The Netherlands have taken the radical decision to move over to the liturgy in the vernacular, the Benedictine abbey at Vaals has opted for the classic Latin liturgy. It is a pillar for support for a wider movement that comes together in the Association for Latin Liturgy. This group argues for maintaining places where the liturgy from after the Second Vatican Council can be celebrated integrally in Latin. Those celebrations in which there is a search for the deepest, individual identity, for the healing of psychological wounds sustained, are other special types. These celebrations are closely connected with certain characteristic qualities of ritual in our culture.[27] Some feminist liturgies can serve as an example of this.

Next, there are types of liturgy which seek an adequate connection with groups or categories of persons. One can not get around the fact that there is in our culture much more attention for the characteristics of separate groups than there was before. Let me focus in on children. In 1955 Van der Meer wrote an magisterial article on the Church and children.[28] He showed that in the past the Church had no interest for children as a separate age group. They simply took part in the liturgy together with their parents. They got lost in the crowd, so to speak. There was no requirement that they be able to follow what was going on. This old attitude toward children was, according to him, the consequence of a great wisdom, because children are sensitive to liturgy as such, and that which is highest and best should not be denied them. Children's Masses, children's prayers and children's songs are 'merely sacrilegious infantilisation

---

[27] See Part 3, Chapter 3, 3.2.
[28] F. VAN DER MEER: 'De kerk en de kinderen', in *Dux* 22 (1955) 41-59.

352   CHRISTIAN RITUAL IN OUR CULTURE

of the mystery of faith.' In answer to Van der Meer Fortmann asked if
the discovery of the child then had not taught us to take the peculiar
nature of children into account. Must one not sometimes give milk to
those who can not yet eat solid food (I Cor. 3:2), and does the Lord himself not tell his disciples, 'I have yet many things to say to you, but you
cannot bear them now' (John 16:12)?[29] There can be adequate adaptations that are not infantilisation. That is an insight of our culture. Consistent with that, we arrived at special children's services. The Directory
for Masses with Children and the new eucharistic prayers for children are
an exemplary model of liturgical inculturation.[30] Furthermore, the way
to adulthood in our culture has become longer and more complicated.[31]
Why then not give special attention to liturgy for the young?[32] This is
also true for other categories: women, students, the mentally challenged,
the elderly. In the previous, absolutely prescribed liturgy from before the
Second Vatican Council, this was not necessary. With a liturgy that
wishes to be inculturated in our culture, it cannot be other.

Giving shape to an adequate liturgy will create a much greater pluriformity in Christian ritual than we have previously been accustomed to. In
light of this, I wish to discuss two further points.

First there is the question of the relation between liturgies for various
categories and groups and the *larger local liturgy*. Is the local community
in which all come together, irrespective of class or rank, of age, category
or peculiar group not irreplaceable? One can answer that by saying that
the renewal of the liturgy of that local community also remains indispensable. This liturgy will necessarily have to keep in mind that children, youth, the handicapped and others will be present, and that half
the community will be comprised of women.[33] But nevertheless, in our

[29] H. FORTMANN: 'De plaats der eucharistische liturgie in de huidige jeugdzielzorg',
in *Dux* 22 (1955) 85.
[30] C.V. JOHNSON: 'The Children's Eucharistic Prayers: A Model of Liturgical Inculturation', in *Worship* 75 (2001) 209-227. The Netherlands witnessed great creativity
with regard to children's services: see among others *Werkcahiers (voor) Vieringen met
kinderen* (1972-1997). After 1997 this publication continued in an annual form under
the title *Een jaar de tijd*.
[31] See in this connection Part 3, Chapter 8, 1.1.2.
[32] For the Netherlands, see among others *Servicemap (voor) Jongerenliturgie* (1971-
1997); after 1997 continued in an annual form under the title *Goed voor een jaar*.
[33] I will return to this dimension of women and liturgy *in extenso* in Chapter 9, 4.

culture local liturgy is often of necessity too global. Moreover, one must realise that in celebrations for one group, those from other groups may also be present. For instance, parents and other adults are generally present at children's services and youth celebrations. Although the accent lies on the children and youth, the others do not have to remain purely passive spectators. Also, in the course of time an interaction will automatically begin to take place between the design of the various types of celebration and the larger local celebration. An example of this at present can be found chiefly in the celebrations for women. One here observes a living process of liturgical influence.[34] The local services will be come less abstract, the special celebrations will become more open to the whole. For the rest, there is at present again a tendency to place less emphasis on categorical celebrations. For instance, the book *Het kind in ons midden* (The child in our midst) recently appeared, in which various essays argued for replacing the children's/family services with celebrations with the child in the midst of the local community.[35] In my opinion, anthropology can also help deepen our reflection here. For example, every family has parties for its children, as well as parties in which everyone participates but where the accent lies on the children, and finally celebrations of adults in which children assume their natural place.

Next, there is the danger of polarisation. More than anyone could have suspected during the Second Vatican Council, in the future we will have to learn to live with a pluriform liturgy. Alongside an ecumenism among the Christian churches there is also an *ecumenism within the church* needed. One will even sometimes find various styles within one and the same liturgy. The funeral of Diana, Princess of Wales, which moved so many, was an example of that. Contemporary church music, old folk music and popular music like Elton John's 'Candle in the Wind' were heard side by side with traditional Anglican church music, constituting a postmodern liturgical whole. I found it striking that a Dutch reporter spoke of this funeral as a unity of liturgical elements combined with pop music. But this last was of course an integral element of the liturgy itself, the element that will apparently longest

[34] In this connection, see the pilot study for the exploration of a multi-disciplinary research project on ritual marginality: POST, PIEPER & NAUTA: 'Om de parochie'.
[35] G. LUKKEN & J. DE WIT (eds.): *Het kind in ons midden* (Liturgie in beweging 5), Baarn 1999.

remain with young people and whole groups of adults. Rather than speaking of the necessity of ecumenism within the church, one might perhaps better draw upon Anglican terminology and speak of the need for 'comprehensiveness'. This word, which denotes sweeping inclusion, is familiar to Anglicans with regard to their own liturgy, and could be particularly valuable for the whole of Christian liturgy in the future.

To close this section: in the design of adequate liturgy there must be attention given to the various levels of faith. But one must guard against defining these levels too much from above, in a reductive manner, or attempting to 'accommodate' them by catechistic introductions during the liturgical celebration. Christian liturgy as such has its own attraction and power, even within a culture in which ever more people are 'illiterate' in a Christian sense. The 'unchurched' are often fascinated by the full-blown Christian rites and actual ritual practices of monasteries and Christian communities, and any introductory catechesis and explanation can only detract from the eloquence of the celebration itself. Christian liturgies appear to have a peculiar and full initiatory function. As such, they have a mystagogical power and attraction. This is also true for young people. One can think, for instance, of the influence of the youth gatherings at Taizé. In this context, sources in France have recently been speaking of the importance of a pastoral strategy of a *proposition de la foi*, a fully-developed presentation of Christian faith which transcends the exclusivity of the pastoral strategy of supply and demand. An authentic and fully-developed Christian liturgy has a special place within such a pastoral strategy.[36]

4. Expression of the 'praeambula fidei'

Inductive liturgy implies that one proceeds along the course of gradualism. On this path lies what classical theology terms the *praeambula fidei* (the 'forecourt' of faith) or the *signa credibilitatis* (signs of credibility). Put simply, this is a way which leads to faith. Attention must be given to that which makes faith humanly acceptable and credible. In this, classical theology notes that there can be no sense of a logical transition between the

---

[36] *Proposer la foi. Renouveler la pastorale*: *La Maison-Dieu* (1998) 216. See also F.P. Prétot: 'Sacraments and Liturgy in the Context of a Pastoral Strategy of 'Invitation to Faith'', in *Studia Liturgica* 32 (2002) 196-221.

praeambula fidei, the *signa credibilitatis*, and faith itself. Between them lies an elusive element. The actual perspective jumps thanks to the *lumen fidei*, the light of faith, which is ultimately a grace: 'No man can come to me, except the Father which hath sent me draw him' (John 6:44). But that in no way excludes a preceding anthropological basis.

The expression of the 'way to faith' is of great importance in inductive liturgy, for two reasons. First, because it is a value in itself; second, because it can contribute to the perspective indeed opening out in the direction of the act of faith, thanks to the *lumen fidei*. Here too it is true that there is no conflict between God and man. An inductive, counselling liturgy, and what it asks in commitment from the participants, are as it were the labour that we must perform for the sake of faith. The opening up of the perspective however extends above us: it is a moment of grace.

In our culture the expression of the in-depth dimensions of man and the world certainly is a part of the *praeambula fidei*. Anyone reading the concentration camp letters and diary of Etty Hillesum will be struck by the way in which she expresses the way to the depth of man and the world.[37] Hillesum died in Auschwitz at the age of 27. Her death was preceded by a period of increasing discrimination against Jews, full of anxiety and uncertainty. Around her she experienced the loss of sense in living, something unbearable. You see her wrestling with this to a growing degree. She will not allow herself to be robbed of the meaning of life. On the contrary, she discovers a new, fuller sense of life. She gradually uncovers the strength of human living: love for all. The Name of God steadily comes into this process more and more, from experiences undergone time after time. Abstractly formulated in this way, this perhaps says little; it is only the concrete story of the diary and camp letters, the inductive story itself, that can function as an expression of *praeambula fidei*. Merely in reading them many have had the experience of encountering themselves, and that this He is closer than my own I.[38] Their life receives new

[37] E. HILLESUM: *A Diary 1941-1943*, London 1983 (English translation of *Het verstoorde leven. Dagboek van Etty Hillesum, 1941-1943*, Bussum 1981); IDEM: *Letters from Westerbork*, New York 1986 (English translation of *Het denkende hart van de barak. Brieven van Etty Hillesum*, Haarlem 1982); see also E. HILLESUM: *Interrupted Life: the Diaries 1941-1943 and Letters from Westerbork*, New York 1996 and K.A.D. SMELIK (ed.): *The letters and diaries of Etty Hillesum 1941-1943: complete and unabridged*, Grand Rapids/Ottawa 2002.

[38] See also L. DUPRÉ: *Transcendent Selfhood. The Loss and Rediscovery of the Inner Life*, New York 1976 – L. DUPRÉ: *Terugkeer naar de innerlijkheid*, Antwerpen/Amsterdam 1982.

meaning. That does not yet produce faith, but it does prepare the way; it makes the field ready so that the seed may perhaps take root.

The expression of the *praeambula fidei* and the *signa credibilitatis* in liturgy is of particularly great importance, because in liturgy we encounter participants with varying degrees of involvement in the church, especially in rituals at life transitions. It is important that the ritual, and that which is being asked, be in harmony. It is a question of performing the rite of passage in an adequate way. This also means that there is a *raison d'être* for more general, low-threshold Christian liturgy. It can have its own independent function; it is meaningful as such. It is also possible to see this threshold liturgy as a phase toward the actual sacrament: the threshold liturgy invites participants to further growth. Certainly, then, the expression of *praeambula fidei* and *signa credibilitatis* is of great importance. Moreover, these threshold liturgies could be considered as a particularisation of inductive liturgy.

Still another aspect is connected with the expression of *praeambula fidei*. Particularly at the performance of rituals involving life transitions there are widely differentiated groups present. Think of the congregations at funerals or weddings. The whole spectrum of society can be present: Christians and non-Christians, believers, doubters, unbelievers. The expression of the *praeambula fidei* there can have a double purpose. For some the expression will be understood in a purely human manner, while the same expression can call up a religious experience for others, or for still others even involve the disclosure of Christian faith. Such ambiguous expressions seem to me to be of great importance in our culture. One finds very good examples of this in the work of Oosterhuis. A free adaptation of Psalm 13, for instance, ends with the words,

> Even then I'll cling to you
> whether you want me or not,
> in your good grace
> or out of it.
> "Save me!" I'll cry to you
> or maybe only
> "Love me."[39]

---

[39] H. OOSTERHUIS, H.: *At Times I See*, London 1974, 2 = H. OOSTERHUIS: *Zien – soms even. Fragmenten over God*, Bilthoven 1972, 33.

Another text reads,

That we fill up with the breath of life and cry: at last we are born.[40]

When this text is sung as a round by the whole congregation, it will be understood according to the context. In a Christian community the objective context is a Christian one. But at the same time the personal context of the participants is always at work. This can lead to the selective perception of a general human or general religious perception. These texts are such that they can also evoke these latter perceptions.

Another striking example was to be found in the memorial service that was held on March 21, 1982, in the Moses and Aaron Church in Amsterdam for four Dutch journalists who were murdered in El Salvador. At the end of the service, the worship leader spoke these words:

> When I invite you for the service of prayer, I am aware that I am issuing an invitation which will be understood in very different ways. I know that there are many among us here this morning for whom prayer is a strange thing, to whom words such as God and faith are foreign. Yet I invite you, because I believe that it is possible to set foot on holy ground with all sorts of feelings and all sorts of opinions, where it is not a matter of statements, nor of superiority, nor of power, nor of who is right, but a matter of deep respect for one another, thinking of one another, being concerned with what awaits us. It is not a matter of being pious, but with our eyes open. We speak their names yet one more time: Koos Koster, Jan Kuiper, Joop Willemsen, Hans ter Laag. We reflect, we pray, we believe that they have not been blotted out, because violence does not have the final word, but rather hope which leads to life. We remember and acknowledge our connection with the members of their families, in powerlessness, in anger, in grief. God, we do not understand. Why, why did you forsake them? Why do we men abandon one another? Why do we inflict pain on and ignore one another? Why do we find having more important than being? Why do we appropriate this world rather than playing in it and caring for it? We are ashamed, because we have made such a perishing mess of things. We are hurt and deeply outraged that violence appears to win time after time, and it appears that the weak must always lose. O God, we will not accept that, because Jesus said that we must stand up, not stand aside.

---

[40] H. OOSTERHUIS: 'Dat wij volstromen', in *Liturgische Gezangen voor de viering van de eucharistie*, Hilversum 1979, 182.

Here we are, then, and let us respect one another, because God has given us each other. He desires that we not leave it at this, that we take over what they have left undone, without being overconfident, without being loud about it, but in deep certainty that this is the way that we are to go. Friends, let us arise and go forth from here. The world waits. We shall not make that world perfect, but we will do what we can't help doing. In the name of God, therefore, do that. Amen.[41]

---

[41] IKON: *Herdenkingsdienst bij de dood van Koos Koster, Jan Kuiper, Joop Willemsen, Hans ter Laag, 21 maart 1982,* Hilversum 1982.

CHAPTER 7

BRENEWED ATTENTION FOR THE PRESENTATIVE
CHARACTER OF RITUAL

One of the major characteristics of our culture is its focus on physicality and sensory experience, which also has its ramifications in ritual.
People today have great difficulty with rituals that are too intellectual,
ethereal or formal. Grimes is correct in observing, 'Although Christian
theologians have thought much about the theology of their rites, they
think very little about the ritual of their rites.'[1] Thus they deprive their
rites of their fundamental physicality and bodiliness, of their basic sensuality and fundamental rootedness in tangible reality, and therefore of
their spirituality. It is important to examine this insight further.

1. THE WORD

In Part 1 I indicated how deeply presentative symbolism in ritual
impacts on us, and how corporality is the source of all ritual.[2] One frequently heard accusation addressed to the renewed Roman Catholic
liturgy is that it is too verbal. This accusation has two sides. The first is
that the accusation sometimes arises from nostalgia for the Catholic
liturgy of the past. In pre-Vatican II liturgy, the senses did play a great
role. There was first of all the space of the church, where there was
much to be seen: the painted walls, the stations of the Cross, numerous
statues, an altar like Mount Calvary, candlesticks and candles, the small,
living flame of the sanctuary lamp in the distance, flowers, decorations,
all sorts of sacred objects. Next, this space was always permeated with
the odour of incense. When incense was in fact being burned, there was
the visible ascension of the smoke. The sense of taste was also addressed:
precisely because the faithful might not touch certain objects, particu-

---

[1] R.L. GRIMES: 'The Initiatory Dilemma: Cinematic Fantasy and Ecclesiastical Rarification', in *Bulletin ET. Zeitschrift für Theologie in Europa* 9 (1998) 2, 161-170.
[2] See Part 1, Chapter 1, 2.5, Chapter 3, 2.7 and Chapter 4, 1.

larly in the Eucharist, an appeal was made to that sense. This was reinforced by the reception of the Host directly on the tongue. Then there
was the ritual itself, which consisted of very balanced motions. Even the
words functioned in a very sensory manner: the use of Latin made these
words into a sort of musical rite. Finally, there was the music itself: from
Gregorian chant to all sorts of polyphony. One could never claim that
this liturgy was lacking in forms of sensory-symbolic interaction and the
presentative symbolism which accompanies this. On the contrary: Yet
this past also was out of balance. The word was short-changed. It was
therefore right that after the Second Vatican Council Latin was replaced
by the vernacular, because the word should remain the word, even if it
is symbolic language. When the word becomes mumbo jumbo, ritual
becomes meaningless and empty. It then remains stuck in its presentative appeal to the senses, and can collapse in on itself. In ritual too there
is always a horizon of understanding, which can in part be expressed in
words. The non-verbal, it is true, has a larger and more radical validity,
but it also is more vague. This vagueness is counterbalanced when
names are given to things. Only then does the non-verbal become integrated in the power of ritual, as here and now, applying to me, to us.
We speak of water, light, fire. We say, 'I bind you in marriage...', 'I baptise you...', 'May this dead body rest in the earth, as a wheat grain that
dies, in order that new life arise.' We perform the gesture and we speak.
In this way we bring things and actions out of their hiddenness, 'illuminate' them, and apply them to our history.[3]
    Restoring the word to its proper place was thus definitely necessary,
both from an anthropological perspective and to protect the evangelical
values of the liturgy. Yet the accusation is not entirely ungrounded,
because in the transition to the vernacular there was a danger that the
word would become all too disconnected from its integral sensory context, at the expense of the ritual.
    This first touches upon the question of the presentative character of
the word. The spoken word is linked with out corporality: with the person, his or her intonation, the timbre of the voice, breathing, the movements of the mouth and face, gestures and other bodily movements, the
place where the speaker is, and the moment at which he or she speaks.
The word is really incarnate, and the gradations of this incarnation run
from that of the abstract, intellectualising word on the one end of the

---

[3] LUKKEN: *De onvervangbare weg van de liturgie.*

spectrum to a full-fledged ritual word on the other. The new liturgy will have to respect this complete embodiment of the word. This has implications not only for the ritual design of the word, but also the elementary demand of well-developed verbal expression, in particular from all who lead in a liturgy.[4] It cannot be denied that worship leaders – and this can include pastoral workers and volunteers too – rather often lack these skills. This touches on matters such as the correct use of a microphone, breathing, intonation, the way in which accents are placed, and so forth. Here liturgy can learn much from theatre studies. But at the same time one must realise that liturgical speaking is not theatrical, but much more restrained, sober and self-effacing. The speaking must leave room, as it were, for the transcendent mystery that is being evoked.[5]

A second question concerns the new liturgical language, a new language for reading, proclamation and prayer. This question touches on both the translation of the Bible and old prayer texts and on the creation of new prayer texts.

With regard to the translation of the Bible, there is always a tension between remaining true to the original text and translation into a contemporary language. A problem with translation is that every language is strongly culturally defined. In its internal structure it has within itself its own way of looking at the world. Thus, as you learn a language you learn and acquire for yourself a particular view of the world, of which the language is the most authentic filter. For instance, the logic and thinking of the Greeks in general is supported by and carried in the grammatical categories of the Greek language. That led to the Greeks thinking and speaking of God in a more abstract manner than the Hebrews. While in the Scripture God is called Father, Son and Holy Spirit, and as such is closely related with actual sacred history, in the Christian confession of faith, which is strongly influenced by Greek thought, the Son is accented as the only-begotten son of God, who is 'begotten, not made, being of one substance with the Father', and the

[4] G. LUKKEN: 'Op zoek naar een nieuwe stijl van voorgaan', in *Analecta aartsbisdom Utrecht* 71 (1998) (May/June), 158-169 and *Tijdschrift voor Liturgie* 82 (1998) 341-351. For verbal expression, see among others J. WIJNGAARDS: *Bijbel voorlezen in de liturgie. Dàn goed verstaanbaar*, Boxtel 1974 and G. SWÜSTE: 'Het voorlezen van een schrifttekst', in G. LUKKEN & J. DE WIT (eds.): *Lezen in fragmenten. De Bijbel als liturgisch boek* (Liturgie in beweging 2), Baarn 1998, 185-191.
[5] See Part 3, Chapter 5, 2.4.

Spirit as the one who 'proceeds from the Father and the Son'. In this connection it is also interesting to note that in the Greek translation of Psalm 139 the expressive images and concrete mythic elements of the original Hebrew text have disappeared.[6] This is undoubtedly connected with the cultural particularity of the Greek language. It is therefore a question whether those things which are specific to a language are not always necessarily lost in translation. In translating the Bible for liturgy there is a further very specific problem, and that is that one must end up with a text that not only can be read well, but also is good when heard. After all, in liturgy the Bible is read out loud, and this imposes other demands than does a printed or written text. There is still much work to be done in this area.[7] Next comes the question of how the Bible can be incorporated in the liturgy a way which on the one hand does justice to the whole Scripture, when on the other hand only small parts can be read at a time. Here one encounters the issues surrounding lectionaries, an area undergoing intense development.[8] Finally, precisely in connection with the 'embodiment' of the word, there is still the question of designing the Bible as a liturgical book, and to rituals in connection with this book.[9]

A peculiar problem area is that of translating old, classic prayer texts.[10] In this connection, I must return to the recent Instruction *Liturgiam authenticam*, regarding the translation of the new Roman liturgy.[11] According to this Instruction, all translations of the new liturgical books

[6] J. HOLMAN: 'Psalm 139 een palimpsest?', in *Schrift* 21 (1989) 124, 148-157.

[7] See among others I. NOWELL: 'The Making of Translations: A Dilemma', in *Worship* 75 (2001) 58-68; G.S. SLOYAN: 'Some Thoughts on Bible Translations', in *Worship* 75 (2001) 228-249; E. DE JONG: 'Bijbelvertaling en liturgie', in LUKKEN & DE WIT (eds.): *Lezen in fragmenten* 100-106; D. MONSHOUWER: 'De verkondiging van het Woord – Johannes 1, 1-18 in vertalingen', in LUKKEN & DE WIT (eds.): *Lezen in fragmenten* 107-118; N. SCHUMAN: 'Schrift, boek, Bijbel, vertaling et cetera', in BARNARD & POST (eds.): *Ritueel bestek* 275-290.

[8] LUKKEN & DE WIT (eds.): *Lezen in fragmenten*; M.A. VRIJLAND: *Liturgiek*, Delft 1987, 272-291; OSKAMP & SCHUMAN (eds.): *De weg van de liturgie* 422-449.

[9] R.T. LAWRENCE: 'The Altar Bible: *Digni, Decori et Pulchri*', in *Worship* 75 (2001) 386-402.

[10] For the sweeping nature of this problem, see among others G. BRÜSKE: 'Plädoyer für liturgische Sprachkompetenz. Thesen zur Sprachlichkeit der Liturgie', in *Archiv für Liturgiewissenschaft* 42 (2000) 317-343; N. MITCHELL: 'The Amen Corner. Once upon a Time', in *Worship* 75 (2001) 469-478.

[11] For this Instruction, see Part 3, Chapter 3, 3.1.

must be revised so that the old Latin liturgy must be passed on as such, as exactly as possible, even in our culture. In terms of both content and form, its texts are normative, explicitly and word for word. With this, the Instruction ignores the problem that the language of the old Latin liturgy in itself, in its internal structure, has its peculiar view of the world, which is alien to many in our culture. The abstract theological precision of the prayers in the Roman Sacramentary lacks the poetic strength to move the hearts of people in our culture.[12] Literal translation therefore only makes sense for those who are steeped in that Roman culture. In any case, translation always means that a text from one culture enters into a different culture, where the language has its own internal structures and its syntactic and semantic coherence. It involves transposing an expression of one culture into an expression of another culture. This always involves larger units of meaning. Translating a text word for word is only the first step in the translation process. Of course one must know exactly what is said in the original. The final, literarily responsible, contemporary translation is however then done on the basis of this. It is a question of on the one hand doing justice to the rich content of the Roman liturgy, and on the other hand providing it with a translated form that makes this rich content accessible for our culture. That has nothing to do with a desire for subjectivism or with expressing purely inner dispositions at the expense of a truth that transcends time and place, as the Instruction suggests (no. 19). Inculturated translations can do thorough justice to the originals. Indeed, through such translations the tradition can be passed on more efficiently than through literal, word for word translations. The document correctly notes that the sacred language is other than everyday language, but it is going too far to make the sacred language of the Roman liturgy as such normative, in the name of this principle. One may not absolutise the Roman sacred language as this document appears to do (no. 27, 47). There is also contemporary liturgical, sacral language. The sacred can definitely be mediated by translation done in a creative manner. One must realise that the sacred is a dynamic concept, which must be given shape anew, in each culture. In this process it obtains that in a new culture certain things (such as, for instance, equality of men and women) can be 'holy' (that is to say, are divinely anchored) that do not have this quality, or have

---

[12] M.E. McGann: 'Timely Wisdom, Prophetic Challenge: Rediscovering Clarence R.J. Rivers' Vision of Effective Worship', in *Worship* 76 (2002) 15-16.

this to a lesser extent, in another culture. I will return to this in the discussion of women in liturgy.[13]

It is thus impossible to translate the classic Roman orisons into a contemporary language in such a way that their peculiar *Anliegen* of succinctness, concision, precision and balanced rhythm – what Augustine calls *mysteria brevia, sed magna* (great mysteries, but very succinctly formulated)[14] – is maintained. The following prayer from the old Sacramentarium Veronense (number 1031) can serve as an example. Translated literally, it reads:

> Lord, thou feedest us with eternal food:
> leave us therefore not without temporal help.

For our culture, such a text is too terse and laconic. Read aloud, the text is over before it gets through to us. For us, it needs to be more verbose. For instance, for our culture this prayer might be translated as follows:

> Thou who art the source of all life,
> in this supper feed us with bread and wine,
> sign of our life beyond death;
> we ask You, who comes so abundantly to our aid,
> to also preserve and watch over
> our vulnerable existence in this world.

This also takes into account the fact that increasing numbers of women in our culture have problems with denoting God with the unambiguously male 'Lord'.

The question is thus whether the wealth of old prayers which are included in the Roman missal and the new rituals should not be translated much more creatively than has been the case to date. However this is answered, the questions posed about the translation of Scripture and old prayer texts all have to do with the physicality of the word, and thus with the possibility of experiencing an approach to the God of salvation, and his appearance to us, in a credible manner.

---

[13] See Part 3, Chapter 9, 4. For a critical comment on the norms of translation in 'Liturgiam authenticam' see also N. MITCHELL: 'The Amen Corner. Liturgical Language: Building a Better Mousetrap', in *Worship* 77 (2003) 250-263; IDEM: 'Croquet with Flamingos', in *Worship* 77 (2003) 457-472.

[14] AUGUSTINE: *Sermo* 9.

There is still the further question of the creative adaptation of old prayer texts and the creation of new prayer texts. This concerns the development of a language for faith which bears within it the tension between below and above, inside and outside, sacred and profane.[15] What is sought is a new language for prayer which is not tendentious, not dominating, and not exclusively masculine, but inductive, narrative, tangible, self-effacing and circumspect. It is a matter of creating a language for prayer which sheds a measure of light on human sorrow and joy, on the search for meaning today, and does so from religious depths, from God, from what happened in Jesus of Nazareth.

A third question touches the issue with regard to the relation between myth and rite which was already discussed in Part 1. In oral cultures the word is subordinate to the ritual act, with all the senses. In written cultures however it is more the opposite. The religions of the book, such as Judaism, Christianity and Islam, belong to the latter. Within Christianity itself one can still point to differences in this. Thus within the Reformation the word has a higher priority than in Catholicism. Although this distinction has become smaller as a result of the ecumenical movement, one can still speak of differing spiritualities.

2. THE SENSUALITY OF THE NON-VERBAL

One must be mindful of what other elements comprise ritual, outside of the word as such. One can first of all think of *silence*. In a certain sense, there is a specific silence within every authentic ritual. But silence is also a component of ritual. This silence can perhaps be a 'filled' silence, with background music. Such a ritual silence is other, thus, than a meditative silence. It is subordinate to the direction of the ritual, and does not have an indeterminate length. It is generally precisely planned, and usually does not last longer than a minute or so, as in the old liturgy, the time of one Our Father.[16]

[15] L. LOOSEN (ed.): *Liturgische gebedstaal: Werkmap (voor) Liturgie* 24 (1990) 3-64.
[16] G. LUKKEN: 'Liturgie en stilte', in *Lijnen* 2 (1985) 38-42; IDEM: 'Sacrale ruimte en stilte', in *Speling* 47 (1995) 1, 48-55. Regarding meditation centres, see Part 3, Chapter 9, 1.

The sensuality of the *odours* can also play an impressive role in contemporary ritual. One can think of the scent of flowers, of incense, and also of aromatic oils. In the Old Testament we read of these oils:

> Moreover, the LORD said to Moses: "Take the finest spices: of liquid myrrh five hundred shekels, and of sweet-smelling cinnamon half as much, that is, two hundred and fifty, and of aromatic cane two hundred and fifty, and of cassia five hundred, according to the shekel of the sanctuary, and of olive oil a hin; and you shall make of these a sacred anointing oil blended as by the perfumer; a holy anointing oil it shall be. And you shall anoint with it the tent of meeting and the ark of the testimony, and the table and all its utensils, and the lampstand and its utensils, and the altar of incense, and the altar of burnt offering with all its utensils and the laver and its base; you shall consecrate them, that they may be most holy; whatever touches them will become holy. And you shall anoint Aaron and his sons, and consecrate them, that they may serve me as priests" (Ex. 30: 22-30).

Fragrant oil: our culture, in which cosmetics play such a large role, is also particularly sensitive to it. Why should we not therefore use fragrant oils in contemporary ritual, for instance their consecration on Maundy Thursday, and in anointing baptisands and the ill?[17]

One can construct a certain ranking of the senses according to the distance between the subject and object which must be bridged. From this perspective, the *eye* is the most superficial of our senses, and taste is the deepest: it brings us into contact with the world in the most intimate way.[18] But at the same time there are also all sorts of syntheses possible. We can 'devour' the world with our eyes, and hear certain tonal 'colours'. It is characteristic of Western culture that in terms of the senses the image, the visual, predominates. In other words, the actual prevailing hierarchy of the senses corresponds with the ranking according to the distance between object and subject. There is to be sure a role for all senses, but at the same time it is true that ours is, before all else, a visual culture. This has important consequences for ritual. It implies that people in our culture can not get around the necessity for visible elements in ritual. Thus it is important to constantly ask whether there

---

[17] With regard to the olfactory in Christian liturgy, see among others J.-P. ALBERT: *Odeurs de sainteté: la mythologie chrétienne des aromates*, Paris 1990.

[18] GREIMAS: *De l'imperfection* 73-74.

is really something to be seen in the space in which the ritual takes place. Are there images, icons, flowers, burning candles, statues? How do the objects that play a role in the ritual look? Colour also belongs to the visual, both the colour of the space and the colour of the objects and the clothing. One can also ask if the word is sufficiently plastic and iconic. Ought one not make more use of slides and film with preaching? Whatever the case, the world of the visual must extend into liturgy. Finally, one must take into account that the visual is connected in a fundamental way with the fact of light.[19] We cannot perceive visually except in and through light. Light plays a fundamental role in our sensory perception. It has many nuances. These changes and nuances in light also play a major rule in liturgy. That is true for the way in which the light falls, and in which it is distributed. One can think here of merely the difference between a Romanesque church and a Gothic cathedral. Then there is the nuance of candle light, and the transition from darkness to light on Easter Saturday night.[20] Light plays an important role in church architecture and the design of the space, but also in the perception of the iconography, clothing, objects, gestures, *acts and movements*. This touches upon a very sensory layer of ritual, and is an area in which there is still a large amount of research to be done.[21]

The hierarchy of senses in Western culture, which is fundamentally a culture of the eye, has also led to 'sight-based' orientation being valorised while touch and other sensual data is regarded as debasing and humanly degrading.[22] In contrast, African and African American cultures are oral and aural in orientation. They are sound-based cultures, in which all the senses are required for apprehending and knowing of the world, and the eye functions integrally with all other senses. Rivers notes that in African and African American-based cultures 'there is a natural tendency for interpenetration and interplay, creating a concert

---

[19] FONTANILLE: *Sémiotique du visible*.
[20] G. LUKKEN: 'Lichtfeier der Osternacht: eine semiotische Analyse', in *Jaarboek voor liturgie-onderzoek* 16 (2000) 69-105.
[21] LUKKEN: "Ik heb geen wortels dan in het licht". See also K. ONASCH: *Lichthöhle und Sternenhaus. Licht und Materie im spätantik-christlichen und frühbyzantinischen Sakralbau*, Dresden/Basel 1993; S. DE BLAAUW: *Met het oog op het licht. Een vergeten principe in de oriëntatie van het vroegchristelijk kerkgebouw*, Nijmegen 2000; M. RENOUÉ: *Sémiotique et perception esthétique. Pierre Soulages et Sainte-Foy de Conques*, Limoges 2001.
[22] MCGANN: 'Timely Wisdom' 17-20.

or orchestration in which the ear sees, the eye hears, and where one both smells and tastes color, wherein all the senses, unmuted engage in every experience'.[23] In this way the world is perceived not through distance but through engagement. The ritual there is very vital and emotionally more involved with what is perceived. The question is whether an inter-cultural dialogue on this between Western culture and African/African American culture might not prove very productive for the viability of liturgy. One must remember here that particularly young people are responsive to the musical rhythm and 'sound' of these cultures.[24]

The expression of liturgy is condensed along the many channels of sensory experience.[25] In this connection, it is interesting to note the observation by Greimas that the multiplication of the level of expression into various 'languages', such as text, music and gesture, causes the mythic object to be experienced as all the more authentic, and giving it maximum efficacy.[26]

The presentativity of ritual also touches the design of acts and movements in space. In ritual the effort is made to return their full human basis to elementary actions. A thoroughgoing process of renewal is underway in all rituals, from birth to death, in this respect. This involves elementary, basic postures and movements which are funda-mental for every person, and which are also being explored in all sorts of experimental rituals in our culture: standing, walking, proceeding, entering, leaving, sitting, praying, bowing, acts involving things as objects with an interior and ultimate worth: earth, water, air, fire, light, ointment, bread, wine. The gestures and actions are on the one hand expressions of oneself, and on the other symbols of the mysterious world of the divine. They stem from Christian tradition, but must be taken up into our culture, there receiving a new, authentic shape. Old actions from Christian liturgy must be reconceived on the basis of contempo-rary anthropology, and thus embedded in our culture. The goal is

---

[23] C.R.J. RIVERS: *The Spirit in Worship*, Cincinnati 1978, 21.

[24] McGANN: 'Timely Wisdom' 18-20.

[25] See also *Liturgy and the Body: Concilium* 26 (1995) no. 3; G. LUKKEN: *Liturgie en zintuiglijkheid. Over de betekenis van lichamelijkheid in de liturgie*, Hilversum 1990 = IDEM: 'Liturgie und Sinnlichkeit. Über die Bedeutung der Leiblichkeit in der Liturgie', in LUKKEN (eds. CASPERS & VAN TONGEREN): *Per visibilia ad invisibilia* 118-139.

[26] GREIMAS: 'Réflexions sur les objets ethno-sémiotiques' 182.

always fully-rounded actions: real ointment with fragrant and healing oils, immersion as more fundamental than sprinkling, laying on of hands, censing, striking light, processing with a venerated image, kissing an icon. New baptismal rituals contain a number of new close-to-life elements: the names of those present are written on the cloth covering the baptised infant as a sign of the child's inclusion in the community; a book is passed around in which felicitations and prayers for the child can be written; the symbolism of the water is enlivened, etc.[27] In this respect, however, there remains much to be done. While the old symbols such as the fire of candles and the hearth, incense and scents, fountains inside and outside – in short, the four basic elements – continue to have an obvious place in everyday life, symbolic expressive elements still often have a difficult time of it in liturgy. This world of images must have its extension in liturgy. For example, it can be asked if in churches the sanctuary should not visually become what it once was, only now filled with changing images that express our contemporary sense of life.[28]

Like verbal expression, authentic physical expression on the part of the worship leader and congregation is by no means an inessential matter, but a fundamental liturgical given that no ritual can do without. Here too there are very practical tasks that involve the search for a new style of leading and celebration. This style can no longer be primarily defined by rubric, by precise rules in liturgical books and their commentaries, as was the case before the Second Vatican Council; what it is about is fully-developed human verbal and physical expression.[29]

With an eye to all this, we should reread authors such as Bachelard and Guardini.[30] Buitendijk's phenomenological reflections offer a unique

---

[27] Numerous examples of the reshaping of old actions from Christian liturgy in the light of contemporary anthropology are to be found in the *Werkmap (voor) Liturgie* and in VRIJDAG: *Zonder beelden sprak hij niet tot hen.*

[28] F. FRIJNS: 'Meer een lijst met vragen', in *Werkmap (voor) Liturgie* 24 (1990) 313-314.

[29] LUKKEN: 'Op zoek naar een nieuwe stijl van voorgaan'.

[30] R. GUARDINI: *Von heiligen Zeichen*, Mainz 1929; G. BACHELARD: *La terre et les rêveries de la volonté: essai sur l'imagination de la matière*, Paris 1988[14]; IDEM: *L'eau et les rêves: essai sur l'imagination de la matière*, Paris 1991[23]; IDEM: *L'air et les songes: essai sur l'imagination du mouvement*, Paris 1990[17]; IDEM: *Psychoanalyse van het vuur*, Meppel 1990; IDEM: *La flamme d'une chandelle*, Paris 1984[7]; IDEM: *La poétique de l'espace*, Paris 1989[4]. See in this connection also H. KIRCHHOFF (ed.): *Ursymbole und ihre Bedeutung für die religiöse Erziehung*, München 1982 and M. JOSUTIS: *Der Weg in das Leben. Eine*

perspective. He writes impressively on the aesthetic side of physical expression.[31] Beautiful human movement is relaxed. At the same time it has the peculiar gradation inherent in gradual movement. In general, slow movements are more gracious than fast ones. Fast movements easily become too linear, brusque and angular. But the movement must also not be too slow. Movements that are too slow appear difficult, like the crawling of a snail. The attention then shifts to the separate components of the movement. The movements must also be regular, but not in such a manner that the rhythm becomes monotonous. In sitting, the body must on the one hand be controlled, but on the other hand left to itself in a relaxed manner. It must sit back without seeking support. The same is true for standing. In our search for a new style of celebration we should, I believe, take his reflections to heart.

In our culture there is a renewed interest in ritual *dance*. One finds attempts to give dance a place of its own in Christian liturgy. This happens in a natural way in Africa, where dance is never purely a form of recreation, but is a way of life. Even demonstrations are held in dance steps. The danced introit procession in the Congolese liturgy then comes across as totally natural. In our Western culture dance has been less integrated in life. Yet it must be asked if that means that dance should not have a place, precisely at the more condensed moments of ritual. Among the ways that this has been given shape in The Netherlands are the spatial services celebrated in Amserfoort.[32]

The presentative character of ritual is also strongly defined by the *space* in which the liturgy takes place. I will address this element separately in Chapter 9.1.

Einführung in den Gottesdienst auf verhaltenswissenschaftlicher Grundlage, München 1991 (regarding basic postures and Ur-actions, including going, sitting, seeing, singing, hearing, eating).

[31] F. BUITENDIJK: *Algemene theorie der menselijke houding en beweging*, Antwerpen 1964, 587-598.

[32] See *Liturgische proeftuinen*: *Rondom het Woord* 27 (1985) no. 2 and *Dansen voor het leven*: *Rondom het Woord* 27 (1985) no. 2 and 31 (1989) no. 2, and VAN AMSTERDAM: *Hoe welkom zijn op de bergen* 107-113; for a description of the spatial services celebrated in Amersfoort, see H. BLANKESTEIJN: 'Dansen in de liturgie', in *Werkmap (voor) Liturgie* 25 (1991) 167-178; IDEM: *Voor wie niet stil kan zitten in de kerk. Liturgie met handen en voeten*, Kampen 2002. See also T. VAN DIJK, & J. PEIJNENBURG: 'Levensdans', in *Werkmap (voor) Liturgie* 25 (1991) 152-166 and W. MEURER: *Volk Gottes auf dem Weg. Bewegungselemente im Gottesdienst*, Mainz 1989.

3. POPULAR PIETY OR RELIGIOUS POPULAR CULTURE

In Part 1 I noted that in religions of the book, there is often a difference in accent between the culture of the people and that of the elite.[33] One must also respect this difference of accent. Popular piety can prevent the word from becoming separated from the full sensory and preconceptual context with which it is connected. As such, it retains the link with the anthropological source of the rite, and is an indispensable corrective that maintains the tension between word and rite.

I propose to go more deeply into the importance of popular piety for liturgy here. The instruction on inculturation is very dismissive with regard to including expressions of popular piety in the liturgy. This course is firmly shut off.[34] It is not impossible that a misconception that one often finds in Church documents plays a part in this rejection. For example, Brückner notes that in these documents popular piety, as *religio carnalis*, is confused – or fused – with the view of popular piety as magic and superstition.[35] The superseded evolutionary concept in comparative religion, which saw a three step progression from superstition through religion to Christianity, as a rising line, plays a role in this.[36] This misconception results in a certain spiritualisation and a negative view of the symbolic-sensory forms of interaction of which Lorenzer speaks, which are an indispensable anthropological foundation for all liturgy.[37] Whatever the case, a rejection as absolute as this was remarkable. It is, after all, rather different if you include popular devotions in liturgy as a whole without further ado, or if you draw upon language and ritual patterns from them to arrive at a more popular and less classical form of liturgy.[38] There is more than enough evidence from the

---

[33] Part 1, Chapter 2, 2.2.

[34] CONGREGATIO DE CULTU DIVINO ET DISCIPLINA SACRAMENTORUM: *De liturgia romana et inculturatione. Instructio quarta* 45. Important is the recent document of the CONGREGATION FOR DIVINE WORSHIP AND THE DISCIPLINE OF THE SACRAMENTS, *Directory on Popular Piety and the Liturgy. Principles and Guidelines*, Vatican City 2001. Although one finds there a more balanced view on the relation between popular piety and liturgy, they are still too much separated. See also P. POST 2004 in Bibliography.

[35] W. BRÜCKNER: 'Zu den modernen Konstrukten 'Volksfrömmigkeit' und 'Aberglauben", in *Jahrbuch für Volkskunde* 16 (1993) 215-218.

[36] POST: 'Religious Popular Culture and Liturgy' 33.

[37] LORENZER: *Das Konzil der Buchhalter*. See also LUKKEN: *Liturgie en zintuiglijkheid* 30-40.

[38] CHUPUNGCO: 'Remarks on the Roman liturgy and inculturation' 275-276.

history of liturgy that popular devotions can enter into liturgy in a productive and mature manner.[39] Through the process of inculturation liturgy and popular religiosity can enter into a dynamic interaction and mutual assimilation with each other's qualities. For churches with a long tradition of popular religious practices inculturation is the only valid solution to liturgical alienation, and the best way to make popular religiosity a vehicle for the gospel. The Puebla document argues for this.[40] Marsili correctly points out that it is not right to determine if the peculiar forms, language and style of popular religion are suitable for liturgy only on the basis of a comparison with the classical qualities of the Roman liturgy.[41] And, according to Chupungco, while the classical Roman liturgy has the qualities of concision, sobriety and directness, Eastern liturgies often have verbose prayer formulae, colourful and dramatic rites and repeated actions in veneration of icons.[42] In other words, there are other authentic liturgical traditions besides the Roman tradition. When the classical Roman rite inculturated into the local Frankish/Germanic culture, the apologias became an important component of this liturgy. As it happens, both the structure and the language of these apologias are completely of devotional origin.

The foremost characteristics of popular religion are festivity, drama, spontaneity and creativity, a personal and at the same time communal character, and an orientation to the other world combined with the deeply human and immediate.[43] The literary genre associated with it is characterised by its picturesque quality. Popular piety loves to use sacred images. It has a predilection for things such as full participation, repetition and communal recitation, and makes use of dramatic forms that are often strongly mimetic and imitative.[44] The gap between popular religiosity and liturgy can and must be bridged. History demonstrates

[39] CHUPUNGCO: *Liturgical Inculturation* 95-133 (under the title 'Popular religiosity and liturgical inculturation').

[40] *Documento de Puebla, La evangelización en el presente y en el futuro de América Latina*, Buenos Aires 1979, 465.

[41] S. MARSILI: 'Liturgia e non-liturgia', in B. NEUNHEUSER a.o. (eds.): *La liturgia momento nella storia della salvezza* (Anamnesis 1), Turijn 1974, 156.

[42] CHUPUNGCO: *Liturgical Inculturation* 111-112.

[43] S. MARSILI: 'Liturgia e non-liturgia', in B. NEUNHEUSER a.o. (eds.): *La liturgia momento nella storia della salvezza* (Anamnesis 1), Turijn 1974, 156.

[44] CHUPUNGCO: *Liturgical Inculturation* 119.

that piety, including popular piety, if it is not sufficiently integrated into liturgy, will establish an independent life of its own alongside liturgy.[45] Popular religiosity should thoroughly be a part of a fully-rounded Christian ritual.

Post demonstrates how important popular religiosity is for the inculturation of contemporary Western liturgy.[46] In the course of this, he points out that the concept of popular piety is in a certain sense outdated, and easily leads to misunderstandings. He prefers to speak of religious popular culture.[47] In fact, important shifts have taken place in ethnology. Since the 1960s and '70s, popular culture is no longer understood as referring to a particular, and specifically lower layer in society. The antithesis between elite and popular has been abandoned. Popular culture is rather the culture which people unconsciously share with one another. It is not the culture of the *kleine Leute*, but culture with a small c, which all share.[48] Religious popular culture is thus a religious culture which touches all.[49] It involves general and everyday forms of religiosity, lived practice, and ritual plays a key role in that. All levels of society participate in this religious popular culture, including the educated and social leaders. Something of the tension between prescribed order and this lived practice always indeed remains, but the earlier dichotomy has been laid to rest.[50] As anthropological qualities of this religious popular

---

[45] M. METZGER: *Histoire de la liturgie. Les grandes étapes*, Paris 1994 = M. METZGER: *History of the Liturgy: the Major Stages*, Collegeville 1997. See also the review of the Italian translation of this book by E. MAZZI: 'A proposito di un libro recente', in *Rivista Liturgica* 82 (1995) 333-340.

[46] POST: 'Religious Popular Culture and Liturgy', in *Questions liturgiques* 79 (1998) 14-59. Further among others POST: 'Traditie gebruiken'; IDEM: 'Het verleden in het spel?'; IDEM: 'De pastor aan de bron'; IDEM: 'Thema's, theorieën en trends in bedevaartonderzoek', in PIEPER, POST & VAN UDEN (eds.): *Bedevaart en pelgrimage* 253-302; IDEM: *Ritueel landschap*; IDEM: 'Van paasvuur tot stille tocht. Over interferentie van liturgisch en volksreligieus ritueel', in *Volkskundig bulletin* 25 (1999) 2/3, 215-234; IDEM: *Het wonder van Dokkum*; POST & PIEPER: *De palmzondagviering*; VAN UDEN, PIEPER & POST (eds.): *Oude sporen, nieuwe wegen*; see also M. VAN UDEN, P. POST & J. PIEPER: *The Modern Pilgrim. Multidisciplinary Explorations of Christian Pilgrimage* (Liturgia condenda 8), Leuven 1998.

[47] See also Part 2, Chapter 2, 1.

[48] POST: 'Religious Popular Culture and Liturgy' 24.

[49] See also L. VOYÉ: 'Uitwissing of nieuwe legitimatie van de volksreligie? Een sociologische benadering', in J. LAMBERTS (ed.): *Volksreligie, liturgie en evangelisatie* 140-141.

[50] POST: 'Religious Popular Culture and Liturgy' 25-29.

culture Post lists the emphasis on the group (through which the spirituality and rituality of the laity come better into view), the close connections with spatial and festive elements, an accent on physicality and sensory experience, emotionality and expressive dramatic strength, a predilection for mediated religiosity (relics, saints, angels, amulets), and a specific attention for nature and the landscape.[51] Religious popular culture touches the corporal craving for the divine that is also characteristic of contemporary culture.[52] In this connection one should reread what was said in the previous section about the importance of an intercultural dialogue with African and African-American cultures.

Presentative symbolism is thus comprehensive, and indispensable in Christian ritual. It penetrates to the deepest layer of human life. It makes faith, hope and love into an integrated human experience. When we burn incense by the coffin on an incense dish during a funeral liturgy, and at the same time pray that all our prayers should rise as incense before the countenance of God, the prayer touches a deeper level in us. Those who bid farewell to the deceased in the cemetery, touching the coffin for the last time, throwing a handful of dirt onto the coffin, and witness its sinking into the ground, close the ritual of burial, and have definitive closure themselves in their farewell. Grimes rightly observes that liturgy must be the most tangible form of ritual. 'In liturgy… the feet cry out to touch the ground.'[53]

---

[51] POST: 'Religious Popular Culture and Liturgy' 55-56.
[52] A.-M. KORTE: 'Een lijfelijke hang naar het goddelijke. De nieuwe culturele belangstelling voor godsgeloof als theologische vraag', in *Tijdschrift voor Theologie* 38 (1998) 227-237; MALLOY: 'The Re-Emergence of Popular Religion' 2-15.
[53] GRIMES: *Marrying and Burying* 224.

CHAPTER 8

NEW RITUALS OF TRANSITION

In our culture Christian rituals marking transitions in life are undergoing radical change. I will first discuss the familiar transitional rituals from birth to death, and then the new transitional rituals which are arising in our culture. In this it is not my intention to paint a full picture of Christian rituals from birth to death. My concern here is only to sketch the new pluriform face of these rituals which is growing in our culture.

1. TRANSITIONAL RITUALS SURROUNDING INITIATION, MARRIAGE, FORGIVENESS AND RECONCILIATION, SICKNESS AND DEATH

Through the last few years there has been enormous creativity in The Netherlands with respect to the rituals accompanying important life transitions, from birth to death.[1] Alongside the Christian sacraments there are new secular, general religious and Christian rituals of transition. This development is particularly marked in regard to initiation, marriage, forgiveness and reconciliation, sickness and death. In the past it was rather frequently the case that people chose a Christian sacrament 'for lack of anything better'. Indeed, until recently there was a paucity of good secular birth rituals, and there were only rather feeble secular rituals for the occasions of marriage and death. Thus it was easy for people to opt for the richer ecclesiastical ritual, though actually it did not precisely fit them. As early as 1984 I therefore argued for designing new transitional rituals. In the future there would have to be a varied selection of rituals for the important transitions in life. I saw their creation as a task for pastoral care, so long as society itself would not provide them. Several years ago, however, the no-man's-land between sacrament and general human life transitions began to disappear. Radical shifts have occurred as a result of the dis-

---

[1] G. LUKKEN: 'Zoeken naar nieuwe overgangsrituelen', in *Werkmap (voor) Liturgie* 24 (1990) 159-166.

appearance of the taboo against ritual, and there is enormous ritual creativity to be found on all sides. With regard to transition rituals, one encounters great multiformity, and this also affects the sacraments in a strict sense. These developments have led to new shape for, and new forms of anchorage of the various sacraments in our culture. In the sections to follow I will sketch the outlines of these developments. They are particularly relevant in connection with the place and form of Christian ritual in our culture.

1.1. Initiation

Before we begin, some clarification is necessary with regard to the term initiation. In its strict sense this word is used for particular rites of transition, namely those rites through which someone becomes a full member of a community.[2] In this context, the term is particularly used for rites at puberty. Initiation involves a separation from a previous situation and a full incorporation into the new community, which is effected through an intermediate stage of certain ordeals. One finds these three phases in Van Gennep: a) the *rites de séparation* or *rites préliminaires*; b) the *rites de marge* or *rites liminaires*; and c) the *rites d'agrégation* or *rites postliminaires*.[3] Van Gennep also uses the term initiation in the sense just noted. On the other hand, he expanded the concept. All sorts of other transitions in human life also have an initiatory character. For both groups and individuals life consists of repeatedly letting go of and working toward, of dying and being reborn. There is constantly a process of acting, pausing, waiting and resting, to act anew, but then in a new manner. Life has a great number of transitions, each of which can be accounted a turning point, and can be accompanied with 'initiatory' rites.[4] Grimes further notes that 'in the

---

[2] GRIMES: *Deeply into the Bone* 117 correctly points out: 'There is no good reason why an occasion has to be *called* initiation in order to *be* initiation. One should look for initiation under other names: orientation, promotion, conversion, confirmation, ordination, and so on. Sororities, fraternities, civic organisations, religious organisations, educational organisations, sport groups, ethnic groups, native groups, and even some business enact rites – some secret, some public – that are initiatory. Such occasions either start (that is, "initiate") a process, or they mark degrees of advancement through the ranks'.

[3] Part 1, Chapter 4, 5.3.

[4] HAMELINE: 'Les *rites de passage* d'Arnold van Gennep' 18-19.

West the model for *all* rites of passage (not just initiations) has been largely initiatory, dependent upon the themes and activities of men's initiation... For this reason *rites of passage* is often used as a synonym for *initiation* ...'[5]

Although it is indeed the case that all transition rituals have numerous initiatory elements, in the following I, like Grimes, will use the word only in the strict sense.[6] That is also the meaning in which it has been used by Christians from the beginning right down to the present day. In connection with initiation one can, following Grimes, further qualify Van Gennep's three-phase structure. Grimes warns against an oversimplification of initiation's complexity into three phases, and at this point presents a list of elements that appear in initiations from various cultures. 'We should be suspicious of threefold sequences, since they too obviously reflect the Western intellectual habit of preferring threes – the doctrine of the Trinity (Father, Son, Holy Ghost), the idea of dialectic (thesis, antithesis, synthesis) and the generic narrative (beginning, middle, end)'.[7] Still, as a rule, particularly with Christian initiation rituals, Van Gennep's tripartite division will be distinctly present (suffering, death, resurrection).

Christian initiation comprises the sacraments of baptism, confirmation and first participation in the Eucharist, through which persons become fully 'incorporated' into the Christian community. In the early church the three phases comprised one large ritual entity, as is now still the case in the Eastern churches. In the West the phases became separated from one another, through which baptism was easily linked with the transitional ritual of birth, and confirmation and first full participation in the Eucharist with that of puberty and becoming adult. In the following I will first deal with the birth rituals, which can be considered as the first step in the initiation, and subsequently with the rituals with regard to becoming adult, which form a second step. With regard to the Eucharist, it will not be dealt with separately, but in the context of the second phase.

---

[5] GRIMES: *Deeply into the Bone* 336.

[6] For Grimes's view with regard to initiation rituals, see GRIMES: *Deeply into the Bone* 87-148 (under the title 'Coming of Age, Joining up') and also IDEM: 'The Initiatory Dilemma'.

[7] GRIMES: *Deeply into the Bone* 103-107, here 107.

1.1.1. Birth

For a long time in our Western culture Christian baptism took the place of an actual birth ritual.[8] Furthermore, in The Netherlands there was rather a paucity of secular rituals accompanying birth. Secular birth rituals were limited to the choosing of a name for the child by the parents, the registration of the child at the Registry Office by the father under that name, sending birth announcements, lying-in visits to the mother, and distribution and consumption of Dutch rusks with blue aniseed candy sprinkles for a boy and pink for a girl. It could justly be said that Christian baptism was the only richer birth ritual.[9] More highly developed secular rituals did not exist. As Christian baptismal ritual fell out of favour – and particularly in The Netherlands that was increasingly the situation over the past decades – a ritual lacunae gradually formed. It is therefore not surprising that people began to take more interest in secular rituals surrounding the birth of a child. For instance, in 1986 the women's magazine *Viva* devoted an issue to the revival of old rituals surrounding birth and the creation of new ones.[10] The years which followed witnessed a flood of creativity with regard to birth ritual.[11] One now has more or less fully developed *secular birth rituals*. 'Ritual agencies' and what are being called 'maternity parties' play a specific role in these.[12]

This creativity has not been limited to secular rituals. Ritual agencies want to also meet demand for *general religious*, and possibly *general Christian birth rituals*. For example, the female director of a ritual agency notes that all kinds of things can go wrong at a 'birth celebration'. She

[8] G. LUKKEN: 'Rituelen rond geboorte en doop: nieuwe ontwikkelingen', in G. LUKKEN & J. DE WIT (eds.): *Nieuw leven. Rituelen rond geboorte en doop* (Liturgie in beweging 1), Baarn 1997, 9-31.

[9] LUKKEN: 'Rituelen rond geboorte en doop: nieuwe ontwikkelingen'; G. LUKKEN: 'Infant baptism in The Netherlands and Flanders. A Christian ritual in the dynamic of the anthropological/theological and cultural context', in POST, ROUWHORST, VAN TONGEREN & SCHEER (eds.): *Christian Feast and Festival* 551-580.

[10] A. BUYSMAN, A.: 'Hoe vier je de geboorte van je kind?', in *Viva* 1986, 20 (16-5-1986) 6-11. P. DE CLERCK: 'Orientations actuelles de la pastorale du baptême', in A. HOUSSIAU a.o., *Le baptême, entrée dans l'existence chrétienne,* Brussel 1983, 124, note 19, notes that in his documentation he has one proposal for a secular birth celebration, that being from the region of Feurs, in France.

[11] In this connection see Part 3, Chapter 2, 2.

[12] Part 3, Chapter 2, 2. and Chapter 3, 2.2. See for instance also *Thebe Visie* (= publication of the Midden Brabant Care Centre) spring 1999, 13.

tells of a couple who did everything they could think of to make the celebration successful: they made sure all the invitations went out, that there were plenty of refreshments, decorations, everything. Still, the parents later felt something had been lacking, although they could not put their finger on what. They ultimately decided that it was because the child, who was in the end what the whole thing was supposed to be about, had slept through the whole affair in its own room, and nobody had gotten to see the baby. 'These people wanted something like a baptism, but not in a church. But in that case, you first must understand what a baptism involves, namely the reception of somebody into a certain community. They wanted to have their child formally included in their family and circle of friends. When all the guests were there, they should have brought the child in, and perhaps recited a poem, played some music or lit a candle, just to let it be seen that the child was there. But it's pretty difficult to think of all that by yourself'.[13]

The rise of *secular birth rituals* like this is not surprising. In a study the Ghent philosopher J. De Visscher, a specialist in culture, described the fundamental anthropological categories that play a depth role in the birth of a child, beyond the purely biological level, in a very impressive manner.[14] A child is born into a community. Therefore its birth is accompanied with a whole web of meanings and expectations: a fabric of stories that is the expression of the philosophy of life and world-views of a community. We regard the child as a unique individual and expect that he or she will develop into an inimitable personality. Already before the birth we prepare the new place at home that the child will fill, and initially that place in the family will be a privileged one. All kinds of things can go wrong at the birth: the child must, as it were, be snatched from capricious and dangerous powers of nature. We therefore experience birth as a leaving behind of an absolute bondage to nature, and see the child as in one way or another a gift and a responsibility, as 'ours'. From the beginning, therefore, we mark that child as a human being, as *our* child. Birth is regarded as a liberation from nature *and* the reception

---

[13] E. VAN HAAREN: 'Het gerommel in je hoofd moet naar buiten', in *Hervormd Nederland* December 21, 1996. See also VOSSEBELD: 'Van confectie naar maatwerk' 20-21.

[14] DE VISSSCHER: *Een te voltooien leven* 26-47. GRIMES: *Marrying and Burying* 160-163, 172-175, 182 points to the importance of participation in the birth itself, and the rituals surrounding it, as the basis for all further birth rituals. Regarding birth rituals see also GRIMES: *Deeply into the Bone* 13-85.

of the child into the world of humans; it has both a negative and a positive pole. We welcome that child into our world, on the one hand seeking to ward off the destructive powers of nature, and on the other hand expressing our desire to make a place for the child in our human world and our history. We give the child a name and express our joy at its arrival in our midst. These common, basic facts of human life play an unmistakable role. Birth is a biological phenomenon which is marked socio-culturally. It is essentially an event which involves the community, because birth is the manner in which the community is perpetuated down through generations. Therefore every culture places it in a socio-cultural context. The new member of the group is acknowledged before the group and by the group in a ritual of naming. The new member's kinship relationships are specified in this way, and the child is acknowledged as a member of the whole community. Thus the ritual of naming is universally the first rite of passage in human life.[15] Indeed, the giving of a name also plays a large role in the new secular birth rituals.[16]

At this point, it is also striking to note that this name-giving is undergoing new developments. For a very long time it was strictly subject to tradition: the child was generally named for a saint, and in any case received a name from the family tradition – perhaps the name of a grandparent or another family member.[17] Until the 1940s, Johannes, Jan and Cornelis were the most common names for boys in The Netherlands, and Maria, Johanna and Anna the most common names for girls. Since the 1960s, however, the nuclear family has become more important, and broader family traditions that were strongly intertwined with the tradition of certain saint's names have been abandoned. Aesthetic considerations have thus gradually assumed the dominant role. The name must be beautiful and pleasant-sounding.[18] Also, even stillborn

---

[15] R. PINXTEN: 'Geboorte en doopsel. Een visie van een antropoloog en vrijzinnige', in L. LEIJSSEN, M. CLOET & K. DOBBELAERE (eds.): *Levensrituelen. Geboorte en doopsel* (Kadoc-Studies 20), Leuven 1996, 47. Also: J.M. JASPARD: 'Geboorte en doopsel vanuit psychofilosofische hoek bekeken', in LEIJSSEN, CLOET & DOBBELAERE (eds.): *Levensrituelen. Geboorte en doopsel* 28-45.

[16] For the ritual of naming, see also GRIMES: *Marrying and Burying* 175 and IDEM: *Deeply into the Bone* 76-82.

[17] M. CLOET: 'Het doopsel in de nieuwe tijd (ca. 1550-ca. 1800)', in LEIJSSEN, CLOET & DOBBELAERE (eds.): *Levensrituelen. Geboorte en doopsel* 87-92.

[18] H. STAAL: 'Kindernamen', in *NRC Handelsblad* November 2, 1999, referring to research by the Meertens Institute and a NIPO survey from 1995.

children are now given names. People have become conscious that it is very important that this giving of a name to stillborn children should also take on a ritual form.[19] In recent years many cemeteries in The Netherlands have erected monuments for unbaptised children who were buried without names. There are rituals by which they can still be given names.[20] The words of the pastor who conducted the service for a new-born baby girl whose body was found alongside a highway, hidden in a refuse bag, as she was given a dignified burial in the children's corner of a cemetery, are apposite here: 'We stand here now at the grave of a child without a name. There is no one here who really grieves for her, although we are all touched by this. The child came into being, apparently, out of the love between two persons. For about nine months she lived under the heart of her mother. What all happened with her mother in the days after her birth, what led her to her act, is unknown to us. She is a nameless little girl, someone to whom no one gave a name, who no one called to, no one knew, who will never be loved, a person who never even received a name. But we may be sure that her name is indeed written in the palm of God's hand, and that she will live on in His love.'[21] Finally, another whole new development is that people can choose to give the family name of the father *or* of the mother to the child, an innovation related to women's emancipation and equality with men. Secular ritual is evolving in all directions.

But there is still more. Many parents experience the birth of their child as a *religiously* charged event. For instance, a father tells how, as he was on his way home after the difficult birth of his first child, he had to stop on the way, so deeply had the event effected him. 'Something so beautiful has got to have something to do with religion,' he said.[22] Another voice calls so complete a little being a miracle: 'There is a driving force

---

[19] W. VOGELS: 'Woord en gebaar rond een doodgeboren kind', in LUKKEN & DE WIT (eds.): *Nieuw leven. Rituelen rond geboorte en doop* 90-97. See also G. RAMSHAW-SCHMIDT: 'Celebrating Baptism in Stages: A Proposal', in M. SEARLE (ed.): *Alternative Futures of Worship. Baptism and Confirmation*, Collegeville 1987, 145-146 (ritual after a miscarriage and when a child is stillborn).

[20] M. VAN DEN BERG: 'Meer nodig dan gedenktekens', in *Een-twee-een* 29 (2001) 20, 23-24.

[21] R. DROST: 'Naamloos vondelingetje sober begraven in Baarle-Nassau', in Dagblad *BN DeStem* August 15, 1998, 1.

[22] SPRUIT & VAN ZOELEN: *Dopen… Ja waarom eigenlijk?* 77-78.

behind it, a little piece of God'.[23] In this case a birth ritual which expresses this religious element, and creates forms for this experience, will be more adequate. Furthermore, it is self-evident that no hard and fast boundary exists between secular and general religious birth rituals.

In The Netherlands one also finds attempts to shape specifically *Christian* birth rituals. These are, to be clear, a rite of passage, placing the birth in a Christian perspective, and not an explicit celebration of baptism proper as Christian *re*birth. One can find suggestions for celebrations of birth of this sort in Kersten's book.[24] He notes that in these it is important to seek out a suitable Bible story or a passage from another source (Christian or otherwise); a poem or song can also function as an extension of this story. In addition, one can also search for adequate symbols. In that search it appears to be better not to make use of the symbol of water, in order to prevent confusion with baptism. But if someone is considering that, it need not be ruled out entirely. De Vries has written a song that could function most strikingly in such a Christian celebration of birth. The song speaks of the child who has left the womb to begin life, and from the beginning is connected with his or her Creator and whose destiny is determined by Him. In literal translation the text of the song reads:

> Knit together in my mother's womb,
> a wonder of creation,
> dedicated to the light,
> Your love has already shaped my life.

> Long before I could know your Word,
> when the day is just begun,
> You dawned as the Sun
> Who will be called my light and life.

> Before I come to that Light,
> You knew me already,
> You have created me,
> and my name is on Your lips.

> In the mouth that can hardly speak yet
> the music is already there,

---

[23] SPRUIT & VAN ZOELEN: *Dopen... Ja, waarom eigenlijk?* 86.
[24] KERSTEN: *Gedoopt voor mensen* 80-81.

the song is already to be found,
that will shatter the silence forever.

You, whose goodness is sung by little ones,
let the song of Your Name
comprise my whole life,
to hold threatening night at bay![25]

These birth rituals can be performed as self-standing rituals. Particularly the general religious and Christian birth rituals can also function, however, as spurs to and steps toward baptism, whether in the shorter or longer term. In that case one could term them catechumenal celebrations. One must realise that infant baptism is not an isolated event, standing entirely by itself. It has, so to speak, a short pre-history of its own. In the *Traditio Apostolica* by Hippolytus (circa 200 AD) one reads, 'When one then selects those who are going to receive baptism, one must investigate their lives. Have they... lived appropriately? Have they had respect for widows? Have they visited the sick? Have they performed all sorts of good works? When those who have supervised them provide affirmative witness, they can give hearing to the Gospel.'[26] In the early Church those to be baptised were selected on the basis of their conduct and for the fact that they were ready to receive the Good News in their life. Before baptism there was a catechumenate. The word 'catechumenate' is related to the word catechesis. In the early Church catechumens were those who received this catechesis – that is to say, an introduction to the faith. This catechumenate was accompanied with ritual moments which prepared them for actual baptism. Of course, one cannot simply transfer the criteria from the *Traditio Apostolica* to infant baptism. After Vatican II, however, the insight has grown that infant baptism too cannot take place without preparation, and this involves particularly the family or milieu in which the child will grow up. Therefore one can speak of there being a certain catechumenate with respect to infant baptism. Thus, after Vatican II what are called 'baptismal instructions' for the parents have very properly been introduced, sometimes individually, sometimes in groups. However, it has not been customary to have ritual moments in this process. Now, if one considers the general religious and Christian celebrations of birth mentioned above as phases on the way to baptism, one could then think of them as catechumenal celebrations. They could well function as such, if infant baptism follows within a short space of time. But they could likewise be a 'mounting-block' for baptism at a later age, for example when the child enters primary school or when he or she reaches adulthood. Some argue for the postponement of baptism to a later time. They would spread the baptism ritual out, as it were, over various phases, and only administer actual baptism at a later age.[27] It could be that this argument rests on a certain view of the child. But also it can be based on an awareness that there are various degrees of involvement in the church, and on the conviction that one must deal circumspectly with the water of baptism. When people are able to be involved with the core of Christianity in a less decisive way, celebrations other than baptism may be experienced as more adequate, and there might be a preference for a gradual approach to baptism.

The above could point the way toward a ritual selection that on the one hand does justice to the pluriform situation of religion in our culture, and on the other to the identity of Christian baptism. The separation of secular, general religious and Christian *birth rituals* and *baptism* serves to do justice to both types of ritual at birth. We have come to realise that through the great interest in the anthropology of ritual in recent decades the *distinction* between transition rituals and sacraments in the strict sense became blurred. Particularly since the Second Vatican Council an approach has arisen that emphasised the coherence between sacraments and rites of passage. In this perspective the sacraments are seen chiefly as *life*-rituals. As examples one can point to theologians such as Kasper, Ratzinger and Boff and to the Louvain *Levensrituelen* series.[28] This is a

[27] See also DE CLERCK: 'Orientations actuelles' 123-146. De Clerck refers to J.Ph. Bonnard, J. Moignt, D. Boureau, H. Denis, Ch. Paliard en P.-G. Trebossen.
[28] W. KASPER: 'Wort und Symbol im sakramentalen Leben. Eine anthropologische Begründung', in W. HEINEN (ed.): *Bild – Wort – Symbol in der Theologie*, Würzburg 1969, 157-175; IDEM: 'Wort und Sakrament', in *Glaube und Geschichte*, Mainz 1970, 285-310; J. RATZINGER: *Die sakramentale Begründung christlicher Existenz*, Meitingen 1966; L. BOFF: *Die Kirche als Sakrament im Horizont der Welterfahrung*, Paderborn 1972, particularly 142, 380-383, 385; IDEM: *Kleine Sakramentenlehre*. For the Louvain series see LEIJSSEN, CLOET & DOBBELAERE (eds.): *Levensrituelen. Geboorte en doopsel*; K. DOBBELAERE, L. LEIJSSEN & M. CLOET (eds.): *Levensrituelen. Het vormsel* (Kadoc-Studies 12), Leuven 1991; R. BURGGRAEVE, M. CLOET, K. DOBBELAERE & L. LEIJSSEN (eds.): *Het huwelijk* (Kadoc-Studies 24), Leuven 2000. These studies are part of a still to be completed series on rituals that mark important moments in the life of a person, and thus stress the relation between transition rites and sacraments.

legitimate approach, but it is important to recognise its limits. The fact is, the danger is not merely theoretical that Christian identity and the anthropological basis are so telescoped into one another that the one will lose out at the expense of the other. The identity of the sacrament will then dominate and manipulate the anthropological basis, or the opposite will happen: the anthropological basis will, as it were, swallow up the identity of the sacrament. After all, the connection between rites of passage and sacraments is not a necessary one.[29] Baptism as rebirth through water and the Spirit does indeed call up associations in one way or another with birth itself, and that birth can play a large role in the liturgical expression of baptism, but baptism does not have to take place at the moment of birth, or soon after it. Adults can also be baptised. In the first centuries, adult baptism was in fact the normal practice. Baptism is thus decidedly more than a Christian celebration of birth. Put in another way: a Christian celebration of birth is not yet Christian baptism per se. Another example is confirmation. This is not connected with a particular age, such as leaving primary school or reaching adulthood. A senior citizen can also be confirmed, and likewise a newborn child, as is customary in Eastern liturgies.

Thus there is no reason that the sacrament should coincide with a turning point in life. An individual's life history does not per se run parallel with the Christian, sacramental salvation history of a believer. The two can run parallel, but that is not essential. There is certainly an analogy between the turning points of a human life and the sacraments. Rebirth in water and Spirit definitely has something to do with birth. But at the same time it is the beginning of an actual new history. It is a matter, according to Paul, of tearing loose and reattaching, a grafting into another stem, for 'you were cut out of an olive tree that is wild by nature, and contrary to nature were grafted into a cultivated olive tree' (Rom. 11:24). This being grafted into Christ brings various people from various times and places together onto a new path, irrespective of rank and class. In this, the ethical dimension of infant baptism also is more clearly delineated. The bonds of the child reach further than those of family or clan.

The sacraments are then intersections in this new life history. The moment and the way in which people come to faith is closely connected with personal choice and experience. It is also related to the situation

[29] LUKKEN: De onvervangbare weg van de liturgie 67-71.

which obtains within their culture. For instance, in a Christian culture the moment of baptism will lie closer to birth than in a non-Christian culture.

Thus in the sacraments an opening up of borders has a place, in the perspective of a *new* life history. This opening reaches still *further*. When one understands the significance of the sacraments too simply in terms of individual life histories, the danger arises that they will close up on themselves. This can lead to subjectivism and privatisation of the sacraments. They will then be seen as only a personal support and comfort in life's critical transitional situations. One remains stuck at the level of the security that the sacrament offers, and they are seen, first and foremost, as family events. But that which is peculiar to a sacrament, that which takes one by surprise in it, is (or in any case should be) precisely that the social dimension is radicalised and universalised. The sacraments are, after all, acts of a new community that breaks through family bonds and knows no ethnic boundaries, a community to whom 'the Jesus affair' happens and must constantly happen. Or, put in other terms, the sacraments place us in the midst of the broad dynamic of Christian sacred history, and therefore, in the midst of the new people of God, who are oriented toward and must focus themselves on the coming of the Kingdom of God, that kingdom of justice and peace which is intended for all. The sacraments are thus about salvation, not as a gift turned in on itself, but as something that reaches much further than the well-being of the individual believer. They aim toward the liberation of mankind. It is the essence of the sacrament that it challenges one to genuine engagement with real problems and with the real world in which we all live.

These theological considerations are extremely fundamental in connection with our topic, because on the basis of the analogy between sacraments and *rites de passage* all sorts of expressions from these *rites de passage* can be taken into the sacraments. The opposite can also happen: on this basis all sorts of expressions from the sacrament are suitable for secular *rites de passage*; a pronounced example of this are the secular transitional rites of Marxism which were mentioned in Part 1.[30] The Christian sacraments were often used as a model in designing these. For example, in the socialist birth ritual one even finds the godfather and

[30] Part 1, Chapter 2, 3.9.

godmother from Christian baptism.[31] But at the same time, there is a difference. When the sacrament is totally absorbed in the expression of a *rite de passage*, it happens at the expense of the true meaning of the sacrament. Baptism then becomes only a Christian celebration of birth within the nuclear and extended family. A sound sacramental theology stands in the field of tension between two poles: that of the anthropological basis and that of what is peculiar to the sacrament. This tension is not purely theoretical; it is constantly present in everyday liturgical practice.

This tension between the anthropological basis and that which is peculiar to the sacrament can however be expressed in entirely different ways. In this connection a comparison between the baptismal practice in The Netherlands and Flanders is especially interesting.[32] The comparison involves one linguistic region, in which Dutch is spoken: The Netherlands and a section of Belgium, namely the Flemish provinces immediately adjoining the Dutch border.[33] Although the two areas abut one another and share a language, it is striking that within this one language region there are two rather distinct tendencies in relation to infant baptism which can be distinguished among Catholics.

According to a Louvain study, in Flanders in 1993 a high percentage of infants were baptised. In that year 80.7% of all live-born children there were baptised in the Catholic Church.[34] This high regard for infant baptism was also highlighted in the European Values Research in 1990.[35] Flemings believe it is important to turn to the Church at pivotal

[31] *Sei Willkommen Kind. Empfehlungen für die Namensweihe*, Zentralhaus für Kulturarbeit, Leipzig 1973; LANE: *The Rites of Rulers*.

[32] LUKKEN: 'Infant baptism in The Netherlands and Flanders' 551-580.

[33] Since 1971 the Belgian Constitution has provided that the country is divided into four language regions, namely the Region of Flanders (Dutch speaking, 55% of the population), the Walloon Region (French speaking), the German-speaking cantons, and the Brussels Region (officially Dutch and French-speaking, although most residents speak French).

[34] LEIJSSEN, CLOET & DOBBELAERE (eds.): *Levensrituelen. Geboorte en doopsel*. Figures from the Interdiocesan Centre, Religious Statistics Service. See A. VAN MEERBEECK: 'Dopen: ja, waarom niet? Een sociologische verkenning van de betekenis van dopen in Vlaanderen', in LEIJSSEN, CLOET & DOBBELAERE (eds.): *Levensrituelen. Geboorte en doopsel* 200 and 216.

[35] A. VAN MEERBEECK: 'The Importance of a Religious Service at Birth: The Persistent Demand for Baptism in Flanders (Belgium)', in *Social Compass* (1995) 47-58; IDEM: 'De praktijk van het doopsel. Een doorlichting van de situatie in Vlaanderen', in *Kultuurleven* 64 (1997) 44-51.

moments in life. With this, however, it must be recognised that the demand for baptism does not always arise from religious considerations. Why, for instance, do people still turn to the Catholic Church at these moments, while they no longer take part in the weekend liturgy and even describe themselves as not religious? Apparently popular customs have become attached to the Catholic ritual of baptism so that it satisfies the need to sacralise the important life-transition that is the birth of a child. That leads to the question of pastoral strategies with regard to infant baptism. It is in this context that the authors of the Louvain collection argue for a liberal policy regarding baptism.[36] They argue that it is best that the Church acts to meet the need for sacralisation felt at the time of the birth of a child, while at the same time making use of the opportunity to lay out requirements. The catechesis that takes place in this context is the moment par excellence for especially stressing the function of Christian religion in providing meaning in life.[37] However, some doubts are also sounded in the concluding observations to the Louvain collection. The editors of the collection observe there that in Flanders baptism is a 'super-valued sacrament', and pose the question, should the Church in the future profile its rituals more strongly, or is it the case that the Church's rituals connect with a universal experience, the interpretation of which expands the potential for deepening the Christian understanding of the meaning of life? They ultimately favour the latter. In our postmodern society, where 'open stories' play so large a role, with sound guidance and catechesis the way can be opened up for further deepening of Christian faith.[38] Leijssen examines the proposal of De Kesel to replace baptism in certain cases by a 'blessing of the children' in which the birth of a child could be celebrated in a pious and religious manner. Prior to that, De Kesel argues for radicalising the baptismal ritual to emphasise its specific Christian power and expression.[39]

---

[36] In addition to the article VAN MEERBEECK: 'Dopen: ja, waarom niet?', see particularly J. GOVAERTS: 'De pastorale begeleiding naar aanleiding van de kinderdoop. Situatie, beleid en vorming', in LEIJSSEN, CLOET & DOBBELAERE (eds.): *Levensrituelen. Geboorte en doopsel* 301-310.

[37] VAN MEERBEECK: 'Dopen: ja, waarom niet?' 215; K. DOBBELAERE: 'Een minderheidskerk? Enkele sociologische bedenkingen', in *Collationes* 18 (1988) 260-268.

[38] L. LEIJSSEN, M. CLOET & K. DOBBELAERE: 'Slotbeschouwingen', in LEIJSSEN, CLOET & DOBBELAERE (eds.): *Levensrituelen. Geboorte en doopsel*, 317-318.

[39] J. DE KESEL: *Omwille van zijn Naam. Een tegendraads pleidooi voor de kerk*, Tielt 1994, 151-155.

Leijssen is however of the opinion that a separation into a blessing of the child as a first step and baptism as a second step is not a good idea. 'Who will decide when the ritual must be limited to the blessing of the child and when the second step can be taken?'[40] P. Pas is even more decisive: 'In the contact surrounding baptism the Church has the role... of a missionary. That role suits the Church perfectly. It is indeed the peculiar commission of the Church, whatever some may argue.' A footnote follows with a reference to De Kesel's book, with the remark, 'In this otherwise interesting book the author views this part of pastoral activity as of less value. Yet precisely this pastoral activity in the coming years will be most important.' He then concludes, 'Statements here about the Church functioning as a religious nursing home imply a terrible arrogance; they would deprive all pastors at the parish level of the courage to continue'.[41] It is a passionate plea for a generous baptismal policy.

The percentage of Catholic infant baptisms in The Netherlands is considerably lower than in Flanders. In 1993 only 24.7% of all live-born children were baptised, thus 56% less than in Flanders.[42] Moreover, it is striking that – as we have seen – a pluriform selection of rituals surrounding birth has gradually developed in The Netherlands.

One can conclude that in Flanders infant baptism is a deeply felt ritual of life marking birth, and that there are no alternative rituals surrounding that event. There are indeed such alternatives in The Netherlands; a pluriform practice is developing in the rituals surrounding birth, and the unique place of infant baptism is more and more emphasised. In this sense, one can speak of the growth of an adequate and more strict practice of baptism in The Netherlands, while in Flanders on the other hand one must speak much more of a widely inclusive practice of baptism. In Flanders it is also argued for accommodating the principle wish of the parents, to perform the baptism exclusively in and for the family circle. After all, as a transition rite, baptism is primarily a family festival. In contrast to that, among Catholics in The Netherlands one finds ever more voices arguing in favour of performing baptism in

[40] L. LEIJSSEN: 'Sacramentologische reflectie op het kinderdoopsel', in LEIJSSEN, CLOET & DOBBELAERE (eds.): *Levensrituelen. Geboorte en doopsel* 271-272.

[41] P. PAS: 'Pastoraal rond het kinderdoopsel', in LEIJSSEN, CLOET & DOBBELAERE (eds.): *Levensrituelen. Geboorte en doopsel* 310.

[42] KASKI: 'Kerncijfers 1994/1995', 16. Unless otherwise indicated, figures for The Netherlands in the remainder of this paper are also derived from the KASKI.

the midst of the congregation, a tradition that comes to the fore particularly in Protestant churches, where the peculiar Christian identity of
infant baptism has always been emphasised.

These differences appear to be related to the different anthropological/
cultural contexts of this ritual. Flanders comes across as a Catholic
region: 70% of the people are Catholic, as opposed to 32% in The
Netherlands. The royal family in Belgium are Catholic too. There is
much that is similar to the Catholic Southern Netherlands, but there are
more little parks with Marian images and Calvaries, Lourdes grottoes
and old pilgrimage sites. Despite modernisation, this popular religious
culture seems to have sustained itself. In Hoogstraten there appears to be
little difficulty in recruiting large numbers of secondary school students
to participate in the Sacred Blood procession. There are many traditional
folk practices surrounding birth which have been maintained, such as,
for instance, the sugar-coated almonds in blue or pink, often in conical
bags tied off with a bow.[43] They are given when a child is born. One
finds all sorts of baptismal presents in the shops. First Communion is
also celebrated more exuberantly than it is on the average in The Netherlands. Around the time of First Communion the stores are chock full of
special Communion clothing and Communion gifts, and after the celebration local photographers show off the pictures of the young commu-
nicants in their display windows. From time to time one can participate
in a festive blessing of the children on a Sunday afternoon, in which,
during the blessing itself, the children are held aloft triumphantly. The
norms for raising children are also stricter. Dutch families along the border sometimes send their children to Belgian schools because the discipline there is better. In some places school uniforms are still required,
and where that is not the case, dress standards are enforced. Prayer still
takes place before lessons begin. Much earlier than in The Netherlands,
Flanders had discovered 'seasonal Christians', present only for occasions
like Ash Wednesday, Palm Sunday and other festivals of the Church.
Flanders has a strong culture of folk festivals and a deeply rooted religious popular culture. In many places the Church in Flanders still functions in conformity with the structures and organisation of a national

---

[43] S. Top: 'Als de ooievaar komt… Volksculturele facetten van zwangerschap,
geboorte en doop (1900-1950)', in Leijssen, Cloet & Dobbelaere (eds.): *Levensrituelen. Geboorte en doopsel* 136.

church. In this, it can rely heavily under the involvement of broadly-based Christian organisations. For years Catholicism has been a dominant political and cultural force.[44] At the same time, it is true that Flanders too is confronted by secularisation and modernisation. As a result, especially since the 1960s there has been a development from a Catholicism rooted in the church to a social-cultural Christianity.[45] The people of God have begun to 'evaporate',[46] but one can still speak of a high degree of cultural Christianity. Secularisation and modernisation thus remain mixed with a Christian infrastructure. In this context Christian rites of passage still always have a rather strong monopoly position. This is referred to explicitly several times in the Louvain study.[47] The Christian rites of passage are very emphatically characterised as 'buttresses' of a 'Catholicism outside the walls of the church'.[48] Draulans and Witte remark: 'Perhaps the monopoly position [of the Church] in the past is today's problem'.[49] In this connection they also refer to theories regarding the 'religious market', as put forward by the North American sociologist Rodney Stark, among others. Analogous with market-economic thought, these theories point to the effects of the principle of competition in religion as well. According to this analysis, pluralism and diversity stimulate involvement in the church and encourage an accent on one's

---

[44] V. DRAULANS & H. WITTE: 'Identiteit in meervoud (I). Nederlands en Vlaams Katholicisme in een veranderende tijd', in *Collationes* 28 (1998) 3, 247-264; IDEM: 'Identiteit in meervoud (II)', in *Collationes* 28 (1998) 265-280; IDEM: 'Initiatie in de vrijwilligerskerk. Verkenningen in vergelijkend perspectief', in L. BOEVE (ed.): *De kerk in Vlaanderen: avond of dageraad?*, Leuven 1999, 167-188.

[45] J. BILLIET & K. DOBBELAERE: *Godsdienst in Vlaanderen: van kerks katholicisme naar sociaal-kulturele kristenheid?*, Leuven 1976; IDEM: 'Les changements internes au pilier catholique en Flandre. D'un Catholicisme d'Eglise à une Chrétienté socio-culturelle', in *Recherches Sociologiques* 14 (1983) 2, 141-184; K. DOBBELAERE: 'Du catholicisme ecclésial au catholicisme culturel', in *Septentrion* 18 (1989) 3, 30-35; IDEM: 'De katholieke zuil nu: desintegratie en integratie', in *Belgisch Tijdschrift voor Nieuwste Geschiedenis* 13 (1982) 1, 119-160.

[46] K. DOBBELAERE: *Het 'Volk-Gods' de mist in? Over de Kerk in België*, Leuven/Amersfoort 1988.

[47] VAN MEERBEECK: 'Dopen: ja, waarom niet?' 204 and 215.

[48] K. DOBBELAERE: 'De 'overgangsrituelen', steunberen van een 'Katholicisme buiten de muren'?', in J. BULCKENS & P. COOREMAN (eds.): *Kerkelijk leven in Vlaanderen anno 2000*, Leuven 1989, 29-38. Also IDEM: *Het 'Volk-Gods' de mist in?* 77-78 and L. VOYÉ: 'Du monopole religieux à la connivence culturelle en Belgique. Un catholicisme 'hors les murs'', in *L'Année sociologique* 38 (1988) 135-167.

[49] DRAULANS & WITTE: 'Initiatie in de vrijwilligerskerk' 170.

own identity, while a monopoly position instead makes the church 'lazy'. The believer can behave rather like a potential customer.[50] This naturally contributes to a permissive practice in the case of rites of passage.

Until the 1960s The Netherlands had a very quiet and traditional society in which the churches played an important role. They stood proud like robust columns, and Christian rituals for transitional moments in life had a certain monopoly position. The Christian churches imprinted their mark on the society, influencing even secular structures. People from outside The Netherlands have always been amazed at the division of radio and television broadcasters into Catholic, conservative and liberal Protestant, and socialist 'columns', but today these are really only the reflection of the earlier traditional society, undergoing severe competition from the 'neutral' commercial broadcasters. In the 1960s a rather abrupt transition took place to an urban, industrialised society. The Netherlands suddenly became a modern, secularised country. Efficiency became the key word. In the course of this transition, the sturdy old columns began to totter.[51] This was accompanied by a rapid increase among those not identifying themselves with any church, as we have seen.[52] Especially among the Catholics in The Netherlands there was, in contrast to Flanders, since the 1960s an acute stream out of the churches.[53] In The Netherlands belonging to a church is in no way

---

[50] DRAULANS & WITTE: 'Initiatie in de vrijwilligerskerk' 171, 178-179. See also T. SCHEPENS: 'De katholieke kerk en de religieuze markt in Nederland', in K.-W. MERKS & N. SCHREURS: De passie van een grensganger. Theologie aan de vooravond van het derde millennium, Baarn 1997, 15-26.

[51] J. THURLINGS: De wankele zuil. Nederlandse katholieken tussen assimilatie en pluralisme, Nijmegen/Amersfoort 1971; T. DUFFHUES, A. FELLING & J. ROES: Bewegende patronen, Baarn 1982.

[52] Part 3, Chapter 1.

[53] DRAULANS & WITTE: 'Initiatie in de vrijwilligerskerk' 263, note with regard to this: 'For decades, in both Flanders and in The Netherlands, in profiling itself in society the Catholic Church could count on the support of a network of its own organisations and institutions. In Flanders the emancipation also led via this network to emancipation at the level of questions of belief... Precisely this point, the personal appropriation of faith, was absent from the emancipation struggle of Dutch Catholics. The reason for this was the very different social context of Catholicism and the very different type of clerical leadership which corresponded with it.' Because of social discrimination against Catholics in The Netherlands, it was necessary to search for an 'identity over against', an emancipation under the leadership of clergy in society in opposition to the threatening environment. When this emancipation was completed, many left the church. In Flanders, in

something which is done as a matter of course. It is rather a matter of true choice. Moreover, Christian ritual gradually lost its monopoly position. There was a search for a new place for Christian ritual in contemporary culture. To an increasing degree it was realised that the peculiar identity of Christian infant baptism was at stake in our secularised culture. And it was in the secular ritual void of birth rituals that new secular and general religious birth-rituals arose, and continue to develop, alongside infant baptism.

The question is whether the Flemish practice perhaps will develop in the direction of Dutch practice. In December 1999, the Flemish newspaper *De Standaard* published a series of articles on 'Geloven in Vlaanderen' (Faith in Flanders).[54] It is noted that for a long time Flanders, along with Ireland and Poland, was a sort of isolated stronghold, but that in recent years it has secularised at an increasing tempo. The church has lost its monopoly position. At the same time, however, it was confirmed that the church still has a disproportionately strong position with regard to the rites of passage such as baptism, marriage and burial, and that as of yet few alternatives exist. Can it be expected that in Flanders too a pluriform culture with regard to the rites surrounding birth will develop? Opinions are divided on this.[55] In any case, Flanders is experiencing a gradual fall in the number of infants baptised (1967, 96.1%; 1993, 80.7%; 1995, 79.1%; 1996, 76.2%; 1998, 73.1%).[56] It appears to me that it is not impossible that the situation in Flanders will come to look like the situation in The Netherlands.

I have discussed at length the tension between transition ritual and sacrament as it presents itself in the rites surrounding birth. It is in fact exemplary for what happens with all the important *rites de passage*. After all, in one way or another the Christian rites at life transitions are similar with those of our culture. But at the same time it is true that the Christian rites break through these in a radical way. That is actually

contrast, the clergy provided positive guidance for the secular engagement of the lay believer, which resulted in various generations of laity who remained critically loyal to the church as an institution.

[54] *De Standaard* December 18-19, 1999, 15; December 18-19 'Weekend', 14-15, 18; December, 20, 5; December 21, 6; December 22, 5.

[55] HELLEMANS: 'Secularization in a religiogeneous modernity' 67-81.

[56] With regard to The Netherlands the decline was as follows: 1993, 26.7%; 1995, 24.4%; 1996, 23.7%, 1998, 21.7%, 2000, 20.5%, 2002, 19.3%.

most clearly to be seen in the rites of initiation, precisely because these involve entry into a completely new community which does not stand entirely in line with genealogical descent and family and ethnic ties, but on the contrary breaks through these. Nevertheless, the gospel is at the same time directed to all who labour and are heavy laden. In that sense it is in no way elitist and extends great religious hospitality.[57] From what has been said above it is clear that various cultures will express this hospitality in various ways.

Bell points out that the transition rites which are not among those that are strictly initiatory, for instance those surrounding marriage and death, are much more intrinsically interwoven with the sphere of the family and tribe.[58] The consequence is that Christianity, from the pastoral perspective, must deal with these transition rites in a much more delicate manner. Yet there too, in a way peculiar to these rites, one must have an eye for the tension discovered here. I shall return to that.

1.1.2. Becoming an adult[59]

The rituals with regard to becoming an adult form a second step within initiation. Here too new ritual directions are defining themselves in our culture.

In his book *Das Mysterium der Wiedergeburt* Mircea Eliade arrestingly describes how youth in all sorts of cultures are incorporated into the full life of their communitie in and by rituals of initiation.[60] The development of the child into a man or woman is a complex process in all cultures. The transition from child to adult is therefore marked in all cultures through initiation ritual that consists of Van Gennep's three phases: a phase of departing from the previous existence, an intermediate stage of testing and initiation into the mysteries of life, and to close,

---

[57] See in this connection also HAMELINE: 'Les *rites de passage d'Arnold van Gennep*' 33-39.

[58] BELL: 'Ritual Tensions'.

[59] I here reprise much of what is to be found in G. LUKKEN: 'Nieuwe vragen rond initiatie', in *Verbum* 64 (1997) 7-8, 119-127.

[60] M. ELIADE: *Das Mysterium der Wiedergeburt. Ihre kulturelle und religiöse Bedeutung*, Zürich/Stuttgart 1961 (= IDEM: *Rites and Symbols of Initiation* (*Birth and Rebirth*), London 1958).

inclusion in the new existence of the adult. In this it is particularly the intermediate phase that is of great importance, so that one can properly speak of a rite of passage.[61] Time and time again this becoming an adult through initiation ritual also appears as a religious event. The divine world plays an important role in it.

At the beginning of his book Eliade notes that in our culture these initiation rituals have disappeared.[62] One can question if this is true, however. Is it not rather a matter of radical changes in our culture that have equally radical consequences for this initiation ritual? Actually, at the end of his book, almost unintentionally Eliade gives some clues. He notes that the theme of initiation lives on in the subconscious of modern man, for instance in literature and film, in which the hero, after all sorts of ordeals. ultimately weathers the crisis and receives a share in mythic immortality.[63] He also notes that subconsciously trials, anxieties, losing and regaining, death and resurrection play a role in every human life. In important crises, people dream of a new and meaningful, higher and better life. In his view, the essential core which leads to religious initiation is to be found in these elements.[64]

It is indeed important to identify the initiation elements that are present in our culture in relation to becoming an adult. But anyone who wishes to get more insight into this must first be aware of the *radical changes* that have taken place with regard to initiation.

First is the fact that the secret of life, and in particular the sacred and religious in our culture, must be constantly rediscovered by the initiate, from the bottom, as it were. In our culture the secret of life is no longer a self-evident, pre-existent truth, but the question must be answered in the middle of our larger and smaller histories, in the middle of our material and sensory world. Of course there is still a certain accepted truth and tradition, but its content must continually be rediscovered in a creative manner. In our culture initiation into the tradition is only possible when there is an active and creative process

---

[61] Thus particularly A. van Gennep and V. Turner. See in this connection K. DOBBELAERE: 'Overgangsrituelen: enkele hypothesen', in DOBBELAERE, LEIJSSEN & CLOET (eds.): *Levensrituelen. Het vormsel* 57-58; V. NECKEBROUCK: 'Initiatie. Een antropologisch voorwoord', in LOMBAERTS & BOEVE (eds.): *Traditie en initiatie* 29-37.

[62] ELIADE: *Das Mysterium der Wiedergeburt* 9.

[63] ELIADE: *Das Mysterium der Wiedergeburt* 227.

[64] ELIADE: *Das Mysterium der Wiedergeburt* 227-229.

of transmission (*tradere*) in and through mutual, critical communication.[65]

Next, in the discovery of the sacral the initiate is faced with a task that is by no means simple. As we noted earlier, our society has been split into separate realms – the economy, science, education, religion – for which religion is no longer the obvious and coordinating source of meaning. Thus people live in various realms, each with their own values, performing various roles. In this fragmented situation the initiate must still attempt to arrive at a coherent source of meaning and an integrated identity, and is forced to chose from various possibilities for doing so. The initiate must assemble his or her own 'meaning package', as it were. In the last analysis, in our culture every coordinating programme of meaning that is found or created will have highly personal features. With all communality there is then constantly a certain syncretism. That does not make being young and becoming adult any simpler.

Finally, there is the fact that contemporary culture is changing quickly. It no longer has the static character and stability of preceding cultures. I have already pointed out that after the Middle Ages one has longer cultural periods, like the baroque and classicism, but that through the emphasis on originality cultural periods have become increasingly short: they last no longer than a generation,[66] and sometimes, one can add, even less than that. Just the older generation living now have seen the most extraordinary changes! I have sometimes remarked that as a teacher every five years I face an entirely different generation of students. One consequence of his constant change is that there can no longer be one initiation ritual with a relatively short transition period. It is no longer possible to make the transition from child to adult in and through one prescribed standard ritual, passed down by tradition. One must be initiated into a culture that is constantly undergoing change, so much so that one must sometimes ask if within such a fast-changing society real ritual has any chance at all. Whatever the case, while in preceding cultures those who underwent the traditional initiation rituals could participate in a full life in a balanced and adult manner, now there is a necessity for a long and complicated initiation

---

[65] My emphasis here is other than that of V. Neckebrouck, who, with archaic culture as the norm, approaches tradition (and in this context initiation) more from continuity than from change, which leads to a pessimistic view of our culture. NECKEBROUCK: 'Initiatie. Een antropologisch voorwoord' 37-41.

[66] Part 3, Chapter 3, 3.1.

process in which there are constantly new transitions from the old to the new. In contemporary culture it is more difficult than ever before for people to develop their own human identity.[67] This is particularly true for a child growing into adulthood, but it is not limited to that. Even one who has finished growing up constantly has much new to learn. This *éducation permanente* is accompanied by *initiation permanente*: more than ever before, at important moments in life, such as entering a long-term relationship, guilt and reconciliation, illness, suffering and death, there are elements of initiation. In this connection I refer to what I said about transition rituals in general in regard to the restrictions on the concept of initiation.[68] Added to all this is the fact that there is no general age pattern with regard to the initiation from childhood to adulthood in its strict sense. It can be that the actual initiation really only takes place long after adolescence has been reached. Grimes's commentary on this is most trenchant. One of the causes which he sees for this is the absence of clear initiation rituals. In our society these are still in the experimental stage that he terms ritualisation.[69] Indeed, we are in a transitional phase. Yet my outlook on this is more positive than that of Grimes, as will appear from what follows.

Possibly the foregoing can be a stimulus to perceiving the *abundance of initiation elements in our culture* within the protracted process of becoming an adult. After birth the child gradually breaks out of the immediate home environment: it is initiated into the world outside the home. First the child leaves the parent's house to return as quickly as possible each time: it plays in the yard and comes back in, as it were. But the separation becomes steadily greater: the day care centre, kindergarten, primary school. Children leave the world of paradisiacal innocence and openness and must find their way in a world of sympathy and antipathy, good and evil, harmony and conflict, joy and grief, the erotic and sexuality, vulnerability, suffering, sickness and mortality. Life encompasses a great many mysteries into which a person must gradually be initiated. They must learn a lot. This is all part of a comprehensive process which is not

---

[67] A. GIDDENS: *Modernity and Self-Identity. Self and Society in the Modern Age*, Cambridge 1991.

[68] See in this Chapter sub 1.1.

[69] GRIMES: *Marrying and Burying* 11-13, 22, 41-45. For the term *ritualization*, see Part 1, Chapter 2, 1.1.

purely cognitive and rational, but also affective and emotional, and completely embedded in material culture, with all its sensory aspects. The initiation includes information that is gained in school and elsewhere, but it
also involves ways of dressing, hair styles, personal ornamentation (from
jewellery through tattoos and piercings), the use of cosmetics, ways of
walking, sitting and standing, decoration of one's own room (including
the identification symbols on the walls, from popular idols to strictly religious symbols), music to be listened to (with the accompanying stars),
conduct on the street and in entertainment venues, one's choice of and
place in groups, travel and vacation destinations, obtaining a driver's
licence and participation in traffic, acquiring the first bicycle, motor bike
or auto, sports and the physical culture that accompanies it, fitness and
survival training, getting a first part-time job (the first step toward economic self-sufficiency) and exploring erotic and sexual relationships as
possible steps toward forming lasting adult relationships. In recent years
technological initiation also has come to play an increasingly important
role: how to handle abstract 'plastic' money in the form of bank passes
and cash cards, communication by mobile telephone, sms and e-mail,
being initiated into the use of databases and the internet. Visual culture
and its technologies, in the form of television, film and video, also play
an important role. Many a soap series is based on an initiatory scheme,
and some television programmes function as an almost pastoral initiation
into forming relations.[70] There is still – generally about the time adulthood is reached – the whole alternative circuit of relational and communications training and of possible initiation into alternative circles, methods and lifestyles. Thus there is clearly an abundance of initiation
elements and identification symbols that focus on discovering one's individual identity in relation to others and to society as a whole. One finds
a jumble of rituals that are essential, that constantly change according to
age, period and trend, but within which nevertheless archetypal constants
of initiation into adulthood are still present. In this, it is also clear that all
these rituals are to some degree controlled by our economic system,
which in part creates, and influences and takes them into its service for
commercial ends. That is also a threat for initiation ritual.[71] The danger
is that unilateral control, and certainly that by a limited, strongly com-

[70] MOL: 'De tv als 'pastor'' 50-57.
[71] B. ROEBBEN: 'Jongeren met veel mogelijkheden maar weinig speelruimte. Initiatie
in een wazige samenleving', in LOMBAERTS & BOEVE (eds.): Traditie en initiatie 191-221.

mercially oriented market economy, will obscure the initiation, and turn the participants in these rituals into dependent consumers rather than independent adults.[72] In this way the rituals could lead to a clouding and evaporation of the I. Therefore one must realise that initiation always implies a certain 'departure', a catharsis and about-face: distancing oneself from superficial consumption, learning the economy of the sufficient, relinquishing the old and an openness to change.

In our culture one thus finds a protracted course of initiation with numerous ritual elements. Quite correctly Neckebrouck notes that in archaic cultures people made a distinction between the process of a child becoming an adult, which occurs slowly and takes time, and the rite of passage itself, which functions as a ritual in which this slow transformation is restructured into a clearly marked scheme.[73] One could consider the initiation elements enumerated above as belonging to this slow and time-consuming process, but with the note that this process contains numerous ritual elements too, and as such a number of small ritual transitions of initiation. The question is then whether within this whole one can point to *central markers* where it can be said there is a demonstrable transition. In other words, can one within this whole point to transitions which are more radical? I suspect that one can, and suggest that these are:

• the age of four to six years, when the child begins to participate in primary school;[74]
• the transition from primary school to secondary school, at the age of about twelve;
• the transition from secondary school to higher education or work, at about eighteen;
• the close of higher education and the transition to a profession at 22 to 24 years of age.[75]

[72] See in this connection also ROEBBEN: 'Jongeren met veel mogelijkheden maar weinig speelruimte'.

[73] NECKEBROUCK: 'Initiatie. Een antropologisch voorwoord' 31-32.

[74] The question remains for me whether, despite having one primary school structure in The Netherlands for children from four to twelve years of age, there is not still a considerable difference between the kindergartener of four years and the child of six, so that I would perhaps rather focus on the upper age.

[75] With regard to the important place of the school as the locus of initiation in our culture, see GRIMES: *Marrying and Burying* 41 and 44-45. What Grimes has to say (*Deeply into the Bone*, 103) also seems to me to be relevant here: 'Because the term

A certain end of the initiation would in any case be reached when economic independence (the point at which a person first really has an income) and a certain stability in relationships (co-habitation or marriage) is achieved. The transitions listed are undoubtedly accompanied with a number of rituals: going to primary school for the first time, graduation rituals from primary school, or other group rituals such as presenting a musical or going to camp together; introduction to secondary school and all sorts of first form rituals; graduation rituals again, and in The Netherlands hanging out the national flag with one's school bag or knapsack on the stock after passing exams; the freshman introductory week at the beginning of university courses, looking for and finding one's own rooms, the hazing and membership in a fraternity or sorority, graduation ceremonies for a university degree, etc. It would be worthwhile to carefully identify and research these secular rituals. In this context, it is interesting to note that what we have termed ritual agencies are beginning to turn their attention to these rituals. I have not done an inventory, but do note that, for instance, the Motiev agency in its brochure lists a 'growth and discovery journey' ('which celebrates how children, with reading, writing and arithmetic can learn to explore the world independently and express their discoveries') in place of a first communion celebration, a 'youth ceremony' ('in which adolescents are introduced into mental and physical adulthood through puberty rites') in place of confirmation, and a 'graduation party' ('when one has successfully completed academic or apprenticeship exams… How ideas and plans can become reality is celebrated in a humorous manner').[76] Finally, one can also ask whether in our culture the experience of radical loss (divorce of parents, death of a loved one) and the confrontation with disasters (with the rituals which accompany them) ought not be

initiation is overloaded, I find it useful to distinguish: *rites of childhood* that follow birth but precede entry into adolescence, *adolescence initiations* that facilitate an exit from childhood and entry into adolescence, and *adult initiations* that negotiate an exit from adolescence and an entry into adulthood. These divisions are necessarily provisional, since they do not reflect every society's way of dividing up the life course'. In a footnote to this (note 88) Grimes appears to then question whether in our culture initiation in the strict sense of the word should not be still further expanded: 'We might also add *rites of middle age*, which follow adult initiation, and *eldering* rites marking entry into old age or elevation to the status of elder'.

[76] *Motiev. Buro voor rituele vormgeving van belangrijke levensmomenten*, Melleveld 15, 4724 EK Wouw.

seen as radical points marked by initiation, if not perhaps in general, but in any case for the person immediately involved.

In our culture the initiation process increasingly also has a *general religious dimension*. Three elements in particular perhaps play a major role in this: the initiate's confrontation with the ultimate questions of meaning in the family and the attitude with regard to all sorts of practices promising meaning, religious and otherwise; the confrontation with philosophical questions which arise in the school situation, which extend (or should extend) beyond cognitive acquaintance;[77] and finally their own experience of the contingency of existence at the crucial moments of life, which in our culture also come to the fore explicitly during decisive transitions. For instance, empirical investigation has established that quite a few young people engage in a certain form of prayer at important moments in their lives.[78] In previous cultural eras at these moments there would have been immediate and almost natural confrontation with the Christian religion, but that self-evidence is departed. In our culture, not only does the initiate come into contact with the other great world religions, but also with many other alternative systems of meaning. It is therefore of importance that there is an opportunity to express the general religious dimension and interreligious communication, particularly in the major transitions. I am convinced that in the field of initiation rituals general religious elements can be integrated into the ritual in an adequate manner. If this can happen, and how it would be possible, deserves further research.

In this context, what can be said on the *Christian rituals of becoming an adult*? To my mind, these find themselves in a new situation.

I have already noted above that in the early Church Christian initiation, with its markers of baptism, confirmation and the Eucharist, was performed as one whole. This took place when the initiate was an adult. Later infant baptism became a general practise, and in the West

---

[77] See among others T. ANDREE: 'Initiatie in geloofstraditie(s). Het inter-religieuze leren', in LOMBAERTS & BOEVE (eds.): *Traditie en initiatie* 123-145; J. BULCKENS: 'Dragen katholieke school en godsdienstonderricht nog bij tot de godsdienstige vorming van jongeren?', in LOMBAERTS & BOEVE (eds.): *Traditie en initiatie* 163-190; A. KLAMER: 'Religie op school', in *Roodkoper* 2 (1997) 6, 12-14.

[78] JANSSEN, DE HART & DEN DRAAK: 'Praying as an indivudualized ritual'. See Part 3, Chapter 4, 2.

the initiation was split into infant baptism and at a later age the more personal choice for confirmation, First Communion, Solemn Communion and, in the Reformation, confession of faith.

With regard to baptism, I have noted the differences between The Netherlands and Flanders. In Flanders there has always been a high percentage with regard to infant baptism, and the percentages for confirmation follow that: in 1989 90% of children in Flanders were still confirmed, generally in the final year of primary school.[79] Here one can ask if the characterisation of baptism as a super-valued sacrament[80] does not also apply to confirmation, and if First Communion does not dovetail with that too. In relation to these sacraments, are some not in a certain sense choosing an option that is too close-fitting? Perhaps they would feel more at ease with a general human or general religious transition ritual, possibly with a certain Christian tint, than with the sacraments of confirmation and the Eucharist, with their real Christian identity. The situation in The Netherlands is, as we saw, different. A pluriform ritual practice in relation to birth exists, or is growing, and the peculiar identity of Christian baptism comes more strongly to the fore. With regard to baptism, a separation has taken place. It is significant that in 2002 the number of First Communions at the age or six or seven was 87.1% of the baptism cohort,[81] and with regard to confirmation, which takes place at the age of 12, in 2002 this involved 58% of the baptismal cohort.[82] Apparently then confirmation and First Communion conjoin with the 'separated' baptism practice. For a while the percentages with regard to Christian initiation after infant baptism were gradually decreasing, even in the 'purified' situation, but in recent years this, like the situation for baptism, appears to have stabilised. At the same time it appears that there is an attempt to have Christian initiation stand out more clearly through services for toddlers,[83] children's

---

[79] DOBBELAERE: 'Overgangsrituelen: enkele hypothesen' 55-56; K. DOBBELAERE a.o.: *Verloren zekerheid. De Belgen en hun waarden, overtuigingen en houdingen*, Tielt 2000.

[80] LEIJSSEN, CLOET & DOBBELAERE: 'Slotbeschouwingen' 315-316; see Part 3, Chapter 8, 1.1.1.

[81] J. SANDERS: 'Kerkcijfers stabiel rond belangrijke levensmomenten', in *Een-twee-een* 30 (2002) 7, 3-5. KASKI: 'Kerncijfers 1994/1995' 12-13.

[82] SANDERS: 'Kerkcijfers stabiel rond belangrijke levensmomenten'.

[83] H. VAN ROOIJ: 'Een eigen plekje voor kinderen in de kerk', in *Bisdomblad* 75 (1997) week 30 (July 25), 4-5 (about the parish of Lucas in Tilburg).

and family services (which can encourage the initiation of parents as well), youth services, youth weekends, theological study groups, hiking tours, Taizé groups, and through explicit attention for developing ongoing catechesis.[84] It is characteristic of the new situation surrounding Christian initiation that in both The Netherlands and Flanders arguments are being made for sliding the age for confirmation to 18 or later.[85] One can compare this with confession of faith at the age of 18, or later, in the Reformation. That crown prince Willem Alexander made his confession of faith at the age of 30 undoubtedly had a certain exemplary function in Dutch society. I have the impression that particularly in The Netherlands a more adequate arrangement with regard to Christian initiation in contemporary culture is developing.

[84] With regard to the ongoing catechesis, see D. ZOUTMAN: 'Bij geloofssocialisatie gaat de kost voor de baat. Interview met Frits Brattinga', in *Praktische Theologie* 23 (1996) 27-29; IDEM: 'Het kerkelijk jaar is een fantastische leidraad voor de levende geloofsgemeenschap', in *Praktische Theologie* 23 (1996) 30-33. With regard to the former German Democratic Republic, since the fall of the Wall 80,000 youth take part in *Jugend-Weihe* celebrations annually. In the GDR period this was obligatory. In place of the devotion to socialism then, it is now an initiation into the capitalist world of consumption. There has been an interesting experiment in Erfurt, where one as a Christian counterpart offers youth from atheist or unchurched families a 'celebration of adulthood'. See C. MODEHN: 'Alternatieve 'Juhgendweihe' in voormalige DDR. Atheïsten worden volwassen in de kerk', in *De Bazuin* 83 (2000) 16 (August 4), 24-26. Also: H.M. GRIESE: *Übergangsrituale im Jugendalter. Jugendweihe, Konfirmation, Firmung und Alternativen. Positionen und Perspektiven am „runden Tisch"* (Jugendsoziologie 2), Münster 2000.

[85] Confirmation at age 18 would then mark the transition from adolescence to adulthood, as that at age 12 marked the transition from child to adolescent; this latter would then obtain as the introduction to a long and vaguely defined transition phase which ultimately would lead to the independence of the adult person. See A. VAN MEERBEECK: 'Het vormsel, een 'rite de passage'?', in DOBBELAERE, LEIJSSEN & CLOET (eds.): *Het vormsel* 68-69. With the decision of the Dutch bishops in 1968 to administer confirmation in the fifth or sixth year of primary school the possibility of opting for a later age was already given to the parents. With regard to this see also H. WEGMAN: 'Het waaien van de Geest', in *Tijdschrift voor Liturgie* 59 (1975) 213-225 and H. ANDRIESSEN: 'Als je gevormd wordt', in *Inzet* 26 (1997) 4, 104-108. For the tendencies in The Netherlands, Belgium German and France see J. BULCKENS: 'Vormselpastoraal en -catechese in de Vlaamse bisdommen sinds de interdiocesane beleidsnota van 1972', in DOBBELAERE, LEIJSSEN & CLOET (eds.): *Levensrituelen. Het vormsel* 141, 148-150, 164-165, and J. LAMBERTS: 'De kwestie van de vormselleeftijd. Een liturgiewetenschappelijke en pastoraaltheologische benadering', in DOBBELAERE, LEIJSSEN & CLOET (eds.): *Levensrituelen. Het vormsel* 182-183.

At the same time one here encounters the problem already noted, that one can not just graft the sacraments, and in particular those of initiation, onto the general anthropology of the transition ritual. Because sacraments have their own identity, they are not linked to phases of life either by their content or by the time of their performance. As baptism is about a rebirth that can take place at any time during a person's life, confirmation is the sacrament of the Spirit, which is about more than attaining the *aetas perfecta* or the maturity of adulthood, and the Eucharist is the full participation in the Christian community, to which children are also entitled. Yet at the same time it remains true that the sacraments have a strong anthropological basis, and that they can be grafted in on this basis. In this it is important on the one hand that the peculiar identity of the sacrament is retained. In this context one can see confirmation as a second step within one Christian initiation, in which a closer connection with the church community is entered into, and the Christian basic metaphor takes shape as a personal realisation of the identity and mission of the church.[86] On the other hand, precisely because of the higher profile of baptism and confirmation, interference can arise with general human and general religious rituals, which makes initiation into the story of Jesus of Nazareth all the more accessible in our culture. With regard to Christian initiation it is therefore important to follow the developments in our culture closely. I suspect that this will to an increasing degree lead to a richer and more varied practice, which will involve not only the split into secular, general religious and Christian initiation rituals, but also a greater pluriformity within Christian initiation itself. In addition to infant baptism one will likely increasingly find baptism at primary school age and in adulthood, possibly preceded by a Christian celebration of birth and/or blessing of children. Moreover, the pressure to administer confirmation at the age of 18 or later will certainly increase. One can in any case question whether confirmation might not have a more meaningful place during the annual Easter celebration in the local congregation. This would more strongly accentuate the supra-familial dimensions of this ritual. An annual celebration of this sort during Eastertide in the local congregation is suggested in a 1974 advice to the Dutch conference of bishops. According to this

---

[86] L. LEIJSSEN: 'La spécificité de la confirmation. Réflexions de théologie sacramentelle (post-moderne)', in *Questions Liturgiques* 79 (1998) 3-4, 260-261. For the term 'basic metaphor', see WORGUL Jr.: 'Inculturation and Root Metaphors'.

advice, confirmation serves to build up and stimulate the local Christian community. One should differentiate the age more, and place it against this background. It is a matter of choosing to participate in the movement of the Spirit, toward the world, in engagement and openness.[87] With regard to First Communion at the age of six, there remain problems that demand further study. Some argue for maintaining *First Communion* at this age as a sort of *rite de passage*.[88] But questions also arise, which Manders quite pointedly posed at the time.[89] Would not some take part as a surrogate for a purely secular or general religious *rite de passage*? Is the peculiar identity of this sacrament not much more than a Christian transitional rite at a particular age? After all, it is really about the fullest participation in the Christian community and the most intense participation in the story of Jesus of Nazareth – and this is not related to the age of six. Can this indeed be tied to a group happening? The proper moment for this can vary: participation can sometimes be meaningful before primary school, and possibly even directly in connection with infant baptism.

In relation to initiation with regard to the *Eucharist* at a later age, it is important to realise that there too a *pluriform design* is possible.[90] This pluriformity does not touch just on the various theologies of the Eucharist, which can have their repercussions on the form of the Eucharist itself, but also touches upon the various intensities with which this basic metaphor can be celebrated as such at the various phases of life.[91] In this pluriform design one can also experience the agapé as a unique form of celebration of community around bread and cup in

---

[87] WEGMAN: 'Het waaien van de Geest'.

[88] So, for instance (though with the requisite conditions and a plea for a cautious pastoral strategy): M. CORVERS: *Doet jouw kind de eerste communie nog? Een beschrijvend onderzoek naar het fenomeen eerste communie en haar toekomst(on)mogelijkheden* (M.A. Thesis Theologische Faculteit Tilburg), Tilburg 1993. Also P. POST & L. VAN TONGEREN: 'Het feest van de eerste communie. Op zoek naar de identiteit van het christelijk ritueel', in MERKS & SCHREURS (eds.): *De passie van een grensganger* 249-264; L. VAN TONGEREN: 'The Celebration of the First Communion. Seeking the Identity of the Christian Ritual', in POST, ROUWHORST, VAN TONGEREN & SCHEER (eds.): *Christian Feast and Festival* 581-598.

[89] H. MANDERS: 'Eerste communie een initiatie? Een partiële pastoraal-theologische meditatie', in *Werkmap (voor) Liturgie* 14 (1980) 7-19.

[90] LUKKEN: 'Op weg naar eenheid in verscheidenheid'.

[91] LEIJSSEN: 'La spécificité de la confirmation' 261-262.

which all can participate, including the dispossessed, the ostracised and victims of discrimination. This agapé can reach further than merely *oecumene* among various Christian churches. It can also be the expression of solidarity with all those in our secularised society who seek ultimate meaning. It can thus in part do justice to the many forms of expression that are possible around the central archetype of the meal.[92]

Although it may not always be possible, in the liturgical/ecclesiological perspective it remains the ideal that as much justice be done to the structural succession of baptism, confirmation and Eucharist as possible. Next, one must take into account that in interference with secular developments new Christian transitional rites may arise. A possible transitional ritual with regard to becoming an adult might be a celebration (possibly ecumenical) of baptismal intentions, to replace what was previously called Solemn Communion, but at an age still to be determined. The French sacramental theologian Chauvet notes that in our time Christian initiation must prove itself in constant interaction with the realm of contemporary human perception and experience. He argues for an existential initiation, that is to say, a personal review of the religious socialisation that the person has already passed through, and which at that time is ratified with the sacramental initiation of baptism, Eucharist and confirmation.[93] His point of departure is thus the initiation that is familiar to us today. From the foregoing discussion, it will be clear that in my view this is one of the possibilities of inculturation, and that variants and supplements to the initiation scheme familiar to us are both possible and necessary.[94]

Probably the developments noted here will lead to a further decline in the percentages of participation in baptism, confirmation and the Eucharist. But on the one hand this will do more justice to the actual situation, and could contribute to people being able to develop their identity in an adequate manner, in part in and through ritual. On the

---

[92] For the agape, see also R. DE WIT: 'Pater is het zaterdag weer mis? Verslag van een samenkomst met bewoners van een forensische kliniek', in *Werkmap (voor) Liturgie* 26 (1993) 261-293.

[93] L.-M. CHAUVET: 'L'initiation chrétienne une fois pour toutes?', in *Catéchèse* (1995) 141, 49-56.

[94] See in this connection also M.E. JOHNSON: 'The Role of Worship in the Contemporary Study of Christian Initiation: A Select Review of the Literature', in *Worship* 75 (2001) 20-35.

other hand it will make it possible to protect the peculiar identity of the sacraments. The basic metaphor in this remains that initiation is always about making the critical transition from child to adult in a meaningful way. It remains a question whether young people in our culture will be able to realise the commission of 'a life to be accomplished'.[95] All of this is in essence about making it through the crisis of old to new, death to resurrection, which can be experienced in so many ways. Christian initiation remains an entirely unique way of doing so, because in Christian ritual the transition from death to resurrection receives shape in a radical and transformative manner.

1.2. Marriage

Toward the end of the 1960s, the phenomenon began to appear in The Netherlands of male and female students starting to live together without wanting – or at least not yet wanting – to get married. This phenomenon spread rapidly, and is now socially accepted – 85% of couples getting married have first cohabited – and is also institutionally regulated: in The Netherlands couples can make a cohabitation contract and register as partners. In this way the economic basis of the cohabitation and the individual rights of the partners are protected. Ritual patterns have also gradually developed around cohabitation, such as sending announcements beforehand, signing the cohabitation contract as such, an inaugural celebration at home when the pair receives visitors, giving gifts to the pair, and their taking days off work. This can be viewed as a search for the design of a new *rite de passage*. There is little data about this *rite de passage*. It deserves further investigation into how far the depth dimension of cohabitation ritual is expressed, and how much of a role religious and Christian elements can play in this.

Officially the Roman Catholic church opposes cohabitation. It is therefore not surprising that the new Roman marriage ritual does not take any account of this new situation. It still assumes that the church marriage is a transition from the families from which the partners come to the first time that the partners will be living together. In this view, the church ceremony still marks the decisive transition to cohabitation. This is rather unrealistic.[96] In point of fact, generally the wedding is no longer the beginning of

---

[95] I borrow this phrase from DE VISSCHER: *Een te voltooien leven.*
[96] See in this connection also WAGNER-RAU: *Segensraum* 197-200.

the partnership and cohabitation. For this reason some are asking if one can still really consider marriage as a transition rite. They observe that marriage ritual in our time is generally more a ritual of confirmation or a ritual in which arrangements are made permanent than a transition ritual.[97] But – allowing for this changed situation – why should one no longer speak of a transition ritual? The performance of a wedding after a period of cohabitation is after all generally still definitely experienced as a transition in the relation. In it the mutual relation between the partners is transformed in a ritual manner from provisional to stable and definitive, and often also from private to public and from informal to institutional. I believe that a careful analysis of contemporary marriage rituals themselves would demonstrate this.[98] One could argue that in our culture this transition ritual is more in stages. While previously one had the phases of betrothal and subsequently marriage, we now have the phases of cohabitation and then marriage. Moreover, one must also note that in anthropology it is not unusual that transition rituals have multiple phases.

But the question of new *rites de passage* with respect to marriage is broader. There is clearly an increasing pluriformity with regard to this ritual. For a long time people in The Netherlands have had recourse to a *secular marriage ritual*: marriage performed at the Registry Office by a city official. Until recently this ritual was rather formal and thin. In recent years it has become considerably richer. There is clearly increased creativity with regard to secular marriage rituals. The new ritual selection is even so large and diverse that one can speak of a ritual 'market' for marriage ritual, which is strongly commercially influenced.[99] There

---

[97] PIEPER & POST: 'Rituele veranderingen met betrekking tot de huwelijkssluiting' 155; G. ROUWHORST: 'Veranderingen in de vormgeving van het huwelijksritueel', in *Praktische Theologie* 25 (1998) 83; C. MENKEN-BEKIUS & J. PIEPER: 'Schipperen tussen leven en leer', in *Praktische Theologie* 25 (1998) 124.

[98] For a model of such a careful analysis, see LUKKEN: 'De nieuwe Romeinse huwelijksliturgie'. See also Part 1, Chapter 3, 2.

[99] Regarding the commercialisation of marriage ritual, particularly in America, see GRIMES: *Deeply into the Bone* 152-153: 'A wedding is the single ritual performance upon which we in the West spend the largest amounts of time, energy, and money...Even though death is inevitable and marriage is optional, the wealth of the wedding industry far exceeds that of the death industry. We complain about the high cost of dying, but between 1990 and 1995 Americans spent an average of 3,742 dollars per funeral ... The average cost of a wedding in the same period was between 19,000 and 22,750 dollars ...Between 1990 and 1995 it (the average family) was spending 48 to 58 percent of a year's income'.

are two special magazines devoted to weddings: *Bruid en bruidegom* (Bride and groom), focusing on etiquette, and *Trouwen* (Marrying), in which one finds articles, advertisements and ideas for the wedding day. The marriage market has become big business. On the average in 2002 a couple in The Netherlands spent € 10, 526 on their wedding.[100] One no longer has to be married in the city hall of the town where one lives; the secular ceremony can take place elsewhere, for instance in a hotel, an historic site, an old church, or at home. In a number of communities the officials from the Registry Office introduce themselves to potential clients in an audio-visual presentation so that the bride and groom can choose the official whose style suits them best. Preliminary interviews are held between the official and the couple, and the official makes a special effort to prepare a personalised marriage charge. He or she wears a gown or other official clothing, and music may be introduced into the ceremony.[101] At the close of the ceremony the couple are presented with a special cover for the marriage certificate, or the pen with which the certificate has been signed. Theme weddings are a possibility. The bridal couple and guests all dress up in costumes from the 1920s, 'fairy tale' weddings are held at the Dutch fairy tale theme park De Efteling, or the marriage is styled on a Venetian ball. Important elements of the ritual include the announcements, the bridal gown, the groom's suit, the bouquets, the wedding rings and other jewellery, bridesmaids, the best man and ushers, the photographic album and the means of transport. For the latter couples can choose a limousine, an antique car, a carriage, an old school bus, a London double-decker, etc. There has been a certain trend toward marriages in other countries; sometimes marriage is combined with a vacation and honeymoon. One travel agency, Extravacanza, specialises in organising such events.[102] Those who remember how in the 1960s some bridal couples would arrive at the Registry Office by bicycle will have to admit that the ritual times have changed considerably.

---

[100] See also G. NANINCK: 'Elke bruid is een ster op haar trouwdag', in *Trouw* October 24, 1996, 32; A. KLOMP: 'De bruid is big business', in *NRC Handelsblad* January 29, 1998, 44.

[101] PIEPER: *Rituele veranderingen met betrekking tot de huwelijkssluiting* 16-20; PIEPER & POST: 'Rituele veranderingen met betrekking tot de huwelijkssluiting' 146-150.

[102] S. KAMERMAN: 'Trouwen in het buitenland: 'Bali is een topper'', in *NRC Handelsblad* August 21, 2001, 8. See also Internet, for instance under 'trouwen buitenland' and 'marrying abroad'.

With regard to marriage ritual, commercialisation unquestionably goes much further than it does with birth ritual. Not everything has been an improvement. The danger is not only that the ritual conceivably becomes all too subjective and that exaggerated emphasis is placed on its emotional and romantic aspects. It is simply a fact that marriage, more so than initiation rituals in a strict sense, are focused on the individual and the 'clan'.[103] As such it is intend to guarantee the continuity of the nuclear family, the extended family and the network of friends and immediate relatives, of which the couple are the centre. But at the same time the ritual must not isolate the couple by themselves, and the broader social aspects must not be lost to sight. This means first of all that the ritual may not disguise the fact that, certainly in our culture, a genuine partnership is more than just a love romance, but also demands effort, altruism and endurance. This was always the case for both partners as individuals, but now applies all the more because there is now less uniformity in culture and tradition. It is not unusual for the two families to represent very different traditions and subcultures. Weddings in our culture mediate ultimate concerns and communities which are different from one another. In this context the wedding ritual has to express the hope that the partners 'will discover and create a common ground with enough solidarity that two ever-changing people can dance on it for a lifetime.'[104] To that must be added the fact that an authentic secular marriage also must be socially oriented; it may not shut itself up in itself and the family/clan, but reaches further. The ritual should also express that. Now that marriage ritual is less fixed than before, the possibility of designing it in a more expressive and adequate manner than before exists, not only in its focus on the partners as individuals, but also on the partners as belonging to different families and circles of friends and relations, and as oriented to the wider society. In the design of a civil ceremony it is generally the official of the Registry Office who plays an important role. But sometimes a 'leader' from the Humanist Society is called upon for secular marriage rituals. For couples who are not religious, but on their marriage day indeed do want to 'do something reflective', this Society offers a humanistic slant. Such ceremonies can be held in the most diverse locations: an art gallery, an orchard, a literary cafe; in place of the Bible, passages are selected from literature.

---

[103] BELL: 'Ritual Tensions' 15-28.
[104] GRIMES: *Deeply into the Bone* 210-214, particularly 214.

'Secular' rituals are also offered by ritual agencies. Whatever the case, it appears to be important that all of the aspects of the marriage ritual discussed here receive sufficient attention in all this creativity.

The pluriformity of the marriage ritual extends still further. Concluding a marriage between a man and a woman is very simply a particularly momentous event. It is not surprising that at this juncture of humanness life approaches us in its full, mysterious depths, and that the moment of marriage is experienced as an encounter with the great mystery of life: 'That day almost everyone believes in God or higher powers, which lifts you out above everyday existence.'[105] People experience the mutual love and the accompanying promise of faithfulness as being grounded in a mysterious and elusive depth. It cannot be excluded that in one way or another this *general religious* dimension also is expressed in a marriage performed by an official at the Registry Office. For instance, a Registry Office official notes that the space that people in this capacity are given for depth and questions of meaning is certainly present.[106] It may be expected that this will be the case more and more now that officials at the Registry Office are beginning to take on a more relational role in the preparatory discussions and collective consultation about the design of the ritual. It is also possible that the general religious dimension will take on form in special celebrations in the City Hall which immediately follow the marriage before the Registrar,[107] or which are held elsewhere. Among the possibilities to accompany civil marriage, ritual agencies expressly provide ways of connecting it with a religious or even Christian marriage celebration. Here and there there are also clergy who will accommodate the wish for such celebrations, less connected with the church.[108]

Entirely new questions arise with regard to *interreligious* marriage rituals. By this I am not referring to marriages between Christians from different

[105] L. THOOFT: 'Ja, ik wil… maar waarom? De beweegredenen en achtergronden van het nieuwe trouwen', in *Opzij* 21 (1993) 13. See PIEPER: *Rituele veranderingen met betrekking tot de huwelijkssluiting* 23; PIEPER & POST: 'Rituele veranderingen met betrekking tot de huwelijkssluiting' 153.

[106] A(NCILLA) BLIJLEVENS: 'Liturgie/pastoraal rond het burgerlijk huwelijk', in *Werkmap (voor) Liturgie* 25 (1991) 247-250.

[107] M. ROMPA: 'Liturgie in een gemeentehuis', in *Werkmap (voor) Liturgie* 28 (1994) 24-27.

[108] BLIJLEVENS: 'Liturgie/pastoraal rond het burgerlijk huwelijk'.

denominations, but marriages of Christians to someone from one of the other great religions. In these one presently chiefly finds cooperation taking place between Islamic and Christian clergy, with an eye to a common celebration of marriage.[109] In the future attention for interreligious rituals will undoubtedly have to be expanded to include other religions.

With regard to *Christian* ritual, here too further differentiation is occurring. I have just referred to the fact that here and there Christian clergy are accommodating the wish for a less church-linked celebration. The Christian dimension of marriage can however definitely also be expressed in such an event. For instance, the marriage ceremony for two young people who were ready to depart for work in a developing country began with a 'travel story'. It was a combination of their life histories, written texts and texts from the Third World: all of this in the perspective of Christian hope. The 'sign' in this service was not the explicit exchange of vows, or rings or a pastoral blessing, but through the collective drinking of wine 'to the future' and to the couple, an intense sung prayer, silence, and an exuberant prothalamion.[110] In this way liturgies are developing for people who wish to go through life together, but are not ready for a strictly 'church' wedding. One also finds services where people implore God's blessing for the union.[111] In the opening words it is expressly said that this is not a celebration of the sacrament of marriage, but of the opportunity to verbally express the marriage union in a Christian manner. The rings are also blessed, after which best wishes are spoken for this covenant. In closing the leader of the ceremony says a prayer, and pronounces a closing benediction. Obviously, there is also congregational singing.[112]

---

[109] G. SPEELMAN: 'Interreligieuze huwelijken: leren leven met verschillen', in *Praktische Theologie* 25 (1998) 43-49.

[110] S. BELLEMAKERS: 'De uitdaging – bij het trouwen van Emmy en Guus', in *Werkmap (voor) Liturgie* 28 (1994) 16-23.

[111] J. ONDERBOOM: 'Journaal', in *Rond de Tafel* 52 (1997) 12.

[112] D. ZIMMERMANN: 'Stufenweise Begleitung zum Sakrament der Ehe. Anregungen aufgrund von Erfahrungen mit dem 'Ehekatechumenat' in Frankreich', in *Lebendige Katechese* 3 (1981) 126-131; L. WERNER: 'Modell eines Ehe-Katechumenats. Ein Versuch der Diözese Autun/Burgund', in *Anzeiger für die Seelsorge* 96 (1987) 182-184; D. ZIMMERMANN: 'Segensfeier statt Trauung', in *Gottesdienst* 31 (1997) 52-53. See also A. EYSINK: 'Experiment in de r.-k. huwelijkspastoraal', in *Praktische Theologie* 9 (1982) 165-173; G. MATHON: 'Mariage – cérémonie ou mariage – sacrement? A propos du mariage des mal croyants. Mariage par étapes ou étapes dans la préparation au mariage', in *Questions Liturgiques* 62 (1981) 21-42; S. DEMEL: *Kirchliche Trauung – unerlässliche Pflicht für die Ehe des katholischen Christen?*, Stuttgart/Berlin/Köln 1993.

The ecumenical service of blessing on Valentine's day for everyone who is involved in a partnership, whether married or unwed, is also interesting, as this has developed from Erfurt in recent years, now spreading into Switzerland too. At the end of the service the couples can come forward for a personal blessing. Non-Christians also take part. 'Everyone ultimately needs comfort and encouragement', says the Reinhard Hauke, who took the initiative in establishing the service. 'We extend our hands over the couple, pray for God's protection and endorsement of their partnership, and bless the man and woman.'[113]

The strictly sacramental celebration of marriage remains a unique form, but also with regard to this ritual one can point to a great wealth of new rituals.[114] It is precisely with respect to this celebration of marriage that the problem of the relation between civil and church marriage presents itself. Under Dutch law, only marriages which are performed by an official of the Registry Office are valid. But the Catholic church acknowledges civil marriage only in exceptional cases. In normal cases what is termed the canonical form of marriage is prescribed, which is to say that the bride and groom must exchange their vows in the presence of the priest, with the assistance of two witnesses. In the past therefore Catholics in The Netherlands considered a marriage 'at city hall' as a marriage of convenience. In our time however this is viewed differently. People take civil marriage seriously. The Protestant churches went down that road long ago. They view the church marriage as a consecration and confirmation. Consecration is here understood in the sense of a service

---

[113] See, also for the ritual order, Internet sub 'Reinhard Hauke' or 'Aktuelles Archiv 2002 Segnungsdienst am Valentinstag'.

[114] L. MEURDERS: 'De Nederlandse huwelijksrituelen', in BLIJLEVENS & LUKKEN (eds.): *In goede en kwade dagen* 54-103; A. SCHEER: 'Peilingen in de hedendaagse huwelijksliturgie. Een oriënterend onderzoek', in *Tijdschrift voor Liturgie* 62 (1978) 259-317. See also BURGGRAEVE, CLOET, DOBBELAERE & LEIJSSEN (eds.): *Het huwelijk* (in this especially: P. POST & L. LEIJSSEN: 'Huwelijksliturgie: inculturatie van een levensfeest' 179-196); P. POST, H. DEGEN & J. STAPS: *Tot zegen aan elkaar gegeven. Over huwelijksliturgie en huwelijkspastoraat* (Liturgische Handreiking 25), Heeswijk 2000; P. POST: 'Trouwen: de mooiste dag van je leven', in BARNARD & POST (eds.): *Ritueel bestek* 174-179. For the history of Christian marriage ritual, see among others: RITZER: *Formen, Riten und religiöses Brauchtum der Eheschliessung*; STEVENSON: *Nuptial Blessing*; P.L. REYNOLDS: *The Christianization of Marriage during the Patristic and Early Medieval Periods*, Leiden/New York/Köln 1994; G. MATHON: *Le mariage des Chrétiens*, 2 Vol., Paris 1993 and 1995; GRIMES: *Deeply into the Bone* 191-205.

with Scripture reading and a sermon, with thanksgiving and prayer for blessing on the marriage performed before civil authorities. When one adds confirmation, one chooses for a compromise: on the one hand civil marriage is acknowledged, on the other hand vows are once again exchanged. The Dutch formula speaks therefore of a declaration that this man (this woman) has taken and takes the partner for a wife (husband) 'before God and this community'.[115] If one wished to be wholly consistent, because of the acknowledgement of the civil marriage one would confine oneself to an ecclesiastical blessing, and the confirmation in which the vows are exchanged a second time would be abandoned. Or, from the standpoint of ritual studies, one must perhaps say that the concern about the second exchange of vows rests on a too rational approach. After all, the church marriage expresses and celebrates the definitive Christian/ecclesiastical dimension of the marriage. However this can take place in various ways. In this case the most harmonious would be for the ecclesiastical celebrant to function as a civil official, as for example in Italy or the Anglican Church in England. Likewise, a harmonious whole would result from limiting the service to an ecclesiastical consecration, in which the exchange of vows is abandoned. Here one can take into account the fact that in the ordination of deacons, bishops and priests the benediction, the epiclesis, is the central performative moment of the celebration. I can however also imagine that the repetition of the vows as such in the context of the church is not experienced as a devaluation of civil marriage, but rather as a performance of them in their Christian depth. The church marriage then expresses that civil marriage has its ultimate ground in the Christian dimension of the Easter mystery. Precisely as a worldly reality, in and through this ritual it is then performed as a Christian sacred mystery.

I am here speaking expressly of performance and performative celebration. In the discussion among the various Dutch Protestant denominations during the process of their unification into the Protestant Church in The Netherlands, the question was raised whether in addition to dropping the term confirmation, the term consecration also ought to be abandoned, because this has a theological and juridical meaning. 'In consecration one is speaking of an ordination or induction

---

[115] When one examines its history, in fact however the expression 'has taken and takes for a wife (husband)' refers not to civil marriage, but to the engagement! See L. BRINK: *De taak van de kerk bij de huwelijkssluiting*, Nieuwkoop 1977, 300.

(*consecratio* or *ordinatio*) by means of a blessing (*benedictio*). But benediction is purely a pastoral/liturgical act, to which no social or juridical
significance whatsoever can be attached.'[116] To the degree that this view
arises from taking civil marriage seriously, I am in agreement with it.
But I have the feeling that this is also related to the Reformation's
wrestling with the deep sacramentality of marriage. 'On the question of
who or what is blessed, the answer will have to be that persons are
blessed, not an institution. It is not the marriage which is blessed, but
persons who enter into marriage.'[117] On the other hand, it is acknowledged that to a certain point blessing is performative: what is spoken is
accomplished in the speaking.[118] The obscurity lies precisely in this 'to a
certain point' performative character. Why should marriage ritual, like
all central transition rituals, not be performative without any reservation? Acknowledging this implies that the visible performance of the
ecclesiastical marriage sacrament really 'accomplishes' something, both
in the vertical depth of this marriage covenant and in the horizontal
dimension. Christian marriage is performed in the middle of the congregation. It is a public and institutional ecclesiastical event, which
extends both to depth and breadth. With regard to the latter, one
realises that in Christian marriage the social dimension is also radicalised. Of course, Christian marriage can not deny that marriage as
such is first and foremost focused on the two partners and the network
of kinsmen and other relatives connected with them. But at the same
time it is true that it reaches further, and looks toward the coming of
the kingdom of God, which gives priority to the poor and dispossessed.

With regard to other forms of cohabitation than those between a man
and a woman, since 1998 in The Netherlands it is possible for two men
or two women to enter into life partnerships with one another.[119] In
addition to men and women, it is possible for two men or women to
make their relationship a registered partnership. This has led to new
creativity in rituals. As early as 1989 the Remonstrant Brotherhood

---

[116] E. HALLEWAS: 'Gezegend samen op weg. Over het zegenen van levensverbintenissen in de verenigde protestantse kerk', in *Praktische Theologie* 25 (1998) 110.

[117] HALLEWAS: 'Gezegend samen op weg' 113.

[118] HALLEWAS: 'Gezegend samen op weg' 112.

[119] For the past, see J. BOSWELL: *Same-Sex Unions in Pre-Modern Europe*, New York
1994 = IDEM: *Marriage of Likeness: Same-Sex Unions in Pre-Modern Europe*, London
1995.

published a portfolio under the title *Verantwoording voor het uitspreken van een zegenbede over een levensverbintenis* (Introduction to pronouncing a blessing on a life covenant).[120] The portfolio contains a ritual in which the blessing on a life covenant between two women or men is included.[121] In 2000 a brochure from the 'Werkverband van katholieke homo-pastores' (Catholic homo-pastors workgroup) appeared, including a number of models for the blessing of the relation between two male or female 'friends'.[122] In various Christian denominations a discussion of Christian rituals for alternative pair-relationships is under way, from which it has become clear that there is a tension between church order and practice at the congregational level.[123]

Moreover, the question of whether one can speak of 'marriage' in such cases also plays an important role in this discussion.[124] In The Netherlands since 1998 civil marriage has been opened up for homosexual and lesbian couples. Institutionally there is thus a full marriage in every sense of the word between two persons of the same sex. Nevertheless, particularly the Christian churches would rather reserve the term 'marriage' for a partnership between a man and a woman. To my mind, the nub of the discussion here is ultimately the question of the performative character of the alternative Christian rituals that involve a partnership between men or women. The core question is whether these rituals actually accomplish something, both in depth and in breadth. I, in any case, would answer in the affirmative. In and through these rituals

---

[120] *Verantwoordingen voor het uitspreken van een zegenbede over een levensverbintenis*, Utrecht 1989.

[121] 'Zegenbeden over een levensverbintenis', in *Werkmap (voor) Liturgie* 24 (1990) 167-172.

[122] WERKVERBAND VAN KATHOLIEKE HOMO-PASTORES: *Tot zegen bereid. Pastorale brief over het vieren van vriendschap*, Baarn 2000.

[123] See CONGRÉGATION POUR LA DOCTRINE DE LA FOI: *Considérations à propos de projets de reconnaissance juridique des unions entre personnes homosexuelles*, Rome, 3 juin 2003; MENKEN-BEKIUS: 'De koster had maar één tafeltje voor het bruidsboeket'; A. VAN ANDEL: 'Vragen om een zegen: daar zeg je toch geen nee tegen. Actuele ervaringen met het zegenen van niet-huwelijkse relaties in een kerkdienst – een verhaal uit de praktijk', in *Praktische Theologie* 25 (1998) 37-42; see also G. VAN DE KAMP: 'Zegening in een trouwviering', in OSKAMP & SCHUMAN: *De weg van de liturgie* 327-331; WAGNER-RAU: *Segensraum* 200-209; T. KALK & C. RIKKERS, *Wij gaan ons echt verbinden. Verbintenisceremonies voor homoseksuele en lesbische stellen*, Amsterdam 2002.

[124] MENKEN-BEKIUS: 'De koster had maar één tafeltje voor het bruidsboeket'; HALLEWAS: 'Gezegend samen op weg'. See also the difference between the titles of the book of Boswell in note 119.

these partnerships indeed become rooted in part in the depth of the Christian sacred mystery, and they in part radicalise the social dimension. One problem involved is then that the ecclesiastical/public acknowledgement of these rituals generally remains limited only to the members of the communities, and does not extent up to the official church.

The rise of *divorce rituals* is entirely new.[125] Because the divorce rate in our culture is considerably higher than in previous eras, a need for transition rituals in this difficult situation has also risen. It is clear that the emphasis lies first and foremost on the separation. A transition must be made from the social status of being publicly linked as a wedded couple to the status of being single and unattached. The civil ritual focuses totally on this. The divorce is pronounced; possessions are divided; a settlement is reached with regard to the children. But a second phase begins after the divorce: that of the intermediate phase on the way to a new situation. The child custody agreement must be put into practice, and should it fail be reviewed. The question arises of whether the partners, now single, should continue to meet one another, and whether new partners will make their appearance. Thus people grow toward a new integration phase, be it as single or remarried, or as cohabiting. The three phases of the transition ritual are thus present, but the emphasis lies on the first alone. Therefore it would appear that the *secular* transition ritual is embedded in a process that undoubtedly has many ritual moments, but that condenses into the ritual of the official pronouncement of the divorce. It is however an open question whether this secular basis is strong enough to be experienced as a transition ritual. In any case, it rather often happens that the ritual has not processed the transition, and

---

[125] LUKKEN: 'Zoeken naar nieuwe overgangsrituelen'; W. KLOPPENBURG: *Trouwring of oorbel?*, IKON-radio, Hilversum 1985, 10-12 (Dutch translation of the ritual 'Recognition of Divorce' of J. WESTERHOFF & W. WILLIMON in *Liturgy and Learning Through the Life Cycle*, New York 1980); NIEUWKOOP: *De drempel over* 142-146 and 184-185; S. DE VRIES: 'Gescheiden wegen', in S. de Vries, *Op liefde gebouwd*, Delft 1987, 19955, 85-91; IDEM: 'Een kring van getuigen; de helende mogelijkheden van een liturgie bij echtscheiding', in *De Bazuin* 70 (1987) 35, 12-13; BAKKER, BOER & LANSER: *Rituelen delen* 70-73 and 128-133; S. DE VRIES: 'Werkelijk 'à Dieu'? Over doel en zin van een ritueel bij echtscheiding', in *Praktische Theologie* 25 (1998) 66-74; R. BOLLINGER (ed.): *Die Umarmung lösen. Grundlagen und Arbeitsmaterialen zur Scheidung in Seelsorge und Gottesdienst*, Gütersloh 1997; A. GROND: 'Huwelijksuitzegening: "Keer je om, je moet verder"', in *De Bazuin* 84 (2001) 9, 10-14; GRIMES: *Deeply into the Bone* 320-323.

that further help from social work or psychotherapy must be called in. This help can take the form of conversations, be they individual, with the two former partners, or in group therapy. But there are also social workers who argue for more attention being paid to the ritual moments around which the separation can condense: the writing of a letter of farewell, throwing the wedding ring (still anxiously kept) into the sea in the presence of others, etc.[126]

This whole receives a new dimension where this sort of social work, including the ritual elements, is performed within the context of pastoral work. R. Nieuwkoop justly remarks that the church does not have a pastoral task only when people lose one another through death.[127] Its task reaches further. With the loss of another with whom one had an intimate relation, it is the task of the church to 'produce a map of the desert, and see how the way to the promised land now can or must be travelled.'[128] This will normally happen in individual pastoral contact, which for the rest reaches beyond the private situation, because the pastor represents the supra-individual and public sphere. He can, after joint conversations weighing up the pros and cons, declare that it is better to separate. I deliberately use the word 'declare', because such a conclusion becomes almost a public ritual moment. This ritual moment can, depending on the circumstances, take the form of prayers and rites of penance, forgiveness and new hope. One also finds the form of a ritual meal involving the pastor and the divorcing (or divorced) couple and their children.[129] Little is known of how things proceed in the individual pastoral situation. Nieuwkoop suggests the writing of a letter (if possible by both partners) to friends and acquaintances, the inclusion of a notice in the Sunday announcements, and attention in the pastoral prayer as possible ritual moments.[130] The most familiar are, however, the publications in recent years of *Christian* transition rituals in which the transition of divorce is performed more or less in public. There is a session in the presence of the children, the

[126] VAN DER HART a.o.: *Afscheidsrituelen in psychotherapie.*
[127] NIEUWKOOP: *De drempel over* 142.
[128] NIEUWKOOP: *De drempel over* 142.
[129] H. MEULINK-KORF & A. VAN RIJEN: 'Bijzondere rituelen van vergeving en verzoening – Gedachten en ervaringen verbonden met individuele pastorale begeleiding', in G. LUKKEN & J. DE WIT (eds.): *Gebroken bestaan. Rituelen rond vergeving en verzoening* 1 (Liturgie in beweging 3), Baarn 1999, 78-85.
[130] NIEUWKOOP: *De drempel over* 144-145.

pastor and possibly the witnesses to the marriage. Depending on whether the circumstances permit, others (family members, friends, representatives of the congregation) can also be present. This gathering is then a ritual that openly closes off a phase that is past, and opens a new phase. It is a transition ritual in which the feelings of the moment are put into words and openly spoken. In this service the feelings of failure and possible guilt can be expressed, and a new perspective can be offered.[131] It must be clear that the performance of such a transition ritual is not possible without an intensive process which precedes it, and the responsibility of completing the process which will follow it. In this manner the integration phase enters the picture.

One major difficulty which arises in the Roman Catholic church with regard to these divorce rituals is that divorce per se is not possible there. But the question remains of what one does pastorally when, in spite of everything, it is an accomplished fact. Moreover, in any case such a ritual would be possible in cases in which an annulment is officially pronounced by a Church court. In the case of divorce, the ritual integration can also occur through a new marriage. Here too one runs up against the friction between what is officially permitted and actual pastoral needs. Where no strictly sacramental celebration is perhaps possible, one must at least bear responsibility for providing an adequate transition ritual.[132]

1.3. Forgiveness and reconciliation

All sorts of developments are occurring with regard to rites involving forgiveness and reconciliation.[133]

One can first survey the *secular* rituals surrounding forgiveness and reconciliation. It has sometimes been argued that the realisation of guilt has disappeared from our society. This is, however, by no means the

---

[131] See the rituals mentioned in note 125.

[132] In this connection see D. ANNAERT-HUYSMANS, L. ANNAERT-HUYSMANS & G.F. FASEUR: 'Liturgische suggesties bij een zegening van trouwe geliefden', in *Tijdschrift voor Liturgie* 81 (1997) 386-392; D. HOEDT (ed.): *"Ik laat u niet gaan, tenzij gij mij zegent." Gebedsvieringen met burgerlijk hertrouwde echtgescheidenen*, Dienst Gezinspastoraal bisdom Brugge, Roeselare 2000; *Directorium voor de Nederlandse Kerkprovincie* 1998 (yearly since 1969) 85.

[133] G. LUKKEN & J. DE WIT (eds.): *Gebroken bestaan. Rituelen rond vergeving en verzoening*, 2 Vol. (Liturgie in beweging 3-4), Baarn 1998-1999.

case. One finds it everywhere: in literature, film, modern art, television programmes, in jurisprudence and discussions of criminality.[134] There are also the confrontations with numerous mass murders, in Armenia, Russia, Germany, Japan, China, Cambodia, Vietnam, El Salvador, Chile, Argentina, Bosnia, Uganda, Angola, Mozambique, Eritrea, Rwanda and Burundi, and the reports from the international tribunals for war crimes. It cannot be denied that there are frequently issues surrounding the concept of guilt. There have however been shifts regarding this concept, and in this context new rituals for forgiveness and reconciliation have been created. Detached observers will note that precisely at this point there has been great creativity. One finds rituals in which, and through which people try to give form to forgiveness and reconciliation, both between individuals and between communities and peoples. I will list only a handful. In forgiveness and reconciliation people extend their hands to one another (a gesture that is already natural in children), or the one gives the other flowers or a gift; they acknowledge guilt to each other, and close this through an embrace or ritual meal. Communities also have rituals of forgiveness and reconciliation. For instance, peoples can be reconciled with one another after a war through gatherings in which the victims are remembered, mutual guilt is acknowledged, compensation is given for possible damage, people shake hands, and look toward a common future. In 1994, on the occasion of the fiftieth anniversary of the Warsaw ghetto uprising against the German occupiers, the President of the Federal Republic of Germany, Herzog, acknowledged, 'I ask forgiveness for that which has done to you by the Germans.' The Polish writer Szczypiorski answered him, 'The Polish people have been waiting forty years for those words.'[135] A ritual of acknowledgement like this is in essence more penetrating than the signing of a treaty. The speech by the then president of the German Federal Republic, Weizsäcker, made to mark the fortieth anniversary of the German capitulation is also worth noting.[136] One can also note the ritual act of Presidents Kohl and Mitterand, who shook hands with each other so impressively at the war cemetery at Verdun. Further, there was the handshake between Arafat and Rabin in Washington in 1993, at the

---

[134] H. STRIJARDS: *Schuld en pastoraat. Een poimenische studie over schuld als thema voor het pastorale groepsgesprek* (serie Zin en Zorg), Kampen 1997, 9.

[135] B. WANNENWETSCH: *Gottesdienst als Lebensform. Ethik für Christenbürger*, Stuttgart/Berlin/Köln 1997, 298-299.

[136] R. VON WEIZSÄCKER: *Von Deutschland aus*, Berlin 1985, 11-35.

prompting of President Clinton, at the signing of the Oslo Accord. Joosse and Rams rightly remark that such gestures are a real symbol of peace and solidarity, and also bring it about.[137] Our culture is also showing more attention for the social side of evil and guilt. We discuss the 'structural or social sin or guilt', a formulation covering every form of support for oppressive or unjust structures. People are also guilty if they have created these structures or maintain them, profit from them, or remain silent as accomplices to them.[138] One can here also think of the call of the churches to combat poverty around the world. Muldoon aptly formulates this structural evil as follows: 'The hands of our children play happily with toys that are made by the hands of people (often women and children) who are exploited in ways that actually reduce them to slaves.'[139] Guilt of this nature can also be expressed in rituals surrounding forgiveness and reconciliation, for instance in the collective confession of a number of individuals or in the public confession of guilt by groups, peoples or institutions, through which new communities are formed.[140]

To this point I have dealt with secular rituals. But in our culture there is also a need for *general religious* rituals surrounding forgiveness and reconciliation. A 'ritual' like the Dutch television programme 'Het spijt me' (I'm sorry) is considered decadent by some,[141] but scientific research indicates that for many it has an orienting effect, that the conversations are carried on with exemplary 'pastoral' expertise, and that this ritual contains authentic elements which are even religiously charged.[142] One also finds rituals of this sort involving forgiveness and reconciliation –

---

[137] J. JOOSSE & W. RAMS: 'Vergeven? – Dat is te doen', in *Inzet* 26 (1997) 3, 97.

[138] L. BOFF & A.L. LIBIANO: *Pecado social y conversion estructural*, Bogota 1978, 30 ff.

[139] M.S. MULDOON: 'Forum: Reconciliation, Original Sin, and Millennial Malaise', in *Worship* 72 (1998) 446.

[140] M. SIEVERNICH: "Social Sin' and its Acknowledgments', in *Concilium* 23 (1987) 2, 55.

[141] DE VISSCHER: *Een te voltooien leven* 84: 'The confessions likewise are made in the very wide publicity of the media, open and stark before the TV camera, in interviews in the gutter press, often not without staged sorrow and regret, as if circumspection and shame henceforth are the greatest of evils, the gravest hypocrisy. Such uninhibited public confessions leave one with an empty and queasy feeling.'

[142] MOL: 'De tv als 'pastor'' 41-58. See also IDEM: *Onze digitale god*, chapter 4, about the program *All you need is love*.

also with religious overtones – in films and even in the much watched television soap operas. The need for such rituals is all the stronger in situations in which the experience of guilt becomes sharper. This can be the case after the death of a loved one. One can note that not a few guilt feelings are 'based on a neglect (real or supposed) of the deceased, for instance a family member with one was not able to achieve reconciliation, who we no longer visited or were concerned about during a long illness and death throes, or who we just left in the lurch because we were just too busy, etc.'.[143] In situations of this sort there is a great need for rituals that can express something of the transcendent. People then desire a certain 'other side' which as it were transcends the limit against which they have run up, and which helps them to go further when life stagnates. Perhaps this happens from time to time in interpersonal relations, and on the general religious level one could here speak of new forms of 'lay confession'. Religious elements can be present in collective ritual too. Was this not the case in the impressive ritual of the Reconciliation Commission under the leadership of Archbishop Tutu in South Africa, in which crimes committed under the apartheid regime were forgiven, and the perpetrators involved reintegrated into the society?

Religious rituals around forgiveness and reconciliation appear to be really effective only if they express the relation to a personal, reconciling God who forgives seventy times seven times. Here one encounters the peculiar strength of the religions of salvation, among them Christianity. The new *Christian* rituals generally are closely connected with the secular and general religious rituals discussed. They place these in the Christian perspective of forgiveness and reconciliation, which ultimately proceeds from God.[144] The fact that God's mercy is greater than all collective and individual human guilt is essential to Christian rituals of penance.[145]

Over the last decades private confession, which occupied a central place among Catholics, has almost disappeared. Some have suggested that the cause for this is the disappearance of a sense of guilt and the weakening of the life of faith. But that is too easy an analysis. The

[143] DE VISSCHER: *Een te voltooien leven* 83.
[144] For examples see LUKKEN & DE WIT (eds.): *Gebroken bestaan* 1999.
[145] See in this connection the detailed and subtle semiotic analysis of rituals of penance by SENGSON: *Research on the Sacramental Process of Penance and Reconciliation.*

matter is much more complex. The church historian Van Laarhoven also points to factors such as the liberation of the laity from the sovereign cleric, through which a number of the additional functions until then fulfilled by the priest have been transferred to more professional (and more expensive!) figures such as psychologists, psychiatrists and doctors; moreover there is the critique long voiced by the Liturgical Movement of the individualistic form of confession, which led to attempts to design collective expressions of penance in which the priest functions more as leader than as judge.[146] With respect to the sense of guilt, as I noted above that has in no way disappeared.

With regard to the most central ritual, which in the past we were accustomed to calling the 'sacrament of confession', it can be asked if we are not standing at the beginning of a new period in the church's mediation of this sacrament, in which the collective observance of penance as a central sacramental ritual is taking shape alongside private confession.[147] Alas, the actual official developments do not respond sufficiently to this fact. Restrictive interventions in the development of the new Ritual of penance and reconciliation, have pushed this ritual increasingly in the direction of a certain monopoly for private confession.[148] Church leaders could not manage to acknowledge communal penance as a full form of the sacrament alongside private confession. The new ritual and the regulations surrounding this ritual remains stuck in a compromise between the old and new eras. The first and normal observance of the sacrament, and also the core of communal penance remains an individual confession and absolution. General confession and absolution are only permitted in exceptional cases. It is an attempt to retain the old private confession as the normal form. Because of this

[146] J. VAN LAARHOVEN: 'Een geschiedenis van de biechtvader', in *Tijdschrift voor Theologie* 7 (1967) 375-422.
[147] L. LEIJSSEN: 'Geschiedenis van de christelijke verzoening in vogelvlucht. Hermeneutische reflecties', in LUKKEN & DE WIT (eds.): *Gebroken bestaan* 1998, 14-33.
[148] E. DE JONG: 'Het rituaal voor boete en verzoening', in LUKKEN & DE WIT (eds.): *Gebroken bestaan* 1998, 35-47; E. SCHILLEBEECKX: 'Over vergeving en verzoening. De kerk als 'verhaal van toekomst'', in *Tijdschrift voor Theologie* 37 (1997) 382, note 11, comments regarding this, 'Anxiety about the disappearance of auricular confession from church life has led to an ossification that has resulted in the church in many places losing not only auricular confession but also the sacramental celebrations of penance. This, while at the beginning of the seventh century the emerging practice of auricular confession could still be termed a 'loathsome usurpation' by a Spanish and South-Gallic council (can.11: J.D. Mansi, Sacr. Conc. Collectio VI, 708).'

the new ritual cannot sufficiently accommodate the new situation. The question however is not to what degree one can revitalise the old, but rather how one can ritualise the new.[149] Precisely holding on too tightly to the old situation leads to unjustified reproaches and to pastoral strategies that are at least in part unfeasible. If communal penance were a fully accepted form, would not the judgements be more positive, and would a more adequate and productive pastoral policy not be possible? In this connection one can note that the recent letter from the Dutch bishops on the sacrament of penance on the one hand is a reflection of the narrowed views on the sacrament of penance, but on the other hand is still written from a broader perspective that makes further development in the future possible.[150] With regard to collective confession, P. Oskamp rightly remarks that it simply deserves a place 'on the church's agenda, analogous to Yom Kippur in the synagogue. Further, such services of penance could be a necessary supplement for the silent processions which have become customary in The Netherlands after fatal street violence.[151] Alongside the justified feelings of impotence and grief for the victims, until now one lacks the voice of protest and conscience.'[152]

For the rest, it is striking that there are arguments in favour of private confession coming precisely from Protestant circles.[153] One argument of this sort from Protestant circles can be found with the Tilburg religious psychologist Nauta.[154] Of course, it is important in our culture to search for a new place and form for individual confession and forgiveness. But

[149] J.A. FAVAZZA: 'Forum: The Fragile Future of Reconciliation', in *Worship* 71 (1997) 242.

[150] NEDERLANDSE BISSCHOPPEN: *God die op ons wacht. Herderlijk schrijven over God de Vader* (Bisschoppelijke brieven 38), Utrecht 1999. See also the letter of the Bishop of Rotterdam A.H. VAN LUYN: "En vergeef ons onze schuld'. Brieven aan mijn petekind', Rotterdam 2001.

[151] For these 'silent processions', see Part 3, Chapter 2, 2.

[152] P. OSKAMP: 'Een protestantse kijk op biecht en boete', in *Tijdschrift voor Liturgie* 86 (2002) 160.

[153] One should read in this connection the fascinating article by J. KRONENBURG: 'Het ritueel van vergeving en verzoening in de reformatie – een verhaal uit de praktijk', in LUKKEN & DE WIT (eds.): *Gebroken bestaan* 1998, 48-59.

[154] NAUTA: 'Rituelen als decor'; J. VAN HOOYDONK: 'De biecht is een fantastisch instrument voor een narcistische cultuur' (interview with R. Nauta), in *De Bazuin* 81 (1998) 14 (July 10), 32. See also P.J. WEIJ: 'Mijn zonden heb ik u gebiecht. Een pleidooi voor de biecht', Zoetermeer 1999; P. OSKAMP: *Vergeef ons onze schulden…Riten om in het reine te komen*, Zoetermeer 2000; IDEM: 'Een protestantse kijk op biecht en boete'.

on the one hand one must with Kronenberg acknowledge that at this moment only a few make use of private confession (in The Netherlands less than 10% of Roman Catholics, most of whom are, moreover, over the age of 60), and on the other hand it is further important to keep in mind that new forms of private confession do exist. Nauta says of these: 'Not in the form of yore, but they do exist... as a form of dialogue between two people who accept each other, each in their own role. The pastor is there as pastor, that is to say, not in his own person, but as the guide for an orderly discussion with yourself. That is what I think a lot of people are seeking.'[155] His colleague, the pastoral theologian Van Knippenberg, notes that in this strongly differentiated society people everywhere can only tell a part of their story, according to the different sectors with which they are involved: law, economy, politics, health care or the private sphere. What in the one sector is a virtue, is in another a weakness. There is nowhere they can tell their whole story. The question is then where they should go to deal with their sense of guilt. What is the right institution for dealing with that? 'Is one then condemned to the private, virtual relation with an internet site such as www.theconfessor.co.uk? On visiting this site texts appear on the screen against a background of blue clouds, with a sunflower in the foreground. There is a space for you to confess your sins. These will not be saved, but forgiven and forgotten, as soon as you have typed them in. A screen with several Bible texts and prayers closes the confession session.'[156]

The ritual of confession can indeed be a part of a wider pastoral discussion in which people can again find space to live. In this connection one can also point to the possibility of restoring 'lay confession' to honour: in a bishops' synod as early as 1983 the South American bishops noted that many people such as doctors, nurses, pastoral workers, congregational leaders and religious leaders fulfil this role, and they deserve acknowledgement.[157]

[155] VAN HOOYDONK: 'De biecht is een fantastisch instrument voor een narcistische cultuur'.

[156] T. VAN KNIPPENBERG: 'Op verhaal komen in de biechtstoel', in *De Bazuin* 83 (2000) (March 3), 19-20.

[157] C. DOOLEY: 'The 1983 Synod of Bishops and the 'Crisis of Confession'', in *Concilium* 23 (1987) 2, 21. For a very particular proposal with regard to the Christian ritual of penance and reconciliation, see W.M. SPEELMAN & H. STRIJARDS: 'Omkeren op de ingeslagen weg. Een heroverweging van het pastoraat van schuld en verzoening', in *Jaarboek voor liturgie-onderzoek* (1998) 197-218.

1.4. Illness

Many in our society have great difficulty in dealing with illness in an adequate manner. We only really realise what illness is when we ourselves are confronted by it.[158] Only someone who has been sick several days realises how greatly illness impinges on our daily life. Suddenly you are out of everyday life. You still hear the sounds of life passing by – but pass you by it does. Suddenly there is a distance from those who stand by your bed with bright faces and lively gestures. Your horizon of time and place suddenly contracts considerably. Illness is a mysterious infringement on life. That is all the more true for a chronic or potentially fatal illness. Each year thousands unexpectedly discover that they are incurably ill. Then life itself is shaken to its foundations. It is the startling experience that death has become an unwelcome guest in your life.

Everyone who becomes ill is also confronted with the *secular* rituals literally surrounding the sickbed. These are primarily rituals of medical care: the resident doctors with their white uniforms, instruments and medical files. The contacts are generally brief and business-like. These are contacts with professionals who 'know about' the illness and are oriented to healing, improvement or palliative care. For the sick person in our culture these rituals have something about them that is mysterious and magical. At the same time it is true that precisely as such they have great limitations. The questions about meaning with regard to illness generally are touched on only tangentially. The agenda of the resident doctor is simply ruled by protocols involving the quality of medical care, implying limits both in respect to time and human scope. This is less true for the rituals of the general practitioner and nursing personnel. The quality of their care is medically oriented, but also focuses on the person of the sick individual. Then there are the rituals of hospital visitation by family and friends. Their concern is directly focused on the sick individual. When a life-threatening condition is involved, this strikes deep into their mutual relationships. Both the sick and the well must then prepare to make a transition to a new life situation. In their relation they then unavoidably encounter questions that touch on the ultimate issues of living and their life together. The new situation

---

[158] See the arresting description in J.H. VAN DEN BERG: *Psychologie van het ziekbed*, Nijkerk 1956.

touches the heart of their being. Countless questions of meaning arise. Dealing with these questions of meaning has its own ritual moments, from the halting conversation, the charged silences while together around the sickbed, listening to music together, the encouraging handshake that expresses sympathy, to the flowers as a sign of the confidence that all will turn out all right.

These can also be religiously charged moments, in which the sick person and those around him or her launch out over the mysterious depths of human existence. There are definitely also *general religious* rituals around the sickbed. This subject deserves further investigation, which could contribute to new designs for them.

Menken-Bekius aptly sketches how *Christians* deal with sickness in their unique way. She opens her book on 'rituals in pastoral care of individuals' with the following account:

In a gallery of the Musée d'Unterlinden in Colmar stands the famous Isenheimer Altar by Matthias Grünewald. It is a triptych on wood showing biblical scenes, centring around the suffering, death and resurrection of Christ. Visitors who come to admire it will perhaps not realise what the import is of the information that this triptych was painted for the hospital church of the St. Anthony monastery at Isenheim, where those excluded from society as plague sufferers were cared for. It was for this church and this group of people that Grünewald painted his triptych between 1512 and 1515. He put all of his compassion into it. In the hospital this church was the place where during the week the ambulant sick could come into their section, which was separated from the rest of the space with latticework, just to be along with themselves and to pray. Through the week the side panels of the altarpiece were closed, so that only the crucified Christ was visible. In an ordinary village church Grünewald's depiction of the Cross with the body of Christ would apparently have generated repugnance rather than religious feelings, because the body has a greenish skin colour and the whole skin is affected with a premature process of decomposition. The man who is depicted here has suffered much more than the suffering that he must have gone through in the hour of death. It is precisely this depiction that made him a figure with whom plague sufferers, for whom there was no hope of recovery, could identify. Her horror can be read on the face of Mary, who faints into the arms of the beloved disciple. She can look no longer.

On Sunday the altarpiece showed another scene. Then the side panels were opened out and the eyes of the churchgoers were comforted by
the scene of the resurrection which had been painted in very warm
colours. The message which radiated from this altar goes right to the
heart: they who now shared in a terrible suffering would after their
death share in a glory beyond imagining, following in the footsteps of
Christ who preceded them. From this the sick could draw courage to
continue to still carry on, strengthened by the bread which they received
in the ritual of Eucharist. To be sure that the sick would understand the
message of the altarpiece, and thus of what the hospital had in mind in
its treatment and nursing, each new patient was brought before the triptych on admission. If the patient feared that his exclusion from society
had also excluded him from the Kingdom of God, he had to realise that
that fear was groundless. Treatment began after this admission ritual.[159]

Here we have a transition ritual that assumed an adequate place in dealing with illness itself. It will not be easy for religious ritual involving illness to obtain such an integrated place in our secularised medical system. Still, in the course of every illness there comes a moment at which
the need arises to give expression in condensed form to the feelings and
questions that occupy the sick person, certainly if it is a life-threatening
illness. It is the moment at which, as it were, the definitive transition is
made to an ultimate surrender to the new life situation. The ritual of
anointing of the sick is focussed just on this moment. For a long time
unction was only administered *in extremis*, at the last moment, close
before death. But since Vatican II unction is regarded as a transition ritual in situations in which the life of the individual reaches a crisis point,
through illness or age, in the inevitable approach of death. One can
think of a life-threatening illness, but also of ageing and serious chronic
illnesses.[160] Sometimes the ritual is also performed on several persons at

---

[159] MENKEN-BEKIUS: *Rituelen in het individuele pastoraat* 3 with reference to W.
FRAENGER: *Matthias Grünewald*, München 1983 and J.F.A. SAWYER: *The fifth Gospel. Isa-
iah in the History of Christianity*, Cambridge 1995, 91. See also the pictures in C. LIMEN-
TANI VIRDIS & E.M. PIETROGIVANNA, *Gothic and Renaissance Altarpieces*, London/New
York 2002. Reproductions of this triptych are also easily found on the internet.

[160] In this context there should also be mention of liturgy with mentally handicapped persons, as this has taken shape in recent years. See among others H. DEGEN, L.
BREZET BROUWER & A. LOOS: 'Liturgie met verstandelijk gehandicapten', in *Werkmap
(voor) Liturgie* 11 (1977) 1-78. See also A. BLIJLEVENS, G. LUKKEN & J. DE WIT (eds.):

the same time, as in the cases of a senior citizens home or for the sick on a pilgrimage to Lourdes. The point at which the ritual is performed can vary; sometimes it will be at the beginning of a process, sometimes near the end. The core of the ritual is in essence that which is expressed in Grünewald's triptych. The ideal would be for anointing of the sick to be given a place in the whole system of care for the sick. That means that in ideal circumstances the community that is closely involved with the sick person, including those caring for them professionally, would be present and play their own role in the ritual. Perhaps the following account can evoke something of the significance of this transition ritual:

For instance, one night last week I was called to be with a dying woman. She had wanted to die at home, but because of all sorts of complications she nevertheless had to be hospitalised. I found her in the vigil room, unconscious, her mouth wry, without dentures, a contorted body with tubes and drips, in a bed like a machine.

The children and grandchildren sat disoriented in the waiting room, sheltering with one another. Right away they told me everything about their mother, who had been a widow for years and had kept a tight grip on the reins herself. The night nurses freed up a large room for all of us. The doctor came to tell what mother's condition was now, and that this would indeed be the farewell. I explained to them what Holy Unction meant, and they agreed to participate in it.

But when their mother was in their midst, almost everyone remained standing, frightened, seeking support along the wall, looking at that unknown person that was their dying mother. I had understood full well what sort of strong woman lay in our midst, and to break the silence I told her what the children had said to me about her, and I took her hand and all prayed with and for her. I anointed her, and the children recalled once again her listening ear, her sharp tongue, her searching eye, her supple hands and the feet on which she had stood alone for so many years.

Liturgie met gehandicapten, Baarn 1997. These liturgical celebrations, which go beyond being strict *rites de passage*, can take on the function of transition rituals. This can be the case particularly when parents and family participate in these liturgies. Transition rituals as such should also have a place in self-help groups with regard to the handicapped; see H. DEGEN: *Gedeelde zorg. Ervaringen van ouders met een zorgenkind. Een handreiking aan oudervenigingen, hulpverleners en pastores*, Hilversum 1976.

After that they came to her one by one, stroked her, kissed her, spoke their thanks, an excuse, a greeting, and remained close by her. They laid a photograph of her next to her on the pillow: that is how she was, how she is.

That hospital room became their living room for two more days, and each felt a pleasant calm with their always busy mother. That night they had conquered their own fear of her death. After she died, one of her daughters said, 'This was just as beautiful as the birth of my child.'[161]

1.5. Death

There has also been great creativity with regard to death, both in secular and in general religious and Christian rituals.[162] This is true not only for the rituals surrounding the leave-taking from the deceased as such, but also for the wider extensions of this transition ritual: one need think only of the new designs of services of remembrance, the construction of memorials and cemetery visits. In what follows I will limit myself to the strict farewell ritual.

After the 1960s this ritual had become seriously impoverished in our culture.[163] There were no longer real rites of piety and closeness. The dead were no longer laid out at home, but in a funeral home, the slow funeral cortege was adapted to speedier traffic, and no longer received right of way. The whole of ritual relating to the dead was strongly formalised. The peculiar characteristics of our economic system exercised great influence on it.

Businesslike conduct, efficiency and uniformity began to be the set the tone. Everything was large-scale, right up to the cemeteries, designed for efficiency with uniform grave markers and crosses. A funeral industry arose that in its advertising sold the funeral as a 'one-size-fits-all, ready to use' package and alluring product. But in recent years considerable changes have taken place. The subject of death is no longer taboo. I previously noted that this changed attitude appeared with the books *Zand erover* (Dust to dust) and *Onder de groene zoden*

---

[161] J. DE VALK: 'De lichamelijkheid van een sacrament', in *De Bazuin* 23 (1987) 1, 15.

[162] LUKKEN: *Op zoek naar een geloofwaardige gestalte van de dodenliturgie*; IDEM: 'Liturgische aspecten: nieuwe tendensen in de uitvaartliturgie'. See there for further literature.

[163] About the American Way of Death, see GRIMES: *Deeply into the Bone* 258-273.

(Six feet under), which appeared in 1989 and 1995, respectively. The subtitles of these publications are typical: that of the first book is 'leave-taking and funerals to one's own discretion' and that of the second 'the personalised funeral'.[164] Both books note that funeral directors, particularly the larger ones, are focused on uniformity, speed and efficiency, and argue for greater involvement on the part of next of kin in the design and organisation of the funeral. While there had been creativity with regard to rituals involving death in the Christian churches since the 1960s, this creativity now spread to *secular* society. People began to resist the funeral industry as it existed, and sought meaningful death rituals. One can remember the reports of the cremation of the Dutch pop singer Klijn in 1993: 'At the singer's request everyone wore white... there were words from the father, friend and carer. The guests all laid a white rose on the white painted casket, and at the end blue balloons were released.'[165] Subsequently people could watch on television how the last wishes of the singer were carried out, and his ashes scattered in New York harbour.[166] New rituals have developed particularly in the circuit of alternative relationships and among AIDS patients.[167] This is undoubtedly related to the fact that in recent years, through an illness like AIDS increasing numbers of young people have been confronted with the standard package from the funeral directors, and as a reaction to it have begun to be creative in designing new rituals. One can also point to new developments with regard to death announcements, the desire for more personal graves, artistic designs for coffins, grave monuments and urns, increasing visitation of cemeteries, and virtual condolence registers.[168] Slowly there are satisfying and authentic secular alternatives to ecclesiastical ritual coming into being. These are also offered by ritual agencies and

[164] See Part 3, Chapter 2, 2. SAX a.o.: *Zand erover*; ENKLAAR: *Onder de groene zoden*. See also P. VAN DEN AKKER: *Het laatste bedrijf. Over waarden, handelingen en rituelen bij sterven, dood en uitvaart*, Tilburg 1995.

[165] M. STEENBERGHE: 'Witte rozen en blauwe ballonnen voor René Klijn', in *Nieuwsblad* September 9, 1993, 3.

[166] See Part 3, Chapter 2, 2.

[167] J. RUIJTER: 'New Rituals Through AIDS', in *Concilium* 29 (1993) 3, 21-29; IDEM: 'Er zijn evenveel begrafenisliturgieën als er uitvaarten zijn', in *Werkmap (voor) Liturgie* 28 (1994) 1, 37-45.

[168] See for instance DERKSEN: *Als het donker wordt* and H. WARREN & M. MOLEGRAAF (eds.): *Ik heb alleen woorden. De honderd meest troostrijke gedichten over afscheid en rouw uit de Nederlandse poëzie*, Amsterdam 1998. See also Part 3, Chapter 2, 2.

the Humanist Society.[169] In Amsterdam six poets developed striking rituals for the burial of the anonimous dead or those without family or friends.[170] At the same time, however, commerce has caught up with the trend for more personal funerals. The phenomenon springs from 'funeral stores' where one can shop for one's final needs: in addition to shrouds, coffins and urns one can find luxurious funeral cards and all sorts of necklaces and bracelets in which one can carry the ashes of their loved one on their person. One can also choose from chic autos or horse-drawn carriages for the cortege. And there are 'funeral stylists' who see to the make-up for the body, select the right clothing and design the solemnities. The trade also has filmmakers who will record the final day, or who can provide striking film images of the deceased for use at the funeral. In the last five years the average amount that people spend on a funeral in The Netherlands has tripled to about 6000 Euro. Despite the commercial influences, about 90% of the Dutch still however opt for a traditional funeral.

Particularly in the confrontation with death there is a need to give form to a general *religious* dimension. Empirical research indicates that death has a high religious quotient.[171] If there is anywhere that religious questions arise, it is there, with the mystery of death. It is as if the mysterious smile that often is seen on the faces of the dead refers to another world. Thus it is a boon that next to secular death ritual there have also been rituals that have come into being in which the general religious dimension is given shape. For instance, in Amsterdam the 'Burial and cremation' workgroup has been established, with the goal of making the leave-taking from the deceased more personal and meaningful.[172] This workgroup prepared a list of churches and annexes in which the survivors could say their farewells in a more personal and peaceful manner. For instance, the Boskapel of the Augustinians in Nijmegen

---

[169] In this connection also A. FRANZ: 'Everything is Worthwhile at the End? Christian Funeral Liturgy amidst Ecclesial Tradtion and Secular Rites', in *Studia Liturgica* 32 (2002) 48-68, especially 56-63.
[170] A. POST: 'Laatste eer voor anoniem gestorvenen. Dichter bij de dood', in *VolZin* 20-23.
[171] A. VERGOTE: *Religie, geloof en ongeloof*, Antwerpen/Amsterdam 1984, 132-168.
[172] J. KOOPMANS: 'Dat je laatste tocht niet opgaat in het ledige', in *De Bazuin* 76 (1993) 41 (Oktober 29), 10-11; IDEM: 'Uitvaart voor niet-kerkelijken: uitdaging voor kerken', in *Kerugma* 37 (1993-1994) 2, 73-80.

also functions in this way.[173] It is a space that is open, and not connected with any parish structures. They can be approached by people who want a service that does not have too much 'churchy' content. They must have a church background or a sense for the religious, but have perhaps become alienated from the church for one reason or another. Experience teaches that a celebration that is able to create open images around death appeals to the basic desire every person has for light on the horizon. In this, visual images can often accomplish more than words. For instance, in the centre of the Boskapel there is often a spotlight directed on a perspectival image by which the viewer is pulled along, as it were, beyond place and time. And for young people songs from the pop world often have more religious import than standard church songs.[174] One can think of the song 'Candle in the Wind' by Elton John at the funeral of Princess Diana: 'And it seems to me you lived your life like a candle in the wind, never fading with the sunset… Now you belong to heaven and the stars spell your name.' The Ur-images of hope for life are always the same with death: the light which appears at the end of a dark tunnel, sunrise, budding spring, the land on the other side, a vast landscape with flowing water, the land that is always greener behind the hills. The question is always the same: do we run up against a wall, or is there something more on the other side?[175] Those who leave that question open encounter religious dimensions that connect the over there and the here. You peer toward the horizon and see the ship slowly disappear from sight. Should you then think that it falls off the edge of the world and disappears into nothingness? Or is it the case that it goes further, to unknown and unsuspected realms? In ritual these images are translated into language, but they are also symbolised in candlelight, in flowers, in fire, in living water. Moreover, it can be that the space on the other side becomes the form of the eternal God who gives space, and eliminates all boundaries… And for some these images from the biblical tradition will be accessible: the city on the mountain, the house of peace, the marriage feast.

Christian faith can open up the existing general religious images to get at their Christian dimensions. In addition to secular and general

---

[173] KOOPMANS: 'Dat je laatste tocht niet opgaat in het ledige' 10.
[174] KOOPMANS: 'Dat je laatste tocht niet opgaat in het ledige'. See also IDEM: 'Uitvaart voor niet-kerkelijken'.
[175] LUKKEN: 'Stoten wij op een muur of is er daarachter meer?'.

religious death ritual there remains a unique place for specifically Christian death ritual. There too there is growing pluriformity.[176] As types for the funerary liturgy one finds celebrations of word and prayer, services of word and prayer with communion rites, and finally the celebration of Eucharist. Moreover, these types themselves are being given shape in various ways. This is also true for church burial and cremation.[177] Bell points out that the rituals surrounding death are strongly focused on the deceased and those who are intimately con-nected with them.[178] Christian rituals surrounding death do not escape this fundamental fact. But at the same time, their reach is broader. They are oriented to the new kingdom of righteousness in which there is room for all, including those who fell short in this life. The inter-cessory prayer in Christian death ritual also focuses on them, express-ing the hope of the new Jerusalem where there are many mansions.

2. TRANSITION RITES IN NEW SITUATIONS

People in our society are confronted with a number of transitional situ-ations for which tradition offers no models for rituals. These involve transitions that do not appear in other cultures, or at least not to the same degree. People generally live longer than before, and moreover in our culture they often stand entirely alone and are inconvenienced by breaks and painful transitions in life. In section 1 I already discussed divorce ritual.[179] One can further list the crises of unemployment, becoming disabled, abortion, adoption, incorporation of new family members after remarriage, mid-life crisis, children moving out of the

---

[176] A. BLIJLEVENS, W. BOELENS & G. LUKKEN (eds.): *Op dood en leven*, 3 Vol., Baarn 1989-1990; L. VAN TONGEREN: 'Over het leven bij de dood. Het leven ter sprake bren-gen bij de uitvaart', in H. BECK & W. WEREN (eds.): *Over leven. Leven en overleven in lagen*, Budel 2002, 133-155; IDEM: 'Individualizing Ritual. The Personal Dimension in Funeral Liturgy', in *Worship* 77 (2003) 117-138.

[177] LUKKEN: 'Het ritueel van de christelijke begrafenis'; J. EGGERMONT: *In het licht van Gods gelaat. Een beschrijving en kritisch-normatieve toetsing van een aantal officiële en niet-officiële Nederlandse rooms-katholieke crematierituelen in historisch perspectief* (M.A. Thesis Theologische Faculteit Tilburg), Tilburg 1987; A. MULDER: "'Naakt kom ik uit de schoot van moeder aarde, naakt keer ik daar terug' (Job 1, 21). Aardesymboliek, Bij-bel en begrafenisliturgie', in *Jaarboek voor liturgie-onderzoek* 12 (1997) 149-165.

[178] BELL: 'Ritual Tensions' 22-25.

[179] For rituals involving divorce, see Part 3, Chapter 8, 1.2.

home, leaving the parent(s) to reorient their lives at a reasonably young age, retirement, and moving into a senior citizens centre. One of the ways one can pursue in processing these transitions is that of self-help groups.[180] One should however also investigate to what extent it is precisely ritual which can be an aid in the transition from one situation to another. In these one should realise that elements from all three phases that Van Gennep and Turner believed were essential for transition rituals could have a place. Thus these do not have to be rituals that happen within a limited space of time. There can be support processes that have moments in them which condense as ritual. These moments may be those of exodus and farewell, but could also be in the ambiguous intermediate phase and in integration. In any case, when all is completed there is something to celebrate. If this aspect is suppressed, there will never be any real completion.[181]

When one speaks of integration with regard to these transition rituals, this could lead to misunderstanding. It may not, for instance, be a case of only integrating the unemployed and disabled in the existing order by means of transition rituals, and quieting their feelings of protest. On the contrary. Worthy transition rituals are oriented on human emancipation and becoming fully adult. They can also express a critical attitude toward the existing society. For example, protest rituals, such as a sit-in in the workplace, could be indispensable components of such rituals. And integration can be oriented to building a countermovement, with a different view of labour and the economy. Ritual can give an irreplaceable voice to those who are without a voice in the world of power and labour. Thus these rituals can also be focused on a new order and new attitudes.

---

[180] LAFAILLE a.o. (eds.): *Zelfhulptechnieken.*

[181] For a description of rituals around abortion and a ritual for the transition into retirement, see for instance GRIMES: *Deeply into the Bone* 310-320 and 323-332.

CHAPTER 9

SEVERAL IMPORTANT DIMENSIONS AND THEMES

In this chapter I will be examining several dimensions and themes which are particularly relevant for Christian ritual in our culture. These involve ritual space, time, music, women and liturgy, liturgy and politics, the theme of feast, the need for more supple liturgical regulations, and the professionalisation of liturgical leaders.

1. SPACE

Space, and how it is organised, is an integrating component of ritual.[1] Heidegger had already called our attention to the considerable degree to which human existence is realised in and through space. He therefore characterised human existence as a *Da-sein* and a *Mit-Dasein*.[2] One must understand these terms as literally meaning a 'being there'. We are inextricably bound up with the space which surrounds us, and our being together is therefore in a fundamental way a 'being there' together. In rituals this effect of space becomes still more condensed, as it were. The space where something is performed and the spatial organisation generally say more than can be expressed in words.[3] The space in which the ritual takes place is therefore in no sense incidental to the ritual. In relation to Christian ritual one can distinguish between the architectural space of the church building and ritual spaces outside it.

1.1. The church building

For a better understanding of rituals it is of the utmost importance to study the history of church buildings, which after all were precisely intended for the performance of the central Christian rituals. Because a

---

[1] LUKKEN: 'Die architektonische Dimensionen des Rituals'; LUKKEN & SEARLE: *Semiotics and Church Architecture* 61-70. See Part 1, Chapter 4, 2.
[2] ETTEMA: *Verbogen taal* 271-273.
[3] LUKKEN: 'Die architektonische Dimensionen des Rituals' 19-36; IDEM: 'Ritueel en ruimte'.

large percentage of the churches now in use consist of monumental buildings from the past, one encounters the question of how one can inculturate Christian ritual through the redesign of these buildings.[4] But more important still is the question of contemporary church architecture. For a long time the primary source for church architecture was the past. There were a succession of neo-styles: neo-classical, neo-baroque, neo-Gothic, neo-Romanesque, neo-Byzantine churches, and until into the 1960s, churches in the style of ancient Roman basilicas. Modern church architecture begins in this century with the churches of Frank Lloyd Wright in the United States. In 1906 he designed the Unity Temple in Chicago. This church deviated from the accepted view that saw a church building as being in a class apart, strongly different from its architectural milieu. He integrated the church building into the general architecture of the age, and returned it to its human scale.[5] The year 1955 marks another turning point. That year the French architect Le Corbusier built the church of Notre-Dame-du-Haut in Ronchamp. Those travelling to the south of France through the Jura must pay a visit to this church. The building expresses a new relation between inside and outside, above and below, between the sacred and profane. The profane

---

[4] See among others R. STEENSMA: *Kerken, wat doe je ermee*, Baarn 1981; A. BLIJLEVENS a.o.: *Ruimte voor liturgie. Opstellen met betrekking tot de restauratie van de Sint-Servaaskerk te Maastricht*, Maastricht 1983; R. STEENSMA: *De geschiedenis van kerkbouw en kerkgebruik*, Groningen 1984; IDEM: *Opdat de ruimten meevieren. Een studie over de spanning tussen liturgie en monumentenzorg bij de herinrichting en het gebruik van monumentale kerken*, Baarn 1992; IDEM: 'Enkele uitgangspunten', in *Functionaliteit en symboliek van het kerkgebouw* (brochure of the diocese Haarlem), Haarlem 1994; IDEM: 'Enkele uitgangspunten bij de (her)inrichting van een katholieke kerk', in *Tijdschrift voor Liturgie* 78 (1994) 332-334; K. RICHTER: *Kirchenräume und Kirchenträume. Die Bedeutung des Kirchenraums für eine lebendige Gemeinde*, Freiburg 1999[2]; R. GILES: *Repitching the Tent. Reordening the Church Building for Worship and Mission*, Norwich 2000 (Revised and expanded edition); J. KROESEN, J.R. LUTH & A.L. MOLENDIJK(eds.): *Religieuze ruimte. Kerkbouw, kerkinrichting en religieuze kunst. Feestbundel voor Regnerus Steensma bij zijn vijfenzestigste verjaardag*, Zoetermeer 2002; P. POST: 'Church Architecture and Liturgy: Current Perspectives for Liturgical Inculturation', in N. SCHREURS & V. PLASTOW (eds.): *Juxtaposing contexts. Doing contextual theology in South Africa and in the Netherlands*, Pietermaritzburg 2003, 162-187; IDEM: *Space for Liturgy between dynamic and static reality. An exploration of the development of the Roman Catholic Liturgical Space in The Netherlands (ca. 1850-present day) with Particular Focus on the Role of Liturgical Booklets, the Microphone and Church Pews* (Netherlands Studies in Ritual and Liturgy), Groningen/Tilburg 2003.

[5] G. BEKAERT: *In een of ander huis. Kerkbouw op een keerpunt*, Tielt/Den Haag 1967, 55-56.

and the sacred are no longer separated by a high threshold, as if the sacral is being lifted out of our world. Inside and outside and below and above continue to exist in a tension that is not abolished. As such, Ronchamp became a new expression of the holy in this world.[6] One can speak of a hidden interior, of what I would term a soft spirituality, of a provisionality and seeing sometimes/just, of a cautious, hesitant and yet focused search for the ultimate. This church is the starting point for modern church architecture – and one must realise that after the Second World War more churches were being built in Europe than ever before.[7]

Particularly through the second half of the 20th century, in new church architecture there was an effort to create church buildings with a human scale and without a high sacred threshold. In this connection Bekaert's 1967 book on modern church architecture, *In een of ander huis. Kerkbouw op een keerpunt* (In one house or another: church architecture at a watershed) is telling.[8] Churches were lower and more less pretentious and lost their commanding presence in the man-made environment. Also, with regard to the interior of the church building, the sacral dimension was given form in a cautious and tentative manner, and there was an effort to retain human scale in the furnishings. The furniture was functional and self-effacing. In these modern churches one no longer finds thrones for the bishop or priests, no absolute separation between the clergy on the sacred side and the congregation in the nave. The articulation of the modern church building makes the roles clear. The church is first and foremost a building for the local congregation, which is the real acting subject in the celebration. After the Second Vatican Council people became more aware of how relationships shaped the basic pattern of the liturgy.[9] There are those with special offices, but they can no longer isolate themselves spatially from the community. As

[6] This is described in an arresting, actually semiotic, manner by J.H. VAN DEN BERG: *Metabletica van de materie. Meetkundige beschouwingen*, Nijkerk 1969[2], 188-193. See also the detailed semiotic analysis of the church of Saints Peter and Paul in Tilburg by M. Searle, in: LUKKEN & SEARLE: *Semiotics and Church Architecture* 75-130.

[7] BEKAERT: *In een of ander huis* 13.

[8] BEKAERT: *In een of ander huis*.

[9] New questions are arising in our culture, because this basic pattern does not fit with the tendencies of individualisation and segmentation. J. van der Ven calls attention to theories with regard to what is termed networking, which can have the effect of creating community. These can furnish more insight into what is or is not feasible in liturgies in this respect, and what can possibly be improved. See VAN DER VEN: *Ecclesiologie in context* 221-224.

such, contemporary church architecture contradicts reactionary movements which seek to restore the absolute dualism between office holders and community. The building itself shows that there is room for only a *relative* bi-polarity, one in front of the community in close solidarity with the community. The place of the priest is in the midst of the congregation, as its servant; there he is a path-breaker and leader, and not a sacred figure set apart. In the old churches men sat on the right and women on the left – something which is still sometimes to be seen in the arrangement of the images of male and female saints. In the new, inculturated church buildings, men and women are equal, and there is no reason that this equality should stop short of the worship leader. The question of admitting women to the offices of the church would appear to be not so much a theological question as an issue of necessary inculturation. I will return to this last matter later.

As the outcome of a Dutch national competition for the design of a church building for the coming millennium, a book entitled *Een ander huis* (Another house) appeared in 1997.[10] This title first is a reference to Bekaert's 1967 book, mentioned above. This book too is about church buildings here and now, in the midst of our contingent history, buildings as 'open stories' in masonry, in which an inductive liturgy can be performed. But at the same time there is a new, different accent which appears in the title of the book. The Dutch title can equally be read as speaking of a *different* house. It calls attention to the fact that in church architecture in recent years a tendency has again appeared to opt for more specific and perhaps more monumental church buildings.[11] This tendency thus moves away from the church building as 'one house or another', and from the all too hesitant expression of the sacred dimension. It seeks a 'different house', a church building which can function as a sacred symbol, and that contrasts somewhat with its environment. It argues for the church building of the future as a specific sacred space, which at the same time is open and hospitable. Various types of Christian ritual must be possible there, and the threshold must also function as a real transition from outside to inside, for instance through walk-in celebrations and offering the space to the city, village or neighbourhood as a general meditation centre.

---

[10] POST (ed.): *Een ander huis* (with an extensive list of literature regarding contemporary church architecture).

[11] P. POST: 'Literatuuroverzicht: liturgie en architectuur', in POST (ed.): *Een ander huis* 20-21 and 25-27.

This new tendency has now been worked out in an impressive manner in De Jonge's recent study of church architecture after 2000.[12] He observes that since the 1960s there has been a uncertainty with regard to the recognisability and peculiar identity of the church building. People really no longer knew how a contemporary church should look. He also notes that among architects at this moment there is interest again in the sacred and spiritual dimension of buildings. In light of this, it is important for architecture and liturgical studies to work together closely. This has happened in a particularly felicitous manner in this study, which came into being as the result of cooperation between the Theological Faculty at Tilburg and the Technical University at Eindhoven. The research is design-oriented and develops and tests typologies for church buildings in the 21st century which break new ground. It focuses on the Dutch situation, which is placed within a broader, international context as a model. The starting point is the inculturation of the church building, with an eye to ritual developments in the church and society, as they have been sketched above. The research also integrates into this the current interest in environmentally friendly construction and the role that such ecologically sustainable technologies can have in church architecture.[13] The author seeks a balance between the exclusively sacral church building as 'God's house' (*Domus Dei*), as sacred space, and the church as a place of assembly (*Domus ecclesiae*). Each church building can have dimensions of both types. Moreover, there can be gradations or various zones of sacrality within one and the same church building. The building must be flexible in order to be able to offer space (literally and metaphorically) for a whole spectrum of contemporary liturgical ritual.[14] It must be a space not only for the weekly celebration of Eucharist, but

[12] S. DE JONGE: *Kerkarchitectuur na 2000. Het ontwikkelen van grensverleggende typologieën vanuit het samenspel tussen liturgie, architectuur en duurzame ontwikkeling*, Eindhoven/Tilburg 2002; P. POST: 'Van Doura tot Vinex: actuele tendenties met betrekking tot liturgische ruimte', in KROESEN, LUTH & MOLENDIJK (eds.): *Religieuze ruimte. Kerkbouw, kerkinrichting en religieuze kunst* 71-89; IDEM: 'Space for Liturgy. Current Perspectives for Liturgical Inculturation', in *Jaarboek voor liturgie-onderzoek* 18 (2002) 45-59; IDEM: *Space for Liturgy between dynamic and static reality*.

[13] See also P. SCHMID: 'Het duurzame 'Huis van verbond", in POST (ed.): *Een ander huis* 62.

[14] See also SCHMID: 'Het duurzame 'Huis van verbond" 61; P. POST: 'Een ander huis: twee kerkontwerpprojecten als signalen van een kenterend getij?', in POST (ed.): *Een ander huis* 15-16; 'De uitslag van de Rotterdamse prijsvraag. Typen en thema's, balans en perspectief, en een afsluitend pleidooi', in POST (ed.): *Een ander huis* 26.

also for others types of celebrations such as services of the word, prayer services, meditative services, children's services and others which might include drama, and for rituals at important life transitions such as birth, baptism, marriage and funerals. There might also be meeting rooms, a meditation centre, a baptistry, a sanctuary in which the congregation might gather around both the altar table and the lectern, and a devotional space. The church building thus facilitates movement, both from outside to inside and vice versa, and also within the interior itself. On the basis of his research, the author comes up with five possible new types. It is impossible to adequately describe these types here. Yet I can hope to sketch something of the direction in which they are moving:

1. The church building as residence or church-house. This involves a modest but easily identified church building which is integrated into a residential neighbourhood: a special corner 'house' that is still not 'domestic', but recognisable by a characteristic identity, and stands out through its unusual materialisation. The concept behind it is the first 'church building' in an extensive new residential subdivision. It is to be used as a welcoming 'walk-in centre' or 'hospitality house' and for liturgical celebrations. With this first option an inventory can be made of what sort of church building will perhaps be possible at a later stage.

2. The church building as play area and clearinghouse. This is an open and hospitable building, particularly suited for rituals at the important events in life. It is centrally located on a square and is oriented to both marginal Christians who occasionally attend church and to the congregation. From the open forecourt to the sequestered sanctuary, there are gradations of sacrality. There are zones that make the building particularly suited for commemorations, meditation, marriages and funerals.

3. The church building as lode and intersection or way of the cross. This building lies on a square or in a park and has facades with plenty of glass so that there is a vigorous interaction between interior and exterior. It is oriented to the community and to marginal Christians in the vicinity. The load-bearing structure of the roof consists of vertical and horizontal crosses that are interconnected with one another. The crosses provide a structure for the division of the building into multiple zones, each with its own character and atmosphere, among others for discussion, catechesis and study, gatherings, meditation, baptism, marriages, lectern, altar and tabernacle.

4. The church building as place of remembrance and beacon. The building stands out through its height and location, and is oriented to both mass ritual celebrations (participants in ritual processions, memorial services, passers-by and occasional churchgoers) and to the celebration of transition rituals (baptism, First Communion, marriages, funerals, etc.).

5. The church building as refuge and crypt/shelter. The building contrasts with the society and is an oasis of calm, stillness, privacy, intimacy and solidarity. It is oriented to core Christians. Specific rituals can be celebrated in various zones.

In this, it is also important to reflect further on the design of existing church buildings. Louis van Tongeren pointed out that the longitudinal design of Gothic and neo-Gothic buildings in itself really has the theatrical effect of producing a sort of division between stage and auditorium, through which what is taking place up front in the church easily comes to be experienced as /letting be seen/ and /making heard/. This even remains the case when the altar is moved forward. As early as the Reformation these Gothic spaces were redesigned along their longitudinal axes. People assembled around a chancel on the longitudinal axis of the nave. This design affords perspectives for a less theatrical use of the Gothic space. When the longitudinal part of these church buildings are redesigned as liturgical spaces – for instance, as an ellipse – the possibilities for active participation by all are increased. Moreover, the space can be made suitable for more dynamic forms of liturgy: the Communion table can be placed at one end of the longitudinal axis of the space, and the lectern at the other, and further the baptismal font can be given its own place. Whatever is done, it makes the space flexible. Among Catholics there are still few examples of such church design within Gothic church buildings. The only example that I know of in The Netherlands is that of St. Dominic's church in Amsterdam, plus efforts to achieve such a design at the cathedral in Breda.[15]

An entirely new development is the rise of the *meditation centre* as such. One finds these in all sorts of places: in the United Nations building in

[15] L. VAN TONGEREN: 'Vers une utilisation dynamique et flexible de l'espace. Une réflexion renouvelée sur le réaménagement d'églises', in *Questions Liturgiques* 83 (2002) 179-195; IDEM: 'The Re-ordering of Church Buildings reconsidered', in SCHREURS & PLASTOW (eds.): *Juxtaposing contexts.* 188-217. See also Th. STERNBERG and L. VAN TONGEREN 2004 in Bibliography

New York, near the Brandenburger Tor in Berlin, at airports, along motorways, in shopping malls, hospitals, psychiatric and psycho-geriatric institutions, nursing homes, prisons, schools and universities.[16] These are sequestered spaces into which people can withdraw in order to pray, meditate, or just enjoy the stillness, and in which, generally, no services are held.[17] In these centres the kaleidoscopic array of alternative philosophical and spiritual paths finds its expression ever more frequently. One can at this moment distinguish three types of meditation centres in The Netherlands.[18] First, one finds the traditional/specific types, that is to say meditation centres that are furnished from a specific faith tradition, for instance Catholic or Islamic. Next, one can find universal centres, without specific content. Symbolism that is not specific to any one religion is chosen for these. They are open to people of all religious or philosophical traditions, and limit themselves to universal/human symbols. Often abstract art is used to create a meditative atmosphere. Finally, there are pan-religious spaces. They provide places for expressions and symbolic language from various religious traditions alongside one another. For instance, the meditation centre in the Academic Hospital at Utrecht, the corners of the ambulatory surrounding a neutral open space are furnished from various religious traditions. Interest in building meditation centres and their actual use is steadily increasing.

1.2. Ritual spaces outside church buildings

From the beginning Christian liturgy has had rituals performed outside the church building.[19] Among these are moving in procession from one

---

[16] C. DE WAELE: 'Een stiltecentrum op de campus', in *Speling* 47 (1995) 40-47; LUKKEN: 'Sacrale ruimte en stilte'; J. HULS: 'Dag Hammarskjöld over de meditatieruimte van de V.N.', in *Speling* 47 (1995) 56-65; J. KROESEN: *Stiltecentra*, Groningen 1997 = J. KROESEN: 'Stiltecentra', in *Jaarboek voor liturgie-onderzoek* 13 (1997) 93-133; P. POST & P. SCHMID: 'Centrum van stilte: een onderzoeksaanvrage', in BARNARD & POST (eds.): *Ritueel bestek* 162-170; DE JONGE: *Kerkarchitectuur na 2000*, 241-243. Practical suggestions for furnishing a meditation space in a city centre can be found in H. BISSELING: 'Niemand komt Jezus voorbij, behalve Cruijff', in *7even. Blad voor mensen die actief zijn in de kerk* 1 (1999) 27-30.

[17] KROESEN: *Stiltecentra* 93.

[18] KROESEN: *Stiltecentra* 112-130.

[19] See here POST: *Ritueel landschap*; *Vieringen (Rituelen) buiten 1 and 2*, in which particularly P. POST: 'Ter inleiding. Rituelen buiten' 4-16. See also ROOIJAKKERS: 'Percepties van bovennatuur'.

church building to another, as in the classic Stations liturgy in Rome, the celebration of Holy Week at various places in Jerusalem, as reported by Egeria at the end of the fourth century,[20] prayer and penitential processions in natural settings on the feast of St. Mark (April 25) and on the Rogation Days (the three days before Ascension), the sacramental procession on Corpus Christi and the celebration of the Eucharist in the open air on that day, marriage in front of the church building,[21] the consecration of the fire on Easter Saturday night, celebrations in the open air at shrines, and the ritual of pilgrimage. From the second half of the 16th century in The Netherlands Roman Catholic rituals were forced to withdraw into the church buildings – to which there were, however, counter-reactions.[22] Although here and there, after the Second Vatican Council there are still 'outside rituals' which have been preserved, since the 1960s these have disappeared in most places. But over the past decade they have begun to return in a new, inculturated manner.

From the earliest times there has been a sacralising of nature. Certain natural sites have become holy places. For instance, in the Old Testament one finds the terebinths at Mamre, and Mount Sinai. One can also think of Stonehenge, Lourdes (a miraculous spring), Fatima (a sun miracle), the holy oak in Oirschot, The Netherlands, Marian and memorial chapels, roadside crosses, crosses on top of mountains and hills, etc. With secularisation and the rise of technology nature was desacralised. Indeed, ever farther-reaching industrialisation and the exploitation of natural resources threaten to destroy nature altogether. This has led to counter-reactions. The environmental movement arose, and industrialised nations now generally have their own Ministries of

---

[20] See among others AUF DER MAUR: *Feiern im Rythmus der Zeit*, I, 78.

[21] One must realise that in the Middle Ages the custom arose of performing a marriage literally *in facie ecclesiae*: the exchange of vows between the bride and groom took place in front of the church building. In rituals from the Middle Ages it is sometimes said that the marriage was performed in the churchyard; because the churchyard lay around the church, it was possible to designate a marriage in front of the church building in this way. See P.A.M. VAN KEMPEN: *Het huwelijksritueel in de Nederlanden voor 1614*, Tilburg 1989; J.M.M. VAN DE VEN: *In facie ecclesiae. De katholieke huwelijksliturgie in de Nederlanden, van de 13ᵉ eeuw tot het einde van het Ancien Regime*, Leuven 2000.

[22] POST: 'Ter inleiding. Rituelen buiten' 7-8; P.J. MARGRY: *Teedere quaesties: religieuze rituelen in conflict. Confrontaties tussen katholieken en protestanten rond de processiecultuur in 19ᵉ-eeuws Nederland*, Hilversum 2000.

the Environment. All kinds of measures have been taken to protect the environment. In our culture one can even detect a general tendency toward experiencing nature and the landscape as sacral zones again.[23] A sacralisation process is under way involving the landscape as such. The landscape itself is becoming a place of celebration, and this leads to new forms of 'topolatry': the veneration of certain locations in nature that are marked as holy places.[24] Along this same line one finds the monuments in the landscape set up in memory of the fallen in war and, at an increasing rate over the last few years, for victims of political and criminal violence, stadium disasters, or traffic fatalities.[25]

In addition to this ritual experience of the landscape there is also a more distanced ritual experience that is growing, one which is related to the tendency toward musealisation. Nature is segregated and demarcated, bought up and 'protected' that way.[26] It becomes a National Park or is administered by a public trust as a site of 'outstanding natural beauty'. Visits to such sites become sacral experiences which substitute for church attendance. Long distance hikes through National Parks become pilgrimages of a kind. The visitors' centres, with their exhibitions, function as temples, churches or chapels of a sort; the small blinds from which people can observe wild animals are also chapels, 'often with their own (post)modern 'intention book' on a chain. In that book, which calls to mind the intention books at pilgrimage sites, the visitors' (post)modern intentions... are recorded, generally in the form of experiences and appeals from the visitors.'[27] Further, in connection with the musealised experience of nature in The Netherlands, one can point to the 'green cathedral' on the outskirts of Almere, opened in 1987 and made from trees that were planted according to the ground plan of the cathedral at Reims, and another cathedral of 112 basalt blocks, also

---

[23] POST: 'Zeven notities over rituele verandering'; IDEM: *Een ander huis* 21-22; IDEM: 'Een idyllisch feest. Over de natuurthematiek in Brabantse oogstdankvieringen', in MULDER & SCHEER (eds.): *Natuurlijke liturgie* 118-139; *Vieringen (Rituelen) buiten 1 and 2*, in which particularly POST: 'Ter inleiding. Rituelen buiten'; S. SHAMA: *Landscape and memory*, New York 1995.

[24] POST: 'Post-modern Pilgrimage'; BELL: *Ritual. Perspectives* 157. As a pronounced example, she cites the pilgrimages to Niagara Falls on the American/Canadian border.

[25] POST: *Ritueel landschap* 42-46.

[26] POST: 'De uitslag van de Rotterdamse prijsvraag' 22.

[27] POST: 'De uitslag van de Rotterdamse prijsvraag' 22.

placed according to the ground plan of Reims, on the former construction island of Neeltje Jans, near the flood tide barrier in Zeeland.[28]

The green Christmas tree in the middle of winter, and the increasing use of this in connection with gifts, lies more in the direction of folklorisation. This tree is also beginning to increasingly function as a 'tree of life', to which people can make their wishes known. For example, several years ago, immediately after St. Nicholas's Day (December 5), the Vroom & Dreesman department store chain set up a large 'Christmas wish tree' in a prominent place in each of their stores. Clients were given cards and hooks with which to hang them in the tree, in the hope that their wish would be fulfilled by the firm. The legend on the card read 'The Wish Tree fulfils some wishes'. It was striking that people not only used these cards for 'lottery wishes', but also for all sorts of immaterial wishes that far exceeded the possibilities of the firm. These particularly involved relationships and health. The Christmas tree functioned as a sort of 'holy' place and as a quasi-ecclesiastical intention book to an invisible benefactor.[29] One finds here a secular layer of popular culture which is reminiscent of pilgrimage sites: a layer which, for the rest, the department store does very well by. More realistic was the Santa Claus who was introduced at the Sportiom in 's-Hertogenbosch in 1998: he arrived from Lapland at the ice rink of the sports complex, and young and old could send Santa their good wishes for others; he was imagined as acting as a mediator. More clearly in the direction of folklorisation are also the rituals such as pilgrimages to shrines for veneration of relics, circumambulations, guild processions, Palm Sunday processions, St. Martin's and Three Kings pageants, the ritual festivities surrounding St. Hubert, etc.[30]

The new experience of outdoor rituals is related to these tendencies. Considerable literature has appeared, particularly regarding the revival

[28] M. BARNARD: 'De conceptuele ruimte van de gothische kathedraal', in BARNARD & POST (eds.): *Ritueel bestek* 87-91; POST: 'De uitslag van de Rotterdamse prijsvraag' 22; IDEM: 'Ruimte voor rituelen', in BARNARD & POST (eds.): *Ritueel bestek* 77-86; F.J. WITTEVEEN: 'Groene kathedralen van de verbeelding. Overpeinzingen bij een openluchtviering in Meerssel-Dreef', in *Werkmap (voor) Liturgie* (Vieringen (Rituelen) buiten 2) 30 (1996) 27-28.

[29] M. STRAATHOF: 'Kerstwensen in de V&D-boom', in *De Bazuin* 81 (1998) (December) 4-6.

[30] POST: *Ritueel landschap* 20-21.

in the ritual of pilgrimage.[31] There are a rising number of open air celebrations: memorial services and grieving at the scene of accidents and
disasters,[32] celebrations during religious walking tours,[33] celebrations on
camping sites, harvest celebrations,[34] massive celebrations marking papal
visits,[35] blessings of the sea,[36] Christmas celebrations,[37] Easter fire consecrations, outdoor wedding celebrations, prayer vigils near prisons for
asylum seekers,[38] nuclear generating plants and military air bases, revival
services.[39] There is also more attention being given to authentic design
for the cortege with the dead to and at the cemetery, and for outdoor
liturgy to accompany the spreading of the ashes of the deceased or the
placement of an urn at a columbarium.[40] At the same time there is a
movement in the other direction. More attention is being given to
nature in indoor liturgy: the use of natural elements as such in church
architecture,[41] through to interest in flower arrangement[42] and nature

[31] See among others PIEPER, POST & VAN UDEN: *Bedevaart en pelgrimage*; VAN
UDEN, PIEPER & POST (eds.): *Oude sporen, nieuwe wegen*; POST, PIEPER & VAN UDEN:
The Modern Pilgrim; P. POST, R. VAN UDEN & J. PIEPER: *Pelgrimage in beweging. Een
christelijk ritueel in nieuwe contexten* (UTP-katern 22), Baarn 1999; P.J. MARGRY & C.
CASPERS (eds.): *Bedevaartplaatsen in Nederland*, 4 Vol., Amsterdam/Hilversum 1997-
2004; J. STOPFORD (ed.); *Pilgrimage explored*, Woodbridge 1999; P. POST & L. VAN
TONGEREN: *Devotioneel ritueel. Heiligen en wonderen, bedevaarten en pelgrimages in
verleden en heden* (Meander 2), Kampen 2001.
[32] POST: *Ritueel landschap* 42-46; VAN DER HEIJDEN: 'Symboliek en ritueel van een
herdenking'; TH. DE WIT & G. TEN BERGE: 'Liturgie buiten, in de open lucht', in
Werkmap (voor) Liturgie (Vieringen (Rituelen) buiten 1) 30 (1996) 23-30.
[33] D. COPPES: 'Voettochten', in R. ADOLFS (ed.): *Buiten-dienst. Informele samenkomsten buiten de kerkmuren*, Baarn 1969, 59-65.
[34] POST: *Ritueel landschap* 32-42; IDEM: 'Een idyllisch feest; J. BIEMANS: 'Oogstdankviering 1995 – Kring de Kempen', in *Werkmap (voor) Liturgie* (Vieringen (Rituelen) buiten 2) 30 (1996) 35-46.
[35] POST: 'Een idyllisch feest' 28-32.
[36] J. CRAEYNEST: 'Liturgie buiten in de open lucht. De zegening van de zee', in
Werkmap (voor) Liturgie (Vieringen (Rituelen) buiten 2) 30 (1996) 30-34.
[37] POST: 'Ter inleiding. Rituelen buiten' 4-5.
[38] C. VAN DE BROEK, & H. HURKENS: 'Wake 'Stop het opsluiten van vreemdelin-
gen'', in *Werkmap (voor) Liturgie* (Vieringen (Rituelen) buiten 1) 30 (1996) 3, 31-41.
[39] See the enumeration in POST: 'Ter inleiding. Rituelen buiten' 10-11.
[40] LUKKEN: 'Het ritueel van de christelijke begrafenis; POST: *Ritueel landschap* 19; A.
MULDER: 'Rituelen buiten: een crematie', in *Werkmap (voor) Liturgie* (Vieringen (Rituelen) buiten 1) 30 (1996) 43-52.
[41] F.J. WITTEVEEN: 'Groene kathedralen van de verbeelding'.
[42] A. VAN TUFFELEN & T. BRUGGE: *Symbolische bloemsierkunst; bloemschikken voor
kerk en woning*, Ede/Antwerpen 1992, 1996²; T. BRUGGE: *Bloemen spreken in stilte. Een*

motifs in the rituals.[43] I have also already noted that in the case of church buildings there is attention being given to the threshold as the transition from outside to inside. That transition between outside and inside is also being accentuated in other ways, for instance where in a crematorium floor to ceiling windows give a view of an always green garden or a surrounding natural landscape, or by connecting a baptismal chapel with an outdoor water source.

The English paediatrician and psychoanalyst D. Winnicott speaks of the indispensability of transitional objects (for instance, stuffed toys) in human development.[44] They have a strong symbolic meaning and contribute to the child on the one hand not losing the connection with its home base, and on the other hand to still being able to receive the outside world as a real, other world. They are a sort of 'intermediate space'. Among adults the transitional objects of childhood disappear. But there still remains a need for such transitional space: the return to the parental house, to the city of one's birth, to one's fatherland. Sacral spaces also have a similar bridge function: they are marked out in our environment as precious places that bring us in contact with the depth dimensions of existence. Just as transitional spaces, they play a very special role in human development toward the profound. It is interesting that in his theory about transitional space Winnicott not only draws connections to later phases of life, but also explicitly involves religious

taal waar woorden niet kunnen spreken, Bloemendaal 1995; IDEM: 'Een taal waar woorden niet kunnen reiken. Bloemen spreken in stilte', in *Tijdschrift voor Geestelijk Leven* 51 (1995) 6, 607-614; IDEM: 'Zorg voor de schepping', in *Werkmap (voor) Liturgie* (Vieringen (Rituelen) buiten 2) 30 (1996) 2-10; IDEM: *Bloemen geven zin. Symbolische bloemsierkunst voor liturgie en bezinning*, Kampen 2002; J. DE WIT: "Men make er geen etalage!'. Over bloemen en liturgie', in *Werkmap (voor) Liturgie* (Vieringen (Rituelen) buiten 2) 30 (1996) 11-18.
[43] For instance BRUGGE: 'Zorg voor de schepping'; M. DE BRUIJNE: 'Een decade vrouwenliederen van 'Eva's lied' tot 'Dag Mens'', in *Werkmap (voor) Liturgie* (Vieringen (Rituelen) buiten 2) 30 (1996) 47-53.
[44] VAN DEN BERK: *Mystagogie* 126-128. See D. WINNICOTT: 'Transitional objects and transitional phenomena', in D. WINNICOTT: *Collected Papers*, London 1958, 229-242; IDEM: 'Transitional objects and transitional phenomena', in D. WINNICOTT: *Playing and Reality*, London/New York 1991, 1-25; HEIMBROCK: *Gottesdienst: Spielraum des Lebens* 47-59; P. VANDERMEERSCH: 'Psychologische lagen in het geloven', in *Tijdschrift voor Theologie* 39 (1999) 399-402 ('De symboliek van de transitionele sfeer'); WAGNER-RAU: *Segensraum* 107-114; N. JONGSMA-TIELEMAN: *Rituelen: speelruimte van de hoop. Wat rituelen (ons) doen*, Kampen 2002.

experience in it. Sacral space functions as transitional space in which the transition can be made to the space of the holy, or the holy One, creatively and in full confidence. Thus the Christian church building, with its own identity, is a space where from birth to death the faithful, in the midst of the many crises of human existence, can find comfort, strength and blessing on their way to their final destination. There Christians can experience that before the God of Jesus of Nazareth, life does not derive its value purely and simply from success, but that in the gospel those who are losers on the social battlefield also have their own identity, and even have a special place. Time after time they will be able to discover God there as the ultimate, loving ground of their being. Therefore it is important that among Christians it receive its shape in an authentic manner.[45] This includes not merely the church building, but also the meditation centres, urban chapels and sacred outdoor sites, the roadside shrines and crosses, monuments, churchyards and pilgrimage sites that are again claiming increasing attention.

2. TIME

In Part 1 we noted that the experience of ritual time is not the same in all cultures. Archaic cultures experience time cyclically. It is important to go more deeply into this in order to then characterise the peculiar Christian experience of time more clearly.[46]

Myths play a fundamental role in primitive societies. These are stories which express the conviction of the community that previously, in the sacred Ur-time (*in illo tempore*), certain preternatural events took place. The myths tell the sacred history of 'gods and heroes' from the Ur-time. These events are regarded as the highest reality, full of vitality, creative force and salvation for the community. People therefore seek contact with these mighty acts from the sacred primal time. This is mediated in the culture's rites. By performing the rites, the community frees itself from the changeable time in which it lives and takes part in the sacred Ur-events. Leaving chronological time they enter into another time, one

---

[45] LUKKEN: 'Mystagogie van de ruimte' 28-41.

[46] Part 1, Chapter 4, 3. About the theme 'time and liturgy', see also L. VAN TONGEREN: *In het ritme van de tijd. Over de samenhang tussen tijd en liturgie*, Baarn 1999 and IDEM: 'Beleving en rituele vormgeving van tijd' 63-68.

which lies at the beginning of all things, but which also can be endlessly repeated. One can think of the Mithraic religion as an example. According to the myth, Mithras was a heroic warrior from the army of the god of light, in the battle against the army of the god of darkness. As a youth he killed the bull, the symbol of fertility and of all good. The community sought contact with this sacred Ur-event through the retelling and re-enactment of the myth. A bull was killed and offered to this god in the initiation to the Mithras cult. The devotees of Mithras were convinced that those who participated actually received a share in the Ur-events, and were born again.[47] It is characteristic of this ritual experience of time that the 'in that time' and the sacred acts which took place then stand outside of the changeable time in which we live. The participants in the ritual leave the present and move to a sort of timelessness. This is termed the myth of the 'eternal return'.

The ritual experience of time in our Western culture is entirely different. It is linear: past, present and future succeed one another. This linear experience of time is characteristic for the Jewish, Islamic and Christian religions. I will now further examine the ritual experience of time involved with Christianity, and its rootage in our culture.

In a certain sense, from its origins the Christian ritual experience of time has been inculturated, as it is embedded in the Western experience of time. It is closely related to the ritual experience of time which I discussed in Part 1. Christians too try to connect past, present and future with one another, and to call up the past as vital in the present, and in tension with the future. The past is brought into the present in order to be able to make the transition to the future. This happens in a focused manner in a rite, in a delineated and concentrated, special time. In Jewish and Christian religion this manner of experiencing ritual time is denoted with the technical term 'anamnesis' or 'remembrance'.[48] This

---

[47] ELIADE: *Das Heilige und das Profane*; IDEM: *Beelden en symbolen*, Hilversum 1963 (= IDEM: *Images and Symbols: Studies in Religious Symbolism*, London 1961); IDEM: *De mythe van de eeuwige terugkeer*, Hilversum 1964 (= IDEM: *Cosmos and History: The Myth of the Eternal Return*, Princeton 1954); IDEM: 'Mythen en mythisch denken', in A. ELIOT a.o.: *Mythen van de mensheid*, Amsterdam/Hasselt 1977, 12-29. About the relation rite-myth in Eliade, see Part 1, Chapter 2, 2.

[48] B. VAN IERSEL: 'Some Biblical Roots of the Christian Sacrament', in *Concilium* 4 (1968) 1, 8 ff; R. BOON: *De joodse wortels van de christelijke eredienst* (Mededelingen Prof. Dr. G. van der Leeuwstichting 40), Amsterdam 1970, 29-56.

'remembrance' is not a mental process of recollection, but of making the past present in time now, as an incentive toward the future. In a certain sense this is the opposite of what the words 'remembering' or 'recalling' normally imply. When we use these words we generally mean that we shift mentally from the present to the past. But anamnesis brings the past into the present as an impetus to new development. What is distant in time is brought close, and becomes present. When Israel is commanded to 'remember' God's mighty acts of liberation from the slavery of Egypt (Deut. 5:15; 8:2; 9:7; 16:3; 24:9; 25:17) it is not purely looking back to what JHWH has done for Israel in the past. No, that event involves *us* just as much. In ritual 'remembrance' what is remembered actually becomes present, with such a reality that according to Deuteronomy 26:6-8 each generation of Israelites can say again, 'The Egyptians mistreated *us* and made *us* suffer, putting *us* to hard labour. Then *we* cried out to the Lord, the God of our fathers, and the Lord heard *our* voice and saw *our* misery, toil and oppression. So the Lord brought *us* out of Egypt with a mighty hand... He brought *us* to this place and gave *us* this land...' (Cf. also Deut. 6:20-25). JHWH has thus brought *us* out of the house of *our* bondage in Egypt. And further, 'it was not with our fathers that the Lord our God made this covenant, but with *us*, with all of *us* who are alive here today. The Lord spoke to *you* face to face out of the fire on the mountain' (Deut. 5:3-4). The degree to which the Jews actively experience anamnesis can be seen in the theatre piece by Silvanus, *Korczak and the Children*. The Polish Jew Korczak, director of a Jewish orphanage since 1911, devoted himself totally to the children in the terrible Warsaw ghetto. In 1942 he, with 200 of his children, were transported to the Maidanek extermination camp, to meet their death. At this gripping moment the rabbi tells Korczak that he is Abraham and Moses. If the children under Korczak's leadership are transported, *they are* the Jewish people who depart from Egypt while the new Moses guides them. Together they sing the song of Moses upon the passage through the Red Sea. Korczak says: 'I will keep in mind how the waters of the Red Sea were parted, opened up for the children of Israel. And the Red Sea is the way to our preservation. I shall think of that – and I will not abandon the children, even as Moses did not abandon his people.'[49] Near Yad Vashem in Israel stands a sculpture by Saktsier,

---

[49] F. FRIJNS: 'Anamnese: in het verleden ligt het heden', in *Tijdschrift voor Liturgie* 56 (1972) 213-214.

depicting a group of children on whose faces death can be read, standing with arms hanging down helplessly. In their midst is the watchful, suffering face of Korczak and his great, protecting hand over the children: an anamnesis in stone.[50]

The Christians continued the Jewish tradition. Remembrance was also central for the followers of Jesus. For them the life of Jesus of Nazareth, from birth to death and resurrection, plays a peculiar role. As in the First Testament that which is recounted in the scriptures unfolds again and again in anamnesis and becomes present, this is also the case in the Second Testament itself, and in the Second Testament in relation to the First Testament. The First and Second Testaments become living reality precisely in liturgical anamnesis, as the anamnesis realises the hidden meaning of earlier stories. In a manner peculiar to them, the salvific acts which took place in that time (*in illo tempore*) become vital within the Christian community in and through its liturgy. However, this is not a full presence. The tension with the future remains. The full reality will only be realised with the return of the Lord, at the end of time. There is thus a linear movement that encompasses past, present and future.

It should be clear that the presence in anamnesis reaches further than the presence which is experienced in theatre or in a museum. There too there is a sense of presence, but it is less radical. In one way or another it remains fictional, or distanced. That is also true for the museal or purely aesthetic experience of a rite. That does not touch the heart of anamnesis. Anamnesis involves a 'real' presence, in one way or another. In this connection, one can speak of a realised eschatology. Salvation is realised in the here and now. It is true that this realisation has been and is experienced in various ways in Christian history. Within the realised eschatology one can emphasise not only the 'actually here', but also the 'not yet'. In some eras and places people accentuate and experience the presence particularly strongly. Then ritual time is experienced so that the divine world is reflected, as it were, in our own history. Especially in the Eastern liturgies anamnesis is experienced as an *epiphania Domini*, an appearance of the Lord. In our culture people are before all else conscious of how tentative, shaky and fuzzy the presence is. For us it is a fragmentary presence, an 'at

[50] C. VISSER: 'Verslindende dood en de weg van Janusz Korczak', in *Dabar-bericht* 1996, 3, 4.

times I see'.[51] People have spoken of an absent presence or a present absence. I will return to that.

The Christian experience of time has left behind countless traces in our Western culture. One can think of the idea of Sunday as a day of rest and as the day of the weekly liturgical gathering, and of feasts such as Christmas, Easter, Ascension and Pentecost, and of saints' days. In this respect there was a sweeping inculturation of the Christian religion. Yet it is precisely at this point that new developments are occurring. The classic Sunday rest and liturgical Sunday observance are increasingly squeezed.[52] It is an ever increasing phenomenon that people celebrate various feasts, without knowing what their original significance is. This is the case especially for Easter, Ascension and Pentecost. When questioned about what is being celebrated with Easter, people will answer that the holiday involves the decoration of Easter eggs because spring has begun. Further, some Christian feasts are not so much celebrated as liturgical ritual, but reflect rather the realm of musealisation and folklore. This is true for instance for Christmas (Christmas gifts, Christmas dinner, Christmas trees, manger scenes) and Easter (Easter egg hunts, and in continental Europe the 'Easter trees', decorated bundles of witch hazel branches). Feasts of saints have also gotten swept up in this trend: St. Valentine's Day, for instance.

In our culture there is a tension between the ritual experience of time and the social experience of time. The social experience is oriented to the greatest possible efficiency in the use of time, and grants itself no rest. Even rites are threatened by the tendency to pure consumerism. In this light, one could even speak of an economic/consumptive oriented

    [51] See the title of the book of OOSTERHUIS: *At Times I See.*
    [52] For a reflection on this problem, see L. VAN TONGEREN: 'De zondag', in BARNARD & POST (eds.): *Ritueel bestek* 69-76 and especially IDEM: 'The Squeeze on Sunday. Reflections on the Changing Experience and Form of Sundays', in POST, ROUWHORST, VAN TONGEREN & SCHEER (eds.): *Christian Feast and Festival* 705-727 and IDEM: 'De christelijke betekenis van de Zondag in kerk en maatschappij', in *Jaarboek voor liturgie-onderzoek* 18 (2002) 101-122; J. DE HART: 'Zondagswijding – Zondagsmijding', in *Praktische Theologie* 30 (2003) 267-283; H. NOORDEGRAAF: 'Een samenleving zonder zondag. Kerken en het debat over de zondag', in *Praktische Theologie* 30 (2003) 284-297; L. VAN TONGEREN: 'De religieuze (ir)relevantie van de zondag. Een liturgiewetenschappelijke reflectie', in *Praktische Theologie* 30 (2003) 298-317.

growth of rites. The economy seems a stimulus for the slogan 'Every day a holiday'.[53] At the same time there is the hegemony of the 24/7 economy exerting control over the society, and suppressing the singularity of Sunday and holy days. It even exercises considerable influence on the disposition of free time as such: this too must be used as efficiently as possible. Ritual time is thus pushed aside. In defiance of this, meditation centres in the midst of shopping malls and airports are an invitation to break through the purely efficient use of time. We now experience the opposite of what happened in previous cultural periods, when ritual and liturgical time was dominant. Over the centuries the number of holy days increased steadily. In the time of Origen (185-253) the holy days were still limited to Easter, Pentecost and Sundays. By the time of the Enlightenment, in the 18th century, the number of holy days on which work was laid aside had reached 120.[54] Their number formed a threat for the economy. Liturgical reformers from the time, for example Winter, therefore argued for a reduction in the number of feast days.[55] Every culture seeks a balance between ritual time and work time in its own way. This is the reason why in our culture there is rising protest against the 24/7 economy. In answer to this protest it is pointed out that for the individual there are more free days than in the recent past. The issue however is about the *collective* balance and the room this balance offers for mutual social intercourse. Also, the observation that the churches support this protest purely out of self-interest is not accurate. There is more at stake than participation in Christian liturgy. Ritual time also includes secular rites and civil religion, general religiosity, and the ritual time of religions such as Judaism, Islam, Hinduism and Buddhism. In essence, the protest is about the 'green space' of rest and free time, which is as essential for our society as parks are for our cities. Only when they are paved over and built on, do we miss them.[56]

---

[53] POST: 'Alle dagen feest'.

[54] J. STEINER: *Liturgiereform in der Aufklärungszeit* (Freiburger theologische Studien 101), Freiburg/Basel/Wien 1976, 36.

[55] STEINER: *Liturgiereform in der Aufklärungszeit* 39.

[56] B. PLAISIER: 'Toespraak bij de start van de actie tegen de 24-uurseconomie', in *Een-twee-een. Kerkelijke documentatie* 26 (1998) 3, 168-169; K. BREEDVELD: *Regelmatig onregelmatig. Spreiding van arbeidstijden en de gevolgen voor vrijetijd en recreatie*, Tilburg 1999; A. VAN DEN BROEK, W. KNULST & K. BREEDVELD: *Naar andere tijden? Tijdsbesteding en tijdsordening in Nederland* (Sociale en culturele studies 29), Den Haag 1999; W.P. KNULST: *Werk, rust en sociaal leven op zondagen sinds de jaren zeventig*, Tilburg 1999.

Another aspect of this tension is that between the ecclesiastical and civil year. Again and again there is the threat of liturgy developing into a purely supra-historical order. For instance, during the siege of Rome by the barbarians, in the prayers of the old *Sacramentarium Veronense* there were very concrete intercessions for protection against enemies, and the concept of mortality was an indication of the prevalence of plague. But gradually these orisons became detached from the concrete circumstances, and were prayed as referring to spiritual enemies and human mortality in general. In the same way the ecclesiastical year has gradually just as much broken free of the history that it unrolled as a unique, self-contained entity, parallel with the annual development of human history. It began to float above the civil year, as it were. Such a development turned the experience of the church year into a sort of cyclic event, which is a threat to the linear experience of time that precisely is so essential for Christian ritual. The new calendar for the ecclesiastical year, through a reassessment of the construction of the church year, has broken through this tendency. But even after these reforms, the task remains of sufficiently rooting the ecclesiastical year in our history itself. It may not ignore what overtakes us in the midst of history. Events such as the Shoah, plagues such as AIDS and contemporary saints deserve their place.[57]

In closing this section, I would want to note the following. Christian time is linear, not cyclic. But this does not mean that, with regard to time, people can not make a distinction between Christian rituals on the linear axis of life and rituals which are actually cyclic, as it were, returning each year or season. Rituals on the horizontal plane of life are first the transitional rituals of birth and death. In every human life there are a number of crucial moments at which, in a more or less radical way

---

[57] Striking is the Invocation of the Saints, in J. BROWN & R. YORK: *The Covenant of Peace. A Liberation Book by the Free Church of Berkeley,* New York 1971, 33-35 See for this also H. SCHMIDT: *Wie betet der heutige Mensch. Dokumente und Analysen,* Einsiedeln/Zürich/Freiburg/Wien 1972, 106-109 and A. STOCK: 'Litanieën', in BARNARD & POST (eds.): *Ritueel bestek* 309-316, particularly 313-315. In addition to classic groups such as confessors, innocents and martyrs, one here finds groups such as peacemakers, children of God and freedom fighters. N. SCHUMAN: 'Nieuwe heiligenkalender', in *Rondom het Woord* 42 (2000) 1, 41-50 mentions for instance Braille and Tolstoi. See also L. VAN TONGEREN: 'De iconografie van moderne heiligen. Op zoek naar een nieuwe typologie', in *Jaarboek voor liturgie-onderzoek* 19 (2003) 127-145.

a transition must be negotiated. This is also true for Christians. They too have *transition rituals* as such. The sacraments also take place against this horizontal plane of life. On the one hand these can be closely interwoven with the general human transition rituals; on the other hand, as I noted above, there is a tension between the two. Also to be found on this horizontal plane – among Christians as well – are the *crisis rituals*. These are rituals which are performed in the face of danger: wars, disasters, accidents, epidemics, etc. But along with the horizontal plane there is also a more cyclic wheel, namely that of the *seasonal rituals and daily rituals*. These are rituals which are not one-off in the lives of people, but which return every season, every month, week or day, and which are a response to recurring needs. But the cyclic recurrence of these rituals does not effect the anamnesis involved in them. Among Christians these are recurring rituals in the linear thrust of sacred history.

With regard to *daily rituals*, Grimes remarks that they are a precondition for the greater rituals. In this connection he speaks of *domestic rituals*. These are of fundamental importance, because they shape our attitude toward ritual.[58] These are thus rituals which in the first instance involve the daily ritual experience of small things. Life itself must be given a ritual value. Both transition and crisis rituals and the cyclical rituals find their foundation there. This is also true for Christian rituals, both with regard to their general anthropological and their specifically religious-Christian basis. In our day the problem has arisen that numerous daily Christian rituals have disappeared. Before the Second Vatican Council the daily life of Christians was full of rituals. In many local history museums, one is impressed by how large the role was in daily life of religious images and statues, in the home, on the street, in school, at work, and in the church building. Daily Christian rituals were just as prolific: morning and evening prayer, praying the rosary, the Angelus at noon, prayers before and after meals. The absence of such a base in contemporary religious culture therefore places new requirements on the performance of larger rituals. For instance, at the beginning of the celebration the leader must realise that more than in the past, those who are going to participate will often have to make a transition to a ritual attitude. He must give them a chance to gradually be carried along in the ritual rhythm. In

[58] GRIMES: *Marrying and Burying* 212 and 216-219.
[59] Part 3, Chapter 6, 2.

this connection, what was said above about adopting a counselling approach at the beginning of the celebration is important.[59]

3. MUSIC

Music is a very primary expression of culture and of meaning in that culture. Music is directed to the ear, but at the same time it involves all of the senses, one's whole corporality. Its place is in the realm of presentative symbolism. In Part 1 I have already noted that music is an integral part of ritual, an essential element of ritual itself, as it is also the Ur-language of religion. It has the power to call up another, deeper world.[60] A re-evaluation of the fundamental role of music in ritual, and the relevance of this for liturgical music, is now under way.[61] Anyone wanting to realise how necessary music is in ritual, and what a deep sensory impact it has, should take the opportunity to participate in a purely spoken Eastern liturgy. What remains is only a skeleton. This is also true for Western liturgy. In the past church music threatened to become independent in relation to the liturgy. The Constitution on Liturgy however rightly emphasises that this music is an integrating component of the liturgy itself (Constitution 112). In a fundamental way, the music defines the shape of the liturgy itself.

With regard to the inculturation of music in Christian ritual, new questions are arising.[62] In our culture there is still a certain distinction between Art with a capital A and the arts with a small a, between elite culture and popular culture, between serious music and popular or pop music.[63] In

---

[60] Because music is such an integrating component of ritual itself, Wilderbeek prefers to speak of ritual music rather than liturgical music. See H. JONGERIUS: 'Op de vierkante meter die je gegeven is doen wat je meent te moeten doen... Een gesprek met Jos Wilderbeek', in *Inzet* 21 (1992) 1, 12

[61] In this connection see VERNOOIJ: *Muziek als liturgisch teken.*

[62] See among others *Music and the Experience of God*: *Concilium* 25 (1989) no. 2 and 'Liturgie et musique', *Congrès de la Societas liturgica Turku, 1997*: *La Maison-Dieu* (1997) no. 212; M.F. MANNION: 'Paradigms in American Catholic Church Music', in *Worship* 70 (1996) 101-128.

[63] For a relativisation of this oppostion, see J. KUNST: 'Pop versus klassiek. Of: Hoe moeten culturen met elkaar omgaan?', in A. VAN ZOEST (ed.): *De macht der tekens. Opstellen over maatschappij, tekst en litteratuur*, Utrecht 1986, 195-203; *Popularmusik und Kirche – kein Widerspruch. Dokumentation des Ersten interdisziplinären Forums 'Popularmusik und Kirche' in Bad Herrenalb vom 28. Februar bis 1. März 2000*, Frankfurt am Main 2001.

SEVERAL IMPORTANT DIMENSIONS AND THEMES 459

relation to this, Huijbers remarks that perhaps the new liturgy offers a possibility of bridging these gaps. 'The solution does not lie in a quantitative domination of the one class over the other… but in quality, of both the popular and classic music'.[64]

Over the last decades, in The Netherlands as elsewhere there has been great creativity with regard to the songs that can be sung by the people. In terms of music the liturgy is enormously in flux. The introduction of the vernacular and restoration of the various roles in the liturgy to honour has resulted in the creation of hundreds of new songs. One finds this reflected in the 1984 collection *Gezangen voor Liturgie* (Songs for liturgy).[65] One radical decision was that of the monastic orders in The Netherlands, which moved to singing the ecclesiastical hours in the vernacular. The *Abdijboek* is an impressive new creation, which undoubtedly in the future will also prove to be inspiring for parish liturgy.[66] With regard to the churches of the Reformation, one finds postwar developments there reflected in the 1973 *Liedboek voor de kerken* (Hymnbook for the churches), which was the result of a unique creative impulse.[67] The Old Catholic Church in The Netherlands came out with a new song book in 1990.[68] Many new liturgical songs have continued to appear after the publication of these collections.[69] In addition to these new songs, which in a certain sense bridge the gap between popular songs and classics, there are still the two poles of classic and popular liturgical music.

[64] B. HUIJBERS: 'Liturgische muziek na Vaticanum II', in *Werkmap (voor) Liturgie* 15 (1981) 381-382.

[65] *Gezangen voor liturgie*, Hilversum 1984, Baarn 1995². See further S. GROOT (ed.): *De lof Gods geef ik stem. Inzichten en achtergronden van de vocale muziek in de rooms-katholieke eredienst*, Baarn 1993; this book provides a good picture of the state of affairs.

[66] INTERMONASTERIËLE WERKGROEP VOOR LITURGIE: *Abdijboek*, Amsterdam 1967 ff. See A. VERNOOIJ: "Hun geluid ging over de hele wereld'. Over de invloed van de kloos-terzang op de Nederlandstalige parochieliturgie', in *Gregoriusblad* 122 (1998) 3, 149-155. With regard to the place of Gregorian music in our culture and in contemporary liturgy, see M. HOONDERT & P. POST: 'De dynamiek van het gregoriaans. Een onder-zoeksperspectief', in *Jaarboek voor liturgie-onderzoek* 15 (1999) 7-26; G. LUKKEN: 'Inculturatie en liturgische muziek', in A. VERNOOIJ (ed.): *Toontaal. De verhouding tussen woord en toon in heden en* verleden (Meander 4), Kampen 2002, 9-43.

[67] *Liedboek voor de kerken*, Den Haag 1973. See W.G. OVERBOSCH (ed.): *Een compendium van achtergrondinformatie bij de 491 gezangen van het Liedboek voor de kerken*, Amsterdam 1978.

[68] *Gezangboek van de Oud-Katholieke Kerk van Nederland*, Hilversum 1990.

[69] GROOT (ed.): *De lof Gods geef ik stem*; OSKAMP & SCHUMAN (eds.): *De weg van de liturgie* 271-279.

On the *classical* side the problem surrounding classic Mass compositions has become obvious. The problem is related to the fact that in previous centuries 'liturgical' music was composed as choral part song (*musica*), including those parts which accrued to the congregation. This choral music includes numerous masterpieces, both from the period of polyphony and from the classic and romantic periods. There is a movement in the church, both at the top and at the congregational level, which passionately defends these gems of ecclesiastical music.[70] But considered from the perspective of liturgy, this music is really no longer usable, because structurally it fails to do justice to the function that the elements of the order of service in question have. Seen liturgically, this music could at the most function as meditative moments – among which one could also consider non-eucharistic celebrations. For the rest, this old music should be allocated to the concert hall. Yet one can also take a less rigid position. In the renewed ritual it is also possible to listen with a high degree of engagement, and thus to participate in this church music. One is in fact left with a sort of hybrid form between concert and liturgy, which from the liturgical perspective is not ideal. Therefore it is obvious that this classical church music cannot just be used as it was before the Second Vatican Council.

Next there is the question of the integration of serious modern music in the liturgy. To date there has been almost no integration of thoroughly innovative styles in liturgical song. Innovation is limited chiefly to the tonal/modern style (Britten, Schröder, Strategier, Toebosch, de Klerk, Pirenne, Vogel, Bartelink, etc.).[71] One noteworthy attempt at far-reaching innovation in The Netherlands was certainly the series of vespers services in Harlingen in 1987 and the follow-up to them.[72] One

---

[70] Since 1963 this movement has been institutionalised as the Consociatio Internationalis Musicae Sacrae (CIMS). On the other hand, since 1962 there has been the Universa laus movement, which considers the music in the liturgy as Christian ritual music. The criteria for church music in this movement are whether it functions in an integrated manner in the Christian ritual as such. For the two movements see G. KOCK: *Tussen altaar en oksaal. Stromingen in de kerkmuziek na Vaticanum II* (M.A. Thesis Theologische faculteit Tilburg), Tilburg 1980. In connection with the contrast between church music as autonomous art and as a component of the liturgy, see VERNOOIJ: *Muziek als liturgisch teken.*

[71] BORNEWASSER: 'Is het waar dat de kerkmuziek van deze eeuw' 243.

[72] K. HOEK, W. OOSTERWAL & H. RUITER: *Nieuwe muziek in de liturgie*, Harlingen 1987.

difficulty is undoubtedly that modern music supposes a strong measure of professionalism. Moreover, public acceptance of modern music lags far behind that of, for example, modern architecture. Is that because people can avoid it more easily than they can avoid a building? Or is it because of the more penetrating character of music? Is it because music constitutes and conditions time, and this is more radical than the constitution and conditioning of space?[73] Or is it because twelve tone music is a more cerebral music, which intends to be nothing more than pure music, and thus can not call upon familiarity and tradition through its emotional implications? Perhaps, according to Vernooij, the possibilities which presented themselves here for a whole new sacred music were not accepted because of the applied character of liturgical music, as an applied art. As such, liturgical music is wary of developments in autonomous music, and is oriented to the taste of the believers, attuned to recognisable sounds.[74] Whatever the case, it remains a question whether far-reaching inculturation in this regard is possible, and if so, on what conditions. Are there new challenges here, certainly in pluriform liturgy? With regard to the inculturation of serious music into the liturgy, this also touches on organ music and other instrumental music. Here more has certainly transpired. One gets the impression that this music is received more quickly. Hameline's observation with regard to this reception is interesting: 'We have all at some time heard wonderful organists who in the liturgy make no concessions whatsoever to technique and the high grammar of their musical language, without this producing any difficulties for the congregation. The condition for this seems to be that the music is in keeping with the possibilities that the liturgy affords at that moment. I remember that Boyer played thirty intervals of a second after a psalm; I can still hear it yet. Those are poetic moments that flash up, and it is the liturgy itself which makes them possible.'[75]

The *opposite pole of popular or pop music* is also seeking its place in contemporary Christian liturgy. Here one is indeed justified in speaking of

---

[73] According to a remark by Anton Vernooij.

[74] VERNOOIJ: 'De taal van de ziel' 236.

[75] J.Y. HAMELINE: 'Actes du colloque 'Création musicale et musique liturgique', jeudi 23 mai 1991', in *Bulletin de l'Institut catholique de Lyon* 99-100 (1992), 90. See P. MARCHAL: 'La participation de l'organiste à la liturgie', in *La Maison-Dieu* (1994) 198, 100.

an authentic ritual way. One can think of the ritual of the pop festival. As I noted before, there is there an intense communication between performers and participants.[76] The participation is more than purely verbal: people clap along, wave their arms, hold each other's hands, sway with the rhythm, sing along on the refrain, wave the flames of their lighters, crowd surf, etc. Here we are dealing with living ritual which, moreover, has a religious charge. There is also vitality and rhythm, which the young identify with. They often find Christian liturgy so boring, even youth liturgy. Then they say, 'You've got to go to a pop concert some time.' Anyway, here you encounter a musical layer of our culture that is of great importance for the inculturation of liturgy. The critique from young people parallels that of Clarence Rivers on the musical culture of the West. McGann summarises Rivers's view clearly as follows:[77]

> Rivers parallels the distinction he makes between ocular and oral cultures with the musical preferences evident in each. He posits that persons shaped by an ocular/linear orientation tend to be melodically oriented, and generally less sophisticated in matters of rhythm – precisely because rhythm is created by breaking the continuity in a musical line. In contrast, African American music, based in the predilections of oral culture, is rhythmically generated, favoring complex and polyrhythmic structures that create a discontinuity in the musical line. This break in the musical line prompts reciprocal, rhythmic movements in the human body. The bias of Western liturgical traditions toward ocular culture, and its concomitant favoring of melodically generated music, had led to a degrading of rhythmic music on moral grounds. Rivers quotes a document circulated at the time of his writing by the Federation of Diocesan Liturgical Commissions.[78] 'Music with an emphasis on beat,' the document posits, elicits 'physical, impulsive and unconscious involvement.' In contrast, music with 'melodic emphasis…leads the listener inwardly to an attitude of interior reflection.' The document continues: 'beat music' establishes a style of worship that highlights its 'horizontal or humanistic' dimensions, while 'melodic music' elicits a worship style that is more 'vertical or spiritually elevating.' The message communicated is that the latter provides a sounder theological basis for liturgical action. This prejudicial view degrades rhythmically-generated music as unserious at best and theologically deficient at worst; and it privileges those styles of worship that may enlighten the mind but may be less able to move the heart.

---

[76] Part 3, Chapter 5, 2.4.
[77] McGann: 'Timely wisdom' 19-20.
[78] Rivers: *The Spirit in Worship* 17.

Thus, in inculturation no musical style whatsoever needs to be excluded, on the condition that it can be integrated into the ritual, and is open for the deeper dimensions of life. As it happens, these deeper dimensions are experienced by youth, and also through older persons, precisely in this music, with all its stylistic variations. Much of this music possesses religious power, and appears suitable for ritual expression.[79]

The tear-jerker and torch song are a whole field of their own. It cannot be denied that these songs can express a primary experience for people, something of their personal and collective history; as such they can be a much loved expression of faith. It would be unfair to bar them from a liturgy that would be a 'people's liturgy'. In a thoroughgoing inculturation of the liturgy into our culture they also deserve a place. The church music historian Kurris rightly observes, 'That is what it is ultimately all about. This deepest (liturgical) function can be operative in both elementary and complex music, in kitsch and in the choicest cultural expressions.'[80]

The 2001 Instruction *Liturgiam authenticam* devoted little attention to liturgical music.[81] Yet the Instruction is less innocent with regard to music than one might think. According to the Instruction, texts to be sung must first and foremost be faithful to the text in the official liturgical source itself. They must be translated in such a way that they are suitable for musical compositions. However, once they are confirmed, one may not paraphrase the translated texts in order to be able to set

---

[79] See also M. ROSSEEUW, P. SCHOLLAERT & J. DE WIT: 'Religieuze muziek: expressie van het onzegbare', in J. HEMELS & H. HOEKSTRA: *Media en religieuze communicatie*, Hilversum 1985, 341-355; R. MES & M. ZAGERS: *Wij zingen de hemel open. Popmuziek in de jongerenliturgie* (UTP-teksten 20), Heerlen 1991. For the breadth and pluriformity of the field of music in youth liturgies, see among others H. EVERS: 'Muziek in jongerenliturgie', in *Werkmap (voor) Liturgie* 21 (1987) 229-239.

[80] A. KURRIS: 'Hoe indringend is het lied?', in *Werkmap (voor) Liturgie* 18 (1984) 14. The argument by WAGNER-RAU: *Segensraum* 181-182 in connection with the funeral liturgy, that *Trivialkultur* and its corresponding musical wishes should be taken seriously, and not considered as deficient but as 'other', also seems to me to be relevant here. Such music belongs to another, but not therefore less important culture. Particularly in 'occasional liturgies', it could express the emotions of large groups in the population and give a religious sense to their lives that is often alien to the high church culture.

[81] For the Instruction, see Part 3, Chapter 3, 3.1. A more extensive commentary in LUKKEN: 'Inculturatie en liturgische muziek' 41-43.

them to music more easily. It is equally forbidden to simply consider songs as equivalent to officially confirmed liturgical texts and use the former in place of the latter (no. 60). The Latin hymns and canticles from the new *editiones typicae*, which in fact only cover a small part of the enormous treasury of the Latin church, must be included in collections of songs in the vernacular. Songs in the vernacular preferably must be derived from Scripture and the treasury of the liturgy (no. 61). Within five years a repertorium with texts for liturgical song must be provided. This document must be submitted to the Congregation for Worship and the Discipline of the Sacraments for approval (*recognitio*) (no. 108). The Instruction appears to want to step hard on the brakes to halt the inculturation of liturgical music as it has developed until now. One gets the impression that the official Roman policy is focused on rectifying or reversing current developments, or at least bringing them under strict control. It would be extremely sad if this Instruction of 'literalness' were to be enforced literally. This would damage the viability of the liturgy, which has been so productive precisely in the realm of liturgical song. Life – and certainly the musical life – does not easily permit itself to be forced into a predetermined and 'approved' structure. It would be disastrous if the further inculturation of liturgical song once again were forced to take place outside the liturgy, as a sort of paraliturgy.

4. WOMEN AND LITURGY

A fundamental process of women's emancipation is under way in our culture. This process has been accompanied with great ritual creativity. Kay Turner is correct in her observation that in general males controlled the rights with regard to rituals. Rituals were the realm in which males could display their authority in the most impressive manner, and they were the most direct form of access to this authority. In most societies, from the primitive to the developed, the performance of ritual is an acknowledgement of the right of males to create and define culture, and by their exclusion a sign that women should remain in their place, a place without real or symbolic marks of power.[82] In terms of ritual, the distinction between the sacred and profane, which plays an essential role

---

[82] K. TURNER: 'Contemporary Feminist Rituals', in B. SPRETNACK (ed.): *Politics of Women Spirituality*, New York 1982, 221.

in anthropology and comparative religion, has served the interests of males. In contrast to women, they had free access to the world of the sacred. It is therefore obvious that in the movement for women's emancipation rituals would have a privileged place, and that they would play an important role in finding, controlling and interpreting the symbolic sources of their traditions and cultures.[83] Numerous new, alternative rituals were developed. According to Grimes three questions especially play a role in this, one which is characteristic for the rising new rituals: the question of how authority must be shaped, the question of to what degree hierarchy can be superseded, and the question of how individual interests can be balanced with social interests.[84]

There is also a women's movement within the churches, and there too ritual plays a primary role. One finds analogous questions there. It cannot be denied that Christian ritual was also reserved for males. Women were only the object of the liturgy. Only males had access to the sacred. The shape of Christian liturgy was determined by patriarchal cultures, in which women were viewed as subordinate to men. We have gradually become aware of the extent to which the masculine dominated Christian liturgy. Here one can say there was need for a radical inculturation of the Christian liturgy, which is still in full swing.[85] This inculturation through the subculture of the women's movement is all the more important, because in the main stream of our culture there is a declining appreciation for 'feminine values'. Masculine characteristics

---

[83] TURNER: 'Contemporary Feminist Rituals' 226.

[84] GRIMES: *Ritual Criticism* 120.

[85] For a bibliography, see T. BERGER: 'Woman and Worship: A Bibliography', in *Studia Liturgica* 19 (1989) 96-110; IDEM: 'Woman and Worship: A Bibliography Continued', in *Studia Liturgica* 25 (1995) 103-117; IDEM: *Liturgie und Frauenseele. Die Liturgische Bewegung aus der Sicht der Frauenforschung*, Stuttgart 1993; IDEM: *Women's Ways of Worship. Gender Analysis and Liturgical History*, Collegeville 1999; T. BERGER & A. GERHARDS (eds.): *Liturgie und Frauenfrage*, St. Ottilien 1990; M. PROCTER-SMITH: *In Her Own Rite. Feminist Liturgical Tradition*, Ohio 1990 (reprint 2000); IDEM: *Praying with Our Eyes Open. Engendering Feminist Liturgical Prayer*, Nashville 1995; D. DIJK: *Een beeld van een liturgie. Verkenningen in vrouwenstudies liturgiek, met bijzondere aandacht voor Marjorie Procter-Smith*, Gorinchem 1999; A. ESSER, B. ENZNER-PROBST, A. BERLIS & C. METHUEN (eds): *Women, Ritual and Liturgy = Yearbook of the European Society of Women in Theological Research* 9 (2001) IV. See further *Liturgie en vrouw: Tijdschrift voor Liturgie* 80 (1996) no. 5, in which especially M. GEURTSEN: 'De andere kant van het glas in lood' 266-280; D. DIJK: 'Developments in Feminist Liturgy in the Netherlands', in *Studia Liturgica* 45 (1995) 120 128; *Vrouwe Leitourgia: Tijdschrift voor Liturgie* 82 (1998) no. 5.

are regarded more highly than feminine, and in general they are also assessed more highly in economic terms.[86] It would be an important correction to this if people were to increase the status of caring, so that care – including care for one's own family – was seen as an economic service to society. At that point new values come into sight. Faxes and deadlines simply become unimportant when a parent takes a child of three for a stroll and pauses by every flower. Esteem for feminine values is only hesitantly finding its stride in our society. The same is true within the institutional church. But despite all the doubts there is great creativity at the congregational level. There the new fact on the ground is appearing, that women are no longer purely and simply the object of liturgical acts, but also their subject, because they are becoming worship leaders and/or joining in preparing the liturgy and giving it shape.[87]

First, there is the new question of whether women can be admitted to the offices of the church. Then there are deep questions regarding the name of God and the predominantly masculine character of the liturgy, involving both the verbal and the non-verbal.

4.1. Women and church offices

The issue of women and ecclesiastical offices hardly ever came up for discussion in Catholic theology until the Second Vatican Council.[88] One also finds no official statements on the matter. Old canon law does indeed contain an ecclesiastical ban on the basis of an almost uncontradicted tradition. In Canon 968,1 one could read that only a baptised man can receive valid holy ordination. This tradition, now in the sense of a long-established custom without further theological basis, is the point of departure for the 1976 statement *Inter insigniores* by the Congregation

---

[86] M. VERDUIJN: 'Vaders in de hoofdrol. Marijke Verduijn in gesprek met Vincent Duindam', in *Roodkoper* 2 (1997) 4, 14-16; M. GRUNELL: *Mannen die zorgen, zijn de kerels van morgen*, Utrecht 1998.

[87] GEURTSEN: 'De andere kant van het glas in lood' 273-275.

[88] W. BOELENS: *Vrouwen in de kerk. Op weg naar behoedzaam leiderschap*, Hilversum 1985, 73-74. Interesting and abundant information on the question of women and church offices is to be found on a very easily used website, www.womenpriests.org by Hans Wijngaards, director of the Housetop Centre in London, which specialises in Christian communication. See H. WIJNGAARDS: 'Toen vrouwen nog diakens waren', in *De Bazuin* 82 (1999) 15, 8-10. Also: I. RAMING: *Priesteramt der Frau. Geschenk Gottes für eine erneuerte Kirche*, Münster 2002 (with bibliography 1974-2001).

for Doctrine, which underscores and substantiates the continued obligation to enforce this ban.[89] The Congregation observes: 'The Church's
tradition in the matter has thus been so firm in the course of the centuries that the Magisterium has not felt the need to intervene in order
to formulate a principle which was not attacked, or to defend a law
which was not challenged.' The Congregation's document was emphatically approved by Pope Paul VI. Therefore, in its canon 1024, the new
book of canon law of 1983 literally retains the old canon 968,1. In
1994 John Paul II returned to the question in his apostolic letter *Ordinatio sacerdotalis*.[90] He emphasises that the Church does not have the
authority to ordain a woman priest, and that the same doctrine, which
is founded on the uninterrupted tradition of the Church, definitely
must be maintained. Shortly thereafter, in 1995, followed a *Responsum*
from the Congregation for Doctrine. It notes that what the apostolic
letter said on this question must be understood as belonging to the articles of faith of the Church and that it is taught infallibly in the ordinary
and general magisterium.[91] With this Rome appeared to close off the
discussion, – wrongly, however. The Perfect of the Congregation,
Ratzinger, himself acknowledged that this was not an *ex cathedra* pronouncement, but the infallible implementation of ordinary and general
magisterium. Unfortunately, an act of ordinary magisterium is only
infallible if it rests on collegiality, and in this question that is not the
case. This means that the arguments can and must be weighed up.[92] The

[89] CONGREGATION FOR THE DOCTRINE OF FAITH: 'Declaratio circa quaestionem
admissionis mulierum ad sacerdotium ministeriale (1976)', in *Acta Apostolicae Sedis* 69
(1977) 98-116 = 'Verklaring aangaande de vraag over het toelaten van vrouwen tot het
ambtelijk priesterschap (1976)', in *Archief van de Kerken* 32 (1977) 282-296 (comment:
917-927).
[90] JOHANNES PAULUS II: *Ordinatio sacerdotalis*, Città del Vaticano 1994.
[91] CONGREGATION FOR THE DOCTRINE OF FAITH: 'Responsum ad dubium circa
doctrinam in Epistola Apostolica "Ordinatio Sacerdotalis" traditam, October 28, 1995',
in *Acta Apostolicae Sedis* 87 (1995) 1114.
[92] H. WALDENFELS: 'Zum Verbindlichkeitsgrad von *Inter insigniores* und *Ordinatio
sacerdotalis* und ihren dogmatischen Positionen', in E. DASSMANN a.o.: *Projekttag.
Frauenordination*, Bonn 1997, 24-25; CATHOLIC THEOLOGICAL SOCIETY OF AMERICA:
'Resolution', in *Bulletin ET. Zeitschrift für Theologie in Europa* 8 (1997) 2, 209-219. See
also 'Dokumentation. Gesellschaft-Wissenschaft-Kirche. Statements zur Tagung der
Deutschen Sektion in Mainz', in *Bulletin ET. Zeitschrift für Theologie in Europa* 8 (1997)
1, 99 and the literature, listed there in note 25; C. THEOBALD: 'The 'Definitive' Discourse of the Magisterium: Why be Afraid of a Creative Reception?', in *Concilium* 35
(1999) 1, 70-76.

German bishops correctly declared after the appearance of *Ordinatio sacerdotalis* that the elucidation of the ecclesiastical magisterium here was neither clear nor satisfactory.[93]

In the discussion one can distinguish three sorts of arguments: an appeal to Scripture, reference to tradition, and considerations on the basis of anthropological data.

The central argument in the Roman documents involves the *Scriptural* account with regard to the conduct of Jesus, followed by the apostles. Precisely because Jesus was more open to women than was customary in his time, their admission to the ranks of the apostles would have been obvious step. The documents involved, however, themselves admit that this argument will not appeal to everyone, and only points in a certain direction. Moreover, it must be realised that shortly before the 1976 declaration *Inter insigniores* from the Congregation, a report had appeared from the papal Bible commission.[94] In this report, which was approved unanimously by the commission, one can read: 'It does not seem that the New Testament by itself alone will permit us to settle in a clear way and once and for all the problem of the possible accession of women to the presbyterate.' That is all the more true today, because gradually, from feminist exegesis, it has become clearer that women also played a role in the shaping of Christian communities.[95]

With regard to *tradition*, it is emphasised that the Church never ordained women to the priesthood, either in the East or in the West. Such ordinations only took place in several heterodox sects, which were rejected by the Church. As a first response to that, one can note that any such argument from a longstanding history of rejection is rather disputable. The fact is, such a rejection could be the result of earlier views that were contingent and culturally determined. One can think of the

---

[93] A. BORRAS & B. POTTIER: *La grâce du diaconat. Questions actuelles du diaconat latin*, Brussel 1998, 178.

[94] PAUSELIJKE BIJBELCOMMISSIE: 'Rapport over de kwestie van de priesterwijding van vrouwen', in *Archief van de Kerken* 31 (1976) 917-927. Source: *N.C. Documentary Service* July 1, 1976.

[95] A. DERMIENCE: 'Femmes et ministères dans l'Eglise primitive', in *Spiritus* 137 (1994) 382-395; UTE E. EISEN: *Amtsträgerinnen im frühen Christentum. Epigraphische und litterarische Studien* (Forschungen zur Kirche- und Dogmengeschichte 61), Göttingen 1996 = UTE E. EISEN: *Woman Officeholders in Early Christianity. Epigraphical and Literary Studies*, Collegeville 2000.

Church's ban on collecting interest, which lasted into the Middle Ages, and the churches' acceptance of slavery, which lasted into the 19th century.[96] The Church can arrive at new insights, in part guided by cultural developments. With regard to views of men and women, I will return to this when I discuss the anthropological grounds. But there are additional problems. The longstanding acceptance of the tradition is itself contestable. The role women played in the growth of Christianity is a particularly interesting phenomenon. They enjoyed considerably higher status within the peculiar subculture of Christianity than pagan women did in the official culture. This involved particularly their position in the family. But they also held positions of leadership in the Church.[97] In part under the influence of feminist theology, new information is being uncovered. Neglected sources are being tapped. This has especially been the case for grave inscriptions. Research into these has already frequently led to a revision of historical views. With regard to women and the early church, the study of grave inscriptions is making it clear that women had an active role in the dissemination and development of Christianity. They exercised the offices of apostle, prophet, teacher, widow, administrator of church property, deacon, presbyter and bishop[98] – even the last three. Regarding the office of deacon, it is generally accepted that in both the East and the West women were admitted to the diaconate.[99] But from grave inscriptions it appears that women also definitely exercised the office of presbyter.[100] On the basis of epigraphic witnesses one can assume that until the fourth century women were active as presbyters in Christian communities in Asia Minor, Greece and Egypt. It was the Synod of Laodicia in the fourth century which wanted to abolish the office of presbyter for women, and tried to ban women from the area around the altar. Developments such as one finds in canon 11 of this synod led to these women no longer receiving the laying on of hands, thereby losing their rootage in the higher ranks of the clergy.

---

[96] BOELENS: *Vrouwen in de kerk* 73-74.

[97] STARK: *De eerste eeuwen* 105-137.

[98] EISEN: *Amtsträgerinnen im frühen Christentum*. Interesting data is also to be found in G. OTRANTO: 'Note sul sacerdozio femminile nell'antichita in margine a una testimonianza di Gelasio I', in *Vetera Christianorum* 19 (1982) 341-360.

[99] BORRAS & POTTIER: *La grâce du diaconat* 158-176; R. GRYSON: *Le ministère des femmes dans l'Église ancienne*, Gembloux 1972; A.M. MARTIMORT: *Les diaconesses. Essai historique*, Rome 1982.

[100] EISEN: *Amtsträgerinnen im frühen Christentum* 112-137.

Nevertheless, it appears that they were not yet completely shut out in the fifth century, and still had a significant role in the community. This is suggested by the fact that according to the *Testamentum Domini* (fifth century) the community explicitly prays for women presbyters.[101] With regard to the West, from the epigraphy one can demonstrate that from the fourth to the sixth century women presbyters were found in Sicily, Southern Italy and Yugoslavia. In addition, it appears from a letter of Pope Gelasius I, from the end of the fifth century, that women in Southern Italy and Sicily were active as priests. That was apparently accepted by the communities themselves, and encouraged by the bishops. It is a custom that Gelasius I (492-496) attacks in his letters.[102] The supposition that women presbyters only were found among heterodox ranks is difficult to maintain, and from this one can also assume that these female presbyters were also entrusted with service at the altar. With regard to the office of bishop, on the basis of epigraphic witnesses it can be assumed that in Rome and the Roman provinces women exercised the office of bishop.[103] As the result of the Catholic paradigm that simply excluded the possibility of women bishops, the female bishops who one finds in the epigraphic witnesses designated as *episcopa* were always considered by researchers to be the wives of bishops. But there are various incontrovertible proofs for female bishops. The female *episcopa* Theodora, to whom there are multiple witnesses in the Zeno chapel of the church of Santa Prassede in Rome, and mother of Pope Paschalis I, was certainly not the wife of a bishop, because it is certain her husband was not a bishop – nor indeed did he hold any other ecclesiastical office. Further Latin inscriptions from Italy and Dalmatia make it probable that women were also active as bishops there in the fifth and sixth centuries.

Finally, there are also the considerations on *anthropological* grounds.[104] For example, it is pointed out that Christ was male, and that this fact touches on the anthropological symbolism of the relation of man and women in their mutual differences and their complementarity. For example, already in the Old Testament the relation between

---

[101] For the text see note 114. See also *Testamentum Domini* II, 35: 'Presbyterae maneant apud episcopam (also this noun is interesting!)) usque ad tempus matutinum, orantes et requiescentes'.

[102] GELASIUS I: *Epistola* 14, 26.

[103] EISEN: *Amtsträgerinnen im frühen Christentum* 193-209.

[104] BORRAS & POTTIER: *La grâce du diaconat* 180-186.

bridegroom and bride plays an important role in the conception of the relation between God and his people. And: particularly during the Eucharist, the priest represents Christ before the community, and in this capacity during the eucharistic prayer repeats the words of institution, 'This is my body.'

To this one can answer that the incarnation is in no sense a matter of becoming a man, but of becoming human. The adage of the Church Fathers which says that which is not taken on is not saved, is relevant here.[105] If the incarnation were a matter of becoming a man, that would mean that only males could be saved. It would thus be wrong to ascribe a privileged place to males on the basis of the incarnation. With regard to the symbolism of representing Christ, one must not take this too realistically. This is not imitation, as in playing a role in theatre, but representation in a ritual manner.[106] Moreover, it can be remarked that the priest acts both *in persona Christi* (the bridegroom) and *in persona ecclesiae* (the bride). There is thus a double representation, male and female.[107]

With respect to anthropological argumentation, one runs into the problem that attitudes about men and women are culturally determined. In the past, particularly the social and cultural views regarding the subordination of women led to women being excluded from priestly office. Rome itself acknowledges that today these views can no longer count as an argument for excluding women from priestly office, because men and women are equal. It was a vision connected with a previous culture that led to women being assigned a subordinate place; in that context they were excluded from priestly office. If that is so, it should equally be true that the equality of men and women in church and society, according to the insights of our culture, should lead to the office of priest being opened up for women.[108] The equal rights of women, reaching so far as the office of priest, has everything to be said for it.

---

[105] See AMBROSE: *Epistola* 48; ATHANASIUS: *Ad epictitum* 7; BASILIUS: *Epistola* 261; CYRIL OF JERUSALEM: *Catecheses* 4, 9; GREGORY OF NAZIANZUS: *Epistola 101 ad cledonium*.

[106] Part 3, Chapter 5, 2.4. See also H.-M. LEGRAND: 'Traditio perpetuo servata? La non-ordination des femmes: tradition ou simple fait historique?', in P. DE CLERCK & E. PALAZZO (eds.): *Rituels. Mélanges offerts à Pierre-Marie Gy, o.p.*, Paris 1990, 411-412; BORRAS & POTTIER: *La grâce du diaconat* 183; T.P. RAUSCH: 'Forum: Priestly Identity: Priority of Representation and the Iconic Argument', in *Worship* 73 (1999) 169-179.

[107] BORRAS & POTTIER: *La grâce du diaconat* 184.

[108] BOELENS: *Vrouwen in de kerk* 74-76; CATHOLIC THEOLOGICAL SOCIETY OF AMERICA: 'Resolution' 213-216.

This is all the more true because our culture is particularly sensitive to the New Testament vision, expressed in Galatians 3:27-28, according to which on the basis of baptism there is no distinction whatever any more between Jew and Greek, slave and free, man and woman. Excluding woman from the priesthood is simply not credible in our culture. However, it is also obvious that the boundary does not lie at the office of priest, but that one can equally argue for the admission of women to the office of bishop.[109] And that is obviously a fortiori true for admitting women to the office of deacon.[110]

This issue of women and office also directly touches on ecumenicity.[111] The possibility for such ordinations has been opened up in various Christian churches. A dialogue among the various Christian churches on this question can therefore be enriching. As there is a shortage of candidates for office in the Catholic Church, one should also realise what the consequences are, both qualitatively and quantitatively, of excluding half of all believers from offices.[112]

In closing I would like to cite two texts from the Christian tradition itself. According to the first text from the *Constitutiones Apostolicae* (about 380) the bishop, laying his hands upon a deaconess, in the presence of the presbytery and of the deacons and deaconesses, prays:

> O Eternal God, the Father of our Lord Jesus Christ,
> Creator of man and of woman,
> who didst replenish with the Spirit Miriam, and Deborah, and Anna, and Huldah;

[109] EISEN: *Amtsträgerinnen im frühen Christentum* 208.

[110] That in spite of this there is still considerable resistance to be overcome, even with respect to the ordination of women to the office of deacon, is demonstrated by recent publications such as that of G.L. MÜLLER: *Der Empfänger des Weihesakraments. Quellen zur Lehre und Praxis der Kirche, nur Männern das Weihesakrament zu spenden*, Würzburg 1999; IDEM: 'Können Frauen die sakramentale Diakonenweihe gültig empfangen?', in: *Notitiae* 39 (2002) no. 7-8 (= no. 432-433), 370-409; INTERNATIONAL THEOLOGICAL COMMISSION: 'Le diaconat: évolution et perspectives', in *La documentation catholique* (19 janvier 2003) 23, 58-107. For a pleading, see for instance PH. ZAGANO: *Holy Saturday. An Argument for the Restoration of the Female Diaconate in the Catholic Church*, New York 2000; IDEM: 'Catholic Women Deacons: Present Tense', in *Worship* 77 (2003) 386-408; WIJNGAARDS: 'Toen vrouwen nog diakens waren' 8-10.

[111] In this connection see A. BERLIS: 'The Ordination of Women: A Test Case for Conciliarity', in *Concilium* (1999) 1, 77-84.

[112] Regarding the power issues, which play a role in this question, see WANNENWETSCH: *Gottesdienst als Lebensform* 177-179.

who didst not disdain
that Thy only begotten Son should be born of a woman;
who also in the tabernacle of the testimony and in the temple,
didst ordain women to be keepers of Thy holy gates, –
do Thou now also look upon this Thy servant,
who is to be ordained to the office of a deaconess,
and grant her Thy Holy Spirit,
and cleanse her from all filthiness of flesh and spirit,
that she may worthily discharge the work which is committed to her
to Thy glory, and the praise of Thy Christ,
with whom glory and adoration be to Thee and the Holy Spirit
for ever.
Amen.[113]

And the prayer for women presbyters by the entire community, as found in the *Testamentum Domini*, is striking. It reads:

For the female presbyters let us beseech,
that the Lord hear their supplications
and in the grace of the Spirit perfectly keep their hearts
and support their labour.[114]

4.2. The name of God and the masculine character of the liturgy

In addition to the issue of offices, there are questions with regard to the name of God and the predominantly masculine nature of the liturgy, with regard to both verbal and non-verbal characteristics.

In liturgy God is addressed as Lord, Father, judge, king, creator, shepherd, commander of the heavenly host, He. Christ is the Son of God, and the Spirit too is generally denoted as He. God is still overwhelmingly regarded as male. It is undoubtedly possible, however, to reinterpret and supplement this masculine image of God from the Bible itself. For instance, we read in Deuteronomy 32:18: 'You deserted the Rock, who fathered you; you forgot the God who gave you birth.' And in Numbers 11:12 Moses complains to God, who is enraged: 'Did I conceive all these people? Did I give them birth?' In Isaiah God is portrayed with feminine images. God in the Bible is also the God who gives birth

---

[113] *Constitutiones Apostolicae* VIII, 19-20.
[114] *Testamentum Domini* I, 35.

to, nourishes, clothes and has pity on her children. Is the Holy Spirit not first and foremost the feminine, the *anima* of God?[115] And God the Father in the Bible is by no means the patriarchal God/Father, but rather the loving and nearby Abba (literally 'pappa').

There are arguments made for more inclusive language with regard to God in the liturgy, in which both the male and female is included.[116] Because the liturgy is always about a way of life, it seems to me important to further concretise this. One can implement this inclusive language in various ways. First, it is possible to designate God with verbal phrases, by linking the word God with a verb (God, who perfects, creates, loves or pities us; God, to whom we can always turn; God, in whose image we are made), or a present or past participle (living God; the risen God). In both cases it is possible to omit the word God (You who create or perfect us; You to whom we turn, You in whose image we are made; the Living One, the Risen One). Next, some argue for alternating the male and female personal and possessive pronouns when speaking of God, in order to in this way stress the androgynous character of God. A third possibility is to use adjectives as proper nouns when speaking of God: God is then denoted as the Merciful, the Loving (One), the Righteous (One). A fourth way is to use ungendered metaphors: One then speaks of God as light, bosom, heart, breath, canopy, spring, fire, warmth, water, lamp, vine, power, comforter, companion on the way: for instance: 'Radiant light that gives direction to our days' or 'Light that finds us in the morning'.[117] Finally, one encounters explicitly female designations of God as Mother. For instance, instead of praying 'Our Father...' people pray 'Our Father and Mother' or 'Thou who art our Father and Mother...', etc. Some feminist theologians argue for integrating the term Goddess into the Jewish and Christian tradition, while others on the contrary want to

---

[115] For the feminine character of the Spirit, see also page 520, note 56.

[116] Among others D. DIJK a.o.: "Ik laat u niet gaan tenzij gij mij zegent'. Over de worsteling met God waarna *Hij* nieuwe namen krijgt', in *Gereformeerd Theologisch Tijdschrift* 85 (1985) 189-212 = D. DIJK a.o.: *Feministisch-Theologische Teksten. Gekozen en ingeleid door Denise Dijk, Fokkelien van Dijk-Hemmes en Catharina J.M. Halkes*, Delft 1985, 76-96; IDEM: 'De waarheid zal u vrijmaken. Over het emancipatoire liturgisch taalgebruik zoals voorgestaan door Marjorie Procter-Smith', in *Jaarboek voor liturgie-onderzoek* 13 (1997) 49-66; R.D. WITHERUP: *A Liturgist's Guide to Inclusive Language*, Collegeville 1996; *Vrouwe Leitourgia: Tijdschrift voor Liturgie* 82 (1998) no. 5; M. GREY: *Introducing Feminist Images of God*, Cleveland, Ohio 2001.

[117] From a song by Huub Oosterhuis; see *Gezangen voor liturgie* 489.

introduce this name as an emphatic break with that tradition. The last term would indeed seem more a break with that tradition than something which could be included in it. Whatever the case, the new creativity with regard to the name of God makes us conscious of how tentative any speaking of and naming of God is. Ultimately God is the One to whom all names bow.[118]

A whole different field is that of the strongly masculine approach to humanity in the liturgy, an approach which is for the rest strongly deter-mined by past culture. This becomes clearest in the English language, where 'mankind' means humanity, and 'man' is the term for human beings collectively. But the problem does not stop there. In its further ramifications language has a strongly masculine character, because males have played a dominant role in it, while women remained in the back-ground or were silenced. This has also been the case in liturgy. Thus there was only 'Let us pray, brothers'. And how often have women had to sing songs like 'Brothers who set out on the way', 'Hear, O sons of men', 'Happy is the man who...', 'Tell my brothers that I live', or 'Lord, bless your bondsman'? Liturgical language was often the language of the men's club of the sons of God.[119] Slowly this use of language is being supplemented. But there often remains a masculine atmosphere, and the experiences of women are too rarely put into words. It is not surprising then that women are beginning to write their own songs.[120] The prob-lem also presents itself in the way in which the liturgy uses the Scripture itself. What appears in the lectionary is necessarily only a selection.[121]

---

[118] See the song by Huub Oosterhuis, 'Jij die voor alle namen wijkt' (You, to whom all names bow), in: H. OOSTERHUIS: *Aandachtig liedboek. 143 teksten om te zingen en ter overweging*, Baarn 1983, 79.

[119] M. CORVERS: 'Taal en beelden in de liturgie', in *Handreiking (aan) Vrijwilligers in het pastoraat* 8 (1987) 1, 301 ff.

[120] K.B. WESTERFIELD TUCKER: 'A Decade of Christian Song: Observations on Recent Hymnals and Songbooks', in *Studia Liturgica* 31 (2002) 193-210, particularly 200-202 (Woman Song in Australia, the United Kingdom and North America). For the Netherlands, see among others W. VAN HILTEN a.o. (eds.): *Eva's lied; 42 liederen door vrouwen*, Kampen 1984 and J. BOEVÉ-VAN DOORN a.o. (eds.): *Eva's lied Twee; 57 geloofs-liederen door vrouwen*, Kampen 1988; the two songbooks are, in a somewhat altered form, published together in: IDEM: *Eva's lied. 99 liederen door vrouwen*, Kampen 1998. See also *Vrouw en liturgie: Werkmap (voor) Liturgie* 19 (1985) 159-231.

[121] M. PROCTER-SMITH: 'Images of Women in the Lectionary', in *Concilium* 21 (1985) 6, 51-62.

This selection has been so male-centred that an article recently appeared with the title 'Het Romeins lectionarium – het grote vergeetboek voor vrouwen' (The Roman lectionary – God's book of oblivion for women).[122] This also touches on the sometimes masculine prejudices in the translation of Scripture.[123] Moreover, one can ask if the way in which women read the Bible might not be an important supplement to an overwhelmingly masculine reading.[124]

It has also been pointed out that the issue of inclusive language in the liturgy extends beyond what has been discussed in the paragraphs above. It involves *all* who have been excluded and discriminated against. There must be a language for prayer which excludes no one. Moreover, it must not only be that the excluded become the object of prayer, but that they can speak for themselves in prayer.[125]

One will find the above considerations nowhere in the recent Roman Instruction *Liturgiam authenticam*. On the contrary. The instruction goes into detail with regard to the use of inclusive language, and rejects it (no. 29 ff). According to this instruction it is the task of catechesis and the homily to provide for the proper inclusive interpretation of texts, so that all prejudices and discrimination on the basis of persons, gender, social condition, race, etc. can be excluded, because after all, these have no foundation in the texts themselves (no. 29). If one moves to inclusive translations, this can negatively affect the exact intentions of the text, or its aesthetic value. The Church must make free decisions about its language system; this must be in the service of its doctrinal mission and must not be subject to liturgical norms imposed from outside (no. 30). The Instruction clearly rejects the criteria for inclusive language use that

---

[122] M. GEURTSEN: 'Het Romeins lectionarium – het grote vergeetboek voor vrouwen?', in LUKKEN & DE WIT (eds.): *Lezen in fragmenten* 5-69. For further literature see there.

[123] Some examples: 'men of stature among the apostles' (Rom. 16:7) while the text literally reads 'who are of note among the apostles', and 'and then shall every man have praise of God' (I Cor. 4:5), while the literal translation is 'then shall *everyone* have praise from God'. See *Een vrouwvriendelijke liturgie in de rooms-katholieke kerk. Advies van de werkgroep Vrouw en Kerk, de Katholieke Raad voor Kerk en Samenleving en de Unie Nederlandse Katholieke Vrouwenbeweging aan de Nederlandse bisschoppen*, Vught 1991, 24.

[124] See among others T. VERSTEGEN: 'Tot zo ver deze lezing. Het lectionarium door vrouwen gelezen', in LUKKEN & DE WIT (eds.): *Lezen in fragmenten* 137-145.

[125] *Vrouwe Leitourgia: Tijdschrift voor Liturgie* 82 (1998) no. 5.

the American bishops have maintained since 1990, by which for instance words such as 'man' and 'mankind' are replaced by 'person', 'people' and 'human family'.[126] The reference to further explanation in catechesis or homily is however less than convincing, precisely from a liturgical stand-point. As it happens, liturgy involves the most primary language: that of prayer, and therefore that of the heart. Precisely in prayer it is a matter of people speaking in their own language, even when it involves a translated euchology. If the task of making the *orthodoxia prima* (primary ortho-doxy, as 'correct praise' in liturgy) accessible is shifted to catechesis (*ortho-doxia secunda*) (cf. nos. 29, 30, 43), one does not do justice to faith. Moreover, in doing this one comes into conflict with the catechetical views from the classic period of the Roman liturgy itself. In the mind of the early Church, catechesis was to be based precisely on the liturgy itself. Before all else, it was a mystagogic catechesis. In no. 3 of the Instruction it is remarked that translations must be free of all ideological influences. One can ask if this does not blow back on this document itself. Is it not governed by certain ideological views: the absolutising of a particular inculturation; the idea that unity is bound up with a certain uniformity, namely that of ecclesiastical Latin of a particular period; the view that unity and pluriformity cannot go together, or do so only with difficulty; the domination of the *lex orandi* by the *lex credendi*; the accent on cate-chesis at the expense of praying in spirit and in truth, from the heart, in the context of one's own culture; the confusion of subjectivity with the right to experience and express the *orthodoxia prima* in one's own, con-temporary sacred language?

But the issue of the strongly masculine approach in liturgy extends still further. It is not only a question of language.[127] It also touches the non-verbal. There too males have left their stamp on our culture. Domi-nance, independence, self-assertion and rationality are placed above sub-ordination, service, affection, fidelity, humility and emotional warmth.

---

[126] *Criteria for the Evaluation of Inclusive Translations of Scriptural Texts Proposed for Liturgical Use* (1990).

[127] For language, see also S. ROLL: 'Language and Justice in the Liturgy', in *Ques-tions liturgiques* 73 (1992) 66-81 = S. ROLL: 'Language and Justice in the Liturgy', in L. LEIJSSEN (ed.): *Liturgie et langage – Liturgy and Language* (Textes et Études Liturgiques/Studies in Liturgy 12), Leuven 1992, 98-121 = S. ROLL: 'Taal en recht-vaardigheid in de liturgie', in L. LEIJSSEN (ed.): *Liturgie en taal*, Leuven/Amersfoort 1992, 99-122. See also WITHERUP: *A Liturgist's Guide to Inclusive Language*.

With regard to liturgy, the masculine priorities are expressed in dominant church buildings, the oppositional design of space, a high chancel,
a 'high' altar, a patriarchal seat for the leader, imposing liturgical clothing, dominant physical poses, etc.[128]

In outline, a liturgy seen from feminist perspectives would have the following characteristics: more of a horizontal relation between worship
leaders and participants, which among other things would be expressed in
a preference for celebration in a circle and leadership as a group; attention
for inclusive language; accentuation of the immanent image of God;
wider attention for symbolism; a positive appreciation of corporality;[129]
and close links with everyday life and the experiences of women.[130]

The exaggerated masculine character of Christian liturgy is a threat to
this liturgy as such. By definition, liturgy is not exclusively male in
nature. It does not master, but watches over. It belongs rather to the
field of what Jung called *anima* (a female principle) than to that of *ani-
mus* (the male principle). To the degree that the voices of women are
heard more in liturgy, ritual as such will be more vital, viable and fertile
in our culture. New accents that penetrate liturgy from the women's
movement are an important contribution to an authentic Christian
form for the liturgy.[131] That authentic form begins with a re-evaluation
of the Old Testament. Maria de Groot has strikingly expressed this in a
song that also gives a place to the matriarch Sarah alongside the patri-
arch Abraham:

> She is a woman famed in Israel.
> She is a woman who will sustain nations.
> She bears her name by divine command:
> Sarah, blessed throughout generations.
> However dark the paths, however narrow,
> women chosen by God will not despair.

---

[128] In this connection see G. MERTENS: 'Als het stereotyp mannelijk is, is het stereotyp mannelijke God. Over de stereotyp mannelijke visuele aspecten van de liturgie', in
Werkmap (voor) Liturgie 22 (1988) 153-159; IDEM: *Beeld en gelijkenis? Een onderzoek
naar nonverbale seksesterotypen in TV Liturgie* (M.A. Thesis Theologische Faculteit
Tilburg), Tilburg 1990; *Een vrouwvriendelijke liturgie in de rooms-katholieke kerk. Advies.*

[129] See in this connection HEIMBROCK: *Gottesdienst: Spielraum des Lebens* 109-118
(Körpererfahrungen mit Ritualen in Frauengruppen).

[130] GEURTSEN: 'De andere kant van het glas in lood' 277.

[131] For a survey of the Dutch liturgies, see GEURTSEN: 'De andere kant van het glas
in lood' 270-273.

Although our search for the word spoken to you
from on high remains in vain,
woman who heard the unheard,
hovering aside, hidden in your tent –
a laugh, a wink, a connection upset,
woman, opened up to a new future.

The Holy One has valued your word highly:
'In all that she says, I will listen to her.'
From you, who suffered for your people,
are kings of nations born.
Foremother Sarah, star on our path,
in whom the glory of Israel may shine.[132]

5. LITURGY AND POLITICS

One frequently hears the remark that churches should keep out of politics. They have their own realm and their own competence, which involves the inner experience of people, the religious dimension of life. For this people rather often appeal to the constitutional separation of church and state in The Netherlands and other modern states. And if this is true for the conduct of churches in general, it is all the more the case for its liturgical acts. Politics does not belong in the church building.

The issue of the political dimensions of liturgy was spotlighted in the 1960s. The context for this was formed by political theologies – black theology, theology of revolution, liberation theology, the critical 'base communities' and Christians for socialism. The *Politiek avondgebed* (Political vespers), which arose in Cologne, exerted huge influence. In 1968 an ecumenical workgroup began there, which was concerned with protest and relief actions for the war zone of Vietnam, and had as its purpose the politicisation of conscience in the liturgy.[133] The key figures in it were D. Sölle and F. Steffensky. On the one hand, they tried to give shape to the political element in liturgy from what was happening in

---

[132] M. DE GROOT: 'Lied van Sara: Zij is een vrouw van Naam', in *Werkschrift voor Leerhuis en Liturgie* 4 (1983) 1, 114.

[133] K. SCHMIDT: 'Das politische Nachtgebet', in W. HERBST: *Evangelischer Gottesdienst. Quellen zu seiner Geschichte*, Göttingen 1992, 298; WANNENWETSCH: *Gottesdienst als Lebensform* 32.

society, and on the other in this way sought to exert influence on society through liturgy. Therefore there was always an element of information included in these celebrations, as was also an element that was focused on action. This *Politiek avondgebed* was particularly influential in The Netherlands.[134] A particular interest was awakened for the political dimension of liturgy.[135] Nor did this attention for the political dimension of liturgy remain limited to practice. There was also explicit reflection on it. For instance, in 1974 Schupp published a critical theory of sacramental praxis.[136] He argues that Christian symbolic language and Christian symbolic actions are only relevant when they make the praxis of social actions transparent and critique it. The Christian symbols are a critique of necessarily alienated and oppressed life, and at the same time a promise: a real utopian anticipation of reconciliation in true life. The tension between the two is peculiar to the symbol. If this is lost, the symbol – even the Christian symbol – loses its reality. The sacramental acts therefore serve as forerunners of the new praxis, according to the example of Jesus, in his Spirit, and stimulate this new praxis. Sacramental acts are thus in the service of liberation, and are subordinate to ethical/social actions.

Schupp's approach is related to that of the *Politiek avondgebed*. It leads to a special type of political liturgy, which is strongly focused on society. That type is undoubtedly important and legitimate. But, in my view, it would be wrong to reduce political liturgy to this 'functional' type, for the question arises whether this subordination of liturgy to ethical/social action does not in the long run take place at the expense of

---

[134] See the almost immediate translation of the Cologne original: D. SÖLLE & F. STEFFENSKY: *Politiek Avondgebed*, 2 Vol., Baarn 1969 and 1972.

[135] Among others H. KNAAPEN: *Liturgie en kosmopolitiek* (M.A. Thesis Theologische Faculteit Tilburg), Tilburg 1974 (treats of the Dutch cosmopolitic celebrations); *Liturgie en maatschappij: Werkmap (voor) Liturgie* 18 (1984) 115-174; *De samenleving in het liturgisch jaar: Werkmap (voor) Liturgie* 22 (1988) 65-128; *Liturgie en maatschappelijke knelpunten: Werkmap (voor) Liturgie* 26 (1992) 1-62; H. VAN REISEN (ed.): *Van gerechtigheid tot liturgie*, Hilversum 1984; VAN DE BROEK & HURKENS: 'Wake 'Stop het opsluiten van vreemdelingen"; see also several liturgies of Huub Oosterhuis, for instance: H. OOSTERHUIS a.o.: *Iemand die recht doet? Brochure bij gelegenheid van de Unctad-zondag 30 april 1972*, Hilversum 1972 and H. OOSTERHUIS: *Vietnamzondag 29 oktober 1972, brochure van de werkgroep Vietnamzondag*, Amsterdam 1972. Also: J. & C. GUICHARD a.o.: *Liturgie et lutte des classes. Symbolique et politique*, Paris 1976.

[136] F. SCHUPP: *Glaube – Kultur – Symbol. Versuch einer kritischen Theorie sakramentaler Praxis*, Düsseldorf 1974.

that which is peculiar to liturgy.[137] One must at least realise that the political dimension of liturgy reaches beyond the function discussed thus far. At this point one can note what sociologists have had to say regarding political liturgies.[138] According to their insights, there are three different circles of church activities: reflection on faith, reflection on the ethical dimensions, and carrying out social and political projects. All three are equally necessary, and one may not just let them merge together. These three core activities must however be kept in touch with one another. They each, however, deserve attention of their own. When the liturgy is burdened with demands that are too heavy with regard to ethical reflection and the carrying out of social and political projects, it deteriorates as liturgy. In the long run this leads to people writing off the liturgy, certainly in respect to its core tasks, as no longer meaningful, and liturgy disappears.

In this connection it is important to realise the degree to which liturgy itself is politically focused. Christian liturgy is in no sense a noncommittal matter. It is a subversive play and a dangerous anamnesis.[139] It is subversive play because a reversal of values takes place in liturgy. In this play the lost can be saved, the poor are satisfied, and the rich go away with empty hands. In this play the first may become the last, and the last first. Thus this play can be threatening to the established order, where the norms are the other way around. Even life and death duel in the liturgy in a miraculous way,[140] so that Paul can write mockingly, 'Where, O death, is your victory? Where, O death, is your sting?' (I Cor. 15:55) Even the Cross becomes a symbol of victory. Metz speaks of

---

[137] This is pointedly expressed in the following observation by Camillo Torres regarding the liturgy: 'I have stopped performing the Mass in order to live from love of my neighbour in the temporal, economic and social order. When my neighbour no longer has anything against me, and the revolution is completed, then I will again perform Mass'. (J.A. GARCIA & C.R. CALLE: *Camillo, Priest en Revolutionary*, New York 1968, 72). Odenthal's observation is also relevant: 'What is salutary in Christian ritual is that it displays the brokenness of human existence, together with its guiltiness, to God, and these are taken up by God' (ODENTHAL: *Liturgie als Ritual* 230).

[138] LUKKEN: *De onvervangbare weg van de liturgie* 144-145; L. LAEYENDECKER & MADY A. THUNG: 'Liturgie in een politiek geëngageerde kerk', in *Tijdschrift voor Theologie* 18 (1978) 53 ff.

[139] LUKKEN: *De onvervangbare weg van de liturgie* 139-146.

[140] See the Easter hymn *Victimae paschali laudes* from the 11th century, in which is sung: *Mors et vita duello conflixere mirando*.

Christian belief as a dangerous remembering of the suffering, death and resurrection of Christ. It is a dangerous remembering, because it assails the existing order.[141] It seems to me that the word remembering here could better be replaced with the liturgical word anamnesis. The political dimension is structurally present precisely in this active liturgical thinking. Christian liturgy cannot be without it: the political dimension is inherent in Christian liturgy *as such*.[142] It is structural for Christian ritual, even as in its own way this is also for ritual as such.[143] Anyone who relegates Christian liturgy to the 'inner', away from society, in order to strip it of its political dimension, will be disappointed. Precisely then he collides full-force with this dimension. Liturgy and politics do not have to be externally linked with one another, as it were, but are intrinsically interwoven with one another. The liturgy celebrates that Christians are residents of a new city (*polis*), indeed as 'fellow citizens with God's people and members of God's household' (Eph. 2:19). In this city there is no distinction between man and woman, between Jew and Greek, no discrimination. The poor and weak have a privileged place. There are no fortifications, so that strangers may not come in, and undocumented aliens are without rights, and are criminalised.[144] On the contrary, they are welcome, unreservedly. Those who are there must first of all be servants. They pray for all, even for those who persecute, hate and are hostile. It is the city where the love of God and one's neighbour and the Beatitudes are the constitution.

Politicians will remind us that concrete politics is a complex affair, one that demands its own competence. That is indeed the case. But that does not detract from the fact that the subversive basic principles of any Christian politics come to life in the liturgy, and that every Christian must act from this liturgical praxis. One here runs up against the fact that the various sectors in our culture have become independent, and that each has its own value system. People must play a different role in each of the different sectors, and each time apply different norms. It is

---

[141] For instance J.B. METZ: 'The future in the Memory of Suffering', in *Concilium* 8 (1972) 6, 9-25.

[142] WANNENWETSCH: *Gottesdienst als Lebensform*.

[143] See what is said about the ethical dimension of ritual in Part 1, Chapter 2, 3.8.

[144] W. VOERMANS: 'Niks misdaan en toch 'gestraft'. Internationaal Congres over vreemdelingenbewaring', in *Kub ter visie. Magazine van de katholieke universiteit Brabant en de stichting professor Cobbenhagen* (1998) 1, 5-7.

difficult to arrive at an integrated identity in this way. Nevertheless, exactly from the Christian liturgy as a way of life, this is possible, and that is of great political significance, precisely in our postmodern culture. Within the various social roles there can be a personal ethical identity, which is constantly actualised on each occasion from the Christian *leitstory* with its own 'constitution', which is celebrated in the liturgy.[145]

Thus it is in every sense justified to supplement the classic adage *lex orandi lex credendi* with the adage *lex orandi lex agendi*.[146]

6. Feast

In Part 1 I referred to the Dutch national research programme (1995-2000) 'Liturgical Movements and Feast Culture'.[147] Within the scope of this study it is impossible to go into the results of this research, which was recently published in a sizeable book of 816 pages.[148] The programme proceeds from the spacious definition of the concept of feast which I gave in Part 1.[149] Here I will only touch on questions which involve the interactions between Christian feast and contemporary feast culture.[150]

Especially since the 1960s there has been a strong resurgence of traditional feast culture, particularly at the regional and local level. This involves commemorations with historical processions and community picnics, guild feasts, the feasts of Carnival and Santa Claus, Christmas markets, pilgrimages, etc. Secular and religious elements are tightly interwoven with each other here. This feast culture touches directly on themes that we have discussed above, such as the folklorisation and musealisation of culture.[151]

---

[145] See in this connection WANNENWETSCH: *Gottesdienst als Lebensform* 210-274, particularly 216-224.

[146] Part 1, Chapter 2, 3.8. See BERGER: 'Lex orandi – lex credendi – lex agendi'.

[147] Part 1, Chapter 4, 6.

[148] POST, ROUWHORST, VAN TONGEREN & SCHEER (eds.): *Christian Feast and Festival*.

[149] Part 1, Chapter 4, 6.

[150] About feast as a central ritual and locus of cultural memory, see particularly J. ASSMANN: 'Der zweidimensionaler Mensch. Das Fest als Medium des kollektiven Gedächtnisses', in IDEM (ed.): *Das Fest und das Heilige. Religiöse Kontrapunkte zur Alltagswelt* (Studien zum Verstehen fremder Religionen 1), Gütersloh 1991, 13-30; IDEM: *Das kulturelle Gedächtnis. Schrift, Erinnerung und politische Identität in frühen Hochkulturen*, München 1997².

[151] Part 3, Chapter 5, 2. For further literature, see POST: 'Liturgical Movements and Feast Culture' 39-40.

Next, one can point to a certain inflation of the authentic feast in our culture. Feast has, as it were, gotten out of balance. At the 'Madonna of the Bijenkorf' symposium which was held in Tilburg in 1997, in the presentation 'Every Day a Feast' reference was made to the constant search in our culture for feast as an escape from reality and the ordinary.[152] What is involved here is chiefly the search for a feeling of freedom, the spontaneous, the provocative and exotic, the intense experience. The stress lies on the happening-character of feast, the kick it provides. One can think of raves and 'house' parties, the exuberant festivities surrounding football championships, the festive excitement of survival courses, etc. In this connection, the distinction between *Fest* and *Feier* made by some authors appears relevant. In a *Feier* the emphasis is primarily on the serious, objective and institutionally linked element of a feast, while in the *Fest* it is on the spontaneous, emotional/ecstatic, detached from the formal-ritual and institutional constraints and obligations.[153] In the concrete feast both elements are present with each other, but in our culture the *feierliche* seems to be being pushed out by the *festliche*. The distinction between *Fest* and *Feier* can indeed somewhat clarify the problem of feast in our culture. Numerous secular feasts are more marked than they were before by characteristics of *Fest*. Even within the Christian liturgy as such one can identify more of an influence of the spontaneous and emotional than there was before. Moreover, in a specific way this is the case in certain types of liturgies such as youth services and the celebrations of the charismatic movement. But in general, in the Christian feasts in our culture *Fest* and *Feier* go together, and a balance between the two is sought. One could also observe with regard to Christian feast culture that 'every day is a feast day'.[154]But that is true in a different sense then the one just discussed, because while it is true that Christian feasts

---

[152] POST: 'Alle dagen feest'.

[153] Among others O.F. BOLNOW: *Neue Geborgenheit. Das Problem einer Überwindung des Essenzialismus*, Stuttgart/Berlin/Köln/Mainz 1979[4]; W. GEBHART: *Fest, Feier und Alltag. Über die gesellschaftliche Wirklichkeit des Menschen und ihre Deutung*, Frankfurt/Bern/New York/Paris 1987, particularly 35-82; IDEM: 'Der Reiz des Aussertäglichen. Zur Soziologie des Festes', in B. CASPAR & W. SPARN (eds.): *Alltag und Transcendenz*, München 1992, 68-71.

[154] SCHILSON: 'Fest und Feier in anthropologischer und theologischer Sicht' 29: 'Für ein Christ ist jeder Tag ein *dies festus*'; quotation with reference to E. SCHOCKENHOFF: *Zum Fest der Freiheit. Theologie des christlichen Handeln bei Origenes*, Mainz 1990, 263.

extend across the whole year, this is not done in the cadence of a constant march in search of the exotic, extravagant, new and sensational.
There is a well thought-out rhythm. The ecclesiastical year has a coherent articulation; there is a order of priority among feasts. The celebration of the Easter mystery is central, with Good Friday, Easter Saturday
and Easter Sunday, followed by a period of fifty days which leads to
Pentecost. Around it are grouped the Sundays of Advent, which lead to
Christmas, and the forty days of Lent which lead up to Easter. Further,
there is the hierarchy of high holy days, feasts and remembrances. Of
course the question is how this richly varied order is in fact experienced
by Christians, and how it gets 'hands and feet' in our present culture.
Many contemporary Christians are more sparing in their participation
in feasts than previous generations were. They select for themselves certain feasts from the ecclesiastical year. In this process, Christmas seems
to be the preference of many. Moreover, popular religious culture often
places the accents elsewhere. Then particular feasts associated with certain holy places or certain saints are experienced as high points of the
ecclesiastical calendar. This poses important questions for inculturation.

The experience of feast is closely connected with the way in which the
relation between everyday work and feast is experienced.[155] In our culture feast belongs to the realm of free time, which stands over against
daily work. In archaic cultures people do not have the distinction
between labour and free time. There work and feast are closely linked.[156]
Feast is in no way a contrast to labour as a social/economic value. That
in no way detracts from the value of feast. On the contrary, feast is
sacred work that makes profane activities possible. It is precisely in and
through feast that the divine work of creation and maintaining the
world is actualised once again; work itself becomes a meaningful element because it is included in this feast. In this way religious feast penetrates into the world of labour. Only in a second phase do feast and
labour come to be opposites to one another. Feast now belongs to the
realm of 'free time'. It no longer penetrates labour, but replaces it. A
third phase begins with the industrial revolution. The economy now

[155] See, also for the following, T. WALTHER-SOLLICH: *Festpraxis und Alltagserfahrung.
Sozialpsychologische Predigtanalysen zum Bedeutungswandel des Osterfestes im 20. Jahrhundert* (Praktische Theologie heute 29), Stuttgart/Berlin/Köln 1997, 67-70.

[156] In light of this, it is interesting that the word 'liturgy' originally meant the 'work
of the people'.

begins to dominate life. Free time becomes closely connected with the world of labour. It is seen as non-work, as a pause in labour, a period of relaxation and re-creation through which further work is possible. Free time begins to be viewed instrumentally.[157] The goods produced by the labour can be consumed in this free time. Consequently, free time remains captive to economic logic: free time is no longer a time to be filled, but a time in which we must undertake something and perform. A recreational industry has arisen which is concerned with exploiting the consumption of free time activities according to the market principles of supply and demand. Feasts are among those activities. Feast as a free time product is instrumentally focused on relaxation from work, and no longer on the experience of transcendent values.

It cannot be denied that many feasts in our secular society are experienced in this way. That is also true of Christian feasts, which have not escaped from this new 'feast culture'. I have already indicated above that Christian feasts can also play a role in the free time economy, and can be enjoyed as consumer goods in the free time market. But nevertheless it remains possible to experience the feast in depth as an occasion which literally 'makes sense' in life. This is true for both secular and religious feasts. As was noted earlier, the celebration of the birth of a child, of Father's Day, Mother's Day and Christmas can be appropriated in both a consumptive and their original festive manner.[158] Whatever the case, it is clear that the authentic feast as such withdraws from the realm of economic benefit, and is more than an interruption of labour. It has meaning in itself. This is true in a very special way for Christian feast.

A personal experience in closing. September, 1997, was a sunny late summer month. We were dining outside in an open air cafe on the Place de la Bastille, in Paris. About 6:30 p.m. we saw Jews passing, whole families, in their Sabbath attire, the men with their yarmulkes on their heads. Slowly it dawned on me that we must be in the neighbourhood of a synagogue, and that they were apparently celebrating a special festival.[159] A glance at my pocket calendar provided the answer: it

---

[157] WANNENWETSCH: *Gottesdienst als Lebensform* 329; E. CORIJN: *Verkenningen in de ontwikkeling van de studie van de vrije tijd. De onmogelijke geboorte van een wetenschap* (Maatschappij en technisch-wetenschappelijke ontwikkelingen 7), Brussel 1998, 189-253.

[158] Part 3, Chapter 3, 2.2.

[159] BELL: *Ritual. Perspectives* 105, correctly points out: 'calendrical distictions are effective in solidifying group identity'.

appeared to be Jewish New Year. We still live in a Christian society – but for how much longer? In our multicultural and multireligious society, in the long run this same sort of experience will present itself with regard to Christian feasts. Bieritz notes that the secular year is becoming increasingly independent of its relationship to the church year, and is developing its own feasts.[160] As examples he names the structuring role of vacations and Bank Holiday weekends, which are quite different from the Christian Sunday. In this way the church year is gradually acquiring the role of a subcultural life structure, which will only still have validity within a social subsystem. It also means that Christians will be living with varying feast codes which overlap one another, and compete with one another. One can try to abolish this competition by adaptations to the civil year. One can also deliberately accept the competition. In the latter instance Christians must sharply accentuate that they know what it is to have, and to live from, another time, which is not the time of the civil year. Once, twice, three times per year one leaves the one time, as it were, to enter another time. Here too, to my mind, there are exciting issues of inculturation. To what extent can archetypal elements of the civil year be included in the church year (for instance, the experience of the seasons), and to what extent should we emphasise the peculiar place and shape of Christian feast within our culture? Whatever the case, for the individual and society feast plays an important, central, and irreplaceable role in mediating meaning.[161] The integrity of feast is ultimately rooted in religious layers. All feasts find their essential vital force in their religious coherence.[162] Christian feast ultimately derives this vital force from the celebration of the Easter mystery: the remembrance of Jesus' suffering, death and resurrection, and the hope of his coming again. A Christian theology of feast can not do without this Easter mystery.[163] I will return to the central place of this Easter mystery in Chapter 10.

---

[160] K.-H. BIERITZ: 'Nächstes Jahr in Jerusalem, Vom Schicksal der Feste', in *Jahrbuch für Liturgik und Hymnologie* (1994/1995) 54-55.

[161] POST: 'Liturgical Movements and Feast Culture' 41.

[162] G. RATSCHOF: 'Die Feste, Inbegriff sittlicher Gestalt', in J. ASSMAN (ed.): *Das Fest und das Heilige. Religiöse Kontrapunkte zur Alltagswelt* (Studien zum Verstehen fremder Religionen 1), Gütersloh 1991, 245.

[163] For a theology of feast see particularly SCHILSON: 'Fest und Feier in anthropologischer und theologischer Sicht' and W. LOGISTER: 'A Small Theology of Feasting', in POST, ROUWHORST, VAN TONGEREN & SCHEER (eds.): *Christian Feast and Festival* 145-166.

7. The need for more supple liturgical regulations

An important part of the 1994 Roman document on inculturation concerns the concrete regulation of the process of inculturation. Indeed, it is even the case that precisely as an 'instruction', this document has a particular juridic value, and concentrates on the concrete regulations of nos. 37 through 40 of the constitution on liturgy.[164] The juridic character becomes clear from the opening words of the instruction: *Varietates legitmae*. Whatever steps are made in inculturation, according to no. 27 of the instruction: 'the liturgy cannot do without legislation and vigilance on the part of those who have received this responsibility in the Church: the Apostolic See and, according to the prescriptions of the law, the episcopal conference for its territory and the bishop for his diocese.' This is repeated in no. 37; there it is added that absolutely no one else, even if he is a priest, may in his own capacity add, omit or change anything in the liturgy. According to this number, inculturation is thus not left to the personal insight of the worship leader – but also not to the collective suggestions of a community. With regard to far-reaching inculturation, according to no. 40 of the constitution the document repeats in nos. 65-69 of the regulation all that was earlier established in the third instruction of 1970 in regard to liturgical experimentation. Proposals for this must be laid before Rome, and after they have been investigated, possible permission may be granted for the experiment during a prescribed period. According to no. 67, among the things to be guarded against during this test are that the prescribed limits in time and place not be exceeded, and that the experiment not become publicly known so that it might already influence the liturgical life of the country. Chupungco correctly observes that this regulation is impractical and unrealistic.[165] I have already referred to that.[166] The provision that the experiment may not become known in such a manner that it would already influence the liturgical life of the country seems to ignore the existence of mass media, and to minimalise the importance of general involvement on the part of the church community.

---

[164] See the official comment: 'Commentarium alla quarta istruzione per una corretta applicazione della costituzione conciliare sulla sacra liturgia', in *Notitiae* 30 (1994) 160-161.

[165] CHUPUNGCO: 'Remarks on the Roman liturgy and inculturation' 269.

[166] Part 3, Chapter 3, 3.2.

But that is not all. In these passages one encounters a practical problem involving liturgical law with regard to inculturation that is very urgent. One gets the impression that the instruction is intended to steer the process of inculturation of the liturgy in a centralised/strategic manner. The document incorporates the achievements of the Second Vatican Council, which returned their liturgical rights to the bishops, but the question is whether it does so adequately, precisely in view of the peculiarities of the problem of inculturation. Inculturation is primarily a matter for the local church itself. The task of inculturation assumes the regionality of the church, and the regionality of the church is necessary to accomplish inculturation.[167] Inculturation is not a process that can be imposed or determined from above by a handful of persons. The best forms of inculturation have therefore always occurred in periods of ecclesiastical vitality.[168] Central direction is in conflict with the essence of inculturation. Of course, the central ecclesiastical authority has a function in it. But in this one must remember how it happened in the first millennium. Jungmann has already noted that Rome in this period only made decisions about liturgy on request, and that these decisions were generally as loose as possible.[169] As early as in the period from 150 to 200, before the first Nicene Council (325), the Church had developed a perfect system of bishops's synods and councils in this respect. Sieben's finding that the structure and the procedure of these synods in sections of the Church were in part, but nonetheless deeply influenced by the socio-cultural context of the day among the peoples and regions where

---

[167] H.J. POTTMEYER: 'Regionale Teilkirchen und 'Zwischeninstanzen' – ihre Wiederentdeckung und ihr ekklesiologischer Rang', in L. BERTSCH (ed.): *Was der Geist der Gemeinden sagt. Bausteine einer Ekklesiologie der Ortskirchen* (Theologie der Dritten Welt 15), Freiburg/Basel/Wien 1991, 168-177. See, also for the following, BERTSCH: 'Entstehung und Entwicklung liturgischer Riten und kirchliches Leitungsamt' 218-238.

[168] J. ALDAZÁBAL: 'Lecciones de la historia sobre la inculturación' 106.

[169] J.A. JUNGMANN: *Gewordene Liturgie. Studien und Durchblicke*, Innsbruck 1941, 4-5; N. MITCHELL: 'The Amen Corner', in *Worship* 69 (1995) 156, notes the attitude of Pope Gregory with regard to inculturation, and how this attitude was related to his ecclesiology and his collegiate view of the office of bishop. For Pope Gregory the Church was neither more nor less than the tangible, visible, historic *communio* of all churches. For him the *sancta universalis ecclesia* was the concrete multiplicity of local churches, each united in faith around a bishop, united with one another *in vinculo caritatis*. Gregory refused to take the title *universalis papa* because, as he wrote, if one bishop is universal, all the rest are superfluous (GREGORY I: 'Letter to Eusebius of Thessalonica', in: *MGH Epistulae* II, 158).

they took place, is interesting in respect to this.[170] It is well to remember that the Second Vatican Council also had the model of the Church as a *communio ecclesiarum* – that is to say, of a church that essentially lives and acts in and through the local churches. Fourty years ago Ratzinger already wrote that the local churches were not administrative units in a cumbersome apparatus, but vital cells each of which comprehended the whole living mystery of the one body of the Church.[171] If inculturation is primarily a matter for the local churches themselves, the principle of subsidiarity must be taken seriously.[172] At this point the dissertation by Leys is particularly interesting, especially for liturgical law as well.[173] He argues for applying the principle of subsidiarity in canon law. The basic concept of the principle of subsidiarity is that the human person and smaller social units may not be deprived of the possibility and means of realising that which they are able to do for themselves. Larger associations must limit their activities to tasks that exceed the strength and capacities of the smaller units. The more inclusive associations must respect the 'hierarchic order' of the various forms of social entities, and aid them, so that they are better able to do for themselves that for which they are fitted.[174] This principle is also of importance for individual churches in their relation to the universal Church. This relation should be fleshed out juridically more fully than the Codex of 1983 does. The competencies must be better defined. The position of the individual church as church in the full sense of the word and as incarnate and inculturated church, apart or in an association such as a bishop's conference,

---

[170] H.J. SIEBEN: *Die Konzilsidee der alten Kirche*, Paderborn 1979, 384-510.

[171] J. RATZINGER: 'Pastoral Implications of Episcopal Collegiality', in *The Church and Mankind* (Concilium Dogma, Vol.1), New Yersey 1965, 44.

[172] Implicitly: H.B. MEYER: 'Liturgietheologische Überlegungen zur Inkulturation – Ein Versuch', in E. VON SEVERUS (ed.): *Ecclesia Lacensis. Beiträge aus Anlass der Wiederbesiedlung der Abtei Maria Laach durch Benediktiner aus Beuron vor 100 Jahren am 25. November 1892 und der Gründung des Klosters durch Pfalzgraf Heinrich II. von Laach vor 900 Jahren 1093*, Münster 1993, 516-528. See the review by B. KRANEMANN: 'Aus der Vergangenheit in der Gegenwart für die Zukunft lernen. Eine Festschrift zum Doppeljubiläum der Abtei Maria Laach', in *Archiv für Liturgiewissenschaft* 35 (1993-1994) 369: 'Meyer insistiert darauf, dass Inkulturation Aufgabe primär der Ortskirchen ist und von der Kirchenleitung nur (kritisch) unterstützt werden kann. Ohne dass dies hier unmittelbar angesprochen wird, ist für die (liturgische) Inkulturation Subsidiarität gefordert'.

[173] A. LEYS: *Ecclesiological Impacts of the Principle of Subsidiarity*, Kampen 1995.

[174] LEYS: *Ecclesiological Impacts* 214.

should be strengthened.[175] In particular, the binding character of the principle of subsidiarity becomes clear from the fact that the Church is a sacrament, and precisely as such is one incarnate and inculturated reality.[176] The importance of this fact is all the greater because in the new ecclesiastical code the liturgy is no longer considered as something that is dependent on ecclesiastical lawgivers, as was the case in the Church code of 1917. Quite to the contrary, one finds there the realisation that the fundamental relationships within the Church are themselves created, deepened and nuanced in the celebration of the liturgy. Put bluntly: it is no longer the case that the liturgy takes its place under church law. The relation is precisely the other way around.[177] All of this therefore means that a more flexible liturgical regulation is necessary than that in the 1994 instruction. It should be much more in the form of a basic framework for liturgy.[178] One must take into account that the inculturation process takes place from the bottom up. The local congregation is therefore the basic unit in the inculturation process.[179]

To my mind, Meyer demonstrates convincingly how much of a basic right for Christians this respect for the process from the bottom up is in inculturation of the liturgy.[180] He notes that in article 14 the constitution, the right and obligation of all believers to actively participate is based in the essence of the liturgy itself and on the sacrament of baptism. If you examine it closely, it is this basic right, founded on baptism, and not the *norma patrum*, the venerable norm of the Fathers, named as such in article 50 and in the foreword of the general introduction to the

[175] LEYS: *Ecclesiological Impacts* 217-218.

[176] LEYS: *Ecclesiological Impacts* 210.

[177] P. HUIZING & B.A. WILLEMS: 'Sacramentele grondslag van het kerkrecht', in *Tijdschrift voor Theologie* 16 (1976) 244-266; R. TORFFS: 'Liefde en recht gaan hand in hand. Een denkoefening over de verhouding tussen theologie en recht', in *Tijdschrift voor Theologie* 36 (1996) 273, note 13, and 281, note 36; LUKKEN: D*e onvervangbare weg van de liturgie* 97-99. See also S. RAU: *Die Feiern der Gemeinden und das Recht der Kirche – Zu Aufgabe, Form und Ebenen liturgischer Gesetzgebung in der katholischen Kirche*, Altenberge 1990.

[178] G. LUKKEN: 'De ontwikkeling van de liturgie sinds Vaticanum II', in A. HOLLAARDT (ed.): *Liturgische oriëntatie na Vaticanum II (Supplement Liturgisch Woordenboek)*, Roermond 1970, 21.

[179] ARBUCKLE: *Earthing the Gospel.*

[180] H.B. MEYER: 'Zur Inkulturation der Eucharistiefeier im Blick auf das deutsche Sprachgebiet', in *Liturgisches Jahrbuch* 41 (1991) 1, 12-13.

Roman missal, article 6, that is the actual and ultimate decisive principle of liturgical reform and the criterion for measures for liturgical reform. This *norma patrum* is indeed of importance with regard to the preservation of authentic tradition, but how this tradition must be guided further, and how the road to the future must be travelled, is to be decided on the principle of the actual participation of the community. That is where the necessity of inculturation finds its legitimacy. This means that inculturation of the liturgy is not only a permanent process, but also something that proceeds from the local churches and their congregations, and that – to my mind – also has its own hermeneutic. The challenge of liturgical inculturation is simply ultimately that not theory alone, but also practice itself must point the way. This is a consequence of the fact that rituals cannot be just conceived and imposed, but also arise and change from the bottom up. Inculturation is a growth process with an experimental character. This is all the more true in our culture, in which change and experimentation are precisely characteristic qualities of ritual.[181] The process of inculturation also has everything to do with the vitality and spirituality of the people, and it is difficult to assign its content in advance. Amalorpavadass observes that inculturation is a lifestyle and a way of living: it is about how people who have encountered Christ accept his gospel, and identify themselves with his cause.[182] The theological, and also the anthropological input would remain purely conceptual and academic unless both arose in part from and found their substance in a deep spiritual experience from the interaction between the gospel and culture. One must therefore also add the spiritual/practical approach to inculturation to the anthropological and theological approaches. Of course experts and theoreticians are also necessary, and the happening of inculturation must in part be formally regulated. There must be guidance that tests and corrects the process. But the regulation must not work out too restrictively, as has been the case until now. Formal regulation does not imply that this must be employed in purely formal ways.[183] Over the past years, has inculturation not often come to be against the rules, regulations and repression?

---

[181] Part 3, Chapter 3, 3.1. and 3.2.

[182] D.S. AMALORPAVADASS: 'Theological reflections on inculturation (Part 1)', in *Studia Liturgica* 20 (1990) 40; IDEM: 'Theological reflections on inculturation (Part 2)', in *Studia Liturgica* 20 (1990) 128-132.

[183] In this connection see B. CLEESON: 'Rubrics versus Creativity in Liturgy', in *Worship* 70 (1996) 128-139.

8. Professionalisation

The growth toward a new form for liturgy and its performance places high new demands on the worship leaders and those who are involved with it as volunteers. One may think of, among other things, the importance of verbal and physical expression, communicative skills and sensitivity for and understanding of the impact of ritual.[184] In our culture people will no longer accept worship leaders purely on the basis of their appointment or ordination. They want expertise with regard to the roles that are to be fulfilled. Inculturation of the liturgy unavoidably brings with it the demand for professionalisation. Moreover, those who give shape to the liturgy and perform it must compete with the high demands that contemporary public communications place on people.

Our culture expects – if I may put it that way – the delivery of a good product, and there is a concern for quality in the provision of liturgical services.[185] Along this line there is also our culture's expectation that people will arrive at policy plans, both locally and regionally, with regard to liturgy.[186] Here one encounters the problem that at the moment professional training in liturgy remains extremely elementary, and is simply insufficient in view of the creative challenges confronting liturgy. Therefore I would argue for training, after the completion of theological studies, in which worship leadership can be taught as a profession.

[184] Part 3, Chapter 7; also W. HAHNE: *De arte celebrandi oder von der Kunst, Gottesdienst zu feiern. Entwurf einer Fundamentalliturgik*, Freiburg/Basel/Wien 1989; J.Y. HAMELINE: 'Observations sur nos manières de célébrer', in *La Maison-Dieu* (1992) 192, 7-24 = J.-Y. HAMELINE, J.Y.: *Une poétique du rituel*, Paris 1997, 35-49; E. KAPELLARI: 'Naar een vernieuwde kunst van het voorgaan in de liturgie', in *ICLZ-Mededelingen* 91 (1997) 790-794 and 92 (1997) 799-802; LUKKEN: 'Op zoek naar een nieuwe stijl van voorgaan'; *L'arte del celebrare. Atti della XXVII Settimana di Studio dell'Associazione Professori di Liturgia. Brescia, 30 agosto – 4 settembre 1998* (Bibliotheca Ephemerides Liturgicae. Subsidia 102), Roma 1999; P. POST: 'Rol en rite: over liturgisch voorgaan', in *Praktische Theologie* 26 (1999) 128-147; M. SCOUARNEC: 'L'art de célébrer', in *La Maison-Dieu* (1999) 219, 119-140; H. JONGERIUS: 'Liturgische vorming of vorming tot liturgie', in *Tijdschrift voor Liturgie* 85 (2001) 231-244; T. PETERS: 'Wie gaat er voor? Over voorgangers in de liturgie en hun vorming', in *Tijdschrift voor Liturgie* 85 (2001) 258-270; *Ars celebrandi*: *Questions Liturgiques* 83 (2002) no. 2-3 = J. LAMBERTS (ed.): *'Ars celebrandi'. The Art to Celebrate the Liturgy. L'art de célébrer la liturgie* (Textes et Études Liturgiques/Studies in Liturgy 17), Leuven 2003.
[185] VAN DER VEN: *Ecclesiologie in context* 373-403.
[186] VAN DER VEN: *Ecclesiologie in context* 318-322.

CHAPTER 10

THE PECULIAR IDENTITY OF CHRISTIAN RITUAL

Part 3 has been about ritual, and in particular Christian ritual in our culture. We have gradually gained more insight into the new place and shape of Christian liturgy. At all points we have seen that there is a close connection between ritual and its development in general on the one side, and Christian ritual on the other. The accent lay on the anthropological basis of Christian ritual.

Yet it gradually emerged that Christian ritual also has an identity peculiar to itself, which is not swallowed up in its anthropological basis. This was particularly the case in the discussion of transition rituals. It is important at the end of this section to examine explicitly the peculiar identity of Christian ritual in our culture.

1. THE RELATION BETWEEN ANTHROPOLOGY AND THEOLOGY OF LITURGY

After the Second Vatican Council liturgical studies and liturgical practice took a turn toward anthropology. Their full attention came to be focused on the anthropological basis of Christian ritual. This interest in the place of mankind in liturgy, with his concrete physicality and, as an extension of that, the material world, had gradually grown through the 20th century. The Liturgical Movement played a large role in this. Among the figures one can think of were Guardini (1891-1957), Pinsk (1891-1957) and Parsch (1884-1954). But the real breakthrough came in 1963 with the Constitution on Liturgy from the Second Vatican Council. The council was above all else a pastoral council. For liturgy this meant that the emphasis came to lie on the adage that the sacraments are for the good of mankind. Only now therefore did people begin on this other side. Moreover, it was precisely at the time of this Council that the social sciences were obtaining great influence. The important questions about the meaning of Christian ritual were thought through again from the standpoint of anthropology. This was so much the case that there was an inclination to see Christian ritual as merely a particularisation of ritual in general. It began to be argued that 'sacramental thinking' is really general human thinking, and that Christian sacramentality is closely connected with it. In concrete terms: the Orpheus mystery and the Osiris mystery, like many myths, are about the primaeval story of life and death, of dying and rising, and the Easter mystery is an extension of these.[1] It is a particularisation of this larger myth. But the question is, then, to what extent is it a particularisation? Is it merely one of many possible variants? Or is there something more? It began to be asked if the anthropological approach was not at the expense of divine transcendence, and if the *Jenseits* of Christian ritual stood out with sufficient clarity. The question then became whether Christian liturgy was not merging too much into anthropology. Sometimes people went to the other extreme and emphasised the transcendent nature of Christian ritual so much that they became too inclined to distrust the anthropological dimensions of liturgy, and didn't really succeed in integrating the dimensions of the behavioural sciences into liturgical studies.[2] Then the danger loomed of Christian liturgy coming to stand at odds with human experience, as this takes shape in general human ritual, and that God and man are played against one another as opponents. A concrete example of this is, for instance, the orthodox Calvinist worship service with a ritual as austere as possible so as not to detract from the Word of God. Such circles prefer worship without any 'frills'. Even within the Catholic tradition one can sometimes find something of this, for instance in the effort of some strict monastic orders to achieve as sober – and in a certain sense, as aesthetically impoverished – a liturgy as possible.

In recent years then the question has increasingly arisen of how the anthropology of liturgy relates to the theology of liturgy. There appears to be a turn toward theology. This theological turn, like the turn to anthropology before it, finds its inspiration in the Second Vatican Council. Already there no. 2 of the Constitution on the Liturgy speaks in a very balanced manner of a liturgy which is 'both human and divine, visible and yet invisibly equipped, eager to act and yet intent on contemplation, present in this world and yet not at home in it; and she is all these things in such wise that in her the human is directed and

---

[1] See in this connection BELL: *Ritual. Perspectives* 3-39.

[2] See for instance M. KUNZLER: *Die Liturgie der Kirche* (Amateca 10), Paderborn 1995.

subordinated to the divine, the visible likewise to the invisible, action to contemplation, and this present world to that city yet to come, which we seek.' The question is thus if, without detracting from the anthropological turn, this anthropology must not equally be broken through from the inside out, in the direction of the unique theological identity. In concrete terms: in the baptismal ritual, for instance, should the horizontal line be transected by the vertical line of self-disclosing Trinitarian depth? This is not just a theoretical question. One equally encounters practical questions that touch on the design of liturgy. We saw this in the discussion of Christian transition rituals.

L. Lies formulates the problem in a balanced manner, as follows: 'Symbol is always an anthropological reality, while sacrament is a theological reality which goes back to God, but which, however, does not lose its anthropological character'.[3] But the question if whether it is possible to be more specific. To clarify this problem I would first want to discuss five authors who have reflected upon the relation between anthropology and theology in liturgy, namely Cornehl, Bieritz, Kohlschein, Neumann and Chauvet. I have chosen these authors, and moreover put them in this order, from didactic considerations. In this way some things will become clear regarding the engagement surrounding a problem, which returns again and again in our culture.[4] Following the last author, I will present my own approach.

[3] LIES: *Eucharistie in ökumenischer Verantwortung* 109.

[4] Other authors grappling with this issue include among others FREYER: *Sakrament – Transitus – Zeit – Transzendenz*; A. HÄUSSLING: 'Die kritische Funktion der Liturgiewissenschaft', in H.B. MEYER (ed.): *Liturgie und Gesellschaft*, Innsbruck 1970, 103-130; IDEM: 'Liturgiewissenschaft, zwei Jahrzehnte nach Konzilsbeginn', in *Archiv für Liturgiewissenschaft* 24 (1982) 1-18; IDEM: 'Kosmische Dimension und gesellschaftliche Wirklichkeit. Zu einem Erfahrungswandel in der Liturgie', in *Archiv für Liturgiewissenschaft* 25 (1983) 1-8; IDEM: 'Liturgiewissenschaftliche Aufgabenfelder vor uns', in *Liturgisches Jahrbuch* 38 (1988) 94-108; IDEM (ed.): *Vom Sinn der Liturgie: Gedächtnis unserer Erlösung und Lobpreis Gottes*, Düsseldorf 1991; R. HEMPELMANN: *Sakrament als Ort der Vermittlung des Heils. Sakramententheologie im evangelisch-katholischen Dialog* (Kirche und Konfession 32), Göttingen 1992; A. KAVANAGH: *On Liturgical Theology*, New York 1985; E.J. LENGELING: 'Liturgie als Vollzug christlichen Lebens', in B. FISCHER, E.J. LENGELING, R. SCHAEFFLER, F. SCHULZ & H.R. MÜLLER-SCHWEFE: *Kult in der säkularisierten Welt*, Regensburg 1974, 63-91; E.J. LENGELING & K. RICHTER: *Liturgie. Dialog zwischen Gott und Mensch*, Freiburg 1981; E. KILMARTIN: *Christian Liturgy; Theology and Practice*, Kansas City, Mo 1988; J. MEYER ZU

The Protestant theologian *Cornehl* arrived at the remarkable distinction between theory and theology of liturgy.[5] Theory of worship occupies itself with scientific reflection on liturgy as a general human phenomenon, using models from anthropology, the social sciences and comparative religion. On the other hand, theology of liturgy starts with biblical and ecclesiastical tradition, and forms a critical corrective. Neither the theory of liturgy or theology of liturgy may be absorbed into the other, because they would then disrupt each other. One must keep theology of liturgy apart from theory of liturgy. It will be clear that theologically this position has little to recommend it. Cornehl does not succeed in holding anthropology and theology together.

The Protestant theologian *Bieritz* gets further.[6] He ties to connect what remains apart in Cornehl, and works out theologically what he has gained in the way of insights from the encounter with the social sciences. He tries to indicate what the content is of the specifically Christian experience. He does this by dynamising the concepts of sacred and

---

SCHLOCHTERN: *Sakrament Kirche. Wirken Gottes im Handeln der Menschen*, Freiburg im Breisgau 1992; D. POWER: *Sacrament: the Language of God's Giving*, New York 1999; G. WAINWRIGHT: *Doxology*; WANNENWETSCH: *Gottesdienst als Lebensform*; A. BRANTS: 'Mens, religie, sacrament. Sacramenten en hun antropologische basis', in *Tijdschrift voor Liturgie* 88 (2004) 24-40.

   Generally the problem involved is concentrated on the question of the relation in the liturgy between human/ecclesiastical acts and divine acts. This is a question in which the churches of the Reformation are also very interested. In this connection see particularly T.B. MURKEN, *Take and Eat, and take the Consequences. How receiving the Lord's Supper is an action that Makes a Difference* (American University Studies VII, Series Theology and Religion 220), New York 2002; further: J. LAMBERTS (ed.): *Hedendaagse accenten in de sacramententheologie*, Leuven 1994 = J. LAMBERTS, (ed.): *Accents actuels en théologie sacramentaire – Current Issues in Sacramental Theology* (Textes et Etudes Liturgiques/Studies in Liturgy 13), Leuven 1994 and *Questions Liturgiques* 75 (1994) 1-2, 1-112; LEVESQUE: 'A Symbolical Sacramental Methodology'; A. VAN EIJK: 'Het pleidooi voor een ruimer sacramentsbegrip', in A. VAN EIJK & H. RIKHOF, *De lengte en de breedte, de hoogte en de diepte. Peilingen in de theologie van de sacramenten*, Zoetermeer 1996, 105-131.

   [5] P. CORNEHL: 'Gottesdienst', in F. KLOSTERMANN & R. ZERFASS: *Praktische Theologie Heute*, München 1974, 449-463; IDEM: 'Theorie des Gottesdienstes. Ein Prospekt', in *Theologische Quartalschrift* 159 (1979) 178-192; IDEM: 'Aufgaben und Eigenart einer Theorie des Gottesdienstes', in *Pastoraltheologische Informationen* (1981) 12-20.

   [6] K.-H. BIERITZ: 'Aussagen zu einer Theorie des Gottesdienstes', in *Theologische Literatur Zeitung* 100 (1975) 721-737; IDEM: 'Anthropologische Grundlegung. 1. Grundlinien liturgischer Anthropologie', in H.-G. SCHMIDT-LAUBER & K.-H. BIERITZ (eds.): *Handbuch der Liturgik* 96-97.

profane, following the lead of Mühlen.[7] Bieritz frees these concepts from their static state, in which they only denote certain well defined realms of reality. With Bieritz the concepts of sacred and profane become relational concepts that effectuate the origin and content of faith. All that is created is both profane and sacred. The more one without reservation takes total reality seriously in its profaneness, not lifting out certain areas of it in the process, the more clearly the sacrality of that reality – that is to say, its involvement with God – can emerge. Conversely, to the degree the theological orientation of reality is taken seriously, to that degree the profaneness of that reality is intensified. What is characteristically Christian is that the new Christian sacrality does not cancel out the profane, but radicalises it and opens it up for the *ganz Neue* of the new covenant. The Christian worship service is the celebration of this *ganz Neue*, thereby distinguishing itself from the inward and hectic search for constantly new and different things and experiences. From this characteristically Christian viewpoint the data of anthropology can be included in the liturgy.

It is clear that Bieritz has come a step further. He succeeds in integrating the anthropology of liturgy into its theology. Yet I am left with the impression that he emphasises one accent too strongly: that of expectations for the future, which in the Christian vision becomes radical eschatology. Thus there is only an impetus to integration from one specific accent.

One finds an interesting approach in *Neumann*.[8] From the correspondences between Reformation and Catholic concepts of the sacraments he develops a model on the basis of which one can clarify the problem of the relation between anthropology and theology through the category of a 'multi-stage structure' (in, with, under) in the relation.[9] Divine and human acts come together in the Christian sacrament: the divine acts of grace take place in the Christian acts. Both aspects are involved, but in a 'multi-stage structure'. The primacy lies with the divine acts, which however do not bypass human acts, but take place in, with and under the human and ecclesiastical ritual acts. Neumann then

---

[7] H. MÜHLEN: *Entsakralisierung. Ein epochales Schlagwort in seiner Bedeutung für die Zukunft der christlichen Kirchen*, Paderborn 1971.

[8] B. NEUMANN: *Sakrament und Ökumene. Studien zur deutschsprachigen evangelischen Sakramententheologie der Gegenwart*, Paderborn 1997, 329-341.

[9] NEUMANN: *Sakrament und Ökumene*, particularly 281-283 and 329-341.

works out further what this means for the relation between anthropology and theology in the Christian sacraments. One can say that the natural symbolism is taken up into the sacrament, precisely in the stages of the structure. First there is the context of creation theology, which deals with the general anthropological/sociological meaning of the rites and the meaning that they have for human beings as such. In addition there is the context of sacred history, which deals with the rootage of the symbolism in the history of God with his people Israel.[10] Neumann argues for speaking of symbolism of creation rather than natural symbolism, because the former, in contrast to the concept of nature, refers as such to the continuing dependence of creation on God as Creator.

The German Catholic theologian *Kohlschein* seeks to arrive at a systematic and integrated theology of liturgy.[11] Like Cornehl he distinguishes a theory and a theology of liturgy. Theory of liturgy involves the anthropology of liturgy, with everything which that implies. Theology of liturgy then concerns the question of whether liturgy in all its dimensions is sufficiently described with the concepts of symbol and communication. His answer is that this is undoubtedly the case, because even before the existence of the collective term liturgy, in the early Church symbol (*sacramentum* and *mysterium*) and communication (*ecclesia*) were the defining liturgical concepts. Liturgical theory is about the question of what symbol and communication mean for liturgy in the more empirical/social sciences sense, while in the theology of liturgy symbol and communication in this empirical/social sciences sense are taken into the service of symbol and communication in the theological sense: the self-communication of God in Christ through his Spirit in the midst of, in and through his church as the assembly of the people of God. Thus the empirical qualities of symbol and communication are transformed into symbolic and communication qualities in the theological sense.

The reflections of Neumann and Kohlschein are quite simply an advance on Bieritz. Yet they run somewhat the risk of becoming stuck in an abstract integration of anthropology into the theology of liturgy. I have the impression that the most mature breakthrough from inside out took place with the French Catholic sacramental theologian *Chauvet*.[12]

---

[10] See also HEMPELMANN: *Sakrament als Ort der Vermittlung des Heils* 209-210.

[11] F. KOHLSCHEIN: 'Symbol und Kommunikation als Schlüsselbegriffe einer Theologie und Theorie der Liturgie', in *Liturgisches Jahrbuch* 35 (1985) 200-218.

[12] CHAUVET: *Du symbolique au symbole*; IDEM: *Symbole et sacrement*; IDEM: 'Ritualité et théologie'; IDEM: *Les sacrements* 1993.

He poses the question of whether after the Second Vatican Council there has not been a too easy and too direct movement from anthropology to theology. Has Christian liturgy not been seen too much as the perfection of general human rituality, in which the human longing for communication with God is experienced? In his view, in the movement between anthropology and theology there is a certain interruption, a break, which is formed by a third term, namely Christology. Christology is the intersection, so to speak, of the ways from below to above and above to below.

Now, this view could lead to a split with the anthropology of ritual. But precisely with Chauvet that is not the case. He continues to respect the anthropology of ritual as much as possible, so much so that I would characterise his approach as that of the breakthrough of anthropology into Christian ritual in a double sense: that of the turn toward anthropology as such, and that of the breaking through of anthropology into theology from the inside out. As it happens, Chauvet points out how at all points (and it is precisely in this that he differs from Bieritz) Christian liturgy repeats the patterns of human ritual. After all, in the symbolic order in which every person grows up there is also a certain self-activation, an *ex opere operatio* of ritual. The elements are also used soberly in that symbolic order: it is not about an abundance of water or bread. In that way they refer to the provisional character of this world, which is rescued, to be sure, but on the other hand still must be delivered into a new world. Rituals have everything to do with 'heterotopy', with references to the Other, so that the expectation of the coming of the kingdom of God and Christian eschatology have deep anthropological roots. Rituals permit us to experience that man does not live by bread alone, and Christians therefore speak of the necessity for the food that gives eternal life. Rituals are also inscribed in human genealogy. They have much to do with tradition and collective memory. That is why people can speak of the 'institution' of rites, and they are characterised by repetition, as is also the case with Christian rites. Within this symbolic equation the Easter mystery is, to be sure, the third term, but not in the sense that it is apart from it. After all, the Easter mystery has its own concrete history leading up to it, the life of Jesus with a particular background, in a certain cultural/political system with its own symbolic order. This life full of faith and trust found its perfection in the entrance into a new existence, in and through the 'break' of the resurrection. This resurrection is in turn most closely connected with our history. Pentecost is the historical expression of the 'for us' of the resurrection. This 'for us' is embodied through the Spirit, who is poured out over the people of God, and who is at work in the Church. There, in the interim history, Christian liturgy is realized, deeply rooted in the anthropology of ritual, until the completion comes in the Parousia.

On the basis of the above I will now go further into the question of the relation between the anthropology and the theology of Christian ritual, in order to identify the peculiar identity of this ritual in our culture.

2. TWO DIRECTIONS WITHIN THE THEOLOGY OF LITURGY

For the sake of a balanced approach to the problem it is important to realise that within theology of liturgy there are two differing basic theoretical options or types in opposition to each other: an anthropologically oriented school, and opposite it a dialectic school that seeks its point of departure in the Christian theology of revelation.[13] The first school moves from the general to the particular, the second from the particular to the general. One might characterise these schools as follows.

The anthropologically oriented school seeks the general human foundation for Christian ritual. According to it, Christian ritual is closely connected with general human rituality, and with the religious rites outside Christianity. It is a deepening and concentration of them. Christian ritual is not something completely new, but has a history leading up to it, and a foundation. Nothing human is alien to Christian ritual. It is a particular form of giving meaning to this life, to this society, to this world. The Bible also has its place 'from the bottom up'. This school

---

[13] See in this connection HEMPELMANN: *Sakrament als Ort der Vermittlung des Heils* 28-32. See also G. LUKKEN: 'De 'overkant' van het menselijk ritueel. Herbezinning vanuit fenomenologie en semiotiek op antropologische en theologische lagen in het christelijk ritueel', in *Tijdschrift voor Theologie* 40 (2001) 145-166 = G. LUKKEN: 'L' 'autre côté' du rituel humain: Reconsidération à partir de la phénoménologie et la sémiotique sur des couches anthropologiques et théologiques dans le rituel chrétien', in *Questions liturgiques* (2001) 1, 68-91; A. GRILLO: 'La "visione antropologica" dei sacramenti e la teologia. Ovvero, come fanno dei ciechi a identificare la verita di un elefante?', in *Ecclesia Orans* 20 (2003) 253-270.

takes into account that the centrality of the Bible is no longer obvious for many in modern culture, particularly in the present day. It points out that there are also other texts, both classic and modern, which speak of the true, good and beautiful and their opposites, of what is humanly tolerable and intolerable, of the origin and meaning of human life.[14] The peculiar place of the Bible, and of the sacred history recounted therein, among the other texts of the great religions is subject to investigation. This approach seeks what is unique about Jewish and Christian history from the context of contemporary culture. It arrives at an inductive Christology: a Christology from the bottom up, which begins with Jesus of Nazareth as a specific man in whom God's form becomes visible and appears to us, which reaches its climax in his suffering, death and resurrection and the sending of the Spirit. In him human life and our creation breaks open to God, an event that will come to completion at the end of time, when the Lord returns; then mankind and this world will definitively be taken up into the divine world. In this perspective the Church is a unique religious community in which Jesus of Nazareth and the sacred history which is focused in him is central. He is the basic sacrament, the pinnacle of creation.[15] Christian ritual breaks general human ritual open to this basic sacrament. There is a movement from present to past and from below to above. Christian ritual is a culmination point of transcendent orientation for general human ritual.

The opposing school begins from the particularity of the Bible and the sacred history revealed in it.[16] Its basis and point of departure is first and foremost what the Bible says about the sacred acts which took place for and in Israel as the chosen people (the first testament) and what is told of Jesus of Nazareth, of his life, of the unique sacred acts of his birth, suffering, death, resurrection, the sending of the Spirit, and his expected return at the end of time (the second testament). There, in an irreducible manner, Christian sacramental ritual finds its origin. It goes back to Scripture, and in particular to the biblical institution narratives for baptism and the Supper. In this view, the fundamental difference between the Christian sacraments and cultic acts outside of Christendom is emphasised. Attention is given to the eschatological aspects. Not

---

[14] L. LAYENDECKER: *Zijn Kerken nog nodig?*, in *Rood Koper* 5 (2000) 6, 12-14.

[15] M.E. BRINKMAN: *Sacraments of Freedom. Ecumenical Essays on Creation and Sacrament – Justification and Freedom*, Zoetermeer 1999.

[16] HEMPELMANN: *Sakrament als Ort der Vermittlung des Heils* 31-32.

the continuity but rather the contrasts with the generally human and general religious are stressed. It is not a matter of the openness to salvation of all that is human and of this world, because on the contrary this view focuses before all else on the eschatological tension between this fallen creation and the promised new creation. There is no organic continuity between the old and new world. Within the world of the sacrament, Jesus Christ is the central gift. He permits mankind to share in the fruits of his death and his resurrection; this is not about human nature from the perspective of created being, but about that nature in its profound lostness. Here the holy is poured out on sinners who repent. The Church appears here as something in opposition to the world. It brings people together and saves them from their destruction.

Both these schools have their previous history in Christian tradition, and they are focused in the opposition between Catholic and Reformation attitudes. The current anthropological approach can be considered as a certain metamorphosis of the traditional metaphysical thinking that played a large role in Catholic sacramental theology. There is, so to speak, an axis: from a metaphysical through an anthropological/transcendental (Rahner) and a phenomenological/anthropological/symbolic approach (Schillebeeckx, Chauvet) to the present of 'ritual studies'. Moreover, it can be noted that scholars within the Reformation's liturgy-theological approach do find anthropological starting points. One can, for instance, point to Schleiermacher (1768-1834) in this connection. In 1799 he published his *Reden über die Religion*, in which under the influence of Romanticism he became aware of the unbalanced, over-rational approach of the Enlightenment and the importance of human experience and feeling and of forms of expression that carry people over boundaries toward wholeness. In this context he refers to the realm of art, and in particular to that of religion. In this manner Schleiermacher arrives at a linkage of anthropology and theology.[17] This liturgy-minded anthropological line now also seems to be breaking through in Reformation tradition. This has much to do with the great advances in ecumenical dialogue.

---

[17] A. WILLEMS: *De actualiteit van Schleiermacher's 'Reden' uit 1799*, in *Tijdschrift voor Theologie* 40 (2000) 341-357, particularly 345-349. Schleiermacher used here the then already passé word 'Apologie' (WILLEMS: *De actualiteit* 345). See N. SCHREURS: *Geloofsverantwoording: Van apologetiek naar een hermeneutische theologie met apologetische inslag*, Nijmegen 1982.

Does that mean that the other school is disappearing from the scene? That is in no way the case. After an extensive analysis of recent authors on both sides, Hempelmann correctly notes that the reception process of ecumenical texts with regard to the subject of the sacraments has not only contributed to clarifying the fundamental consensus, but has also made the issue of a continuing fundamental distinction timely. This fundamental distinction closely coincides with a difference in the 'interpretation horizon' that results from an historically developed overall view.[18] There is an antithesis that one constantly encounters in the history of thinking about the sacraments. The tension between the two schools ultimately involves a fundamental theological problem, that of the relation between nature and revelation, between God and our world, between creation and eschaton.[19] It is clear that there is a tension in the relationship between anthropology and theology of liturgy.[20] Both schools must deal with the fundamental question of how one should handle the tension between anthropology and theology of liturgy. The concern of those who take theology as their point of departure is before all else that the other school regards anthropology too much as the foundation of sacramental theology. This could lead to the misunderstanding that a noetic way to the sacraments is possible, outside of faith in the gospel.[21] Those departing from theology, emphasize that there can be no logical step from anthropology to theology, but only a leap to another level, another realm, a realm that rather inversely is a 'revelation' of an anthropology that is completely in the service of the theological dimension.[22]

[18] HEMPELMANN: *Sakrament als Ort der Vermittlung des Heils* 202.

[19] E. JÜNGEL: 'Das Sakrament – Was ist das?', in E. JÜNGEL & K. RAHNER: *Was ist ein Sakrament?*, Freiburg/Basel/Wien 1971, 29.

[20] For a recent approach to this problem from an almost exclusively systematic sacramental theological angle, see *The Presence of God in a Postmodern Context: the Sacramental Contours of a God Incarnate*: *Questions Liturgiques* 81 (2000) no. 3-4; L. BOEVE & L. LEIJSSEN: *Sacramental Presence in a Postmodern Context* (Bibliotheca Ephemeridum Theologicarum Lovaniensium 160), Leuven 2001; IDEM: *Sacramental Contours of a God incarnate* (Textes et Études Liturgiques/Studies in Liturgy 16), Leuven 2001; *Life Cycle Rituals and Sacramentality: Between Continuity and Discontinuity*: *Questions Liturgiques* 83 (2002) no. 1; L. BOEVE, S. VAN DEN BOSSCHE, G. IMMINK & P. POST (eds.): *Levensrituelen en sacramentaliteit. Tussen continuïteit en discontinuïteit* (Meander 5), Baarn 2003.

[21] HEMPELMANN: *Sakrament als Ort der Vermittlung des Heil* 210.

[22] Paul Post observes that the integrated anthropological aim and openness of research in liturgical studies, and the important role that ritual studies can play for that reason, has been under increasing pressure lately. For instance, according to Meßner the

3. ANTHROPOLOGICAL PROLEGOMENA OF THE FRACTURE BETWEEN
ANTHROPOLOGY AND THEOLOGY OF LITURGY, AND THE RAPPROCHE-
MENT BETWEEN THE TWO DIRECTIONS

In the preceding I have continually opted for the anthropologically oriented school, which seeks the general human foundation for Christian
ritual. In the first section of this chapter, it emerged that anthropology
and theology of liturgy do not join up perfectly with one another. Ultimately there is a 'gap' between anthropology and theology of liturgy.
But it would be wrong to isolate anthropology and theology of liturgy
from each other because of this gap. On the contrary: it is precisely on
the basis of this 'gap' that they are closely connected with one another.
In fact, it is extremely important to realise that this gap between anthropology and theology of liturgy also has its own anthropological prolegomena. It is possible to bring the two opposing basic theological
options closer together along this line. In what follows I will on the one
hand clarify to what degree there is a rational approach, and wider yet,
a fully human approach, and on the other hand how full justice can be
done to faith in the gospel.

3.1. A philosophical approach: man as 'animal rationale'

The pronouncement of the First Vatican Council that man is able to
know God from created reality 'by the natural light of human reason' is
well known.[23] Thus according to Vatican I man as *animal rationale* has
by nature the capacity to arrive at knowledge of God. In saying this the
Council is not making any pronouncement about actual fact. Indeed, it
also adds that 'it can be ascribed to divine revelation that in the divine

concept of the symbol can only be defined theologically, and theology and anthropology
should not be mixed. Liturgy can only be understood within itself. (See R. MEßNER:
'Was ist systematische Liturgiewissenschaft? Ein Entwurf in sieben Thesen', in *Archiv für
Liturgiewissenschaft* 40 (1998) 257-274; G. WINKLER & R. MEßNER: 'Überlegungen zu
den methodischen und wissenschaftstheoretischen Grundlagen der Liturgiewissenschaft', in *Theologische Quartalschrift* 178 (1998) 141-172). In work in liturgical
studies *katabasis* and *anabasis* are sometimes mistakenly played against each other, so
that the turn toward anthropology that proved so stimulating for liturgy is discredited,
according to POST: 'Personen en patronen' 99 and 'Interference and Intuition' 53.
    [23] Vaticanum I, see H. DENZINGER & H. SCHÖNMETZER: *Enchiridion Symbolorum*,
Barcelona 1963, 1785; IDEM: *Enchiridion Symbolorum* 2145 (antimodernist oath).

which is not inaccessible in itself for human reason, even in the present state of the human race can easily be known by all with sure certainty and without admixture of error'.[24] The anthropology of Vatican I was also not all that optimistic either. Undoubtedly this is related to the conviction that human existence is a wounded, hurt and broken existence. But what is important is that Vatican I has pronounced its trust in human rationality as an access to the divine. In this, Vatican I was responding to fideism, according to which the divine world is only accessible by means of faith (de Lamennais, de Bonald, Bautain). One also finds this view in the new *Catechism of the Catholic Church*, from 1993, and in the 1998 encyclical *Fides et ratio*.[25] It is a typically Catholic view.

This rational *Vorstufe* of Christian faith has been enunciated in a surprising manner over recent decades by the French philosopher/theologian Jean-Luc Marion, professor at the Sorbonne in Paris.[26] In his 1982 book *Dieu sans l'être* Marion proceeds from Husserl's phenomenology, which he rereads and updates in his own way. Husserl's motto was that philosophy must return '*zu den Sachen selbst*'. Husserl wished to describe reality from human consciousness, without presuppositions, and precisely as it revealed itself. Phenomenology is the science of phenomena, that is to say, of that which shows itself, that which appears. One must perceive the phenomena impartially and open-mindedly,

---

[24] DENZINGER & SCHÖNMETZER: *Enchiridion Symbolorum* 1786.

[25] *Catechism of the Catholic Church* 156-159, 286; JOHANNES PAULUS II: *Fides et ratio*, Città del Vaticano 1998.

[26] J.-L. Marion (b. 1946) is also director of the Centre d'Etudes Cartésiennes at the Sorbonne. Further, he teaches at the University of Chicago as successor to Paul Ricoeur. See R. WELTEN (ed.): *God en het denken. Over de filosofie van Jean-Luc Marion* (Annalen van het Thijmgenootschap, 88, 2), Nijmegen 2000, in which particularly R. WELTEN: 'God en het Denken. Een inleiding in de filosofie van Jean-Luc Marion' (7-44) and S. VAN DEN BOSSCHE: 'God verschijnt toch in de immanentie. De fenomenologische neerlegging van de theologie in Jean-Luc Marions Étant donné' (128-153). For the oeuvre of Marion, see WELTEN (ed.): *God en het denken* 37-40. Marion's three most important works are: J.-L. MARION: *Dieu sans l'être*, Paris 1982 (translation: *God Without Being*, Chicago 1995); IDEM: *Étant donné. Essai d'une phénoménologie de la donation*, Paris 1997 (translation: *Being Given. Toward a Phenomenology of Giveness*, Palo Alto 2002); IDEM: *De surcroît. Études sur les phénomènes saturés*, Paris 2001 (translation: *In Excess. Studies of Satured Phenomena*, New York 2002). See also VAN DEN BOSSCHE: *Presentie in differentie: Vier Essays over de Godsontmoeting in een postmoderne context* (Doctoral Thesis), Leuven 2000.

without preceding theories or views (*zurück zu den Sachen selbst!*). In this sense there is deconstruction – a scrapping, a destruction of the preceding concepts and premises, construction coming only after that. Impartial observation is only possible through cutting back, *epochè* or *Einklammerung*. The knowledge of the world as we perceive it daily must be set apart between brackets and suspended. One must start from the consciousness of the subject in his or her intentionality, ultimate orientation to what shows itself, what appears. In this, Husserl places a strong emphasis on the intentional orientation of the subject. Marion takes the view that through this neither the reduction nor the phenomena are sufficiently served. If you only understand phenomena from the intentionality of the subject, as with Husserl, then there is still the danger of bias, of a determination beforehand. Then what appears still is correlated with my focused perception, and correlation – co-relation – means that you will make what appears conform to your own perception.[27] That too must be reduced or demolished. According to Marion, phenomenology must go further. It must drop the primacy of intentionality. Phenomenological reduction must deal with a phenomenality *that gives itself*. Put simply, the flesh of an apple shows itself when the rind is peeled away. The flesh then gives itself. There is a coincidence of the peeling of the rind and the self-giving of the flesh. Or in other words: the reduction of the peeling and the self-giving of the flesh are one and the same. Now, by stripping God of our metaphysical speculations, of our wishes and desires, we find the God who gives himself, as He is.[28] Thus here one cannot say that there is a self-giving of God *from* my intentionality. His self-giving does not show itself because I have focused on it or because I expected it. God reveals himself in such an overwhelming and abundant way that this cannot be just a fulfilling of my desires. Marion speaks here of a saturated phenomenon. Reality is like a screen through which the Other appears to us, watches us. Marion thus opts for a Giver who precedes the given reality. Whatever we do, we always respond to what is first given to us.

In recent years Marion has gone still further. In his 1997 book *Étant donné* his thought has taken a radical turn. In this latest book, more

---

[27] This is not correlation in the real sense, because there is no equal relation, but a relation in which the completely other is illuminated. See about this also H. BERGER: *Tegen de negatieve filosofie. Dionysius – Kant – Derrida*, Leende 2000, especially 285 ff.

[28] WELTEN: *God en het Denken. Een inleiding* 22.

than in *Dieu sans l'être*, he emphasises the pure gift as such within phe-nomenality. Within phenomenality, immanent in it and to it, is the structure of *givenness*. The *immanent other* that is characteristic of phe-nomenality thus has the possibility in itself of a real divine immanence and presence. That is an important development. Marion here distances himself from *theology* by placing *radical alterity* as a possibility within immanence. In other words, God, as *possibility*, as self-giving, is dis-cernible by human reason, but nevertheless, to arrive at faith a leap is necessary. However, that leap is not a leap into the unknown as it is in fideism. This is not a totally irrational leap, but a leap which is anthro-pologically anchored. This leap has, so to speak, its own anthropological prolegomenon, its own anthropological *praeambulum*.[29] God as the complete Other is still discernible here and now, in one way or another, as *possibility*. Marion's expansion of phenomenology consists in his expansion of immanence to a level that on the one hand is discernible as phenomenon, but on the other hand is at the same time not visible, to wit, as a level on which reality *gives itself*, and thus is really gratuitous, before it appears. The paradox of phenomenology is that it takes *the ini-tiative in order to ultimately lose it*.[30] All particular input is ultimately lost. As his example here Marion uses the painting as phenomenon.[31] As phenomenon, a painting is ultimately an instance of pure givenness, *giv-ing and revealing itself*. I can only hope that the painting will give itself to me, that it will address me and make me committed to it. The self-giving precedes my looking. It is the same as in the case of a gift. What counts is not the object, but the gesture behind it and which makes it a pure gift.[32]

This givenness as abundant, saturated gift now becomes still richer when the endless numbers of subdivisions of reality give themselves maximally. Then there is a copious, a doubly saturated phenomenality. Marion speaks of a saturation in the second degree in this case. And in such a case, according to Marion, you encounter revelation as a *possi-bility*. You encounter a prolegomenon, a *praeambulum* of Christian rev-elation.

---

[29] The term *praeambulum fidei* does not have to be understood chronologically, per se. One can also interpret it in the sense of 'foundation'.

[30] VAN DEN BOSSCHE: 'God verschijnt toch in de immanentie' 134.

[31] VAN DEN BOSSCHE: 'God verschijnt toch in de immanentie' 135-139.

[32] VAN DEN BOSSCHE: 'God verschijnt toch in de immanentie' 141.

It should be clear that Marion's phenomenology is extremely challenging for the anthropological side of theology. Van Den Bossche correctly observes that Marion has for the first time resolved the conflict between *theologia rationalis* and *theologia revelata*, between the God of the philosophers and the God of Abraham, Isaac and Jacob. Both rational phenomenology and revealed theology find the same God. That is to say, rational phenomenology finds God as *possibility* and revealed theology finds God as a *fact of faith*. According to Van Den Bossche, Marion 'rediscovers' 'the standpoint of Vatican I on "natural knowledge of God"'.[33] The reader will agree with me that the emphasis that Marion places on phenomenality as the manifestation of pure givenness, and this in abundance, can considerably soften the sharp distinction between the anthropological direction in sacramental theology and the dialectical direction. Yet I suspect that this philosophical approach will still be insufficient, simply because it is purely philosophical and departs from man as *animal rationale*. For a real liturgical anthropological approach a more integrated approach is necessary. That must begin from man as *animal symbolicum*.

3.2. An integrated human approach: man as 'animal symbolicum' and the 'other side' of ritual

In the preceding parts and chapters of this book I have constantly emphasised how greatly, according to more recent sacramental theology, liturgical studies and ritual studies, religion and faith in particular are permeated by the human capacity for symbolisation. This capacity for symbolisation was always the point of departure for my approach to ritual. I have just indicated that it is possible to begin on this side, with man as an *animal rationale*, and at the same time do justice to the priority of the divine 'other side'. It is possible to speak of a rational prolegomenon for faith. The question is now, is this also more broadly true? After all, man is more than *ratio*. Faith is about confessing God as a completely gratuitous gift with our mind, but also with all our heart and all our strength and senses. Does *this* confession also have its prolegomenon, its *praeambulum*?

I believe that this is indeed the case, and would now develop this further from semiotics. For this my starting point will be the paintings of

---

[33] VAN DEN BOSSCHE: 'God verschijnt toch in de immanentie' 152-153.

the American painter Mark Rothko.[34] Rothko was born in 1903 in Dvinsk, Russia, as the son of Jewish parents. When he was ten his family fled the pogroms to the United States. He died in New York in 1970. In the last twenty years of his life Rothko painted nothing other than rectangular fields against an almost monochrome background.[35] Contrary to expectations, Rothko did not term these images abstract, but realistic. According to Rothko, 'These new forms say what (previously) symbols said'.[36] You can undoubtedly regard Rothko's paintings as symbols. Standing in front of these paintings you can not escape the impression that you are being confronted with something that appears to us from *within* the space of these paintings. The rectangular figures are placed in the middle of the paintings and fill almost the whole space. They evoke a maximum of restfulness. The object will show itself to us, entirely and as close as possible. You get the feeling that it desires to make contact with you, yes, even that it is watching you closely. It is as if this manifestation is advancing toward you out of an infinite space, wanting to say something. Light plays an important role in these paintings. What Rothko shows us stands in a space of light and is itself a source of light, even where the source radiates a dark light. That strongly evokes the effect of the appearance of an existing reality. The object that Rothko presents appears to us as coming from another world, as something that lies on the other side of subjectivity, a revelation of the other side of our existence. In viewing such a painting there is a great tension, a tension between the viewer and the painting. This

---

[34] At this point I would want to draw attention to the innovative initiatives toward a sacramental theology from a theology of images. The sensory/visual reality dimension of the sacraments is being thought through anew with the aid of concrete art works. See A. STOCK: *Poetische Dogmatik*, 4 Vol., Paderborn 1995-2001; C. GÄRTNER: *Gegenwartsweisen in Bild und Sakrament. Eine theologische Untersuchung zum Werk von Thomas Lehnerer*, Paderborn 2002; see also: P. SCHMIDT: *In de handen van mensen: 2000 jaar Christus in kunst en cultuur*, Leuven 2000.

[35] T. VAN DER STAP: *Over het religieuze in de kunst. Naar aanleiding van Rembrandt en Mark Rothko*, in VAN SPEYBROECK (ed.): *Kunst en religie* 95-99. For reproductions of two of his paintings, see VAN SPEYBROECK (ed.): *Kunst en religie* 39-40. See also GROUPE MU a.o.: *Approches sémiotiques sur Rothko: Nouveaux Actes Sémiotiques* 6 (1994) no. 34-36 (illustration at the end of no. 34-36) and MARION: *De surcroît* 65-98 (reproduction at the beginning of this book). Reproductions of paintings by Rothko from this period are also easily found on Internet under the subject 'Rothko', which will turn up references for numerous locations.

[36] VAN DER STAP: *Over het religieuze in de kunst* 96-97.

tension has much to do with our physicality, our senses, our heart, our emotions. I said that for good reason: you get the *feeling* that the painting wants to make contact with you, that the light touches you in an intense way and overcomes you. There is not only cognitive perception, but also a sensory/corporeal perception. In the words of Greimas: in perception here there is also proprioceptivity coming into play, the internal sensory/physical perception. The perception of these paintings is thus a very physical and sensory event. Perception of these paintings outside of me (exteroceptivity) is cognitively internalised (interoceptivity), but this cognitive discovery of meaning takes place through the perception of one's own physicality (proprioceptivity). What is important then is not the cognitive end result of assigning meaning, but the primary origin and experience thereof. In the semiotic description of this perception contemporary French semiotics reaches back in its own peculiar way to phenomenology, especially that of Merleau-Ponty.[37] According to this French semiotics, in the dynamics of this perception there is a change between 'ordinary' and 'extraordinary' perception. It can be termed a shift of isotopy. A *break* appears, a split, a discontinuity. The perspective jumps. All bounds are transcended. In his book *De l'imperfection* Greimas was the first to arrestingly describe this occurrence.[38] The transcending of bounds has to do with the experience of great tension between what one sees outwardly (the 'appearance') and the manifestation of that which is the essential quality of the painting. The 'imperfection' of the figurative 'appearance' produces an intentionality in the subject. The subject begins to exert themselves in order, beginning from the figurative screen of the external appearance, to touch the actuality of the figurative phenomenon, that which ultimately appears and is revealed in and through the outward manifestation. The occurrence of this crossing of boundaries, of this break, is accompanied by a moment of encounter between the subject and that which ultimately appears. In this a second, extremely penetrating change takes place, for at the same time a change takes place in the *orientation* of the

---

[37] See especially M. MERLEAU-PONTY: *Phénoménologie de la perception*, Paris 1945. See, also for the following, particularly: D. BERTRAND: *Précis de sémiotique littéraire*, Paris 2000, 148-164; J. FONTANILLE: *Sémiotique et littérature. Essais de méthode*, Paris 1999, 223-257.

[38] GREIMAS: *De l'imperfection*; see also H. PARRET: *Semiotiek en esthetica*, in W. VAN BELLE a.o.: *De betekenis als verhaal. Semiotische opstellen* (Semiotisch perspectief 1), Amsterdam 1991, 213-235.

relation between the perceiving subject and that which ultimately appears. This relation is reversed.[39] Let me concretise this with our paintings. The I breaks open the figurative screen, as it were, to the other world of the ultimate source of light, but the I is thereby at the same time so affected by this light that the object becomes an active subject that takes over all initiative. The orientation within the dynamic tension is thus radically reversed. The painting, or rather the light that it evokes, is the true source and the I that looks is the target (*cible*) on which the light is directed. Thus it could be said that all the initiative passes to the other side. One could also say that ultimately all my intentionality ultimately proves to have been awakened and borne by this other side.

As has been said, one can regard Rothko's paintings as a prototype of the symbol, symbolic language and symbolic action. In our symbolisation too, by means of symbol, symbolic acts and symbolic language, there is also such a sensory/physical perception, in which the screen of figurativity is broken open to that which ultimately appears and in which at the same time relations are reversed. One could speak of the *allocentric* character of the symbol. The symbol directs the perceiving and committed subject to what is given, what is already-given, to what was and is given. This produces a reversal, so that it would be more correct to say that the I is directed by that other, and that the initiative ultimately lies with the other. This all touches directly on ritual. After all, ritual is not only functional, but also symbolic. Precisely to the extent that ritual is about symbolism, what has been said here applies to ritual.

Through semiotics we here discover a particular *praeambulum fidei*. Thus the 'gap' between anthropology and theology of liturgy, *precisely as a 'gap'*, also has its own anthropological prolegomenon. There is not only a rational anthropological prolegomenon which touches the *orthodoxia secunda* (cognitive theology, 'right' doctrine), but likewise a prolegomenon to the *orthodoxia prima* ('right' praise): it involves the whole of man and therefore has to do with *integral* anthropology. Thus general human ritual touches in a unique way on the credibility of Christian ritual, and the theology of liturgy appears to be deeply anchored in the anthropology of ritual. Because this is involved with both the possibility of the gap and the reversal of the initiative to the other side, it also brings the anthropological school of liturgy very close to the dialectical.

---

[39] See in this connection also FONTANILLE: *Sémiotique du discours* 137-180.

Anabasis and *katabasis* touch each other.[40] Moreover, it seems clear to me that in this prolegomenon one encounters what I have outlined as the general religious layer of ritual, the design of which is so important in our time, and which speaks to so many in our culture.

4. THE BREAK AND REVERSAL IN CHRISTIAN RITUAL

It would be incorrect to say that the break and reversal which occurs in and through ritual in general anthropological terms is identical to that of Christian ritual. That break and that reversal doe not automatically lead to Christian ritual, and it is also insufficient to say that Christian ritual is the culmination of the break and reversal in question. No, Christian ritual is rooted in general human ritual in an impressive manner, but at the same time it is true that the break and reversal are radicalised in Christian ritual.[41] The break and the reversal take the name of the personal God from the first and second testaments, who commits himself to us and who graciously watches over and frees us. In Christian ritual the perspective jumps in a radical way to what was and is poured out by God, to what is pure givenness and grace, in Jesus of Nazareth, through his Spirit.

Now, it is precisely at this point that there is a danger of prematurely suspending the anthropologically oriented line. After all, one could now

---

[40] Thus it is not necessary to stress the *katabasis* at the expense of the *anabasis*, as this happens in Kunzler; see for instance KUNZLER: *Die Liturgie der Kirche*. For the search for balance, see G. IMMINK: 'Een dubbele beweging', in OSKAMP & SCHUMAN: *De weg van de liturgie* 67-89. P. POST: 'Life Cycle Rituals: A Ritual-Liturgical Perspective', in *Questions Liturgiques* 83 (2002) 25 remarks in this connection: 'Here we touch upon the double movement of *katabasis* and *anabasis* for which we can use the principle of the *synkatabasis*, a telling, though little known patristic term from the Vaticanum II documents. The term was coined by John Chrysostom and is really untranslatable.... Literally the term can be translated as "go down with someone to the place where he or she is staying." This attitude is attributed to God and may therefore be referred to as "God's humaneness." Liturgy is inextricably linked to the anthropological, ritual and cultural environment.' See also IDEM: 'Introduction and Application' 70.

[41] I have already noted that in the 'dialectical' school of the theology of liturgy the stress does not lie so much on the reality of creation as on fallen creation. The 'imperfection' thus does not only involve creation as such, but at the same time implies the wounded creation and unavoidable sinful human failure. But the anthropological vision is also relevant from this perspective. The *l'imperfection* then becomes the *condition humaine* in the sense of a wounded and broken existence.

begin from the incarnation as the third element between anthropology and theology, indeed understanding this in the sense of the Nicene Council, according to which divine and human nature are united into one person in Christ. We would then have a Christology from above. The incarnation would be seen as the basic model for Christian liturgy. As the divine and human worlds meet each other in Christ, and there is a descending line from above and a rising line from below, so too that would be the case for liturgy. One then stresses that the sacramental salvific order has revealed itself most tangibly in the incarnation of Christ. Yet this approach has its imbalances. First, in this model the descending line is more strongly accented than the rising line. Liturgy is much more experienced as the *epiphania Domini*, the appearance of the Lord, as is the case in the East. Now, it cannot be denied that the Eastern liturgy still remains especially sensitive to the anthropological basis of liturgy: as human nature was taken up in Christ in a full manner, so is that the case with regard to the world of men and things in the liturgy. But it remains a fact that in our culture people prefer to begin from the human side, and that this is a very legitimate point of departure for liturgy. Then, if one takes the incarnation as a theological/liturgical starting point, there is a danger that this will be at the expense of the dynamic of history. Seen from the fullness of the incarnation, it would appear that what follows is just an anticlimax. This can lead to a static liturgy, in which the accent falls on the fullness of grace. The liturgy becomes like heaven on earth. Here too it is important to hold onto the integration of the anthropological. The life of Jesus was intensely anchored in our history. It had its own human and dramatic course.

Over against this Christology from above stands a *Christology from the bottom up*.[42] Drawing upon a terminology introduced earlier in this book, one might call it an inductive Christology. This Christology proceeds from the earthly Jesus and his message. It bestows attention in the con-

[42] A. SCHILSON: 'Perspektiven gegenwärtiger Christologie. Ein Situationsbericht', in G. BITTER & G. MILLER (eds.); *Konturen heutiger Theologie. Werkstattberichte*, München 1976, 161-175; S. BELLEMAKERS: *Lees: het zinsverband van woord en vlees. Het belang van de 'close reading' methode bij het bestuderen en beoordelen van liturgische teksten, aan de hand van een onderzoek naar de christologie in enkele tafelgebeden van Huub Oosterhuis* (M.A. Thesis Theologische Faculteit Tilburg), Tilburg 1985, 250-252. See in this connection also A.E. LEWIS: *Between Cross and Resurrection. A theology of Holy Saturday*, Michigan/Cambridge 2001, 53-56.

crete life of Jesus, and is historical/dynamic. His life is connected with the long previous history of the First Testament and unfolds gradually as a stirring, messianic life to the climax of his suffering, death and resurrection. The 'breaking point' then lies in the paradox of the Easter mystery.

5. THE PARADOX OF THE EASTER MYSTERY

Despite all progress, we live in a history in which there is still enormous suffering and massive and senseless death. The countless war cemeteries in Europe and mass graves around the world bear witness to this. In our postmodern culture there is justifiably renewed attention for the tragedy of evil, suffering and death.[43] It is however wrong to attribute all these imperfections of the creation, all suffering death, purely and simply to a sinful decline, either in the beginning or in our further history.[44] Modern biology sees death as something that is inherent in all life. 'Strife and suffering belong to nature. Floods and earthquakes are part of the same reality to which majestic mountains and fertile valleys belong'.[45] The Scripture also sometimes flatly denies an identifiable connection between sin and suffering (Job, Luke 13:1-5, John 9:3). On the other hand, more often this connection is strongly asserted in the Bible. This latter expresses just as much what is in fact close to our experience. We

---

[43] For instance R. SAFRANSKI: *Das Böse oder das Drama der Freiheit*, München 1997 = R. SAFRANSKI: *Het kwaad, of Het drama van de vrijheid*, Amsterdam 1998. In recent years new studies on 'original sin' have begun appearing, a theme around which there had been silence for some considerable time: G. LUKKEN: *Original Sin in the Roman liturgy. Research into the theology of Original Sin in the Roman sacramentaria and the early baptismal liturgy*, Leiden 1973; G. NIJHOFF: *La confusion des arbres. Essai d'une revalorisation du dogme du péché originel*, Vérossaz 1995; L. PANIER: *Le péché originel. Naissance de l'homme sauvé*, Paris 1996; G.-H. BAUDRY: *Le péché dit originel* (Théologie Historique 113), Paris 2000; G. LUKKEN: 'Doopliturgie en ons gekwetste bestaan', in *Inzet* 28 (1999) 3, 85-89; G. MINOIS: *Les origines du mal. Une histoire du péché originel*, Paris 2002. See also M. HEWITT SUCHOCKI: *The Fall to Violence: Original Sin in Relational Theology*, New York 1994; MULDOON: 'Forum: Reconciliation, Original Sin, and Millennial Malaise'; VAN WOLDE: *A Semiotic Analysis of Genesis 2-3*. In the period after the Second Vatican Council people had little interest in these negative sides of (Christian) existence: see J. COURTÉS: 'Sémiotique et théologie du péché', in PARRET & RUPRECHT (eds.): *Exigences et perspectives de la sémiotique* 863-903; IDEM: 'Sémiotique et théologie du péché'.
[44] BRINKMAN: *Sacraments of Freedom* 46-54.
[45] BRINKMAN: *Sacraments of Freedom* 46.

are all too conscious of the decisive role our guilty deeds play in the destruction of nature and humanity. 'In many cases... it is nearly impossible to distinguish between the consequences of our sins and the capricious character of nature itself.'[46] Whatever the case, there is enormous collective tragedy in creation, also, and particularly, in our present culture. One hears people speak of 'modern plagues' in our society[47] and 'new forms of evil'.[48] Equally undeniable is the drama of individual suffering: a handicapped child, broken relationships, the loss of a loved one, the death of an innocent person, misfortune, illness, infirmity, guilt, anxiety, uncertainty, loneliness, not being accepted, sorrow about the transitoriness of life. The life of Jesus was every bit as dramatic. He, who began his life as a displaced person and constantly stood up for the poor and those deprived of their rights, who was betrayed by a kiss from one of his friends; through religious intrigues among his own people he was given over to the occupiers for trial; he was condemned by a cynical and opportunistic Roman governor, Pontius Pilate: he was disposed of in the most degrading manner, nailed to the pillory of the cross, between two murderers. During his death struggles he was mocked. He died in an abject manner, in a remote corner of the world. That drama is still central in Christian faith. It is characterised by the cross as its central symbol. Those who realise that it was a degrading instrument of torture and execution, and in no sense an ornament, know that such a central symbol is a *skandalon*, a stumbling block. How often is suffering seen precisely as evidence that God cannot exist, or does not intervene in this world? Was Jesus of Nazareth not right when he cried out in the midst of his suffering, 'My God, my God, why have you forsaken me?'? *The* great paradox of Christianity is therefore the Easter mystery. *The* short circuit with our anthropology, *the* theological moment, occurs where suffering and death prove to be a way to resurrection. There you encounter an unbridgeable chasm. That gulf is expressed in a striking way in the *Hohe Messe* by Bach: after the falling motif of the *crucifixus* and *sepultus est* follows a silence, and only then follows, in constantly rising motifs, the *et resurrexit*.[49] The enigma of Easter, with its mysterious reversal, defines the deepest

---

[46] BRINKMAN: *Sacraments of Freedom* 47.

[47] *The Return of the Plague*: *Concilium* 33 (1997) no. 5.

[48] *The Fascination of Evil*: *Concilium* 34 (1998) no. 1.

[49] W. DERKSE: 'Kleine dingen in de muziek', in DE VISSCHER (ed.): *Mosterdzaadjes van het bestaan* 59.

essence of the identity of Christianity.[50] It characterises Christian ritual in general and each Christian ritual in particular. The liturgy of Holy Week, which Augustine felicitously characterised as the three day celebration of the crucified, dead and resurrected One (*sacratissimum triduum crucifixi, sepulti, suscitati*) is central in every year.[51]

Precisely here, in the Easter mystery, God takes on a name, and his face lights up as the completely other. The Easter mystery imposes boundaries on the metaphysical and onto-theological speculations about the divine world. God is no longer the *explanatory* final word of the liturgy.[52]

As such, one could call the story of Jesus a postmodern story. With the death of Jesus you stand before an open end, a story that is unfinished, and that we, people, can in no way whatsoever fill up. Only there is the leap of faith possible that breaks through all that is culturally defined, even that in postmodernity. This has its repercussions for all of Christian ritual. For a long time people were inclined to emphasise primarily the identity aspect of the symbol: the veiled *presence* (epiphany) of the divine. That perception is still to be found, and it has its right to exist. But in our culture there is much more of an inclination to place the emphasis on the diversity aspect of the symbol: on its concealment, on the fact that the world that it evokes ultimately is and remains hidden and completely other. One speaks then – and this is not pure word games – of 'not-present absence' or even the 'not-absent absence'.[53]

---

[50] I. PAHL: 'Le mystère pascal essentiel pour la forme de la liturgie', in *La Maison-Dieu* (1995) 204, 51-70; W. RORDORF: 'Remarques sur le mystère pascal', in *La Maison-Dieu* (1995) 204, 71-82.

[51] AUGUSTINE, *Epistola 55*, 14, 24.

[52] CHAUVET: *Symbole et sacrement*; D. POWER: *Eucharistic Mystery. Revitalizing the Tradition*, Dublin 1992, 312, 325; BLOECHL & VAN DEN BOSSCHE: 'Postmoderniteit, theologie en sacramententheologie'; S. VAN DEN BOSSCHE: 'Geen wijn in water veranderen: De onherleidbare particulariteit van het christelijk geloof', in *Tijdschrift voor Theologie* 38 (1998) 109-119; BOEVE & RIES (eds.): *The Presence of Transcendence*. For further literature see the authors cited here, and for background, among others: H. VAN VEGHEL: 'God en de roos. Heidegger en de god van de filosofie', in R.J. PEETERS a.o. (eds.): *De onvoltooid verleden tijd. Negen bijdragen tot een bezinning op traditie*, Tilburg 1992, 51-67; H. VAN DEN BOSCH: 'It is (un)finished. Mark C. Taylor over Thomas J.J. Altizer', in PEETERS a.o. (ed.): *De onvoltooid verleden tijd* 99-118. See also A. HOUTEPEN: *God, een open vraag. Theologische perspectieven in een cultuur van agnosme*, Zoetermeer 1997.

[53] For an overview of the way the tradition of negative theology is given meaning in contemporary philosophy of culture, see BULHOF & TEN KATE (eds.): *Flight of the Gods*; L. BOEVE, A. VAN HARSKAMP & L. TEN KATE: 'Van een God die niet bestaat en de ondoorgrondelijke dingen die Hij doet', in *Tijdschrift voor Theologie* 41 (2001) 337-355.

Whatever the case, the symbol is seen rather as something that points away from itself, as it were. God is the one for whom all names stand aside. He is ultimately the Nameless One whose life ends up at the open grave: symbol that points away from itself to a space that cannot be bridged by men, namely that of the resurrection.

Thus the accent here is other than what one finds in current Christology (what is termed the 'third wave'), which concentrates on the historical Jesus.[54] Of course such research has its value. But at the same time it is true that it is often very objective in nature, and frequently leaves one with the impression that it has too little realisation that any search for the 'historical Jesus' in fact is still another interpretation and construction. One can simply not separate the figure of Jesus from the context of the practice of faith as it exists, neither at the origins, nor in the course of the history of Christianity. Contemporary practice strongly experiences the stories of Jesus as an open question about God himself, who in Jesus' life, and in particular in the Easter mystery, is illuminated as the totally Other, the inscrutable. I find what the liturgist Al has written to be apropos here: 'My reality is that Jesus died, an historical fact. For me it is also reality that He lives. I have no clear insight into what precisely happened. But I know that he lives... As Paul says, "I know that my redeemer lives", which I see concretised in church history, in which the power of the Spirit is present, in very many people, unknown people, but also great men who stand out, the Spirit who gives life. The Spirit who also raised Jesus from the dead, as Paul says, has also given us life.'[55]

Beyond the unbridgeable space of the resurrection, the Christians' story, their *Leit-story*, goes further. What the prophet Joel wrote – 'I will pour my Spirit on all people' and that 'everyone who calls on the name of the Lord will be saved' (Acts 2:17-21) – was fulfilled. Pentecost is inseparably linked with Easter. The Pentecost mystery is an integral part of the Easter mystery itself. In this way Jesus' resurrection is in turn connected again most closely

---

[54] W. WEREN: 'Weer op zoek naar de ware Jezus', in MERKS & SCHREURS (eds.): *De passie van een grensganger* 92-109. The first wave, extending from 1778 to 1906, was that of the historical/critical method. The second wave began in 1953; the purely historical interest in the earthly Jesus was replaced by a pure theological interest in the divine Jesus, as he was proclaimed as the Christ by the first Christian community. The third wave began in the 1980s, and concentrates again on research into the historical Jesus.

[55] H. LUYTEN & C. VISSER: 'De totale onkenbaarheid van God. Een gesprek met Piet Al, norbertijn', in *Dabar-bericht* (1998) 4, 24.

with our history. Pentecost is the historical expression of the 'for us' of the resurrection. Precisely this 'for us' is embodied through the Spirit who is poured out over the people of God, and who is at work in the Church. There it is operative in the intermediate history of the Christian liturgy, deeply rooted in the anthropology of ritual, until it comes to fulfilment in the Parousia. It is important to go more deeply into this.

Thanks to Easter the Spirit, of whom no one knows whence He comes and where He goes, broke through all social barriers, privileges and language divisions. The dynamism of the Easter mystery, that secret of suffering, death and resurrection, henceforth is actualised in and through the Spirit who is given. The unbridgeable chasm and the name-lessness of God are now bridged by God in the form of the breath of life, of a soft breeze, a tongue of fire, from inside. In the midst of all suf-fering and death He appears not to be the hard hand of the masculine tyrant, the rigid ideology, but rather the mild, sheltering hand that pro-tects us. The Spirit is like a bird that as it were hovers above us praying: the hovering of a falcon is in French termed *le voler du Saint Esprit*. It was not for nothing that the Jewish Christians in the new Church were convinced that the Spirit was female.[56] She will not break the bruised reed nor cause her voice to call out to us in the street' (Isaiah 42:2). This Spirit is the heart, the dynamism inside the community that celebrates the liturgy.[57] She has no patriarchal reticence, and is one of the factors that accomplishes the shaping of the liturgy in various cultures.[58] This Spirit also belongs to the paradox of the Easter mystery. In the old (12th or 13th century) hymn *Veni Sancte Spiritus*, this Spirit is sung of as father of the poor, light of our hearts, choicest comforter, sweet guest of our soul, rest in all labour, coolness in the heat, comfort in all tears. She cleanses what is foul and unclean, waters what is barren, heals what is wounded, makes supple what is rigid, and sets on the right way those who have strayed.[59]

---

[56] B. QUISPEL: 'The Birth of the Child', in *Eranos* 40 (1971) 304-305; see also E. MOLTMANN-WENDEL: *Die weiblichkeit des Geistes. Studien zur Feministischen Theologie*, Gütersloh 1995.

[57] LUKKEN: *De onvervangbare weg van de liturgie* 81-85; IDEM: 'Church and Liturgy as Dynamic Sacrament of the Spirit', in LUKKEN (eds. CASPERS & VAN TONGEREN); *Per visibilia ad invisibilia* 140-157.

[58] Regarding the Spirit and inculturation of the liturgy, see TRIACCA: "Incultur-azione e liturgia': eventi dello Spirito Santo'.

[59] 'Veni Sancte Spiritus': *Analecta hymnica* 54 (1922) 234.

The absolute love of God comes to light in the paradox of the Easter mystery: the *inaestimabilis dilectio caritatis* of which the Easter hymn *Exsultet* speaks.[60] There one finds the core of the radical break and reversal. In and through his resurrection from the dead Jesus of Nazareth became the prototype of the new man, in whom the Spirit of God breaks through completely and becomes visible. In this risen, pneumatological man the tension of the break between anthropology and theology is resolved. God's grace appears in an unconcealed manner in his imperishable corporality. He is the ultimate, the eschatological man in whom the divine light of the other side shines clearly, 'light of light' (*lumen de lumine*). His Spirit-filled corporality recognises no boundaries and no barriers of space and time. He is that Lord, filled by the Spirit, who is revealed in and through Christian ritual. It is inseparable from the Easter mystery that he is now already pouring out his Spirit over all flesh and that this Spirit is renewing the face of the earth. As such his new existence touches the figurative screen of ritual itself and opens it up for the Christian dimension. In the screen of Christian ritual one can thus say there is a *break and reversal of the second degree*.

The Easter mystery will only come to full completion with the resurrection of the dead, at the end of time. Here we encounter the mystery of *our resurrection*, which calls up questions on the part of many today. Because these questions are so essential for the experience of the Easter mystery as the core of Christian ritual, it is important to go into this further.

Questions regarding the resurrection directly touch on our own future. We experience that most pointedly whenever we are confronted with death. What has happened to the deceased person will happen to us all. Each time that again raises the question: what is after that? One finds quite a few basic images that also appear in the Scripture and Christian liturgy. I listed them above: the light that dawns, daybreak, burgeoning spring, the land on the other shore, a vast landscape with flowing water, the land that is always greener behind the hills.[61] One

---

[60] For the *Exsultet*, see among others: H.-J. AUF DER MAUR: 'Die österliche Lichtdanksagung. Zum liturgischen Ort und zur Textgestalt des Exsultet', in *Liturgisches Jahrbuch* 21 (1971) 38-52; G. FUCHS & H.M. WEIKMAN: *Das Exsultet. Geschichte, Theologie und Gestaltung der österlichen Lichtdanksagung*, Regensburg 1992; LUKKEN: 'Lichtfeier der Osternacht'; IDEM: 'Das Osterlob als Vollzug des Paschamysteriums', in *Jaarboek voor liturgie-onderzoek* 17 (2001) 73-106.

[61] See above Part 3, Chapter 8, 1.5.

can add to these, the city set upon the hill, the house of peace, the marriage feast, the land where the lion lies down with the lamb and the
child plays safely next to the adder's den, paradise, the grain of wheat
that falls into the earth and dies, thus bringing forth fruit, seeing our
loved ones again, the worship of the Lamb by the elect, clad in white
robes, entry into the heavenly Jerusalem.

Our future is always conceived in symbols of all sorts. Some would
say that these are *just* symbols, that the future we conceive is essentially
an unreal world, our projection and fantasy. But then one does not take
the symbolic world seriously enough. Symbols refer to a reality that can
only be expressed in and conceived through images. Of course it is true
that on the last day (itself already a metaphor) no angels will sound
trumpets, and that the elect will not be literally to the right and the
reprobate to the left of a throne. And yet, these images touch in an
arresting way on what this is all about: the reality of the merciful judgement of God is difficult to conceive other than through these images.[62]
We are constantly finding new images. Here I would have you reread
the quote from the Dutch writer Van het Reve that I cited in Part 1:

> I would hope that after this it is sufficiently clear to you that I travel to get
> somewhere, and by no means for the pleasure of the trip itself. If God for
> once is going to be 'all in all', it seems to me that must imply that every-
> one will be within walking distance, so that, in a manner of speaking, you
> never have to go anywhere any more. That will be the most amazing thing
> yet that we, in giving up our separation from Him, will get to see: the
> Kingdom of God will look surprisingly like a village, not much bigger
> than Schoorl: calm weather; making small talk; a man smoking his pipe at
> the back door; watching the clouds go by. Peace, no quarrels: there is
> already so much trouble in the world. As I said.[63]

As I said. Reve felicitously expresses in images what the Kingdom of
God is all about. Yet thinking more reflectively about our resurrection
can also be enlightening.[64] The Bible speaks of the resurrection of the
flesh and the resurrection of the body. What is meant by this? In the
Bible flesh and body do not mean the biological cells of the human
body, pure and simple. In the Jewish world both the term flesh and the

---

[62] FORTMANN: *Hoogtijd* 106-107.
[63] VAN HET REVE: *Op weg naar het einde* 68-69.
[64] See, also for the following, L.-M. CHAUVET: 'Sur quelques difficultés actuelles de
l' 'au-delà", in *La Maison-Dieu* (1998) 213, 33-58.

term body stood for the whole of the human person, subject to suffering and death. The Jewish view of our corporality lies close to that of
contemporary anthropology, which no longer speaks dualistically of the
soul as that which is immortal and the body as a mortal prison of the
soul. It instead sees man in his integrity as a corporeal being which, precisely as such, is connected with others in the past and present and with
the cosmos. Without this connection one cannot be human. Thus resurrection of the flesh or of the body is about me, myself, as a unique
corporeal individual in connection with others and the cosmos. It is as
such that a person is resurrected from the dead after death, and lives further in God. This is a living on of the I, including countless relations
with others and the world. There is thus both continuity and discontinuity with personal existence here and now: continuity, because it is
about the same unique person, and not about being dissolved in God or
in the great All and Nothing of Nirvana at the end of a long series of
reincarnations, as in Buddhism; discontinuity, because it involves a real
new existence. This is aptly expressed in an anecdote which is told of
someone who had undergone a near-death experience, but returned to
life. When asked what it was like there, he answered 'Entirely different.'
    In Christian faith, the concepts of personal and general judgement
are inextricably linked with the passage from death to resurrection. Both
touch on the image of God as judge. Is that idea not in conflict with the
concept of God as love? One can say three things at this point. First, it
would be strange that the passage for a murderer would be the same as
that of his victim. Justice is inseparably connected with our being
human. Next, what is at issue here is justice, not revenge. And finally, it
would be evidence of imperfection if God did not take human responsibility seriously.
    Now, judgement affects one first as an individual. At the end of life
everybody will separately judged on their love for their brothers and sisters. One should read the beatitudes in Matthew 25. After death and the
purification that possibly must take place (the essence of the classic image
of purgatory is a loving purification in the face of God's holiness), there is
in a sense already an individual resurrection. But resurrection also has a
collective side. It remains in process so long as history is not yet complete.
In that sense the resurrection of the individual after his or her death is not
yet complete, precisely because we are corporeal beings connected in a
fundamental way with others and with the cosmos. This is expressed
in the image of general judgement at the end of time. So long as sacred

history is not entirely complete, heaven continues to grow. That is also
true for the Lord himself, the first-born among the dead. Although He
rose on Easter, it is also true that his resurrection is still unfinished. Thus
it is true that the dead are raised after their death (the personal aspect),
but at the same time it is true that they still await their resurrection (the
social aspect). The individual's bliss is not apart from that of all. There still
remains the difficult question of whether one can still speak of a hell: the
individual who for all time will be completely imprisoned in himself. Personally, I have just as much difficulty with that dark side of the Easter
mystery as Origen, who in the third century spoke of the possibility of
only a temporary hell. Others, however, see hell as the tragic metaphor for
human freedom, and speak of their hope that hell will be empty.

6. WHAT IS UNIQUE ABOUT CHRISTIAN RITUAL

When one asks about the peculiar place and shape of Christian ritual in
our pluriform culture, one must begin with the observation that Christian
ritual can penetrate this culture deeply. It has the characteristics of all ritual, including the ritual of our contemporary culture. It stands open to,
and includes the shape of our culture. Through this openness to and
rootage in contemporary culture it takes on a face which is recognisable
for, and can be experienced by believers today. Christian ritual cannot
retain its identity by jumping over culture. It is always incarnate in a particular culture. Therefore Christian ritual has a changing shape, and we in
our culture are in search of a new shape for this ritual. Moreover, we in
our culture have become aware that there are many systems of meaning.
It is no longer the case that people can defend the peculiar nature of
Christianity by excluding other religions and systems of meaning. Christian ritual does not derive its peculiar identity from excluding other meaningful rituals. The question is no longer so much whether Christ is so
unique that He must be termed exclusive, so much so that outside of Him
no salvation is possible. It is impermissible to speak of an exclusive Christology. One must be careful with absolutising pronouncements about
Christianity.[65] 'Who in fact accepts that all those other religions, particu-

[65] SCHILLEBEECKX: 'Cultuur, godsdienst en geweld' 387-404, particularly 401; W.
LOGISTER: 'Voorbij de apartheid. Enkele gedachten over interreligieus leren en leven', in
Werkmap (voor) Liturgie 28 (1994) 320-327.

larly those old, honourable religions with their rich past, have nothing to do with our God? Those other religions that we encounter every day, on the street and on television; they have become a very nearby reality for us. (…) For countless people, Hinduism or Islam appear to be the way to God. Must we not leave it to God how He puts people on his track?'[66] In our culture we have also become aware that Christian ritual may not exclude any authentic contemporary ritual that helps people make sense of life. One should recognise these other rituals in their individuality and contextual authenticity. Christian ritual has absolutely no hegemony over other rituals which impart meaning, and can not decree how these must be. On the contrary: Christian ritual has its place and shape in the midst of all other rituals. The unobtrusiveness of Christian ritual also fits in our pluriform culture. But at the same time it is true that it does not merge into these other rituals, or that there is a radical ritual pluralism.[67] The books about Jesus cannot just be indiscriminately put next to all sorts of other books about religious figures or books about Celestine promises or other do-it-yourself religious books.[68] Socrates and Jesus both represent ways of dealing with transcendence, but you can not resolve these two completely different ways of being human into one another. Accepting and taking seriously other particular ways of thinking in no way has to exclude Christian faith being a serious and entirely unique alternative in the midst of the others.[69] The same is true for Christian rituals. In the

[66] J. BLUYSSEN: *Gebroken wit. Vrijmoedige herinneringen*, Baarn 1995, 303. See also LOGISTER: 'Voorbij de apartheid'; INTERNATIONAL THEOLOGICAL COMMISSION: *Christianity and the World Religions*, Città del Vaticano 1997 = 'Het christendom en de godsdiensten, Rome 1996', in *Een-twee-een. Kerkelijke documentatie* 25 (1997) 7.

[67] In this connection see T. MERRIGAN: 'De geschiedenis van Jezus in haar actuele betekenis. De uitdaging van het pluralisme', in *Tijdschrift voor Theologie* 34 (1994) 407-429. For the discussion in connection with radical pluralism in theology see further, among others: C. CORNILLE & V. NECKEBROUCK (eds.): *A Universal Faith? Cultures, Religions and the Christ*, Leuven 1992; CH. GILLIS: *Pluralism. A New Paradigm for Theology*, Leuven 1993; R. HILLE & E. TROEGER (eds.): *Die Einzigartigkeit Jesu Christi als Grundfrage der Theologie und missionarische Herausforderung*, Wuppertal/Zürich/Giessen/Basel 1993.

[68] G. VAN OYEN: '"Jezus redt… alle mensen opgelet'. Over de band tussen christologie en onderzoek naar Jezus', in *Tijdschrift voor Theologie* 37 (1997) 332; VAN DEN BOSSCHE: 'Geen wijn in water veranderen'. Van den Bossche properly critiques the book by DE VISSCHER: *Een te voltooien leven* on this point. See also P. POST: 'Rijke oogst: literatuurbericht liturgiewetenschap', in *Praktische Theologie* 26 (1999) 100-102.

[69] Van den Bossche: 'Geen wijn in water veranderen'. Sometimes the discontinuity is then still so strongly stressed that, in my opinion, the 'in the midst of other rituals' fades too much. For the discussion surrounding the subject, see *The Presence of God in*

midst of other rituals they have their own irreplaceable identity: that of
the paradox of the Easter mystery. In Christian ritual the perspective
jumps radically to what was and is poured out by God, to what is pure
givenness and grace, centrally in Jesus of Nazareth through his Spirit. In
Christian ritual human intentionality is ultimately determined by a new
attraction from above: 'No one can come unto me unless the Father who
sent me draws him' (John 6:44).[70] It is the Spirit, who according to an old
prayer 'illuminates our heart and our senses', which is definitive: the
power of attraction from above reaches deep into human affectivity. In
every Christian ritual there is the history of the Easter mystery as the radical revelation of God's love, of the new man as a pure gift. It is in that
which Christians find the ultimate, decisive meaning of their life. In the
midst of the here and now there is the absolute breakthrough of divine
initiative. The rising line which is also essential for Christians is here broken in a radical way by the divine initiative of the descending line.
Already at the birth of a child, that the child will not be irretrievably lost
in a world of suffering and death, but is included in the mystery of suffering, death and resurrection is confessed and celebrated in baptism. 'Or
don't you know that all of us who were baptised into Christ Jesus were
baptised into his death? We were therefore buried with him through baptism into death in order that, just as Christ was raised from the death
trough the glory of the Father, we too may live a new life. If we have been
united with him like this in his death, we will certainly also be united
with him in his resurrection' (Rom. 6:3-5). The anamnesis of the Easter
mystery will repeat itself again and again in Christian ritual, in its own
way and with its own accent in each ritual.

---

a Postmodern Context; *Life Cycle Rituals and Sacramentality: Between Continuity and Discontinuity*. The discontinuity is stressed by H. GEIJBELS: 'Algemeen menselijk of eigen
christelijk. Rituelen en de identiteit van religies', in *Tijdschrift voor Theologie* 41 (2001)
3, 221-230 and G. DANNEELS: 'Rituelen in, sacramenten out?', in *Tijdschrift voor
Liturgie* 86 (2002) 306-322.

[70] See in this connection what E. Schillebeeckx writes in his article 'Naar een
herontdekking van de christelijke sacramenten' regarding the relation between *opus
operatum* and *opus operantis*: 'The *opus operantis* is an essential part of the *opus operatum*, and not something which is added to it, because the whole of both aspects is precisely the performance that is the mediator of Gods gracious approach. The *opus operantis is the opus operatum ...*' (p. 178). Further on in the same article: 'The
meaningful ritual whole as human expression and vehicle for the vitalisation of faith
for all who take part, as a church and as individuals, *is* the concrete gift of grace' (p.
180).

If Christian rituals from birth to death are able to inculturate themselves, they will remain a distinctive system of providing meaning, one for which there is no possible replacement, in the midst of others. Particularly in and through the Easter and Pentecost mystery general human ritual receives a new dimension. It becomes like the window of a Gothic cathedral – transfiguring windows, as it were, in which Christian sacred history is illuminated. The transparency of these windows is in all degrees. Divine presence manifests itself in eucharistic ritual, in the eucharistic performance, the eucharistic transfiguration, in a more penetrating way than in a simple gesture of blessing.[71] There can also be all sorts of differences in emphasis in other ways. Sometimes in Christian ritual the stress will be on 'realised eschatology', the eschatological in the present, on the 'now already' of participation in the Easter mystery. But a 'non-realised eschatology' can equally be stressed, an 'only barely seeing sometimes' and a 'not yet'. This will emerge precisely in the shaping of the ritual itself among believers. In the case of an accent on realised eschatology, people will strive to make the 'filmy mirror' of the ritual as clear and transparent as possible, so to speak. Think of the ceremony of light on Easter Saturday night, in which in a very impressive way the new light gradually is intensified, and ultimately, when all the candles are lit, the words of the *Exsultet* are sung in a lyric manner, '*This is the night* that shines like day', 'O truly blessed night, that reconciles heaven and earth, that binds God and man'.[72] As was noted earlier, realised eschatology can also be characteristic for certain liturgies. Think of Eastern liturgies, in comparison to those of the West, and think of the medieval liturgy in comparison with current liturgy, which undoubtedly rather emphasises the opacity of the figurative screen.

7. THE AMBIGUITY OF CHRISTIAN RITUAL

In Part 1 I discussed at length the strength and weakness of ritual, including Christian ritual in that discussion.[73] Christian ritual does not

---

[71] In this context the approach to eucharistic presence through concepts such as transfiguration and transfinalisation is more adequate than the concept of transubstantiation. Central to the Eucharist is an optimal transfiguration.

[72] LUKKEN: 'Lichtfeier der Osternacht' and IDEM: 'Das Osterlob als Vollzug des Paschamysteriums'.

[73] See Part 1, chapter 3, 7.

escape the ambiguity which characterises all ritual. It was precisely for this reason that the prophets strongly criticised ritual. Have you never read Amos (5:21-26): 'I hate, I despise your religious feasts; I cannot stand your assemblies. Even though you bring me burnt offerings and grain offerings, I will not accept them. Though you bring choice fellowship offerings, I will have no regard for them. Away with the noise of your songs! I will not listen to the music of your harps. But let justice roll on like a river, righteousness like a never-failing stream!' Do we not hear this again and again? (See Hosea 6:1-6; Micah 6:5-8; Isaiah 1:10-16; 29:13-15; 58:1-8; Jeremiah 6:20; 7:1-15; Ecclesiasticus 34:18-26 etc.) And did not Jesus himself drive the money-changers and sellers of animals for offerings from the temple (Mark 11:15-17)? Indeed, Christian liturgy can also function in a negative way. But this does not detract from the fact that in and through an authentic liturgy and genuine participation, sacred history develops in the most impressive manner. Where the liturgy is celebrated with a sincere heart, it is pleasing to JHWH, and it is a blessing for Israel (Ecclesiasticus 35:1-10). For Jesus the temple was the house of the Father (John 2:16), where he teaches (Luke 19:47, 21:37, 22:53; John 7:14, 10:24, 18:20). And, according to the New Testament, the congregation of the elect is first and foremost a liturgical community, in which people are included through baptism (Acts 2:38-41, 47, 8:1, 10:48, 19:16, 22:16), and which as such reaches its climax in the breaking of the bread (Acts 2:42, 46, 20:7, 11).

In part for the sake of the authenticity of Christian ritual, there is a necessity for a *liturgia semper reformanda*: a liturgy which constantly must be renewed and tested for its authenticity.

8. TOWARD UNITY IN DIVERSITY

From the beginning there was great diversity in Christian liturgy. It was marked by the peculiar qualities of the local churches. That was the case not only in the East, but also in the West. There one had, for instance, the Gallic, Celtic, Ambrosian and Old Spanish or Visigothic liturgies. Ultimately however one liturgy gained the upper hand in the West: the Roman, which blended with others to become the Roman-Frankish-Germanic liturgy, which however also had its variants from city to city, and even from church to church. But slowly this Western liturgy was brought into uniformity, which reached its apex in the 16th century (Council of Trent). Only after the Second Vatican Council would this liturgy gradually take on greater pluriformity again.

Yet this is only a partial story, because one can only speak of uniformity in liturgy between Trent and Vatican II if one only considers the Catholic Church. The fact of the matter is that precisely in the same period of uniformity there arose other Christian liturgies. In its inception the uniform Roman liturgy was defined by the split in Western Christianity, which in the course of the 16th century fell into Catholic and Protestant factions. Thus the diversity did not disappear. On the contrary, new Christian liturgies appeared which bore the fundamental stamp of the Reformation confessions; these were chiefly the liturgies of the Lutheran, Reformed and Anglican churches. Thus diversity continued to exist, but the tragedy was that it was a diversity which was accompanied by a shattered unity. The differences became unbridgeable dividing lines.

Only in our own century did a movement get under way that strove for the restoration of this broken unity. The realisation grew that the division of the churches, precisely as communities that mutually excluded one another in their liturgies, did unimaginable harm to the credibility of Christian liturgy. Both innovative theological reflection and changes in liturgical practice stimulated the efforts toward a new unity. With regard to The Netherlands, an important step toward unity was taken in the 1960s. The controversy which arose around the conditional rebaptism of Princess Irene by Cardinal Alfrink hastened the process considerably. Beginning in 1967 the Catholic and Protestant churches arrived at a mutual recognition of the validity of each other's baptism: in 1967 with the Dutch Reformed Church, in 1968 with the Reformed Churches in The Netherlands and the Evangelical Lutheran Church, and in 1974 with the Remonstrant Brotherhood. That laid the fundamental basis for growth toward further liturgical unity. After the mutual recognition of baptism the questions of intercommunion and church offices became central. Gradually people began to realise that the liturgical structure of the Eucharist as such really implied the acknowledgement and acceptance of communion with all other Christian communities which celebrated Eucharist. Disunity in this respect is even *de jure* intolerable because precisely on the basis of the Eucharist Christians lay claim to unity and solidarity. One can only speak of real unity when members of various churches also have the right to participate in one another's liturgy, and clergy also have the right to preside in the other church. Internationally the theological harmony took form in the declaration on baptism, Eucharist and ministry from the Commission on Faith and Order of the World Council of Churches (Lima, Peru, 1982).[74] It is clear that the intellectual dialogue on Eucharist and ministry is already far advanced. This is also true for The Netherlands, where the *Eindrapport van de commissie Maaltijd des Heren en kerkelijk ambt* (Final report of the committee on the Lord's Supper and ecclesiastical office) appeared in 1989.[75] This document makes it clear that a large measure of agreement exists with regard to central liturgical core concepts.[76] On some points the dialogue is not entirely conclusive. This is particularly the case for discussion on the sacrifice, on the relation between human and divine action, the continuing presence in the Eucharist, and ordination and offices. Recent international literature however reveals that on these points too the parties are coming to better understanding of one another.[77] The process will undoubtedly be carried further. The question in all of this is whether the time has not slowly come to acknowledge that one must also do justice to the various theological spiritualities which are related to various traditions and religious subcultures. For instance, the one will emphasise God's transcendence more, while the other His immanence, and that obviously has repercussions for thinking about relation between the divine and human/ecclesiastical liturgical acts. This often involves more differences of accent that reflect the characteristic spirituality.

---

[74] WORLD COUNCIL OF CHURCHES: *Baptism, Eucharist and Ministry* (Faith and Order Papers 111), Geneva 1982.

[75] COMMISSIE MAALTIJD DES HEREN EN KERKELIJKE AMBT: 'Eindrapport, analyse van de liturgische teksten aangaande maaltijd en ambt, een studie', in *Een-twee-een. Kerkelijke documentatie* 17 (1989) 1.

[76] In this context, what A. Bodar wrote in *Trouw* on June 13, 1998, under the title 'Eet en drinkt U geen oordeel' (Do not eat and drink judgement upon yourself) is all the more remarkable: 'If you still desire to participate in the Eucharist while you are a Protestant, simply become a member of the Church of Rome.'

[77] W. PANNENBERG (ed.): *Lehrverurteilungen – kirchentrennend?*, III: *Materialien zur Lehre von den Sakramenten und vom kirchlichen Amt*, Freiburg/Göttingen 1990. With regard to the presence of Christ in the Eucharist, the doctrine of transubstantiation and what is being called transfinalisation, from the Protestant side see N. SLENCZKA: *Realpräsenz und Ontologie. Untersuchungen der ontologischen Grundlagen der Transsignifikationslehre*, Göttingen 1993 and from the Catholic side FITZPATRICK: *In Breaking the Bread*.

More important yet than the theological overtures is the mutual recognition of one another in the liturgical form of the Eucharist itself. In the design of the Eucharist Christian churches are moving toward one another in surprising ways, so much so that the Lord's Supper and Eucharist are beginning to visibly and concretely resemble one another. The Catholic altar has become a table, while the Protestant communion table has become a place of honour. Catholics are beginning to receive both bread *and* cup again, while the Reformer's pulpit is brought more in balance with the communion table. It is relevant in this context that on the basis of the Lima report *Baptism, Eucharist and Ministry* a liturgy has been designed that in its plan does not really differ from the Catholic Eucharist celebration.[78] In The Netherlands there is intensive ongoing discussion on the lectionary, and the churches are beginning to use one another's prayers and songs more and more. A joint *Dienstboek* (Liturgy) appeared for the Samen-op-Weg churches (now formally united as the Protestant Church in The Netherlands), in which all the eucharistic prayers have the basic structure of our common tradition.[79] Thus the mutual recognition and acknowledgement has reached all the way to the most central text of the Eucharist, the eucharistic prayer. From this perspective it is not surprising that believers have arrived at the point where they have begun to participate in each other's eucharistic celebrations. This happens frequently at the congregational level. In the experience believers in a certain sense unerringly intuit the correspondence between their own faith and that which the celebration itself expresses. It was therefore remarkable when in 1998, on the occasion of the marriage of Prince Maurits and Marilène van den Broek, the participation in the Catholic Eucharist by members of the Protestant Dutch royal house, caused so much of a commotion in official ecclesiastical circles.[80] This is all the more true because it was nothing new for them. For years Prince Bernhard had received communion whenever he was visiting his mother,

---

[78] See the appendix of WORLD COUNCIL OF CHURCHES: *Baptism, Eucharist and Ministry.*

[79] *Dienstboek. Een proeve: Schrift, Maaltijd, Gebed,* Zoetermeer 1998. See G. LUKKEN: 'Het nieuwe dienstboek van de Samen-op-Weg-kerken: een onvervangbare weg voor de oecumene', in *Praktische Theologie* 26 (1999) 4. Particularly relevant for this liturgical ecumenism is the appearance of the manual by OSKAMP & SCHUMAN (eds.): *De weg van de liturgie.* See in this connection P. POST: 'De synthese in de huidige liturgiewetenschap. Proeve van positionering van *De weg van de liturgie*', in *Jaarboek voor liturgie-onderzoek* 14 (1998) 141-172.

[80] G. LUKKEN: 'Vorstelijke oecumene', in *Eredienstvaardig* 14 (1998) 4, 106-109.

Princess Armgard, who had converted to Catholicism and lived in The Netherlands, and Queen Juliana and Prince Bernhard received not only at the marriage of their daughter Christina with Guillermo, but also when they participated with them or with their daughter princess Irene in a Catholic liturgy. Moreover, Reformed clergy themselves also participated in Catholic celebrations of the Eucharist, when the opportunity presented itself, and priests, for their part, had participated in Protestant Lord's Supper services. At the marriage of Prince Maurits and Marilène the Catholic and Reformed worship leaders had waived a joint active role in the eucharistic prayer. This goes further than open communion, in the sense that the issue becomes whether two churches permit their worship leaders to mutually administer the Eucharist or Lord's Supper – what is termed intercelebration. Although to a lesser degree than open communion, this intercelebration also takes place at the congregational level too. Sometimes it even occurs very publicly. For instance, during the German Catholic Days at Mainz in 1998 a Catholic priest and a Lutheran pastor jointly led an ecumenical Eucharist celebration. Whatever the case, within the Catholic church neither open communion nor intercelebration is officially permitted. With regard to open communion, while a number of denominations in The Netherlands descended from the Reformation have and promote open participation in the Supper, that is not the case from the Catholic side. The judgement of the Catholic Church is that participation in the Eucharist for Protestants will only be possible if and when the eucharistic dialogue is concluded (including dialogue on ordained offices) and Catholics also must not participate in the Supper. According to the Catholic Church eucharistic communion must be an expression of full unity, and cannot be regarded as a possible way toward that unity.[81] Only in exceptional cases can a bishop give Protestants permission to receive communion – and this is limited at this moment to, for instance, the Protestant groom at the celebration of a 'mixed marriage'.[82] On the

---

[81] This standpoint was once again emphatically formulated in the encyclical of JOHANNES PAULUS II: *Ecclesia de Eucharistia*, Città del Vaticano 2003.

[82] See in this connection for instance: CATHOLIC BISHOP'S CONFERENCES OF ENGLAND & WALES, IRELAND, AND SCOTLAND: *One Body, A Teaching Document on the Eucharist in the Life of the Church and the Establishment of General Norms on Sacramental Sharing*, London/Dublin 1998, no. 111; NEDERLANDSE BISSCHOPPENCONFERENTIE: Verklaring over intercommunie, in *Een-twee-een. Kerkelijke documentatie* 27 (1999) no. 7, 33-34; RAAD VAN KERKEN IN NEDERLAND: *Intercommunie. Het assymetrische geloofsgesprek tussen protestanten en katholieken*, Zoetermeer 1999.

point of eucharistic participation, according to this standpoint unity is only possible when theological-noetic and institutional unity is also achieved. This institutional attitude leads to violation of the rules at the congregational level in the Church. Hopefully the rules will be further adapted. The commotion surrounding the marriage of Prince Maurits and Princess Marilène could be a stimulus for faster progress in ecumenism, as was the case after the provisional rebaptism of Princess Irene. This then touches on the theological approaches and further adjustments in the rules. But it reaches further. We must arrive at a new accent in ecumenism. The fact is that the standpoint that one must first wait for complete unanimity in the theological dialogue or the achievement of full ecclesiastical/institutional community is certainly open to dispute.[83] Alongside the intellectual/institutional approach there is the liturgical approach, and this undoubtedly has solid precedents in Christian tradition. One can note that in five of the current official Roman Eucharistic Prayers the Holy Spirit is asked to draw us closer to one another and heal divisions precisely through the very sharing of the eucharistic bread and wine.[84] Alas, in recent centuries the noetic approach has often prevailed over the liturgical path. We lost sight of the fact that the liturgy is a unique and irreplaceable source for theology. Secondary orthodoxy (correct doctrine) has prevailed over primary orthodoxy (correct praise – for that is the original meaning of the word 'orthodoxy'). But the most primary way within the Christian church in our day too is primary orthodoxy: the liturgical way of life. Is it not much better to celebrate the Eucharist together and on the basis of that experience continue our thinking? It is then a matter of ecumenical re-flection in the chronological sense, too. This liturgical conviction touches on the broader insight from contemporary philosophy that 'the symbol itself makes you think' (Ricoeur). One can quite rightly ask if we do not often stand closer to one another in worship than is expressed in the formulation of doctrinal pronouncements.[85] Should we not then first take our liturgical traditions and

---

[83] MEYER: *Eucharistie* 479. See also the discussion on the occasion of the 50th anniversary of the St. Willibrord Association on June 12, 1998. Only a small minority endorsed the proposition 'Liturgy is *not* a means toward unity.'

[84] M.E. JOHNSON: 'A Response to Gerard Austin's "Identity of a Eucharistic Church in an Ecumenical Age"', in *Worship* 72 (1998) 39-40; for G. AUSTIN: 'Identity of a Eucharistic Church in an Ecumenical Age', see *Worship* 72 (1998) no. 1, 26-35.

[85] K. SCHLEMMER (ed.): *Gottesdienst – Weg zur Einheit. Impulse für die Ökumene*, Freiburg/Basel/Wien 1989.

contemporary liturgical practice as our point of departure more than we usually do? One here encounters a decidedly weak point in the ecumenical discussion.

The growth of liturgical unity will in no way say that all differences in liturgical forms will disappear. As in the realm of intellectual debate there will remain various theologies that are all legitimate, so the form of the liturgy itself will remain pluriform. The goal is unity in diversity.

9. TO FIND SALVATION AND HEALING

From time immemorial the classic Roman prefaces have begun with the words 'To find salvation and healing...'. Salvation and healing: that is the familiar theme in the classic Roman liturgy.

Particularly in the second and third centuries the young church developed a view of salvation in which the figure of Christ as physician took a central place. This development paralleled the veneration of Aesculapius, the pagan saviour and physician, which had spread across the Roman empire. In a certain sense, the influence of Aesculapius reaches down to our time: the red snake coiled around a staff, which is the identifying symbol for medical doctors, is derived from the cult of Aesculapius. Over against Aesculapius the Christians placed Christ as the true physician. Harnack remarks that the gospel came into the world as a message of salvation for the whole of a person, and that in the first centuries the Christians considered the church as a great healing institution, as a hospital for mankind, in which the Church's actions were accounted the remedies.[86] In the fourth and fifth centuries the medical model for salvation had become passé, but Augustine revived this terminology by connecting it with the group of words surrounding *salus* (save), to which the medical significance still adhered. This set up interference: the words with salvation took on a more concrete content through the medical terms, and the medical words took on a more Christian depth

---

[86] A. HARNACK: *Medizinisches aus der ältesten Kirchengeschichte* (Texte und Untersuchungen 8), Leipzig 1892; revised edition in A. HARNACK: *Mission und Ausbreitung des Christentums in den ersten drei Jahrhunderten, Vol. 1: Die Mission im Wort und Tat*, Leipzig 1906², 87-107; M. ELLEBRACHT: *Remarks on the Vocabulary of the Ancient Orations in the Missale Romanum* (Latinitas christianorum primaeva 18), Nijmegen 1963, 178; P. EYKENBOOM: *Het Christus-Medicusmotief in de preken van Augustinus*, Assen 1960, XVI-XIX.

through the 'salvation' terminology.[87] Because of this, often when the classic Roman liturgy speaks of our 'salvation' happening in our present circumstances, or of our 'healing' in and through the liturgy, this has a comprehensive significance. Both words imply the health of the whole of a human being. Oosterhuis was quite correct then in translating the word *salutare*, which appears in the invariable introductory formula of all the Roman prefaces, with 'in order to find salvation and healing'. That is in the spirit of the old liturgy. Christian liturgy is not purely about an esoteric and intangible salvation, apart from mankind. It is about salvation that permeates the whole of a person. It is about a salvific healing or a healing salvation, because Christian ritual touches the depths of a person's injured being, and returns them to integrity. It also has to do with our psychological wellbeing. Fortmann observes that ancient religion never made the distinction between the health that it expected from surrender to the divinity and that which we today would call psychological health. It was about the restoration of inward unity, the healing of the divisions in the person.[88] Today Christian ritual is still oriented to this restoration of inward unity.

This has important consequences for the relation between Christian liturgy and the anthropology of ritual. Here again it appears that there is no competition between the two. What we said about the beneficial effect of ritual in general and about the salubrity of Christian ritual mesh with each other. The anthropology of ritual is a necessary basis for Christian ritual. In that sense too it is true that the grace supposes nature (*gratia supponit naturam*). But it is also true that genuine Christian ritual can contribute to a more decent life and a more humane society. Precisely the peculiar identity of Christian ritual can contribute to that. One must take in what was said about the political dimension of Christian ritual and the dynamic of the Spirit. Also, the creative shaping itself of the liturgy within a particular culture is of significance for that culture in general. That is patiently obvious for the past, as will appear from the current musealisation of Christian culture. One can expect that giving shape to the liturgy in contemporary culture will also bear its fruit for this culture in general, probably in a more modest way than before, but perhaps in an all the more essential way. In the midst of the abundance of rituals there is an intensive interaction, but at the same

---

[87] EYKENBOOM: *Het Christus-Medicusmotief.*
[88] H. FORTMANN: *Als ziende de onzienlijke*, part 3b, 88.

time it is true that in the midst of the abundance Christian ritual continues to search for its own identity.

AFTERWORD

Our term 'church' comes from the Greek *ekklèsia*. This Greek word originally referred to the public meeting of free citizens of a city. This secular/Hellenistic background remains present in the biblical word 'church' as the term for the concrete local community of Christians who come together.[89] The idea of a city (*polis*) is thus included in the characterisation of the church precisely as the community which assembles in liturgy. With that there is also a specific eschatological accent, which alludes to the city that is to come, in the awareness that we do not have an enduring city here (Heb. 13:14). But there is something of that future here already, for we have come already to the heavenly Jerusalem, the city of the living God... the joyful assembly of the firstborn (Heb. 12:22-23).

The future city of which today's community coming together in liturgy is a prefiguration, is sketched as the ideal Hellenistic city. It will always be bright there, for the glory of God himself will give it light (Rev. 21:23-24; 22:5). There are no clouds, the sky is always clear. It is the perfection of the ideal of Hellenistic urban planning and architecture. The walls of this heavenly city have gates that are always open (Rev. 21:25). There is no need to bolt gates shut for the sake of safety. The gaze is turned inward, to life within the city walls. While in Eastern and Greek cities the shrine or shrines lay in the centre of the city, and the city was oriented to them, the Hellenistic city was a secular city. It was defined by its population. With its streets and squares it was a place where people assembled and communicated with one another. The new Jerusalem is an open, democratic city.[90] For us, living in an urban society, it is not difficult to respond to this utopian image of the future city. We could in our own way sketch the ideal variants defined

---

[89] WANNENWETSCH: *Gottesdienst als Lebensform* 153-154, and the literature, listed there.

[90] WANNENWETSCH: *Gottesdienst als Lebensform* 155, with reference to D. GEORGI: 'Die Visionen vom himmlischen Jerusalem in Apk. 21 und 22', in D. LÜHRMANN & G. STERCKER: *Kirche. Festschrift für Günther Bornkamm*, Tübingen 1980, 353-372.

by our culture. Whatever the case, the urban liturgical community is a foreshadowing of this future urbane society. It too is an open, democratic, pluriform community, collected out of all nations, brought together harmoniously from all possible economic, political and social contexts. They are already realising now something of our future – which at the same time implies that all that we do and create is but for the interim: the liturgy of the past and present is, to put it in the words of Augustine, only the scaffolding of the heavenly city that is our hope.[91]

---

[91] AUGUSTINE: *Sermo* 362, 7: PL 39, 1615.

BIBLIOGRAPHY

ACHTERBERG, G.: *Ode aan Den Haag*, 's-Gravenhage 1953

ACHTERBERG, G.: *Verzamelde gedichten*, Amsterdam 1985

ADOLFS, R. (ed.): *Buiten-dienst. Informele samenkomsten buiten de kerkmuren*, Baarn 1969

AIXALA, J. (ed.): *Other Apostolates Today: Selected Letters and Adr.*, St. Louis 1981

AKKER, P. VAN DEN: *Het laatste bedrijf. Over waarden, handelingen en rituelen bij sterven, dood en uitvaart*, Tilburg 1995

ALBERT, J.-P.: *Odeurs de sainteté: la mythologie chrétienne des aromates*, Paris 1990

ALDAZÁBAL, J.: 'Lecciones de la historia sobre la inculturación', in *Phase* (1995) 96-100

ALEXANDER, B.C.: 'Ritual and Current Studies of Ritual', in S.D. GLAZIER: *Anthropology of Religion: a Handbook*, Westport Conn./London 1997, 139-160

ALLEN, J.L., Jr.: 'Rome', in *National Catholic Reporter*, November 16, 2001

ALTIZER, T.J.J.: *The Gospel of Christian Atheism*, Philadelphia 1966

ALTIZER, T.J.J. & W. HAMILTON: *Radical Theology and the Death of God*, Indianapolis/New York/Kansas City 1966

AMAFILI, L.: 'Inculturation: its Etymology and Problems', in *Questions Liturgiques* 73 (1992) 170-188

AMALORPAVADASS, D.S.: 'Theological reflections on inculturation (Part 1)', in *Studia Liturgica* 20 (1990) 36-54

AMALORPAVADASS, D.S.: 'Theological reflections on inculturation (Part 2)', in *Studia Liturgica* 20 (1990) 116-136

AMSTERDAM, M. VAN: *Hoe welkom zijn op de bergen de voeten van de vreugdebode (Jesaja 52, 7)... Dans binnen de liturgie...?* (Liturgie in perspectief 4), Baarn 1995

AMSTERDAM, M. VAN: 'Over lichamelijkheid en dans', in M. BARNARD & P. POST (eds.): *Ritueel bestek. Antropologische kernwoorden van de liturgie*, Zoetermeer 2001, 104-109

ANALECTA HYMNICA: *Analecta hymnica medii aevi*, Vols. 1-55, Leipzig 1886-1922

ANBEEK, C., C. BAKKER, L. MINNEMA & C. MENKEN-BEKIUS (eds.): *Geloven in de interreligieuze dialoog: Praktische Theologie* 29 (2002) no. 1

ANDEL, A. VAN: 'Vragen om een zegen: daar zeg je toch geen nee tegen. Actuele ervaringen met het zegenen van niet-huwelijkse relaties in een kerkdienst – een verhaal uit de praktijk', in *Praktische Theologie* 25 (1998) 37-42

ANDEL, P. VAN: 'Uitvaart op de fiets', in *NRC Handelsblad* 2 Oktober 1998, 20

ANDERSON, E. & B. MORRILL (eds.): *Liturgy and the Moral Self: Humanity at Full Strectch Before God*, Collegeville 1998

ANDRADE, M.: *The History of the Elevation of the Host in the Mass of the Roman Rite* (Doctoral Thesis San Anselmo), Rome 1995

ANDREE, T.: 'Initiatie in geloofstraditie(s). Het inter-religieuze leren', in H. LOMBAERTS & L. BOEVE (eds.): *Traditie en initiatie. Perspectieven voor de toekomst*, Leuven 1996, 123-145

ANDRIESSEN, H.: 'Als je gevormd wordt', in *Inzet* 26 (1997) 4, 104-108

ANDRIEU, M.: *Les Ordines Romani du haut moyen-âge* (Spicilegium Sacrum Lovaniense 23), Leuven 1948

ANDRINGA, L. & B. GOUDZWAARD: 'Economie in dienst van het leven', in *Een-twee-een* 30 (2002) no. 9, Section 3-21

ANGENENDT, A.: *Liturgik und Historik. Gab es eine organische Liturgie-Entwicklung?* (Quaestiones disputatae 189), Freiburg/Basel/Wien 2001

ANGES: 'Les anges dans nos campagnes', in *L'actualité religieuse* 139 (1995) 17-37

ANNAERT-HUYSMANS, D., L. ANNAERT-HUYSMANS & G.F. FASEUR: 'Liturgische suggesties bij een zegening van trouwe geliefden', in *Tijdschrift voor Liturgie* 81 (1997) 386-392

APOSTEL, L.: 'Relationaliteit in ritueel en mystiek. Over Frits Staal', in *Ons erfdeel* 37 (1994) 3, 393-404

AQUILI, E.G. D': 'The Myth-Ritual Complex: A Biogenetic Structural Analysis', in *Zygon* 18 (1983) 3, 247-269

AQUILI, E. D' & C. D. LAUGHLIN: 'The biophysical determinants of religious ritual behaviour', in *Zygon* 10 (1975) 32-57

AQUILI, E. D' & C.D. LAUGHLIN: 'The neurobiology of myth and ritual', in E. D'AQUILI, C.D. LAUGHLIN & J. MCMANUS: *The Spectrum of Ritual. A Biogenetic Structural Analysis*, New York 1979

AQUILI, E.G. D', C.D. LAUGHLIN & J. MCMANUS: *The Spectrum of Ritual. A Biogenetic Structural Analysis*, New York 1979

ARBUCKLE, G.A.: Earthing the Gospel: An Inculturation Handbook for the Pastoral Worker, New York 1990

ARIÈS, P.: 'Les rituels de mariage', in *La Maison-Dieu* (1975) 121, 143-150.

ARIÈS, P.: 'La naissance du mariage occidental', in *La Maison-Dieu* (1982) 149, 107-112

ARKUSH, R.D. & L.O. LEE (eds.): *Land without Ghosts. Chinese Impressions of America from the Mid-Nineteenth Century to the Present*, Berkeley 1989

ARRIVÉ, M. & J. COQUET: *Sémiotique en jeu. A partir et autour de l'œuvre d'A. J. Greimas*, Paris/Amsterdam/Philadelphia 1987

ARTS, W., J. HAGENAARS & L. HALMAN: *The Cultural Diversity of European Unity*, Leiden/Boston 2003

ARS CELEBRANDI: *Ars celebrandi*: *Questions Liturgiques* 83 (2002) no. 2-3 = J. LAMBERTS (ed.): *'Ars celebrandi'*. *The Art to Celebrate the Liturgy. L'art de célébrer la liturgie* (Textes et Études Liturgiques/Studies in Liturgy 17), Leuven 2003

ARTE DEL CELEBRARE: *L'arte del celebrare. Atti della XXVII Settimana di Studio dell'Associazione Professori di Liturgia. Brescia, 30 agosto – 4 settembre 1998* (Bibliotheca Ephemerides Liturgicae. Subsidia 102), Roma 1999

ASAD, T.: 'Toward a Genealogy of the Concept Ritual', in T. ASAD: *Genealogies of Religion. Discipline and Reasons of Power in Christianity and Islam*, Baltimore 1993, 55-79

ASAD, T.: *Genealogies of Religion. Discipline and Reasons of Power in Christianity and Islam*, Baltimore 1993

ASSMANN, J.: 'Der zweidimensionaler Mensch. Das Fest als Medium des kollektiven Gedächtnisses', in IDEM (ed.): *Das Fest und das Heilige. Religiöse Kontrapunkte zur Alltagswelt* (Studien zum Verstehen fremder Religionen 1), Gütersloh 1991, 13-30

ASSMAN, J. (ed.): *Das Fest und das Heilige. Religiöse Kontrapunkte zur Alltagswelt* (Studien zum Verstehen fremder Religionen 1), Gütersloh 1991

ASSMANN, J.: *Das kulturelle Gedächtnis. Schrift, Erinnerung und politische Identität in frühen Hochkulturen*, München 1997[2]

AUBERT, R.: *The Christian Centuries. A New History of the Catholic Church*, Vol. 5: *The Church in a Secularized Society*, London 1978

AUF DER MAUR, H.-J.: 'Die österliche Lichtdanksagung. Zum liturgischen Ort und zur Textgestalt des Exsultet', in *Liturgisches Jahrbuch* 21 (1971) 38-52

AUF DER MAUR, H.-J.: *Feiern im Rythmus der Zeit, I: Herrenfeste in Woche und Jahr* (Gottesdienst der Kirche. Handbuch der Liturgiewissenschaft 5), Regensburg 1983

AUGUSTUS-KERSTEN, A.: 'Liturgie in het hol van de leeuw?', in *Eredienstvaardig* 16 (2000) 84-88

AUNE, M.B. & V. DEMARINIS: *Religious and Social Ritual: Interdisciplinary Explorations*, New York 1996

AUSTIN, D.J.: 'Born again... and again: Communitas and Social Change among Jamaican Pentecostalists', in *Journal of Anthropological Research* 37 (1981) 3, 226-246

AUSTIN, G.: 'Identity of a Eucharistic Church in an Ecumenical Age', in *Worship* 72 (1998) 26-35

AUSTIN, G. (ed.): *Fountain of Life*, Washington 1991.

AYER, A.: *The Central Questions of Philosophy*, London 1973

AZEVEDO, M.C. DE: *Inculturation and the Challenges of Modernity*, Rome 1982

BAAREN, P. VAN: 'The Flexibility of Myth', in A. DUNDES: *Sacred Narrative: Readings in the Theory of Myth*, Berkeley 1984

BACHELARD, G.: *La poétique de la rêverie*, Paris 1971

BACHELARD, G.: *La flamme d'une chandelle*, Paris 1984[7]

BACHELARD, G.: *La terre et les rêveries de la volonté: essai sur l'imagination de la matière*, Paris 1988[14]

BACHELARD, G.: *La poétique de l'espace*, Paris 1989[4]

BACHELARD, G.: *L'air et les songes: essai sur l'imagination du mouvement*, Paris 1990[17]

BACHELARD, G.: *Psychoanalyse van het vuur*, Meppel 1990.

BACHELARD, G.: *L'eau et les rêves: essai sur l'imagination de la matière*, Paris 1991[23]

BÄRSCH, J.: 'Das Dramatische im Gottesdienst. Liturgiewissenschaftliche Aspekte der Osterfeiern und Osterspiele im Mittelalter', in *Liturgisches Jahrbuch* 46 (1996) 1, 41-66

BAHR, H.E. (ed.): *Religionsgespräche. Zur gesellschaftlichen Rolle der Religion*, Darmstadt 1975

BAKKER, L., L. BOER & A. LANSER: *Rituelen delen. Een verzameling ideeën om geloven vorm te geven*, Kampen 1995

BAL, L., M. VAN DIJK-GROENEBOER & C. MENKEN-BEKIUS: 'De stille tocht van Gorinchem. Een sociologische analyse', in *Praktische Theologie* 28 (2001) 278-291

BANCK, G. (ed.): *Gestalten van de dood. Studies over abortus, euthanasie, rouw, zelfmoord en doodstraf*, Baarn 1980

BANTON, M. (ed.): *The Relevance of Models in Social Anthropology*, London 1965

BARNARD, M.: *Liturgiek als wetenschap van christelijke riten en symbolen*, Amsterdam 2000

BARNARD, M.: 'Beeld en ritueel', in M. BARNARD & P. POST (eds.): *Ritueel bestek. Antropologische kernwoorden van de liturgie*, Zoetermeer 2001, 115-122

BARNARD, M.: 'De conceptuele ruimte van de gothische kathedraal', in M. BARNARD & P. POST (eds.): *Ritueel bestek. Antropologische kernwoorden van de liturgie*, Zoetermeer 2001, 87-91

BARNARD, M.: 'Dynamiek van cultus en cultuur', in M. BARNARD & P. POST (eds.): *Ritueel bestek. Antropologische kernwoorden van de liturgie*, Zoetermeer 2001, 47-62

BARNARD, M.: 'Een kerkdienst in een museum', in M. BARNARD & P. POST (eds.): *Ritueel bestek. Antropologische kernwoorden van de liturgie*, Zoetermeer 2001, 56-62

BARNARD, M. & P. POST (eds.): *Ritueel bestek. Antropologische kernwoorden van de liturgie*, Zoetermeer 2001

BARNARD, M., M. VAN LEEUWEN, N.A. SCHUMAN & J.H. UYTENBOGAARDT (eds.): *Nieuwe wegen in de liturgie. De weg van de liturgie – een vervolg*, Zoetermeer 2002

BARNARD, M. & N. SCHUMAN, *Nieuwe wegen in de liturgie. De weg van de liturgie*, Zoetermeer 2001

BARTHES, R.: *Le système de la mode*, Paris 1967

BAUDRILLARD, J.: *Pour une critique de l'économie politique du signe*, Paris 1972

BAUDRILLARD, J.: *L'échange symbolique et la mort*, Paris 1976

BAUDRY, G.-H.: *Le péché dit originel* (Théologie Historique 113), Paris 2000

BAUERNFEIND, H.: *Inkulturation der Liturgie in unsere Gesellschaft: eine Kriteriensuche, aufgezeigt an den Zeitzeichen Kirche heute, Esoterik/New Age und modernes Menschsein* (Studien zur Theologie und Praxis der Seelsorge 34), Würzburg 1998

BAUMER, I.: 'Interaktion – Zeichen – Symbol', in *Liturgisches Jahrbuch* 1 (1981) 25-30

BAUMSTARK, A.: *Vom geschichtlichen Werden der Liturgie* (Ecclesia Orans 10), Freiburg im Breisgau 1923

BAUMSTARK, A.: *Liturgie comparée. Conférences faites au Prieuré d'Amay*, Chevetogne 1939

BAUMSTARK, A.: *Liturgie comparée. Principes et méthodes pour l'étude historique des liturgies chrétiennes*, Chevetogne 1953[3] (edition revised by B. BOTTE)

BAUMSTARK, A.: *Comparative Liturgy*, London 1958 (English edition of the previous publication)

BAZAN, A.: 'Realtà liturgica e comunicazione ciberspaziale. Verso una nuova liturgia?', in *Rivista liturgica* 87 (2000) 137-144

BECK, H. & W. WEREN (eds.): *Over leven. Leven en overleven in lagen*, Budel 2002

BECKER, H.J.: 'Liturgie in Dienst der Macht. Nationalsozialistischer Totenkult als säkularisierte christliche Paschfeier', in *'Totalitarismus' und 'Politische Religionen'. Konzepte des Diktaturvergleichs* 2 A, Paderborn 1997, 37-73

BECKER, J.W.: *De vaststelling van de kerkelijke gezindte in enquêtes*, Sociaal en Cultureel Planbureau, Den Haag 2003

BECKER, J.W. & J.W.R. VINK: *Secularisatie in Nederland 1966-1991* (Sociale en culturele studies 19), Den Haag 1994

BECKER, J.W. & J. DE WIT: *Secularisatie in de jaren negentig*, Sociaal en Cultureel Planbureau, Den Haag 2000.

BECKER, J.W., J. DE HART & J. MENS: *Secularisatie en alternatieve zingeving in Nederland*, Den Haag 1997

BECKERS-DE BRUIN, R.: 'Van verlangen naar beweging. Van beweging naar groene politiek', in H. GEERTS (ed.): *Maakbaarheid, macht en matigheid. Korte beschouwingen over het natuurdebat* (Annalen van het Thijmgenootschap 86 (1998) 3), Nijmegen 1998, 71-75

BEENDER, E.: 'Een vonk kan overspringen. Kerkelijke vieringen in het museum', in *Vieren. Tijdschrift voor wie werkt aan liturgie* 1 (2003) 4, 8-12

BEENTJES, P., J. MAAS & T. WEVER: *Gelukkig de mens. Opstellen over Psalmen, exegese en semiotiek aangeboden aan Nico Tromp*, Kampen 1991

BEKAERT, G.: *In een of ander huis. Kerkbouw op een keerpunt*, Tielt/Den Haag 1967

BELGISCHE: 'Belgische kerkcijfers', in *Een-twee-een* 26 (1998) 5, 15

BELL, C.: 'Ritual, Change, and Changing Rituals', in *Worship* 63 (1989) 31-41

BELL, C.: *Ritual Theory, Ritual Practice*, New York/Oxford 1992

BELL, C.: 'The Authority of Ritual Experts', in *Studia Liturgica* 23 (1993) 98-120

BELL, C.: *Ritual. Perspectives and Dimensions*, Oxford 1997

BELL, C.: 'Ritual Tensions: Tribul and Catholic', in *Studia Liturgica* 32 (2002) 15-28 (French: 'Tensions à l'intérieur du rite: tribal et catholique', in *La Maison-Dieu* (2001) 228, 41-61).

BELLE, W. VAN a.o.: *De betekenis als verhaal. Semiotische opstellen* (Semiotisch perspectief 1), Amsterdam 1991

BELLEMAKERS, S.: *Lees: het zinsverband van woord en vlees. Het belang van de 'close reading' methode bij het bestuderen en beoordelen van liturgische teksten, aan de hand van een onderzoek naar de christologie in enkele tafelgebeden van Huub Oosterhuis* (M.A. Thesis Theologische Faculteit Tilburg), Tilburg 1985

BELLEMAKERS, S.: 'De uitdaging – bij het trouwen van Emmy en Guus', in *Werkmap (voor) Liturgie* 28 (1994) 16-23

BELLIGER, A. & D.J. KRIEGER (eds.): *Ritualtheorien. Ein einführendes Handbuch*, Wiesbaden 1998.

BENTURQUI, D.: *Couples islamo-chrétiens: promesse ou impasse?*, Lausanne 1990

BERG, J.H. VAN DEN: *Psychologie van het ziekbed*, Nijkerk 1956

BERG, J.H. VAN DEN: *Metabletica*, Nijkerk 1957[3]

BERG, J.H. VAN DEN: *Metabletica van de materie. Meetkundige beschouwingen*, Nijkerk 1969[2]

BERG, M. VAN DEN: 'Meer nodig dan gedenktekens', in *Een-twee-een* 29 (2001) 20, 23-24

BERGAMINI, A.: 'Culto', in D. SARTORE & A.M. TRIACCA (eds.): *Nuovo dizionario di liturgia*, Rome 1984, 333-340

BERGER, H.: *Tegen de negatieve filosofie. Dionysius – Kant – Derrida*, Leende 2000

BERGER, H. a.o.: *Tussentijds. Theologische Faculteit Tilburg. Opstellen bij gelegenheid van haar erkenning*, Tilburg 1974

BERGER, J.: *Ways of seeing*, Londen 1972

BERGER, T.: 'Lex orandi – lex credendi – lex agendi', in *Archiv für Liturgiewissenschaft* 27 (1985) 425-432

BERGER, T.: 'Woman and Worship: A Bibliography', in *Studia Liturgica* 19 (1989) 96-110

BERGER, T.: *Liturgie und Frauenseele. Die Liturgische Bewegung aus der Sicht der Frauenforschung*, Stuttgart 1993

BERGER, T.: 'Woman and Worship: A Bibliography Continued', in *Studia Liturgica* 25 (1995) 103-117

BERGER, T.: *Women's Ways of Worship. Gender Analysis and Liturgical History*, Collegeville 1999

BERGER, T. & A. GERHARDS (eds.): *Liturgie und Frauenfrage*, St. Ottilien 1990

BERGER, W.: 'Preken en counselen', in *Tijdschrift voor Pastorale Psychologie* 4 (1972) 35-38

BERGER, W.: 'Uitvaart na zelfdoding. Een vraaggesprek met de voorganger', in *Praktische Theologie* 7 (1980) 347-353

BERGER, W.: 'Opdat wij niet, na anderen gepredikt te hebben, zelf verloren gaan', in *Praktische Theologie* 8 (1981) 244-249

BERGKAMP, N.: 'Huub Oosterhuis, 'Een lijk verbranden is vreselijk'', in *De Gelderlander,* Saturday October 21, 1972, 4

BERK, T. VAN DEN: *Mystagogie. Inwijding in het symbolisch bewustzijn*, Zoetermeer 1999

BERLIS, A.: 'The Ordination of Women: A Test Case for Conciliarity', in *Concilium* (1999) 1, 77-84

BERTRAND, D.: *Précis de sémiotique littéraire*, Paris 2000

BERTSCH, L. (ed.): *Was der Geist der Gemeinden sagt. Bausteine einer Ekklesiologie der Ortskirchen* (Theologie der Dritten Welt 15), Freiburg/Basel/Wien 1991

BERTSCH, L.: 'Entstehung und Entwicklung liturgischer Riten und kirchliches Leitungsamt', in L. BERTSCH (ed.): *Der neue Messritus im Zaire. Ein Beispiel kontextueller Liturgie* (Theologie der dritten Welt 18), Freiburg/Basel/Wien 1993, 209-256

BERTSCH, L. (ed.): *Der neue Messritus im Zaire. Ein Beispiel kontextueller Liturgie* (Theologie der dritten Welt 18), Freiburg/Basel/Wien 1993

BESEMER, J.: 'Ieder speelt zijn rol – ieder geeft zijn deel', in J. DE WIT a.o.: *Leve(n) de liturgie*, Baarn 1995, 56-67

BESEMER, J.: 'Theater en liturgie', in P. POST: *Een ander huis. Kerkarchitectuur na 2000* (Liturgie in perspectief 7), Baarn/Berne 1997, 49-54

BEURMANJER, R.: 'Ritueel en dans: de eerste stap', in M. BARNARD & P. POST (eds.): *Ritueel bestek. Antropologische kernwoorden van de liturgie*, Zoetermeer 2001, 110-114

BIEMANS, J.: 'Oogstdankviering 1995 – Kring de Kempen', in *Werkmap (voor) Liturgie* (Vieringen (Rituelen) buiten 2) 30 (1996) 35-46

BIERITZ, K.-H.: 'Aussagen zu einer Theorie des Gottesdienstes', in *Theologische Literatur Zeitung* 100 (1975) 721-737

BIERITZ, K.-H.: 'Nächstes Jahr in Jerusalem, Vom Schicksal der Feste', in *Jahrbuch für Liturgik und Hymnologie* (1994/1995) 37-57

BIERITZ, K.-H.: 'Anthropologische Grundlegung. 1. Grundlinien liturgischer Anthropologie', in H.-G. SCHMIDT-LAUBER & K.-H. BIERITZ (eds.): *Handbuch der Liturgik. Liturgiewissenschaft in Theologie und Praxis der Kirche*, Leipzig/Göttingen 1995, 96-127

BIERITZ, K.-H.: 'Das Kirchenjahr', in H.-C. SCHMIDT-LAUBER & K.-H. BIERITZ (eds.): *Handbuch der Liturgik. Liturgiewissenschaft in Theologie und Praxis der Kirche*, Leipzig/Göttingen 1995, 453-489.

BILLIET, J. & K. DOBBELAERE: *Godsdienst in Vlaanderen: van kerks katholicisme naar sociaal-kulturele kristenheid?*, Leuven 1976

BILLIET, J. & K. DOBBELAERE: 'Les changements internes au pilier catholique en Flandre. D'un Catholicisme d'Eglise à une Chrétienté socio-culturelle', in *Recherches Sociologiques* 14 (1983) 2, 141-184

BISSELING, H.: 'Niemand komt Jezus voorbij, behalve Cruijff', in *7even. Blad voor mensen die actief zijn in de kerk* 1 (1999) 27-30

BITTER, G. & G. MILLER (eds.); *Konturen heutiger Theologie. Werkstattberichte,* München 1976

BLAAUW, S. DE: *Met het oog op het licht. Een vergeten principe in de oriëntatie van het vroegchristelijk kerkgebouw,* Nijmegen 2000

BLANKESTEIJN, H.: 'Dansen in de liturgie', in *Werkmap (voor) Liturgie* 25 (1991) 167-178.

BLANKESTEIJN, H.: *Voor wie niet stil kan zitten in de kerk. Liturgie met handen en voeten,* Kampen 2002

BLIJLEVENS, A. a.o.: *Ruimte voor liturgie. Opstellen met betrekking tot de restauratie van de Sint-Servaaskerk te Maastricht,* Maastricht 1983

BLIJLEVENS, A., W. BOELENS & G. LUKKEN (eds.): *Op dood en leven,* 3 Vols., Baarn 1989-1990

BLIJLEVENS, A. & G. LUKKEN (eds.): *In goede en kwade dagen,* Baarn 1991

BLIJLEVENS, A., G. LUKKEN & J. DE WIT (eds.): *Liturgie met gehandicapten,* Baarn 1997

BLIJLEVENS, A(NCILLA): 'Liturgie/pastoraal rond het burgerlijk huwelijk', in *Werkmap (voor) Liturgie* 25 (1991) 247-250

BLOCH, D.: 'Uit-eten voor een vruchtbare toekomst', in *NRC Handelsblad. Agenda* April 11, 1996, 3

BLOECHL, J. & S. VAN DEN BOSSCHE: 'Postmoderniteit, theologie en sacramententheologie. Een onderzoeksproject toegelicht', in *Jaarboek voor liturgie-onderzoek* 13 (1997) 21-48

BLUYSSEN, J.: *Gebroken wit. Vrijmoedige herinneringen,* Baarn 1995

BOEF, A.H. VAN DEN: *Nederland seculier! Tegen religieuze privileges in wetten, regels, praktijken, gewoonten en attitudes,* Amsterdam 2003

BOEKE, R.: *Dit zal u een teken zijn,* 's-Gravenhage 1987

BOELENS, W.: *Vrouwen in de kerk. Op weg naar behoedzaam leiderschap,* Hilversum 1985

BOEVE, L.: 'Theologie na het christelijke grote verhaal. In het spoor van Jean-François Lyotard', in *Bijdragen. Tijdschrift voor filosofie en theologie* 55 (1994) 269-295

BOEVE, L.: *Spreken over God in 'open verhalen'. De theologie uitgedaagd door het postmoderne denken* (Doctoral Thesis), Leuven 1995

BOEVE, L.: 'Een postmoderne theologie van het 'open verhaal'', in *Onze Alma Mater* 50 (1996) 210-238

BOEVE, L.: 'Initiatie en traditie in een postmoderne samenleving. Een theologische verheldering', in *Verbum* 64 (1997) 7-8, 128-135.

BOEVE, L. (ed.): *De kerk in Vlaanderen: avond of dageraad?*, Leuven 1999

BOEVE, L.: 'Method in Postmodern Theology. A Case Study', in L. BOEVE & J.C. RIES (eds.): *The Presence of Transcendence. Thinking Sacrament in a Postmodern Age*, Leuven 2001, 3-17

BOEVE, L. & L. LEIJSSEN: *Sacramental Presence in a Postmodern Context* (Bibliotheca Ephemeridum Theologicarum Lovaniensium 160), Leuven 2001.

BOEVE, L. & L. LEIJSSEN: *Sacramental Contours of a God incarnate* (Textes et Études Liturgiques/Studies in Liturgy 16), Leuven 2001

L. BOEVE & J.C. RIES (eds.): *The Presence of Transcendence. Thinking Sacrament in a Postmodern Age*, Leuven 2001

BOEVE, L., A. VAN HARSKAMP & L. TEN KATE: 'Van een God die niet bestaat en de ondoorgrondelijke dingen die Hij doet', in *Tijdschrift voor Theologie* 41 (2001) 337-355

BOEVE, L., S. VAN DEN BOSSCHE, G. IMMINK & P. POST (eds.): *Levensrituelen en sacramentaliteit. Tussen continuïteit en discontinuïteit* (Meander 5), Baarn 2003

BOEVÉ-VAN DOORN, J. a.o. (eds.): *Eva's lied Twee; 57 geloofsliederen door vrouwen*, Kampen 1988

BOEVÉ-VAN DOORN, J. a.o.: *Eva's lied. 99 liederen door vrouwen*, Kampen 1998

BOFF, L.: *Die Kirche als Sakrament im Horizont der Welterfahrung*, Paderborn 1972

BOFF, L.: *Kleine Sakramentenlehre*, Düsseldorf 1976

BOFF, L. & A.L. LIBIANO: *Pecado social y conversion estructural*, Bogota 1978

BOLKESTEIN, F.: 'Normloosheid is liberalisme vreemd', in *NRC Handelsblad* March 29, 1997, 7

BOLLINGER, R. (ed.): *Die Umarmung lösen. Grundlagen und Arbeitsmaterialen zur Scheidung in Seelsorge und Gottesdienst*, Gütersloh 1997

BOLNOW, O.F.: *Neue Geborgenheit. Das Problem einer Überwindung des Essenzialismus*, Stuttgart/Berlin/Köln/Mainz 1979[4]

BOMMER, J.: 'Die Verkündigungsaufgabe der Kasualien Taufe, Hochzeit und Beerdigung', in F. FURGER a.o.: *Liturgie als Verkündigung* (Theologische Berichte 6), Zürich/Einsiedeln/Köln 1977, 167-199

BOON, A.L. (= Kees Fens): 'Een sterfelijk, zondig mens', in *De Tijd* April 14, 1989, 40

BOON, R.: *De joodse wortels van de christelijke eredienst* (Mededelingen Prof. Dr. G. van der Leeuwstichting 40), Amsterdam 1970

BORG, M. TER: 'Publieke religie in Nederland', in O. SCHREUDER & L. VAN SNIPPENBURG (eds.): *Religie in de Nederlandse samenleving. De vergeten factor*, Baarn 1990, 165-184

BORNEWASSER, K.: 'Is het waar dat de kerkmuziek van deze eeuw weinig of niets heeft meegenomen van de muzikale ontwikkelingen buiten de kerk?', in *Werkmap (voor) Liturgie* 26 (1992) 239-245

BOROBIO, D. (ed.): *La celebracion en la Iglesia, I Liturgia y sacramentologia fundamental* (Lux mundi 57), Salamanca 1985, 413-434

BORRAS, A. & B. POTTIER: *La grâce du diaconat. Questions actuelles du diaconat latin*, Brussel 1998

BOSCH, H. VAN DEN: 'It is (un)finished. Mark C. Taylor over Thomas J.J. Altizer', in R.J. PEETERS a.o. (ed.): *De onvoltooid verleden tijd. Negen bijdragen tot een bezinning op traditie*, Tilburg 1992, 99-118

BOSSARD, J.H.S. & E.S. BOLL: *Why marriages go wrong*, New York 1958

BOSWELL, J.: *Same-Sex Unions in Pre-Modern Europe*, New York 1994 = IDEM: *Marriage of Likeness: Same-Sex Unions in Pre-Modern Europe*, London 1995

BOTTE, B.: 'Le problème de l'adaptation en liturgie', in *Revue du Clergé Africain* 18 (1963) 307-330

BOUDEWIJNSE, B.: 'The Ritual Studies of Victor Turner. An Anthropological Approach and its Psychological Impact', in H.-G. HEIMBROCK & B. BOUDEWIJNSE (eds.): *Current Studies on Rituals. Perspectives for the Psychology of Religion*, Amsterdam 1990, 1-32

BOUDEWIJNSE, B.: 'The Conceptualisation of Ritual. A History of its Problematic Aspects', in *Jaarboek voor liturgie-onderzoek* 11 (1995) 31-56

BOURDIEU, P.: *Rede und Antwort*, Frankfurt am Main 1992

BOUT, J. VAN DEN a.o. (eds): *Handboek Sterven, Uitvaart en Rouw*, Maarssen 2001

BRADSHAW, P.: 'Difficulties in Doing Liturgical Theology', in *Pacifica* 11 (June 1998) 181-194

BRANTS, A.: 'Mens, religie, sacrament. Sacramenten en hun antropologische basis', in *Tijdschrift voor Liturgie* 88 (2004) 24-40

BRAUN, W. & R.T. MCCUTCHEON (eds.): *Guide to the Study of Religion*, London/New York 2000

BREDERODE, D. VAN: *Ave verum corpus*, Amsterdam 1994

BREEDVELD, K.: *Regelmatig onregelmatig. Spreiding van arbeidstijden en de gevolgen voor vrijetijd en recreatie*, Tilburg 1999

BREEKBAAR: *Breekbaar als glas. Over de broosheid van symbolen en riten*: *Tijdschrift voor Geestelijk Leven* 54 (1998) no. 2

BREUKELEN, H. VAN: *Het Engeltje van Hans van Breukelen*, Hoornaar 1989

BRINGÉUS, N.-A. (ed.): *Religion in Everyday Life. Papers Given at a Symposium in Stockholm 1993*, Stockholm 1994

BRINK, L.: *De taak van de kerk bij de huwelijkssluiting*, Nieuwkoop 1977

BRINKMAN, M.E.: *Sacraments of Freedom. Ecumenical Essays on Creation and Sacrament – Justification and Freedom*, Zoetermeer 1999

BROEK, A. VAN DEN, W. KNULST & K. BREEDVELD: *Naar andere tijden? Tijds-besteding en tijdsordening in Nederland* (Sociale en culturele studies 29), Den Haag 1999

BROEK, C. VAN DE & H. HURKENS: 'Wake 'Stop het opsluiten van vreemdelin-gen", in *Werkmap (voor) Liturgie* (Vieringen (Rituelen) buiten 1) 30 (1996) 3, 31-41

BROERS A. a.o.: *De nieuwe katholieken*, Gorinchem 2000

BROM, L. VAN DEN: 'Geloof gaat langs de afgrond', in *Rondom het woord* 38 (1996) 4, 18-24

BROWN, J. & R. YORK: *The Covenant of Peace. A Liberation Book by the Free Church of Berkeley*, New York 1971

BRÜCKNER, W.: 'Zu den modernen Konstrukten 'Volksfrömmigkeit' und 'Aber-glauben", in *Jahrbuch für Volkskunde* 16 (1993) 215-218

BRÜSKE, G.: 'Plädoyer für liturgische Sprachkompetenz. Thesen zur Sprach-lichkeit der Liturgie', in *Archiv für Liturgiewissenschaft* 42 (2000) 317-343

BRUGGE, T.: *Bloemen spreken in stilte. Een taal waar woorden niet kunnen spreken*, Bloemendaal 1995

BRUGGE, T.: 'Een taal waar woorden niet kunnen reiken. Bloemen spreken in stilte', in *Tijdschrift voor Geestelijk Leven* 51 (1995) 6, 607-614

BRUGGE, T.: 'Zorg voor de schepping', in *Werkmap (voor) Liturgie* (Vieringen (Rituelen) buiten 2) 30 (1996) 2-10

BRUGGE, T.: *Bloemen geven zin. Symbolische bloemsierkunst voor liturgie en bezinning*, Kampen 2002

BRUIJN, J. DE: 'Huwelijk bevestigt het mystieke verbond van God, Nederland en Oranje', in *NRC Handelsblad* February 3, 2002, 9

BRUIJNE, M. DE: 'Een decade vrouwenliederen van 'Eva's lied' tot 'Dag Mens", in *Werkmap (voor) Liturgie* (Vieringen (Rituelen) buiten 2) 30 (1996) 47-53

BUGNINI, A.: 'Progresso nell'ordine', in *L'Osservatore Romano* December 12, 1973

BUITENDIJK, F.: *Algemene theorie der menselijke houding en beweging*, Antwerpen 1964

BUITENDIJK, F.: 'Taal en samenleven', in *Taal en gezondheid* (Serie Geestelijke Volksgezondheid 40), Utrecht 1969, 9-16

BULCKENS, J.: 'Vormselpastoraal en -catechese in de Vlaamse bisdommen sinds de interdiocesane beleidsnota van 1972', in K. DOBBELAERE, L. LEIJSSEN & M. CLOET (eds.): *Levensrituelen. Het vormsel* (Kadoc-Studies 12), Leu-ven 1991, 135-165

BULCKENS, J.: 'Dragen katholieke school en godsdienstonderricht nog bij tot de godsdienstige vorming van jongeren?', in H. LOMBAERTS & L. BOEVE (eds.): *Traditie en initiatie. Perspectieven voor de toekomst*, Leuven 1996, 163-190

J. BULCKENS & P. COOREMAN (eds.): *Kerkelijk leven in Vlaanderen anno 2000*, Leuven 1989

BULHOF, I.N. & L. TEN KATE (eds.): *Flight of the Gods: Philosophical Perspectives on Negative Theology*, New York 2000

BULHOF, I.N. & J. DE VALK (eds.): *Postmodernisme als uitdaging*, Baarn 1990

BURGGRAEVE, R., M. CLOET, K. DOBBELAERE & L. LEIJSSEN (eds.): *Het huwelijk* (Kadoc-Studies 24), Leuven 2000

BURKERT, W.: *Kulte des Altertums. Biologische Grundlagen der Religion*, München 1998

BUYSMAN, A.: 'Hoe vier je de geboorte van je kind?', in *Viva* 1986, 20 (16-5-1986) 6-11

CALDECOTT, S. (ed.): *Beyond the Prosaic. Renewing the Liturgical Movement*, Edinburgh 1998

CANDA, E.R.: 'Therapeutic Transformation in Ritual, Therapy and Human Development', in *Journal of Religion and Health* 27 (1988) 3, 205-220

CASCOIGNE, B.: *De christenen. Geschiedenis van een wereldreligie*, Amsterdam/Brussel 1977

CASPAR, B. & W. SPARN (eds.): *Alltag und Transzendenz*, München 1992

CASPERS, C.: *De eucharistische vroomheid en het feest van Sacramentsdag in de Nederlanden tijdens de late Middeleeuwen*, Leuven 1992

CASPERS, C. & M. SCHNEIDERS (eds.): *Omnes circumadstantes. Contributions towards a history of the role of the people in the liturgy*, Kampen 1990

CASPERS, C. a.o. (eds.): *Bread of Heaven. Customs and Practices Surrounding Holy Communion. Essays in the History of Liturgy and Culture* (Liturgia condenda 3), Kampen 1995

CASSIRER, E.: *Philosophie der symbolischen Formen*, 3 Vols., Berlin 1923 and further

CASSIRER, E.: *An Essay on Man: An Introduction to a Philosophy of Human Culture*, New Haven 1944

CATECHISM: *Catechism of the Catholic Church*, Città del Vaticano 1994

CATHOLIC BISHOP'S CONFERENCE OF ENGLAND AND WALES: *The Common Good and the Catholic Church's Social Teaching*, Manchester 1996 = BISSCHOPPENCONFERENTIE VAN ENGELAND EN WALES: 'Verklaring: Het algemeen welzijn en de sociale leer van de katholieke kerk', in *Een-twee-een. Kerkelijke documentatie* 25 (1997) 2/3, 23-24

CATHOLIC BISHOP'S CONFERENCES OF ENGLAND & WALES, IRELAND, AND SCOTLAND: *One Body, A Teaching Document on the Eucharist in the Life of the Church and the Establishment of General Norms on Sacramental Sharing*, London/Dublin 1998, no. 111

CATHOLIC THEOLOGICAL SOCIETY OF AMERICA: 'Resolution', in *Bulletin ET. Zeitschrift für Theologie in Europa* 8 (1997) 2, 209-219

CHAUVET, L.-M.: *Du symbolique au symbole. Essai sur les sacrements*, Paris 1979

CHAUVET, L.-M.: 'L'avenir du sacramentel', in J. MOINGT: *Les sacrements de Dieu*, Paris 1987, 81-106

CHAUVET, L.-M.: *Symbole et sacrement. Une relecture sacramentelle de l'existence chrétienne*, Paris 1988

CHAUVET, L.-M.: 'Ritualité et théologie', in J. MOINGT, *Enjeux du rite dans la modernité* (Recherches de Science Religieuse 78 (1990) 4, 535-564), Paris 1991, 198-226

CHAUVET, L.-M.: *Les sacrements, parole de Dieu au risque du corps*, Paris 1993

CHAUVET, L.-M.: 'L'initiation chrétienne une fois pour toutes?', in *Catéchèse* (1995) 141, 49-56

CHAUVET, L.-M.: 'Sur quelques difficultés actuelles de l' 'au-delà'', in *La Maison-Dieu* (1998) 213, 33-58

CHICHLO, B.: 'Le pouvoir des rites en U.R.S.S.', in J. MOINGT, *Enjeux du rite dans la modernité* (Recherches de Science Religieuse 78 (1990) 4, 513-534) Paris 1991, 171-192

CHILDERS, J.: *Performing the Word. Preaching as Theatre*, Nashville, NT 1998

CHUPUNGCO, A.: *Cultural Adaptation of the Liturgy*, New York 1982

CHUPUNGCO, A.: *Liturgical Inculturation. Sacramentals, Religiosity, and Catechesis*, Collegeville 1992

CHUPUNGCO, A.: 'Liturgical Inculturation', in *East Asian Pastoral Review* 30 (1993) 2, 108-119

CHUPUNGCO, A.: 'Remarks on the Roman liturgy and inculturation', in *Ecclesia Orans* 11 (1994) 3, 269-277

CHUPUNGCO, A. (ed.): *Handbook for Liturgical studies*, Vol. 2: *Fundamental Liturgy*, Collegeville 1998

CHUPUNGCO, A.: 'Liturgy and Inculturation', in A. CHUPUNGCO (ed.): *Handbook for Liturgical studies*, Vol. 2: *Fundamental Liturgy*, Collegeville 1998, 337-375

CLAES, E.: *Het netwerk en de nevelvlek. Semiotische studies* (Argo-studies 1), Leuven 1979

CLEESON, B.: 'Rubrics versus Creativity in Liturgy', in *Worship* 70 (1996) 128-139

CLERCK, P. DE: 'Orientations actuelles de la pastorale du baptême', in A. HOUSSIAU a.o., *Le baptême, entrée dans l'existence chrétienne*, Brussel 1983, 113-146

CLERCK P. DE & E. PALAZZO (eds.): *Rituels. Mélanges offerts à Pierre-Marie Gy, o.p.*, Paris 1990

CLITEUR, P.: 'Alleen oecumenisch humanisme brengt licht', in NRC Handelsblad December 22, 2001, 7

CLOET, M.: 'Het doopsel in de nieuwe tijd (ca. 1550-ca. 1800)', in L. LEIJSSEN, M. CLOET & K. DOBBELAERE (eds.): *Levensrituelen. Geboorte en doopsel* (Kadoc-Studies 20), Leuven 1996, 87-92

COBBAN, A.: *A History of Modern France*, Vol. 2: *From the first Empire to the second Empire 1799-1871*, Hammondsworth 1965

COHEM, A.P.: 'Coercing the Rain Deities in Ancient China', in *History of Religions* 17 (1978) 3-4

COHEN, D.: *De cirkel van het leven. Menselijke rituelen uit de hele wereld*, Utrecht/Antwerpen 1991

COMMENTARIUM: 'Commentarium alla quarta istruzione per una corretta applicazione della costituzione conciliare sulla sacra liturgia', in *Notitiae* 30 (1994) 152-166

COMMISSIE MAALTIJD DES HEREN EN KERKELIJKE AMBT: 'Eindrapport, analyse van de liturgische teksten aangaande maaltijd en ambt, een studie', in *Een-twee-een. Kerkelijke documentatie* 17 (1989) 1

CONGREGATIO DE CULTU DIVINO ET DISCIPLINA SACRAMENTORUM: *De liturgia romana et inculturatione, Instructio quarta 'ad executionem Constitutionis Concilii Vaticani secundi de Sacra Liturgia recte ordinandum (ad Const. Art. 37-40)*, Città del Vaticano 1994 = *Acta Apostolicae Sedis* 87 (1995) 288-314 and *Notitiae* 30 (1994) 80-115 = *De Romeinse liturgie en de inculturatie. Vierde instructie voor de juiste toepassing van de constitutie over de liturgie van het Tweede Vaticaans concilie (bij de nummers 37-40)*, in *Een-twee-een. Kerkelijke documentatie* 23 (1995) 1, 30-46

CONGREGATIO DE CULTU DIVINO ET DISCIPLINA SACRAMENTORUM: *De usu linguarum popularum in libris liturgiae romanae edendae. Instructio quinta 'ad exsecutionem constitutionis Concilii Vaticani Secundi de sacra liturgia recte ordinandum' (Ad Const. art. 36)*, in *Notitiae* 37 (2001) no. 3-4 (= no. 416-417), 120-174

CONGREGATION FOR DIVINE WORSHIP AND THE DISCIPLINE OF THE SACRAMENTS, *Directory on Popular Piety and the Liturgy. Principles and Guidelines*, Vatican City 2001

CONGREGATION FOR THE DOCTRINE OF FAITH: 'Declaratio circa quaestionem admissionis mulierum ad sacerdotium ministeriale (1976)', in *Acta Apostolicae Sedis* 69 (1977) 98-116 = 'Verklaring aangaande de vraag over het toelaten van vrouwen tot het ambtelijk priesterschap (1976)', in *Archief van de Kerken* 32 (1977) 282-296 (comment: 917-927)

CONGREGATION FOR THE DOCTRINE OF FAITH: 'Responsum ad dubium circa doctrinam in Epistola Apostolica "Ordinatio Sacerdotalis" traditam), October 28, 1995', in *Acta Apostolicae Sedis* 87 (1995) 1114.

CONGRÉGATION POUR LA DOCTRINE DE LA FOI: *Considérations à propos de projets de reconnaissance juridique des unions entre personnes homosexuelles*, Rome, 3 juin 2003

COPPES, D.: 'Voettochten', in R. ADOLFS (ed.): *Buiten-dienst. Informele samenkomsten buiten de kerkmuren*, Baarn 1969, 59-65

COPPET, D. DE (ed.): *Understanding Ritual*, Londen/New York 1992

CORIJN, E.: *Verkenningen in de ontwikkeling van de studie van de vrijetijd. De onmogelijke geboorte van een wetenschap* (Maatschappij en technisch-weten-schappelijke ontwikkelingen 7), Brussel 1998

CORNEHL, P.: 'Gottesdienst', in F. KLOSTERMANN & R. ZERFASS: *Praktische Theologie Heute*, München 1974, 449-463

CORNEHL, P.: 'Theorie des Gottesdienstes. Ein Prospekt', in *Theologische Quartalschrift* 159 (1979) 178-192

CORNEHL, P.: 'Aufgaben und Eigenart einer Theorie des Gottesdienstes', in *Pastoraltheologische Informationen* (1981) 12-20

CORNILLE, C. & V. NECKEBROUCK (eds.): *A Universal Faith? Cultures, Religions and the Christ*, Leuven 1992

CORVERS, M.: 'Taal en beelden in de liturgie', in *Handreiking (aan) Vrijwilligers in het pastoraat* 8 (1987) 1, 299-310

CORVERS, M.: *Doet jouw kind de eerste communie nog? Een beschrijvend onderzoek naar het fenomeen eerste communie en haar toekomst(on)mogelijkheden* (M.A. Thesis Theologische Faculteit Tilburg), Tilburg 1993

COULT, T. & B. KERSHAW: *Engineers of the Imagination: the Welfare State Handbook*, London 1983

COURTÉS, J.: 'Sémiotique et théologie du péché', in H. PARRET & H.-G. RUPRECHT (eds.): *Exigences et perspectives de la sémiotique. Recueil d'hommages pour A.J. Greimas*, Amsterdam/Philadelphia 1985, 863-903

COURTÉS, J.: *Sémantique de l'énoncé: applications pratiques*, Paris 1989

COURTÉS, J.: 'Sémiotique et théologie du péché', in J. COURTÉS: *Sémantique de l'énoncé: applications pratiques*, Paris 1989, 178-224

COURTÉS, J.: *Analyse sémiotique du discours. De l'énoncé à l'énonciation*, Paris 1991

COURTÉS, J.: *Du lisible au visible. Initiation à la sémiotique du texte et de l'image*, Brussel 1995

COUWENBERG, S.W. (ed.): *Westerse cultuur: model voor de hele wereld*, Kampen 1994

COX, H.: *The Seduction of the Spirit*, New York 1973 = H. COX: *De verleiding van de geest. Persoonlijke overdenkingen over gebruik en misbruik van de religie*, Bilthoven 1973

CRAEYNEST, J.: 'Liturgie buiten in de open lucht. De zegening van de zee', in *Werkmap (voor) Liturgie* (Vieringen (Rituelen) buiten 2) 30 (1996) 30-34

CRITERIA: *Criteria for the Evaluation of Inclusive Translations of Scriptural Texts Proposed for Liturgical Use* (1990)

CRONACA: 'Cronaca dei lavori della 'plenaria' 1991', in *Notitiae* 27 (1991) 82-83

CRUMLIN, R.: *Images of religion in Australian art*, Kensington 1988

CRUMLIN, R. & A. KNIGHT: *Aboriginal art and spirituality*, North Blackburn 1991

CULTE: *Culte et culture*: *La Maison-Dieu* (1984) no. 159

DANEN, L.: *Uit goede bron. Literatuurlijst van liturgisch materiaal en achter-grondinformatie* (Liturgische Handreikingen 13), Breda 1987

DANEN, L. & J. JOOSSE: *Literatuuroverzicht liturgie* (Liturgische Handreikingen 24), Breda 1999

DANNEELS, G.: 'Rituelen in, sacramenten out?', in *Tijdschrift voor Liturgie* 86 (2002) 306-322

DANSEN: *Dansen voor het leven*: *Rondom het Woord* 27 (1985) no. 2 and 31 (1989) no. 2

DASSMANN, E. a.o.: *Projekttag. Frauenordination*, Bonn 1997

DAVIES, J.G. (ed.): *A New Dictionary of Liturgy and Worship*, Londen 1986

DEFOORT, C.: 'Riten als dijken. Het Chinese Boek der Riten', in *Kultuurleven* 64 (1997) 38-43

DEGEN, H.: *Gedeelde zorg. Ervaringen van ouders met een zorgenkind. Een handreiking aan ouderverenigingen, hulpverleners en pastores*, Hilversum 1976

DEGEN, H., L. BREZET BROUWER & A. LOOS: 'Liturgie met verstandelijk gehandicapten', in *Werkmap (voor) Liturgie* 11 (1977) 1-78

DEGEN, H.J.F. a.o. (eds.): *Herinneringen aan de toekomst. Pastoraat in de geest van Vaticanum II*, Baarn 1991

DEMEL, S.: *Kirchliche Trauung – unerlässliche Pflicht für die Ehe des katholischen Christen?*, Stuttgart/Berlin/Köln 1993

DENZINGER, H. & H. SCHÖNMETZER: *Enchiridion Symbolorum*, Barcelona 1963

DERKSE, W.: 'Het nieuwe heilige?', in *Brabantia nostra. Tijdschrift voor kunst en cultuur* 40 (1991) 3-5

DERKSE, W.: 'Het nieuwe heilige? Over de opbloei van geestelijke muziek in een geseculariseerde tijd', in D. VAN SPEYBROECK (ed.): *Kunst en religie*, Baarn 1991, 43-57

DERKSE, W.: 'Kleine dingen in de muziek', in J. DE VISSCHER (ed.): *Mosterdzaadjes van het bestaan. De waarde van de kleine dingen*, Baarn 1996, 52-61

DERKSEN, L.: *Als het donker wordt, wat zal ik dan nog zeggen... Een verzameling rouwpoëzie*, Naarden 1992

DERMIENCE, A.: 'Femmes et ministères dans l'Eglise primitive', in *Spiritus* 137 (1994) 382-395

DESSAUR, C.: *De droom der rede. Het mensbeeld in de sociale wetenschappen. Een poging tot criminosofie*, Den Haag 1982

DEVISCH, R.: 'Des forces aux symboles dans le rite bantou: l'interanimation entre corps, groupe et monde', in R. DEVISCH a.o.: *Le rite, source et ressources*, Brussel 1995, 11-82

DEVISCH, R. a.o.: *Le rite, source et ressources*, Brussel 1995

DIENSTBOEK: *Dienstboek. Een proeve: Schrift, Maaltijd, Gebed*, Zoetermeer 1998

DIJK, D.: 'Developments in Feminist Liturgy in the Netherlands', in *Studia Liturgica* 45 (1995) 120-128

DIJK, D.: 'De waarheid zal u vrijmaken. Over het emancipatoire liturgisch taalgebruik zoals voorgestaan door Marjorie Procter-Smith', in *Jaarboek voor liturgie-onderzoek* 13 (1997) 49-66

DIJK, D.: *Een beeld van een liturgie. Verkenningen in vrouwenstudies liturgiek, met bijzondere aandacht voor Marjorie Procter-Smith*, Gorinchem 1999

DIJK, D. a.o.: "Ik laat u niet gaan tenzij gij mij zegent'. Over de worsteling met God waarna *Hij* nieuwe namen krijgt', in *Gereformeerd Theologisch Tijdschrift* 85 (1985) 189-212 = D. DIJK a.o.: *Feministisch-Theologische Teksten. Gekozen en ingeleid door Denise Dijk, Fokkelien van Dijk-Hemmes en Catharina J.M. Halkes*, Delft 1985, 76-96

DIJK, B. VAN: *Zoek het Levend Water waar het zich vinden laat: in bronnen. Een studie naar het gebruik van de liturgie als zoek- en vindplaats in de bilaterale dialoog tussen de Lutherse Wereld Federatie en de Rooms-Katholieke Kerk* (M.A. Thesis Theologische Faculteit Tilburg), Tilburg 1991

DIJK, T. VAN & J. PEIJNENBURG: 'Levensdans', in *Werkmap (voor) Liturgie* 25 (1991) 152-166

DIJN, H. DE: *De herontdekking van de ziel. Voor een volwaardige kwaliteitszorg* (Annalen van het Thijmgenootschap 87, 3), Nijmegen 1999

DINGEMANS, G.D.J., J. KRONENBURG & R. STEENSMA: *Kaïn of Abel. Kunst in de kerkdienst: twee vijandige broeders?*, Zoetermeer 1999

DIRECTORIUM: *Directorium voor de Nederlandse Kerkprovincie* (yearly since 1969)

DIXON, J.W.: *The Physiology of Faith. A Theory of Theological Relativity*, San Francisco 1979

DOBBELAERE, K.: 'De katholieke zuil nu: desintegratie en integratie', in *Belgisch Tijdschrift voor Nieuwste Geschiedenis* 13 (1982) 1, 119-160

DOBBELAERE, K.: 'Een minderheidskerk? Enkele sociologische bedenkingen', in *Collationes* 18 (1988) 260-268.

DOBBELAERE, K.: *Het 'Volk-Gods' de mist in? Over de Kerk in België*, Leuven/Amersfoort 1988

DOBBELAERE, K.: 'De 'overgangsrituelen', steunberen van een 'Katholicisme buiten de muren'?', in J. BULCKENS & P. COOREMAN (eds.): *Kerkelijk leven in Vlaanderen anno 2000*, Leuven 1989, 29-38

DOBBELAERE, K.: 'Du catholicisme ecclésial au catholicisme culturel', in *Septentrion* 18 (1989) 3, 30-35

DOBBELAERE, K.: 'Overgangsrituelen: enkele hypothesen', in K. DOBBELAERE, L. LEIJSSEN & M. CLOET (eds.): *Levensrituelen. Het vormsel* (Kadoc-Studies 12), Leuven 1991, 53-61

DOBBELAERE, K., L. LEIJSSEN & M. CLOET (eds.): *Levensrituelen. Het vormsel* (Kadoc-Studies 12), Leuven 1991

DOBBELAERE, K. a.o.: *Verloren zekerheid. De Belgen en hun waarden, overtuigingen en houdingen*, Tielt 2000

DOCUMENTO: *Documento de Puebla, La evangelización en el presente y en el futuro de América Latina*, Buenos Aires 1979

DÖLGER, F.: *Der Exorzismus im altchristlichen Taufritual. Eine religionsgeschichtliche Studie*, Paderborn 1909

DOKUMENTATION: 'Dokumentation. Gesellschaft – Wissenschaft – Kirche. Statements zur Tagung der Deutschen Sektion in Mainz', in *Bulletin ET. Zeitschrift für Theologie in Europa* 8 (1997) 1, 92-128

DOOLEY, C.: 'The 1983 Synod of Bishops and the 'Crisis of Confession'', in *Concilium* 23 (1987) 2, 11-20

DORRESTEIN, R.: *Want dit is mijn lichaam*, Amsterdam 1997

DOUGLAS, M.: *Purity and Danger. An Analysis of Concepts of Pollution and Taboo*, New York 1966

DOUGLAS, M.: *Natural Symbols. Explorations in Cosmology*, New York 1973

DRAULANS, V. & H. WITTE: 'Identiteit in meervoud (I). Nederlands en Vlaams Katholicisme in een veranderende tijd', in *Collationes* 28 (1998) 3, 247-264

DRAULANS, V. & H. WITTE: 'Identiteit in meervoud (II)', in *Collationes* 28 (1998) 265-280

DRAULANS, V. & H. WITTE: 'Initiatie in de vrijwilligerskerk. Verkenningen in vergelijkend perspectief', in L. BOEVE (ed.): *De kerk in Vlaanderen: avond of dageraad?*, Leuven 1999, 167-188

DREYFUS, H.L. & P. RABINOW (eds.): *Michel Foucault: Beyond Structuralism and Hermeneutics*, Chicago 1983[2]

DRIESSEN, J. & H. DE JONGHE (eds.): *In de ban van de betekenis. Proeven van symbolische antropologie*, Nijmegen 1994

DROST, R.: 'Naamloos vondelingetje sober begraven in Baarle-Nassau', in Dagblad *BN De Stem* August 15, 1998, 1

DUBACH, A. a.o.: *Religiöse Lebenswelt junger Eltern*, Zürich 1989

DUBY, G.: *Le temps des cathédrales. L'art et la société de 980 à 1420*, Paris 1976

DUBY, G.: *Le chevalier, la femme et le prêtre. Le mariage dans la France féodale*, Paris 1981

DUFFHUES, T., A. FELLING & J. ROES: *Bewegende patronen*, Baarn 1982

DUNDES, A.: *Sacred Narrative: Readings in the Theory of Myth*, Berkeley 1984

DUNK, H. VON DER: 'Nederland wordt een fluwelen regelstaat', in *NRC Handelsblad* September 7, 1993, 8

DUPRÉ, L.: *Transcendent Selfhood. The Loss and Rediscovery of the Inner Life*, New York 1976 = L. DUPRÉ: *Terugkeer naar de innerlijkheid*, Antwerpen/Amsterdam 1982

DURAND, G.: *L'imagination symbolique*, Paris 1964

EBBERS, J.: 'Een bevrijding van knellende banden', in O. VAN DER HART a.o.: *Afscheidsrituelen in psychotherapie*, Baarn 1981, 43-52

EBERHARD, D.: *Kult und Kultur. Volksreligiosität und kulturelle Identität am Beispiel der Maria-Lionza-Kultes in Venezuela* (Beiträge zur Soziologie und Sozialkunde Lateinamerikas 23), München 1983

EGGERMONT, J.: *In het licht van Gods gelaat. Een beschrijving en kritisch-normatieve toetsing van een aantal officiële en niet-officiële Nederlandse roomskatholieke crematierituelen in historisch perspectief* (M.A. Thesis Theologische Faculteit Tilburg), Tilburg 1987

EIJK A. VAN & H. RIKHOF, *De lengte en de breedte, de hoogte en de diepte. Peilingen in de theologie van de sacramenten*, Zoetermeer 1996

EIJK, A. VAN: 'Het pleidooi voor een ruimer sacramentsbegrip', in A. VAN EIJK & H. RIKHOF, *De lengte en de breedte, de hoogte en de diepte. Peilingen in de theologie van de sacramenten*, Zoetermeer 1996, 105-131

EISEN, UTE E.: *Amtsträgerinnen im frühen Christentum. Epigraphische und litterarische Studien* (Forschungen zur Kirche- und Dogmengeschichte 61), Göttingen 1996 = UTE E. EISEN: *Woman Officeholders in Early Christianity. Epigraphical and Literary Studies*, Collegeville 2000

ELFSTEDENTOCHT: 'Elfstedentocht', in *NRC Handelsblad* 6 januari 1997, 7

ELIADE, M.: *Das Heilige und das Profane*, Hamburg 1957 (= IDEM: *The Sacred and the Profane: The Nature of Religion*, London 1959 and *Het gewijde en het profane*, Hilversum 1962)

ELIADE, M.: *Das Mysterium der Wiedergeburt. Ihre kulturelle und religiöse Bedeutung*, Zürich/Stuttgart 1961 (= IDEM: *Rites and Symbols of Initiation* (*Birth and Rebirth*), London 1958)

ELIADE, M.: *Beelden en symbolen*, Hilversum 1963 (= IDEM: *Images and Symbols: Studies in Religious Symbolism*, London 1961).

ELIADE, M.: *De mythe van de eeuwige terugkeer*, Hilversum 1964 (= IDEM: *Cosmos and History: The Myth of the Eternal Return*, Princeton 1954)

ELIADE, M.: 'Mythen en mythisch denken', in A. ELIOT a.o.: *Mythen van de mensheid*, Amsterdam/Hasselt 1977, 12-29

ELIAS, N.: *Die höfische Gesellschaft*, Darmstadt 1977

ELIOT, A. a.o.: *Mythen van de mensheid*, Amsterdam/Hasselt 1977

ELLEBRACHT, M.: *Remarks on the Vocabulary of the Ancient Orations in the Missale Romanum* (Latinitas christianorum primaeva 18), Nijmegen 1963

ELSBREE, L.: *Ritual Passages and Narrative Structures*, Bern 1991

ENG, T. VAN & B. SENTIUS: 'Skript-interview met Willem Frijhoff', in *Skript. Historisch tijdschrift* 6 (1984) 237-252

ENGELS, L.: 'Een bisschopswijding en de afwezigheid van de plaatselijke kerk', in *Tijdschrift voor Liturgie* 56 (1972) 218-240

ENGEMANN, W.: 'Semiotik und Theologie – Szenen einer Ehe', in W. ENGEMANN & R. VOLP: *Gib mir ein Zeichen. Zur Bedeutung der Semiotik für theologische Praxis- und Denkmodelle*, Berlin/New York 1992, 3-28

ENGEMANN, W. & R. VOLP: *Gib mir ein Zeichen. Zur Bedeutung der Semiotik für theologische Praxis- und Denkmodelle*, Berlin/New York 1992, 3-28

ENKLAAR, J.: 'In het rijk van SCI is de dood koning', in *NRC Handelsblad* August 9, 1991

ENKLAAR, J.: *Onder de groene zoden. De persoonlijke uitvaart. Nieuwe rituelen in rouwen, begraven en cremeren*, Zutphen 1995

ENKLAAR, J.: 'Nederlandse uitvaartbranche volgt voorbeeld van 'Mcdeath'-multinationals', in *NRC Handelsblad* September 5, 2002, 16

ERRICO, F. D' a.o.: 'Neanderthal Acculturation in Western Europe? A Critical Review of the Evidence and its Interpretation', in *Current Anthropology* 39 (1998) Supplement 1-44

ESSER, A., B. ENZNER-PROBST, A. BERLIS & C. METHUEN (eds): *Women, Ritual and Liturgy* = *Yearbook of the European Society of Women in Theological Research* 9 (2001) IV

ESTER, P., L. HALMAN & R. DE MOOR (eds.): *The Individualizing Society: Value Change in Europe and North America*, Tilburg 1993

ETTEMA, H.: *Verbogen taal. Verplaatste tekens. Semiotische beschouwingen van taal in relatie met psychopathologie*, Groningen 1998

EVERS, G. a.o.: 'Annoted Bibliography on Inculturation', in *Theologie in Context. Supplements*, Aachen 1984

EVERS, H.: 'Muziek in jongerenliturgie', in *Werkmap (voor) Liturgie* 21 (1987) 229-239

EYKENBOOM, P.: *Het Christus-Medicusmotief in de preken van Augustinus*, Assen 1960

EYSINK, A.: 'Experiment in de r.-k. huwelijkspastoraal', in *Praktische Theologie* 9 (1982) 165-173

FALSINI, R.: 'Lo spirito della liturgia da R. Guardini a J. Ratzinger', in *Rivista liturgica* 88 (2001) 3-7

FASCINATION: *The Fascination of Evil: Concilium* 34 (1998) no. 1

FAVAZZA, J.A.: 'Forum: The Fragile Future of Reconciliation', in *Worship* 71 (1997) 210-220

FÉDÉRATION LUTHÉRIENNE MONDIALE: *Culte et culture en dialogue. Consultations internationales de Cartigny (Suisse, 1993) et de Hong Kong (1994)*, Département des études, Genève 1995.

FENS, K.: 'God is geur, muziek en licht', in *NCR Handelsblad* December 24, 1996, 24

FERRY, L.: *L'homme-Dieu, ou le sens de la vie*, Paris 1996

FINNEGAN, R.: 'How to Do Things with Words. Performative Utterances Among the Limba of Sierra Leone', in *Man* 4 (1969) 537-552

FISCHER, B., E.J. LENGELING, R. SCHAEFFLER, F. SCHULZ & H.R. MÜLLER-SCHWEFE: *Kult in der säkularisierten Welt*, Regensburg 1974

FITZPATRICK, P.J.: *In Breaking the Bread. The Eucharist and Ritual*, Cambridge 1993

FLEW, A. & A. MACINTYRE: *New Essays in Philosophical Theology*, London 1955

FONTANILLE, J.: *Sémiotique du visible. Des mondes de lumière*, Paris 1995

FONTANILLE, J.: *Sémiotique du discours*, Limoges 1998

FONTANILLE, J.: *Sémiotique et littérature. Essais de méthode*, Paris 1999

FONTANILLE, J. & C. ZILBERBERG: *Tension et signification*, Sprimont 1998

FORTMANN, H.: 'De plaats der eucharistische liturgie in de huidige jeugdziel-zorg', in *Dux* 22 (1955) 74-98

FORTMANN, H.: *Als ziende de onzienlijke*, 3 Vols., Hilversum 1965-1968

FORTMANN, H.: *Hoogtijd. Gedachten over feesten en vasten*, Utrecht 1966

FORTMANN, H.: 'Latijnse uitvaart', in H. FORTMANN: *Hoogtijd. Gedachten over feesten en vasten*, Utrecht 1966, 103-124

FORTMANN, H.: *Heel de mens. Reflecties over de menselijke mogelijkheden*, Bilthoven 1972.

FORTMANN, H.: 'De primitief, de dichter en de gelovige', in H. FORTMANN: *Heel de mens. Reflecties over de menselijke mogelijkheden*, Bilthoven 1972, 261-265

FORTMANN, H.: 'Zonder het woord wordt alles zinloos', in H. FORTMANN: *Heel de mens. Reflecties over de menselijke mogelijkheden*, Bilthoven 1972, 72-78

FORTUIN, J.: 'Op verzoek van de overledene... Een onderzoek naar de uit-vaartgewoonten aan de hand van overlijdensadvertenties', in G. BANEK (ed.): *Gestalten van de dood. Studies over abortus, euthanasie, rouw, zelfmo-ord en doodstraf*, Baarn 1980

FOUCAULT, M. (ed. C. GORDON): *Power/Knowledge: Selected Interviews and Other Writings 1972-1977*, New York 1980

FOUCAULT, M.: 'The subject of Power', in H.L. DREYFUS & P. RABINOW (eds.): *Michel Foucault: Beyond Structuralism and Hermeneutics*, Chicago 1983[2], 208-226

FRAENGER, W.: *Matthias Grünewald*, München 1983.

FRANZ, A.: 'Everything is Worthwhile at the End? Christian Funeral Liturgy amidst Ecclesial Tradtion and Secular Rites', in *Studia Liturgica* 32 (2002) 48-68

FRANZEN, F.: *Adres-Wijzer voor de Alternatieve Gezondheidszorg voor Zuid Ned-erland, Periode 1997*, Eindhoven 1997

FREITAG, W. & C. POLL (eds.): *Das dritte Reich im Fest. Führermythos, Feier-laune und Verweigerung in Westfalen 1933-1945*, Bielefeld 1997

FREYER, T.: *Sakrament – Transitus – Zeit – Transzendenz. Überlegungen im Vor-feld einer liturgisch-ästhetischen Erschliessung und Grundlegung der Sakra-mente* (Bonner Dogmatische Studien 20), Würzburg 1995

FRIEDRICH, M.A.: *Liturgische Körper. Der Beitrag der Schauspieltheorien und -techniken für die Pastoralästhetik*, Stuttgart 2001

FRIESE, S.: 'A Consumer Good in the Ritual Process: The Case of the Wedding Dress', in *Journal of Ritual Studies* 11 (1997) 2, 47-58

FRIJHOFF, W.: 'Toeëigening: van bezitsdrang naar betekenisgeving', in *Trajecta* 6 (1997) 2, 99-118.

FRIJNS, F.: 'Een bruiloftsfeest. Proeve van een huwelijksviering', in *Tijdschrift voor Liturgie* 55 (1971) 370-377

FRIJNS, F.: 'Anamnese: in het verleden ligt het heden', in *Tijdschrift voor Liturgie* 56 (1972) 209-217

FRIJNS, F.: 'Meer een lijst met vragen', in *Werkmap (voor) Liturgie* 24 (1990) 310-318

FRIJNS, F.: *Rituelen. Rituelen in het dagelijks leven van mensen in het bijzonder van mensen met een verstandelijke handicap*, Best 1996

FRÜHWALD, W.: 'Zwischen Märtyrerdrama und politischem Theater. Vom spannungsvollen Verhältnis der Kirche zur Theaterkultur', in *Theologie und Glaube* 85 (1995) 35-46

FUCHS, G. & H.M. WEIKMAN: *Das Exsultet. Geschichte, Theologie und Gestaltung der österlichen Lichtdanksagung*, Regensburg 1992

FULGHUM, R.: *From Beginning to End. The Rituals of Our Lives*, London 1996

FURGER, F. a.o.: *Liturgie als Verkündigung* (Theologische Berichte 6), Zürich/Einsiedeln/Köln 1977

GABRIEL, K.: 'Sehnsucht nach Religion im säkularen Europa', in *Bulletin ET. Zeitschrift für Theologie in Europa* 7 (1996) 2, 185-196

GÄRTNER, C.: *Gegenwartsweisen in Bild und Sakrament. Eine theologische Untersuchung zum Werk von Thomas Lehnerer*, Paderborn 2002

GAMBER, K.: *The Reform of the Roman Liturgy. Its Problems and Background*, San Juan Capistrano 1993

GARCIA, J.A. & C.R. CALLE: *Camillo, Priest and Revolutionary*, New York 1968

GASE N'GANZI, N.: 'Débat autour des matières eucharistiques en contexte africain: état de la question', in B. HALLENSLEBEN & G. VERGAUWEN (eds.): *Praedicando et docendo. Mélanges offerts à Liam Walsh o.p.* (Cahiers œcuméniques 35), Freiburg 1998, 49-73

GASE N'GANZI, N.: *Les signes sacramentels de l'Eucharistie dans l'Eglise latine. Etudes théologiques et historiques*, Freiburg 2001

GEBHART, W.: *Fest, Feier und Alltag. Über die gesellschaftliche Wirklichkeit des Menschen und ihre Deutung*, Frankfurt/Bern/New York/Paris 1987

GEBHART, W.: 'Der Reiz des Aussertäglichen. Zur Soziologie des Festes', in B. CASPAR & W. SPARN (eds.): *Alltag und Transcendenz*, München 1992

GEERTS, H. (ed.): *Maakbaarheid, macht en matigheid. Korte beschouwingen over het natuurdebat* (Annalen van het Thijmgenootschap 86 (1998) 3), Nijmegen 1998

GEERTZ, C.: 'Impact of the Concept of Culture on the Concept of Man', in J.R. PLATT (ed): *New Views of the Nature of Man*, Chicago 1965

GEERTZ, C.: 'Religion as a Cultural System', in M. BANTON (ed.): *The Relevance of Models in Social Anthropology*, London 1965, 1-46

GELOOF: *Geloof in levensstijl: een empirisch onderzoek onder de Nederlandse jeugd*, Rotterdam 1998

GENNEP, A. VAN: *Les rites de passage*, Paris/Den Haag 1969 (first edition 1909)

GEORGI, D.: 'Die Visionen vom himmlischen Jerusalem in Apk. 21 und 22', in D. LÜHRMANN & G. STERCKER: *Kirche. Festschrift für Günther Bornkamm*, Tübingen 1980, 353-372

GERHARDS, A.: 'Review', in: *Herder-Korrespondenz* 54 (2000) 263-268

GERHOLM, T.: 'On Ritual: a Postmodernist View', in *Ethnos* 3-4 (1988) 190-203

GERTLER, M.K.J.: *Fernsehgemeinde: Erfahrung von Kirche durch Gottesdienstübertragungen*, Köln 1999

GERTLER, M.K.J.: 'Wenig Feierlichkeit auf dem Bildschirm. Gottesdienstübertragungen im deutschen Fernsehen', in P. POST, G. ROUWHORST, L. VAN TONGEREN & A. SCHEER (eds.): *Christian Feast and Festival. The Dynamics of Western Liturgy and Culture* (Liturgia condenda 12), Leuven 2001, 747-774

GESPRINT, A.: *L'objet comme procès et comme action. De la nature et de l'usage des objets dans la vie quotidienne*, Paris 1995

GEURTSEN, M.: 'De andere kant van het glas in lood', in *Tijdschrift voor Liturgie* 80 (1996) 266-280

GEURTSEN, M.: 'Het Romeins lectionarium – het grote vergeetboek voor vrouwen?', in G. LUKKEN & J. DE WIT (eds.): *Lezen in fragmenten. De bijbel als liturgisch boek* (Liturgie in beweging 2), Baarn 1998, 5-69

GEIJBELS, H.: 'Algemeen menselijk of eigen christelijk. Rituelen en de identiteit van religies', in *Tijdschrift voor Theologie* 41 (2001) 3, 221-230

GEZANGBOEK: *Gezangboek van de Oud-Katholieke Kerk van Nederland*, Hilversum 1990

GEZANGEN: *Gezangen voor liturgie*, Hilversum 1984, Baarn 1995²

GIBSON, P.: 'Eucharistic Food. May We Substitute?', in *Worship* 76 (2002) 445-455

GIDDENS, A.: *Modernity and Self-Identity. Self and Society in the Modern Age*, Cambridge 1991

GIJSWIJT-HOFSTRA, M.: *Vragen bij een onttoverde wereld* (Amsterdamse Historische Reeks, kleine serie 37), Amsterdam 1997

GILES, R.: *Repitching the Tent. Reordening the Church Building for Worship and Mission*, Norwich 2000 (Revised and expanded edition)

GILL, S. & J. FOX: *The Dead Good Funerals Book*, Ulverston 1996

GILLES, B.: *Durch das Auge der Kamera. Eine liturgie-theologische Untersuchung von Gottesdiensten im Fernsehen*, Münster 2001

GILLIS, CH.: *Pluralism. A New Paradigm for Theology*, Leuven 1993

GLAZIER, S.D.: *Anthropology of Religion: a Handbook*, Westport Conn./London 1997

GLOBALIZATION: *Globalization and its Victims: Concilium* 37 (2001) no. 5

GOETHALS, G.T.: 'Ritual and the Representation of Power in High and Popular Art', in *Journal of Ritual Studies* 4 (1990) 2, 149-177 = G.T. GOETHALS: 'Ritual und die Repräsentation von Macht in Kunst und Massenkultur', in A. BELLIGER & D.J. KRIEGER (eds.): *Ritualtheorien. Ein einführendes Handbuch*, Wiesbaden 1998, 303-322

GOLDAMMER, K.: *Die Formenwelt des Religiösen. Grundriss der systematischen Religionswissenschaft*, Stuttgart 1960

GOODY, J.: *The Interface Between the Written and the Oral*, Cambridge 1987

GOUDZWAARD, B. & H.M. DE LANGE: *Genoeg van te veel, genoeg van te weinig. Wissels omzetten in de economie*, Baarn 1991 (third revised and augmented edition)

GOVAART, TH.: 'Het liturgisch experiment in Nederland. Informaties en inzichten', in *Tijdschrift voor Liturgie* 50 (1966) 331-342

GOVAERTS, J.: 'De pastorale begeleiding naar aanleiding van de kinderdoop. Situatie, beleid en vorming', in L. LEIJSSEN, M. CLOET & K. DOBBELAERE (eds.): *Levensrituelen. Geboorte en doopsel* (Kadoc-Studies 20), Leuven 1996, 278-310

GREENBLATT, S.: 'Filthy Rites', in *Daedalus* 111 (1982) 3, 1-16

GREIMAS, A.J.: 'Conditions d'une sémiotique du monde naturel', in A.J. GREIMAS: *Du sens. Essais sémiotiques*, Paris 1970, 49-91

GREIMAS A.J.: *Du sens. Essais sémiotiques*, Paris 1970

GREIMAS, A.J.: 'Introduction', in A.J. GREIMAS (ed.): *Essais de sémiotique poétique*, Paris 1972, 6-24.

GREIMAS, A.J. (ed.): *Essais de sémiotique poétique*, Paris 1972

GREIMAS, A.J.: 'Réflexions sur les objets ethno-sémiotiques', in A.J. GREIMAS, *Sémiotique et sciences sociales*, Paris 1976, 175-185

GREIMAS, A.J.: *Sémiotique et sciences sociales*, Paris 1976

GREIMAS, A.J.: *De l'imperfection*, Périgueux 1987

GREIMAS, A.J. & J. COURTÉS: *Sémiotique. Dictionnaire raisonné de la théorie du langage*, Tome 1, Paris 1979 = A.J. GREIMAS & J. COURTÉS: *Semiotics and Language. An Analytical Dictionnary*, Bloomington 1982 = A.J. GREIMAS & J. COURTÉS: *Analytisch woordenboek van de semiotiek*, Vol. 1, Tilburg 1987

GREIMAS, A.J. & J. FONTANILLE: *Des états de choses aux états d'âmes. Essais de sémiotique des passions*, Paris 1991 = A. J. GREIMAS & J. FONTANILLE: *The Semiotics of Passions. From States of Affairs to States of Feelings*, Minneapolis/London 1993

GREY, M.: *Introducing Feminist Images of God*, Cleveland, Ohio 2001

GRIESE, H.M.: *Übergangsrituale im Jugendalter. Jugendweihe, Konfirmation, Firmung und Alternativen. Positionen und Perspektiven am „runden Tisch"* (Jugendsoziologie 2), Münster 2000.

GRILLO, A.: 'La "visione antropologica" dei sacramenti e la teologia. Ovvero, come fanno dei ciechi a identificare la verita di un elefante?', in *Ecclesia Orans* 20 (2003) 253-270

GRIMES, R.L.: *Beginnings in Ritual Studies,* Washington 1982

GRIMES, R.L.: *Research in Ritual Studies. A Programmatic Essay and Bibliography,* Metuchen 1985

GRIMES, R.L.: *Ritual Criticism: Case Studies in its Practice, Essays on its Theory,* Columbia 1990

GRIMES, R.L.: 'Liturgical Supinity, Liturgical Erectitude: on the Embodiment of Ritual Authority', in *Studia Liturgica* 23 (1993) 51-69

GRIMES, R.L.: *Reading, Writing, and Ritualizing. Ritual in Fictive, Liturgical, and Public Places,* Washington DC 1993

GRIMES, R.L.: *Marrying and Burying. Rites of Passage in a Mans Life,* San Francisco/Oxford 1995

GRIMES, R.L.: 'The Initiatory Dilemma: Cinematic Fantasy and Ecclesiastical Rarification', in *Bulletin ET. Zeitschrift für Theologie in Europa* 9 (1998) 2, 161-170

GRIMES, R.L.: *Deeply into the Bone. Re-inventing rites of passage* (Life Passages 1), Berkeley/Los Angeles/London 2000.

GRIMES, R.L.: 'Ritual', in W. BRAUN & R.T. MCCUTCHEON (eds.): *Guide to the Study of Religion,* London/New York 2000, 259-270 (ch. 18)

GROND, A.: 'Het museum is geen tempel', in *De Bazuin* 81 (1998) (April 3), 32

GROND, A.: 'Huwelijksuitzegening: "Keer je om, je moet verder" ', in *De Bazuin* 84 (2001) 9, 10-14

GROOME, T.: 'Inculturation. How to Proceed in a Pastoral Context?', in *Concilium* 30 (1994) 2, 120-133

GROOT, M. DE: 'Lied van Sara: Zij is een vrouw van Naam', in *Werkschrift voor Leerhuis en Liturgie* 4 (1983) 1, 114

GROOT, S. (ed.): *De lof Gods geef ik stem. Inzichten en achtergronden van de vocale muziek in de rooms-katholieke eredienst,* Baarn 1993

GROTOWSKI, J.: *Towards a Poor Theatre,* New York 1968.

GROUP OF LISBON: *Limits of Competition,* Cambridge, Mass. 1995

GROUPE MU a.o.: *Approches sémiotiques sur Rothko*: *Nouveaux Actes Sémiotiques* 6 (1994) no. 34-36

GRÜN, A.: *Geborgenheit finden. Rituale feiern: Wege zu mehr Lebensfreude,* Stuttgart 1997 = A. GRÜN: *Een veilige schuilplaats. Meer levensvreugde door rituelen,* Baarn 1997

GRUNELL, M.: *Mannen die zorgen, zijn de kerels van morgen,* Utrecht 1998

GRYSON, R.: *Le ministère des femmes dans l'Église ancienne,* Gembloux 1972

GUARDINI, R.: *Von heiligen* Zeichen, Mainz 1929

GUARDINI, R.: *Vom Geist der Liturgie* (Reihe Romano Guardini Werke), Mainz/Paderborn 1997 (original edition 1917)

GUICHARD, J. & C. a.o.: *Liturgie et lutte des classes. Symbolique et politique*, Paris 1976

GUSDORF, G.: *La parole*, Paris 1968[6]

GUWY, F.: 'Religie zonder geloof in God. France Guwy in gesprek met de filosoof Luc Ferry', in *Roodkoper* 2 (1997) 2, 6-10

GY, P.M.: 'The Inculturation of the Christian Liturgy in the West', in *Studia Liturgica* 20 (1990) 8-18

GY, P.M.: 'L'esprit de la liturgie du cardinal Ratzinger est-il fidèle au concile ou en réaction contre?', in *La Maison-Dieu* (2002) 229, 171-178

HAAKMAN, S. (ed.): *Rituelen* (Studium Generale), Utrecht 1989

HAAREN, E. VAN: 'Het gerommel in je hoofd moet naar buiten', in *Hervormd Nederland* December 21, 1996

HAARS, J.: *Kansanderen. Liefhebben vanuit de marge*, Averbode 2000

HAAS, G. DE: *Publieke religie. Voorchristelijke patronen in ons religieus gedrag*, Baarn 1995

HABERMAS, J.: 'Habermass', in H.E. BAHR (ed.): *Religionsgespräche. Zur gesellschaftlichen Rolle der Religion*, Darmstadt 1975

HÄRING, H.: 'Tussen 'civiele religie' en godsdienstkritiek', in *Tijdschrift voor Theologie* 24 (1984) 348-354

HÄRING, H.: 'De Schriften, 'ziel van de theologie': Pleidooi voor een herontdekking van de Bijbel', in *Tijdschrift voor Theologie* 38 (1998) 280-300

HÄRING, H.: 'The Theory of Evolution as a Megatheory of Western Thought', in *Concilium* 36 (2000) 1, 23-34

HÄUSSLING, A.: 'Die kritische Funktion der Liturgiewissenschaft', in H.B. MEYER (ed.): *Liturgie und Gesellschaft*, Innsbruck 1970, 103-130.

HÄUSSLING, A.: 'Liturgiewissenschaft, zwei Jahrzenhnte nach Konzilsbeginn', in *Archiv für Liturgiewissenschaft* 24 (1982) 1-18.

HÄUSSLING, A.: 'Kosmische Dimension und gesellschaftliche Wirklichkeit. Zu einem Erfahrungswandel in der Liturgie', in *Archiv für Liturgiewissenschaft* 25 (1983) 1-8.

HÄUSSLING, A.: 'Liturgiewissenschaftliche Aufgabenfelder vor uns', in *Liturgisches Jahrbuch* 38 (1988) 94-108

HÄUSSLING, A. (ed.): *Vom Sinn der Liturgie: Gedächtnis unserer Erlösung und Lobpreis Gottes*, Düsseldorf 1991

HÄUSSLING, A.: 'Der Geist der Liturgie. Zu Joseph Ratzingers gleichnamiger Publikation', in *Archiv für Liturgiewissenschaft* 43/44 (2001-2002) 362-395

HAHN, A.: *Religion und der Verlust der Sinngebung. Identitätsprobleme in der modernen Gesellschaft*, Frankfurt 1974

HAHN, A.: 'Kultische und säkulare Riten und Zeremonien in soziologischer Sicht', in A. HAHN a.o.: *Anthropologie des Kults, Die Bedeutung des Kults für das Ueberleben des Menschen*, Freiburg 1977

HAHN, A. a.o.: *Anthropologie des Kults. Die Bedeutung des Kults für das Ueberleben des Menschen*, Freiburg 1977

HAHN, J.G.: *Liturgie op televisie of 'televisie-liturgie'*, Amsterdam 1992

HAHNE, W.: *De arte celebrandi oder von der Kunst, Gottesdienst zu feiern. Entwurf einer Fundamentalliturgik*, Freiburg/Basel/Wien 1989

HALLENSLEBEN, B. & G. VERGAUWEN (eds.): *Praedicando et docendo. Mélanges offerts à Liam Walsh o.p.* (Cahiers œcuméniques 35), Freiburg 1998

HALLEWAS, E.: 'Gezegend samen op weg. Over het zegenen van levensverbintenissen in de verenigde protestantse kerk', in *Praktische Theologie* 25 (1998) 103-121

HALMAN, L.: *Waarden in de Westerse Wereld. Een internationale exploratie van de waarden in de westerse samenleving*, Tilburg 1991

HALMAN, L.: *The European Values Study: A Third Wave. Source Book of the 1999/2000 European Values Study Surveys*, Tilburg 2001

HALMAN, L., F. HEUNKS, R. DE MOOR & H. ZANDERS: *Traditie, secularisering en individualisering. Een onderzoek naar de waarden van de Nederlanders in een Europese context*, Tilburg 1987

HAMELINE, J.Y.: 'Relire van Gennep... Les rites de passage', in *La Maison-Dieu* (1972) 112, 133-143

HAMELINE, J.Y.: 'Actes du colloque 'Création musicale et musique liturgique', jeudi 23 mai 1991', in *Bulletin de l'Institut catholique de Lyon* 99-100 (1992)

HAMELINE, J.Y.: 'Observations sur nos manières de célébrer', in *La Maison-Dieu* (1992) 192, 7-24 = J.-Y. HAMELINE, J.Y.: *Une poétique du rituel*, Paris 1997, 35-49

HAMELINE, J.Y.: *Une poétique du rituel*, Paris 1997

HAMELINE, J. Y.: 'Les *rites de passage* d'Arnold van Gennep', in *La Maison-Dieu* (2001) 228, 7-39

HAMMAD, M.: 'Définition syntaxique du topos', in *Le Bulletin* 3 (1979) 10, 25-27

HAMMAD M.: 'L'architecture du thé', in *Actes Sémiotiques. Documents* 9 (1987) no. 84-85, 1-50.

HARNACK, A.: *Medizinisches aus der ältesten Kirchengeschichte* (Texte und Untersuchungen 8), Leipzig 1892; revised edition in A. HARNACK: *Mission und Ausbreitung des Christentums in den ersten drei Jahrhunderten*, Vol. 1: *Die Mission im Wort und Tat*, Leipzig 1906², 87-107

HART, J. DE: 'Bijgeloof – bij geloof? Christelijke religiositeit en 'New Age'-stromingen onder Nederlandse jong-volwassenen', in *Tijdschrift voor Theologie* 33 (1993) 166-176

HART, J. DE: 'Een bespreking van recente godsdienstsociologische boeken', in *Praktische Theologie* 24 (1997) 334-356

HART, J. DE: 'Kerkelijke en niet kerkelijke religie', in *Praktische Theologie* 26 (1999) 277-296

HART, J. DE: 'Zondagswijding – Zondagsmijding', in *Praktische Theologie* 30 (2003) 267-283

HART, O. VAN DER: 'Relaties en rituelen', in K. VAN DER VELDEN a.o.: *Directieve therapie*, Deventer 1977

HART, O. VAN DER: 'Therapeutische rituelen: twee voorbeelden', in K. VAN DER VELDEN a.o.: *Directieve therapie*, Deventer 1977

HART, O. VAN DER: *Overgang en bestendiging: Over het ontwerpen en voorschrijven van rituelen in psychotherapie*, Deventer 1978

HART, O. VAN DER: *Rituelen in psychotherapie. Overgang en bestendiging*, Deventer 1984 (second and augmented edition of the previous book)

HART, O. VAN DER a.o.: *Afscheidsrituelen in psychotherapie*, Baarn 1981 (English edition: *Coping with Loss. The Therapeutic Use of Leave-Taking Rituals*, New York 1987; revised edition: *Afscheidsrituelen in psychotherapie. Achterblijven en verdergaan*, Lisse 2003)

HARTZINGER, W.: *Religion und Brauch*, Darmstadt 1992

HARSKAMP A. VAN a.o.: *De religieuze ruis in Nederland. Thesen over versterving en de wedergeboorte van de godsdienst*, Zoetermeer 1998

HASSELMAN, C.: 'Chicago Global Ethic Declaration (1993)', in *Concilium* 36 (2000) 4, 26-37

HASTINGS, A.: 'Western Christianity Confronts other Cultures', in *Studia Liturgica* 20 (1990) 19-27

HAUGG, W.: *Kritik der Warenästhetik*, Frankfurt 1971

HAUSREITHER, J.: *Semiotik des liturgischen Gesanges. Ein Beitrag zur Entwicklung einer integralen Untersuchungsmethode der Liturgiewissenschaft* (Liturgia condenda 16), Leuven 2004

HEFFELS, B.: 'De Matthäuspassion: opgetrokken rond de kruiskreet van Christus', in *Univers* 27 (1996) 10-11

HEGEL, G.W.F.: *Phänomenologie des Geistes*, Hamburg 1952

HEIJDEN, J.O. VAN DER: 'Symboliek en ritueel van een herdenking', in *Werkmap (voor) Liturgie* (Vieringen (Rituelen) buiten 1) 30 (1996) 17-22

HEIJERMANS, H.H.: *Snikken en Smartlapjes*, Baarn 1981

HEIMBROCK, H.-G.: *Gottesdienst: Spielraum des Lebens. Sozial- und kulturwissenschaftliche Analysen zum Ritual in praktisch-theologischem Interesse* (Theologie en Empirie 15), Kampen/Weinheim 1993

HEIMBROCK, H.-G. & B. BOUDEWIJNSE (eds.): *Current Studies on Rituals. Perspectives for the Psychology of Religion*, Amsterdam 1990

HEINEN, W. (ed.): *Bild – Wort – Symbol in der Theologie*, Würzburg 1969

HEINZ, A. & H. RENNINGS: *Gratias agamus. Studien zum Eucharistischen Hochgebet für Balthasar Fischer*, Freiburg 1992

G. HEITINK & H. STOFFELS: *Niet zo'n kerkganger. Zicht op buitenkerkelijk geloven*, Baarn 2003

HELLEMANS, S.: 'Secularization in a religiogeneous modernity', in R. LAERMANS, B. WILSON & J. BILLIET: *Secularization and Social Integration. Papers in honor of Karel Dobbelaere*, Leuven 1998, 67-81

HELLEMANS, S.: 'Veranderende religie, veranderende kerken', in *Praktische Theologie* 26 (1999) 315-326

HEMELS, J.: 'Liturgie en massamedia. Na de discussie over televisietoneel is nu ook die over de televisieliturgie ons deel geworden', in *De Bazuin* 65 (1982) 46, 1-2 and 6-7

HEMELS, J. & H. HOEKSTRA: *Media en religieuze communicatie*, Hilversum 1985

HEMPELMANN, R.: *Sakrament als Ort der Vermittlung des Heils. Sakramententheologie im evangelisch-katholischen Dialog* (Kirche und Konfession 32), Göttingen 1992

HENAU, E.: 'Verscheidenheid in kerkbetrokkenheid. Een pastorale uitdaging', in E. HENAU & L. HENSGENS (eds.): *Een pastorale uitdaging. Verscheidenheid in kerkbetrokkenheid*, Tielt/Bussum 1982, 13-58

HENAU, E. & L. HENSGENS (eds.): *Een pastorale uitdaging. Verscheidenheid in kerkbetrokkenheid*, Tielt/Bussum 1982

HENAU, E. & F. JESPERS (eds.): *Liturgie en kerkopbouw. Opstellen aangeboden aan Ad Blijlevens*, Baarn 1993

HENTEN, J.W. VAN & A. HOUTEPEN (eds.): *Religious Identity and the Invention of Tradition. Papers Read at a Noster Conference in Soesterberg, January 4-6, 1999* (Studies in Theology and Religion 3), Assen 2001

HERBST, W.: *Evangelischer Gottesdienst. Quellen zu seiner Geschichte*, Göttingen 1992

HERMANS, H. (ed.): *De echo van het ego. Over het meerstemmige zelf* (Annalen van het Thijmgenootschap 83, 2), Baarn 1995

HERMANS, J.: *Benedictus XIV en de liturgie*, Brugge/Boxtel 1979

HERT, I. D' & J. VANDIKKELEN: 'Overgave om niet. Antropoloog Rik Pinxten over riten en sacrale drama's', in *Tijdschrift voor Geestelijk Leven* 51 (1995) 6, 597-606

HERZBERG, J.: *Doen en laten. Een keuze uit de gedichten*, Amsterdam 1994

HEWITT SUCHOCKI, M.: *The Fall to Violence: Original Sin in Relational Theology*, New York 1994

HILHORST, H.: 'De godsdienstsociologie op zoek naar nieuwe vormen van religie', in P. STOUTHARD & G. VAN TILLO (ed.): *Katholiek Nederland na 1945*, Baarn 1985, 114-130

HILLE, R. & E. TROEGER (eds.): *Die Einzigartigkeit Jesu Christi als Grundfrage der Theologie und missionarische Herausforderung*, Wuppertal/Zürich/Giessen/Basel 1993

HILLESUM, E.: *A Diary 1941-1943*, London 1983 (English translation of *Het verstoorde leven. Dagboek van Etty Hillesum, 1941-1943*, Bussum 1981).

HILLESUM, E.: *Letters from Westerbork*, New York 1986 (English translation of *Het denkende hart van de barak. Brieven van Etty Hillesum*, Haarlem 1982).

HILLESUM, E.: *Interrupted Life: the Diaries 1941-1943 and Letters from Westerbork*, New York 1996

HILTEN, W. VAN a.o. (eds.): *Eva's lied; 42 liederen door vrouwen*, Kampen 1984

HOBSBWAM, E.: 'Introduction. The Invention of Tradition', in E. HOBSBWAM & T. RANGER (eds.): *The Invention of Tradition*, Cambridge 1983, 1-14

HOBSBWAM, E. & T. RANGER (eds.): *The Invention of Tradition*, Cambridge 1983

HOEDT, D. (ed.): *"Ik laat u niet gaan, tenzij gij mij zegent." Gebedsvieringen met burgerlijk hertrouwde echtgescheidenen*, Dienst Gezinspastoraal bisdom Brugge, Roeselare 2000

HOEK, K., W. OOSTERWAL & H. RUITER: *Nieuwe muziek in de liturgie*, Harlingen 1987

HOEKSTRA, E.G. & R. KRANENBORG (eds.): *Rituelen in religieus Nederland. Gebruiken van joden, christenen, moslims, hindoes en boeddhisten in belangrijke levensfasen*, Baarn 2001

HOENDERDAAL, G.J.: *Riskant spel. Liturgie in een geseculariseerde wereld*, Den Haag 1977

HOFFMAN, L.A.: 'How Ritual Means: Ritual Circumcision in Rabbinic Culture and Today', in *Studia Liturgica* 23 (1993) 78-97

HOLLAARDT, A. (ed.): *Liturgische oriëntatie na Vaticanum II (Supplement Liturgisch Woordenboek)*, Roermond 1970

HOLLEMAN, T.: *De Neanderthaler. Een verguisde pionier*, Amsterdam 1998

HOLMAN, J.: 'Psalm 139 een palimpsest?', in *Schrift* 21 (1989) 124, 148-157

HOLMES, U.T.: 'Liminality and Liturgy', in *Worship* 47 (1973) 286-297

HONKA, L. (ed.): *Science of Religion. Studies in Methodology*, New York 1979

HOONDERT, M. & P. POST: 'De dynamiek van het gregoriaans. Een onderzoeksperspectief', in Jaarboek voor liturgie-onderzoek 15 (1999) 7-26

HOORNIK, E.: *Journalistiek proza en brieven*, Amsterdam 1974

HOOYDONK, J. VAN: 'Trouwen in het bos?', in *De Bazuin* 80 (1997) 22, 32

HOOYDONK, J. VAN: 'De biecht is een fantastisch instrument voor een narcistische cultuur' (interview with R. Nauta), in *De Bazuin* 81 (1998) 14 (July 10), 32

HOUSSIAU, A. a.o., *Le baptême, entrée dans l'existence chrétienne*, Brussel 1983

HOUTEPEN, A.: *God, een open vraag. Theologische perspectieven in een cultuur van agnosme*, Zoetermeer 1997

HOUTMAN, A., M. POORTHUIS & J. SCHWARTZ (eds.): *Sanctity of Time and Space in Tradition and Modernity*, Leiden 1998

HUIJBERS, B.: 'Liturgische muziek na Vaticanum II', in *Werkmap (voor) Liturgie* 15 (1981) 369-388

HUIJBERS, B.: *Aan Gij voorbij. Het mysterie bezongen*, Hilversum 1989

HUIZING, P. & B.A. WILLEMS: 'Sacramentele grondslag van het kerkrecht', in *Tijdschrift voor Theologie* 16 (1976) 244-266

HUIZINGA, J.: *The Waning of the Middle Ages. A Study of the Forms of Life, Thought, and Art in France and the Netherlands in the Fourteenth and Fifteenth Centuries* (Pelican Books A 307), London/Tonbridge 1955

HULS, J.: 'Dag Hammarskjöld over de meditatieruimte van de V.N.', in *Speling* 47 (1995) 56-65

HUMPHREY, C. & J. LAIDLAW: *The Archetypal Actions of Ritual. A Theory of Ritual Illustrated by the Jain Rite of Worship* (Oxford Studies in Social and Cultural Anthropology), Oxford 1994

HURTH, E.: *Zwischen Religion und Unterhaltung. Zur Bedeutung der religiösen Dimensionen in den Medien*, Mainz 2001

HUXLEY, J.: 'Introduction. A Discussion on Ritualisation of Behavior', in J. HUXLEY (ed.): 'A Discussion on Ritualisation of Behavior of Animals and Man', in *Philosophical Transactions of the Royal Society*, Series B, 251 (1966) 249-271

HUXLEY, J. (ed.): 'A Discussion on Ritualisation of Behavior of Animals and Man', in *Philosophical Transactions of the Royal Society*, Series B, 251 (1966)

HYMNBOOK: *The Hymnbook*, Richmond, etc. 1955

IERSEL, B. VAN: 'Some Biblical Roots of the Christian Sacrament', in *Concilium* 4 (1968) 1, 4-11

IERSEL, B. VAN: 'Bible and Evolution: Two Codes – Two Messages', in *Concilium* 36 (2000) 1, 102-111.

IKON: *Herdenkingsdienst bij de dood van Koos Koster, Jan Kuiper, Joop Willemsen, Hans ter Laag, 21 maart 1982*, Hilversum 1982

IMBER-BLACK, E. & J. ROBERTS: *Rituals for Our Times. Celebrating, Healing, and Changing our Lives and Relationships*, New York 1992

IMMINK, G.: 'Een dubbele beweging', in P. OSKAMP & N. SCHUMAN: *De weg van de liturgie. Traditties, achtergronden, praktijk*, Zoetermeer 1998, 67-89

INTERMONASTERIËLE WERKGROEP VOOR LITURGIE: *Abdijboek*, Amsterdam 1967 and further

INTERNATIONAL THEOLOGICAL COMMISSION: *Christianity and the World Religions*, Città del Vaticano 1997 = 'Het christendom en de godsdiensten, Rome 1996', in *Een-twee-een. Kerkelijke documentatie* 25 (1997) 7

INTERNATIONAL THEOLOGICAL COMMISSION: 'Le diaconat: évolution et perspectives', in *La documentation catholique* (19 janvier 2003) 23, 58-107

INTERRELIGIEUS: *Interreligieus vieren: Werkmap (voor) Liturgie* 28 (1994) 273-327

IRWIN, K.: *Liturgical Theology: A Primer*, Collegeville Minnesota 1990

IRWIN, K.: *Context and Text: Method in Liturgical Theology*, Collegeville Minnesota 1994

ISAAC, J.: *Arendt, Camus and Modern Rebellion*, Yale 1992

ISAMBERT, F.: 'Fête', in *Encyclopedia Universalis* VI, Paris 1970

JAKOBSON: R., *Essais de linguistique générale*, Paris 1963

JAKOBSON, R. & C. LÉVI-STRAUSS: '"Les chats" de Beaudelaire', in R. JAKOBSON a.o.: *Questions de poétique*, Paris 1973

JAKOBSON, R. a.o.: *Questions de poétique*, Paris 1973

JANSSEN, J.: 'Religie: privé-bezit of sociaal kapitaal', in *De Bazuin* 84 (2001) 25, 23-33

JANSSEN J. & M. PRINS: "Let's reinvent Gods'. De religie van Nederlandse jongeren in een Europese context', in J. JANSSEN, R. VAN UDEN & H. VAN DER VEN (eds.): *Schering en inslag. Opstellen over religie in de hedendaagse cultuur. Aangeboden aan Jan van der Lans bij zijn afscheid als hoogleraar godsdienstpsychologie aan de Katholieke Universiteit Nijmegen*, Nijmegen 1998, 123-138

JANSSEN, J., J. DE HART & C. DEN DRAAK: 'Praying as an individualized ritual', in H.-G. HEIMBROCK & B. BOUDEWIJNSE: *Current Studies on Rituals. Perspectives for the Psychology of Religion*, Amsterdam/Atlanta 1990, 71-85

JANSSEN, J., R. VAN UDEN & H. VAN DER VEN (eds.): *Schering en inslag. Opstellen over religie in de hedendaagse cultuur. Aangeboden aan Jan van der Lans bij zijn afscheid als hoogleraar godsdienstpsychologie aan de Katholieke Universiteit Nijmegen*, Nijmegen 1998

JAQUEN, R.: *L'Eucharistie du mil. Languages d'un people, expressions de la foi*, Paris 1995

JASPARD, J.M.: 'Geboorte en doopsel vanuit psychofilosofische hoek bekeken', in L. LEIJSSEN, M. CLOET & K. DOBBELAERE (eds.): *Levensrituelen. Geboorte en doopsel* (Kadoc-Studies 20), Leuven 1996, 28-45

JEFFERY, P.: 'A Chant Historian Reads *Liturgiam Authenticam*. 1: The Latin Liturgical Traditions, 2: The Bible in the Roman Liturgy, 3.: Languages and Cultures, 4: Human and Angelic Tongues', in *Worship* 78 (2004) 2-24, 139-164, 236-265, 309-341.

JENNINGS, T.: 'On Ritual Knowledge', in *Journal of Religion* 62 (1982) 111-127

JENNINGS, T.: 'Ritual Studies and Liturgical Theology. An invitation to dialogue', in *Journal of Ritual Studies* 1 (1987) 35-56

JENSEN, A.E.: *Das religiöse Weltbild einer frühen Kultur*, Wiesbaden 1949

JENSEN, A.E.: *Mythos und Kult bei Naturvölker. Religionswissenschaftliche Betrachtungen*, Wiesbaden 1951

JEROENSE, J.: *De speelse kerk. Een pleidooi voor theater in de kerk*, Zoetermeer 1995

JESPERS, F. & E. HENAU (eds): *Liturgie en kerkopbouw. Opstellen aangeboden aan Ad Blijlevens*, Baarn 1993

JETTER, W.: *Symbol und Ritual. Anthropologische Elemente im Gottesdienst*, Göttingen 1978

JOHANNES PAULUS II: *Centesimus annus*, Città del Vaticano 1991

JOHANNES PAULUS II: *Ordinatio sacerdotalis*, Città del Vaticano 1994

JOHANNES PAULUS II: *Fides et ratio*, Città del Vaticano 1998

JOHANNES PAULUS II: *Ecclesia de Eucharistia*, Città del Vaticano 2003

JOHNSON, C.V.: 'The Children's Eucharistic Prayers: A Model of Liturgical Inculturation', in *Worship* 75 (2001) 209-227

JOHNSON, M.E.: 'A Response to Gerard Austin's "Identity of a Eucharistic Church in an Ecumenical Age"', in *Worship* 72 (1998) 35-43

JOHNSON, M.E.: 'Can We Avoid Relativism in Worship? Liturgical Norms in the Light of Contemporary Liturgical Worship', in *Worship* 74 (2000) 135-155

JOHNSON, M.E.: 'The Role of Worship in the Contemporary Study of Chritian Initiation: A Select Review of the Literature', in *Worship* 75 (2001) 20-35

JONG, E. DE: 'Bijbelvertaling en liturgie', in G. LUKKEN & J. DE WIT (eds.): *Lezen in fragmenten. De Bijbel als liturgisch boek* (Liturgie in beweging 2), Baarn 1998, 100-106

JONG, E. DE: 'Het rituaal voor boete en verzoening', in G. LUKKEN & J. DE WIT (eds.): *Gebroken bestaan. Rituelen rond vergeving en verzoening* 1 (Liturgie in beweging 3), Baarn 1998, 35-47

JONG, M. DE: 'Het gebaar als spiegel van de middeleeuwse ziel', in *NRC Handelsblad* March 21, 1992, Zaterdags bijvoegsel (Saturday Supplement), 4

JONGE, S. DE: *Kerkarchitectuur na 2000. Het ontwikkelen van grensverleggende typologieën vanuit het samenspel tussen liturgie, architectuur en duurzame ontwikkeling*, Eindhoven/Tilburg 2002

JONGERIUS, H.: 'Op de vierkante meter die je gegeven is doen wat je meent te moeten doen... Een gesprek met Jos Wilderbeek', in *Inzet* 21 (1992) 1, 11-15

JONGERIUS, H.: 'Liturgische vorming of vorming tot liturgie', in *Tijdschrift voor Liturgie* 85 (2001) 231-244

JONGSMA-TIELEMAN, N.: *Rituelen: speelruimte van de hoop. Wat rituelen (ons) doen*, Kampen 2002

JOOSSE, J.: *Eucharistische gebeden in Nederland. Een documentaire studie over de ontwikkeling van de vertaalde en 'eigen' Nederlandse eucharistische gebeden (1963-1979)* Tilburg 1991

JOOSSE, J.: 'Symboliseren, rituelen, ritueel en cultuur', in *Liturgiewetenschap*, Vol. 2 (Open Theologisch Onderwijs), Kampen 1991, 8-58

JOOSSE, J. & P. DE MAAT: 'Semiotische analyse van de opening van het 'Amsterdamse doopritueel'', in *Jaarboek voor liturgie-onderzoek* 1 (1985) 2-67

JOOSSE, J. & P. DE MAAT: 'Semiotische analyse van de tussenzang van het 'Amsterdamse doopritueel'', in *Jaarboek voor liturgie-onderzoek* 2 (1986) 86-118

JOOSSE, J. & W. RAMS: 'Vergeven? – Dat is te doen', in *Inzet* 26 (1997) 3, 94-97

JOSUTIS, M.: *Der Weg in das Leben. Eine Einführung in den Gottesdienst auf verhaltenswissenschaftlicher Grundlage*, München 1991

JOUNEL, P. a.o. (eds.): *Liturgia opera divina e umana; Studi sulla riforma liturgica offerti a S.E. Mons. Annibale Bugnini in occasione del suo 70 compleanno*, Rome 1982

JOUSSE, M.: *L'anthropologie du geste*, Vol. 1, Paris 1974

JOUSSE, M.: *L'anthropologie du geste*, Vol. 2, *La manducation de la parole*, Paris 1975

JOUSSE, M.: *L'anthropologie du geste*, Vol. 3, *Le parlant, la parole et le souffle*, Paris 1978

JÜNGEL, E.: 'Das Sakrament – Was ist das?', in E. JÜNGEL & K. RAHNER: *Was ist ein Sakrament?*, Freiburg/Basel/Wien 1971

JÜNGEL, E. & K. RAHNER: *Was ist ein Sakrament?*, Freiburg/Basel/Wien 1971

JUNG, C.G.: *Psychologische Typen*, Zürich 1921

JUNG, C.G.: *Symbole der Wandlung*, Zürich 1952

JUNGMANN, J.A.: *Gewordene Liturgie. Studien und Durchblicke*, Innsbruck 1941

JUNGMANN, J.A.: *Missarum sollemnia*, Wien 1958[4]

JUNGMANN, J.A.: *The Mass of the Roman Rite*, New York 1961

JUNGMANN, J.A.: *Pastoral Liturgy*, London 1962

JUNG MO SUNG: 'Evil in the Free Market Mentality', in *Concilium* 33 (1997) 5, 24-32

KABASELE, F.: 'Eucharistiefeier in Schwarzafrika', in L. BERTSCH (ed.): *Der neue Messritus im Zaire. Ein Beispiel kontextueller Liturgie* (Theologie der dritten Welt 18), Freiburg im Breisgau 1993, 123-183

KACZYNSKI, R.: 'Angriff auf die Liturgiekonstitution? Anmerkungen zu einer neuen Übersetzer-Instruktion', in *Stimmen der Zeit* 126 (2001) 651-668

KACZYNSKI, R.: 'Anmerkungen zu den nachkonziliaren liturgischen Büchern', in M. KLÖCKENER & B. KRANEMANN (eds.): *Liturgiereformen. Historische Studien zu einem bleibenden Grundzug des christlichen Gottesdienstes* (Liturgiewissenschaftliche Quellen und Forschungen 88), Münster 2002, 1003-1016

KAGIE, R.: 'Topsport en geluksrituelen', in *NRC Handelsblad* April 5, 1991, 18

KALK, T. & C. RIKKERS, *Wij gaan ons echt verbinden. Verbintenisceremonies voor homoseksuele en lesbische stellen*, Amsterdam 2002

KALSE, M. & P. TIMMERS: 'Veranderende rituelen rond dood en begraven', in *Studio* 72 (1998) 42 (October 10-16), 6-7

KAMERMAN, S.: 'Trouwen in het buitenland: 'Bali is een topper'', in *NRC Handelsblad* August 21, 2001, 8

KAMP, G. VAN DE: 'Zegening in een trouwviering', in P. OSKAMP & N. SCHUMAN: *De weg van de liturgie. Tradities, achtergronden, praktijk*, Zoetermeer 1998, 327-331

KAMPENHOUT, D. VAN: *Rituelen. Essentie, uitvoering en begeleiding*, Amsterdam 1993

KAPELLARI, E.: 'Naar een vernieuwde kunst van het voorgaan in de liturgie', in *ICLZ-Mededelingen* 91 (1997) 790-794 and 92 (1997) 799-802

KASKI: 'Kerncijfers 1994/1995. Uit de kerkelijke statistiek van het R.-K. Kerkgenootschap in Nederland', in *Een-twee-een. Kerkelijke documentatie*

23 (1995) no. 9 = KASKI: *Kerncijfers uit de kerkelijke statistiek 1994/1995 van het R.-K. Kerkgenootschap in Nederland* (Memorandum no. 291), Den Haag 1995

KASPER, W.: 'Wort und Symbol im sakramentalen Leben. Eine anthropologische Begründung', in W. HEINEN (ed.): *Bild-Wort-Symbol in der Theologie*, Würzburg 1969, 157-175

KASPER, W.: 'Wort und Sakrament', in *Glaube und Geschichte*, Mainz 1970, 285-310

KAVANAGH, A.: *On Liturgical Theology*, New York 1985

KAVANAGH, A.: 'Textuality and Deritualisation: the Case of Western Liturgical Use', in *Studia Liturgica* 23 (1993) 70-77

KELLEHER, M.M.: 'Liturgy: An Ecclesial Act of Meaning', in *Worship* 59 (1987) 482-497.

KELLEHER, M.M.: 'Liturgy and the Christian Imagination', in *Worship* 66 (1992) 125-147.

KELLEHER, M.M.: 'Hermeneutics in the Study of Liturgical Performance', in *Worship* 67 (1993) 292-318

KEMPEN, P.A.M. VAN: *Het huwelijksritueel in de Nederlanden voor 1614*, Tilburg 1989

KENNEDY, E.C.: 'The Contribution of Religious Ritual to Psychological Balance', in *Concilium* 7 (1971) 2, 53-58.

KERNER, H. (ed.): *Gottesdienst und Kultur. Zukunftsperspektiven*, Leipzig 2004

KERSTEN, TH.: *Gedoopt voor mensen. Werkboek voor katechese en liturgie*, Nijmegen 1983

KESEL, J. DE: *Omwille van zijn Naam. Een tegendraads pleidooi voor de kerk*, Tielt 1994, 151-155

KILMARTIN, E.: *Christian Liturgy; Theology and Practice*, Kansas City, Mo 1988

KILSDONK, J. VAN: 'Groeten in Amsterdam', in *De Bazuin* 65 (1982) 15 (April 9), 2

KILSDONK, J. VAN: *Met het licht van jouw ogen ... zegen mij*, Amstelveen 1982

KILSDONK, J. VAN: *Met het licht van jouw ogen ... zegen mij. Toespraken*, Heeswijk 2000

KIRCHHOFF, H. (ed.): *Ursymbole und ihre Bedeutung für die religiöse Erziehung*, München 1982

KLAMER, A.: 'Religie op school', in *Roodkoper* 2 (1997) 6, 12-14

KLAUSER, TH.: *Kleine abendländische Liturgiegeschichte*, Bonn 1965

KLERCK, B. DE: 'Het museum een kathedraal', in *NRC Handelsblad* September 26, 1997, 43

KLÖCKENER, M. & B. KRANEMANN (eds.): *Liturgiereformen. Historische Studien zu einem bleibenden Grundzug des christlichen Gottesdienstes* (Liturgiewissenschaftliche Quellen und Forschungen 88), Münster 2002

KLÖCKENER, M. a.o. (eds.): *Gottes Volk feiert... Anspruch und Wirklichkeit gegenwärtiger Liturgie*, Trier 2002

KLOMP, A.: 'De bruid is big business', in *NRC Handelsblad* January 29, 1998, 17

KLOOS, P.: *Culturele antropologie. Een inleiding*, Assen 1995 (sixth revised edition)

KLOSTERMANN, F. & R. ZERFASS: *Praktische Theologie Heute*, München 1974

KLOPPENBURG, W.: *Trouwring of oorbel?*, IKON-radio, Hilversum 1985, 10-12 (Dutch translation of the ritual *'Recognition of Divorce'* of J. WESTERHOFF & W. WILLIMON in *Liturgy and Learning Through the Life Cycle*, New York 1980)

KNAAPEN, H.: *Liturgie en kosmopolitiek* (M.A. Thesis Theologische Faculteit Tilburg), Tilburg 1974

KNIPPENBERG, T. VAN: 'Op verhaal komen in de biechtstoel', in *De Bazuin* 83 (2000) (March 3), 18-20

KNULST, W.P.: *Werk, rust en sociaal leven op zondagen sinds de jaren zeventig*, Tilburg 1999

KOCH, K.: 'Liturgie und Theater. Theologische Fragmente zu einem vernachlässigten Thema', in *Stimmen der Zeit* 120 (1995) Heft 1 (Bnd.213), 3-16

KOCK, G.: *Tussen altaar en oksaal. Stromingen in de kerkmuziek na Vaticanum II* (M.A. Thesis Theologische faculteit Tilburg), Tilburg 1980

KOESTER, A.Y. & B. SEARLE (eds.): *Vision. The Contributions of Mark Searle to Liturgical Renewal*, Collegeville 2004

KÖSTLIN, K.: 'Die Wiederkehr der Engel', in N.-A. BRINGÉUS (ed.): *Religion in Everyday Life. Papers Given at a Symposium in Stockholm 1993*, Stockholm 1994, 79-96

KOHLSCHEIN, F.: 'Symbol und Kommunikation als Schlüsselbegriffe einer Theologie und Theorie der Liturgie', in *Liturgisches Jahrbuch* 35 (1985) 200-218

KOHNSTAMM, R.: 'Beschutting van ritualen', in *NRC Handelsblad* April 11, 1998

KOK, H.: *De geschiedenis van de laatste eer in Nederland*, Lochem 1970

KOK, K.: 'Esthetisch katholicisme. Kees Kok in gesprek met Edward Schillebeeckx', in *Werkschrift voor Leerhuis en Liturgie* 10 (1990) 4, 16-18

KOK-ESCALLE, M.-C.: *Instaurer une culture par l'enseignement de l'histoire de France 1876-1912. Contribution à une sémiotique de la culture*, Berne/ Frankfurt am Main/New York/Paris 1989

KOLAKOWSKI, L.: *Geist und Ungeist christlicher Traditionen*, Stuttgart 1971

KOOLSBERGEN, N.: 'Macht over de dood', in *Het Nieuwsblad* September 17, 1993, 25

KOOPMANS, J.: 'Dat je laatste tocht niet opgaat in het ledige', in *De Bazuin* 76 (1993) 41 (October 29), 10-11

KOOPMANS, J.: 'Uitvaart voor niet-kerkelijken: uitdaging voor kerken', in *Kerugma* 37 (1993-1994) 2, 73-80

KOORDANSER: *Koördanser. Informatieblad voor persoonlijke groei* (2002) (May), no. 198.

KORTE, A.-M.: 'Een lijfelijke hang naar het goddelijke. De nieuwe culturele belangstelling voor godsgeloof als theologische vraag', in *Tijdschrift voor Theologie* 38 (1998) 227-237

KOTTMAN, P.: 'Paul de Leeuw maakte gedenkwaardige televisie', in *NRC Handelsblad* November 29, 1993, 15

KRANEMANN, B.: 'Aus der Vergangenheit in der Gegenwart für die Zukunft lernen. Eine Festschrift zum Doppeljubiläum der Abtei Maria Laach', in *Archiv für Liturgiewissenschaft* 35 (1993-1994) 366-373

KRIEGER, D.J. & A. BELLIGER: 'Einführung', in A. BELLIGER & D.J. KRIEGER (eds.): *Ritualtheorien. Ein einführendes Handbuch*, Wiesbaden 1998, 7-33

KROEBER, A.F. & C. KLUCKHOHN: *Culture. A Critical Review of Concepts and Definitions* (Papers of the Peabody Museum, 1952, 47), New York 1995

KROESEN, J.: *Stiltecentra,* Groningen 1997 = J. KROESEN: 'Stiltecentra', in *Jaarboek voor liturgie-onderzoek* 13 (1997) 93-133

KROESEN, J., J.R. LUTH & A.L. MOLENDIJK (eds.): *Religieuze ruimte. Kerkbouw, kerkinrichting en religieuze kunst. Feestbundel voor Regnerus Steensma bij zijn vijf en zestigste verjaardag*, Zoetermeer 2002

KRONENBURG, J.: 'Het ritueel van vergeving en verzoening in de reformatie – een verhaal uit de praktijk', in G. LUKKEN & J. DE WIT (eds.): *Gebroken bestaan. Rituelen rond vergeving en verzoening* I (Liturgie in beweging 3), Baarn 1998, 48-59

KUNST, J.: 'Pop versus klassiek. Of: Hoe moeten culturen met elkaar omgaan?', in A. VAN ZOEST (ed.): *De macht der tekens. Opstellen over maatschappij, tekst en litteratuur*, Utrecht 1986, 195-203

KUNZLER, M.: *Die Liturgie der Kirche* (Amateca 10), Paderborn 1995

KURRIS, A.: 'Hoe indringend is het lied?', in *Werkmap (voor) Liturgie* 18 (1984) 6-25

KURVERS, G.: 'Liturgisch drama in de Middeleeuwen: lessen voor nu', in *Tijdschrift voor Liturgie* 79 (1995) 178-196

KUYPER, E. DE: *Pour une sémiotique spectaculaire* (Doctoral Thesis EHSS), Paris 1979

LAARHOVEN, J. VAN: 'Een geschiedenis van de biechtvader', in *Tijdschrift voor Theologie* 7 (1967) 375-422

LAARHOVEN, J. VAN: 'Het boek van de Middeleeuwen', in *Kohelet. Faculteitsblad Theologische Faculteit Tilburg* 5 (1988) 1, 6-12

LACAN, J.: *Écrits*, Paris 1966

LAERMANS, R., B. WILSON & J. BILLIET: *Secularization and Social Integration. Papers in honor of Karel Dobbelaere*, Leuven 1998

LAEYENDECKER, L.: 'De keerzijde wordt zichtbaar – Problematische kanten van de moderniteit', in S.W. COUWENBERG (ed.): *Westerse cultuur: model voor de hele wereld*, Kampen 1994, 40-47

LAEYENDECKER, L.: 'Kerk en tegencultuur', in *Praktische theologie* 23 (1996) 255-270

LAYENDECKER, L.: *Zijn Kerken nog nodig?*, in *Rood Koper* 5 (2000) 6, 12-14

LAEYENDECKER, L.& MADY A. THUNG: 'Liturgie in een politiek geëngageerde kerk', in *Tijdschrift voor Theologie* 18 (1978) 49-71

LAFAILLE, R. a.o. (eds.): *Zelfhulptechnieken. Wat het individu zelf kan doen aan zijn lichamelijk en geestelijk welzijn*, Deventer/Antwerpen 1981

LAMBERIGTS, M. & L. KENIS: *Vatican II and its legacy*, Leuven 2002

LAMBERTS, J.: 'De kwestie van de vormselleeftijd. Een liturgiewetenschappelijke en pastoraaltheologische benadering', in K. DOBBELAERE, L. LEIJSSEN & M. CLOET (eds.): *Levensrituelen. Het vormsel* (Kadoc-Studies 12), Leuven 1991, 167-193

LAMBERTS, J. (ed.): *Hedendaagse accenten in de sacramententheologie*, Leuven 1994 = J. LAMBERTS, (ed.): *Accents actuels en théologie sacramentaire – Current Issues in Sacramental Theology* (Textes et Etudes Liturgiques/Studies in Liturgy 13), Leuven 1994 and *Questions Liturgiques* 75 (1994) 1-2, 1-112

LAMBERTS, J. (ed.): *Liturgie en inculturatie. Verslagboek van het twaalfde liturgiecolloquium van het Liturgisch Instituut van de K.U. Leuven – oktober 1995* (Nikè-reeks 37), Leuven/Amersfoort 1996 = J. LAMBERTS (ed.): *Liturgie et inculturation. Liturgy and Inculturation* (Textes et Études Liturgiques/ Studies in Liturgy 14), Leuven 1996

LAMBERTS, J. (ed.): *Popular Religion and Liturgy: Questions Liturgiques* 79 (1998) no. 1-2. = J. LAMBERTS (ed.): *Religion populaire, liturgie et évangélisation – Popular Religion. Liturgy and Evangelization* (Textes et Études Liturgiques/Studies in Liturgy 15), Leuven 1998 = J. LAMBERTS (ed.): *Volksreligie, liturgie en evangelisatie* (Nikè-reeks 42), Leuven/Amersfoort 1998

LANDOWSKI, E.: 'En deçà ou au-delà des stratégies, la présence contagieuse', in *Nouveaux Actes Sémiotiques* 83 (2002) 5-44

LANE, C.: *The Rites of Rulers. Ritual in Industrial Society – The Soviet Case*, Cambridge 1981

LANGE-SNELDERS, M. DE: 'Een pleidooi voor rituelen', in R. LAFAILLE a.o. (eds.): *Zelfhulptechnieken. Wat het individu zelf kan doen aan zijn lichamelijk en geestelijk welzijn*, Deventer/Antwerpen 1981, 1-12

LANGER, S.: *Philosophie auf neuem Wege*, Frankfurt 1965 (English original: IDEM: *Philosophy in a New Key. A Study in the Symbolism of Reason, Rite, and Art*, New York 1942)

LANSER, A.: "Geef dat het van ons leert te kijken'. De functie van thuisrituelen in de religieuze socialisatie', in *Praktische Theologie* 23 (1996) 426-438

LATHROP, G.: *Holy Things. A Liturgical Theology*, Minneapolis 1993.

LATHROP, G.: *What are the Essentials of Christian Worship?*, Minneapolis 1994

LAUGHLIN, C.D.: 'Ritual and the Symbolic Function. A Summary of Bio-genetic Structural Theory', in *Journal of Ritual Studies* 4 (1990) 1, 15-39

LAUGHLIN, C., D.J. MCMANUS & E. D'AQUILI: *Brain, Symbol and Experience*, New York 1990

LAWLER, M.: *Symbol and Sacrament. A Contemporary Sacramental Theology*, Mahwah 1987

LAWRENCE, R.T.: 'The Altar Bible: *Digni, Decori et Pulchri*', in *Worship* 75 (2001) 386-402

LEARY, S. O': 'Cyberspace as Sacred Space: Communicating Religion on Computer Networks', in *The Journal of the American Academy of Religion* 64 (1996) 781-808

LEEUW, G. VAN DER: *Wegen en grenzen*, Amsterdam 1948²

LEGRAND, H.-M.: 'Traditio perpetuo servata? La non-ordination des femmes: tradition ou simple fait historique?', in P. DE CLERCK & E. PALAZZO (eds.): *Rituels. Mélanges offerts à Pierre-Marie Gy, o.p.*, Paris 1990, 399-416

LEIJSSEN, L. (ed.): *Liturgie et langage – Liturgy and Language* (Textes et Études Liturgiques/Studies in Liturgy 12), Leuven 1992 = L. LEIJSSEN (ed.): *Liturgie en taal*, Leuven/Amersfoort 1992

LEIJSSEN, L.: 'Sacramentologische reflectie op het kinderdoopsel', in L. LEIJSSEN, M. CLOET & K. DOBBELAERE (eds.): *Levensrituelen. Geboorte en doopsel* (Kadoc-Studies 20), Leuven 1996, 261-277

LEIJSSEN, L.: 'Geschiedenis van de christelijke verzoening in vogelvlucht. Hermeneutische reflecties', in G. LUKKEN & J. DE WIT (eds.): *Gebroken bestaan. Rituelen rond vergeving en verzoening* 1 (Liturgie in beweging 3), Baarn 1998, 14-33

LEIJSSEN, L.: 'La spécificité de la confirmation. Réflexions de théologie sacramentelle (post-moderne)', in *Questions Liturgiques* 79 (1998) 3-4, 249-264

LEIJSSEN, L., M. CLOET & K. DOBBELAERE: 'Slotbeschouwingen', in L. LEIJSSEN, M. CLOET & K. DOBBELAERE (eds.): *Levensrituelen. Geboorte en doopsel* (Kadoc-Studies 20), Leuven 1996, 310-318

LEIJSSEN, L., M. CLOET & K. DOBBELAERE (eds.): *Levensrituelen. Geboorte en doopsel* (Kadoc-Studies 20), Leuven 1996

LEIJSSEN, L., P. MOYAERT & L. BOEVE: 'Samenspraak. Rituelen, sacramenten en liturgieën', in *Kultuurleven. Tijdschrift voor cultuur en samenleving* 64 (1997) 5-15

LEKTOREN IN ST. AUGUSTIN (ed.): *In verbo tuo. Festschrift zum 50jährigen Bestehen des Missionspriesterseminar St. Augustin bei Siegburg, Rheinl. 1913-1963*, St. Augustin 1963

E.J. LENGELING: 'Liturgie als Vollzug christlichen Lebens', in B. FISCHER, E.J. LENGELING, R. SCHAEFFLER, F. SCHULZ & H.R. MÜLLER-SCHWEFE: *Kult in der säkularisierten Welt*, Regensburg 1974, 63-91

LENGELING, E.J. & K. RICHTER: *Liturgie. Dialog zwischen Gott und Mensch*, Freiburg 1981

LEVER, J.: 'Klein, onzienlijk, onvoorstelbaar', in J. DE VISSCHER (ed.): *Moster-dzaadjes van het bestaan. De waarde van de kleine dingen*, Baarn 1996, 22-37

LEVESQUE, P.: 'A Symbolical Sacramental Methodology: An Application of the Thought of Louis Dupré', in *Questions Liturgiques* 76 (1995) 161-181

LEWIS, A.E.: *Between Cross and Resurrection. A theology of Holy Saturday*, Michi-gan/Cambridge 2001

LEYS, A.: *Ecclesiological Impacts of the Principle of Subsidiarity*, Kampen 1995

LIEDBOEK: *Liedboek voor de kerken*, Den Haag 1973

LIES, L.: *Eucharistie in ökumenischer Verantwortung*, Graz/Wien/Köln 1996

LIESHOUT, J. VAN & M. MERCX: *Spelenderwijs revolutie maken. Volkstheater in Nicaragua*, Nijmegen 1986

LIFE: *Life Cycle Rituals and Sacramentality: Between Continuity and Discontinu-ity*: *Questions Liturgiques* 83 (2002) no. 1

LIGT: 'Ligt u lekker?', in *NRC Handelsblad* July 8, 1995, Zaterdags bijvoegsel (Saturday Supplement), 2

LIMENTANI VIRDIS, C. & E.M. PIETROGIVANNA, *Gothic and Renaissance Altar-pieces*, London/New York 2002.

LINN, E.: *Preaching as counseling. The unique Method of Hary Emerson Fosdick*, Valley Forge 1966

LITURGIE: *Liturgie en maatschappij*: *Werkmap (voor) Liturgie* 18 (1984) 115-174

LITURGIE: *Liturgie en theater*: *Werkmap (voor) liturgie* 25 (1991) 129-192

LITURGIE: *Liturgie en maatschappelijke knelpunten*: *Werkmap (voor) Liturgie* 26 (1992) 1-62

LITURGIE: *La liturgie, un théâtre?*: *La Maison-Dieu* (1999) no. 219

LITURGIE: *Liturgie en vrouw*: *Tijdschrift voor Liturgie* 80 (1996) no. 5

LITURGIE: 'Liturgie et musique'. *Congrès de la Societas liturgica Turku, 1997*: *La Maison-Dieu* (1997) no. 212

LITURGIE: *La liturgie, un théâtre?*: *La Maison-Dieu* (1999) no. 219

LITURGISCHE: *Liturgische Gezangen voor de viering van de eucharistie*, Hilversum 1979

LITURGISCHE: *Liturgische proeftuinen*: *Rondom het Woord* 27 (1985) no. 2

LITURGY: *Liturgy and the Body*: *Concilium* 26 (1995) no. 3.

LOGISTER, W.: 'Voorbij de apartheid. Enkele gedachten over interreligieus leren en leven', in *Werkmap (voor) Liturgie* 28 (1994) 320-327

LOGISTER, W.: 'A Small Theology of Feasting', in P. POST, G. ROUWHORST, L. VAN TONGEREN & A. SCHEER (eds.): *Christian Feast and Festival. The Dynamics of Western Liturgy and Culture* (Liturgia condenda 12), Leuven 2001, 145-166

LOMANS, P.: 'Symbolen in de samenleving. Tussen hakenkruis en hostie', in *Het Nieuwsblad* October 22, 1991, 19

LOMBAERTS, H.: 'Weerbaar of weerloos? Godsdienstige tradities in de hedendaagse maatschappij', in H. LOMBAERTS & L. BOEVE (eds.): *Traditie en initiatie. Perspectieven voor de toekomst*, Leuven/Amersfoort 1996, 79-108

LOMBAERTS, H.: 'Kunst zonder religie? Religie zonder kunst?', in H. LOMBAERTS, J. MAAS & J. WISSINK (eds.): *Beeld en gelijkenis. Inwijding, kunst en religie*, Zoetermeer 2001, 17-27

LOMBAERTS, H. & L. BOEVE (eds.): *Traditie en initiatie. Perspectieven voor de toekomst*, Leuven 1996

LOMBAERTS, H., J. MAAS & J. WISSINK (eds.): *Beeld en Gelijkenis. Inwijding, kunst en religie*, Zoetermeer 2001

LOOF, D. DE: 'A Comparison of Selected German and American Emblems', in *Kodikas Code* 3 (1981) 101-102

LOOR, H. DE & J. PETERS: 'Een vergelijkende sociologische analyse van de katholieke en de hervormde kerk sedert 1945', in P. STOUTHARD & G. VAN TILLO (eds.): *Katholiek Nederland na 1945*, Baarn 1985, 144-168

LOOSE, D.A.A.: *Vergeten Ithaka. De odyssee van de moderne tijd*, Vught 1995

LOOSEN, L. (ed.): *Liturgische gebedstaal: Werkmap (voor) Liturgie* 24 (1990) 3-64

LORENZ, K.Z.: 'Evolution of Ritualization in the Biological and Cultural Spheres', in *Philosophical Transactions of the Royal Society*, Series B, 251 (1966) 273-284

LORENZER, A.: *Das Konzil der Buchhalter. Die Zerstörung der Sinnlichkeit. Eine Religionskritik*, Frankfurt 1981

LÜBBE, H.: 'Der Fortschritt und das Museum', in *Dilthey Jahrbuch* 1 (1983) 39-56

LÜHRMANN, D. & G. STERCKER: *Kirche. Festschrift für Günther Bornkamm*, Tübingen 1980

LUIJPEN, W.: 'De erwtensoep is klaar', in *Streven* 22 (1969) 510-526

LUIJS, J.: 'Taal, teken, ritueel. Humanisten in dubio', in *Werkmap (voor) Liturgie* 25 (1991) 244-246

LUKKEN, G.: 'Enkele kanttekeningen over het exorcisme', in *Tijdschrift voor Liturgie* 52 (1968) 254-260

LUKKEN, G.: 'De ontwikkeling van de liturgie sinds Vaticanum II', in A. HOLLAARDT (ed.): *Liturgische oriëntatie na Vaticanum II (Supplement Liturgisch Woordenboek)*, Roermond 1970, 19-24

LUKKEN, G.: *Original Sin in the Roman liturgy. Research into the Theology of Original Sin in the Roman Sacramentaria and the Early Baptismal Liturgy*, Leiden 1973

LUKKEN, G.: 'The Unique Expression of Faith in the Liturgy', in *Concilium* 2 (1973) 9, 11-21

LUKKEN, G.: 'De liturgie als onvervangbare vindplaats van de theologie. Methoden van theologische analyse en verificatie', in H. BERGER a.o.: *Tussentijds. Theologische Faculteit Tilburg. Opstellen bij gelegenheid van haar erkenning*, Tilburg 1974, 317-332 = G. LUKKEN: 'La liturgie comme lieu théologique irremplaçable. Méthodes d'analyse et vérification théologiques, in *Questions liturgiques* 56 (1975) 317-322 and (with additions) G. LUKKEN (eds. C. CASPERS & L. VAN TONGEREN): *Per visibilia ad invisibilia. Anthropological, Theological and Semiotic Studies on the Liturgy and the Sacraments* (Liturgia condenda 2), Kampen 1994, 239-255

LUKKEN, G.: 'Kernvragen rond de christelijke dodenliturgie', in *Tijdschrift voor Liturgie* 64 (1980) 146-164

LUKKEN, G.: *De onvervangbare weg van de liturgie*, Hilversum 1980, 1984²

LUKKEN, G.: *Geen leven zonder rituelen. Antropologische beschouwingen met het oog op de christelijke liturgie* (Tweede serie Geestelijke Volksgezondheid 2-24), Baarn 1984, Hilversum 1986², 1988³

LUKKEN, G.: 'Het binnengaan in de kerk in de Romeinse huwelijksliturgie. Een semiotische analyse', in *Jaarboek voor liturgie-onderzoek* 1 (1985) 69-89

LUKKEN, G.: 'Liturgie en stilte', in *Lijnen* 2 (1985) 38-42

LUKKEN, G.: 'De nieuwe Romeinse huwelijksliturgie', in SEMANET (ed. G. LUKKEN): *Semiotiek en christelijke uitingsvormen. De semiotiek van A.J. Greimas en de Parijse school toegepast op bijbel en liturgie*, Hilversum 1987, 155-226

LUKKEN, G.: 'De semiotiek van de Parijse school', in SEMANET (ed. G. LUKKEN): *Semiotiek en christelijke uitingsvormen. De semiotiek van A.J. Greimas en de Parijse school toegepast op bijbel en liturgie*, Hilversum 1987, 8-54

LUKKEN, G.: 'Semiotische analyse van de huwelijkssluiting in het post-tridentijnse Rituale Romanum', in *Jaarboek voor liturgie-onderzoek* 3 (1987) 41-85

LUKKEN, G.: 'Semiotics and the Study of Liturgy', in W. VOS & G. WAINWRIGHT (eds.): *Gratias Agamus. An ecumenical collection of essays on the liturgy and its implications. On the occasion of the twenty fifth anniversary of Studia liturgica (1962-1987)* (Studia liturgica 17), Rotterdam 1987, 108-117

LUKKEN, G.: 'De plaats van de vrouw in het huwelijksritueel van het Rituale Romanum en van Vaticanum II. Van ondergeschiktheid van de vrouw naar een zekere evenwaardigheid van man en vrouw', in *Jaarboek voor liturgie-onderzoek* 4 (1988) 67-89 = G. LUKKEN: 'Die Stellung der Frau im

Trauungsritus des *Rituale Romanum* und nach Vaticanum II. Von der Unterordnung der Frau zu einer gewissen Gleichwertigkeit von Mann und Frau', in G. LUKKEN (eds. C. CASPERS & L. VAN TONGEREN): *Per visibilia ad invisibilia. Anthropological, Theological and Semiotic Studies on the Liturgy and the Sacraments* (Liturgia condenda 2), Kampen 1994, 311-334

LUKKEN, G.: 'Ritueel en menselijke identiteit', in A. DE RUIJTER a.o.: *Totems en trends. Over de zin van identificatiesymbolen*, Hilversum 1988, 20-34

LUKKEN, G.: 'Die architektonische Dimensionen des Rituals', in *Liturgisches Jahrbuch* 39 (1989) 19-36 = IDEM: 'Les dimensions architectoniques du rituel', in *Sémiotique et Bible* 16 (1991) 5-21 and IDEM (eds. C. CASPERS & L. VAN TONGEREN): *Per visibilia ad invisibilia. Anthropological and Semiotic Studies on the Liturgy and the Sacraments* (Liturgia condenda 2), Kampen 1994, 360-374

LUKKEN, G.: 'De constituering van het subject in het ritueel discours', in *Versus. Tijdschrift voor film en opvoeringskunsten* 4 (1989) 2, 34-42

LUKKEN, G.: 'Un chant liturgique néerlandais analysé comme objet syncrétique', in *Jaarboek voor liturgie-onderzoek* 6 (1990) 135-154

LUKKEN, G.: 'Les transformations du rôle liturgique du peuple. La contribution de la sémiotique à l'histoire de la liturgie', in CH. CASPERS & M. SCHNEIDERS (eds.): *Omnes circumadstantes. Contributions towards a history of the role of the people in the liturgy*, Kampen 1990, 15-30 (= *Sémiotique et Bible* 18 (1994) 27-48)

LUKKEN, G.: *Liturgie en zintuiglijkheid. Over de betekenis van lichamelijkheid in de liturgie*, Hilversum 1990 = G. LUKKEN: 'Liturgie und Sinnlichkeit. Über die Bedeutung der Leiblichkeit in der Liturgie', in G. LUKKEN (eds. C. CASPERS & L. VAN TONGEREN): *Per visibilia ad invisibilia. Anthropological, Theological and Semiotic Studies on the Liturgy and the Sacraments* (Liturgia condenda 2), Kampen 1994, 118-139

LUKKEN, G.: 'Zoeken naar nieuwe overgangsrituelen', in *Werkmap (voor) Liturgie* 24 (1990) 159-166

LUKKEN, G.: 'De 'doorbraak' van de antropologie in de liturgie', in H.J.F. DEGEN a.o. (eds.): *Herinneringen aan de toekomst. Pastoraat in de geest van Vaticanum II*, Baarn 1991, 167-176

LUKKEN, G.: 'De geschiedenis in vogelvlucht', in A. BLIJLEVENS & G. LUKKEN (eds.): *In goede en kwade dagen*, Baarn 1991, 41-43 (= *Werkmap (voor) Liturgie* 12 (1978) 369-373)

LUKKEN, G.: 'Ritueel en ruimte', in *Werkmap (voor) Liturgie* 25 (1991) 132-140

LUKKEN, G.: 'Stoten wij op een muur of is er daarachter meer?', in *Hervormd Nederland* 48 (1992) 34, Section *Voorlopig: Dood en begraven*, 7-8

LUKKEN, G.: *Ontwikkelingen in de liturgiewetenschap: balans en perspectief* (Liturgie in perspectief 1), Baarn 1993

LUKKEN, G.: 'Op weg naar eenheid in verscheidenheid. Modellen van gemeenschapsvorming rondom brood en beker', in E. HENAU & F. JESPERS (eds.): *Liturgie en kerkopbouw. Opstellen aangeboden aan Ad Blijlevens*, Baarn 1993, 92-104

LUKKEN, G.: 'Church and Liturgy as Dynamic Sacrament of the Spirit', in G. LUKKEN (eds. C. CASPERS & L. VAN TONGEREN); *Per visibilia ad invisibilia. Anthropological, Theological and Semiotic Studies on the Liturgy and the Sacraments* (Liturgia condenda 2), Kampen 1994, 140-157

LUKKEN, G.: *Inculturatie en de toekomst van de liturgie* (Liturgie in perspectief 3), Heeswijk-Dinther 1994 = G. LUKKEN: 'Inculturation et avenir de la liturgie', in *Questions Liturgiques* 75 (1994) 113-134

LUKKEN, G.: *Op zoek naar een geloofwaardige gestalte van de dodenliturgie* (Liturgische Handreikingen 19), Breda 1994

LUKKEN, G.: 'Semiotics of the Ritual. Signification in Rituals as a Specific Mediation of Meaning', in G. LUKKEN (eds. C. CASPERS & L. VAN TONGEREN): *Per visibilia ad invisibilia. Anthropological, Theological and Semiotic Studies on the Liturgy and the Sacraments* (Liturgia condenda 2), Kampen 1994, 269-283

LUKKEN, G. (eds.: C. CASPERS & L. VAN TONGEREN): *Per visibilia ad invisibilia. Anthropological, Theological and Semiotic Studies on the Liturgy and the Sacraments* (Liturgia condenda 2), Kampen 1994

LUKKEN, G.: 'Liturgische ruimte en haar vormgeving: ter inleiding', in *Werkmap (voor) Liturgie* 29 (1995) 2-5

LUKKEN, G.: 'New Rites around Communion in Present-day Western Culture', in C. CASPERS a.o. (eds.): *Bread of Heaven. Customs and Practices Surrounding Holy Communion. Essays in the History of Liturgy and Culture* (Liturgia condenda 3), Kampen 1995, 215-229

LUKKEN, G.: 'Sacrale ruimte en stilte', in *Speling* 47 (1995) 1, 48-55

LUKKEN, G.: 'De bijdrage van de semiotiek aan de praktische theologie', in G. LUKKEN & J. MAAS: *Luisteren tussen de regels. Een semiotische bijdrage aan de praktische theologie*, Baarn 1996, 8-31

LUKKEN, G.: "Ik heb geen wortels dan in het licht' (Hans Andreus). Een semiotische beschouwing over het licht in de liturgie', in A. MULDER & T. SCHEER (eds.): *Natuurlijke liturgie* (Liturgie in perspectief 6), Baarn/Heeswijk-Dinther 1996, 68-90

LUKKEN, G.: 'Inculturatie van de liturgie. Theorie en praktijk', in J. LAMBERTS (ed.): *Liturgie en inculturatie. Verslagboek van het twaalfde liturgiecolloquium van het Liturgisch Instituut van de K.U. Leuven – oktober 1995* (Nikè-reeks 37), Leuven/Amersfoort 1996, 15-56 = G. LUKKEN: 'Inculturation de la liturgie. Théorie et pratique', in *Questions Liturgiques* 77 (1996) 1-2, 10-39 and in J. LAMBERTS (ed.): *Liturgie et inculturation.*

Liturgy and Inculturation (Textes et Études Liturgiques/ Studies in Liturgy 14), Leuven 1996, 10-39.

LUKKEN, G.: 'Het ritueel van de christelijke begrafenis. Een semiotisch-theologisch onderzoek', in *Jaarboek voor liturgie-onderzoek* 12 (1996) 113-135

LUKKEN, G.: 'Semiotische analyse van de Schrift in homiletisch perspectief. Semiotische vragen aan de (bijbel)tekst', in G. LUKKEN & J. MAAS: *Luisteren tussen de regels. Een semiotische bijdrage aan de praktische theologie*, Baarn 1996, 32-70

LUKKEN, G.: 'Wat heeft de liturgie met theater te maken? Een verheldering vanuit de semiotiek van de verschillen, overeenkomsten en raakvlakken', in G. LUKKEN & J. MAAS; *Luisteren tussen de regels. Een semiotische bijdrage aan de praktische theologie*, Baarn 1996, 134-166

LUKKEN, G.: 'Liturgiewetenschappelijk onderzoek in culturele context. Methodische verhelderingen en vragen', in *Jaarboek voor liturgie-onderzoek* 13 (1997) 135-148

LUKKEN, G.: 'Liturgische aspecten: nieuwe tendensen in de uitvaartliturgie', in J. MAASSEN (ed.): *Uitvaarten – een last en een lust voor pastores*(DPC-bundel 4), Rotterdam 1997, 43-64

LUKKEN, G.: 'Nieuwe vragen rond initiatie', in *Verbum* 64 (1997) 7-8, 119-127

LUKKEN, G.: 'Rituelen rond geboorte en doop: nieuwe ontwikkelingen', in G. LUKKEN & J. DE WIT (eds.): *Nieuw leven. Rituelen rond geboorte en doop* (Liturgie in beweging 1), Baarn 1997, 9-31

LUKKEN, G.: 'Op zoek naar een nieuwe stijl van voorgaan', in *Analecta aartsbisdom Utrecht* 71 (1998) (May/June), 158-169 and *Tijdschrift voor Liturgie* 82 (1998) 341-351

LUKKEN, G.: 'Symbool als grondcategorie van de liturgie. Enkele aanvullende verhelderingen vanuit de semiotiek', in *Jaarboek voor liturgie-onderzoek* 14 (1998) 87-97

LUKKEN, G.: "Zo spreekt de Heer'. De Schrift als levend boek', in *Schrift* 30 (1998) 178, 119-122

LUKKEN, G.: 'Vorstelijke oecumene', in *Eredienstvaardig* 14 (1998) 4, 106-109

LUKKEN, G.: 'Doopliturgie en ons gekwetste bestaan', in *Inzet* 28 (1999) 3, 85-89

LUKKEN, G.: 'Hoe krijgt de ruimte betekenis in het ritueel?', in J. MAAS & A. SMEETS (eds.): *Werktekeningen. Semiotische constructies in blauwdruk*, Tilburg 1999, 39-52

LUKKEN, G.: 'Het nieuwe dienstboek van de Samen-op-Weg-kerken: een onvervangbare weg voor de oecumene', in *Praktische Theologie* 26 (1999) 4

LUKKEN, G.: 'Semiotik des Raums in Theater und Rituell: Unterschiede, Übereinkünfte und Berühungsebenen', in TH. NISSLMÜLLER & R. VOLP: *Raum als Zeichen. Wahrnehmung und Erkenntnis von Räumlichkeit*, Münster 1999, 55-70

LUKKEN, G.: 'Lichtfeier der Osternacht: eine semiotische Analyse', in *Jaarboek voor liturgie-onderzoek* 16 (2000) 69-105.

LUKKEN, G.: 'Het christelijke dodenritueel in onze geseculariseerde en multi-culturele samenleving', in *Speling* 53 (2001), 1, 83-90

LUKKEN, G.: 'Implantatie versus inculturatie? Een nieuwe Instructie over het ver-talen van de Romeinse liturgie', in *Eredienstvaardig* 17 (2001) 4, 127-131

LUKKEN, G.: 'Infant baptism in The Netherlands and Flanders. A Christian rit-ual in the dynamic of the anthropological/theological and cultural con-text', in P. POST, G. ROUWHORST, L. VAN TONGEREN & A. SCHEER (eds.): *Christian Feast and Festival. The Dynamics of Western Liturgy and Culture* (Liturgia condenda 12), Leuven 2001, 551-580

LUKKEN, G.: 'Het kerkgebouw als 'totaal kunstwerk': verbondenheid van kunst en cultus', in J. MAAS (ed.): *Beeld en gelijkenis. Bundel voordrachten gehouden bij het afscheid aan de Katholieke Theologische Universiteit te Utrecht van dr. Tjeu van den Berk*, Utrecht 2001, 27-38

LUKKEN, G.: 'Mystagogie van de ruimte', in H. LOMBAERTS, J. MAAS & J. WISSINK (eds.): *Beeld en Gelijkenis. Inwijding, kunst en religie*, Zoetermeer 2001, 28-41

LUKKEN, G.: 'Nieuwe ontwikkelingen in het uitvaartritueel', in J. VAN DEN BOUT a.o. (eds): *Handboek Sterven, Uitvaart en Rouw*, Maarssen 2001, III 4.4, 1-16

LUKKEN, G.: 'Das Osterlob als Vollzug des Paschamysteriums', in *Jaarboek voor liturgie-onderzoek* 17 (2001) 73-106

LUKKEN, G.: 'De 'overkant' van het menselijk ritueel. Herbezinning vanuit fenomenologie en semiotiek op antropologische en theologische lagen in het christelijk ritueel', in *Tijdschrift voor Theologie* 40 (2001) 145-166 = G. LUKKEN: 'L'autre côté' du rituel humain: Reconsidération à partir de la phénoménologie et la sémiotique sur des couches anthropologiques et théologiques dans le rituel chrétien', in *Questions liturgiques* (2001) 1, 68-91

LUKKEN, G.: 'Inculturatie en liturgische muziek', in A. VERNOOIJ (ed.): *Toon-taal. De verhouding tussen woord en toon in heden en verleden* (Meander 4), Kampen 2002, 9-43

LUKKEN, G.: 'Gottesdienst als kulturelles Phänomen. Zukunftsperspektiven: Gottesdienst und Theater', in H. KERNER: *Gottesdienst und Kultur. Zukun-ftsperspektiven*, Leipzig 2004, 83-105

LUKKEN, G.: 'Rituelen in het spanningsveld van herhaling en vernieuwing', in *Tijdschrift voor Geestelijk Leven* 60 (2004) 377-389

LUKKEN, G. & J. MAAS: *Luisteren tussen de regels. Een semiotische bijdrage aan de praktische theologie*, Baarn 1996

LUKKEN, G. & M. SEARLE: *Semiotics and Church Architecture. Applying the Semiotics of A.J. Greimas and the Paris School to the Analysis of Church Buildings* (Liturgia condenda 1), Kampen 1993

LUKKEN, G. & J. DE WIT (eds.): *Nieuw leven. Rituelen rond geboorte en doop* (Liturgie in beweging 1), Baarn 1997

LUKKEN, G. & J. DE WIT (eds.): *Lezen in fragmenten. De Bijbel als liturgisch boek* (Liturgie in beweging 2), Baarn 1998

LUKKEN, G. & J. DE WIT (eds.): *Gebroken bestaan. Rituelen rond vergeving en verzoening*, 2 Vols. (Liturgie in beweging 3-4), Baarn 1998-1999

LUKKEN, G. & J. DE WIT (eds.): *Het kind in ons midden* (Liturgie in beweging 5), Baarn 1999

LUTHERAN WORLD FEDERATION; 'Nairobi Statement on Worship and Culture. Contemporary Challenges and Opportunities', in *Studia Liturgica* 27 (1998) 88-93

LUTHERAN WORLD FEDERATION: 'Chicago Statement on Worship and Culture: Baptism and Rites of Life Passage', in *Studia Liturgica* 28 (1998) 244-252

LUTHERAN WORLD FEDERATION (ed. S.A. STAUFFER): *Baptism, Rites of Passage, and Culture*, Genève 1999

LUTTIKHUIS, P.: 'Musica sacra zorgt voor verdeeldheid in Maastrichtse kerken', in *NRC Handelsblad* September 19, 1994, 8

LUYN, A.H. VAN: "En vergeef ons onze schuld'. Brieven aan mijn petekind', Rotterdam 2001

LUYTEN, H. & C. VISSER: 'De totale onkenbaarheid van God. Een gesprek met Piet Al, norbertijn', in *Dabar-bericht* (1998) 4, 21-26

LYOTARD, F.: *Le différend*, Paris 1983

MAAS, J. (ed.): *Beeld en gelijkenis. Bundel voordrachten gehouden bij het afscheid aan de Katholieke Theologische Universiteit te Utrecht van dr. Tjeu van den Berk*, Utrecht 2001

MAAS, J. & A. SMEETS (eds.): *Werktekeningen. Semiotische constructies in blauwdruk*, Tilburg 1999

MAAS, J. & H.-G. ZIEBERTZ: 'Over breukvlakken en bruggenhoofden', in *Tijdschrift voor Theologie* 37 (1997) 384-404

MAASSEN, J. (ed.): *Uitvaarten – een last en een lust voor pastores* (DPC-bundel 4), Rotterdam 1997

MAERTENS, J.TH.: *Ritologiques*, Paris 1978, 5 Vols.: 1. *Le dessin sur la peau. Essai d'anthropologie des inscriptions tégumentaires; 2. Le corps sexionné. Essai d'anthropologie des inscriptions génitales; 3. Le masque et le miroir. Essai d'anthropologie des revêtements faciaux; 4. Dans la peau des autres. Essai d'anthropologie des inscriptions vestimentaires; 5. Le jeu du mort. Essai d'anthropologie des inscriptions du cadavre*

MAGGIANI, S.: 'Festa/Feste', in D. SARTORE & A.M. TRIACCA (eds.): *Nuovo dizionario di liturgia*, Rome 1984, 555-581

MAGGIANI, S.: 'Rito/Riti', in D. SARTORE & A.M. TRIACCA (eds.): *Nuovo dizionario di liturgia*, Rome 1984, 1224-1225

MAHIEU, W. DE: 'Anthropologie et théologie africaine', in *Revue du Clergé Africain* 25 (1970) 378-387

MALINOWSKI, B.: *Argonauts of the Western Pacific*, Londen 1922

MALINOWSKI, B.: *A Scientific Theory of Culture and Other Essays*, Chapel Hill 1944

MALINOWSKI, B.: *Magic, science, and other essays*, Glencoe 1948

MALLOY, P.L.: 'The Re-Emergence of Popular Religion Among Non-Hispanic American Catholics', in *Worship* 72 (1998) 2-25

MANDERS, H.: 'Eerste communie een initiatie? Een partiële pastoraal-theologische meditatie', in *Werkmap (voor) Liturgie* 14 (1980) 7-19

MANNION, M.F.: 'Paradigms in American Catholic Church Music', in *Worship* 70 (1996) 101-128

MARANDA, P.: 'Semiotik und Anthropologie', in *Zeitschrift für Semiotik* 3 (1983) 2/2, 227-249

MARCHAL, F.: 'La participation de l'organiste à la liturgie', in *La Maison-Dieu* (1994) 198, 71-105

MAREAN, C. & S. YEUN KIM: 'Mousterian Large – Mammal Remains from Kobeh Cave: Behavioral Implications for Neanderthals and Early Modern Humans', in *Current Anthropology* 39 (1998) Supplement 79-113

MARGRY, P.J. (ed.): *Goede en slechte tijden: het Amsterdamse Mirakel van Sacrament in historisch perspectief*, Aardenhout 1995

MARGRY, P.J.: 'Accomodatie en innovatie met betrekking tot traditionele rituelen. Bedevaarten en processies in de moderne tijd', in M. VAN UDEN, J. PIEPER & P. POST (eds.): *Oude sporen, nieuwe wegen. Ontwikkelingen in bedevaartonderzoek* (UTP-katern 17), Baarn 1995, 169-201

MARGRY, P.J.: *Teedere quaesties: religieuze rituelen in conflict. Confrontaties tussen katholieken en protestanten rond de processiecultuur in 19e-eeuws Nederland*, Hilversum 2000

MARGRY, P.J. & C. CASPERS (eds.): *Bedevaartplaatsen in Nederland*, 4 Vols., Amsterdam/Hilversum 1997-2004

MARION, J.-L.: *Dieu sans l'être*, Paris 1982 (translation: *God Without Being*, Chicago 1995)

MARION, J.-L.: *Étant donné. Essai d'une phénoménologie de la donation*, Paris 1997 (translation: *Being Given. Toward a Phenomenology of Giveness*, Palo Alto 2002).

MARION, J.-L.: *De surcroît. Études sur les phénomènes saturés*, Paris 2001 (translation: *In Excess. Studies of Satured Phenomena*, New York 2002)

MARSILI, S.: 'Liturgia e non-liturgia', in B. NEUNHEUSER a.o. (eds.): *La liturgia momento nella storia della salvezza* (Anamnesis 1), Turijn 1974, 137-156

MARTIMORT, A.M.: *Les diaconesses. Essai historique*, Rome 1982

MARTIN, M.: *Fest und Alltag*, Stuttgart 1973

MARTINEZ, G.: 'Cult and culture. The Structure of the Evolution of Worship', in *Worship* 64 (1990) 406-433

J. MASSON (ed.): *Mission et cultures non-chrétiennes*, Brugge 1959

MASSON, J.: 'L'église ouverte sur le monde', in *Nouvelle revue théologique* 84 (1962) 1032-1043

MATHON, G.: 'Mariage – cérémonie ou mariage – sacrement? A propos du mariage des mal croyants. Mariage par étapes ou étapes dans la préparation au mariage', in *Questions Liturgiques* 62 (1981) 21-42

MATHON, G.: *Le mariage des Chrétiens*, 2 Vols., Paris 1993 and 1995

MAZZI, E.: 'A proposito di un libro recente', in *Rivista Liturgica* 82 (1995) 333-340

MCGANN, M.E.: 'Timely Wisdom, Prophetic Challenge: Rediscovering Clarence R.J. Rivers' Vision of Effective Worship', in *Worship* 76 (2002) 2-24

MCMANUS, F.: 'Back to the Future: The Early Christian Roots of Liturgical Renewal', in *Worship* 72 (1998) 386-403

MEER, F. VAN DER: 'De kerk en de kinderen', in *Dux* 22 (1955) 41-59

MEERBEECK, A. VAN: 'Het vormsel, een 'rite de passage'?', in K. DOBBELAERE, L. LEIJSSEN & M. CLOET (eds.): *Het vormsel* (Kadoc-Studies 12), Leuven 1991, 63-83

MEERBEECK, A. VAN: 'The Importance of a Religious Service at Birth: The Persistent Demand for Baptism in Flanders (Belgium)', in *Social Compass* (1995) 47-58

MEERBEECK, A. VAN: 'Dopen: ja, waarom niet? Een sociologische verkenning van de betekenis van dopen in Vlaanderen', in L. LEIJSSEN, M. CLOET & K. DOBBELAERE (eds.): *Levensrituelen. Geboorte en doopsel* (Kadoc-Studies 20), Leuven 1996, 199-216

MEERBEECK, A. VAN: 'De praktijk van het doopsel. Een doorlichting van de situatie in Vlaanderen', in *Kultuurleven* 64 (1997) 44-51

MENKEN-BEKIUS, C.: 'Als het hart een moordkuil wordt... Een ritueel als pastorale hulpverlening', in *Werkmap (voor) Liturgie* 25 (1991) 108-116

MENKEN-BEKIUS, C.: 'Een angstige bedevaartganger. Tussen pastoraat en psychotherapie', in M. VAN UDEN, J. PIEPER & E. HENAU (eds.): *Bij Geloof. Over bedevaarten en andere uitingen van volksreligiositeit* (UTP-katern 11), Heerlen 1991, 125-138

MENKEN-BEKIUS, C.: 'Een kanaal voor onze emoties. Rituelen rond de dood', in *Rondom het woord* 38 (1996) 2, 30-37

MENKEN-BEKIUS, C.: 'Rituelen houden niet op bij de begrafenis', in *Rondom het woord* 38 (1996) 2, 357-364

MENKEN-BEKIUS, C.: 'De koster had maar één tafeltje voor het bruidsboeket', in *Praktische Theologie* 25 (1998) 29-36

MENKEN-BEKIUS, C.: *Rituelen in het individuele pastoraat. Een praktisch theologisch onderzoek*, Kampen 2000.

MENKEN-BEKIUS, C.J.: *Werken met rituelen in het pastoraat*, Kampen 2001

MENKEN-BEKIUS, C. & J. PIEPER: 'Schipperen tussen leven en leer', in *Praktische Theologie* 25 (1998) 122-128

MENKEN-BEKIUS, C., L. BAL & M. VAN DIJK-GROENEBOER: 'De kerk en stille tochten tegen geweld. Praktisch-theologische overwegingen bij een nieuw ritueel', in *Praktische Theologie* 28 (2001) 272-277

MENKEN-BEKIUS, C., L. BAL & M. VAN DIJK-GROENEBOER: 'De beleving van de stille tocht van Gorinchem', in *Praktische Theologie* 28 (2001) 292-301

MENNEKES, F.: *Kein schlechtes Opium. Das Religiöse im Werk von Alfred Hrdlicka*, Stuttgart 1987

MENNEKES, F.: *Faith. Das Religiöse im Werk von James Brown*, Stuttgart 1989

MENNEKES, F.: *Altarbild, Geist und Körper. Eine Wettbewerbsausstellung des 90. Deutschen Katholikentags*, Berlin 1990

MENNEKES, F. & J. RÖHRING: *Peter Drake*, Köln 1990

MENNEKES, F. & J. RÖHRING: *Crucifixus. Das Kreuz in der Kunst unserer Zeit*, Freiburg/Basel/Wien 1994

MERKS, K.-W. & N. SCHREURS (eds.): *De passie van een grensganger. Theologie aan de vooravond van het derde millennium*, Baarn 1997

MERLEAU-PONTY, M.: *Phénoménologie de la perception*, Paris 1945

MERRIGAN, T.: 'De geschiedenis van Jezus in haar actuele betekenis. De uitdaging van het pluralisme', in *Tijdschrift voor Theologie* 34 (1994) 407-429

MERTENS, G.: 'Als het stereotyp mannelijk is, is het stereotyp mannelijke God. Over de stereotyp mannelijke visuele aspecten van de liturgie', in *Werkmap (voor) Liturgie* 22 (1988) 153-159

MERTENS, G.: *Beeld en gelijkenis? Een onderzoek naar nonverbale seksesterotypen in TV Liturgie* (M.A. Thesis Theologische Faculteit Tilburg), Tilburg 1990

MERTENS, H.: 'Religie als ervaring van de werkelijkheid', in *Tijdschrift voor Theologie* 14 (1974) 117-129

MES, R. & M. ZAGERS: *Wij zingen de hemel open. Popmuziek in de jongerenliturgie* (UTP-teksten 20), Heerlen 1991

MESSNER, R.: 'Was ist systematische Liturgiewissenschaft? Ein Entwurf in sieben Thesen', in *Archiv für Liturgiewissenschaft* 40 (1998) 257-274

METZ, J.B.: 'The future in the Memory of Suffering', in *Concilium* 8 (1972) 6, 9-25

METZGER, M.: *Histoire de la liturgie. Les grandes étapes*, Paris 1994 = M. METZGER: *History of the Liturgy: the Major Stages*, Collegeville 1997

MEULINK-KORF, H. & A. VAN RIJEN: 'Bijzondere rituelen van vergeving en verzoening – Gedachten en ervaringen verbonden met individuele pastorale begeleiding', in G. LUKKEN & J. DE WIT (eds.): *Gebroken bestaan. Rituelen rond vergeving en verzoening* 1 (Liturgie in beweging 3), Baarn 1999, 78-85

MEURDERS, L.: 'De Nederlandse huwelijksrituelen', in A. BLIJLEVENS & G. LUKKEN (eds.): *In goede en kwade dagen*, Baarn 1991, 54-103

MEURER, W.: *Volk Gottes auf dem Weg. Bewegungselemente im Gottesdienst,* Mainz 1989

MEYER, H.B. (ed.): *Liturgie und Gesellschaft,* Innsbruck 1970

MEYER, H.B.: *Eucharistie. Geschichte, Theologie, Pastoral* (Gottesdienst der Kirche. Handbuch der Liturgiewissenschaft 4), Regensburg 1989

MEYER, H.B.: 'Zur Inkulturation der Eucharistiefeier im Blick auf das deutsche Sprachgebiet', in *Liturgisches Jahrbuch* 41 (1991) 1, 7-23

MEYER, H.B.: Liturgietheologische Überlegungen zur Inkulturation – Ein Versuch', in E. VON SEVERUS (ed.): *Ecclesia Lacensis. Beiträge aus Anlass der Wiederbesiedlung der Abtei Maria Laach durch Benediktiner aus Beuron vor 100 Jahren am 25. November 1892 und der Gründung des Klosters durch Pfalzgraf Heinrich II. von Laach vor 900 Jahren 1093,* Münster 1993, 516-528

MEYER-FORTES, R.: 'Religious Premises and Logical Technique in Divinatory Ritual', in J. HUXLEY (ed.): 'A Discussion on Ritualisation of Behavior of Animals and Man', in *Philosophical Transactions of the Royal Society,* Series B, 251 (1966)

MEYER ZU SCHLOCHTERN, J.: *Sakrament Kirche. Wirken Gottes im Handeln der Menschen,* Freiburg im Breisgau 1992

MICHELS, T.: *Liturgical Innovation in the Practice of a Marriage Rite and the Sacramental Theology of Chauvet* (M.A. Thesis Theologische Faculteit Tilburg), Tilburg 1996

MILLER, D. (ed.): *Unwrapping Christmas,* Oxford 1993

MINOIS, G.: *Les origines du mal. Une histoire du péché originel,* Paris 2002

MITCHELL, N.: 'The Amen-Corner: the Coming Revolution in Ritual Studies', in *Worship* 67 (1993) 74-81

MITCHELL, N.: 'The Amen Corner', in *Worship* 69 (1995) 154-163

MITCHELL, N.: 'Emerging Rituals in Contemporary Culture', in *Concilium* 3 (1995) 3, 121-129

MITCHELL, N.: 'The Amen Corner. Rereading Reform', in *Worship* 71 (1997) 462-470

MITCHELL, N.: 'The Amen Corner. Reform the Reform?', in *Worship* 71 (1997) 555-563.

MITCHELL, N.: 'The Amen Corner. Smells and Bells', in *Worship* 72 (1998) 539-547

MITCHELL, N.: 'The Amen Corner. Back to the Future', in *Worship* 73 (1999) 60-69

MITCHELL, N.: 'The Amen Corner. Ritual as *Ars Amatoria*', in *Worship* 75 (2001) 250-259

MITCHELL, N.: 'The Amen Corner. Once upon a Time', in *Worship* 75 (2001) 469-478

MITCHELL, N.: 'The Amen Corner. Brave New World', in Worship 76 (2002) 67-77

MITCHELL, N.: 'The Amen Corner. Liturgical Language: Building a Better Mousetrap', in *Worship* 77 (2003) 250-263.

MITCHELL, N.: 'Croquet with Flamingos', in *Worship* 77 (2003) 457-472

MODEHN, C.: 'Alternatieve 'Juhgendweihe' in voormalige DDR. Atheïsten worden volwassen in de kerk', in *De Bazuin* 83 (2000) 16 (August 4), 24-26

MODERNITY: *The Debate on Modernity: Concilium* 28 (1992) no. 6

MOINGT, J.: *Les sacrements de Dieu*, Paris 1987

MOINGT, J.: *Enjeux du rite dans la modernité* (Recherches de Science Religieuse 78 (1990) 4), Paris 1991

MOL, D.: *Onze digitale god. Religieuze en pastorale kanten van televisie* (Zin-Speling), Kampen 1997

MOL, D.: 'De tv als 'pastor'', in *Praktische Theologie* 24 (1997) 41-58

MOLIN, J.B. & P. MUTEMBE: *Le rituel du mariage en France du XII au XVI siècle* (Théologie historique 26), Paris 1974

MOLTMANN-WENDEL, E.: *Die weiblichkeit des Geistes. Studien zur Feministischen Theologie*, Gütersloh 1995

MONSHOUWER, D.: 'De verkondiging van het Woord – Johannes 1, 1-18 in vertalingen', in G. LUKKEN & J. DE WIT (eds.): *Lezen in fragmenten. De Bijbel als liturgisch boek* (Liturgie in beweging 2), Baarn 1998, 107-118

MOOIJ, A.: *Taal en verlangen*, Meppel 1975

MOOR, R. DE: 'Globalisering van de cultuur en nationale identiteit', in J.J.M. DE VALK (ed.): *Nationale identiteit in Europees perspectief*, Baarn 1993, 21-45

MOORE, R.L.: 'Contemporary Psychotherapy as Ritual Process: An Initial Reconnaissance', in *Zygon* 18 (1983) 3, 126-143

MOORE, R.L.: 'Ministry, Sacred Space and Theological Education: the Legacy of Victor Turner', in *Theological Education*, autumn 1984, 87-100

MOORE, R.L.: 'Space and Transformation in Human Experience', in R.L. MOORE & F. REYNOLDS (eds.): *Anthropology and the Study of Religion*, Chicago 1984, 126-143

MOORE, R.L. & F. REYNOLDS (eds.): *Anthropology and the Study of Religion*, Chicago 1984

MORESON, M.: 'Symbolen en riten in de vredesliturgie', in *Tijdschrift voor Liturgie* 70 (1986) 218-226

MORRIS, B.: *Anthropological Studies of Religion: an Introductory Text*, Cambridge 1987

MORRIS, CH.W.: *Foundations of the Theory of Signs*, Chicago 1939

MORRIS, CH.W.: *Signs, Language, and Behavior*, New York 1946

MOSSEL, D. & C.B. STRUIJK: 'De macht van het kleine. Verrukking en vrees in balans', in J. DE VISSCHER (ed.): *Mosterdzaadjes van het bestaan. De waarde van de kleine dingen*, Baarn 1996

MOYAERT, P.: 'Het ik en zijn identificaties', in A. DE RUIJTER a.o.: *Totems en trends. Over de zin van identificatiesymbolen*, Hilversum 1988, 52-77

MÜHLEN, H.: *Entsakralisierung. Ein epochales Schlagwort in seiner Bedeutung für die Zukunft der christlichen Kirchen*, Paderborn 1971

MÜLLER, G.L.: *Der Empfänger des Weihesakraments. Quellen zur Lehre und Praxis der Kirche, nur Männern das Weihesakrament zu spenden*, Würzburg 1999.

MÜLLER, G.L.: 'Können Frauen die sakramentale Diakonenweihe gültig empfangen?', in *Notitiae* 39 (2002) 370-409

MULDER, A.: *Pastoraat en ritueel. Verslag van een verkennend onderzoek naar het gebruik en effect van therapeutische rituelen, beschreven binnen het concept van communicatief pastoraat* (M.A. Thesis Theologische Faculteit Tilburg), Tilburg 1991

MULDER, A.: 'Op zoek naar de ware pelgrim. Over pelgrimage en toerisme', in M. VAN UDEN, J. PIEPER & P. POST (eds.): *Oude sporen, nieuwe wegen. Ontwikkelingen in het bedevaartonderzoek* (UTP-katern 17), Baarn 1995, 15-52

MULDER, A.: 'Rituelen buiten: een crematie', in *Werkmap (voor) Liturgie* (Vieringen (Rituelen) buiten 1) 30 (1996) 43-52

MULDER, A.: "Naakt kom ik uit de schoot van moeder aarde, naakt keer ik daar terug' (Job 1, 21). Aardesymboliek, Bijbel en begrafenisliturgie', in *Jaarboek voor liturgie-onderzoek* 12 (1997) 149-165

MULDER, A. & T. SCHEER (eds.): *Natuurlijke liturgie* (Liturgie in perspectief 6), Baarn/Heeswijk-Dinther 1996

MULDOON, M.S.: 'Forum: Reconciliation, Original Sin, and Millennial Malaise', in *Worship* 72 (1998) 445-452

MUNACHI EZEOGU, E.: 'The Jewish Response to Hellenism: a Lesson in Inculturation', in *Journal of inculturation theology* 1 (1994) 2, 144-155

MURKEN, T.B.: *Take and Eat, and take the Consequences. How receiving the Lord's Supper is an action that Makes a Difference* (American University Studies VII, Series Theology and Religion 220), New York 2002

MUSIC: *Music and the Experience of God: Concilium* 25 (1989) no. 2

NAAR: 'Naar een verinheemsing van het christelijk huwelijksritueel. Document van het symposion van de bisschoppenconferenties van Afrika en Madagascar, Acara September 15, 1976', in *Archief van de Kerken* 32 (1977) 725-729. Source: *Documentation Catholique* April 17, 1977

NANINCK, G.: 'Elke bruid is een ster op haar trouwdag', in *Trouw* 24 oktober 1996, 32

NATIONALE RAAD VOOR LITURGIE: Het huwelijk (Liturgie van de sacramenten en andere kerkelijke vieringen 7), Hilversum 1977

NAUTA, R.: 'Rituelen als decor. Over het geheim van de leegte', in P. POST & W.M. SPEELMAN (eds.): *De Madonna van de Bijenkorf* (Liturgie in perspectief 9), Baarn 1997, 73-95

NECKEBROUCK, V.: 'Initiatie. Een antropologisch voorwoord', in H. LOM-
BAERTS & L. BOEVE (eds.): *Traditie en initiatie. Perspectieven voor de
toekomst*, Leuven 1996, 29-37.
NECKEBROUCK, V.: 'Progressistische theologie en inculturatie', in J. LAMBERTS
(ed.): *Liturgie en inculturatie. Verslagboek van het twaalfde liturgiecolloquium van het Liturgisch Instituut van de K.U. Leuven – oktober 1995*
(Nikè-reeks 37), Leuven/Amersfoort 1996, 75-109 = V. NECKEBROUCK:
'Théologie progressiste et inculturation de la liturgie', in *Questions
Liturgiques* 77 (1996) 1-2, 52-76 = V. NECKEBROUCK: 'Théologie progressiste et inculturation de la liturgie', in J. LAMBERTS (ed.): *Liturgie et incul-
turation. Liturgy and Inculturation* (Textes et Études Liturgiques/ Studies
in Liturgy 14), Leuven 1996, 52-76
NEDERLANDSE: 'Nederlandse jeugd geloviger dan gedacht', in *Een-twee-een* 26
(1998) 9, 332
NEDERLANDSE BISSCHOPPEN: *God die op ons wacht. Herderlijk schrijven over God
de Vader* (Bisschoppelijke brieven 38), Utrecht 1999
NEDERLANDSE BISSCHOPPENCONFERENTIE: Verklaring over intercommunie, in
Een-twee-een. Kerkelijke documentatie 27 (1999) no. 7, 33-34
NEUMANN, B.: *Sakrament und Ökumene. Studien zur deutschsprachigen evange-
lischen Sakramententheologie der Gegenwart*, Paderborn 1997
NEUNHEUSER, B. a.o. (eds.): *La liturgia momento nella storia della salvezza*
(Anamnesis 1), Turijn 1974
NIATI, J.P.: *La messe zaïroise: efforts d'une église africaine en vue d'une litur-
gie inculturée* (M.A. Thesis Theologische Faculteit Tilburg), Tilburg
1994
NIEUWKOOP, R.: *De drempel over. Het gebruik van (overgangs)rituelen in het pas-
toraat*, Den Haag 1986
NIJHOFF, G.: *La confusion des arbres. Essai d'une revalorisation du dogme du
péché originel*, Vérossaz 1995
NIJK, A.: *Secularisatie. Over het gebruik van een woord*, Rotterdam 1968
NISSLMÜLLER, TH. & R. VOLP: *Raum als Zeichen. Wahrnehmung und Erkennt-
nis von Räumlichkeit*, Münster 1999
NOORDEGRAAF, H. & S. GRIFFIOEN (eds.): *Bewogen realisme. Economie, cultuur,
oecumene*, Kampen 1999
NOORDEGRAAF, H.: 'Een samenleving zonder zondag. Kerken en het debat over
de zondag', in *Praktische Theologie* 30 (2003) 284-297
NOTAE: *Notae morales et canonicae ad tractatum de sacramentis in genere*, Sint-
Michielsgestel 1947
NOUVEAU: *Le nouveau Petit Robert. Dictionnaire alphabétique et analogique de la
langue française*, Paris 1994
NOWELL, I.: 'The Making of Translations: A Dilemma', in *Worship* 75 (2001)
58-68

NUGTEREN, T.: 'De nieuwe kleren van de keizer? Enkele notities over context, inhoud en verwerking van alternatieve zingevingssystemen in Nederland', in B. VEDDER a.o. (eds.): *Zin tussen vraag en aanbod. Theologische en wijsgerige beschouwingen over zin*, Tilburg 1992

ODEN, T.: *Kerygma and counseling*, Philadelphia 1966

ODENTHAL, A.: *Liturgie als Ritual. Theologische und psychoanalytische Überlegungen zu einer praktisch-theologischen Theorie des Gottesdienstes als Symbolgeschehen*, Stuttgart 2002

ONASCH, K.: *Lichthöhle und Sternenhaus. Licht und Materie im spätantik-christlichen und frühbyzantinischen Sakralbau*, Dresden/Basel 1993.

ONDERBOOM, J.: 'Journaal', in *Rond de Tafel* 52 (1997) 12

OOSTERHUIS, H.: *Bid om vrede*, Utrecht 1966

OOSTERHUIS, H.: *In het voorbijgaan,* Utrecht 1968

OOSTERHUIS, H.: *Your Word is near. Contemporary Christian Prayers*, New York 1968 (partial translation of *Bid om vrede*, Utrecht 1966)

OOSTERHUIS, H. a.o.: *Iemand die recht doet? Brochure bij gelegenheid van de Unctad-zondag 30 april 1972*, Hilversum 1972

OOSTERHUIS, H.: *Vietnamzondag 29 oktober 1972, brochure van de werkgroep Vietnamzondag*, Amsterdam 1972

OOSTERHUIS, H.: *At Times I See,* London 1974 = H. OOSTERHUIS: *Zien – soms even. Fragmenten over God*, Bilthoven 1972

OOSTERHUIS, H.: *Aandachtig liedboek. 143 teksten om te zingen en ter overweging*, Baarn 1983

OOSTERHUIS, H.: *Israël, Volhard in hem. Een nieuwe liturgie voor Goede Vrijdag*, Hilversum 1986 = *Werkschrift voor Leerhuis en Liturgie* 4 (1983) 1

OOSTROM, F. VAN: 'Niets nieuws sinds Jacob van Maerlant. De waarde van het boek', in *NRC Handelsblad* February 12, 1994, Boeken, 3

OOSTROM, F. VAN: *De waarde van het boek*, Leiden 1994

OOSTROM, F. VAN: *Handgeschreven wereld: Nederlandse literatuur en cultuur in de Middeleeuwen*, Amsterdam 1995

OOSTVEEN, T.: 'De schoonheid van de liturgie zonder alle rechtse praatjes', in *De Tijd* March 9, 1984, 53-58

ORTIGUES, E.: *Le discours et le symbole*, Aubier-Montaigne 1962

OS, H. VAN: *Een kathedraal voor de kunst*, Amsterdam 1997

OSKAMP, P.: *Vergeef ons onze schulden...Riten om in het reine te komen*, Zoetermeer 2000

OSKAMP, P.: 'Een protestantse kijk op biecht en boete', in *Tijdschrift voor Liturgie* 86 (2002) 149-160

OSKAMP, P. & N. SCHUMAN (eds.): *De weg van de liturgie. Traditie, achtergronden, praktijk*, Zoetermeer 1998, third revised edition 2001

OTNES C. & M.A. MCGRATH: 'New Research on Consumption Rituals', in *Journal of Ritual Studies* 11 (1997) 2, 35-44

OTRANTO, G.: 'Note sul sacerdozio femminile nell'antichita in margine a una testimonianza di Gelasio I', in *Vetera Christianorum* 19 (1982) 341-360

OVERBOSCH, W.G. (ed.): *Een compendium van achtergrondinformatie bij de 491 gezangen van het Liedboek voor de kerken*, Amsterdam 1978

OYEN, G. VAN: "Jezus redt... alle mensen opgelet'. Over de band tussen christologie en onderzoek naar Jezus', in *Tijdschrift voor Theologie* 37 (1997) 331-342

PAHL, I.: 'Le mystère pascal essentiel pour la forme de la liturgie', in *La Maison-Dieu* (1995) 204, 51-70

PALAZZO, E.: *Le Moyen Age. Des origines au XIIIe siècle*, Paris 1993

PANIER, L.: *Le péché originel. Naissance de l'homme sauvé*, Paris 1996

PANNENBERG, W. (ed.): *Lehrverurteilungen – kirchentrennend?*, III: *Materialien zur Lehre von den Sakramenten und vom kirchlichen Amt*, Freiburg/Göttingen 1990

PARRET, H.: *Semiotiek en esthetica*, in W. VAN BELLE a.o.: *De betekenis als verhaal. Semiotische opstellen* (Semiotisch perspectief 1), Amsterdam 1991, 213-235

PARRET, H. & H.-G. RUPRECHT (eds.): *Exigences et perspectives de la sémiotique. Recueil d'hommages pour A.J. Greimas*, Amsterdam/Philadelphia 1985

PAS, P.: 'Pastoraal rond het kinderdoopsel', in L. LEIJSSEN, M. CLOET & K. DOBBELAERE (eds.): *Levensrituelen. Geboorte en doopsel* (Kadoc-Studies 20), Leuven 1996, 301-310

PASCAL, B.: *Les pensées de Pascal* (ed. F. KAPLAN), Paris 1982 = B. PASCAL: *Gedachten. I. Tekst*, Amsterdam 1997

PASTORAL: *Pastoral Constitution on the Church in the Modern World Gaudium et Spes*, Città del Vaticano 1965.

PATER, W.A. DE: 'Het postmodernisme nog eens uitgelegd', in *Nederlands Theologisch Tijdschrift* 50 (1996) 3, 177-202

PAULUS VI: *Mysterium fidei: Acta Apostolicae Sedis* 57 (1965) 753-774

PAULUS VI: *Evangelii nuntiandi*, Città del Vaticano 1975

PAULUS VI: 'Damaged Church', in *The Catholic Messenger*, Davenport, IA Vol. 115: 17 (April 24, 1997) 1, 10

PAUSELIJKE BIJBELCOMMISSIE: 'Rapport over de kwestie van de priesterwijding van vrouwen', in *Archief van de Kerken* 31 (1976) 917-927. Source: *N.C. Documentary Service* July 1, 1976

PAVIS, P.: *Problèmes de sémiologie théâtrale*, Montréal 1976

PEETERS, H.: *Over deugden en ondeugden. Vroeger en nu*, Nijmegen 1996

PEETERS, R.J. a.o. (ed.): *De onvoltooid verleden tijd. Negen bijdragen tot een bezinning op traditie*, Tilburg 1992

PEPERSTRATEN, F. VAN: *Samenleving ter discussie. Een inleiding in de sociale filosofie*, Bussum 1995[3]

PERRON, P. & J. FABBRI: 'Foreword', in A.J. GREIMAS. & J. FONTANILLE: *The semiotics of passions. From States of Affairs to States of Feelings*, Minneapolis/London 1993, I-XVI

PESCHKE, K.-H.: 'Die Sünde in den Traktaten über die Sakramente', in LEKTOREN IN ST. AUGUSTIN (ed.): *In verbo tuo. Festschrift zum 50jährigen Bestehen des Missionspriesterseminar St. Augustin bei Siegburg, Rheinl. 1913-1963*, St. Augustin 1963, 235-246

PETERS, J.: 'Religie in meervoud', in O. SCHREUDER & L. VAN SNIPPENBURG (eds.): *Religie in de Nederlandse samenleving. De vergeten factor*, Baarn 1990, 42-65

PETERS, J., G. DEKKER & J. DE HART: *God in Nederland 1966-1996*, Amsterdam 1997

PETERS, T.: 'Wie gaat er voor? Over voorgangers in de liturgie en hun vorming', in *Tijdschrift voor Liturgie* 85 (2001) 258-270

PETRELLA, R. a.o.: *Grenzen aan de concurrentie*, Amsterdam 1994

PHILIPSE, H.: *Atheïstisch manifest*, Amsterdam 1995

PIEPER, J.: *Rituele veranderingen met betrekking tot de huwelijkssluiting. Een onderzoeksvoorstel Wetenschapswinkel Katholieke universiteit Brabant*, Tilburg 1996

PIEPER, J. & P. POST: 'Rituele veranderingen met betrekking tot de huwelijkssluiting', in *Jaarboek voor liturgie-onderzoek* 12 (1996) 136-163

PIEPER, J., P. POST & M. VAN UDEN: *Bedevaart en pelgrimage. Tussen traditie en moderniteit* (UTP-katern 16), Baarn 1994

PIEPER, J., P. POST & M. VAN UDEN: *Pelgrimage in beweging. Een christelijk ritueel in nieuwe contexten*, Baarn 1999

PIJFFERS, J.: 'De godsdealers. Het eigenlijke thema van de boekenweek is koopmanschap', in *De Bazuin* 80 (1997) 5, 16-19

PINXTEN, R.: 'Geboorte en doopsel. Een visie van een antropoloog en vrijzinnige', in L. LEIJSSEN, M. CLOET & K. DOBBELAERE (eds.): *Levensrituelen. Geboorte en doopsel* (Kadoc-Studies 20), Leuven 1996, 46-53

PLAISIER, B.: 'Toespraak bij de start van de actie tegen de 24-uurseconomie', in *Een-twee-een. Kerkelijke documentatie* 26 (1998) 3, 167-171

PLASCHAERT, J.N.E.: 'Het gemeentehuis', in *Burgerzaken en recht* (1995) 2, 29-31

PLATT, J.R. (ed): *New Views of the Nature of Man*, Chicago 1965

PLATTEL, M. & C. RIJK: 'Het geseculariseerd mens- en wereldbeeld in verband met het godsdienstig verschijnsel', in *Werkmap Katholieke Studentendagen 1969 Tilburg*, Tilburg 1968

PLATVOET, J. & K. VAN DER TOORN (eds.): *Pluralism and Identity: Studies in Ritual Behaviour* (Studies in the History of Religions 67), Leiden 1995

POLISH, D. (ed.): *Rabbi's Manual*, New York 1988

POPPE, E.: 'De toeschouwer en het spektakel', in *Versus. Tijdschrift voor film en opvoeringskunsten* 4 (1989) 2, 7-33

POPPE, E.: 'Omtrent 25 jaar semiotiek van de film', in *Versus. Tijdschrift voor film en opvoeringskunsten* 7 (1992) 2, 88-108

POPULARMUSIK: *Popularmusik und Kirche – kein Widerspruch. Dokumentation des Ersten interdisziplinären Forums 'Popularmusik und Kirche' in Bad Herrenalb vom 28. Februar bis 1. März 2000*, Frankfurt am Main 2001

POST, A.: 'Laatste eer voor anoniem gestorvenen. Dichter bij de dood', in *VolZin* 20-23

POST, J.: *Optische effecten in de film. Aanzetten tot een semiotische analyse*, Leuven 1998

POST, P.: 'Traditie gebruiken. Sint Hubertus in Muiderberg', in M. VAN UDEN, J. PIEPER & E. HENAU (eds.): *Bij geloof. Over bedevaarten en andere uitingen van volksreligiositeit* (UTP-katern 11), Hilversum 1991, 191-211

POST, P.: 'Het verleden in het spel? Volksreligieuze rituelen tussen cultus en cultuur', in *Jaarboek voor liturgie-onderzoek* 7 (1991) 79-124

POST, P.: 'De pastor aan de bron: over de opbloei van Dokkum als Bonifatiusstad', in F. JESPERS & E. HENAU (eds): *Liturgie en kerkopbouw. Opstellen aangeboden aan Ad Blijlevens*, Baarn 1993, 240-268

POST, P.: 'Pelgrims tussen traditie en moderniteit. Een verkenning van hedendaagse pelgrimsverslagen', in J. PIEPER, P. POST & M. VAN UDEN (eds.): *Bedevaart en pelgrimage. Tussen traditie en moderniteit* (UTP-katern 16), Baarn 1994, 23-30

POST, P.: 'Thema's, theorieën en trends in bedevaartonderzoek', in J. PIEPER, P. POST & M. VAN UDEN (eds.): *Bedevaart en pelgrimage. Tussen traditie en moderniteit* (UTP-katern 16), Baarn 1994, 253-302

POST, P.: 'De creatie van traditie volgens Eric Hobsbawm', in *Jaarboek voor liturgie-onderzoek* 11 (1995) 77-101

POST, P.: 'Goede tijden, slechte tijden: devotionele rituelen tussen traditie en moderniteit', in P.J. MAGRY (ed.): *Goede en slechte tijden: het Amsterdamse Mirakel van Sacrament in historisch perspectief*, Aardenhout 1995, 62-80

POST, P.: *Ritueel landschap: over liturgie-buiten. Processie, pausbezoek, danken voor de oogst, plotselinge dood* (Liturgie in perspectief 5), Baarn 1995 = P.

POST: 'Paysage rituel: liturgie et plein air, la visite du pape, action de grâce pour la moisson, rites autour d'une mort subite', in *Questions Liturgiques* 77 (1996) 174-190 and 240-256

POST, P.: 'Zeven notities over rituele verandering, traditie en (vergelijkende) liturgiewetenschap', in *Jaarboek voor liturgie-onderzoek* 11 (1995) 1-30

POST, P.: 'Een idyllisch feest. Over de natuurthematiek in Brabantse oogstdankvieringen', in A. MULDER & T. SCHEER (eds.): *Natuurlijke liturgie* (Liturgie in perspectief 6), Baarn 1996, 118-139

POST, P.: 'Ter inleiding. Rituelen buiten', in *Werkmap (voor) Liturgie* (Vieringen (Rituelen) buiten 1) 30 (1996) 4-16

POST, P.: 'Liturgische bewegingen en feestcultuur. Een landelijk liturgieweten-schappelijk onderzoekprogramma', in *Jaarboek voor liturgie-onderzoek* 12 (1996) 21-55

POST, P.: 'The Modern Pilgrim. A Christian Ritual between Tradition and Post-Modernity', in *Concilium* 32 (1996) 4, 1-9

POST, P.: 'Rituelen buiten', in *Werkmap (voor) Liturgie* (Vieringen (Rituelen) buiten 1) 30 (1996) 4-16

POST, P.: 'Alle dagen feest, of: de ritencrisis voorbij. Een verkenning van de markt', in P. POST & W.M. SPEELMAN (eds.): *De Madonna van de Bijenkorf: bewegingen op de rituele markt* (Liturgie in perspectief 9), Baarn 1997, 11-32

POST (ed.): *Een ander huis. Kerkarchitectuur na 2000* (Liturgie in perspectief 7), Baarn 1997

POST, P.: 'Een ander huis: twee kerkontwerpprojecten als signalen van een ken-terend getij?', in P. POST (ed.): *Een ander huis. Kerkarchitectuur na 2000* (Liturgie in perspectief 7), Baarn 1997, 10-17

POST, P.: 'Literatuuroverzicht: liturgie en architectuur', in P. POST (ed.): *Een ander huis. Kerkarchitectuur na 2000* (Liturgie in perspectief 7), Baarn 1997, 96-101

POST, P.: 'De uitslag van de Rotterdamse prijsvraag. Typen en thema's, balans en perspectief, en een afsluitend pleidooi', in P. POST (ed.): *Een ander huis. Kerkarchitectuur na 2000* (Liturgie in perspectief 7), Baarn 1997, 18-29

POST, P.: 'Post-modern Pilgrimage. Christian ritual between Liturgy and 'Topo-latry'', in A. HOUTMAN, M. POORTHUIS & J. SCHWARTZ (eds.): *Sanctity of Time and Space in Tradition and Modernity*, Leiden 1998, 299-315

POST, P.: 'Religious Popular Culture and Liturgy. An illustrated Argument for an Approach', in *Questions liturgiques* 79 (1998) 14-59 and in J. LAMBERTS (ed.): *Religion populaire, liturgie et évangélisation – Popular Religion. Liturgy and Evangelization* (Textes et Études Liturgiques/Studies in Liturgy 15), Leuven 1998 = P. POST: 'Religieuze volkscultuur en liturgie. Geïllustreerd pleidooi voor een benadering', in J. LAMBERTS (ed.): *Volksre-ligie, liturgie en evangelisatie* (Nikè-reeks 42), Leuven/Amersfoort 1998, 19-77

POST, P.: 'Rituals and the Function of the Past: Rereading Eric Hobsbawm', in *Journal of Ritual Studies* 10 (1998) 85-107

POST, P.: 'De synthese in de huidige liturgiewetenschap. Proeve van positioner-ing van *De weg van de liturgie*', in *Jaarboek voor liturgie-onderzoek* 14 (1998) 141-172

POST, P.: 'Van paasvuur tot stille tocht. Over interferentie van liturgisch en volksreligieus ritueel', in *Volkskundig bulletin* 25 (1999) 2/3, 215-234

POST, P.: 'Rijke oogst: literatuurbericht liturgiewetenschap', in *Praktische The-ologie* 26 (1999) 94-117

POST, P.: 'Rol en rite: over liturgisch voorgaan', in *Praktische Theologie* 26 (1999) 128-147

POST, P.: 'Interference and Intuition: on the Characteristic Nature of Research Design in Liturgical Studies', in *Questions Liturgiques* 81 (2000) 48-65

POST, P.: *Het wonder van Dokkum. Verkenningen van populair religieus ritueel,* Nijmegen 2000

POST, P.: 'The Creation of Tradition: Rereading and Reading beyond Hobsbawm', in J.W. VAN HENTEN & A. HOUTEPEN (eds.): *Religious Identity and the Invention of Tradition. Papers Read at a Noster Conference in Soesterberg, January 4-6, 1999* (Studies in Theology and Religion 3), Assen 2001

POST, P.: 'Engel, bode, advocaat et cetera', in M. BARNARD & P. POST (eds.): *Ritueel bestek. Antropologische kernwoorden van de liturgie,* Zoetermeer 2001, 259-274

POST, P.: 'Feest', in M. BARNARD & P. POST (eds.): *Ritueel bestek. Antropologische kernwoorden van de liturgie,* Zoetermeer 2001, 171-180

POST, P.: 'Introduction and Application: Feast as a Key Concept in a Liturgical Studies Research Design', in P. POST, G. ROUWHORST, L. VAN TONGEREN & A. SCHEER (eds.): *Christian Feast and Festival. The Dynamics of Western Liturgy and Culture* (Liturgia condenda 12), Leuven 2001, 47-77

POST, P.: 'Liturgical Movements and Feast Culture. A Dutch Research Program', in P. POST, G. ROUWHORST, L. VAN TONGEREN & A. SCHEER (eds.): *Christian Feast and Festival. The Dynamics of Western Liturgy and Culture* (Liturgia condenda 12), Leuven 2001, 3-43

POST, P.: 'La marche silencieuse: perspectives rituelles et liturgiques sur de nouveaux rites populaires aux Pays Bas', in *La Maison-Dieu* (2001) 228, 143-157

POST, P.: 'Overvloed of deritualisering. Lukken en Grimes over het actuele ritueel-liturgische milieu', in *Jaarboek voor liturgie-onderzoek* 17 (2001) 193-212

POST, P.: 'Personen en patronen. Literatuurbericht liturgiewetenschap', in *Praktische Theologie* 28 (2001) 86-110.

POST, P.: 'Ruimte voor rituelen', in M. BARNARD & P. POST (eds.): *Ritueel bestek. Antropologische kernwoorden van de liturgie,* Zoetermeer 2001, 77-86

POST, P.: 'Trouwen: de mooiste dag van je leven', in M. BARNARD & P. POST (eds.): *Ritueel bestek. Antropologische kernwoorden van de liturgie,* Zoetermeer 2001, 174-179

POST, P.: 'Life Cycle Rituals: A Ritual-Liturgical Perspective', in *Questions Liturgiques* 83 (2002) 10-29

POST, P.: 'Van Doura tot Vinex: actuele tendenties met betrekking tot liturgische ruimte', in J. KROESEN, J.R. LUTH & A.L. MOLENDIJK (eds.): *Religieuze ruimte. Kerkbouw, kerkinrichting en religieuze kunst. Feestbundel voor Regnerus Steensma bij zijn vijf en zestigste verjaardag,* Zoetermeer 2002, 71-89

POST, P.: 'Programm und Profil der Liturgiewissenschaft. Ein niederländischer Beitrag', in W. RATZMANN (ed.): *Profile und Perspektiven der Liturgiewissenschaft*, Leipzig 2002, 81-100

POST, P.: 'Space for Liturgy. Current Perspectives for Liturgical Inculturation', in *Jaarboek voor liturgie-onderzoek* 18 (2002) 45-59

POST, P.: 'Church Architecture and Liturgy: Current Perspectives for Liturgical Inculturation', in N. SCHREURS & V. PLASTOW (eds.): *Juxtaposing contexts. Doing contextual theology in South Africa and in the Netherlands*, Pietermaritzburg 2003, 162-187

POST, P.: *Space for Liturgy between dynamic and static reality. An exploration of the development of the Roman Catholic Liturgical Space in The Netherlands (ca. 1850-present day) with Particular Focus on the Role of Liturgical Booklets, the Microphone and Church Pews* (Netherlands Studies in Ritual and Liturgy), Groningen/Tilburg 2003

POST, P.: 'Ritual Studies. Einführung und Ortsbestimmung im Hinblick auf die Liturgiewissenschaft', in *Archiv für Liturgiewissenschaft* 45 (2003) 21-45

POST, P.: 'Het Directorium over volksvroomheid en liturgie: Drie evaluerende notities', in *Tijdschrift voor Theologie* 44 (2004) 386-407

POST, P.: 'Over de historische referentie in de rooms-katholieke 'Hervorming-van-de-hervormingsbeweging'', in *Jaarboek voor liturgie-onderzoek* 20 (2004) 73-88

POST, P. & L. LEIJSSEN: 'Huwelijksliturgie: inculturatie van een levensfeest', in R. BURGGRAEVE, M. CLOET, K. DOBBELAERE & L. LEIJSSEN (eds.): *Het huwelijk* (Kadoc-Studies 24, serie Levensriten), Leuven 2000, 179-196

POST, P., H. DEGEN & J. STAPS: *Tot zegen aan elkaar gegeven. Over huwelijksliturgie en huwelijkspastoraat* (Liturgische Handreiking 25), Heeswijk 2000

POST, P., R.L. GRIMES, A. NUGTEREN, P. PETERSON & H. ZONDAG: *Disaster Ritual. Explorations of an Emerging Ritual Repertoire* (Liturgia condenda 15), Leuven/Paris/Dudley MA 2003.

POST, P., A. VAN NUGTEREN & H. ZONDAG: *Rituelen na rampen. Verkenning van een opkomend ritueel repertoire* (Meander 3), Kampen 2002

POST, P. & J. PIEPER: *De palmzondagviering. Een landelijke verkenning*, Kampen 1992

POST, P., J. PIEPER & R. NAUTA: 'Om de parochie: het inculturerend perspectief van rituele marginaliteit. Verkenning van een onderzoeksperspectief', in *Jaarboek voor liturgie-onderzoek* 14 (1998) 113-140

POST, P., J. PIEPER & M. VAN UDEN: *The Modern Pilgrim. Multidisciplinary Explorations of Christian Pilgrimage* (Liturgia condenda 8), Leuven 1998.

POST, P., G. ROUWHORST, L. VAN TONGEREN & A. SCHEER (eds.): *Christian Feast and Festival. The Dynamics of Western Liturgy and Culture* (Liturgia condenda 12), Leuven 2001

POST, P. & P. SCHMID: 'Centrum van stilte: een onderzoeksaanvrage', in M. BARNARD & P. POST (eds.): *Ritueel bestek. Antropologische kernwoorden van de liturgie*, Zoetermeer 2001, 162-170

POST, P. & W.M. SPEELMAN (eds.): *De Madonna van de Bijenkorf: bewegingen op de rituele markt* (Liturgie in perspectief 9), Baarn 1997

POST, P., & L. VAN TONGEREN: 'Het feest van de eerste communie. Op zoek naar de identiteit van het christelijk ritueel', in K.-W. MERKS & N. SCHREURS (eds.): *De passie van een grensganger. Theologie aan de vooravond van het derde millennium*, Baarn 1997, 249-264

POST, P. & L. VAN TONGEREN: *Devotioneel ritueel. Heiligen en wonderen, bedevaarten en pelgrimages in verleden en heden* (Meander 2), Kampen 2001

P. POST, P., R. VAN UDEN & J. PIEPER: *Pelgrimage in beweging. Een christelijk ritueel in nieuwe contexten* (UTP-katern 22), Baarn 1999

POSTMODERNISME: 'Het postmodernisme voorbij', Supplement of *Werkschrift voor Leerhuis en Liturgie* 13 (1993) 1, 1-52

POTEL, J.: *Les funérailles une fête*, Paris 1973

POTTMEYER, H.J.: 'Regionale Teilkirchen und 'Zwischeninstanzen' – ihre Wiederentdeckung und ihr ekklesiologischer Rang', in L. BERTSCH (ed.): *Was der Geist der Gemeinden sagt. Bausteine einer Ekklesiologie der Ortskirchen* (Theologie der Dritten Welt 15), Freiburg/Basel/Wien 1991, 168-177

POWER, D.: 'Cult to Culture. The Liturgical Foundation of Theology', in *Worship* 54 (1980) 482-495

POWER, D.: *Eucharistic Mystery. Revitalizing the Tradition*, Dublin 1992

POWER, D.: *Sacrament: the Language of God's Giving*, New York 1999

POWER, D.: 'Foundation for Pluralism in Sacramental Expression: Keeping Memory', in *Worship* 75 (2001) 194-209

PRESENCE: *The Presence of God in a Postmodern Context: the Sacramental Contours of a God Incarnate*: *Questions Liturgiques* 81 (2000) no. 3-4

PRÉTOT, F.P.: 'Sacraments and Liturgy in the Context of a Pastoral Strategy of 'Invitation to Faith'', in *Studia Liturgica* 32 (2002) 196-221

PROCTER-SMITH, M.: 'Images of Women in the Lectionary', in *Concilium* 21 (1985) 6, 51-62

PROCTER-SMITH, M.: *In Her Own Rite. Feminist Liturgical Tradition*, Ohio 1990 (reprint 2000)

PROCTER-SMITH, M.: *Praying with Our Eyes Open. Engendering Feminist Liturgical Prayer*, Nashville 1995

PROPOSER: *Proposer la foi. Renouveler la pastorale*: *La Maison-Dieu* (1998) 216

QUISPEL, B.: 'The Birth of the Child', in *Eranos* 40 (1971) 304-305

RAAD VAN KERKEN IN NEDERLAND: *Intercommunie. Het assymetrische geloofsgesprek tussen protestanten en katholieken*, Zoetermeer 1999

RAKOWSKI, H.: 'Literaturbericht zum Thema 'Gottesdienstübertragungen im Fernsehen'', in *Communicatio socialis* 20 (1987) 250-265

RAMING, I.: *Priesteramt der Frau. Geschenk Gottes für eine erneuerte Kirche*, Münster 2002

RAMSHAW-SCHMIDT, G.: 'Celebrating Baptism in Stages: A Proposal', in M. SEARLE (ed.): *Alternative Futures of Worship. Baptism and Confirmation*, Collegeville 1987, 137-155

RAND, M.: *Ritueel* (Magnum Images 1), Amsterdam 1990

RAPPAPORT, R.: *Ecology, Meaning and Religion*, Richmond 1979.

RAPPAPORT, R.: 'The obvious Aspects of Ritual', in R. RAPPAPORT: *Ecology, Meaning and Religion*, Richmond 1979 = R. RAPPAPORT: 'Ritual und performative Sprache', in A. BELLIGER & D.J. KRIEGER (eds.): *Ritualtheorien. Ein einführendes Handbuch*, Wiesbaden 1998, 191-211

RAPPAPORT, R.: *Ritual and Religion in the Making of Humanity* (Cambridge Studies in Social and Cultural Anthropology 110), Cambridge/New York/Melbourne/Madrid 1999

RATSCHOF, G.: 'Die Feste, Inbegriff sittlicher Gestalt', in J. ASSMAN (ed.): *Das Fest und das Heilige. Religiöse Kontrapunkte zur Alltagswelt* (Studien zum Verstehen fremder Religionen 1), Gütersloh 1991, 13-30

RATZINGER, J.: 'Pastoral Implications of Episcopal Collegiality', in *The Church and Mankind* (Concilium Dogma, Vol.1), New Yersey 1965

RATZINGER, J.: *Die sakramentale Begründung christlicher Existenz*, Meitingen 1966

RATZINGER, J.: *Der Geist der Liturgie: eine Einführung*, Freiburg 2000

RATZINGER, J.: 'Um die Erneuerung der Liturgie. Antwort auf Reiner Kaczynski', in *Stimmen der Zeit* 126 (2001) 837-843

RAZTINGER, J.: 'L'Esprit de la liturgie ou la fidélité au Concile. Réponse au père Gy', in *La Maison-Dieu* (2002) 230, 114-120

RATZMANN, W. (ed.): *Profile und Perspektiven der Liturgiewissenschaft*, Leipzig 2002

RAU, S.: *Die Feiern der Gemeinden und das Recht der Kirche – Zu Aufgabe, Form und Ebenen liturgischer Gesetzgebung in der katholischen Kirche*, Altenberge 1990

RAUSCH, T.P.: 'Forum: Priestly Identity: Priority of Representation and the Iconic Argument', in *Worship* 73 (1999) 169-179

RECLAIMING: *Reclaiming our rites: Studia Liturgica* 23 (1993) no. 1

REES, W. & M. WACKERNAGEL: *Our Ecological Footprint. Reducing Human Impact on the Earth*, Gabriola Island BC 1998

REICH, K.H.: 'Rituals and social structure: the moral dimension', in H.-G. HEIMBROCK & B. BOUDEWIJNSE (eds.): *Current Studies on Rituals. Perspectives for the Psychology of Religion*, Amsterdam 1990, 121-134

REISEN, H. VAN (ed.): *Van gerechtigheid tot liturgie*, Hilversum 1984

RENOUÉ, M.: *Sémiotique et perception esthétique. Pierre Soulages et Sainte-Foy de Conques*, Limoges 2001

RETURN: *The Return of the Plague: Concilium* 33 (1997) no. 5

REVE, G.K. VAN HET: *Op weg naar het einde*, Amsterdam 1963

REVE, Gerard: *Verzamelde gedichten*, Amsterdam 1987
REY-MERMET, TH.: *Ce que Dieu a uni… Le mariage chrétien hier et aujourd'hui*, Paris 1974
REYMOND, B.: *Théâtre et christianisme*, Genève 2002
REYNOLDS, P.L.: *The Christianization of Marriage during the Patristic and Early Medieval Periods*, Leiden/New York/Köln 1994
RICHTER, K.: *Kirchenräume und Kirchenträume. Die Bedeutung des Kirchenraums für eine lebendige Gemeinde*, Freiburg 1999²
RICHTER, K.: 'Review', in *Theologische Revue* 96 (2000) 4, 324-326
RICOEUR, P.: *Finitude et culpabilité*, Paris 1963
RICOEUR, P.: *Le conflit des interprétations. Essais d'herméneutique*, Paris 1969
RIDDER, B. & L. WOLTERING: *Rituelen spelen. Rituelen helen*, Oost-Soeburg 1995
RIPHAGEN, E.: *Kinderen en rituelen. Het belang van vaste gewoonten voor opgroeiende kinderen*, Kampen 1997
RITUAL: *Ritual and Power: Journal of Ritual Studies* 4 (1990) no. 2
RITUELEN: *Rituelen: Skript. Historisch tijdschrift* 6 (1984) no. 4
RITUELEN: *Rituelen: Op Schrift. Maandschrift van de RVU educatieve omroep* 3 (1985) no. 8
RITUELEN: *Rituelen en religie: Kultuurleven. Tijdschrift voor cultuur en samenleving* 64 (1997) no. 6
RITUELEN: *Rituelen in je leven: Humanist. Maandblad over humanisme en wereld* 52 (1997/1998) no. 12/1
RITUELEN: *Rituelen schenken levenskracht. Liturgie met ouderen in de praktijk* (DPC-brochure Rotterdam), Rotterdam 1998
RITZER, K.: *Formen, Riten und religiöses Brauchtum der Eheschliessung in den christlichen Kirchen des ersten Jahrtausends* (Liturgiewissenschaftliche Quellen und Forschungen 38), Münster 1982²
RIVERS, C.R.J.: *The Spirit in Worship*, Cincinnati 1978
ROEBBEN, B.: 'Jongeren met veel mogelijkheden maar weinig speelruimte. Initiatie in een wazige samenleving', in H. LOMBAERTS & L. BOEVE (eds.): *Traditie en initiatie. Perspectieven voor de toekomst*, Leuven/Amersfoort 1996, 191-221
ROEBBEN, B.: 'Spiritual and Moral Education in/and Cyberspace: Preliminary Reflections', in *Journal of Education and Christian Belief* 3 (1999) 85-95
ROLL, S.: 'Language and Justice in the Liturgy', in *Questions liturgiques* 73 (1992) 66-81 = S. ROLL: 'Language and Justice in the Liturgy', in L. LEIJSSEN (ed.): *Liturgie et langage – Liturgy and Language* (Textes et Études Liturgiques/Studies in Liturgy 12), Leuven 1992, 98-121 = S. ROLL: 'Taal en rechtvaardigheid in de liturgie', in L. LEIJSSEN (ed.): *Liturgie en taal*, Leuven/Amersfoort 1992, 99-122
ROMPA, M.: 'Liturgie in een gemeentehuis', in *Werkmap (voor) Liturgie* 28 (1994) 24-27
ROOIJ, H. VAN: 'Een eigen plekje voor kinderen in de kerk', in *Bisdomblad* 75 (1997) week 30 (July 25), 4-5

ROOIJAKKERS, G.: *Rituele repertoires. Volkscultuur in oostelijk Noord-Brabant 1559-1853*, Nijmegen 1994

ROOIJAKKERS, G.: 'Percepties van bovennatuur. Continuïteit en verandering in de Zuidnederlandse rite-praktijk', in *Jaarboek voor liturgie-onderzoek* 11 (1995) 103-125

ROOIJAKKERS, G.: 'De kerststal tussen kerk en VVV', in *De Bazuin* 83 (2000) (December 22), 10-13

RORDORF, W.: 'Remarques sur le mystère pascal', in *La Maison-Dieu* (1995) 204, 71-82

ROSSEELS, C.: *Rituelen vandaag*, Antwerpen 1995

ROSSEEUW, M., P. SCHOLLAERT & J. DE WIT: 'Religieuze muziek: expressie van het onzegbare', in J. HEMELS & H. HOEKSTRA: *Media en religieuze communicatie*, Hilversum 1985, 341-355

ROUILLARD, P.: 'Liturgies en Afrique', in *La Maison-Dieu* (1977) 130, 129-146

ROUWHORST, G.: 'Herman Wegman. Een terugblik op zijn leven en werk', in *Jaarboek voor liturgie-onderzoek* 12 (1996) 6-20

ROUWHORST, G.: 'Inculturatie en verandering in de westerse cultuur', in *Inzet* 25 (1996) 5, 108-115

ROUWHORST, G.: 'Liturgie voor onze tijd: inculturatie van de rooms-katholieke liturgie in de moderne westerse samenleving', in *Analecta aartsbisdom Utrecht* 69 (1996) 214-224

ROUWHORST, G.: 'A la recherche du christianisme primitif', in *Bulletin ET. Zeitschrift für Theologie in Europa* 8 (1997) 2, 181-195

ROUWHORST, G.: 'Veranderingen in de vormgeving van het huwelijksritueel', in *Praktische Theologie* 25 (1998) 75-89

ROUWHORST, G.: '"Ritual Studies": drie benaderingen van een complex verschijnsel...', in *Tijdschrift voor Liturgie* 86 (2002) 266-280

ROUWHORST, G.: 'Bronnen van liturgiehervorming tussen oorsprong en traditie', in *Jaarboek voor liturgie-onderzoek* 20 (2004) 7-23

RUDD, N.A.: 'Cosmetics Consumption and Use among Women: Ritualized Activities that Construct and Transform the Self', in *Journal of Ritual Studies* 11 (1997) 59-78

RUIJTER, A. DE a.o.: *Totems en trends. Over de zin van identificatiesymbolen*, Hilversum 1988

RUIJTER, J.: 'New Rituals Through AIDS', in *Concilium* 29 (1993) 3, 21-29

RUIJTER, J.: 'Er zijn evenveel begrafenisliturgieën als er uitvaarten zijn', in *Werkmap (voor) Liturgie* 28 (1994) 1, 37-45

RUPRECHT, H.-G.: 'Ouvertures métasémiotiques: entretien avec Algirdas Julien Greimas', in *Recherches Sémiotiques/Semiotic Inquiry* 4 (1985) 1, 1-22

SAFRANSKI, R.: *Das Böse oder das Drama der Freiheit*, München 1997 = R. SAFRANSKI: *Het kwaad, of Het drama van de vrijheid*, Amsterdam 1998

SALLNOW, M.J.: 'Communitas Reconsidered: The Sociology of Andrean Pilgrimage', in *Man (N.S.)* 16 (1981) 163-182

SAMENLEVING: *De samenleving in het liturgisch jaar: Werkmap (voor) Liturgie* 22 (1988) 65-128

SANDERS, J.: 'Kerkcijfers stabiel rond belangrijke levensmomenten', in *Een-twee-een* 30 (2002) 7, 3-5

SANTE, C. DI: 'Cultura e liturgia', in D. SARTORE & A.M. TRIACCA (eds.): *Nuovo dizionario di liturgia*, Rome 1984, 71-92

SARTORE, D. & A.M. TRIACCA (eds.): *Nuovo dizionario di liturgia*, Rome 1984

SAWYER, J.F.A.: *The fifth Gospel. Isaiah in the History of Christianity*, Cambridge 1995

SAX, M. a.o.: *Zand erover. Afscheid en uitvaart naar eigen inzicht*, Amsterdam 1989

SCHAEFFLER, R.: 'Kultisches Handeln. Die Frage nach Proben seiner Bewahrung und nach Kriterien seiner Legitimation', in A. HAHN a.o., *Anthropologie des Kults*, Freiburg 1977, 9-50

SCHECHNER, R.: *Essays on Performance Theory 1970-1976*, New York 1977

SCHECHNER, R.: *Between Theater and Anthropology*, Philadelphia 1985

SCHECHNER, R.: *Performance Theory*, New York/London 1988

SCHECHNER, R.: *Theater – Anthropologie. Spiel und Ritual im Kulturvergleich*, Reinbeck 1990

SCHECHNER, R.: *The Future of Ritual*, London/New York 1993

SCHECHNER, R. & W. APPEL (eds.): *By means of Performance: Intercultural Studies of Theatre and Ritual*, Cambridge 1995

SCHEER, A.: 'Peilingen in de hedendaagse huwelijksliturgie. Een oriënterend onderzoek', in *Tijdschrift voor Liturgie* 62 (1978) 259-317

SCHEER, A.: 'Het dilemma: cultuur-cultus', in *Jaarboek voor liturgie-onderzoek* 7 (1991) 159-168

SCHEER, A.: 'Liturgiewetenschap: cultus en cultuur in dialectiek', in *Praktische Theologie* 22 (1995) 80-99

SCHEER, A.: 'Liturgische taalvernieuwing als culturatievraagstuk', in *Tijdschrift voor Liturgie* 82 (1998) 289-302

SCHEER, A.: 'Ut duo sint … A theory of acts approach to marriage liturgy', in P. POST, G. ROUWHORST, L. VAN TONGEREN & A. SCHEER (eds.): *Christian Feast and Festival. The Dynamics of Western Liturgy and Culture* (Liturgia condenda 12), Leuven 2001, 599-644

SCHEPENS, T.: 'De katholieke kerk en de religieuze markt in Nederland', in K.-W. MERKS & N. SCHREURS: *De passie van een grensganger. Theologie aan de vooravond van het derde millennium*, Baarn 1997, 15-26

SCHILLEBEECKX, E.: *The Eucharist*, New York 1968

SCHILLEBEECKX, E.: *Marriage: Human Reality and Saving Mystery*, London/New York 1976

SCHILLEBEECKX, E.: 'Cultuur, godsdienst en geweld. Theologie als onderdeel van een cultuur', in *Tijdschrift voor Theologie* 36 (1996) 387-404

SCHILLEBEECKX, E.: 'Ruptures dans les dogmes chrétiens', in *Bulletin ET. Zeitschrift für Theologie in Europa* 8 (1997) 1, 11-38

SCHILLEBEECKX, E.: 'Over vergeving en verzoening. De kerk als 'verhaal van toekomst'', in *Tijdschrift voor Theologie* 37 (1997) 368-383

SCHILLEBEECKX, E.: 'Naar een herontdekking van de christelijke sacramenten. Ritualisering van religieuze momenten in het alledaagse leven', in *Tijdschrift voor Theologie* 40 (2000) 164-187

SCHILSON, A.: 'Perspektiven gegenwärtiger Christologie. Ein Situationsbericht', in G. BITTER & G. MILLER (eds.); *Konturen heutiger Theologie. Werkstattberichte*, München 1976, 161-175

SCHILSON, A.: 'Fest und Feier in anthropologischer und theologischer Sicht', in *Liturgisches Jahrbuch* 44 (1994) 1, 4-32

SCHILSON, A.: 'Den Gottesdienst fernsehgericht inszenieren? Die Verantwortung der Liturgie angesichts des 'Medienreligiösen'', in *Stimmen der Zeit* 8 (1996) 534-546

SCHILSON, A.: 'Das neue Religiöse und der Gottesdienst. Liturgie vor einer neuen Herasuforderung?', in *Liturgisches Jahrbuch* 46 (1996) 2, 94-109

SCHILSON, A.: 'Musicals als Kult. Neue Verpackung religiöser Symbolik?', in *Liturgisches Jahrbuch* 48 (1998) 3, 143-167

SCHILSON, A.: 'Liturgie(-Reform) angesichts einer sich wandelnden Kultur. Perspektiven am Ende des 20. Jahrhunderts', in M. KLÖCKENER & B. KRANEMANN (eds.): *Liturgiereformen. Historische Studien zu einem bleibenden Grundzug des christlichen Gottesdienstes* (Liturgiewissenschaftliche Quellen und Forschungen 88), Münster 2002, 965-1002.

SCHILSON, A.: ,Der Geist der Liturgie – von Guardini bis Ratzinger, in M. KLÖCKENER a.o. (eds.): *Gottes Volk feiert... Anspruch und Wirklichkeit gegenwärtiger Liturgie*, Trier 2002, 92-117

SCHINELLER, P.: *A Handbook on Inculturation*, New York 1990

SCHIWY, G.: *Zeichen im Gottesdienst*, München 1976

SCHLEIFFER, R.: *A.J. Greimas and the nature of meaning. Linguistics, semiotics and discourse theory*, London/Sidney 1987

SCHLEMMER, K. (ed.): *Gottesdienst – Weg zur Einheit. Impulse für die Ökumene*, Freiburg/Basel/Wien 1989

SCHMID, P.: 'Het duurzame 'Huis van verbond'', in P. POST (ed.): *Een ander huis. Kerkarchitectuur na 2000* (Liturgie in perspectief 7), Baarn 1997, 59-63

SCHMIDT, H.: *Introductio in liturgiam occidentalem*, Rome 1959

SCHMIDT, H.: 'Language and its Function in Christian Worship', in *Studia Liturgica* 8 (1970-1971) 1-25

SCHMIDT, H.: *Wie betet der heutige Mensch. Dokumente und Analysen*, Einsiedeln/Zürich/Freiburg/Wien 1972

SCHMIDT, K.: 'Das politische Nachtgebet', in W. HERBST: *Evangelischer Gottesdienst. Quellen zu seiner Geschichte*, Göttingen 1992, 298-307

SCHMIDT, P.: *In de handen van mensen: 2000 jaar Christus in kunst en cultuur*, Leuven 2000

SCHMIDT-LAUBER, H.-C & K.-H. BIERITZ (eds.): *Handbuch der Liturgik.*
Liturgiewissenschaft in Theologie und Praxis der Kirche, Leipzig/Göttingen
1995; third revised edition Göttingen 2003
SCHMITT, J.-C.: *La raison des gestes dans l'occident médiéval,* Paris 1990
SCHOCKENHOFF, E.: *Zum Fest der Freiheit. Theologie des christlichen Handeln bei*
Origenes, Mainz 1990
SCHOENMAKER, T.: 'Vieren 'Met de dood in de ogen", in *Jaarboek voor liturgie-*
onderzoek 8 (1992) 153-168
SCHOOTS, E.: 'Het goede afscheid nemen', in *NRC Handelsblad* November 26,
1993, Weekagenda, 1
SCHREITER, R.: 'Inculturation of Faith or Identification with Culture?', in *Con-*
cilium 30 (1994) 2, 15-24
SCHREUDER, O.: 'De religieuze traditie in de jaren tachtig', in O. SCHREUDER
& L. VAN SNIPPENBURG (eds.): *Religie in de Nederlandse samenleving. De*
vergeten factor, Baarn 1990, 17-41
SCHREUDER, O. & L. VAN SNIPPENBURG (eds.): *Religie in de Nederlandse samen-*
leving. De vergeten factor, Baarn 1990
SCHREURS, N.: *Geloofsverantwoording: Van apologetiek naar een hermeneutische*
theologie met apologetische inslag, Nijmegen 1982
SCHREURS, N. & V. PLASTOW (eds.): *Juxtaposing contexts. Doing contextual the-*
ology in South Africa and in the Netherlands, Pietermaritzburg 2003
SCHUMAN, N.: 'Nieuwe heiligenkalender', in *Rondom het Woord* 42 (2000) 1,
41-50
SCHUMAN, N.: 'Gedenken', in M. BARNARD & P. POST (eds.): *Ritueel bestek.*
Antropologische kernwoorden van de liturgie, Zoetermeer 2001, 181-193
SCHUMAN, N.: 'Schrift, boek, Bijbel, vertaling et cetera', in M. BARNARD & P.
POST (eds.): *Ritueel bestek. Antropologische kernwoorden van de liturgie,*
Zoetermeer 2001, 275-290
SCHUPP, F.: *Glaube – Kultur – Symbol. Versuch einer kritischen Theorie sakra-*
mentaler Praxis, Düsseldorf 1974
SCHWALL, H.: 'Engelen: het overschot van ons tekort', in *Tijdschrift voor*
geestelijk leven 52 (1996) 1, 37-52
SCHWIBBE G. & I. SPIEKER: 'Virtuelle Friedhöfe', in *Zeitschrift für Volkskunde*
95 (1999) 220-245
SCOUARNEC, M.: 'L'art de célébrer', in *La Maison-Dieu* (1999) 219, 119-140
SEARLE, M. (ed.): *Alternative Futures of Worship. Baptism and Confirmation,*
Collegeville 1987
SEARLE, M.: '*Fons vitae*: A Case Study in the Use of Liturgy as a Theological
Source', in G. AUSTIN (ed.): *Fountain of Life,* Washington 1991, 217-242
= A.Y. KOESTER & B. SEARLE (eds.): *Vision. The Contributions of Mark*
Searle to Liturgical Renewal, Collegeville 2004, 208-253
SEARLE, M.: 'Tussen énoncé en enunciatie: naar een semiotiek van gebeds-
teksten', in P. BEENTJES, J. MAAS & T. WEVER: *Gelukkig de mens. Opstellen*

over Psalmen, exegese en semiotiek aangeboden aan Nico Tromp, Kampen 1991, 193-211

SEARLE, M.: 'Semiotic Analysis of Roman Eucharistic Prayer II', in A. HEINZ & H. RENNINGS: *Gratias agamus. Studien zum Eucharistischen Hochgebet für Balthasar Fischer*, Freiburg 1992, 469-487

SEGAL, R.A.: *The myth and ritual theory: an anthology*, Malden Mass. 1998

SEGURA, R.P.: 'L'initiation, valeur permanente en vue de l'inculturation', in J. MASSON (ed.): *Mission et cultures non-chrétiennes*, Brugge 1959

SEI: *Sei Willkommen Kind. Empfehlungen für die Namensweihe*, Zentralhaus für Kulturarbeit, Leipzig 1973

SEMANET (ed. G. LUKKEN): *Semiotiek en christelijke uitingsvormen. De semiotiek van A.J. Greimas en de Parijse school toegepast op bijbel en liturgie*, Hilversum 1987

SENGSON, N.M.: *Research on the Sacramental Process of Penance and Reconciliation. Semiotic Approach to the Orationes of Medieval Rites of Penance* (Thèse de doctorat, Institut Supérieur de Liturgie, Paris), Paris 2001

SERNÉ, M.: *Ritueelbegeleiding, hulp bij het maken van een persoonlijke viering*, Vught (Capellebosdreef 13) without year

SEVERUS, E. VON (ed.): *Ecclesia Lacensis. Beiträge aus Anlass der Wiederbesiedlung der Abtei Maria Laach durch Benediktiner aus Beuron vor 100 Jahren am 25. November 1892 und der Gründung des Klosters durch Pfalzgraf Heinrich II. von Laach vor 900 Jahren 1093*, Münster 1993

SEXSON, S.: *Gewoon heilig. De sacraliteit van het alledaagse*, Zoetermeer 1997

SHAMA, S.: *Landscape and memory*, New York 1995

SHORTER, A.: *Towards a Theology of Inculturation*, Londen/New York 1988

SIEBEN, H.J.: *Die Konzilsidee der alten Kirche*, Paderborn 1979

SIEVERNICH, M.: "Social Sin' and its Acknowledgments', in *Concilium* 23 (1987) 2, 52-63

SINTERKLAAS: *Sinterklaas en de kerstman: concurrenten of collega's? Rituelen – commercie – identiteiten: Volkskundig Bulletin* 22 (1996) no. 3

SLENCZKA, N.: *Realpräsenz und Ontologie. Untersuchungen der ontologischen Grundlagen der Transsignifikationslehre*, Göttingen 1993

SLOMP, J.: 'Met moslims bidden? Een interreligieuze liturgische vraag', in *Werkmap (voor) Liturgie* 27 (1993) 117-125

SLOYAN, G.S.: 'Some Thoughts on Bible Translations', in *Worship* 75 (2001) 228-249

SMELIK, K.A.D.(ed.): *The letters and diaries of Etty Hillesum 1941-1943: complete and unabridged*, Grand Rapids/Ottawa 2002

SMYTH, M.: 'Une avancée oecuménique et liturgique. La note romaine concernant l'Anaphore d'Addaï et Mari', in *La Maison-Dieu* (2003) 233, 137-154

SNIPPENBURG, L. VAN (ed.): *Religie in de Nederlandse samenleving*, Baarn 1990

SNOEK, G.: *Medieval Piety from Relics to the Eucharist: A Process of Mutual Interaction* (Studies in the History of Christian Thought), Leiden 1995 = G. SNOEK: *Eucharistie- en reliekverering in de Middeleeuwen*, Amsterdam 1989

SOBRINO, J. & G.F. WILFRED: 'Globalization and its Victims. Introduction; The Reasons for Returning to this Theme', in *Concilium* 37 (2001) 5, 11-15

SÖLLE, D.: 'The Repression of the Existential Element, or Why So Many People Become Conservative', in *Concilium* 17 (1981) 1, 69-75

SÖLLE, D. & F. STEFFENSKY: *Politiek Avondgebed*, 2 Vols., Baarn 1969 and 1972

SOHIER, A.: 'Inculturation dans le monde chinois', in J. MASSON, *Mission et cultures non-chrétiennes*, Brugge 1959

SPECTRE: *The Spectre of Mass Death*: *Concilium* 29 (1993) no. 3

SPEELMAN, G.: 'Kerstfeest in een interreligieuze school', in *Begrip Moslims-Christenen*, November 1991, 106

SPEELMAN, G.: 'Interreligieuze huwelijken: leren leven met verschillen', in *Praktische Theologie* 25 (1998) 43-49

SPEELMAN, G. a.o. (eds.): *Ik ben christen, mijn partner is moslim*, Kampen 1995

SPEELMAN, W.M.: 'The plays of our culture. A formal differentiation between theatre and liturgy', in *Jaarboek voor liturgie-onderzoek* 9 (1993) 65-91

SPEELMAN, W.M.: *The Generation of Meaning in Liturgical Songs* (Liturgia condenda 4), Kampen 1995

SPEELMAN, W.M.: 'Een lied van een geborene', in *Inzet* 26 (1997) 22-26

SPEELMAN, W.M.: 'Het ware licht. Theologie van de liturgie in de media', in *Jaarboek voor liturgie-onderzoek* 16 (2000) 167-186

SPEELMAN, W.M.: 'The Feast of Diana's Death', in P. POST, G. ROUWHORST, L. VAN TONGEREN & A. SCHEER (eds.): *Christian Feast and Festival. The Dynamics of Western Liturgy and Culture* (Liturgia condenda 12), Leuven 2001, 775-801

SPEELMAN, W.M.: 'Televisie en liturgie', in M. BARNARD & P. POST (eds.): *Ritueel bestek. Antropologische kernwoorden van de liturgie*, Zoetermeer 2001, 123-130

SPEELMAN, W.M.: *Liturgie in beeld. Over de identiteit van de Rooms-katholieke liturgie in de elektronische media* (Netherlands Studies in Ritual and Liturgy 3), Groningen/Tilburg 2004

SPEELMAN, W.M. & H. STRIJARDS: 'Omkeren op de ingeslagen weg. Een heroverweging van het pastoraat van schuld en verzoening', in *Jaarboek voor liturgie-onderzoek* (1998) 197-218

SPERBER, D.: *Rethinking symbolism*, Cambridge 1975

SPEYBROECK, D. VAN (ed.): *Kunst en religie. Sporen van reële aanwezigheid* (Annalen van het Thijmgenootschap 79, 1), Baarn 1991

SPINKS, B.D.: 'Review', in *The Journal of Theological Studies* 46 (1995) 808

SPIRO, M.: 'Symbolism and Functionalism in the Anthropological Study of Religion', in L. HONKA (ed.): *Science of Religion. Studies in Methodology*, New York 1979, 323-329

SPRETNACK, B. (ed.): *Politics of Women Spirituality*, New York 1982

SPRUIT, L. & H. VAN ZOELEN: *Dopen... Ja waarom eigenlijk? Onderzoek naar de motieven die ouders hebben om hun kind al dan niet te laten dopen in de katholieke kerk*, Hilversum 1980

STAAL, F.: 'The Meaninglessness of Ritual', in *Numen* 26 (1975) 1, 2-22 = F. STAAL: 'De zinloosheid van het ritueel', in F. STAAL: *Over zin en onzin in filosofie, religie en wetenschap*, Amsterdam 1986, 295-321

STAAL, F: *Over zin en onzin in filosofie, religie en wetenschap*, Amsterdam 1986

STAAL, F.: *Rules without Meaning. Ritual, Mantras and the Human Sciences*, Bern 1989

STAAL, H.: 'Kindernamen', in *NRC Handelsblad* November 2, 1999

STANDAERT, N.: 'L'histoire d'un néologisme. Le terme 'inculturation' dans les documents romains', in *Nouvelle Revue Théologique* 110 (1988) 555-570

STAP, T. VAN DER: *Over het religieuze in de kunst. Naar aanleiding van Rembrandt en Mark Rothko*, in D. VAN SPEYBROECK (ed.): *Kunst en religie. Sporen van reële aanwezigheid* (Annalen van het Thijmgenootschap 79, 1), Baarn 1991, 95-99

STARK, R.: *De eerste eeuwen. Een sociologische visie op het ontstaan van het christendom*, Baarn 1998

STAUFFER, S.A. (ed.): *Worship and Culture in Dialogue*, Genève 1994

STAUFFER, S.A. (ed.): *Christian Worship. Unity in cultural diversity*, Genève 1996

STAUFFER, S.A.: 'Worship and Culture. A Select Bibliography', in *Studia Liturgica* 27 (1997) 102-128.

STEENBERGHE, M.: 'Witte rozen en blauwe ballonnen voor René Klijn', in *Nieuwsblad* September 9, 1993, 3

STEENBRINK, K.: 'Moslims en de kerken. Contacten en dialoog als onderdeel van kerkelijk handelen', in *Tijdschrift voor Theologie* 3 (1997) 56-72

STEENSMA, R.: *Kerken, wat doe je ermee*, Baarn 1981

STEENSMA, R.: *Opdat de ruimten meevieren*, Baarn 1982

STEENSMA, R.: *De geschiedenis van kerkbouw en kerkgebruik*, Groningen 1984

STEENSMA, R.: 'De receptie van de tentoonstelling 'Met de dood in de ogen' in de Grote Kerk te Leeuwarden', in *Jaarboek voor liturgie-onderzoek* 8 (1992) 169-204

STEENSMA, R.: *Opdat de ruimten meevieren. Een studie over de spanning tussen liturgie en monumentenzorg bij de herinrichting en het gebruik van monumentale kerken*, Baarn 1992.

STEENSMA, R.: 'Enkele uitgangspunten', in *Functionaliteit en symboliek van het kerkgebouw* (brochure bisdom Haarlem), Haarlem 1994

STEENSMA, R.: 'Enkele uitgangspunten bij de (her)inrichting van een katholieke kerk', in *Tijdschrift voor Liturgie* 78 (1994) 332-334

STEINER, J.: *Liturgiereform in der Aufklärungszeit* (Freiburger theologische Studien 101), Freiburg/Basel/Wien 1976

STEKETEE, H.: 'God in Nederland is verhuisd', in *NRC Handelsblad* November 14, 1997, 3

STERNBERG, TH.: 'Räume für die heilige Versammlung. Funktionale und theologische Probleme des Kirchenbaus', in *Jaarboek voor liturgie-onderzoek* 20 (2004) 89-105

STEVENSON, K.: *Nuptial Blessing. A Study of Christian Marriage Rites*, Londen 1982

STOCK, A.: 'Tempel en tolerantie. Over de musealisering van de religie', in *Werkschrift voor Leerhuis en Liturgie* 15 (1996) 98-101

STOCK, A.: 'Litanieën', in M. BARNARD & P. POST (eds.): *Ritueel bestek. Antropologische kernwoorden van de liturgie*, Zoetermeer 2001, 309-316

STOCK, A.: *Poetische Dogmatik*, 4 Vols., Paderborn 1995-2001

STOKS, H.: 'Review' of J. PLATVOET a.o. (eds.): *Pluralism and Identity: Studies in Ritual Behaviour* (Studies in the History of Religions 67), Leiden/New York/ Köln 1995, in *Tijdschrift voor Theologie* 36 (1996) 3, 325-326

STOPFORD, J. (ed.); *Pilgrimage explored*, Woodbridge 1999

STOSUR, D.A.: 'Liturgy and (Post)Modernity: A Narrative Response to Guardini's Challenge', in *Worship* 77 (2003) 22-41

STOUTHARD, P. & G. VAN TILLO (ed.): *Katholiek Nederland na 1945*, Baarn 1985

STRAATHOF, M.: 'Kerstwensen in de V&D-boom', in *De Bazuin* 81 (1998) (December) 4-6

STRIJARDS, H.: *Schuld en pastoraat. Een poimenische studie over schuld als thema voor het pastorale groepsgesprek* (serie Zin en Zorg), Kampen 1997

STRINGER, D.: 'Liturgy and Anthropology: the History of a Relationship', in *Worship* 63 (1989) 503-520

STRINGER, M.D.: *On the Perception of Worship. The Ethnography of Worship in Four Cristian Congregations in Manchester*, Birmingham 1999.

STROEKEN, K.: 'Afrikaanse initiatieriten', in *Kultuurleven* 64 (1997) 58-63

SWAAN, W.: *Glorie der gotiek*, Amerongen 1977

SWINKELS, T. & P. POST: 'Beginnings in Ritual Studies according to Ronald Grimes', in *Jaarboek voor liturgie-onderzoek* 19 (2003) 215-238

SWÜSTE, G.: 'Het voorlezen van een schrifttekst', in G. LUKKEN & J. DE WIT (eds.): *Lezen in fragmenten. De Bijbel als liturgisch boek* (Liturgie in beweging 2), Baarn 1998, 185-191

SYMBOLEN: *Symbolen en riten*: Tijdschrift voor Geestelijk Leven 51 (1995) no. 6

TAFT, R.: 'The Structural Analysis of Liturgical Units: An Essay in Methodology', in *Worship* 52 (1978) 314-329 = R. TAFT: *Beyond East and West. Problems in Liturgical Understanding*, Washington 1984, 151-164

TAFT, R.: 'Comparative Liturgy Fifty Years after Anton Baumstark (d.1948): A Reply to Recent Critics', in *Worship* 73 (1999) 521-540

TAFT, R.: 'A Generation of Liturgy in the Academy', in *Worship* 75 (2001) 46-58

TAFT, R.: 'Mass Without the Consecration? The Historic Agreement on the Eucharist between the Catholic Church and the Assyrian Church of the East Promulgated 26 October 2001, in *Worship* 77 (2003) 482-509

TAFT, R. & G. WINKLER: *Acts of the International Congress Comparative Liturgy fifty years after Anton Baumstark (1972-1948)* (Orientalia Christiana Analecta 265), Roma 2001.

TAMBIAH, S.J.: 'The Magical Power of Words', in *Man* 3 (1968) 2, 175-208

TENBRUCK, F.H.: 'Geschichtserfahrung und Religion in der heutigen Gesellschaft', in *Spricht Gott in der Geschichte*, Freiburg 1972

TENNEKES, J.: *De Bierkaai en de Bron. Antropologische kanttekeningen bij hedendaags christendom*, Kampen 2000

TERRIN, A.: 'Antropologia culturale', in D. SARTORE & A.M. TRIACCA (eds.): *Nuovo dizionario di liturgia*, Rome 1984, 71-92

THALER, A.: 'Inkulturation der Liturgie. Am Beispiel der Mahlelemente', in *Diakonia* 20 (1989) 172-179

THEOBALD, C.: 'The 'Definitive' Discourse of the Magisterium: Why be Afraid of a Creative Reception?', in *Concilium* 35 (1999) 1, 70-76

THISELTON, A.C.: 'Sign, Symbol', in J.G. DAVIES (ed.): *A New Dictionary of Liturgy and Worship*, Londen 1986, 491-492

THOOFT, L.: 'Ja, ik wil... maar waarom? De beweegredenen en achtergronden van het nieuwe trouwen', in *Opzij* 21 (1993) 8-15

THUISZORG: 'Thuiszorg neigt steeds meer naar 'stopwatch-zorg'', in *NRC Handelsblad* 20 maart 1997, 8

THURLINGS, J.: *De wankele zuil. Nederlandse katholieken tussen assimilatie en pluralisme*, Nijmegen/Amersfoort 1971

TIENEN, F.J. VAN: 'Een verterend vuur', in *Praktische Theologie* 8 (1981) 240-243

TODOROV, T.: *Théories au symbole*, Paris 1977

TOFFLER, A. & H.: *Creating a New Civilization. The Politics of the Third Wave*, Atlanta 1994

TONGEREN, L. VAN: 'Analyse d'un rituel: Introduction dialoguée de la préface romaine', in *Sémiotique et Bible* 9 (1983) no. 32, 19-26

TONGEREN, L. VAN (ed.): *Toekomst, toen en nu. Beschouwingen over de ontwikkeling en de voortgang van de liturgievernieuwing* (Liturgie in perspectief 2), Heeswijk-Dinther 1994

TONGEREN, L. VAN: 'De inculturatie van de liturgie tot (stil)stand gebracht? Kanttekeningen bij een Romeins document over liturgie en inculturatie', in *Jaarboek voor liturgie-onderzoek* 12 (1996) 164-186

TONGEREN, L. VAN: 'Liturgie in context. De vernieuwing van de liturgie en de voortgang ervan als een continu proces', in *Tijdschrift voor Liturgie* 81 (1997) 178-198

TONGEREN, L. VAN: 'Een onafscheidelijk driespan. Liturgie en kerkbouw in de context van de cultuur', in P. POST (ed.): *Een ander huis. Kerkarchitectuur na 2000* (Liturgie in perspectief 7), Baarn/Berne 1997, 30-38

TONGEREN, L. VAN: *In het ritme van de tijd. Over de samenhang tussen tijd en liturgie*, Baarn 1999

TONGEREN, L. VAN: 'Beleving en rituele vormgeving van tijd', in M. BARNARD & P. POST (eds.): *Ritueel bestek. Antropologische kernwoorden van de liturgie*, Zoetermeer 2001, 63-68

TONGEREN, L. VAN: 'The Celebration of the First Communion. Seeking the Identity of the Christian Ritual', in P. POST, G. ROUWHORST, L. VAN TONGEREN & A. SCHEER (eds.): *Christian Feast and Festival. The Dynamics of Western Liturgy and Culture* (Liturgia condenda 12), Leuven 2001, 581-598

TONGEREN, L. VAN: 'The Squeeze on Sunday. Reflections on the Changing Experience and Form of Sundays', in P. POST, G. ROUWHORST, L. VAN TONGEREN & A. SCHEER (eds.): *Christian Feast and Festival. The Dynamics of Western Liturgy and Culture* (Liturgia condenda 12), Leuven 2001, 705-727

TONGEREN, L. VAN: 'De zondag', in M. BARNARD & P. POST (eds.): *Ritueel bestek. Antropologische kernwoorden van de liturgie*, Zoetermeer 2001, 69- 76

TONGEREN, L. VAN: 'De christelijke betekenis van de Zondag in kerk en maatschappij', in *Jaarboek voor liturgie-onderzoek* 18 (2002) 101-122

TONGEREN, L. VAN: 'Liturgical Renewal Never Ends', in M. LAMBERIGTS & L. KENIS: *Vatican II and its legacy*, Leuven 2002, 365-384

TONGEREN, L. VAN: 'Over het leven bij de dood. Het leven ter sprake brengen bij de uitvaart', in H. BECK & W. WEREN (eds.): *Over leven. Leven en overleven in lagen*, Budel 2002, 133-155

TONGEREN, L. VAN: 'Vers une utilisation dynamique et flexible de l'espace. Une réflexion renouvelée sur le réaménagement d'églises', in *Questions Liturgiques* 83 (2002) 179-195

TONGEREN, L. VAN: 'De iconografie van moderne heiligen. Op zoek naar een nieuwe typologie', in *Jaarboek voor liturgie-onderzoek* 19 (2003) 127-145

TONGEREN, L. VAN: 'De religieuze (ir)relevantie van de zondag. Een liturgie-wetenschappelijke reflectie', in *Praktische Theologie* 30 (2003) 298-317

TONGEREN, L. VAN: 'The Re-ordering of Church Buildings reconsidered', in N. SCHREURS & V. PLASTOW (eds.): *Juxtaposing contexts. Doing contextual theology in South Africa and in the Netherlands*, Pietermaritzburg 2003, 188-217

TONGEREN, L. VAN: 'Individualizing Ritual. The Personal Dimension in Funeral Liturgy', in *Worship* 77 (2004) 117-138

TONGEREN, L. VAN: 'De ruimtelijke dispositie van de gemeenschapsliturgie', in *Jaarboek voor liturgie-onderzoek* 20 (2004) 107-133

TOP, S.: 'Als de ooievaar komt... Volksculturele facetten van zwangerschap, geboorte en doop (1900-1950)', in L. LEIJSSEN, M. CLOET & K. DOBBELAERE (eds.): *Levensrituelen. Geboorte en doopsel* (Kadoc-Studies 20), Leuven 1996, 123-146

TORFFS, R.: 'Liefde en recht gaan hand in hand. Een denkoefening over de verhouding tussen theologie en recht', in *Tijdschrift voor Theologie* 36 (1996) 270-289

TRAN-VAN-KHA, F.: 'L'adaptation liturgique telle qu'elle a été réalisée par les commissions nationales liturgiques jusqu'à maintenant', in *Notitiae* 25 (1989) 864-883

TRIACCA, A.M.: "Inculturazione e liturgia': eventi dello Spirito Santo. A proposito di alcuni principi per il progresso dell'approfondimento degli studi su 'liturgia e culture", in *Ecclesia Orans* 15 (1998) 1, 59-89.

TRIACCA A.M. & A. PISTOIA (eds.): *Liturgie et cultures* (Bibliotheca Ephemerides Liturgicae 90), Rome 1997

TUFFELEN, A. VAN & T. BRUGGE: *Symbolische bloemsierkunst; bloemschikken voor kerk en woning*, Ede/Antwerpen 1992, 1996²

TURNER, K.: 'Contemporary Feminist Rituals', in B. SPRETNACK (ed.): *Politics of Women Spirituality*, New York 1982

TURNER, V.: *The Forest of Symbols. Aspects of Ndembu Ritual*, Ithaca 1967

TURNER, V.: *The Drums of Affliction. A Study of Religious Processes among the Ndembu of Zambia*, Oxford 1968

TURNER, V.: *The Ritual Process. Structure and Anti-structure*, Chicago 1969

TURNER, V.: *Dramas, Field and Metaphors. Symbolic Action in Human Society*, Ithaca 1974

TURNER, V.: 'Ritual, Tribal and Catholic', in *Worship* 50 (1976) 504-526

TURNER, V.: 'Social Dramas and Stories About Them', in *Critical Analysis* 7 (1980) 141-168

TURNER, V.: *The Anthropology of Performance*, New York 1987

TURNER, V.: *Das Ritual. Struktur und Anti-Struktur*, Frankfurt am Main 1989

TURNER, V.: *Vom Ritual zum Theater. Der Ernst des menschlichen Spiels*, Franfurt/Main 1989

UDEN, M. VAN: *Rouw, religie en ritueel*, Baarn 1988

UDEN, M. VAN, J. PIEPER & E. HENAU (eds.): *Bij geloof. Over bedevaarten en andere uitingen van volksreligiositeit* (UTP-katern 11), Hilversum 1991

UDEN, M. VAN, J. PIEPER & P. POST (eds.): *Oude sporen, nieuwe wegen. Ontwikkelingen in bedevaartonderzoek* (UTP-katern 17), Baarn 1995

UDEN, M. VAN, P. POST & J. PIEPER: *The Modern Pilgrim. Multidisciplinary Explorations of Christian Pilgrimage* (Liturgia condenda 8), Leuven 1998

UKPONG, J.S.: 'Towards a Renewed Approach to Inculturation Theology', in *Journal of Inculturation Theology* 1 (1994) 8-24

ULEYN, A.: 'Drie idealen waardoor groepen zich laten leiden', in *Speling* 27 (1975) 88-99

URSPRUNG: O.: *Die katholische Kirchenmusik*, Potsdam 1931

VAESSEN, J.: *Musea in een museale cultuur. De problematische legitimering van het kunstmuseum*, Zeist 1986

VALK, J. DE: 'De lichamelijkheid van een sacrament', in *De Bazuin* 23 (1987) 1, 15

VALK, J.J.M. DE (ed.): *Nationale identiteit in Europees perspectief*, Baarn 1993

VAN DEN BOSSCHE, S.: 'Geen wijn in water veranderen: De onherleidbare particulariteit van het christelijk geloof', in *Tijdschrift voor Theologie* 38 (1998) 109-119

VAN DEN BOSSCHE, S.: 'God verschijnt toch in de immanentie. De fenomenologische neerlegging van de theologie in Jean-Luc Marions Étant donné', in R. WELTEN (ed.): *God en het denken*. *Over de filosofie van Jean-Luc Marion* (Annalen van het Thijmgenootschap, 88, 2), Nijmegen 2000, 128-153

VAN DEN BOSSCHE, S.: *Presentie in differentie: Vier Essays over de Godsontmoeting in een postmoderne context* (Doctoral Thesis), Leuven 2000

VANDERMEERSCH, P.: 'Psychotherapeutic and Religious Rituals: The Issue of Secularisation', in H.-G. HEIMBROCK & B. BOUDEWIJNSE (eds.): *Current Studies of Ritual. Perspectives from the Psychology of Religion*, Amsterdam/Atlanta 1990, 151-164 = P. VANDERMEERSCH: 'Psychotherapeutische Rituale', in BELLIGER, A. & D.J. KRIEGER (eds.): *Ritualtheorien. Ein einführendes Handbuch*, Wiesbaden 1998, 435-447 = P. VANDERMEERSCH: 'Psychotherapeutische en religieuze rituelen', in *Werkmap (voor) Liturgie* 25 (1991) 79-91.

VANDERMEERSCH, P.: 'Psychologische lagen in het geloven', in *Tijdschrift voor Theologie* 39 (1999) 381-407

VEDDER, B. a.o. (eds.): *Zin tussen vraag en aanbod. Theologische en wijsgerige beschouwingen over zin*, Tilburg 1992

VEER, L. VAN DER: 'Een pastorale week. Verslag van een gecomprimeerde vorm van pastorale hulpverlening, waarin gebruik gemaakt wordt van rituelen', in *Praktische Theologie* 8 (1981) 230-239

VEGHEL, H. VAN: 'God en de roos. Heidegger en de god van de filosofie', in R.J. PEETERS a.o. (eds.): *De onvoltooid verleden tijd. Negen bijdragen tot een bezinning op traditie*, Tilburg 1992, 51-67

VELDEN, K. VAN DER a.o.: *Directieve therapie*, Deventer 1977

VELTHAUSZ, A.: 'Bij de baby op de borrel', in *De Twentsche courant Tubantia* January 4, 1997, 'Leven', 1

VEN, J. VAN DER: *Ecclesiologie in context*, Kampen 1993

VEN, J. VAN DER: 'Het Planbureau versimpelt het godsgeloof', in *NRC Handelsblad* June 27, 1997, 7

VEN, J. VAN DER: 'Faith in God in a Secularised Culture', in *Bulletin ET. Zeitschrift für Theologie in Europa* 9 (1998) 1, 21-45

Ven, J.M.M. VAN DE: *In facie ecclesiae. De katholieke huwelijksliturgie in de Nederlanden, van de 13ᵉ eeuw tot het einde van het Ancien Regime*, Leuven 2000

VEN, P. VAN DER: 'Religieus ritueel is geen gereedschap voor de therapeut', in *Trouw* February 1989

VERANTWOORDINGEN: *Verantwoordingen voor het uitspreken van een zegenbede over een levensverbintenis*, Utrecht 1989

VERDUIJN, M.: 'Vaders in de hoofdrol. Marijke Verduijn in gesprek met Vincent Duindam', in *Roodkoper* 2 (1997) 4, 14-16

VERGOTE, A.: *Het huis is nooit af. Gedachten over mens en religie*, Antwerpen/Utrecht 1974

VERGOTE, A.: 'Christian Misreadings of the Human', in *Concilium* 18 (1982) 5, 16-22

VERGOTE, A.: *Religie, geloof en ongeloof*, Antwerpen/Amsterdam 1984

VERHELST, M. a.o.: *Met rituelen het leven spelen. Initiatie – welkom – dank-verzoening – feest*, Kapellen/Brussel 1988

VERHOEVEN, C.: *Rondom de leegte*, Utrecht 1967

VERKUYTEN, M.: *Symbool en samenleving. Over symbolen en hun rol in het sociale leven*, Zeist 1990

VERNOOIJ, A.: "Dan danst de kreupele als een hert…' (Jesaja 35, 6). Over de toekomst van de gemeenschapsliturgie', in L. VAN TONGEREN (ed.): *Toekomst, toen en nu. Beschouwingen over de ontwikkeling en de voortgang van de liturgievernieuwing* (Liturgie in perspectief 2), Heeswijk-Dinther 1994, 57-76

VERNOOIJ, A.: "Hun geluid ging over de hele wereld'. Over de invloed van de kloosterzang op de Nederlandstalige parochieliturgie', in *Gregoriusblad* 122 (1998) 3, 149-155

VERNOOIJ, A.: *Muziek als liturgisch teken* (Liturgie in perspectief 10), Baarn/Heeswijk 1998.

VERNOOIJ, A.: 'De taal van de ziel', in *Jaarboek voor liturgie-onderzoek* 14 (1998) 219-237.

VERNOOIJ, A.: 'Musiceren en luisteren', in M. BARNARD & P. POST (eds.): *Ritueel bestek. Antropologische kernwoorden van de liturgie*, Zoetermeer 2001, 145-154

VERNOOIJ, A. (ed.): *Toontaal. De verhouding tussen woord en toon in heden en verleden* (Meander 4), Kampen 2002

VERSTEGEN, T.: 'Tot zo ver deze lezing. Het lectionarium door vrouwen gelezen', in G. LUKKEN & J. DE WIT (eds.): *Lezen in fragmenten. De bijbel als liturgisch boek* (Liturgie in beweging 2), Baarn 1998, 137-145

VERWEIJ, J.: *Secularisering tussen Feit en Fictie. Een internationaal vergelijkend onderzoek naar determinanten van religieuze betrokkenheid*, Tilburg 1998

VEYNE, P.: *L'inventaire des différences*, Paris 1976

VIERINGEN: *Vieringen (Rituelen) buiten 1 and 2: Werkmap (voor) Liturgie* 30 (1996) no. 3-4

VISSCHER, J. DE: 'Alsof Genesis 3 niet had plaatsgehad. Het postmodernisme in de hedendaagse schilderkunst en sculptuur', in I. BULHOF & J.M.M. DE VALK (eds.): *Postmodernisme als uitdaging*, Baarn 1990, 98-113

VISSCHER, J. DE: 'Kunst en religie. Van manifeste verbondenheid naar verborgen verwantschap', in D. VAN SPEYBROECK (ed.): *Kunst en religie. Sporen van reële aanwezigheid* (Annalen van het Thijmgenootschap 79, 1), Baarn 1991, 100-112

VISSCHER, J. DE: *Een te voltooien leven. Over rituelen van de moderne mens*, Kampen 1996

VISSCHER, J. DE (ed.): *Mosterdzaadjes van het bestaan. De waarde van de kleine dingen*, Baarn 1996

VISSCHER, J. DE: 'Geherbergd in een traditie. Symbolen en rituelen dienen tot niets', in *Tijdschrift voor Geestelijk Leven* 54 (1998) 113-122

VISSCHER, J. DE a.o.: *Hannah Arendt en de moderniteit*, Kampen 1992

VISSER, C.: 'Verslindende dood en de weg van Janusz Korczak', in *Dabar-bericht* 1996, 3, 4

VISSER, H.: *Leven zonder God. Elf interviews over ongeloof*, Amsterdam 2003

VOERMANS, W.: 'Niks misdaan en toch 'gestraft'. Internationaal Congres over vreemdelingenbewaring', in *Kub ter visie. Magazine van de katholieke universiteit Brabant en de stichting professor Cobbenhagen* (1998) 1, 5-7

VOGELS, W.: 'Woord en gebaar rond een doodgeboren kind', in G. LUKKEN & J. DE WIT (eds.): *Nieuw leven. Rituelen rond geboorte en doop* (Liturgie in beweging 1), Baarn 1997, 90-97

VOLL, P.: 'Religion im Alltag', in A. DUBACH a.o.: *Religiöse Lebenswelt junger Eltern*, Zürich 1989, 262-300

VOLP, R.: *Liturgik. Die Kunst, Gott zu feiern*, Vol. 2, Gütersloh 1994

VOLP, R. a.o.: *Zeichen. Semiotik in Theologie und Gottesdienst*, München/Mainz 1982

VOS, W. & G. WAINWRIGHT (eds.): *Gratias Agamus. An ecumenical collection of essays on the liturgy and its implications. On the occasion of the twenty fifth anniversary of Studia liturgica (1962-1987)* (Studia liturgica 17), Rotterdam 1987

VOSSEBELD, J.: 'Van confectie naar maatwerk. Keuze uit een keur aan kwaliteit op de markt van uitvaart, huwelijk en aanverwante artikelen', in *Mara* 9 (1996) 4, 12-21

VOYÉ, L.: 'Du monopole religieux à la connivence culturelle en Belgique. Un catholicisme 'hors les murs'', in *L'Année sociologique* 38 (1988) 135-167

VOYÉ, L.: 'Le rite en question', in R. DEVISCH a.o.: *Le rite, source et ressources*, Brussel 1995, 105-136

VOYÉ, L.: 'Uitwissing of nieuwe legitimatie van de volksreligie? Een sociologische benadering', in J. LAMBERTS (ed.): *Volksreligie, liturgie en evangelisatie* (Nikè-reeks 42), Leuven/Amersfoort 1998, 129-151

VRIES, S. DE: 'Gescheiden wegen', in S. DE VRIES, *Op liefde gebouwd*, Delft 1987, 1995^5, 85-91

VRIES, S. DE: 'Een kring van getuigen; de helende mogelijkheden van een liturgie bij echtscheiding', in *De Bazuin* 70 (1987) 35, 12-13

VRIES, S. DE: 'Werkelijk 'à Dieu'? Over doel en zin van een ritueel bij echtscheiding', in *Praktische Theologie* 25 (1998) 66-74

VRIJDAG, H.: *Zonder beelden sprak hij niet tot hen*, 3 Vols., Baarn 1988-1991

VRIJLAND, M.A.: *Liturgiek*, Delft 1987

VROUW: *Vrouw en liturgie*: *Werkmap (voor) Liturgie* 19 (1985) 159-231

VROUWE: *Vrouwe Leitourgia*: *Tijdschrift voor Liturgie* 82 (1998) no. 5

VROUWVRIENDELIJKE: *Een vrouwvriendelijke liturgie in de rooms-katholieke kerk. Advies van de werkgroep Vrouw en Kerk, de Katholieke Raad voor Kerk en Samenleving en de Unie Nederlandse Katholieke Vrouwenbeweging aan de Nederlandse bisschoppen*, Vught 1991

WAAROM: *Waarom lopen de kerken leeg? Over de oorzaken van afgenomen kerkbezoek en kerkverlating in Nederland tussen 1937 en 1995*: *Sociale Wetenschappen* (1998) no. 2

WAELE, C. DE: 'Een stiltecentrum op de campus', in *Speling* 47 (1995) 40-47

WAGNER-RAU, U.: *Segensraum. Kasualpraxis in der modernen Gesellschaft* (Praktische Theologie heute 50), Stuttgart/Berlin/Köln 2000

WAINWRIGHT, G.: *Doxology. The Praise of God in Worship, Doctrine and Life. A Systematic Theology*, Westminster 1982[2]

WALDENFELS, B.: *Stachel des Fremde*, Frankfurt 1990

WALDENFELS, H.: 'Zum Verbindlichkeitsgrad von *Inter insigniores* und *Ordinatio sacerdotalis* und ihren dogmatischen Positionen', in E. DASSMANN a.o.: *Projekttag. Frauenordination*, Bonn 1997, 24-25

WALRAVE, M.: 'Religieuze symbolen in de reclame. Rage of postmoderne trend?', in *Tijdschrift voor Geestelijk Leven* 54 (1998) 2, 197-205

WALTHER-SOLLICH, T.: *Festpraxis und Alltagserfahrung. Sozialpsychologische Predigtanalysen zum Bedeutungswandel des Osterfestes im 20. Jahrhundert* (Praktische Theologie heute 29), Stuttgart/Berlin/Köln 1997

WANNENWETSCH, B.: *Gottesdienst als Lebensform. Ethik für Christenbürger*, Stuttgart/Berlin/Köln 1997

WARNINK, G.: *Lezen over vieren: Literatuurwijzer ten dienste van werkgroepen liturgie*, een uitgave van de deputaten voor de eredienst van de Gereformeerde Kerken in Nederland (Postbox 202, 3830 AE Leusden), 1981

WARREN, H. & M. MOLEGRAAF (eds.): *Ik heb alleen woorden. De honderd meest troostrijke gedichten over afscheid en rouw uit de Nederlandse poëzie*, Amsterdam 1998

WEAKLAND, R.G.: 'Liturgy in the United States these Past 25 Years', in *Worship* 75 (2001) 5-12

WEAKLAND, R.: 'The Liturgy as Battlefield', in *Commonweal* (New York) January 11, 2002 = IDEM: 'Liturgie zwischen Erneuerung und Restauration', in *Heiliger Dienst* 56 (2002) 83-93 and *Stimmen der Zeit* 220 (2002) 475-487.

WEAKLAND, R.: 'The Right Road for the Liturgy', in *The Tablet* (London) February 2, 2002, 10-13

WEERDENBURG, H. VAN: 'Een rode kist in een witte lijkauto', in *De Bazuin* 76 (1993) 36, 8-10

WEGMAN, H.: 'Het waaien van de Geest', in *Tijdschrift voor Liturgie* 59 (1975) 213-225

WEGMAN, H.: 'The rubrics of the Institution Narrative in the Roman Missal 1970', in P. JOUNEL a.o. (eds.): *Liturgia opera divina e umana; Studi sulla riforma liturgica offerti a S.E. Mons. Annibale Bugnini in occasione del suo 70 compleanno*, Rome 1982, 329-338

WEGMAN, H.: *Liturgie in de geschiedenis van het christendom*, Kampen 1991

WEGMAN, H.: 'Liturgie en lange duur', in L. VAN TONGEREN (ed.): *Toekomst, toen en nu. Beschouwingen over de ontwikkeling en de voortgang van de liturgievernieuwing* (Liturgie in perspectief 2), Heeswijk-Dinther 1994, 11-38

WEIGL, A.M.: *Schutzengeschichten heute*, Altöting 1973⁹

WEIJ, P.J.: 'Mijn zonden heb ik u gebiecht. Een pleidooi voor de biecht', Zoetermeer 1999

WEIMA, J.: *Reiken naar oneindigheid. Inleiding tot de psychologie van de religieuze ervaring*, Baarn 1981

WEIZSÄCKER, R. VON: *Von Deutschland aus*, Berlin 1985, 11-35

WELLINGA, K. (ed.): '... *Om Nicaragua te bevrijden...' Poëzie van Ernesto Cardenal*, Amsterdam 1978

WELTEN, R.: 'God en het Denken. Een inleiding in de filosofie van Jean-Luc Marion', in R. WELTEN (ed.): *God en het denken. Over de filosofie van Jean-Luc Marion* (Annalen van het Thijmgenootschap, 88, 2), Nijmegen 2000, 7-44

WELTEN, R. (ed.): *God en het denken. Over de filosofie van Jean-Luc Marion* (Annalen van het Thijmgenootschap, 88, 2), Nijmegen 2000

WELTERS, R.: 'De prijs van de markt (Interview with Henk Tieleman)', in *De Bazuin* 78 (1995) (January 20), 8

WENGER, A.: 'La nouvelle campagne antireligieuse en URSS', in *La Croix* 85 (1964) February 17-19

WEREN, W.: 'Weer op zoek naar de ware Jezus', in K.-W. MERKS & N. SCHREURS (eds.): *De passie van een grensganger. Theologie aan de vooravond van het derde millennium*, Baarn 1997, 92-109

WERKVERBAND VAN KATHOLIEKE HOMO-PASTORES: *Tot zegen bereid. Pastorale brief over het vieren van vriendschap*, Baarn 2000

WERNER, H.: *Einführung in die Entwicklungspsychologie*, München 1953

WERNER, L.: 'Modell eines Ehe-Katechumenats. Ein Versuch der Diözese Autun/Burgund', in *Anzeiger für die Seelsorge* 96 (1987) 182-184

WESSELS, A.: *Kerstening en ontkerstening van Europa. Wisselwerking tussen evangelie en cultuur*, Baarn 1994

WEST, F.: *Anton Baumstark's Comparative Liturgy in its Intellectual Context I* (Dissertation Notre Dame University, promotor Marc Searle), Ann Arbor 1988

WEST, F.: *The Comparative Liturgy of Anton Baumstark* (Joint Liturgical Studies 31), Nottingham 1995

WESTERFIELD TUCKER, K.B.: 'A Decade of Christian Song: Observations on Recent Hymnals and Songbooks', in *Studia Liturgica* 31 (2002) 193-210

WESTERHOFF, J. & W. WILLIMON: 'Ritual: Recognition of Divorce', in J. WESTERHOFF & W. WILLIMON: *Liturgy and Learning Through the Life Cycle*, New York 1980, 125-128.

WESTERHOFF, J. & W. WILLIMON: *Liturgy and Learning Through the Life Cycle*, New York 1980

WHEELOCK, W.: 'The Problem of Ritual Language: From Information to Situation', in *Journal of the American Academy of Religion* 50 (1982) 1, 49-71

WHIT, D.R.: '*Varietetates legitimae* and an African-American Liturgical Tradition', in *Worship* 71 (1997) 504-537

WHITE, J.F.: 'How Do We Know It Is Us?', in E. ANDERSON & B. MORRILL (eds.): *Liturgy and the Moral Self: Humanity at Full Strectch Before God*, Collegeville 1998, 55-65

WIJERS, C.: *Prinsen en clowns in het Limburgse Narrenrijk. Het carnaval in Simpelveld en Roermond 1945-1992*, Amsterdam 1995

WIJNGAARDS, J.: *Bijbel voorlezen in de liturgie. Dàn goed verstaanbaar*, Boxtel 1974

WIJNGAARDS, J.: 'Toen vrouwen nog diakens waren', in *De Bazuin* 82 (1999) 15, 8-10

WILLEMS, A.: *De actualiteit van Schleiermacher's 'Reden' uit 1799*, in *Tijdschrift voor Theologie* 40 (2000) 341-357

WINKLER, G. & R. MEßNER: 'Überlegungen zu den methodischen und wissenschaftstheoretischen Grundlagen der Liturgiewissenschaft', in *Theologische Quartalschrift* 178 (1998) 141-172

WINNICOTT, D.: 'Transitional objects and transitional phenomena', in D. WINNICOTT: *Collected Papers*, London 1958

WINNICOTT, D.: *Collected Papers*, London 1958

WINNICOTT, D.: 'Transitional objects and transitional phenomena', in D. WINNICOTT, *Playing and Reality*, London/New York 1991

WINNICOTT, D.: *Playing and Reality*, London/New York 1991

WIT, J. DE: "Men make er geen etalage!'. Over bloemen en liturgie', in *Werkmap (voor) Liturgie* (Vieringen (Rituelen) buiten 2) 30 (1996) 11-18

WIT, R. DE: 'Pater is het zaterdag weer mis? Verslag van een samenkomst met bewoners van een forensische kliniek', in *Werkmap (voor) Liturgie* 26 (1993) 261-293

WIT, TH. DE & G. TEN BERGE: 'Liturgie buiten, in de open lucht', in *Werkmap (voor) Liturgie* (Vieringen (Rituelen) buiten 1) 30 (1996) 23-30

WITHERUP, R.D.: *A Liturgist's Guide to Inclusive Language,* Collegeville 1996

WITTE, H.: 'Kerken kunnen té geïncultureerd zijn', in *Een-twee-een* 22 (1994) 23-24

WITTENBERG, D.: 'Big business. Het uitgekiende ondernemingsbeleid van PSV', in *HP/De Tijd* May 20, 1988, 16-19

WITTEVEEN, F.J.: 'Groene kathedralen van de verbeelding. Overpeinzingen bij een openluchtviering in Meerssel-Dreef', in *Werkmap (voor) Liturgie* (Vieringen (Rituelen) buiten 2) 30 (1996) 19-29

WOLDE, E.J. VAN: *A Semiotic Analysis of Genesis 2-3. A Semiotic Theory and Method of Analysis Applied to the Story of the Garden of Eden* (Studia Semitica Neerlandica 25), Assen 1989

WOLFORD, L. & R. SCHECHNER (eds): *The Grotowski Sourcebook*, London 1997

WORGUL, G.S., Jr.: 'Inculturation and Root Metaphors', in *Questions Liturgiques* 77 (1996) 40-51 and in J. LAMBERTS (ed.): *Liturgie et inculturation. Liturgy and Inculturation* (Textes et Études Liturgiques/ Studies in Liturgy 14), Leuven 1996 = G.S. WORGUL, Jr.: 'Inculturatie en basismetaforen', in J. LAMBERTS (ed.): *Liturgie en inculturatie. Verslagboek van het twaalfde liturgiecolloquium van het Liturgisch Instituut van de K.U. Leuven – oktober 1995* (Nikè-reeks 37), Leuven/Amersfoort 1996, 57-74

WORKUM, J. VAN: 'Acht aardes, en nóg niet genoeg', in *Roodkoper* 2 (1997) 5, 8-9

WORLD: *World Christian Encyclopedia*, Oxford 2001

WORLD COUNCIL OF CHURCHES: *Baptism, Eucharist and Ministry* (Faith and Order Papers 111), Geneva 1982.

ZACHARIAS, W. (ed.): *Zeitphenomen Musealisierung: das Verschwinden der Gegenwart und die Konstruktion der Erinnerung*, Essen 1990

ZAGANO, PH.: *Holy Saturday. An Argument for the Restoration of the Female Diaconate in the Catholic Church*, New York 2000

ZAGANO, PH.: 'Catholic Women Deacons: Present Tense', in *Worship* 77 (2003) 386-408

ZEGENBEDEN: 'Zegenbeden over een levensverbintenis', in *Werkmap (voor) Liturgie* 24 (1990) 167-172

ZIJDERVELD, A.C.: *Staccato cultuur. Flexibele maatschappij en verzorgende staat*, Utrecht 1991

ZIJDERVELD, A.C.: 'Katholiek reveil', in *NRC Handelsblad* June 8, 1996, 9

ZIMMERMANN, D.: 'Stufenweise Begleitung zum Sakrament der Ehe. Anregungen aufgrund von Erfahrungen mit dem 'Ehekatechumenat' in Frankreich', in *Lebendige Katechese* 3 (1981) 126-131

ZIMMERMANN, D.: 'Segensfeier statt Trauung', in *Gottesdienst* 31 (1997) 52-53

ZITNIK, M.: *Sacramenta. Bibliographia internationalis*, I-IV, Rome 1992

ZOEST, A. VAN (ed.): *De macht der tekens. Opstellen over maatschappij, tekst en litteratuur*, Utrecht 1986

ZOUTMAN, D.: 'Bij geloofssocialisatie gaat de kost voor de baat. Interview met Frits Brattinga', in *Praktische Theologie* 23 (1996) 27-29

ZOUTMAN, D.: 'Het kerkelijk jaar is een fantastische leidraad voor de levende geloofsgemeenschap', in *Praktische Theologie* 23 (1996) 30-33

ZSIFKOVITS, V.: *Wirtschaft ohne Moral?*, Innsbruck/Wien 1994

ZUIDGEEST, P.: 'Mensen leven van beelden', in *Praktische Theologie* 8 (1981) 291-308

ZUMTHOR, M.: 'Le texte médiéval entre oralité et écriture', in H. PARRET & H.-G. RUPRECHT (eds.): *Exigences et perspectives de la sémiotique. Recueil d'hommages pour Algirdas Julien Greimas*, Amsterdam 1985, 826-843

ZWAGERMAN, J.: *Colga van God. Portretten en polemieken*, Amsterdam 1993

INDEX OF NAMES

INDEX OF SUBJECTS

PRINTED ON PERMANENT PAPER • IMPRIME SUR PAPIER PERMANENT • GEDRUKT OP DUURZAAM PAPIER - ISO 9706

N.V. PEETERS S.A., WAROTSTRAAT 50, B-3020 HERENT